Derek
Jarman

Derek
Jarman

TONY PEAKE

LITTLE, BROWN AND COMPANY

A *Little, Brown* Book

First published in Great Britain in 1999
by Little, Brown and Company

Copyright © 1999 by Anthony Peake

The moral right of the author has been asserted.

A CIP catalogue record for this book
is available from the British Library.

ISBN 0 316 64466 8

Typeset in Goudy by M Rules
Printed and bound in Great Britain by
Clays Ltd, St Ives plc

Little, Brown and Company (UK)
Brettenham House
Lancaster Place
London WC2E 7EN

Contents

Prologue

The picture on the front page of the *Independent* was of an unequivocally bespectacled man photographed against a hazy bank of flowers
in Monet's garden at Giverny. Wearing a cap, scarf and rumpled
tweed jacket, he had a book clasped tightly in his left hand, a walking stick in the other, and was confronting the camera with a steady
gaze subtly suggestive of a smile.

The caption read: 'Gay champion dies on eve of new age.' It
might have added a number of other epithets: painter, designer, film-
maker, writer and gardener. The 'new age' (prematurely announced)
was a reference to the parliamentary vote being taken that evening,
21 February 1994, to give homosexuals parity with heterosexuals by
lowering the age of consent for homosexual sex to sixteen.

Later that night, as Parliament settled on a compromise age of
eighteen, disappointed protesters on the pavement outside fell
momentarily silent in the dead man's honour. The doorstep of
Phoenix House, the block of flats in Charing Cross Road where
Derek Jarman had latterly lived when in London, was adorned with
candles, as was the exterior of the nearby Waterstones bookshop,
where copies of *Chroma*, Jarman's most recent book, graced the

window. Shipley's, a bookshop that took particular care to stock everything he had ever written, created a small shrine to his memory. So did Maison Bertaux, the coffee shop in Greek Street where he had been a devoted regular, and Presto in Old Compton Street, where he often ate. Soho was saluting one of its denizens – though, as coverage in the national papers indicated, Jarman's fame stretched far beyond the nexus of streets where he had lived. By the time his other home, a simple cottage at the tip of Romney Marsh, came to witness his funeral, news of his death had circled the world.

It was 2 March 1994, the most perfect of early spring days. The sky was clear, the viridescent fields dotted with tentative lambs and occasionally splashed with the red of budding willows. Those who arrived in good time went first to Dungeness where, on the windswept shingle between the looming ugliness of the nearby power station, the fishing huts and the slate-grey sea, Jarman had famously created a sculptural garden of great unusualness and beauty. Passing through the cottage's dark wooden rooms, more redolent of a Russian dacha than of anything English, one arrived at the newly constructed 'west wing', a plain room overlooking the rear garden. The drapes were drawn, candles guttered, a small grapefruit tree filled the air with its scent. One of Jarman's most treasured possessions – a plaster cast of the head of Mausolus, the ancient king whose tomb gave the world the word 'mausoleum' – locked unseeing eyes with the room's central occupant. The plain oak coffin was open. Jarman was dressed in a robe of glittering gold. The cap on his head proclaimed him a 'controversialist'. People came and stood in silence over the coffin. They hugged and spoke quietly with Keith Collins, Jarman's companion, and with Howard Sooley, the photographer friend who had faithfully recorded the last years of Jarman's life. Earlier that day, Collins had placed a number of carefully chosen effects in the coffin. The designer Christopher Hobbs, one of Jarman's oldest friends, now added a small brass wreath similar to the one he had last fashioned as a prop for Jarman's filmic account of the painter Caravaggio. The actress Jill Balcon, who had appeared in two of Jarman's later films, *Edward II* and *Wittgenstein*, supplied a second wreath, of laurel. As the mourners left this temporary mausoleum, they encountered another line of people in the passage outside, queuing to use the bathroom, whose walls of blue stood testament to Jarman's final film, an imageless journey into a blue void.

In the garden people wondered whether the silent, sightless, shrunken form in the coffin could possibly be Jarman. The face was familiar and, no doubt, the feet – absurdly huge and pale in comparison with the tenuous, umber features above them. Yet the talkative, excitable Jarman had never been that small, that Mandarin-like, that still. The only thing that felt right was that he should be the centre of so much attention.

Spilling from the garden into the road, groups of black-clad people came and went, talking in hushed tones. Many had ribbons on their lapels, some red to acknowledge support for AIDS-related charities, the majority blue, the colour of that final film: acknowledgement less of a disease than of a particular victim. Equally unusual were the flapping habits of the Sisters of Perpetual Indulgence, men who dressed as nuns in order to expiate homosexual guilt and promulgate universal joy. Three years previously, these same sisters had come to Prospect Cottage to canonise Jarman. Then, the occasion had been a party and some of the sisters had taken their new saint for a paddle in the sea. Today there was no paddling. It had not been easy for Jarman, an avowed atheist and relative newcomer to the area, to obtain permission to be buried locally. When permission was obtained, it was on condition that proprieties were observed. The Sisters of Perpetual Indulgence were on notice to behave with uncharacteristic decorum.

To those more familiar with the rebellious side of Jarman's persona, the controversialist in him as opposed to the traditionalist, the service that followed was as puzzling as it was inappropriate. Conducted by Canon Peter Ford in the Church of St Nicholas in nearby New Romney, it consisted of prayers, readings and two hymns, both chosen by Jarman: George Herbert's 'Teach Me, My God and King' and 'Abide With Me'. Also at Jarman's request there were four addresses. Nicholas Ward-Jackson, the producer of *Caravaggio*, remembered the almost feverish excitement with which Jarman had made the announcement that he was HIV positive. Norman Rosenthal of the Royal Academy recalled the dead man's gift for friendship. Sarah Graham, herself a political activist, detailed his contribution to the cause of gay politics. The journalist and critic Nicholas de Jongh referred memorably to the 'significant mischief' inherent in Jarman's attitude to life.

Since it was Lent, there were no flowers in the church, but Jarman's sister Gaye had supplied a single bouquet of mimosa, a flower of particular importance to her brother. This lay on the now sealed coffin and, as the coffin was carried from the church after the closing hymn, its scent hung in the still air.

The congregation dispersed, some covertly complaining that they had not been invited to join the immediate family and select coterie of friends who made the short journey to Old Romney and the small churchyard of St Clement, where final prayers were said and the coffin was lowered into the ground in the shade of the ancient and venerable yew tree of which Jarman had been so fond.

Had he died seven years previously, on completion of *Caravaggio*, although almost as many people might have attended his funeral, and from as many walks of life, he would never have made the front page of a national newspaper. Then, if he was known at all, it was principally to dedicated filmgoers and cognoscenti of the artistic avant garde. In the interim, his diagnosis as HIV positive and his decision to be open about his disease, his ineluctable Englishness and the extraordinary grace and courage with which he faced death, all led to his achieving iconic status in the eyes not only of his most obvious constituency, gay men, but of almost anyone with a care for the human spirit.

The commemorations continued, one within days of the funeral. *Glitterbug*, a compilation of Jarman's super-8 footage put together for BBC 2's *Arena*, was hastily scheduled for broadcast on 5 March. Channel 4 responded with *A Night with Derek*, a repeat of a profile entitled *You Know What I Mean*, plus four of Jarman's features. There were three exhibitions, the first in Portland at the Chesil Gallery and Portland Lighthouse, the second at Manchester's Whitworth Gallery, the third at the Drew Gallery in Canterbury. A dramatisation of Jarman's journal *Modern Nature* was performed at the Edinburgh Festival. Richard Salmon, Jarman's art dealer, produced a limited edition of the text of *Blue*. There was a season of his films at the National Film Theatre. Making magnificent use of Howard Sooley's photographs, Thames and Hudson published *derek jarman's garden*. The steady trickle of visitors to Dungeness become a flow. Keith Collins began to joke darkly about establishing a company called Prospect Products.

As in life, eulogy was tempered by controversy. Even before the funeral, Christopher Tookey, film critic of the *Daily Mail*, was writing a rebuttal of Jarman under the heading: 'HOW CAN THEY TURN THIS MAN INTO A SAINT?'[1] A piece by Ed Porter in the *Modern Review* asked: 'Had Derek Jarman not been gay, would his home videos have been shown on Channel 4?'[2] Arguing that if he had 'not taken the HIV test or drugs like AZT, he could be alive today', a letter in the *Pink Paper*[3] wondered whether his death was not 'self-willed'. Behind the scenes, there were fierce arguments between Collins and the local parish council over the exact form of Jarman's gravestone, erected in June 1997.

In May 1996, a comprehensive retrospective of Jarman's work was mounted at the Barbican. Thames and Hudson published *Derek Jarman: A Portrait*, a collection of essays complementing the exhibition. The critic Brian Sewell gave the work on display a decided drubbing and concluded: 'Without the alchemist, there is no alchemy.'[4]

He may well be right. Only time will tell. It is certainly true that Jarman's undoubted gift for turning dross to gold lay as vividly in his persona as it did in his work. Genius is a much overused word, but if Jarman had genius, it resided as much in the sheer incandescence with which he existed as it did in the fruits of that existence.

'Do you know what I mean?' had always been his catchphrase, endlessly punctuating the excited flow of his talk. The hope of this book is to give some sense of what he did mean, to capture the complicated sweetness of honey produced from the lion's mouth.

In an interview containing an attack on, among other things, the Bloomsbury Group, Jarman said of biography:

> I have a horror of Bloomsbury in an odd sort of way. I can't bear it. But then it was all literary based, wasn't it? My environment isn't. That's why it's perpetuated through our culture through the *TLS* and everything because it's all

novels. I don't know any novelists, thank God. Otherwise we would be stuck like that; there would be endless biographies. It's a whole industry, isn't it? It's extraordinary. It's so uninteresting. I mean it's so genuinely dull.[5]

The subject of this biography could not have been dull if he tried.

1

Family Mythology

In *Dancing Ledge*, the first of his published journals, Derek Jarman titles his brief account of his family background 'A Short Family Mythology'. The Viceroy's Ball, Great-Aunt Doris and her rubber roses, grandmother Moselle – or Mimosa, as he called her – a daffodil bell hanging from a lychgate. The clips are short but telling, scenes snipped from an expert's home movie; and there is an actual home movie, complete with inter-titles, to complement the journal: severely bonneted toddlers at play in the twenties, Moselle stepping eagerly from a biplane at Le Bourget, a family lunch.

The family thus featured are the Puttocks, Jarman's forebears on his mother's side. There is no equivalent memorial to the Jarmans,[1] only written records of how the family, based in Devon, moved about the county as work or marriage dictated until, in 1814, Elias, a tanner, married Mary Elworthy, whose family owned the manorial rights to the village of Uplowman, a scattering of houses and tiny farms on the steep hills to the north-east of Tiverton. Here the couple settled, taking over the management of a modest farm at Middle Coombe.

With only two exceptions, the eight children of Elias's and Mary's

third son, John, forsook Devon for New Zealand. The last to leave
was the eldest, also John, who set sail in 1888 and eventually
acquired a smallholding in Riccarton, now a suburb of
Christchurch.

It was in this most English of colonial cities that the second of
John's four sons, Hedley Elworthy, met and married Mary Elizabeth
Chattaway Clarke, a carpenter's daughter. Hedley worked for the
Tramway Board, first as a clerk, finally as general manager. In his
spare time he played the violin in the Christchurch Symphony
Orchestra, sang in the church choir, acted as churchwarden. He was
a Rotarian and Grand Master of the Riccarton Masonic Lodge, devi-
ating from this civic-mindedness only to indulge his passion for
dancing the waltz.

The second of Hedley and Lizzie's five children was a son,
Lancelot Elworthy, born on 17 August 1907. Obliged from a relatively early age to make his own way in the world, Lance left school
at fifteen to become an engineering apprentice with the
Christchurch Tramway Board. Meanwhile he attempted to improve
his prospects by embarking on a part-time course in mechanical and
electrical engineering. In October 1928, underwritten by money
scraped together by his family, he sailed for England aboard the SS
Ionic to pursue his engineering career in the Royal Air Force.

Regular letters home provide a vivid picture of Lance's first ten
years away from the certainties of New Zealand. Of his first
encounter with an official at the Air Ministry, he wrote: 'They do
not like New Zealanders being trained unless they are going to live
permanently in England.'[2] Although he was almost immediately
granted a temporary commission as a pilot officer in the RAF, at his
second training school, where he acquitted himself admirably, the
comment was: 'A very conscientious and hard worker Colonial who
has brains and power of application.'

The praise is fulsome, the subtext unmistakable – certainly to
anyone who has suffered the insularity of the English. It was an insularity Lance felt keenly. To counter it, he set about reinventing
himself. He changed his name to Mike[3] and, by October 1933, just
five years after his arrival, was writing to his mother: 'I only hope
that when I return home my speech will appear normal to you, as

[a friend] remarked that I had no colonial accent at all.' He had entered that pernicious no-man's-land occupied by many such colonials, where, in self-defence, he began to nurture an idealised and fiercely conservative vision of the country to which he pretended.

For all her 'stiff-necked conventions', England nevertheless offered Lance unrivalled opportunities. On receiving a permanent commission in the RAF, he had been posted to Palestine, flown over large swathes of East Africa and danced at every opportunity: 'I have done so much dancing lately I am becoming a super snake at it, rivalled only by the gigolo we saw in the cabaret at Mombasa.' His aunt Emily (one of the two children of her generation not to emigrate to New Zealand) was still alive, her Exeter home providing a family base of sorts. He had a small but close circle of friends and the time and funds to indulge his various passions: cars, sailing, swimming, sunbathing and photography. He was having fun, more fun than many: 'Last Wednesday I had a day out in London and saw some of the unemployed riots in Trafalgar Square. Things looked very ugly for a time until a charge from the mounted police damped the hunger strikers' enthusiasm a bit . . . I had a dancing lesson in the afternoon and in the evening went to the Palladium to hear Paul Robeson.'[4]

By mid-1938, now elevated to the rank of squadron leader, Lance was a less enthusiastic dancer than in his twenties. All the same, come the final mess ball of the season, he invited several guests, including 'two girls from Northwood'. On 16 November he wrote: 'I motored over to Northwood, North London and stayed the evening there.' A month later his letter enclosed 'several snaps, some . . . with the daughter of the house at Northwood where I stay sometimes at weekends'. Northwood was where the Puttocks lived and the 'daughter of the house' is almost certainly the twenty-year-old Elizabeth Evelyn, or 'Betts', as she was known.

It is a testament to Lance's strength of character – and to the enduring love that soon developed between him and Betts – that he was able to spend as much time as he did at Northwood. Betts' parents, Moselle and Harry Litten Puttock, were neither rich nor particularly well connected, but they had in their time enjoyed the trappings of a quite splendid lifestyle. Snobbish Moselle wanted more for her daughter than marriage to the son of a New Zealand clerk eleven years Betts' senior, however fit and handsome he might be.

It is not known when or where Moselle, also called May, or 'Girlie', and her flamboyant sister Doris, also called Sophia, were born; probably between 1885 and 1890 in either South Africa or India. Their father, Isaac Fredric Reuben, was, as his name suggests, Jewish. Tall, dashing and moustachioed, with a fondness for oysters and Guinness, he was an army officer, though in which regiment, even which army, is not recorded. His wife Flora died when the two girls were very young, leaving them to the principal care of a series of governesses who brought them up as Christians.

Although Doris was the more extreme of the two, Moselle was not without dash. Intrepid, vivacious and exceptionally extravagant, she was dark-eyed and dark-haired, glamorous in a decidedly un-English way. She dressed exquisitely, usually in pastel shades, and always made sure that the silk tips of her cigarettes matched the colour of her clothes. By contrast, Harry Litten Puttock, despite a shock of red hair, was as mild and inoffensive as his background. The son of a commercial clerk, he was born in uninspiring Stoke Newington in 1883. As a young man, he had joined the firm of Harrisons & Crosfield, the tea and rubber merchant, thereby quitting Stoke Newington for more exotic Calcutta, where he made a steady but unspectacular climb from tea-taster to manager.

The couple had three children: Edward Colin Litten (Teddy), Elizabeth Evelyn (Betts), and Moyra Litten. Teddy was born in 1915 in London; Betts, on 8 August 1918, and Moyra, seven years later, in Calcutta. Until the age of seven, London and Calcutta would signify the contrasting poles of the children's environment: innumerable servants, the endless tennis and garden parties, of what Jarman would later term 'subcontinental suburbia'[5] alternating, in due course, with boarding-school life back in England.

For families such as the Puttocks, the interwar years were an extraordinary time. Their existence bore scant relation either to their own particular histories or to a changing world. How often in the past – or the future – would a girl like Betts, at the age of sixteen, have the opportunity to 'come out', as she did in Calcutta during the Christmas season of 1934, and attend not only a plethora of garden parties, but even the Viceroy's Ball – where, fittingly, all the decorations, even the tablecloths and sweet wrappings, were imperial purple?

To turn the pages of most family photograph albums is to risk experiencing a sense of loss. In the case of the Puttocks, whose yellowing photos are enhanced by their home movies, that sense is particularly acute. Toddlers at play on the beach at Bexhill, Moselle stepping eagerly from that biplane at Le Bourget, the uniformed girls returning to school at the end of the summer holidays, the caption that joshingly informs us the girl squinting shyly at the camera is the 'always smiling Betty' – the flickering images record a way of life that has vanished forever; a lost Eden, but an Eden, too, that is haunted by the spectre of what lay behind it. Little wonder that when Jarman came to pick up a camera of his own, his work should be steeped in a sense of paradise lost, a paradise which, even as he yearned for it, he mistrusted, because he knew that somewhere, somehow, it was poisoned.

In 1935 Harry suffered a minor stroke. It forced him to take early retirement. A friend from Calcutta had settled in Northwood, still a village on the outskirts of London. Here the Puttocks moved, staying first at the Château de Madrid, a residential hotel that would later become the headquarters of Coastal Command, then at Manor Cottage, 9 Watford Road, a pretty, if unremarkable, Edwardian dwelling with an ample garden. Harry's early retirement meant a disastrous withering of income, his poor health a flood of medical bills. There were still family holidays in Cornwall and Bexhill, and a whiff of imperial excitement seeing Teddy off to India, where he was due to join a tea firm, but taking the waters at Contrexville and attending the Viceroy's balls were now a thing of the past.

Betts briefly attended the Harrow Art School with her friend Verity Shierwater. She studied dress design, then found work as an assistant to Norman Hartnell. The job was hardly exalted, paying barely enough to cover her fare into London, but it did have the benefit of glamour. There were clothes to prepare for royal tours, film stars to flatter, fashion shows to announce. In future, Betts would always be able to make her own, exceptionally stylish outfits.[6]

Less glamorous – though it did involve excitement of a sort – was
the Voluntary Aid Detachment (VAD), which Betts had joined in
1936, again with her friend Verity, plus two friends of Moselle's, the
Aunties Orr – Phil and Vi – two 'small and birdlike'[7] spinster sisters
who lived in an old Northwood house called Langlands. The growth
of the VAD was one of many pointers towards the deteriorating
international situation. Another was the number of young men in
the forces for whom, when they were at play, consorts were needed.
Harry Puttock was an old-fashioned man, and Betts was not allowed
out unless he and Moselle had vetted her beau; but because the
evening had been proposed by friends, who would be in attendance,
in late 1938 she was given permission to accompany a man she had
never met – Squadron Leader Jarman – to a dance at a nearby air-
field.

Four months later, in March 1939, Harry died of a stroke. In the
summer, Moselle, Betts and Moyra moved into 10 Chester Place, a
modest, two-bedroomed flat in a newly built, three-storey block in
Green Lane, just around the corner from the station and above a
parade of shops. It was a further reduction in circumstances, and
one that it fell to the efficient Betts to oversee. About its only positive aspect was that Moselle was now less able to turn up her nose at
her daughter's suitor.

Exactly a year after Harry's death, on 31 March 1940, Lance and
Betts were married at Holy Trinity Church, Northwood. The vicar's
wife made a wedding bell of daffodils which hung on the lychgate.
As the dashing squadron leader paused underneath it to gaze ador-
ingly at the smiling bride on his arm, the moment was caught by the
camera. The photograph appeared in no fewer than seven papers.

Within a week, the reality of war had reasserted itself. Lance was
in the air again, reconnoitring the Danish coast. Three months later
he was transferred as chief flying instructor to a training unit in the
remote Scottish fishing village of Lossiemouth. In July 1940 he was
invested with the Distinguished Flying Cross, and that December he
was promoted to the rank of wing commander. A year later he was
transferred to Lichfield, this time as commanding officer.
Meanwhile, Betts had become pregnant. In January 1942, after a
tense few months in which it was feared she might miscarry, she

returned home to give birth. A friend had been put on notice to save enough petrol to drive her to the hospital, which he did, through heavy snow, on the night of the 30th. The next morning Moselle and Moyra sent a card to the Royal Victoria Nursing Home, Pinner Hill. It read: 'Congratulations on a happy landing.' Not long afterwards, Betts and Lance were sending out a card of their own: a drawing of baby Derek assailing the blue in a single-engined plane.

He was Derek from the start, though when he was christened two months later, on 28 March, at Holy Trinity Church, Northwood, it was as Michael Derek Elworthy.

In June 1942, in the same month as he was mentioned in dispatches, Lance was transferred from Lichfield to Eggington as senior air staff officer. In April 1943 he went to Kirmington to command No. 166 Squadron. In October came a further move, to RAF Wyton, also as commanding officer. Although Betts and baby Derek joined him on each of these postings, they spent as much time at 10 Chester Place, not least because Betts was again pregnant and again fearful of miscarriage. In the event, the pregnancy passed without incident and, on 18 September 1943, she gave birth to Elisabeth Gaye Elworthy, who, like her brother, would always be known by her second name.

Meanwhile, Lance's war had taken a venturesome turn. Having volunteered as a Pathfinder, a position which involved flying ahead of the bomber squadrons and dropping flares to illuminate the targets, in June 1944 he was posted to Italy as a senior air staff officer with the Mediterranean Allied Air Forces.

This meant that for the last year of the war, Betts and the children were forced to remain in England on their own. As soon as hostilities ended, Betts returned to Northwood, where her mother was able to supply her with accommodation: after Harry's death Moselle had put Manor Cottage, the old family home, on the market, but before it found a buyer, war had been declared and the house had been requisitioned by the army. It was now returned to Moselle, who divided it into two flats, one of which she offered Betts.

During Lance's final English posting, at RAF Wyton, Betts had acquired help in the form of a young girl from nearby Huntingdon called Joany. Betts brought Joany with her to Northwood to help with house and children. When, in early 1946, she was finally able to join Lance in Italy, it was again with Joany in tow. They travelled by train in the first wave of service families to venture on to the continent. The journey was not easy, but for four-year-old Derek it was a huge adventure. To be quitting their 'bleak wartime married quarters with their coke stoves and mildew'[8] felt like a liberation. The journey's end was magical: family reunion, sunlight and warmth. Filmically speaking, they were switching from black and white into colour.

2

Beautiful Flowers and How to Grow Them

'Roses. There is a charm about a beautiful Rose garden which appeals irresistibly to every lover of flowers. It is not necessary to win a prize at a Rose show to enjoy Roses when they are used in free, informal, natural ways. There is a wide gulf between exhibiting and gardening.'[1] Published in 1926, *Beautiful Flowers and How to Grow Them* is a substantial work. A mere thirty-two colour plates illustrate 400 pages of dense text. Even so, the Jarmans deemed it an appropriate gift for their four-year-old son, to whom it was given on 25 April 1946, shortly after the family's reunion in Italy.

At Manor Cottage, little Derek, or 'Dekky' as his doting grandmother called him, had wandered into the garden which, owing to the neglect of war, had become hopelessly overgrown. He picked nearly every flower in sight, studying each one with intense pleasure as he did so. 'These spring flowers,' he would later write, 'are my first memory, startling discoveries; they shimmered briefly before dying, dividing the enchantment into days and months, like the gong that summoned us to lunch, breaking up my solitude . . . In that precious time I would stand and watch the garden grow, something imperceptible to my friends.'[2]

After Northwood, Italy was a fabulous floral crescendo. The gardens of the villa where the family spent their first summer were, in Jarman's words, 'a cornucopia of cascading blossom, abandoned avenues of mighty camellias, old roses trailing into the lake, huge golden pumpkins, stone gods overturned and covered with scurrying green lizards, dark cypresses, and woods full of hazel and sweet chestnut'.[3] Very much a product of England, and a war-torn England at that – his first reaction on seeing the Coliseum was to comment on how badly it had been bombed – little Dekky was ravished, in imagination if not in reality, by the vividness of the colours, textures, sounds and scents which Italy presented him.

> The dawn would bring Cecilia the housekeeper bustling into
> my bedroom – with a long feather duster to shoo out the
> swallows that flitted through the windows to build their nests
> in the corners of the room . . . After breakfast Davide, her
> handsome eighteen year old nephew, would place me on the
> handlebars of his bike, and we'd be off down country lanes –
> or out on the lake in an old rowing boat, where I would
> watch him strip in the heat as he rowed round the headland
> to a secret cove, laughing all the way. He was my first love.[4]

The image is splendidly romantic, splendidly romanticised, and was of such importance to its somewhat precocious author that, love-struck, he would return to it a number of times in his writings and films.

Lance was based in Rome, a city which, for all its splendours, is simply too hot in high summer. With Lance flying up for weekends, Betts, Joany, Derek and Gaye found themselves billeted with a number of other air force families in the villa with the magnificent gardens, the swallows, Cecilia and Davide. Situated on the shore of Lake Maggiore, the Villa Zuassa had been requisitioned by the Allied Commission from a Fascist whose wife, 'a sinister figure with a string of alsatians',[5] was still in residence. Her baleful, witch-like presence in the other half of the villa could cast a shadow across this Italian Eden as dark and alarming as the stormclouds that occasionally gathered across the lake.

There were other shadows. In most respects little Dekky was a model child, impeccably turned out, well-mannered and cheerful. In matters prandial, however, he was proving something of a rebel. Usually it fell to Joany to feed the recalcitrant child. 'Eat this for little Joany,' she would croon – until Betts' sister, Moyra, who happened to be staying, could stand it no longer. 'For God's sake,' she snapped, 'eat that for bloody little Joany.' Thus did 'Bloody Little Joany' acquire a nickname and Jarman a reputation for being difficult at table. It was a reputation that would soon bring him into fierce conflict with his father, who up to now had seen very little of his son.

That winter, after a brief stint in Venice, the family took up residence in Rome, a city then remarkable for its emptiness: 'There were very few cars, everyone travelled on bicycles. Limbless soldiers and maimed children begged in the streets and lived in the ruins on the Via Appia, a quiet little lane that wound into the countryside. At every turning there were priests like flocks of crows, scurrying busily about their work.'[6] They were billeted in a cavernous nineteenth-century flat in the Via Paisiello, not far from the Borghese Gardens – another of Jarman's Edens.

The flat, requisitioned from Admiral Count Costanzo Ciano, the father of Mussolini's son-in-law, was cruelly cold; unless packing cases could be found to burn in its many grates, the only warm room was the kitchen. For Dekky, however, its art-deco grandeur more than compensated for its chill. He was overawed by the echoing marble, the parquet floors, the tiger-skin rug, the copy of Titian's *Sacred and Profane Love*, the suits of armour. He adored the attic, where there was a further treasure-trove of astounding objects: a small glass dome which, when shaken, produced a snowstorm; a violin, a doll, a collection of ceramic donkeys, old ballgowns and 'two circular ostrich-feather fans with handles, sown with hummingbirds, a tinsel Christmas tree, and letters to the Admiral from Mussolini scattered across the floor'.[7]

In an adult notebook, Jarman once compiled the following list:

curriculum vitae Art History self portrait romance
1) the swallow who flew into room at Largo mas

2) the red glass ball with the snow that broke
3) the castles on the appian way with the roses in May
4) the cupboard with the white fans
5) looking for pine kernels in Borghese gardens
6) riding on tiger skin
7) a particular mean nada Zigarnatan etc.[8]

The list provides a key to Jarman's entire aesthetic. The manner in which the sparseness of his RAF beginnings caused a handful of objects to shimmer with such totemic potency that they acquired an almost magical allure is echoed down the years by his appreciation of single items of great beauty or personal significance, which he placed with ritualised care in all the spaces he ever inhabited, as well as in his paintings and films.

Rome crucially prefigured the future in two further ways. The flat was shared with a family of Yugoslavian refugees. While the children provided Jarman with playmates, the mother afforded him an early artistic example. When not at the kitchen table singing 'rousing Yugoslav partisan songs',[9] Nada Ziganovitch[10] (the 'particular mean nada Zigarnatan' of Jarman's list) spent most afternoons combing the streets of Rome for a spot to erect her easel. In her footsteps followed a fascinated Jarman.[11]

Then came the afternoon his parents took him to the cinema for the first time, to a matinée showing for forces children of *The Wizard of Oz*. Because the outing interrupted the feeding of his tortoise, one of the few pets his peripatetic childhood allowed, he had not been keen to go, and there were moments that afternoon when he wished he had not. The film so utterly transported him that at one point he ducked under his seat 'with a terrified wail', then bolted, only to be 'captured by the usherette and handed back along the row to [his] embarrassed parents'. The Kansas farm, the spiteful neighbour, Dorothy and her dog, Toto, the tornado that lifted her house clear into the sky, the glorious technicolour of what lay over the rainbow, Dorothy's trio of friends, a yellow brick road, the Wicked Witch of the West and her frightening cohort of flying monkeys, a wizard who 'frankly admits his incompetence'[12] – the images were so real to Dekky that he would never forget their impact. 'I took part in . . . [the film], rather than merely watched it, and am grateful to this day that it had a happy ending.'[13]

The wonder of gardens, aesthetic appreciation of a Latinate young man and of other objects of beauty, the power of painting, of cinema, wizardry and witchcraft – Jarman's Italian sojourn was short but of great importance, providing him with a template, a 'curriculum vitae Art History self portrait romance', from which can be traced virtually his entire artistic future.

3

Buried Feelings

By 1947, although the war had been over for two years, its effects were still being strongly and unpleasantly felt in England. Despite victory and the determination of the recently elected Labour government to start a new social chapter in the country's history, the process of adapting to peace was slow and painful. It is a mere detail, but not long after the Jarmans returned from Italy, Lance was invited to lunch at Blenheim Palace. That evening, Betts and the children were agog to know what it had been like. What had he been given to eat? The answer was distressingly simple: Spam.

The family had travelled back from Italy on a 'storm-tossed troop ship'.[1] With Bloody Little Joany still in attendance, they had gone to stay in Northwood with Moselle. They were not the only prodigals returning home. After a war spent presumed missing, but actually enduring unspeakable horrors in a Japanese POW camp, Betts' brother Teddy was also back in Northwood, married to his first wife Pegs. Moyra was working for her flamboyant Aunt Doris in a boarding house behind Harrods, later moving to nearby Mount Vernon Hospital, where she would meet her first husband. For the first time in almost ten years, the Puttock family were reunited and able to bear witness to the after-effects of the war as they related to Lance.

Lance's ascent through the ranks of the RAF was continuing unabated. On his return to England in July 1947, a month before his fortieth birthday, he had been promoted to group captain and given a posting to RAF Oakington near Cambridge, where he was put in charge of transport. Yet although the future held some exciting challenges, the particular excitements of youth and war were a thing of the past. Lance was now shouldering the responsibilities of a young family on RAF pay and in the bleak surroundings of life on the 'patch'. Italian opulence had been supplanted by a mildewed Nissen hut 'filled with thick suffocating coke fumes and running with . . . condensation',[2] Lake Maggiore by an old yellow dinghy on the lawn, smelling strongly of rubber and filled with hose water.

As Jarman later explained, with no forays to make into enemy territory, Lance's temper, never placid, spilled into the domestic arena. The person with whom he most often clashed was his son; 'so elegant', according to his Aunt Pegs, 'so full of fun with his little twinkle in his eye; a really go-ahead little boy'. Their fights were principally over food. Jarman's persistent refusal to eat certain things maddened his father beyond endurance. It was the start of a titanic clash of wills. Though the father, with his military bearing, was the more obviously powerful of the two, there was an equal, if more subtle, thread of steel running through the 'elegant' son. Mealtimes became skirmishes that could also involve Gaye. The story is sometimes told about Jarman but, as Aunt Pegs remembers it, it was Gaye, then four, who was fiddling with the salt cellar when Lance told her to stop. She refused. Although it was winter, he lifted her out of the window and left her in the cold until sufficiently chastened. Then came the night Jarman's ear was hurting. He was in bed, crying. There were guests for dinner. His wails disturbed them. Lance strode down the passage and beat the child until he fell silent. The next day, Derek was still in pain and the doctor was called. It was discovered he had an abscess in his ear which needed to be etherised and drained.

In the Puttock home-movie footage of a family meal, if one looks carefully one can see that the film is inadvertently running backwards: food is being regurgitated instead of ingested. The images we have of Jarman family life need similarly careful scrutiny if one is to appreciate the darkness lying behind a generally bland and blameless façade; to see that little Dekky was being traumatised by his clashes with his father; that doting Moselle sensed this and would never forgive her son-in-law for his actions; that it fell to the 'always smiling Betty' to keep the family peace, a role at which she became painfully adept over the years.

In January 1948, Lance was posted as commanding officer to RAF Abingdon near Oxford. Gaye and Derek were taken out of their school, Kimway, where they had spent only a couple of terms, and put into a local convent school, St Helen and St Katharine.

In an adult diary, Jarman provides a vivid account of life on the Abingdon 'patch'. He skilfully sketches their desolate, camouflaged house, the uneven lawn bounded by barbed wire, the concrete rockery made from the remains of an old air-raid shelter. It is an account that encompasses both the normality and the chilling abnormality of the Jarman home.

> In the corner of the garden some wild cats bred in a pile of logs, and I lay in wait to trap the kittens, which bit and scratched . . . the house next door had been bombed, the garden had gone wild, we'd play there . . . Dad took me out shooting rabbits and hares at night, by the headlights of his car on the empty airfield, I hated that – I starved rather than eat those rabbits. I was very difficult with food, virtually lived on suet pudding, 'canary' pudding, and of course I was very artistic. I drew endlessly, which was a great source of pride to my mother . . . flowers and Tudor villages, sunsets with geese flying, copies from biscuit tins . . . Plants fascinated me, I remember standing mesmerised in front of a huge horsechestnut in full flower in a field . . . I watched the tree grow until called home. In the evening my mother would take out her Vogue Pattern book and make clothes, she was always immaculately dressed, the most stylish of the mums, I was very aware of that . . . I was always asked to thread the needle in the Singer sewing machine . . . My parents would

go out in the evening, and we would wait breathlessly to see
them off. Mum appeared in her latest dress like a dazzling film
star . . . Dad would be in his full mess kit. They were
impressive, almost other worldly, at these moments . . . Living
behind barbed wire, we were set apart, we knew we were
different. I still feel this to this day . . . I don't understand the
sloppiness of civvy street. You see we clicked to attention
when we had to. Dad was being saluted continuously . . . he
seemed even more alien when the two of us took off alone,
flying the Chipmunk trainer . . . playing hide and seek
through the motionless cumulo nimbus clouds that hang
above the butterfly fields of Oxfordshire. He frightened us
with his sudden outbursts of violent temper, he would fix on
some small mannerism . . . 'hands in the pockets' or 'pardon',
that was belted out of me, often I felt terribly sad and dreamt
of vengeance, but then mum seemed to love him so he had to
be all right. I never unleashed my fury. I was too frightened,
and later, as I grew up, my mother contracted cancer so we all
behaved out of deference to her illness. We buried our
feelings and stuck it out . . .'[3]

At Kimway School, Jarman had attained straight As. St Helen
and St Katharine would report that while he took good care of Gaye,
and his drawing and handwork showed consistent originality, he was
too excited, restless or careless to do well at his other subjects. It was
the start of a long and worrying scholastic decline in a child whose
quick intelligence should have led him to shine. In Italy, he had
become reasonably fluent in Italian, to the extent that Betts and
Moyra had used him as an interpreter. Now, when asked by his parents to demonstrate his linguistic prowess at a party, this most
performance-orientated of children, who loved nothing better than
'to act things out', was overcome by sudden shyness and found that
the language had deserted him. His natural extroversion was trans-
muting into energy of a more jittery nature. He began to develop
characteristics which would dog him for the rest of his life: a slight
clicking sound in his throat when he talked, a restless hopping from
foot to foot, a flapping of his arms. Although physically robust, he

became gradual prey to a clutch of ailments usually considered nervous in origin: asthma, eczema and, for a while, hayfever. Two contradictory impulses, extroversion and introversion, were developing side by side in the boy, which is doubtless why, as a grown-up, despite being the most warm and open of people, and the least secretive, there would always be a part of him one sensed one could never know.

In January 1948, on turning six, he had to contend briefly with another convent: St Juliana's in Oxford, within easy reach of Lance's new posting to Kidlington.[4] The nuns here were particularly gruesome: 'automata', Jarman called them, who 'hacked my paradise to pieces like the despoilers of the Amazon – carving paths of good and evil to Heaven, Hell and Purgatory'.[5] But a grown-up school was being sought, one which Lance, still intent on assimilating, hoped would mould his son into the sort of Englishman to bring credit to his parents. As Jarman put it: 'After the war he [Lance] no longer played the piano or did other creative work. He just had to bury his whole past and this took a terrible toll on him. He retreated into a kind of shell . . . he became more English than the English, yet at the same time, he hated them. He turned my sister and me into middle class English product . . . We were part of his fitting in . . .'[6]

In early 1948, Jarman was accepted for the May 1950 intake by Hordle House, a family-owned prep school on the outskirts of Milford-on-Sea. In the summer of that year, as if in an effort to familiarise themselves with the area, the family's holiday allegiance switched from prewar Bexhill to postwar Swanage. Swanage spelled August, a boarding house and – until she left to get married – Bloody Little Joany to assist if Lance could not get away. On the drive there, it meant passing Bournemouth, and 'a prize of sixpence'[7] for the first child to see the grey stone fingers of Corfe Castle pointing dramatically skywards, followed soon thereafter by a first glimpse of the sea sparkling in the distance between the Purbeck Hills. It meant an enclosed bay, a small, almost apologetic stretch of sandy beach, an old stone harbour bobbing with boats, a pier, a high street. It meant sandcastles, 'buckets, spades and candy floss',[8] trips to the caves at nearby Tilly Whim, where 'you could imagine yourself as a smuggler',[9] and bracing walks along the gull-haunted cliffs at Dancing Ledge.

For Jarman, it was the start of a lifelong love affair with what he called 'the twilit England':[10] that island within an island, the Isle of Purbeck, with its range of hills and sweeping stretch of down at Lulworth that tumbles to the sea in huge folds like petrified breakers; its bewildering tracery of winding lanes, small villages uniformly built of grey Purbeck stone and scattered, lonely farms; its patches of scrubby, blackened heath and gorse; its Ministry of Defence firing ranges; the village of Worth Matravers. In time, these places would come to signify a very personal geography, a geography of the soul; a map less of 'twilit England' than of the heart; a magical alternative to the often harsh and unpalatable realities of the outside world.

4

School House and Manor House

The fifties are frequently seen as an age of wide-eyed innocence. The Festival of Britain, a young Elizabeth, Supermac, net petticoats, Brylcreem, quiffs, salad days. They were also a time of great stress and unease – the end of empire, Cold War, Suez. One of the ways people coped was by pretending that nothing had changed. By turning their backs on the outside world. By clinging to old certainties. Nowhere was this more evident than in certain public schools.

Hordle House, Jarman's prep school, and Canford, his public school, were in the business – and it was a business – of providing the country with future leaders. They believed this was best done by adhering to tradition, fearing God and encouraging manliness. In the clumsy-sounding Latin of the Hordle motto: *Move Te Ipsum* – Bestir Thyself! Though in Hordle's case, sternness was tempered by genuine concern for its youthful charges; by a determination to foster an alternative 'family'.

Since its inception in 1926, the school had occupied a brick-built, ivy-clad house bestriding some thirty acres of ground on the cliffs overlooking the Solent, the long low hump of the Isle of Wight and the three Needles.[1] It is a particularly windswept part of

Hampshire, and the house, into two wings of which, one senior, one junior, eighty boarders were crammed, could be extremely cold in winter. Existence there in the early fifties was fairly spartan. Rationing was still in force, which meant that despite the efforts of the school cook, the diminutive but doughty Mrs Monger, responsible for such delights as 'Mrs Monger's toenails: tough apple cores swimming in a sour translucent mush',[2] school meals relied heavily on bread spread with margarine and watery strawberry jam. On this meagre fare – supplemented only by what treats they kept in their tuck boxes in the Nissen hut on the front lawn, or their Saturday ration of sweets – the boys were expected to engage in a plethora of outdoor activities: football, rugby, cricket, rifle practice, squash, boxing, athletics and, thanks to the school's location, sailing and swimming. Each and every day during the summer months the entire school would descend the cliffs. Avoiding the remnants of the squat, concrete tank defences on the beach, the boys would plunge into the sea, no matter what the temperature, while the long-suffering under-matrons stood up to their waists in the waves, acting as markers. If anyone was found shirking, or in any way misbehaving, it was off to the headmaster's study to be tanned.

Anything less congenial to someone of Jarman's sensibilities would be hard to imagine. The picture suggested by his arrival at the school in May 1950 is heartrending. A brusque father, a mother loath to be sending her son away so young, a sympathetic aunt. A sparsely furnished dormitory, uninspiringly named after one of the school's founder members. Serried ranks of beds, and – since this is a junior dormitory – a teddy bear upon each pillow. Taking charge of the new arrivals, the fearsome Miss Barbara Nickal, known as Ma Nick, 'a great grey bulk of musty pullovers and thick woolly stockings and steel-capped walking-shoes that clicked like the deathwatch'. Ma Nick lived at the top of the house and instilled such terror in her charges that she was rumoured to be a male German spy. The 'cast iron hairstyle with steely ringlets'[3] was, the boys whispered, a cunning disguise, the lighthouse on the Needles a sinister means of flashing coded messages to Ma Nick at night.

In this environment the otherwise bright and intelligent Jarman began to founder. He dropped to the bottom of the class. His lack of co-ordination became more acute, never more so than when in the grip of some excitement. Then, unable to keep still, he would leap around gesticulating wildly, much to the amusement, sometimes scorn, of his fellow pupils. The obligatory sports – boxing in particular – became an enormous trial.

He responded by withdrawing further into himself and by throwing himself with even greater absorption into his painting. 'I started to paint in order to defend myself from this world.'[4] His first sketch pad was a lined HMSO notebook. In its pages he extended his repertoire from the flowers and flying geese he had been copying from his precious *Beautiful Flowers and How to Grow Them*, or the lids of biscuit tins, to dinosaurs lifted from a 'King Penguin "inspired" by Conan Doyle's *Lost World*',[5] plus his 'own world of cities of white timberwork houses',[6] over which he created complicated 'aerial battles'[7] between Stukas and Spitfires. The mediaeval townscape was suggested by Trevelyan's *Illustrated English Social History*, a recent and treasured gift. 'I'd fallen in love with the pictures,' he wrote, 'particularly . . . of a young man, who leans lovesick against a tree.'[8]

Another consolation was the school garden. This was a walled area by the chapel where, among gnarled fruit trees, herbaceous borders and a pergola of 'blousy pink cabbage roses'[9] which shed their petals like confetti, the boys were allotted plots. Here the child who stood aloof from school competitiveness could subtly allow his character to blossom alongside the flowers he tended. Every summer there was a competition and a prize for the best plot. Jarman was soon winning, and valued his supremacy to such an extent that he could not bear for it to be threatened. Over the years there was a gradual shift from the frippery of flowers to vegetables. Eventually the inevitable happened, and the 'showy perfection'[10] of Jarman's deluge of lobelias and pansies lost out to a vegetable patch. The erstwhile champion was livid. In retaliation, he stole some salt from the kitchen and sprinkled it liberally over the dreary vegetables.[11]

As the sanctuary of the school garden indicates, life at Hordle was not all miserable. Ma Nick might have been fearsome, but her presence was ameliorated by the gentler under-matrons. The school calendar was dotted with picnics. In summer, Friday lunch was taken on the beach, Sunday lunch on the lawns in front of the house. There was an annual picnic in the New Forest, to which the entire school was ferried in a couple of overloaded cars and a lumbering bus. Cherries were doled into the floppy 'squishers' the boys had to wear against the sun. Then, hats in place, they would hunt for butterflies, something of a school obsession. As Jarman later recalled, more than a little ruefully: 'I hunted among the beech trees for white admirals, but never caught sight of the elusive emperor, whose capture would have made me a king.'[12]

There were games of marbles and of 'touch and flee' in the dormitories after dark. There were pillow fights and trips to look at the wreck of the *Lamorna*, 'grounded one stormy night at the foot of the cliffs at Barton on its way to the South Seas'.[13] There were the dens constructed in 'Monkey Town', the undergrowth in the tangled pathway between the playing fields, where the boys could create their own world. 'In the cornfield we hollowed out a nest, and ate the green ears, pretending to be field mice; and sharpened lethal peashooters from the stalks of wild cow parsley, using the verdigris ivy berries as ammunition.'[14]

There were school plays and concerts. Philip Howard, the elegant English master, adopted the nom-de-plume of Bobby Loony Ravingsoon to write the 'fearful dramatic thriller'[15] *Kidnabbed*. Jarman was the Aga of Nutty Slack. He also played Frederick in the school's version of *Shockheaded Peter*[16] and Clarence, the captain of school, in the annual Christmas concert:

> *I'm Cuthbert, the senior prefect.*
> *I'm Clarence, the Captain of the School.*
> *I'm Claud the Bad lad, who is never so glad*
> *As when he is playing the fool.*
> *So next time you feel sad,*
> *Just drop in for tea*
> *And a bit of a spree*
> *With Cuthbert and Clarence and Claud.*

There was even drag. In each dormitory there was a raised central section for the boys' washing bowls. This formed a natural stage where Jarman would organise private end-of-term plays. 'Dressed up in a sheet',[17] he would invariably play the female.

In 1951, during Jarman's second year at Hordle, the dormitory witnessed drama of a more frightening kind. That February, his parents went on an extended trip to New Zealand. Given the difficulties he had been experiencing at school, the prolonged absence of Lance and Betts, of Betts in particular, could well have been what prompted Jarman to seek companionship in the bed of another nine-year-old boy – to catastrophic and long-lasting effect.

He gave varying accounts of the incident. The first is in *Dancing Ledge*, published in 1984:

> At nine I discovered that sleeping with someone was more fun than sleeping alone and climbed into my mate Gavin's bed. Cuddling each other alleviated some of the isolation of boarding school. This wholly innocent affair was destroyed by a jealous dormitory captain who crept out one morning and informed the headmaster's wife. She descended on us like a harpy and, in her fury, pulled the mattress right off the bed, turning us onto the floor. The headmaster whipped us both, and afterwards commended the sneak and threatened to tell our parents of this horrible crime; before calling us out of the class and denouncing us in front of the other boys.[18]

Then, in a passage not included in the published book, he concludes: 'This was the moment that I grew to hate and mistrust the grown-up world which had cruelly destroyed my sexuality, sowing the terrible seeds of doubt and self-hate and starting a trail of destruction through my adolescent life.'[19]

Writing three years later in *The Last of England*, he provides substantially the same account, though here his 'first confrontation with oppression' is given a more detailed envoi: 'I became detached and dreamy, spent hours alone painting or watching the flowers grow, had a physical aversion to chumminess and sexual innuendo, organised games, and school showers. I was set apart.'[20]

In *Modern Nature*, the event is treated in a more poetic, though decidedly less innocent way: 'Skinny nine year olds, we explored the contours of forgotten landscapes. The imaginary worlds of Prester John – and of Big Foot, Tight Arse, Stiff Cock. An orgy of little devils swarming across the tympani, in the shadow of hell fire. We dug deep in King Solomon's mines, flirted with strange tribal initiations. Warmth and giggles before reveille.'[21]

Finally, in *At Your Own Risk*, the account is at its most brutal and angry. 'I was unsuccessfully trying to fuck the boy in the bed next to mine – quite unaware that I was doing anything out of the ordinary – when the sky fell in as we were ripped apart like two dogs.'[22]

As an adult, Jarman would constantly tell and retell his own story, mythologising it in the process, reinventing, polishing, holding first this facet, then another, to the light. It was a way of validating his existence. In this case, it was the means of reclaiming an event that might otherwise have been subject to a conspiracy of silence. Interestingly, the headmasters of Hordle deny any knowledge of it, as does the boy into whose bed Jarman crept. Other than Jarman's own accounts, the only proof of what happened that night is a single line of typically English understatement in his housemaster's report for the Easter term: 'His conduct in his dormitory has not been above criticism.'

In 1951, Lance qualified as a jet pilot and was briefly posted to Yorkshire as station commander of RAF Full Sutton, an advanced training unit for the pilots of jet aircraft, and the family moved to the nearby market town of Pocklington. Jarman contracted jaundice that year, and spent a great deal of the summer in York General Hospital, 'on a fat-free diet – dry toast and yellow sponge pudding. Canary pudding. Pretty as a picture with bright yellow jaundice.'[23] At around the same time the removal of his tonsils found him in an RAF hospital 'alone in a ward full of young men, who had been dreadfully maimed by the [Korean] war'. One of their number 'coughed up blood continuously'.[24] The experience so affected the young Jarman that he was ever after 'allergic to hospitals'.[25]

Yorkshire heralded a sudden oasis of happiness. That December, after only seven months at Full Sutton, Lance was asked to set up an entirely new station to train officers to fly De Havilland jet aircraft at RAF Merryfield. Accommodation was of a grander kind than usual: the Elizabethan manor house at Curry Mallet, near Taunton

and Yeovil, a most imposing house and the focal point of the tiny village. Built of weathered grey stone around a small central courtyard
and dating variously from the fourteenth, sixteenth and nineteenth
centuries, Curry Mallet Manor boasts leaded windows, high, twisting
Tudor chimney pots and a large, secluded garden hidden behind a
high stone wall. Rooks caw in the trees, doves coo; beyond the walls,
lush countryside stretches alluringly to distant hills.

It was a happy time for the entire family. Lance was master of a
manor house – the ultimate reward for a colonial desperate for assimilation – and Betts at last had a dwelling of style and substance in
which to entertain and play the part of a station commander's wife.
The children, meanwhile, were gifted an endless succession of
upstairs rooms, fabulous four-poster beds, a spiral staircase in a stone
tower, a 'mediaeval A-frame hall'[26] with a minstrel's gallery, wood-
panelled living rooms with low ceilings, a cavernous inglenook,
stone flagging, plus acres of overgrown garden spreading out from a
yew said to date from the Domesday Book. There was an active
ghost and, in one corner of the property, beyond a formal arrangement of box hedges, an old burial ground. Playing there, the children
dug up bones. Over the wrought-iron gates and protective walls lived
old Miss Pilkington, who babysat on occasion, and in whose garden
Jarman loved to roam. There was an actual farmer Giles with an
apple-laden loft, where wild bees buzzed in the stones: 'this attic of
honeyed memory'. Here too was a dressing-up box, crammed with
'bonnets [and] silky top hats [and] fragile crinolines'.[27]

Like the house on Lake Maggiore, Curry Mallet Manor had a
lasting impact on Jarman's imagination. It is no coincidence that the
period of English history most central to his aesthetic is the
Elizabethan age. In *The Angelic Conversation*, a section of which was
filmed in the nearby, and similarly Elizabethan, Montacute House,
one of the characters sits dreaming at a leaded window. It is easy to
imagine the ten-year-old Jarman doing likewise, listening to the
rooks, staring down at the box hedges and the spreading yew, utterly
under the spell of house and garden, dreaming himself a million
miles from the twentieth-century horrors of Hordle House.

Sadly, the spell was soon broken. In September 1952, after a mere
nine months in Curry Mallet Manor, Lance was dispatched to the

Royal Pakistan Air Force Headquarters as chief of staff, a posting at the level of air commodore, where he was responsible, among other things, for converting the RPAF to a jet force before it was transferred to local command. At the end of the year Betts, left by Lance to cope alone with packing up the house, sailed with the children to join her husband in Karachi.

5

Pakistan

Although Jarman's trips to Pakistan to visit his parents affected and marked him less intensely – certainly less obviously – than his earlier sojourn in Italy, it would be wrong to dismiss their effect entirely. Witnessing at first hand the sometimes surreal spectacle of a once splendid colonial power glorying in its past and traditions even as it stepped from the stage gave the young Jarman a training in, and a taste for, pinpointing the pomposities and ironies of sovereignty that would never desert him – even if, as many observers maintain, he was not always the most political of animals.

On his first voyage east he was granted a never-to-be-forgotten glimpse of exotic Egypt, later a source of considerable fascination, both aesthetic and spiritual. Betts and the children went ashore at Port Said, stepping from a ship suddenly 'a-bustle' with 'conjuring guly-guly men' who could produce 'live chicks out of eggs',[1] or tear banknotes in half before restoring them. Back on board ship, as the children placed bets on the probable colour of the Red Sea, they emerged from the Suez Canal 'into a beautiful rosy sunset mirrored in the calmest sea' Jarman had ever seen. He 'had pillaged the Christmas tree for silver balls when it was taken down', and he now 'tied one on a piece of cotton and gently lowered it over the side of the liner where it bounced along in the wake. A tiny, glittering spark in the sunset.'[2]

The kaleidoscope of experience offered by the ship's journey – a stormy Bay of Biscay, vibrant Port Said, a truly Red Sea – was repeated, albeit in a different guise, in Pakistan. A bleakly functional army camp in the Sindh Desert, 'a wasteland of dry stone gullies and thorn scrub',[3] gave way to a gracious dwelling in the centre of Karachi. Surrounded by verandahs and lush garden, there were punkahs in every room and a small army of immaculately uniformed servants. 'You woke up in the morning,' Jarman wrote, 'to find your clothes neatly folded, the toothpaste already on the toothbrush, and breakfast laid.'

This 'subcontinental suburbia' was not a milieu in which the boy felt comfortable. After a 'tea party of obnoxious, precocious eleven-year-olds . . . given by the sons of the prime minister and the grandsons of Jinnah, the founder of Pakistan . . . [where a] bearer stood behind every second spoilt child',[4] he threw a tantrum and flatly refused to attend another such event. Preferring small things ('butterflies, my fish tank') to the larger picture, what he valued about Pakistan was the chance to have his mother almost entirely to himself, with a minimum of militaristic intervention on the part of his largely absent father – and it was perhaps in protest at the values and strictures of his father's world that he reacted as he did to the stifling hierarchies and petty hypocrisies of colonial society.

The remainder of his time at prep school – during which, because of Pakistan, he was invariably without the comfort of his mother – forms a series of tableaux, some dazzling, some troubling, whereby the now adolescent boy was instructed in the puzzling, often frightening, ways of the adult world. In the summer of 1953 came the arrest of Lord Montagu of Beaulieu, accused with a friend of indecent assault on a pair of boy scouts in a beach hut on the peer's estate. The New Forest was suddenly home to something less innocent than cherries and the pursuit of butterflies. Jarman, who was familiar with the Montagu seat because a friend lived in its shadow, began to look 'with excitement tinged with fear at the walls of the wicked palace'.[5] Although terrified of the way his inner life was developing, secretly he wished it had been him, not the boy scouts, who had been in that hut on the beach at Milford.

He had graduated to a senior dormitory where the air was awash with testosterone and it was customary to be introduced to the 'facts of life' by the other seniors.

> After lights out, the boys jerked off in a competition to see who could come first – it makes you blind and saps the moral fibre and did you know it can make you grow hair on the palms of your hands?
>
> Already the dormitory was divided into three groups: those who would report you – future guardians of morality; those who enjoyed themselves – myself; and the rest, frightened by their own come, and probably destined for the cloth.[6]

The above was written towards the end of Jarman's life, when it was a point of honour with him to be defiantly positive about his sexuality. As an adolescent he was cruelly torn between desires which, on the one hand, felt quite natural and, on the other, he was told were abhorrent. Ever since he had been discovered by the headmaster's wife in the bed of another boy, sex had posed problems; nor did it sit easily with him that dormitory masturbation and exhibitionism were acceptable purely because they 'only involved yourself'.[7] Jarman's instinct was for a partner, though if he was to indulge this instinct he needed the hedgerow leading down to the cliffs, where he had discovered a 'secret garden' of purple violets – and where, as he writes in *Modern Nature*: 'I brought him, sworn to secrecy, and then watched him slip out of his grey flannel suit and lie naked in the spring sunshine. Here our hands first touched; then I pulled down my trousers and lay beside him. Bliss that he turned and lay naked on his stomach, laughing as my hand ran down his back and disappeared in the warm darkness between his thighs. He called it "the lovely feeling" and returned the next day, inviting me into his bed that night.' Later still the two of them would lie in their secret burrow and plan to dig 'to the other side of the world, far away from the bullying sports masters and the bells that marked out our lessons'.[8] As far, in fact, as fantasy could take them – maybe already had, for there is more than a touch of wish-fulfilment in the lyricism of these Arcadian trysts.

His contemporaries termed it 'queering'. For Jarman, there was as yet no language to describe his complex emotions, nor to bridge the gap between Lord Montagu's 'offence' and 'the lovely feeling'; between his desire for intimacy and the need to keep one's masturbation both solitary *and* public. It was a dichotomy which would shape the development of his entire sexual and emotional life.

With his parents in Pakistan, sources of adult solace were few and far between. Normally his beloved grandmother would have been on hand to protect him, but during 1953 she suffered a series of distressing strokes which led to her death that November. Jarman's sense of desolation was profound. Not only had Moselle always adored her Dekky, she had also been able to withstand the fierceness of his father in a way his mother never could. Her tiny flat, with its store of treasured ornaments, had been his truest 'home', as much of a sanctuary and an Aladdin's cave as Ciano's flat in the Via Paisiello.

Almost all the key figures in Jarman's early life were female, strong influences who provided him with a measure of protection from his father, with whom, of course, he could never identify as closely as he undoubtedly wished. As an adult, Jarman tended to look on women not as equals, but as angels and protectors, or as a source of flamboyance. He would set them apart on a pedestal, where they could be worshipped; or, by the same token, subtly ignored. In his attitude to women, reverence and an unconscious misogyny combine. Its genesis can be traced to these early years.

Until she emigrated to South Africa in 1954, it frequently fell to Jarman's Aunt Moyra to meet him off the school train at the end of term, see him on to the plane for Pakistan, even to put him up for the holiday. A second, less welcome surrogate home was Langlands, residence of the Aunties Orr. Though charming and, in essence, gentle souls, to a boy forced against his will to holiday with them, the elderly, birdlike sisters with their 'high Victorian morality' loomed as large, as austere and forbidding as the 'enormous gloomy pile' that was their house. Later, Jarman impishly dubbed Langlands 'Castle of the Sleeping Princesses'.[9] Then, he simply dreaded staying there.

A less terrifying, though no less eccentric figure was his Great-Aunt Doris. Exoticism personified, she was one of the first people in Jarman's life to provide him with a role model for the flaunting of convention. When Moselle had married Harry, she settled for a life of convention. By contrast, the ample, adventurous, artistic and entrepreneurial Doris sailed through life like a battleship, alienating family with her constant demands for money and hatching ever wilder schemes to improve her lot. She was reputedly the first woman to play polo in India and would later offer herself to the Russians as an astronaut for Sputnik. She also, as just one of a line of 'inventions' ranging from a folding coathanger to a pudding recipe, came up with the idea of manufacturing artificially perfumed rubber roses, the first bouquet of which she presented to Queen Mary in order to gain the seal of royal approval. The stories about Doris are legion, and Jarman relished them all.

One escapade that caused particular trouble was the Dorchester episode. Doris's son Ian, who was engaged to the daughter of the Guatemalan ambassador, was having difficulty finding somewhere appropriate for a New Year's Eve dinner. Everywhere was fully booked. Having unsuccessfully tried the Dorchester once, Ian rang the hotel again, this time pretending to be secretary to a maharajah. Miraculously, the hotel now had a table. Ian attired himself in an elaborate brocade jacket and used a tablecloth as a turban; Doris likewise improvised a sari. Because royalty do not carry money, it fell to Moyra to join the deceit and return to the hotel a few days later to settle the bill. The Dorchester inquired solicitously after their recent and honoured guests who, in the meantime, had decided to fund their meal by selling their story to a national newspaper. It made the front page. Moselle was scandalised, and did her utmost to distance her family from her unprincipled sister.

Moselle could not, however, prevent all meetings, and Doris was able to slip her starstruck great-nephew a vast silver handbag which, she claimed, had been given to her by Queen Mary at the Delhi Durbar. It was a gift Jarman particularly treasured. He kept it for years and later used it as a prop in several of his films.[10]

The boy's final, and favourite, surrogate home was in Kilve, a scattered and peaceful village on the Somerset coast, where he used to stay as the guest of John Kennedy, a contemporary at Hordle. Jarman would later remember these holidays as 'the happiest part'[11] of his childhood. '*Oklahoma* on the gramophone, blue cotton dresses with polka dots, maidenhair ferns watered with cold tea, a cat and a boxer puppy, bulb catalogues, scented balsam poplars, a vegetable garden.'[12] Kennedy's mother Isobel shared Jarman's keenness for things horticultural, antique and artistic, giving the boy much-needed encouragement in these pursuits. Concentrating fiercely, his mouth opening and shutting unconsciously, Jarman would pore over any art book he could lay his hands on, or over Isobel's collection of old Russian coins; he visited churches and studied the wording on the tombstones; he went for long walks along the deserted and boulder-strewn beach, where he would construct 'driftwood sculptures for the incoming tide to sweep away'.[13] Returning, he would enthuse about the sunset over Bridgwater Bay, or the view towards the Quantock Hills – in time the subject of his first landscape paintings. He honed his considerable talents as a storyteller, never allowing too much attention to truth to undermine a good narrative. He indulged his passion for dressing up, swathing himself in Isobel's clothes and winding old bedspreads into elaborate turbans decorated with Isobel's jewellery.

Yet even in secluded Kilve, male disapproval could and did intrude upon the idyll. John Kennedy found all this 'theatrical behaviour' so hard to cope with that in the end he lost patience and gave his supposed friend a black eye.

In 1954, as his time at Hordle drew to a close, Jarman was made a sub-prefect. This somewhat surprising recognition of his qualities – whether they were of leadership or force of personality is not recorded – was not echoed in his school reports. His drawing, although criticised for being 'slapdash' or 'too easily satisfied', usually drew praise, as did his dancing, writing and history. But his maths, divinity and French were simply weak. The general comment was that he did not have 'a sufficiently robust attitude to his work'.

That summer Jarman and his sister flew to Pakistan for the last time. While Lance sailed, the children passed lazy days swimming in Karachi Harbour and evenings 'on the beach at Bilagi, where the turtles lumbered out of the phosphorescent surf to lay improbable numbers of ping-pong eggs in the sand'.[14] In August Lance took the family on a tour of north Pakistan in a De Havilland Dove. They stayed in Peshawar, as guests of the governor of the north-west frontier province, from where they made a trip up the Khyber to the Afghan border. Ever the transgressor, and keen to have a suitably thrilling tale to tell at school, Jarman stepped over the white line on the road. 'As I did so,' he later recalled, 'a sentry came smartly to attention [and] my mother screamed, thinking I was going to be shot and bayoneted.' There followed a memorable picnic with the governor

> on the banks of the river Jhelum. There were three lorries, one of them fortified, with troops in it, followed by two others and a fleet of cars. When we got to the picnic spot . . . all the troops deployed out of the first lorry and set up discreet machine gun posts around us. Out of the second lorry came the entire living room furniture – carpets, chairs, sofa and tables, and they were all set up, just as they had been in the living room . . . Out of the third lorry came all the bearers with their gold hats, and they served a meal with several courses. It was . . . an almost surreal experience.[15]

On 17 January 1955, Lance was posted back to England as a staff member on the Ministry of Defence Research Policy Committee in Whitehall. He and Betts returned to Northwood, where the headquarters of Coastal Command, with which the air commodore would be closely associated, were based. Meanwhile, Jarman junior faced a posting of his own. After suffering such an acute attack of nerves when sitting his Common Entrance that he did not achieve the necessary grades for Radley, where Lance had hoped to send him, Hordle's close links with nearby Canford, which imposed less rigorous standards, were called into play, and it was to Canford that Jarman was sent, with a valedictory report from Hordle to say how much they would miss him. In return Jarman gave the school a parting gift that clearly spelled out what he had most valued in his time there: a number of rose bushes, used by Hordle to start a rose garden in the walled area by the chapel where, over the years, he had so assiduously tended his own small plot.

6

A Subtle Terror Rules

The house assigned to Lance and Betts on their return to Northwood was still in the process of being built, which meant that for the first few months they had to lodge with Betts' brother Teddy and his wife Pegs. If the wait in any way whetted their appetites for their new home, they were in for a disappointment. The house was as dreary and unprepossessing as all the patch's other brick-built, two-storey residences, all standing to predictable architectural attention in row upon neat row, all filled with identical furniture: the single settee and two armchairs, the oak table, the regulation glasses, cutlery and brown lino.

Although Lance's work was not without importance or excitement – in April 1955 he was in Nevada as 'official observer at eight atomic explosions at Yucca Flats . . . including the atomic explosion to trigger the Hydrogen bomb'[1] – he seldom flew any more and being deskbound did not suit his temperament. With only the fierce weekend sailing of his Firefly on the Welsh Harp, the Neasden lake that was the nearest strip of water, to compensate, he began to close in on himself, building such a high fence around the new house – a virtual palisade – that he earned himself the nickname 'Davy Crockett'.

As a housewife, and someone who had never been a fan of Northwood, Betts was even more cruelly affected by the move, which must have felt like a repeat of her childhood return from colourful Calcutta to the relative impoverishment of Manor Cottage and 10 Chester Place. Acquaintances noticed that, despite her sunny disposition, like her husband, she kept herself pretty much to herself.

The main beneficiaries of the move were Derek and Gaye. After years of rootlessness, they once again had a ready-made community of children with whom to play, and – most important, this, certainly for Jarman – there was the added attraction of a garden. Taking his inspiration jointly from Miss Pilkington of Curry Mallet, who had had an *Aloe variegata* on her windowsill, and the final chapter of *Beautiful Flowers and How to Grow Them*, Jarman was soon turning his back on the lobelias and pansies of early childhood and using the unpromisingly clay-like Northwood soil for the cultivation of a new, more grown-up obsession: cacti.

In equally grown-up fashion, he was packing his trunk with a new set of uniforms and boarding the train for Canford.

Situated some five miles inland from Poole, surrounded by what had originally been three extensive deer parks and flanked by the River Stour, Canford Hall – home of the school since its foundation in 1923 – had grown up over many years. At its core was the mediaeval John of Gaunt's building, part of the manor house of Thomas de Monteacute, Earl of Salisbury. Buttressing this were various substantial Victorian additions: some by Edward Blore, architect of Buckingham Palace, others by Charles Barry, who turned his attention from designing the Houses of Parliament to adding, among other flourishes, a most impressive tower.

Opinions on the architecture of Canford Hall vary considerably. For Pevsner, the tower is 'is one of the best things Barry ever designed'.[2] Jarman, a future pupil of Pevsner's, is less flattering: 'a mad jumble of ambition and folly, with ornate ceremonial staircases, smoking rooms, billiard rooms, panelled and painted in the Assyrian, Roman, Tudorbethan, Gothic and Modern styles. And the heart of the building, deep in the kitchen: rows and rows of bells, still numbered and named.'[3]

As a school, Canford had had something of a chequered history. In the thirties, under the relaxed headmastership of the Reverend C.B. Canning, it had been regarded as little more than a dumping ground for the Common Entrance rejects of other, more illustrious institutions. Known as 'Canning's Country Club', its principal recommendation had been the quality of its horse riding. After the war, a new headmaster made a determined effort to raise standards. John Hardie was a formidable figure – the boys nicknamed him Yahweh – who entered the school in a gruelling race to better itself.

Within this driven and cocooned environment, Jarman had the misfortune to find himself in Monteacute House. One of the lowliest of seven houses, Monteacute had no distinct territory of its own. It shared the Beaufort building, built around the time of the school's foundation, with the house of that name, then spilled over into some of the less prized parts of the main building. The housemaster was Tony Shorland-Ball, a sporting fanatic who placed as much importance on the weekly manoeuvres of the Combined Cadet Force (CCF) as he did on his classes. Shorland-Ball believed it was only on the playing field that his house could hope to gain parity with its competitors. If Canford as a whole was poorly suited to someone of Jarman's character and sensibilities, Monteacute was the proverbial straw that could be expected to break the camel's back.

The importance of hierarchy – and of unquestioning obedience – was enshrined in every sphere of school life. On arrival you were given a number, which then went up or down depending on your behaviour and achievements. As a form of initiation, you had to learn by heart the school's blue book, which listed all 400 boys and their various offices. If you were in the junior common room, you did not dare lift your eyes as you walked past the senior common room and glance inside; if you did, and were observed, you faced swift and terrible retribution. The surrounding park, dotted with huge and magnificent trees, had been left to grow wild and would have been a marvellous place in which to roam – except that it was out of bounds. Bells rang constantly to announce lessons, chapel, inspections and interminable afternoons of obligatory, interhouse sport: rugby, cricket, hockey, rowing, or cross-country runs across the bleak expanse of Canford Heath.

If lowly, you were a 'dreg' or a 'skivvie'. You fagged for the prefects (or, in Canford parlance, 'curated' for the 'pigs'). This involved polishing their shoes, cleaning their studies, or 'lodges', and washing up after their endless fry-ups in the stone sink next to the 'grubber', or tuck shop, where there was scant hot water and the wind always seemed at its keenest. Every day after house prayers there was an inspection in the senior common room. The juniors would file past under the eagle eyes of the house prefects and other seniors. If there was so much as a speck of dust on your shoes it meant scrubbing and polishing the long oak tables in the senior common room, or cleaning the windows and buffing their brass fittings. More serious offences would merit the cane, or the 'dap', a cut-down plimsoll with a knife handle strapped inside it to give it added resilience.

All of which was fuelled, as at Hordle, on insufficient food. You ate by house at long tables in the august surroundings of the main hall. The meal was served to each table on a tray, and unless you were close to it, or suitably agile, you seldom received your fair share. It was a culinary jungle. Only the fittest survived. It is little wonder that as an adult Jarman never showed much interest in food, always regarding it as something to be bolted simply in order to keep the body functioning. 'I still gulp it quickly,' he would write later, 'as a penance.'[4]

Predictably, Jarman's junior years at Canford were fairly miserable. He was given an IQ test on arrival and scored a dismal 95,[5] with the result that ever afterwards, Shorland-Ball regarded him as educationally subnormal. Nor did he excel at sport. He rowed and played passable games of tennis and hockey, but in general he was 'hopeless at all the communal activities, particularly ball games'.[6] And when it came to the CCF on Wednesday afternoons, he was more of a misfit than ever: his kit was invariably untidy, his awkwardness on the parade ground a sight to behold.

The eccentricity of his physical movements, in particular the way he would flap his arms and jump about when excited, soon became the cause of widespread teasing. The other boys loved to deride the fact that he was not a fighter, that he talked with such unnatural enthusiasm about his garden at home, that even his colouring was odd. He was an exceptionally swarthy child, and before long, amid fevered speculation as to whether Betts was Anglo-Indian, he was given the nickname 'Wog'.

As an adult, Jarman described Canford with a hatred made potent by the years. 'The school is bleak and soulless, dominated by bells, prayers, bullying, and everything that brings a chill; a huge shadow cast over life, distilled into a distressing muscular Christianity . . . A subtle terror rules, thoughtfully preparing us for the outside world. I feel threatened, isolated and friendless . . .'[7] In an aside, he added that he went so far as to contemplate suicide. 'I plan to do this by jumping in the Stour.'[8] It was an environment he reacted against with an intensity that would mark his thinking for life: 'I can't abide the English system that has everyone queuing except those that have no need to – as they jumped it long ago. Nor can I abide the values of this repression, its false houses, marriages, families, the Church of England, sport, all the rotten paraphernalia, the anger fizzes on below the surface waiting to explode.'[9]

There can be no denying the passion of those words. Yet, as a thirteen-year-old, he seems to have borne his vicissitudes with remarkable fortitude, even cheerfulness. His reaction to his nickname provides an excellent example of how, when faced with the choice of being ashamed of his differences or of glorying in them, Jarman would instinctively follow the latter course. Of course he wished to be like his peers – why else the overwhelming desire to prove himself? – but after studying an old family photograph of his father's family, he decided his paternal aunts looked like Maoris and for a while went around boasting of Maori blood. His father 'was speechless, he was so shocked',[10] and soon put paid to this fanciful notion. Undeterred, Jarman promptly sought evidence of exoticism on his mother's side. It was not the darkness of Moselle's complexion that he fixed upon, but her Jewish surname. So excitedly would he hint at Jewish ancestry and talk about his colourful past that in later life more than one friend was convinced that his upbringing had been entirely Jewish.

Although home provided solace, the summer holidays did not. In July 1955, Lance represented the RAF in the Inter-Services Sailing Championships which took place at Seaview on the Isle of Wight, and was so seduced by the island town with its splendidly active

yacht club and sparkling views across the Solent that he returned a
few weeks later with the entire family for the whole of August. They
returned every August thereafter.

Less entranced than his father by charming but sleepy Seaview –
and certainly less enamoured of Lance's endless sailing – Jarman
later remembered these holidays thus:

> My sister and I dreaded those afternoons when he insisted we
> crew for him. The more the sea crashed over the bows, the
> happier he was. He always won the race, and if he didn't he
> blamed us, shouting, 'Not that way you bloody idiot!' . . . I
> did everything I could to be out of the way, making myself as
> scarce as possible, which increased his moodiness.
>   'Why do you think I brought you on this bloody holiday?
> To sit around and build sandcastles?' Everything about the
> yacht club was a humiliation: ghastly middle-aged men in
> shorts, their wives deserted on the verandah, making do.[11]

As the peacemaker, Betts would drive the children around the
island. They visited Blackgang Chine, then no more than a bramble-
covered fissure in the chalky cliffs where Jarman loved to hunt for
fossils. Or they might visit the island's antique shops, where an
equally feverish hunt was conducted for artifacts less ancient but
just as prized – the start for Jarman of a lifelong obsession with collecting old things.

Like Canford, Seaview had its hierarchies. You were either 'bay' or
'yacht club', 'bay' being preferable. If, like the Jarmans, you were
'yacht club' and only visited once a year, you were subtly made to feel
you did not belong. At home in Northwood, the isolation Jarman
was experiencing at school was again compounded, and again in the
subtlest of manners, by the fact that the 'patch' was so clearly at one
remove from the rest of the world, into which, if you wanted to
experience it, you had to make purposeful forays: cycling trips to
swim at the nearby reservoir, bus trips to Watford or going ice-
skating at Wembley.

At Northwood, a friendship was developing with a new next-
door neighbour: Dorothy (Dab) Bargh. Hopping from foot to foot,

Jarman would present himself at the Barghs' house immediately after breakfast to outline whatever project he had dreamed up for that day's amusement. Although his exaggerated, nervy physical tics could give the impression that he was uncomfortable in his own skin, and although his gentleness and sensitivity made him seem an unlikely ringleader, his sheer enthusiasm was so infectious it always carried others with him.

In the woods behind the patch, Jarman, Dab and Gaye constructed a camp out of grass and clay bricks which Jarman carefully measured and fashioned. No one was allowed in the camp except by invitation, though these were regularly issued to Betts and Mrs Bargh, who were treated to meals of beans and sausages cooked over a makeshift fire. The building of the camp, presumably because it was a suitably manly activity, marked the one occasion when Lance was seen actively to support his son. There were plans afoot to enlarge the headquarters of Coastal Command, and the children were told they would have to dismantle their refuge. They were devastated, Jarman especially. Lance stepped in to make sure that the destruction of the camp was left until everyone had returned to school.

Other activities would have found less favour. Mrs Bargh used to take the children into Watford to spend their pocket money at the market. Jarman would make a beeline for the make-up and, back at the Barghs' house, would paint his face and drape himself in whatever materials or clothes were to hand. Sensing that thus attired he would be less than ever the sort of son an air commodore craved, Mrs Bargh ensured that he did his dressing up in the safety of her spare bedroom and that his face was scrubbed clean by the time he returned home. This, it seemed to her, he was often reluctant to do.

Jarman was equally loath to return to Canford at the end of the summer holidays, as the letters he started to write to Dab in the autumn of 1955 demonstrate.

October. Dear Dab, Last sunday Mummy and Daddy came
down to take me out. I found two Rhododendron bushes wich
were about 6" high growing in a wood near here, and mummy
has planted [them] near the front door. I have been told that

the grass is coming up so we should have a bit of a lawn next holidays . . . I have tryed making some pottery, at the art school, but the kiln has broken down and none of the things we have made have been able to be fired. I have finished fagging for the next 3 weeks, so I have some free time for once. Nearly half the term has finished now thank heavens.

December. Dear Dab . . . I can't wait to get home, there is such a lot to see. I wonder if our brussel sprouts are ready for eating . . . let's hope this holidays are the best we have ever had.

A poem is attached to the letter:

GUESS WHO?

Dark of hair, with eyes so gay
Out of bed by nine each day
Round to the J's by ten o'clock
And showing Gaye a nice new frock
Then to our camp in woods so green
Here, with a fir the room she'll clean
You'll never guess of who I mean
Beside the pool she walked and ran
And joined in games of kit the can
Round O.M.Q.'s she used to play
Gradually drew on that fatal day
Herewith to school, and let us say
The Moral is Do not Despare
As we next hols will be back there
Believe in god and well you'll fare

March 1956. Dear Dab, I had a letter from Mummy today . . . They are making garages between the houses, and at the moment there are bulldozers ruining our lawns! The first of the crocuses we planted are coming out, and that bowl of bulbs I made with you, remember?, are all out . . . Only two more weeks – wonderful! I am reading a book by Buchan called 'Mr Standfast', it is very good. I have only got one more week of fagging now.

June. Dear Dab, On Wednesday, the school was given a whole holiday, and we were all allowed to go and see the royal counties show, which was about a mile from the school buildings . . . the exhibits were wonderful, and included things like forestry, bees, spinning, weaving, fire safety, hundreds of farming machines, cars, horse jumping, painting, and all sorts of kitchen gadgets. It was most interesting and I brought back about 30 different leaflets and books which were free.

July. Dear Dab . . . On the Sunday I took another boy out and we went to Corfe castle, a famous beauty spot near here and had lunch, after which we went to the Tillwhim caves, old smugglers caves near swanage. Please excuse the rough block paper, but some how I have more inspiration writing on it, than I do on normal paper. I have done quite a bit of swiming and guess what, I can dive, it all came about in a miraculous way, when we were all forced to dive in at the begining of a race!! I managed to dive in somehow and nearly drowned in the attempt! . . . I have done a bit of art in the last week or so but I just can't find any inspiration here, its so monotonous.

He ends this letter with a drawing, under which he adds, as a post-script: 'Can't you see I am a budding artist.'

Because Monteacute was pushed for space, in the middle common room a group of about fifteen boys would sleep in Moortown, Shorland-Ball's house at the far end of the school grounds. So that they could cycle to and from the main buildings, the boys were issued with numbered bicycles, the front mudguards of which were painted yellow, the house colour. After the summer holiday of 1956, Jarman moved into Moortown for a year.

October. Dear Dab . . . I think the song 'lay down your arms'[12] etc is quite good compared with one or two of the records you

hear here. Every time Rock 'n Roll goes on the air the whole
Common Room stages a riot . . . I wonder if we will be able to
get to a dance this hols, you beter help me brush up one or
two dances in case we can . . . incidentally, I don't like blonds
quite as blonde as M[arilyn] M[onroe]. Bridgette Bardot or
Glynis Johns for me! . . . The trees here are lovely, all reds
and yellows, it won't be long before the leaves fall now . . .
Happy Rock 'n Roll dreams.

November. Dear Dab . . . I have been following the papers
this week, have you? I think the reds should be beaten up a
bit and have a bit of their own stuff. Our collection today was
for the Hungarian relief funds. My bike has been out of
action for the past week after a smash up, in which I bust
several spokes.

Dear Dab, Thank you very much for the lovely confirmation
card. Mummy and Daddy came down for the service on
Saturday before lunch, the Bishop of Salisbury took it . . .
Mummy and Daddy gave me a beautiful pair of gold cuff links
with the school crest and colours on them . . . On Sunday I
was up early to go to communion in our chapel, Mummy and
Daddy came. After we had breakfast we went for a motor ride
till lunch, which we cooked over a charcoal fire on the heath
again, sausages chops ect. They had to go back at four, after
an early tea.

Dab, who was at a Quaker school, was considered somewhat 'fast':
the first person Gaye knew to wear false eyelashes and dye her hair.
Now she was suggesting that perhaps she and Jarman might become
romantically involved.

December. Dear Dab . . . I am writing this as you can
probably guess, under the red hot coals of 'CAT' the duty
prefect who is taking prep . . . Yesterday we had a whole day
exercise in corps on our heath, lugging rifles about that are
so antiquated (1910), that they won't fire anything, it was

boiling and most exhausting . . . I don't think Quaker and C. of E. would quite mix, there would be religious arguments ALL day.

January 1957. Dear Dab . . . What do you think of B. Haley's comet curl. I could follow that style, or what about Yul Brynner bristle style or Elvis the pelvis streamlined.

Dear Dab, Thank you very much for your letter. I will not forget Valentines day feb 14th.

His valentine was home-made, a letter written on heart-shaped paper:

Dear Dab, I am very sorry but the school have stopped selling Valentine cards this year, but I hope this is a permisable substitute! We are all most annoyed!!! . . . I didn't know that young ladies at an ancient, and honourable school, especially with a Quaker headmistress, wanted to go to a film like 'Baby Doll' . . . its the film all of us sex maniacs here want to see!

Though on one level these letters are quite ordinary, reading between the lines one glimpses the sombre reality underscoring the stoical schoolboy banter. At one point he writes airily that his bike 'is still going strong' in spite of 'ambushes, and two crooked wheels'. Later, as we have seen, he remarks, almost in passing, that the 'bike has been out of action for the past week after a smash up'. Ambushes between Moortown and the school were not infrequent and could be extremely serious. On at least one occasion, Jarman was the victim of a wire stretched across the path, causing him to fly over his handlebars. Then there was the small matter of sex. Only his oblique remark to Dab that their religious differences might make them incompatible alerts one to the fact that the role of heterosexual sex maniac and rock 'n' roll-loving Lothario was not one that came naturally to Jarman, however dutifully and convincingly he might have played it.

'It is a well worn myth,' Jarman wrote in an adult diary,

that boys in English public schools jump into bed with each other at the slightest provocation. If they did of course it might be one of the few things to say in favour of these deadly institutions. At Canford this never happened. The school was run like a concentration camp, an atmosphere which was not conducive to sex. Perhaps I was shy. Sex was the main topic of conversation but friendships remained platonic. This, as far as I know, was the rule, except for one unfortunate boy in my house . . . who had written a love letter to another boy, which had fallen into the authorities' hands. He disappeared mysteriously in a Stalinist-style purge, without even saying goodbye . . . At eighteen, when I left Canford, I was still a virgin with a secret I had been unable to share.[13]

There was no help or cure for this 'secret', not even from the 'well-thumbed expurgated copy of *Lady Chatterley* falling to pieces in our grubby hands',[14] nor the 'sex manual with lurid colour photographs' left in his bedroom by his parents and which he guiltily imagined must belong to one of his friends. He was 'so embarrassed' by this manual that 'I burnt it on a bonfire, as I thought my parents might stumble upon it'.[15] Least help of all was the Dickensian figure of Dr Matthews, sex educator extraordinaire, who regularly came to lecture the inmates of Canford. The doctor would rummage

in his battered Gladstone bag, pulling out ancient slides as if from a lucky dip at a gymkhana. Silver hair awry, eyes glistening, [he] eyed up his blushing audience who squirmed with embarrassment as their innermost secrets were revealed to them – huge images of private parts, 20ft pubescent and pre-pubescent cocks, balls dropping, huge lost sperms wandering into a slide rather than the fallopian . . . After it was all over the good doctor gave private sessions to any boy who thought he had a 'problem'; but I never went, knew my 'problem' was so encompassing it could never be solved by him, even if that had been my wish.[16]

It is telling that the word 'secret' should recur so regularly. Jarman hated secrets. The moment he was able, he turned the tables on Dr Matthews and his ilk by shouting his 'secret' from the rooftops. Yet despite his subsequent openness about his sexuality, there was one Canford incident of which he never wrote and hardly spoke. 'Wog' was not his only nickname. He had a clutch of others, more widely used, deriving from his house's fascination with, and envy of, a certain part of his anatomy: 'Snake', 'Snakeman' and 'Hose'. The incident in question involved him being cornered by a group of his contemporaries, held down, stripped, then brought to public orgasm by the stroking of a feather duster up and down the length of his legendary 'snake'.[17]

Yet the fact that Jarman never wrote openly or directly about this incident is an indication of the extent to which it may have traumatised and marked him. He writes about his experience at the hands of the headmaster's wife at Hordle. He writes about his sexual fantasies. He writes about Dr Matthews. He never writes about being pinned down by a group of hostile, probably curious boys and being brought to orgasm for their sport.

If we fast-forward to the mid-seventies and his first feature film, an account of the treatment of St Sebastian at the hands of a garrison of Roman soldiers in a far-flung outpost of the empire, we can read the saint's abasement and eventual martyrdom as a recreation of this adolescent torment. Were one to dress the Roman soldiers in the uniforms of Canford, their antics would have an all-too-familiar schoolboy ring. Scrolling on through Jarman's oeuvre, we would then encounter other echoes of sadomasochism, of what it is like to be in sexual thrall to those who overpower you.

It is not difficult to appreciate why Jarman should have considered suicide 'by jumping in the Stour'. That he did not – or that at the very least he did not run away – can be attributed to his natural optimism, a fear of what his father would have said and an ability, like his father's, to fly a steady path through the flak. That and the easily overlooked fact that for all its bleak, bell-dominated harshness, Canford did have a gentle side. In addition to the light relief provided by various societies, the school play, visiting speakers or the occasional film, the school set great store by music. There was an active school choir in which Jarman sang, and in Monteacute the Reverend Crowder, then house tutor, regularly invited boys into his study to listen to his collection of classical records. Most importantly of all for Jarman, at the far end of the school grounds, past the assembly hall and the armoury and immediately behind the fives court, there was the art shack, domain of a master whose ethos ran splendidly counter to much of what Canford stood for.

7

Every Man is a Special Kind of Artist

A spry figure with a distinctive goatee and a shock of unruly hair, Robin Noscoe had been in charge of art at Canford for some five years when Jarman arrived at the school. A silversmith, potter, furniture-maker, painter and keen student of architecture, Noscoe did not value one sphere of artistic activity over another, nor did he pretend that as the teacher he had all the answers. As humble as he was eclectic, he allowed his pupils to follow their own enthusiasms and carry him with them when appropriate. In his own words, he often found himself being 'pushed from behind' rather than 'leading by the nose'.

He was the proud owner of a vintage open-topped Rolls–Royce called Percy, which he had partly – and rather eccentrically – built himself. Hand on horn, Noscoe would bowl along the country lanes in Percy, broadening the aesthetic horizons of his charges by taking them to the Stanley Spencer Chapel at Burghclere, nearby Montacute House, Longleat, Oxford, Salisbury, or Bath. He also haunted the bombsites of Poole where, with the help of his pupils, he scavenged for doors, windows and floorboards to use in the house he was building for himself on the outskirts of nearby Wimborne Minster.

Noscoe's profound influence on Jarman is evidenced in almost every sphere of Jarman's work as an adult artist: in the fluid way in which he would move between disciplines – painting, collage, design, film; in his appreciation of things architectural; in his wide-ranging and improvisatory use of found objects; in his tendency to emphasise and favour the practical rather than the theoretical nature of art; in his instinctive questioning of authority; in the sheer, almost childish delight he took in his work. Usually, when discussing the major influences on Jarman's art, critics and historians cite William Morris, Nash, Rauschenberg, Schwitters, Warhol, to name but some of the most obvious. Noscoe predates them all.

Equally influential was the location of the shack where Noscoe ran his extracurricular classes. The adult Jarman would almost always operate on the fringe. As a painter he hardly ever exhibited in a West End gallery. As a film-maker he eschewed mainstream cinema. As a sexual being he embraced his position on the margins of conventional society. When, towards the end of his life, he came to buy his first house, he chose a cottage on an isolated shingle spit at the far end of Romney Marsh. In the context of Canford, the art shack was similarly at one remove from the centre of the school; a universe unto itself.

Standing on the furthest edge of the overgrown park, the shack was a ramshackle building, riddled with neglect. A brick base supported wooden slatted walls. There were extensive windows on three sides. The fourth wall backed on to the fives court, which supported the entire structure. Inside there was an 'old coke stove, broken and comfortable furniture, books and drawers full of postcards'.[1] Above the windows ran a frieze which read:

AN ARTIST IS NOT A SPECIAL KIND OF MAN,
BUT EVERY MAN IS A SPECIAL KIND OF ARTIST.

The words are Eric Gill's. They could have been Jarman's. Perhaps, by the end of his schooldays, he imagined they were. He certainly made the art shack his own, the very centre of his schoolboy life; an absolute 'defence against an everyday existence that was awry'.[2]

Jarman began visiting the shack in his first year, often in the company of Jonathan Ionides, then a constant companion. Although, as a new boy, he was still uncharacteristically and painfully shy – 'pale-faced, quiet and lost'[3] – and although it would be a while before he would make his mark in this new-found haven, after a mere two terms at Canford Shorland-Ball would grudgingly report: 'Rugger does not seem much up his street, but he has spent profitable hours in the Art Room.'

In the spring term of 1956, the art shack underwent an expansion. It acquired a pottery wheel, plus a lean-to shed to house it. Jarman took immediate advantage of this, moving Noscoe to report: 'some of his clay models are most lively and interesting'. He was also starting to paint, and to paint furiously: landscapes primarily, but also self-portraits and still lifes, works which were variously figurative, impressionistic, cubist, abstract, expressionistic. As flamboyantly colourful and energetic as their creator, and taking their inspiration from either the postcards of famous paintings in Noscoe's drawer or his own surroundings – seldom from his imagination – these early works were happily and undiscriminatingly eclectic, plundering every known artist as merrily as they plundered the different 'schools': Claude Lorrain, Van Gogh, Gauguin, Monet, Braque, Spencer, William Scott, Jackson Pollock. At times it could seem as if Jarman painted as a direct extension of his restless energy. He simply fixed a brush in his hand, and the way his arms flailed through the air when he was excited translated that energy on to the canvas.

Such was the fledgling painter's boundless enthusiasm that he managed to fall foul even of his easygoing teacher. The boys had instituted a competition to see who could cover the most canvases during the course of a single afternoon. Outperforming everyone, Jarman completed about fifteen. Noscoe was furious. To a man forced to run his art department on a mere £10 a term, this profligate use of materials was little short of scandalous.

Jarman was discovering that painting was not only an escape and a release, but a possible future. 'At around the age of twelve I became aware that painting was a real profession. I began to read romantic books about van Gogh and . . . I started to paint van Goghs and . . . tried to pass them off as my own.'[4] Signing himself 'Michael Jarman', he threw up a barrier of canvases to protect himself from the bulk of his contemporaries. Painting became his 'secret garden . . . an escape out of Heterosoc'.[5] He made a vow that he was 'never going to work with these tyrants and dead souls, who are to be the industrialists, politicians and "thinkers" that the headmaster is forming in this land of the living dead'.[6] It was a vow he kept: as an adult he never held down a conventional job.[7]

In time the art shack replaced its electric kiln with a more substantial, wood-fired model. When the new kiln needed to be fired, Noscoe would appoint a 'firing party', who would obtain overnight leave from the house in order to stay in the shack and keep the fire at the correct temperature by feeding it logs gathered from the grounds. While the rest of the school slept, the firing party would watch mesmerised as the logs burst into flames the instant they met the heat. They would talk, laugh, make endless rounds of toast and listen repeatedly to their handful of classical records.[8]

In the art shack and among the like-minded boys who congregated there, Jarman never seemed less than outgoing, confident, carefree, brimming with enthusiasm, immensely kind and sensitive to the feelings of others. Any sign of the profound unhappiness and reclusiveness he refers to in his own adult accounts of Canford is impossible to detect – unless one takes into account the obsessiveness of his involvement with painting to suggest a certain loneliness and feelings of inadequacy. Nevertheless, while accepting that 'Michael Jarman' might have been unstoppable, we must also acknowledge that Derek Jarman was more fragile, and view the remainder of his time at Canford in a double light. Every moment, however positive, is shadowed by a potential negative. The coin has two sides.

As a junior, he had struggled under the stigma of his dismal IQ. Although unfailingly polite and co-operative, and reasonably proficient in history and geography, all his other subjects (maths in particular) left much to be desired, as did his powers of concentration. It was only by means of fierce study that he managed to pass his O-Levels. As Shorland-Ball never tired of reminding him, his academic future looked far from bright. Until, that is, the Monteacute house tutor rode gloriously to his rescue.

Andrew Davis was much younger than Robin Noscoe, but no less eccentric and self-assured. Brimming with enthusiasm for his subject, which was English, he had 'an easy ironic humour'[9] and a passion both for painting and the collecting of rare books. He also had the knack of fostering the talents of those in whom he believed.

In Davis's sixth form tutorial group, Jarman wrote an essay on Cleopatra as the Egyptian goddess Isis which so impressed Davis that he singled it out for particular praise, kindling in Jarman the confidence in class he had hitherto lacked. It was a turning point. The essays and assignments that now flowed from Jarman's already distinctive hand were suddenly tackled with an enthusiasm once reserved solely for painting.

Painting, meanwhile, was itself beginning to earn him accolades. In 1958, the school's Art Cup was won by Monteacute, *The Canfordian* recording: 'Monteacute has had a steadily developing painting tradition for several years now, and has occupied a definite "corner" in the pottery department. Geddes . . . and Miller, D.A. . . . are the leaders of this band. Campbell, D.N. and Jarman were prolific in their painting.' Jarman's report adds: 'He has been a most prolific painter this term, with a lively and vigorous style with oil paints.'

A year later, Jarman won the Canning Prize for painting. *The Canfordian* was again approving. It loved his 'exuberant handling of oils (with an original abstraction of a tawny self-portrait to vary the florid view)', and added sagely that his best work showed 'just enough restraint to avoid restless verticals'. That winter, the magazine further complimented the work emanating from the art shack, which, it said, 'particularly under the Monteacute "Fauvists", ranges from "Realism" to "Cubism", "Tachism", "Impressionism" and many other "isms" of art. Jarman is one of the more adaptable painters.' Noscoe agreed: 'His work is developing very well indeed. He is still full of vigorous and experimental ideas, and in every painting he sets out to tackle something new. His drawing is bold and lively.' The only caveat: '[He] needs more careful observation from life.'

Jarman's work was included in a joint exhibition of local schools.[10] It even attracted buyers. In 1959 he used the proceeds of his first sale[11] to purchase a copy of Frank Elgar's biography of Van Gogh. More sales followed: to parents, teachers, even to 'Yahweh' Hardie himself. The budding Van Gogh started to keep a black notebook in which he made proud and careful note of each and every transaction.

Yet there remained two figures whose approval he felt he had not obtained; two figures whose approval was crucial. Even as *The Canfordian* lavished praise on him, Shorland-Ball was writing: 'Having more than a touch of the artistic temperament, he does not find it easy to exercise authority or to enforce orderly habits on others . . . the old criticism still remains, that he will work at what interests him, but cannot be bothered with what does not.'

This 'old criticism' has the ring of truth. Throughout his life, Jarman would work only at what interested him and then only for as long as his interest lasted. He darted from project to project, from enthusiasm to enthusiasm, often with dizzying speed. Still, that did not make the 'old criticism' any the more palatable, for Shorland-Ball's comments went hand in hand with what Jarman perceived as an equal lack of support from his father.

In later life, Jarman was able to understand his father's complex personality, realising that while Lance took 'immense pride in the fact that he was seeing me through a public school . . . his attitude was strangely mixed; as a New Zealander who had worked his passage to England he could at times scarcely conceal his dislike for a system in which he was an outsider'.[12] At the time, however, all the boy saw was that whereas paternal criticism was frequent, paternal praise was virtually non-existent.

A case in point is Jarman's involvement in the CCF. As a senior, he had graduated from the general corps to the RAF section, which he could only have chosen over the navy or army sections in order to please his father. It was certainly not out of interest. A friend once witnessed him instructing a group in field work. They were in the park and, instead of the required drill, Jarman was teaching his group the Latin names of all the trees. Then came the day when he was actually singled out for commendation. Was Lance pleased? Possibly, but he never said a word. Jarman confided despairingly to a friend: 'I've just realised. My father is exactly like Shorland-Ball. It's terrible.'

He fought back in two distinct ways. First, by subtly adjusting history, he blew his own trumpet louder than an entire battalion of fathers. For instance, although his individual talents were never in question, the art shack's pre-eminence was not due only to him. He was very much part of a group that included, among others, his friends David Miller, who sculpted, Dugald Campbell, whose speciality was architectural drawing, and Robin McIver, a potter nicknamed 'Earthy'. Yet in his journals and elsewhere Jarman writes about winning the Art Cup for Monteacute as if he alone were responsible. He would even say that until he won the cup, Monteacute's trophy cupboard had always stood empty – not the case at all.

Secondly, he withdrew as comprehensively as was possible from any area of activity favoured by his father or Shorland-Ball. On holiday in Kilve with John Kennedy, he had happily begun learning to drive Isobel's car in the fields above the cliffs leading down to the beach. He had also flown dual-training Chipmunks with his father. In late 1957, in a Dakota, the two of them had even flown as far as Gibraltar, with Jarman 'in the cockpit most of the way with my hands on the controls'.[13] Now he decided he should never again even drive a car, let alone fly a plane, a resolution he stuck to. Faced with the incontrovertibility of his father's expertise in the area of things mechanical, he sought to establish his own identity by eschewing such expertise. He began to take perverse pride in his technical incompetence. Even as an adult film-maker, and a technically innovative one at that, he would never come wholly to grips with the intricacies of the camera. He preferred to let others worry about such mechanical niceties.

The same held true for television which, in Jarman's view, almost always

> reinforced the tyranny of the family as a parent usually
> controlled the switch. In our house the weather forecast grew
> like a demon god – absolute silence and concentration was
> demanded by my father as the announcer pushed the sun and
> clouds over a map of England, pronouncing weather fair or
> foul like an oracle of the gods.[14]

Coming to believe that this new medium had replaced the hearth where the household gods, the fire and the family stories should reside,

Jarman decided that he would never watch television again and made
the reinstatement of that hearth one of his prime objectives.

Yet Jarman's desire to proclaim his independence from the mili-
tarism of Lance and Shorland-Ball did not preclude an equal and
entirely natural need to run with the crowd, to be 'one of the boys'.

On the trip to Gibraltar he had been billeted with a group of
young men doing their national service. It was a mesmerising and
troubling experience. Fascinated by sleeping with the young men, he
persuaded his father to 'leave me behind for a few extra days when he
returned to England. I ate in the seamen's mission, swam all day at
Nelson's Cove and returned in the evening to the barracks to listen
to their stories and fantasies about their girlfriends.'[15] The uniformed
figure of the swaggering soldier would feature often in Jarman's films,
and to highly charged erotic effect.

Jarman and his sister Gaye also formed part of a teenage group
that twice went skiing in Austria over the Christmas holidays.
Jarman never stood aloof from the activities of the group. He danced
with the others on the train to and from Austria, proved himself a
proficient skier, sampled his fair share of schnapps and certainly did
not complain when, wearing only her nightie, one of the girls
appeared in the doorway of the boys' room to spend five minutes in
each of their beds before crying, 'Your time's up,' and moving on to
the next one. In other school holidays at Northwood he consoli-
dated the friendships he had made at Canford by inviting his cronies
home and throwing himself wholeheartedly into their joint games
and projects.

Changes were afoot at Northwood, some welcome, some not.
Betts' health was showing signs of deterioration. She had already
developed the pronounced tremble in her hands that would plague
her for the rest of her life. After an alarming episode of unexpected
and extensive haemorrhaging, she was forced to undergo a hysterec-
tomy. That Lance adored his wife was never in question; yet not
once did he let her illness interfere with his weekends – currently
spent sailing on the Welsh Harp with a new-found crew member, a
young German woman called Yana Spence, whose ubiquity provoked a degree of fascinated (and unwarranted) speculation from the
children. Betts made equal light of her problems. In February 1957,

writing to Dab Bargh, whose family had moved away from Northwood, Jarman remarked: 'Mummy is at Halton hospital for 5 days having a check up, which I think she enjoys as it means no housework, and a nice warm ward.' One suspects the soothing words belonged as much to Betts as they did to her son.

Less worryingly, in March 1957 Lance was transferred from the Ministry of Defence to the Northwood headquarters of Coastal Command, his final posting. Thinking he would stand a better chance of finding civilian employment at forty-nine than at fifty, he applied for early retirement from the RAF and, in July 1958, became administrative director of the Engineering Industries Association, a body charged with safeguarding the interests of engineering firms up and down the country. With the new job came a London office and a new identity, that of city gent, with its corresponding uniform: sober suit, bowler hat, black umbrella. There was also a new house: the first the family could truly call its own.

Throughout the fifties Northwood's large old houses with their rambling gardens were being demolished to make way for clusters of small, modern closes. What had once been an indisputable village, surrounded by fields, was being slowly subsumed by Metroland. Submitting to the march of time, Lance bought a plot of land in an old apple orchard at 42 Murray Road and on it built his dream home: an aggressively modern, two-storey house set sideways to the road and well back from it at the top of a steep drive. About the only nod towards Northwood's past were 'Phil' and 'Vi', two rose bushes which Betts planted by the front door and named for the Aunties Orr. Inside, the downstairs area was open-plan. Upstairs were four small bedrooms. There was also a newfangled system of air-ducted central heating which never quite worked properly. The name Lance chose for his new house was another nod at the past: Merryfield, scene of his happiest posting. Though in comparing the Elizabethan splendour of the manor at Curry Mallet with the bleak and unrelenting modernity of Merryfield, furnished as it was almost solely by reproduction pieces from Maples, it is poignant to note how little resemblance the old bore to the new.

Despite all this and the combination of Lance's fierceness and Betts' mania for tidiness, which could, on occasion, make the atmosphere in the house slightly edgy, in the main Merryfield meant only welcome. Jarman's schoolfriends from Canford would frequently visit, along with new local friends. Principal among these were Penny Jenkins, whose parents had met the Jarmans in Pakistan; Una Gray, who lived across the road and had watched Merryfield being built; Ann and John Colligan; Diana Edmunds, whose parents ran the True Lovers' Knot, a local pub; and the somewhat mysterious Barry, whom Gaye and her friend Caroline Green gigglingly thought might be a gigolo.

At school, Shorland-Ball would lament of Jarman: 'He gets on with things in his own quiet way, following his interests and making the most of his talents; not a leader, at present anyhow.'[16] In Northwood, the opposite held true. Here Jarman was anything but quiet and very much the leader: spirited Pied Piper to the rest of the gang. He it was who invariably initiated their expeditions: swimming, ice-skating, going to the cinema or the Proms, combing the junk shops of Watford, or, at Christmas, serenading the local residents with a selection of carols. In summer, the gang would gather under the apple trees in what remained of the old orchard or, when the weather was poor, troop indoors and up the stairs to the privacy of Jarman's room, where they would flop on to the bed or squeeze around the heavy mahogany and brass reading chair – which, to his parents' horror, he had picked up in a junk shop for 25 shillings – talking and listening to classical music. Poor Gaye: she would have preferred to listen to Elvis, but it was her brother who set the musical agenda.

Across the orchard from Merryfield lived a childless couple, Donald and Güta Minton. They soon befriended Jarman and offered him the use of their attic in which to paint. They were an interesting couple. Donald was clerk of convocation at the University of London. Güta had fenced for England in the 1936 Olympics. Their large Edwardian house, set in a fine and well-tended garden, was full of beauty, for Güta was descended, or so she said, from the mistress of a Danish king and had inherited a stunning collection of late eighteenth- and early nineteenth-century furniture, most of it made in Paris. Here was beauty and sanctuary combined; and to it Jarman had his very own key, given him by Güta so that he could come and go as he pleased. Throughout his final years at school and well into his time at university, whenever possible he would dart to the attic, where – with paints bought at Brodie & Middleton in Long Acre, with canvas upon canvas stacked against the wall, and with some suitably inspiring classical music playing in the background – he would paint as feverishly as he painted at the art shack.[17]

Part of the reason for Jarman's feverishness might have been the fact that, as he ventured more deeply into the 'secret garden' of painting, he came to realise that the garden contained as many challenges as it did answers. As he would later say: 'About the age of fifteen I began to realise that as a painter I was actually in competition with the past and that I had to discover myself. This was a problem. The older I got the more I realised that everyone was becoming individuals and that I was only joining the masses.'[18] Intriguingly, it was a dilemma to which his eventual solution was already being hinted at in an article written at around this time by the painter John Minton: 'Painting is outdated, like the horse and cart. Modern art is getting nowhere. Traditional art – it's all been done before. The cinema, the theatre, possibly television, are the mediums in which painters must express themselves.'[19]

This notwithstanding, it was towards a confrontation with the issue of discovering himself as a painter that Jarman was heading. He had decided he wanted to study art and, largely because William Coldstream, then head of the Slade, had once been a visiting teacher at Canford, the Slade seemed the obvious, if not the only place to which to apply. Jarman's referees were Tony Shorland-Ball and Andrew Davis. Their recommendations, and those of the headmaster, were seconded by a fulsome letter from Robin Noscoe: 'He is the most prolific artist I have ever known here, full of enthusiasm and energy and never at a loss for ideas and for new things, and ways that he wants to paint.'[20] In February 1960, the Slade responded with the offer of a place for the October of that year.

Lance, meanwhile, was adamant that Jarman should attend university. In March 1959, he had written to Shorland-Ball suggesting Oxbridge. Shorland-Ball repeated his old refrain: Jarman was not of scholarship standard. Undaunted, Jarman applied to King's College, London, where, as by the Slade, he was readily accepted. Climbing the stairs to Shorland-Ball's forbidding study to inform him of this wondrous fact was one of the high points of Jarman's life at Canford.

A choice had to be made. Jarman struck a bargain with his father. He would attend King's on condition that, as long as he got a degree, Lance would then put him through the Slade. In later life, Jarman would sometimes resentfully imply that he was 'forced' into making this bargain by a father who did not understand his needs. This is far from certain. Not unreasonably, Lance argued that, without any other qualifications, Jarman might experience difficulty supporting himself as an artist. Andrew Davis was in complete agreement, and thought at the time that what Lance was offering was extremely generous. As others would observe, Lance might not have known how best to express it, but he *was* proud of his son and, in his own way, even supportive.

The Slade confirmed that although they could not commit themselves to accepting Jarman once he had finished at King's, they would certainly consider it. They also offered him 'an hour or so each week to do some drawing'.[21]

Thus, as a new decade dawned, Jarman was able to fling himself into his final term at school with his immediate future secure. He was made a house prefect, with the attendant privilege of moving out of the dormitory and into a lodge with two other 'pigs'. After years of being a fag himself, he now had a 'curator' of his own. He took care not to abuse his new-found position, though in every other respect – studies for his forthcoming A-Levels permitting – he made the most of the privileges suddenly on offer.

He also had fun designing and painting the set for the annual school play: a modern-dress production of *Julius Caesar*. The backdrop was a line of flats on which, in tones of ochre and pink intended to convey a sense of Mediterranean heat, Jarman painted two columns, one on either side of the stage. David Miller, who played Caesar, supplied a white bust of himself meant to make him look like De Gaulle, his character's modern-day alter ego. This Jarman placed on a plinth centre stage where it could dominate proceedings.

In this first, decidedly schoolboy attempt to create an appropriate ambience for the action of a play there are in embryo certain notions to which Jarman would return in his adult work. The symmetry of statuary set against an architectural background would become something of a trademark, as would the use of anachronism and modern dress to bring out the contemporary relevance of the past. In *Caravaggio*, Jarman's film of the painter's life, the critic Baglione sits Marat-like in his bath and types his slanders against Caravaggio on an old typewriter. In the Canford production of *Julius Caesar*, Artemidorus similarly used a typewriter to tap out his warning to Caesar.

Desmond Vowles, who produced the play, was well aware of Jarman's reputation as an oddball. Accordingly, he cast him as Casca. Jarman decided to play the part as a dandy. He designed his own costume: a flamboyant suit and bow tie, a monocle, a silver-topped cane. As a finishing touch, he added a small goatee, perhaps to thank the goatee-wearing Robin Noscoe for so powerfully shaping his life at Canford.[22]

Noscoe, meanwhile, was busy organising the school's annual art exhibition. Surveying the paintings that had been hung on the walls of the fives court, Jarman suddenly announced that there were too many of them. 'What we need,' he cried, 'is a vertical structure!' Grabbing dental plaster, wire mesh and newspaper, he devoted the next two days to making such a structure. It was a monolithic figure, taller than its creator, one arm bent towards its head, the other pointing magisterially at the horizon. It was dubbed 'The Frink' after the sculptor Elisabeth Frink.

Jarman's vertical structure and the varied paintings he had chosen to show at the exhibition drew praise from F.E. Courtney, principal of the Bournemouth College of Art. 'Jarman's large plaster figure was a tremendous accomplishment for one so relatively inexperienced,' wrote Courtney. 'It was, however, in painting that he excelled: I picked out several of his for mention, and especially his still-life with bottles. He has good design and colour, he tackles a variety of subjects, and is capable in large canvases; he had abstract paintings, two of which were extraordinarily subtle and mature . . . There were several really good portraits, with Jarman again notable.'[23]

That Speech Day, Jarman won the Art Essay prize, plus, for the second year running, the Canning Prize for painting. He was also singled out for a brief mention in the headmaster's speech. 'M.D.E.

Jarman,' said Hardie, 'goes to the Slade.' Only one hurdle remained: the exam results, which, when they came, considerably sweetened the dubious delights of the summer holiday. M.D.E. Jarman had passed his A-Levels in English, history and art.[24]

Towards the end of Jarman's life, long after he had bought his cottage in Dungeness and made his garden there, he contributed to another sculptural garden, that of his near neighbour Brian Yale. In Yale's garden there is a piece about time: various epithets from various sources, all written on slate. Jarman's contribution is a phrase lifted from *Modern Nature*: 'the timeless sadness of childhood'.[25]

Was his childhood sad? The answer has to be yes – certainly as recounted by its protagonist. Yet at eighteen, the age at which he left Canford, he was full of hope. The future stretched before him, rich with possibility. So rich, in fact, that he and the potter McIver made a pact. Snake and Earthy promised, when they turned eighty, to treat themselves to a slap-up dinner at the Savoy.

8

Metroland Student

In one of the interviews that formed the basis for his first volume of autobiography, Jarman claimed not to remember much about King's, saying only that it 'seemed rather grey and colourless'. Yet his three years there were crucial to his development. Grey it may have been, but within the rabbit warren of rooms that led off its underground corridors, or above ground in its grand chapel and hall, firm foundations were laid for the future.

Founded in 1829 to remedy the lack of theology on offer from a secular University of London, King's was decidedly unbohemian in outlook. The majority of students were either sombrely gowned theologians and lawyers, or more hearty medics and engineers. They were predominantly male, predominantly conservative. There was, of course, debate about the issues of the day – CND, Biafra, the Congo, South Africa, the Berlin Wall, the Cuban crisis; but there was more consistent concern for the welfare of 'Reggie', the college mascot, a plaster lion painted in the college colours who occupied a sacred plinth in the Great Hall. It was an environment in which, as late as 1963, *King's News*, the college newspaper, could without a flicker of irony run the following editorial:

TROUSERS FOR WOMEN?

Whether a person dresses to defy convention, or as a guard
against the harsh winter, it should not be necessary to remind
them that a moderate standard of dress exists at King's – and
trousers are out for women.

Besides this manifestation which has recently become
prevalent, one also gets the occasional abhorrent character
who makes a bizarre attempt to shock or defy convention by
his manner of dress. This must not be confused with
'Individual Style', which has taste, imagination and colour.

It is not just a matter of keeping the status of King's, or to
keep the College 'twee', but a moderate standard of dress
helps to preserve the atmosphere of an academic institution.[1]

It is a vanished world that retained strong links with even earlier
times. At the college's southernmost limit is a wide terrace overlooking the Thames, in those days still a working river plied by
barges and lined with busy warehouses. To the north stood soot-
covered St-Mary's-le-Strand, while along Fleet Street and in the
alleys off it, antediluvian shops served the surrounding newspapers
and legal firms in Lincoln's Inn. The area was redolent with the
smell of hot metal and printer's ink. On occasion, visibility was
reduced to zero by the last of London's pea-souper fogs. Dickens
would not have felt entirely out of place. Jarman was powerfully
affected by it. If many of the Arcadian elements in his 'private' landscape were supplied by the Isle of Purbeck and the Dorset coast,
London's grimy Victorian heart now supplied an urban counterpoint.

Unlike the more usual and possibly more demanding Honours,
which required specialisation in a single subject, Jarman's choice of
degree, the soon to be discontinued BA General, consisted of three
separate courses; in his case, English, history and the history of art.
History attracted him largely because of his experiences in Pakistan,
where his brush with the Raj had so impressed and disturbed him
that he wanted to look in more detail at the processes by which
countries grow to what passes for maturity. He was fascinated by
what the present owes the past and hoped to carry this fascination

into the future. The same holds true of English. His study of old and middle English, of mediaeval and Elizabethan texts, would provide him with a multifaceted literary compass with which to navigate the coming years. *Piers Plowman*, Chaucer, Donne, Marlowe, Shakespeare all profoundly influenced his thought and in many cases fed directly into subsequent projects.[2] As Andrew Davis would later remark: 'I'm sure your years at London Univ have given you more ballast and sharpened up your THOUGHT; so many . . . artists get lost in mere sensations . . . the best always seem to be able to go beyond their immediate perceptions.'[3]

The third aspect of his studies was the one most obviously allied to his field of interest: the history of art. It was a subject not directly on offer at King's, and its weekly lectures, attended by students from a number of University of London colleges, were held at Birkbeck. They were given principally by Nikolaus Pevsner, a man whose name is synonymous with the study of architecture. To Jarman, already schooled in an appreciation of old buildings by Robin Noscoe, Pevsner's weekly lectures and accompanying walks were a revelation: 'With Pevsner, architecture became a passion. We would travel to the cathedrals – Lincoln, Winchester, Canterbury – and spend the entire day leaving no stone unturned. At Lincoln we clambered through the roofs; the timbered forest above the crazy vaults was spectacular, with great beams radiating in every direction like the spokes of a wheel.'[4] Pevsner was as attuned to the modern as he was to the ancient. 'He passed before the Daily Mirror building in High Holborn and praised the great blank wall at its end as if he had stumbled on Rheims.'[5]

Before long, Jarman was aping his lecturer by taking his friends on excited walks through the city, pointing out and detailing his favourite buildings. It was a pattern of behaviour that would last his entire life and could either enthral or irritate. Ernst Chin, fresh from Malaysia, would always be grateful to Jarman for explaining the proportions of Georgian architecture to his untutored eye, thus helping him appreciate what had at first seemed merely plain. Keith Collins, Jarman's companion in his final years, was less enamoured of the way in which, on their frequent bus rides to Camden Lock Market, a favourite haunt, Jarman would dip into the 'encyclopaedia of

architectural detail'[6] that he carried in his mind in order to lecture
on the passing buildings. Each journey would call forth the same
enthusiastic speech, to which the self-appointed guide brooked no
interruption.

In addition to his weekly sessions at Birkbeck College, Jarman was
also occasionally taking up the invitation extended him by the Slade
and attending their life classes. Throughout his time at King's, no
matter what the demands of his degree, he never stopped painting.
The sight of him striding energetically through Northwood, painting
paraphernalia tucked under one arm, became a familiar one.

In the October of that year, exhibiting under the name of Michael
Jarman, he had his first one-man show of twenty-five paintings in
the unlikely setting of the True Lovers' Knot, the Northwood pub
run by the parents of his friend Diana Edmunds. The range of styles
on display created quite a stir – and not a little confusion – among
the regulars. As the head barmaid commented drily: 'The paintings
certainly make people talk. And around closing time they begin to
understand . . . what they're all about.' Undeterred by this bemused
reaction to his work, Jarman defended the eclecticism of his style to
a local reporter. 'A lot of the vitality and imagination tends to go out
of painting when there is too much realism,' he said, adding an early
and utterly characteristic plea for the artist to be integrated into
society: 'In Renaissance times, the artist was treated more as a crafts-
man – an integral and useful member of society . . . I don't like
picture galleries. I'd like to see architects giving the artist work to do
in the decoration of buildings.'[7]

A short time later, two of his paintings[8] were exhibited in the
sixth International Amateur Art Exhibition in Warwick Square,
and in May 1961 came his finest hour yet. For the previous five
years, the University of London Union, sponsored by the *Daily
Express*, had held an annual art exhibition in the Assembly Hall.
The exhibition was open to students from all the colleges, art schools
and hospitals within the union. It allowed two classes of entrant:
amateur (students whose first subject was not art) and professional
(those studying art and planning to make it their career). In the
1961 exhibition, out of some 350 entrants, seventy-three of them
amateur, David Hockney, then at the Royal College of Art, won

the first prize of £25 in the professional class with *The Most Beautiful Boy in the World*. In tandem with David Kunzle of the Courtauld Institute, Jarman was voted joint winner of the amateur section, for which they each received £20. The painting Jarman had entered was *We Wait*, a Lowryesque study of a queue at a bus stop.[9]

This triumph was followed within a fortnight by a second one-man exhibition, again under the name of Michael Jarman. It comprised as many as forty paintings and was held in an upstairs room at the Watford Public Library. True to Jarman's perception of the dangers inherent in 'too much realism', abstracts predominated, giving rise to a reaction which, although on the whole complimentary, was in some quarters as guarded as that at the True Lovers' Knot. 'Some of his works,' wrote the *Watford Observer*, '. . . are a little hard to determine, but one soon realises they are done skilfully.'[10]

During Jarman's first two years at King's, Northwood remained the hub of his universe. He was still living at home and, like many another Metrolander, commuting on a daily basis into the centre of London in the company of either Donald Minton or his father. 'We travelled,' he wrote, '. . . in silence, he with his bowler and furled umbrella, I in a duffel coat and black polo-necked sweater; he reading the Annual Report and I immersed in *Ulysses* – which I read from end to end with little comprehension.'[11]

The tableau suggests a poignant mix of rebellion and conformity: the duffel coat and *Ulysses* ranged against a dutiful compliance with Father's wishes. That Jarman did not rebel more markedly when, as he would later write, he felt so repressed by his situation, is in part due to the times. In that first year of the decade, the sixties were far from swinging. There was, too, an even more crucial and insidious factor at work: Betts had been found to have cancer of the breast. She never let either of her children know quite how seriously her health was threatened but, even so, her illness soon became impossible to ignore. She was not operated on immediately, which possibly allowed the cancer to take a greater hold than might otherwise have been the case, and when the first operation was eventually performed, only one breast was removed. By the time her other breast was operated on the cancer had moved into the bone. Though she still had eighteen years to live, they were to be years of an increasingly gruelling and futile battle against her disease. 'I've often wondered,' wrote Jarman, 'what effect my mother's long illness had in keeping me from breaking out and rebelling at this time. I think I may have been storing it up for later.'[12]

It was a common complaint at King's that there was nothing to do in the evenings. Come the end of the day, the college pretty much dropped its shutters, forcing Metroland to compensate. As Jarman started to make friends at King's, so he introduced them to the swimming, the ice-skating, the carol-singing, the visits to the Proms, exhibitions, the cinema, the junk shops in Watford, the reading of poetry and plays (a relatively new pursuit); drinking at the True Lovers' Knot or Moor Park Golf Club; his taste in music, art, architecture and literature; parties; and, of course, the talk, the endless, excited talk.

The new arrivals came mainly from the King's Drama Society, which Jarman had joined in his first term. Among their number were Michael Ginsborg, studying medicine; his girlfriend Robby Nelson, who was in the zoology department; Dennis Brown, who read English, and Roger Jones, one of the college's many theologians. With his restless energy and all-consuming enthusiasm, his intellectual curiosity, the breadth of his knowledge as to what to read and see, his lack of arrogance and delight in introducing others to his passions, his ability to make you feel special, Jarman was still very much Pied Piper to this expanded, maturing gang. If confirmation, however slight, is to be sought for the insecurity and repression he claimed to be suffering, it is at King's, where, although he certainly stood out from the crowd, he was more of a team member than leader, even within the confines of the Drama Society.

It was as part of this team that he helped paint Moira Tait's sets for Lorca's *Blood Wedding*, the society's December production for 1960. Other productions Jarman worked on – as designer in both cases – were Arthur Miller's *The Crucible*, which the society toured through northern Germany in the summer of 1962, and Ibsen's *The Pillars of Society*. He added a further feather to his artistic cap with his collaged posters for such college events as the Arts Faculty Ball and, in the last term of his second year, he became a diligent and innovative arts editor of *Lucifer*, the college magazine. In it, he flippantly (but not inaccurately) described himself as: 'Second year General Arts. Hopes to paint. Likes the Portobello and Caledonian, Wren churches and Stilton. Dislikes the Shell building and all who disagree.' He also contributed two pieces of writing. The first was an assured, if rather dry, account of the primacy of the 'Gothic linear tradition of Northern Europe' in English art.[13] The second was the more poetic and characteristic 'Notes Found on the Body of a BA General Student'. He was, then as later, as much for anonymity in art as for the integration of the artist into society. Affecting to scorn those of his contemporaries who fretted about receiving proper credit for their work, he insisted that his piece be published anonymously. Even so, it is not hard to see, in its combination of swooning romanticism and almost scientific precision, the way it darts from image to image and from thought to thought, a foreshadowing of the journals he would keep in later life:

> It's cold this morning.
> Very cold.
> Geraniums all killed by frost.
> Pity
> Yes good ones as well as purple type from Watford market.[14]

The tour of Germany with *The Crucible* was Jarman's third student foray on to the continent. Three months previously, in the April of 1962, he had hitch-hiked with a friend to Rome. They travelled through France, stopping on the way in Paris, Lyons and Provence, where an obliging French artist showed them Aix, Avignon, Orange, Les Baux, St Remy and Nice. In Italy they visited Assisi, Rome, Florence and Siena – 'seeing all my buildings', as Jarman, very much under Pevsner's spell, pronounced in a postcard to his mother. A year earlier, in the summer vacation of 1961, he had made an even longer trip, again hitch-hiking, this time with his schoolfriend David Miller, a student of architecture, and two other students, Peter Facey and Simon Holding. The quartet went from hostel to hostel in a trajectory that took them through Aachen, Heidelberg, Munich, Salzburg and Venice before dropping down through Yugoslavia into mainland Greece and thence to Crete. In addition to the opportunity it gave

Jarman to visit a string of magnificent cathedrals, the trip was most notable for the briefest of stops in Colmar, where he was able to see the famed Issenheim altarpiece, a profound influence on painters as diverse as Sutherland and Bacon. 'I ran through the gallery past startled visitors, reaching the hall with four minutes to view the picture . . . I was thrown into a terrible state of agitation. Breathless from the run I was surprised by the scale of the work . . . The colours blazed forth in great flaming haloes with shimmering rainbow edges, and the participants in the drama were transfigured by an assurance of their place in the late-medieval world.'[15] As a schoolboy at Canford, Jarman had pored over the postcards in the art shack. Now he was seeing for himself what the cards could only hint at: the Middle Ages brought to vast, vivid and disturbing life. And since the trip ended in Crete, he was soon enthusing about all things Greek: sleeping under the stars, the ice-cream (ice-cream came a close second to cathedrals in his affections) and, of course, the light. After the trip to Germany with *The Crucible*, he had returned with the inspiration for a new painting: the cast leaving the set and walking towards the viewer. After Greece, it was not just new images he carried in his head, but new colours and a new sense of light. Although William Scott and Paul Nash, who had succeeded Stanley Spencer in his affections, still informed Jarman's work, their influence was now tempered by the myriad influences of the Mediterranean. Childhood memories of Rome had been reawakened and reinforced.

Despite the air of cosmopolitan sophistication he was acquiring from his forays on to the continent, by the end of his second year at King's Jarman's sexuality was still in the state of suspended animation to which his experiences at school had consigned it. Indeed, so frozen were his feelings that no one in his circle had the slightest inkling that anything was amiss. True, he did not have a girlfriend as such, but then neither did many others; and anyway, the gang always went around as a group, not in a series of pairings. Nor was it as if Jarman did not get on with women. The intense and sometimes flirtatious friendship he had enjoyed with Dab Bargh was reprised with Una Gray from across the road, now also at King's; and, to a lesser extent, with Gaye's friend Caroline Green. The dinner-jacketed Jarman looked no more awkward than any other twenty-year-old when caught by the camera escorting a beaming Una, whom he called his bird of paradise, to a dance. And if, when Caroline and Jarman found themselves paired off on the evenings in Northwood when the gang tired of talk and turned off the lights, their rather desultory exploration of each other was anything but earth-shattering for Caroline, she did not question this. Talk was more important, and Jarman such an endlessly fascinating person with whom to bandy words.

Perhaps if sex had featured as a topic of conversation, things might have been different. Perhaps then he might have been able to express some of the turmoil he was experiencing. As it was he had to hide what he felt when, on arrival at King's, he encountered 'one handsome young man . . . in the dining room [and] used to hang around hoping we might get talking', or when, one evening on the train, 'a business man exposed himself in the carriage'.[16] Then came a particularly brutal encounter on his way home from Crete. Having separated for some reason from his travelling companions, he was on his own in Switzerland when he was given a lift by a 'tough-looking middle-aged man'. Suddenly, 'without warning, my lift drove off the road and ground to a halt in the trees. Without a moment's hesitation, he grasped me around the shoulder and tried to kiss me, while with the other hand he unzipped his flies. Before I took in what was happening, he had my hand in an armlock and was trying to make me suck his cock.'[17]

Such a savage encounter might have set back his sexual clock by any number of years; instead it seems to have forced the shaken Jarman to examine and question those parts of his psyche he was more used to keeping under lock and key. It would not be long before he finally managed to blurt out the shameful fact that he thought he might be attracted to other men.

9

If You're Anxious for to Shine

At the close of the summer of 1962 and the start of his final year at King's, Jarman moved with Michael Ginsborg and his schoolfriend Dugald Campbell, now studying architecture at the Regent Street Polytechnic, into a purpose-built block of flats in Coram Street, just north of Russell Square. Three months shy of his twenty-first birthday and 'free of parental guidance for the first time',[1] he was finally bidding adieu to 'the never-ending boredom'[2] of Metroland and stepping properly on to the road to adulthood.

Although the tensions at Merryfield remained well hidden from Jarman's friends, Betts confided to her brother Teddy's first wife that she could not bear the atmosphere generated at home by the two men in her life. And when, through the offices of Teddy, who lived in the block and could therefore keep an eye on the youngsters, Jarman and his two flatmates obtained a year-long lease on 11 Witley Court, Betts' words to Pegs were: 'It's better, darling.'

A typical example of early 1930s architecture – square, spare and functional – Witley Court tended to house sedate academics, making it less than ideal for students. Nevertheless, the trio lost no time in stamping their personalities on the flat: 'At Witley Court we began to redefine our living space . . . we were very aware of the look of our rooms, after those of our suburban parents . . . White paint blotted out the past. The fifties fad of painting every wall a different colour was obliterated.'[3] Jarman's newly painted walls were a blank canvas against which he could artfully arrange his antique reading chair; his books; his paintings; two gold candlesticks of carved wood bought in the flea market in Rome; the 'friendship' plant he had been given by Güta Minton; and, of course, the wind-up easel which had come to him from his Aunt Pegs.

Money was tight and the three flatmates did not go out a great deal; to concerts always; to films occasionally, especially continental films and what was showing at the Everyman; less often to the theatre; least often, certainly in Jarman's case, to the pub. With the exception of rare invitations to join Uncle Teddy and his wife, meals were invariably prepared at home and eaten by candlelight. More important, though, than either the food or the lighting, or the classical music invariably playing in the background, was the talk. There was a youthful rivalry between the friends that resulted in an endless and excited exchange of ideas as they jockeyed to establish and define their personae.

A revealing and earnest diary entry gives a flavour of what exercised Jarman's mind during these conversational marathons:

I believe great artists paint solely for themselves and the idea
of audience participation is irrelevant to the act of creation.
Witness van Gogh . . . the artist's life is one of self revelation
and destruction, he destroys his identity and is consumed by
some ungovernable force, he might wish to lead a normal life
but is incapable unless he destroys that which is his own
existence . . . I would like to think I believed in nothing
except the sanctity of life, and my own personal experience,
[yet] I am muddled . . . and I am afraid to become
unmuddled . . . You know you are alone when you paint, you
know it is a solitary experience, you know it depends for its
end on you alone, yet you are still afraid of whether or not
you are noticed or the judgment of the passer by – this is the
weakness, van Gogh overcame it . . . It is only when you have

had the courage to sacrifice the opinion of yr audience, to
produce a painting which you believe to be true in the face of
opposition and to cling to it as yr only hope that the isolation
is complete, the way is open. Pity the day you have a
retrospective; you know you are in the grave. Roger believes
in Christ, I cannot, the step is too great, it needs complete
denial of self to suprahuman concepts, I believe only in my
own experience . . . and at this stage I can only feel failure at
my own inability to release this self.[4]

In *Modern Nature*, Jarman paints a vivid, detailed, yet oddly
impersonal picture of his year at Witley Court. The nurses' home
opposite, on which Michael Ginsborg trained a naval telescope; the
decayed Georgian terrace in Marchmont Street where they shopped.
The minimal choice of food on offer there: 'Mushrooms were still a
luxury; the first delicatessens had only just opened. Few had seen an
avocado.'[5] The way the vegetable market at Covent Garden would
come to life as the theatres closed. The bombsites, the last of the
London smogs. The heavy snows that fell that winter: 'An eerie
silence descended on the city – the only time in my life when you
could hear a pin drop in the West End.'[6] Visits to the Festival Hall
and the Albert Hall – where, memorably, they attended the first
London performance of Benjamin Britten's *War Requiem*. The Indian
restaurant where, on special occasions, they enjoyed the novel sensation of eating out.

As Jarman later put it, at Witley Court 'London could hardly be
said to "swing".' There were no discos or pubs with music to speak of.
Instead, they made do with coffee bars, the occasional jukebox, college balls, or the meetings of Habags – the Honorary Association of
BA General Students, whose main purpose was to give that somewhat embattled minority the opportunity to meet out of college
hours. In 1963, Jarman was president. Over coffee and biscuits, he
chaired their meetings. Caffeine apart, there were no drugs – no cigarettes, no marijuana – though a medical friend of Ginsborg's did
experiment with mescalin, while another went to the extreme of
swallowing an entire packet of Morning Glory seeds before a Prom.
Nor had sex as a leisure activity yet achieved 'listings' status. There

was no *Gay News*, no small ads. 'Life was much simpler, pleasures fewer and perhaps for that more intense.'[7]

Equally intense was the imminence of change. Slowly but inexorably, this relatively provincial, unsophisticated society was catching up with the twentieth century. There was hunger for the new. The Euston Arch was demolished and few protested. European and American influences were starting to make themselves felt: Genet, Cocteau, Miller, Pound – the very productions, indeed, that the Drama Society was choosing to mount, the very films being shown by the Film Society. Ginsborg's schoolfriend Peter Asher, also at King's, 'had befriended the Beatles and had taken to twanging his guitar in Michael's room'.[8] Jarman himself was profoundly unimpressed by Asher's famous friends, even when McCartney and Lennon were in the immediate vicinity; even so, he could not ignore the fact that London was beginning to dance to a different tune.

Nowhere was this more evident than in the sphere of politics. 'Politics at Witley Court was a secondary preoccupation,' Jarman wrote. '. . . The agenda was personal – how we were "to lead our lives".'[9] All the same, there was no avoiding the outside world. In the minds of most people, the pivotal moment from this era is Kennedy's assassination.[10] Equally traumatic, if not more so, was the global apprehension in October 1962 that the future of the entire world depended on a single finger not pressing a single button. During the Cuban crisis, although the flatmates did not go so far as to join the demonstrations outside the American Embassy, they still 'shivered the nights away, felt our time was up, discussed our last moments'.[11] They treated themselves to a meal, then walked all the way from the Inns of Court to Docklands to see the city for one last time before the impending holocaust.

In that moment, the twin spectres of post-war austerity and the Cold War came to a head. Nothing would ever be the same again. The scales were tipped – fell, too, from the eyes of a whole generation – and before long that generation would baulk at America's involvement in the Vietnam War, dress to defy their elders, sing new songs, turn on, tune in and drop out. Politics, music and fashion were about to fuse in a way the world had never seen before. For Jarman, this global convulsion was echoed in a series of personal events, some negligible, others less so, that would force him into as momentous an individual revolution as the universal one on his doorstep.

In January 1963 he turned twenty-one. He celebrated not at Witley Court, but at Northwood, where, in the company of his friends, he danced a vigorous Charleston with Gaye (Dugald Campbell says Jarman used to dance a 'Jarman number one', a Groucho Marx-like 'corrupted tango'). Despite the season and his antipathy to sport, he even ventured into the garden to captain a game of cricket. He was bowled by the first ball. His father bowled something at him too, every bit as deadly as any googlie. He was presented with 'the account, my school report and bills, the cost of an education to make me "an Englishman".'[12] It was not that Lance was ungenerous: in fact, he was supplementing Jarman's County Award, which covered tuition fees and gave the student an allowance of just under £100, with an extra £150 per year.[13] But he did need Jarman to be aware of what was at stake in the transaction, of what he owed his father and society. Play up, was the instruction, play up and play the game.

Hot on the heels of this coded message came another which, because it struck with even deadlier force at how Jarman viewed himself, must have sent him reeling. Having reapplied the previous November for entry to the Slade, on 6 February he was informed they did not have a place for him. 'I am extremely sorry to have to let you know that, because of the very severe competition, the examiners have not felt able to offer you a place here next season,' wrote the secretary. 'I think you are aware that we have in fact had over 530 people to consider for only about 50 places. Much of the work submitted has been of a very high standard.'

Luckily, the crisis was of short duration. Six days later the secretary was writing in a very different vein:

I am so very sorry that we have made this awful mistake about
your place here . . . The truth was that everyone felt your
work to be only just below interview standard this time; but
as we had so many to consider, the line had to be drawn
somewhere. I am afraid that I myself completely forgot to
remind everyone that we had already promised to keep a

place open for you when we last wrote to you in 1960 . . . I
am now writing to confirm that we have kept a place for you
for October, 1963 . . .

In fact, in 1960 the Slade had not 'promised' him a place – they had
merely said they would reconsider him. Jarman, however, was not
about to quibble and replied gushingly: 'Thank you very much for
your letter . . . I am so sorry I have caused you so much trouble . . . I
am looking forward to coming next October, and intend to use the
summer in an attempt to make up the leeway I have lost during my
three years at King's.'[14]

At Canford Jarman had on occasion felt that in his battle to discover himself as a painter he was 'only joining the masses'. Since
then, however, his exhibitions and the admiration of friends had by
and large protected him from artistic self-doubt. 'DEREK JARMAN –
ARTIST' was the bold and flattering headline of the feature that King's
News ran in January 1963. Underneath a suitably pensive photograph of himself, taken at Witley Court with one of his paintings and
his Roman candlesticks conspicuous in the background, the artist
gave free rein to his credo:

Reluctant though he is to sell his paintings, Derek is ever
eager to communicate his sort of art to all . . . Artificiality is
something repulsive to him; honest and outspoken opinions
are what count. He feels there is a reluctance to be
provocative, aggressive – indeed a fear to say what one
honestly believes . . . Above all, he dreads the ever-increasing
effects of commercialisation – forcing individual effort into a
common mould.

Despite all, Derek considers certain great talent cannot be
forever suppressed; and surely he is a fitting testament to this
faith.[15]

Now the Slade was telling him his talent was neither that great
nor that certain; that there was 'a line that had to be drawn' and no
guarantee he would always be able to cross it. He was good; but not
that good.

This blow to his self-confidence was exacerbated a few months later by competition from a most unlooked-for source. Michael Ginsborg – almost entirely as a result of Jarman's example, it has to be said – had also started painting, and entered a work for the University of London Union art exhibition. Jarman's entry that year had taken him a considerable amount of time. Ginsborg completed his painting in a matter of moments and then won the prize, while Jarman's offering went unnoticed. Jarman was furious. As he fumed to a friend: 'There are no objective standards left in art!'[16]

It was not only in art that he was being challenged. Both Ginsborg and Campbell were heterosexual, both had girlfriends. There was no intended rivalry in this, no conscious oneupmanship, but Jarman must have felt rather isolated as he watched the telescope trained on the nurses' home opposite the flat, the smuggling of girlfriends past the uniformed doormen in the lobby, the giggling excuses made to the self-same doormen for the number of calls that came through on the phone downstairs from people whom the lease impelled Ginsborg and Campbell to pretend were sisters or cousins. All Jarman had was his music, his painting, his studies and his burgeoning collection of antique artifacts: Georgian glass picked up on early-morning forays to Bermondsey Market, plus the *Boy's Own* adventure stories he had started to accumulate for their covers. Though even here, given that he had yet to grow into his own saturnine and exotic looks (his head still seemed too large for his gangling body), the idealised images of clean-cut, square-jawed masculinity adorning his book collection must have represented another line he was unable to cross.

There is a hint of masochism here that will find its echo in much of his later work, especially film. He was already obsessed by the image of St Sebastian, who features in the Issenheim altarpiece. He was drawn to the work of Caravaggio. During his year at Witley Court, in addition to landscapes, still lives, numerous portraits of friends and paintings featuring the metal grids of the window to his room, he essayed a number of stark crucifixions. Of course, these can be explained in purely artistic terms. The painting of crucifixions, particularly for an artist drawn to the past, is par for the course. But, just as the paintings of his grid-like window suggest a subliminal

sense of imprisonment, so might the image of the cross equate with
him flagellating himself for not living up to what was expected and
required.

The volcano of repressed and knotted sexuality on which Jarman
had been uneasily but determinedly sitting was ready to erupt.
Crossing Russell Square one day, he encountered what at first sight
looked like one of his book covers brought to life; the cover, moreover, of a rather unorthodox story into whose pages Jarman was
about to step.

Roger Ford had been a Canford contemporary, since when he had
matured into the very image of confident masculinity: thick black
hair, green eyes, broad shoulders, slim hips. Belying this unequivocal
exterior, while still at school, he had been taken up by an older
man, a teacher called Michael Harth, who had been not only a
father figure but also his lover. 'Fordy' had then done a foundation
year at Bournemouth Art School and was now studying industrial
design at the Central. Harth – not yet out of his forties, but of independent means – had retired from teaching, bought a one-bedroom
basement flat at 16a Gloucester Crescent in Camden Town and was
attempting to establish himself as a writer. Harth and Fordy were no
longer lovers, but they still lived together, making Gloucester
Crescent home to an amiably bohemian – and tightly knit – menage.
Harth retained the back bedroom, while Fordy slept on a put-you-up
in the living room with Brenda Lukey, whom he had met at
Bournemouth and who was now in London working as a designer for
Associated Book Publishers.

Although sex was seldom discussed there and few references were
made to Fordy and Harth's joint past, this tiny flat held possibilities
undreamed of at Witley Court. Jarman became an eager and constant visitor. The crush he developed on Fordy was by and large
sublimated in talk and boyish wrestling matches on the sofa, but
there was an ever-present chorus in the form of Harth to provide a
running commentary on the coded drama being enacted in his living
room. He 'would sit at his piano singing the songs he composed for
unperformable musicals about buggery, and . . . every now and then
he'd spin round on his piano stool and rag me. I would blush and he
would pounce: "Blushing, you're blushing."'[17]

There was at the same time another Roger in Jarman's life, equally
handsome, equally a crush. This Roger – Roger Jones, the theology
student, who had played Proctor in *The Crucible* – lived at a mission
in the East End where students could take rooms in return for involving themselves in the mission's work. In Jones' case, this meant the
youth club. Having once joined forces with Ginsborg and Robby
Nelson to help Jones stage a poetry reading-cum-exhibition for his
youth club, Jarman subsequently became as regular a visitor to the
mission as he was to Gloucester Crescent. 'Almost every Sunday I
would take off without an A-Z into the unknown – and like a homing
pigeon arrive by instinct some two hours later at [Roger's] door.'[18]

In addition to being good-looking, Jones was a good listener, and
Jarman was able to indulge himself in what he liked doing best: talking nineteen to the dozen. They talked about religion; about
Jarman's impending finals, which were weighing heavily on his
mind. Jarman then found the courage to admit that something else
was worrying him.

> After weeks of self-debate, I sat with him one evening and
> told him I thought I was homosexual. I was terrified that this
> revelation might destroy our friendship. He was very
> sympathetic, but had no real solution. I told him about my
> Swiss experience, and he said we must approach the whole
> thing with caution. The telling helped, but the whole subject
> seemed as obscure and remote as my Anglo-Saxon studies. So
> I returned home and while my flatmates went out to the pub,
> played myself to sleep with Gregorian chant.[19]

He had taken a first, tentative step towards lifting himself off his own
particular cross.

The long, harsh winter had ended, and it was in a heatwave – 'we
sat sweating it out in our shirtsleeves'[20] – that Jarman took his
dreaded finals. Successfully, too; on 27 July he was able to write to
Andrew Davis: 'Have just heard that I've got an upper 2, so those
coffee sessions seem to have had some effect.'

With the help of Robin McIver, who had a van, he moved his
things out of Witley Court and back to Northwood. In a gesture that

would become increasingly common and later infuriate his art dealer, he offered to pay McIver with either money or a painting. McIver, being a penniless student, opted for money.

Jarman had hated Canford and yet, by the end of his time there, he was making the most of what the school had to offer him. The same was true of King's. If he resented his father for sending him there, he never seemed to resent King's itself – certainly not at the time. Indeed, in *Modern Nature* he notes: 'After finals, there was a great feeling of anticlimax – three years of relationships evaporated.'[21] One is reminded of the words of W. S. Gilbert, himself an alumnus of King's:

> *If you're anxious for to shine in the high aesthetic line as a man of*
>   *culture rare,*
> *You must get up all the germs of the transcendental terms, and*
>   *plant them everywhere.*
> *You must lie upon the daisies and discourse in novel phrases of*
>   *your complicated state of mind,*
> *The meaning doesn't matter if it's only idle chatter of a*
>   *transcendental kind.*
>   *And everyone will say,*
>   *As you walk your mystic way,*
> *'If this young man expresses himself in terms too deep for me,*
> *Why, what a very singularly deep young man this deep young man*
>   *must be!'*[22]

Setting aside the scorn and flippancy inherent in the song, Gilbert's satirical portrait of Wilde (whose name had been invoked in Jarman's confession to Jones) fits Jarman like a glove.

10

Meeting Mr Wright

At the end of the 1963 summer holidays, during which he kept himself in pocket money with a series of odd jobs,[1] Jarman returned to
London to look for digs with Noël Hardy, another Drama Society
friend from King's. Their search led them to Kentish Town and a
house at 2 Healey Street, immediately south of the shabby Victorian
terraces of Prince of Wales Road. As an area, Kentish Town was
both poverty-stricken and colourful. It boasted a myriad businesses,
from piano-manufacturers to the Greek bakeries which served the
local Cypriot community. Along Chalk Farm Road, one encountered 'a string of shops that sold old electrical equipment and cheap
second hand furniture stacked in unloved piles and spilling on to the
street. The last train had just left the Roundhouse.'[2]

The house was owned by a couple who could have stepped
straight from an episode of Granada's recently launched *Coronation
Street*. He was a postman who greeted the dawn in his Royal Mail
livery. She was a housewife, her dress domestic: a floral pinny accessorised with a duster. Their name was Luff, though Jarman swiftly
nicknamed them Mr and Mrs Lust. He and Hardy set about re-
arranging the accommodation to their liking. They had taken the

top floor – a front room and kitchen at the rear, with shared use of the bathroom on the half-landing. Jarman occupied the front room and covered the floral carpet with polythene so as not to fall foul of Mrs Lust when he started using the room as a studio. Hardy had the kitchen, in which they also ate, and which he draped from floor to ceiling with muslin in a desperate attempt to mask the ferociously jolly seaside scenes on the bright blue wallpaper.[3]

Less easily masked was Jarman's continuing jumpiness. Hardy's girlfriend, Winnow Colyer, remembers Jarman at this time as extremely tense. Plagued by spots and boils and given to swallowing vitamins by the mouthful, he was anything but easy in his casing of post-adolescent skin. Although finally at art school, where he had always wanted to be, he was finding that the Slade, like his sexuality, was something of a minefield.

To the fulsome letter of recommendation that had accompanied Jarman's original application to the Slade, Robin Noscoe had added a rider: 'His drawing is bold and vigorous and would respond well, I think, to the discipline an art school could give it.'[4] The reverse was proving true. Although Jarman professed horror to Roger Jones at how sloppily everyone at the Slade was dressed ('There are no standards,' he wailed), he was far more disconcerted by the discovery that in fact there were standards, quite rigorous standards, against which he was now being measured and frequently found wanting. Already under siege from his worries about his sexuality, the seemingly confident 'artist' of the King's News feature, for whom 'honest and outspoken opinions are what count', could not bear confrontation in the one area which had, until now, been sacrosanct: his art. In his own, despairing words, he found the Slade 'an alien, competitive world. Art had never been that way for me before.'[5]

One department among many at University College, London and 'located in that slightly decaying academic atmosphere of Bloomsbury, 18th-century publishing houses and students' hostels',[6] the Slade was as cold, grey and forbidding as the courtyard of which it formed the north face. It was also peculiarly without focus. Was it an art school, and therefore bohemian, or was it part and parcel of the university, and as such pedagogic? It had, in just over a hundred years of existence, been paterfamilias to Wyndham Lewis, Paul Nash,

Stanley Spencer, David Bomberg, Mark Gertler, Dora Carrington, Augustus John. Yet undermining this proud and very English heritage, there was, in the mid-sixties, enormous uncertainty as to how to move forward and marry the Slade's figurative tradition with the new developments dashing themselves against the rocks of artistic orthodoxy.

Since 1949 the Slade had been run by the soberly suited, patrician figure of Sir William Coldstream, founder with Claude Rogers and Victor Pasmore of the Euston Road School of Art. This school was famous – or infamous, depending on your opinion – for its view of the artist as little more than a humble observer whose principal function, by means of characteristic marks on the canvas, was to reproduce accurately the image being recorded there. The Euston School was rigorously opposed to the Parisians, expressionism and any hint of self-indulgence or self-consciousness of style.

Though this was not to say that Coldstream, for all the Calvinism of his demeanour and outlook, was intent on holding the twentieth century at bay. His staff formed a not unreasonable cross-section of artistic endeavour. Set against Keith Vaughan, for instance, or Euan Uglow, an exponent of the Euston School, or the equally figurative Jeffery Camp, who taught in the life room, there was the expressionism of Frank Auerbach and the experimentalism of Harold Cohen. Visiting lecturers ranged from Lowry and Henry Moore to R.B. Kitaj and Francis Bacon. And in 1960, Coldstream – who had worked with the GPO Film Unit before the war – decided the moment had come to acknowledge that newest of all art forms, the cinema, by starting a film department.

By the same token, the requirements for the Diploma in Fine Art were, in Jarman's time, made slightly less rigorous and specific than they had been earlier. You still had to take a major and a subsidiary subject – in Jarman's case, painting and drawing alongside stage design – and the first year was still largely given over to an introductory course devoted to drawing, run by Patrick George. There were obligatory courses in anatomy, in geometry and perspective, in the history of art. There was the life room, where you had to draw or paint from the model. There was the antique room, where, in addition to a model, you could work from an array of classical statuary.

You had to sign in on a regular basis. But over and above that, the portfolio of twenty drawings and ten paintings you were required to produce for your finals could be done in your own time and in whatever style you preferred.

Jarman's tutor was Maurice Feild, a gentle, avuncular man appropriately nicknamed 'uncle'. Equally appropriately, given his age and Edwardian demeanour, Feild was based in the antique room, where he drew from the model, peered at his students through gold-rimmed spectacles and assiduously watered the many plants that vied for space with the statues. Feild's first report on Jarman, still styling himself Michael, set the tone of much that was to follow. Being a gentle man, Feild was careful to coat the kernel of his report in sugar but, even so, his summing up ('Perfectly satisfactory start here') could not disguise his criticism of Jarman's drawing skills ('very alive but rather haphazard'), nor of Jarman's work in the perspective class ('rather difficult').

For his part, Jarman detested being taught formally. On his first day, Patrick George instructed his students to draw an apple, an exercise Jarman found unbearable. He was used to being left to his own devices, to working in his own way, and seldom from life. Although he had painted his share of portraits and still lives, in general his work tended towards the abstract, to exploring the geometric essence of his subjects. He also liked to work quickly, dashing off his paintings at great speed and with a minimum of reworking. Scholarly rigour and censure were anathema to him, as was the process of 'building' a picture, something by which the Slade set great store.

He had started to keep a notebook, in which his inner turmoil was translated into a series of furious scribbles:

> The arts have been ossified into respective spheres . . . There
> can be no possible future for the rigid structures – e.g. a
> national theatre – they are dead even in their conception. I
> am unable with honesty to say that I am affected by any so
> called modern painting . . . except on the level of visual
> titillation . . . I am not moved by Johns, Rauschenberg etc.
> Creative people not painters sculptors etc should come
> together . . . the event must form a unity.[7]

It was through this search for 'unity' that Jarman found a way forward. Although in his notebook he dismissed modern painting, and Rauschenberg with it, it was an aspect of Rauschenberg's work that, in early 1964, provided him with the inspiration for that term's major project. Bryan Robertson, director of the influential Whitechapel Gallery, had recently mounted an exhibition of Rauschenberg's *Dante Drawings*. The literary content of these illustrations presented Jarman with a way of escaping how inadequate the Slade made him feel by falling back on the academic legacy of Canford and King's.

'Construction . . . collage . . . or any form of junk yard art,' he wrote in his notebook, 'enables one to bypass the abstraction which seems the inevitable form in which "competent" painting appears in the early 60's – it has characteristics akin to the cinema and has the ability to make literary ideas pictorial.'[8] The result, as described by Feild in his April report, was 'a large album with collages of both literary and decorative content using photographs, old prints and some drawing: an entertaining and tasteful scrapbook'.

At Canford and King's, if Jarman had seen himself in any one role, it was that of painter. Yet within two terms of being at the Slade, although still producing a stream of 'semi-abstract' paintings, the project that most excited him was one where he was able to mix disciplines. It was an intimation of the multifaceted artist he would become, one who would work equally with collage, with found objects, in scrapbooks as well as on canvas, in film and in design; an artist who would avoid being pinned down – and therefore sidestep unwelcome criticism for specific weaknesses – by being as nonspecific as possible; by breaking down the 'rigid structures'. Although Maurice Feild did not exactly let his student have his head – he still insisted on a day of drawing on Mondays, plus a day with Euan Uglow's class on Fridays – Jarman was beginning to put out feelers towards a 'structureless' future which he could claim as his own, towards that moment when he would start using his usual name, when Michael Jarman would become Derek Jarman.

Another field of activity was creative writing. Jarman's art and his jottings on the subject were not enough to express all that bubbled inside him. He needed additional means of making sense of existence, of reconciling the past with the present, the classical with the modern. Accordingly, his notebooks filled with lyric poetry and fragments of plays. His calligraphy was still somewhat childlike, but the confident way his pen chased itself across the page prefigures the elegant script that would become an adult hallmark, while the small notebooks, interleaved as they are with postcards and newspaper cuttings that complement his writings, presage the larger, more elaborate workbooks that would be such a feature of later years.[9]

In exchanging Witley Court for Healey Street, Jarman had moved to within fifteen minutes' walk of Gloucester Crescent, where he remained a regular visitor and took considerable delight in reading his work aloud to the captive and somewhat bemused audience of Michael Harth, Brenda Lukey and Roger Ford. Harth was sharing his bed with a young Canadian student by the name of Ron Wright, who had taken a year off university in order to tour Europe. Wright had a magnetic, some would say narcissistic, physical presence, a mouth as seductive as it was sulky, and a temperament to match. His effect on Jarman on the fateful evening when the two of them met while Harth was away would be as long-lasting as it was explosive:

I missed the last bus and Brenda said to me, 'Why don't you stay in Michael's bed tonight, it's very late and he's not coming home.' As I was falling asleep Ron crossed the room and got into bed with me. It was so unexpected. I didn't acquaint Queer people with youth. I thought they were middle-aged as the papers said.

When Ron got into bed, I was so startled I just lay in his arms. Next morning when I woke, he'd gone. Were we going to see him in the evening? 'Yes,' Brenda said, 'he's going to come back.' I thought – shall I ring him? Better not, I'll wait.

I wandered aimlessly round London – couldn't face going to work at the Slade. That evening we had all been invited to a party in a flat behind the Middlesex Hospital by one of Brenda's friends; Ron never appeared. In my panic, I consumed a whole bottle of whiskey. I was carried home, almost unconscious.

The next day Ron still didn't appear. I was in a terrible state. He was the only Queer lad in the world. A blind rage of

self-destruction overtook me. Roger had always collected my
paintings; they were all over the flat. I took Brenda's dress-
making scissors and threatened suicide. Fortunately I didn't
harm myself but the whole household was in turmoil as I
carved into these paintings – it's quite difficult to hack a
painting to pieces. Brenda was in tears, Roger quite ashen-
faced. They tracked Ron down and brought him over. This
time he stayed.[10]

As with many of the seminal events in Jarman's life, his account
of it would vary with the telling. But whatever the details, what
cannot be gainsaid is that, by sharing a bed with Wright, the part of
Jarman which had been frozen since the last time he had shared
another boy's bed, at Hordle, suddenly thawed and transfigured him
forever. In thus 'destroying' himself, he was making way for a new
self. It was a moment of true catharsis.

Sadly, the course of Jarman's first love ran neither true nor
smooth. In their different ways, both men were perhaps more in
love with love itself than with each other. To quote Wright's own
assessment: 'Wrapped away from the world in what seemed to me
almost a glass case, Derek lived in a world completely of his own creation. We became sexually involved, and although I found him
remote physically and very rigid, he became deeply in love with
me . . . I . . . found myself keeping a guarded distance.' Certainly as
far as the sex was concerned, the affair was hopelessly onesided and,
as a consequence, short-lived.

Jarman behaved, however, as if he were completely unaware of
Wright's lack of commitment. Not for a minute was he going to let
anything dampen the exhilaration he felt at having at last found
someone to whom he could open up. A new poem was added to the
notebook:

POEM I
in the common silence
of the world
the white poppies of
my love are dancing[11]

Jarman took Wright to meet his parents, marched him round London, swept him off to the West Country – where he did nothing to contradict Wright's assumption on being shown the manor house at Curry Mallet that Jarman was of aristocratic descent. Then came the Easter holiday and a three-week hitch-hiking trip to Italy, achieved on a total of £20 each.

Back at home, Jarman succumbed to suspected chicken pox and was confined to bed at Northwood, where his mother could nurse him. When he returned to London, 'Michael [Harth] danced a polka on his piano and said to me: "Right, none of this shilly-shallying, we're all going to the 'Willy' in Hampstead." I was horrified at the thought of going to a Queer pub, but there was safety in numbers.' What Jarman fails to mention is that the William IV was not the only form of Hampstead 'willy' Harth was proposing: an old heath hand, Harth was equally evangelical about the delights of late-night sex in the bushes behind Jack Straw's Castle. It is not recorded whether Jarman was prepared for this further degree of initiation. He found the William IV, with its clientele of 'elderly models and artistic antique dealers',[12] daunting enough. All we know for certain is that soon he was a regular of the pub, deftly avoiding the offers of 'My place for a cup of coffee, dear?', befriending Stanley Spencer's mistress, who held court alongside the middle-aged men, and even managing to meet others of his own age.

Down the hill in Healey Street, Jarman still could not bring himself to say much more to Noël Hardy than that he had met a fantastic guy. Like everyone else in those pre-Wolfenden days, he was acutely aware of the fact that his sexuality was a criminal offence. But at least he was no longer hostage to the utter and despairing secrecy of his adolescence. However confusingly, and whatever the see-saw of his emotions, the word had finally been made flesh.

Wright's year in Europe was drawing to a close, with the result that no sooner had the two of them returned from Italy than Jarman was hatching plans to spend his summer vacation in Canada and America. As he somewhat disingenuously told his mother, 'Now is the time to see as much of the world as possible.'[13] It is peculiarly fitting that Jarman's first affair should have pointed him where it did, in the direction of the New World and what he ambiguously termed 'the Billboard Promised Land'. It was a world towards which, for a variety of reasons, both personal and professional, he had been attracted for some time.

> Growing up in the 1950s we dreamed the American dream.
> England was grey and sober . . . Over the Atlantic lay the
> land of cockaigne; they had fridges and cars, TV and
> supermarkets. All bigger and better than ours . . . The whole
> daydream was wrapped up in celluloid, and presented nightly
> at the 'Odious' at the end of every high street in the land.
> How we yearned for America! And longed to go west.
>   In 1960 every young English artist had an eye across the
> Atlantic.[14]

Like the affair with Wright, Jarman's relationship with the Billboard Promised Land would not run smoothly. Intoxicating and multifaceted though the liberation America offered undoubtedly was, the country's essential brashness was always at odds with Jarman's essential Englishness, and the tension thus engendered would echo fitfully throughout his life. Artistically and sexually, the promises on the billboard were as loaded as Jarman's very Ginsbergian phrase.

The phrase – one he would use repeatedly in his poetry and stories during the sixties and into the seventies – has its roots in his time at King's, where he experienced a vivid introduction to the literature of the Billboard Promised Land from one of his tutors, the academic, poet and jazz expert Eric Mottram. Mottram taught a course in American literature which Jarman took as a special subject in his second and third years. Under Mottram's enthusiastic tutelage, Jarman discovered the Beats – Ginsberg, Burroughs, Kerouac, Ferlinghetti.

Like most young men whose sexuality is in question, Jarman was desperate for role models and validation. He found Ginsberg's fevered verse a revelation and would later relate strongly to his espousal of a 'gay succession', in which Ginsberg slept with Dean Moriarty, who had slept with Gavin Arthur, who had slept with Edward Carpenter, who had slept with Walt Whitman.[15] The Beats supplemented his already voracious reading of anything European that had a homosexual content: Cocteau, Genet, the sonnets of Michelangelo, Marlowe's *Edward II*, with its much earlier reference to another gay lineage:

> *The mightiest kings have had their minions –*
> *Great Alexander lov'd Hephestion;*
> *The conquering Hector for Hylas wept;*
> *And for Patroculus stern Achilles droop'd.*
> *And not kings only, but the wisest men –*
> *The Roman Tully lov'd Octavius;*
> *Grave Socrates, wild Alcibiades.*[16]

It was not merely Ginsberg's openness about his sexuality that Jarman relished. He was also drawn to the Beats' hatred of capitalism, consumerism and the military-industrial complex; plus, of course, their celebration of experimentalism, of spontaneity, of the value of 'madness' as a response to an age – the atomic age – itself deranged. Their fluid transformation of the sexual and the social into the political was an alchemy that Jarman, despite the classicism to which he was equally committed, could and did embrace wholeheartedly. When he came to make *The Last of England*, it was not an English poem he used to set the tone of the film, but the opening line of Ginsberg's *Howl*: 'I saw the best minds of my generation destroyed by madness.'

Throughout his time at King's, Jarman read a great deal, 'the sort of reading you do at university, and in a sort of way directed by other people'.[17] At the Slade he often spent whole days in his antique reading chair, poring over some aspect of art history, or some new play. Thereafter, his reading would be less wide-ranging and, while still eclectic, tended to centre on specific subjects: *The Devils of Loudun*, for example, because he was designing *The Devils*; or the history of Rome as it pertained to St Sebastian, because that was what he wanted to film. The foundations, though, had been laid, not only for a formidable bank of knowledge, but for what was at the root of his talent. His ability 'to be directed by other people', to be susceptible (sometimes naïvely) to their opinions and to the vagaries of fashion, to absorb and then live out these opinions and fashions, meant that he was acutely attuned to his times; a kind of litmus paper that changed colour in accordance with its surroundings. Although perfectly capable of original thought, it was largely Jarman's openness to others as filtered through the lens of his undoubted self-obsession that allowed him to mirror and comment on his times with the vividness that he did.

By 1964, these times were, in the words of Bob Dylan, 'a-changin''. The impingement of things American on the local artistic, cultural and social scene was growing daily and would have the effect on Jarman of 'shattering' the English tradition in which he had been working. The previous November, at a Guy Fawkes party, he had met Peter Orlovsky, the American writer and companion of Ginsberg. Orlovsky, shoeless and dressed in a dhoti and cap embroidered with little mirrors, had walked with Jarman back to his room in Healey Street. Jarman had – in his own, rather rueful words – worn 'elastic sided Chelsea boots and . . . a sensible duffel coat against the November chill'.[18] The Chelsea boots might have been fashionable, but they were as nothing compared to bare feet; besides, they were fatally compromised by the duffel coat.

Seven months later, in June 1964, as he boarded the student charter flight that would finally take him to New York, Jarman had acquired some more appropriate plumage: a highly desirable Edwardian yachting cap of the kind favoured by the Beatles. He also carried a ninety-nine-day Greyhound ticket and every intention of experiencing to the full whatever America might throw at him.

11

The Billboard Promised Land

In later years, Jarman would put a jaunty gloss on his recollections of his first transatlantic trip – a gloss perhaps not entirely in keeping with the underlying facts.

Through Roger Jones he had been given the name of a New York priest who might offer him a place to stay. The instant they met, the priest 'piled' Jarman into a cab. 'We'd hardly gone a block before his hand was on my crotch. I decided the best course was to pretend it wasn't happening, and stared resolutely at the architecture whizzing by, hoping that the taxi driver wouldn't notice. At the mission in Henry Street I found all the priests were after me, all of them unbelievably forward. I felt as though I were a lottery ticket.'[1]

A few months earlier, the Beatles had been mobbed by hysterical girls on their arrival at Idlewild Airport. Now Jarman, suitably attired in his 'Beatles hat', was being subjected to a similar experience by a group of ecstatic priests in the most unecclesiastical of garb: tight jeans and T-shirts. Although to a certain extent flattered by their attentions and highly amused by the service the next day at 'an Episcopalian church which they called "Mary on the Verge", where the altar boys were all strikingly good-looking, and spent the entire service cruising the all-male congregation, winking at them through clouds of incense and lace',[2] Jarman was in fact far from ready for a 'priestly gang bang'.[3] If he had come to America for sex, it was sex with Wright. As soon as he could, he fled by Greyhound to Calgary, scribbling ersatz Ginsberg as he went:

> MANHATTAN LOWER EAST SIDE
> *these fooly wastes teasing mortality*
> *dethical streets*
> *wailing the sirens knell*
> *for oediple Europe's distracted sons*
> *leaving paternal warehouses*
> *singing a new world song*[4]

Jarman found Wright working as a swimming-pool supervisor. He himself landed a job measuring abattoirs. Their free time was spent either at Wright's pool or on trips to the Rockies, where on one memorable occasion they took off their clothes to sunbathe in a cutting by the railway. As the Canadian–Pacific rumbled past, they threw their arms around each other and defiantly embraced within sight of the observation cars. 'It was a moment of naked triumph,'[5] Jarman would later write, purloining (and misremembering) the title of a Hockney painting in order to give the moment mythic weight: 'we two boys clinging together'.

Wright's account is markedly less mythic:

A letter arrived from Derek announcing that he would shortly be arriving for a visit. Since his feelings for me were not mutual (he was so stiff in his body, almost frozen solid, that sensuality was difficult), I felt somewhat uncomfortable. Would his expectations overwhelm me?

He arrived in early July, all bright and enthusiastic, with his box of oil paint and a roll of canvas. Mom and Dad quite willingly provided him with a room and Derek was off on this 'Canadian Adventure' with a somewhat dubious Ron in tow. I have to admit that Derek was already one of my cultural icons at age 21. Unlike myself and most of the people I knew

who basically accepted the terms by which the world
presented itself, or complained that it should change, Derek
gleefully and energetically saw the world as a giant playroom
inviting him to dismantle and reconstruct as he moved along.
He produced a dizzying painting in oils of a circus world
where the characters seemed to be spinning on a carousel, or
flying about like phantoms in a dream . . . A party was in
order, Derek decided. I was enthusiastic at first, but perplexed
when he began decorating the living room with plant stems,
not attractive plum blossom-type plants either, but weeds,
rhubarb leaves, potato tops standing in jars. He decorated the
mantelpiece with boxes of detergent and bottles of bleach. I
have absolutely no memory about the party, just the decor.

The peak of our visit, literally, was a hike up a rock slide
area to the top of a mountain in Yoho National Park . . . In
his first autobiography, Derek described this visit. The pivotal
words for his experience seemed to be 'outrageous', 'daring'.
The hinge of his memory was an incident I don't even recall,
but am certain that if it occurred, he exaggerated, of he and I
'making out' by the CPR railroad as a trainload of shocked
passengers rushed by. The carnival. The circus.

So much is questionable, particularly whether they even had sex.
Not only did Wright have a girlfriend at the time, but Jarman himself seems unsure. In some accounts he says they did, in others that
they did not. What they did have was rows – lots of them – and
when, in late August, Jarman boarded the Greyhound for San
Francisco, he was saying goodbye to Wright as a love object.

This last leg of Jarman's trip had as its prime goal something of a
holy grail: the City Lights Bookshop in San Francisco. More perhaps
than Wright, it was this bookshop that had attracted Jarman to
America in the first place. Here he could buy his own copies of
Howl, *The Naked Lunch* and the novels of Kerouac – books which
were either banned or unavailable in London and which he
devoured like a man starved.

Helped by his hat, which made him 'the most desirable of for-
eigners – an inhabitant of swinging London,'[6] he acquired new

friends to show him the West Coast sights. He heard Bob Dylan sing and went to a party in Cannery Row. He visited Big Sur, San Simeon, even Los Angeles, where he stayed with Rhoda Robinson, a friend of his mother's. He visited Monterey, attending an anti-Goldwater concert given by Joan Baez and a Hell's Angels convention, where he took his first trip of a non-geographic nature.

Notes taken after marijuana . . . first attempt rolled inexpert cigarettes . . . feelings of nausea probably because unused to smoking also apprehensive of results . . . no use fighting the effects attempt to relax . . . overcome by immobility . . . I was soon concentrating on colour. A red bk cast shadow on copper kettle the shadow came alive congealed oozed down the side of kettle. Khaki green ceiling turned emerald as if projected from a magic lantern, unable to stand owing to instability of objects . . . the ivy still as a Vermeer . . . the bks on the shelves are united in an endless embrace. Handel sounds just as he should nothing but . . . [next day] and what remains chiefly that to look back at these same things they still retain a lustre which would normally go unnoticed . . . I am now aware of the copper red shadow on the kettle . . . it no longer floats this morning but remains luminous . . .[7]

By now it was mid-September – time for the newly inducted hippy to return to New York, where America had one final 'gift' in store for him.

When I got into the Greyhound terminal I was exhausted after the non-stop ride from San Francisco. I tossed a coin for which of the Reverends I'd ring – the least obnoxious, as Ron would say – and decided on Tom, who without hesitating invited me round. When I got to his place, he told me there was no time to unpack as we were going to a party. All I wanted to do was to go to sleep, but he wouldn't leave me behind. So we arrived at a small flat which was so packed that people were hanging out of the windows. In the centre of the room a gang of black drag queens were swishing around announcing they were the most 'glamorous', and when some weedy-looking white drag queen took them on in the beauty stakes, the room divided, and it nearly started a fight in which someone pulled a knife. I took refuge in a bedroom with a black boy, Marshall Hill, who was at art college – painting. We curled up on the floor and made love.

Afterwards, I was so drunk and exhausted, deprived of food and sleep, he offered to drive me back as Tom had disappeared, leaving me stranded. Tom hadn't arrived home, so we lay on the carpet outside the front door and fell asleep in each other's arms. When Tom arrived back at 4.30 I asked him if Marshall could come in and stay. He began shouting, telling us we were a disgrace and threw me and my luggage into the hallway and slammed the door. So much for Christian charity – Marshall and I spent the rest of the day sightseeing, then he took me out to the airport in the evening more dead than alive.[8]

As the 'kodak dream' of 'screaming manhattan' receded, Jarman found himself, with a notebook full of poems that encapsulated his many experiences, back in 'time sapped Europe', a complete wreck. 'What have you been up to?' cried his mother. The answer was not long coming. America's final gift turned out to itch furiously and to have taken up residence in Jarman's pubic hair. Blissfully unaware of what it might be, he innocently told his parents. His father – typically – said nothing; his mother, either as innocent as her son or, for his sake, pretending to be, laughingly speculated that 'Derek's nits' were the legacy of either hotel bedding or Rhoda Robinson's cats. The family doctor pronounced otherwise. He 'eyed me with suspicion, took out an enormous book . . . and flicked the pages slowly and deliberately as if to prolong the agony. Finally he said, "The cure is really dangerous, it's mercury. Have you been sleeping with prostitutes, Derek?" I was tongue-tied, it hadn't occurred to me these monsters were transmitted by fucking. I looked at him and the words froze in my mouth; then in desperation I blurted: "Yes."'[9]

Jarman had come of age as a sexual being. In the space of three months, he had had his first experiences of a failed relationship, of casual sex, and of some of the consequences of the latter. 'The thaw'[10] was how he termed it.

As ever, the proselytising Michael Harth stood on the sidelines to urge Jarman forward as he cautiously but determinedly explored the London pubs and coffee bars in which, because homosexuality was still illegal, the language whereby one man signalled his desire for another was, if verbal, often 'polari', the gay slang. To 'varda a bona feely homme' was, if you feared being overheard, safer than staring at a handsome youth. Another comrade in arms was Peter Docherty, a fellow student at the Slade, who lived off the King's Road, then undergoing its transformation from a conventional 'high street with bread shops, paper shops, cafés and a sprinkling of art and antique shops'[11] into a mecca for the fashion-conscious, the famous and the louche. These denizens of the demimonde would frequently gather at Keith Lichtenstein's restaurant, the Casserole, below which, down a narrow flight of stairs, was a nightclub, the Gigolo – or *les tombeaux*, as Jarman was soon calling it. While the likes of the Beatles and the Rolling Stones led the passing parade at street level, underground an altogether less newsworthy group gyrated keenly on the tiny dance floor, propped up the bar drinking Coke and Nescafé (none of the clubs were licensed; if you needed a stronger stimulus than caffeine, you carried a stash of Purple Hearts), or were drawn to the small, raised area at the back where 'everyone had their flies undone . . . and you might find yourself blown in a dark corner'.[12] In relative peace, too – the management turned a blind eye to what went on at the back – unless you were unlucky enough to be present on a night when passing football supporters threatened to torch the place, or when the police came to call. Then you might wonder why the club was so *very* full of pretty men, only to have your question answered when, on propositioning one of them, you found yourself under arrest.

On warm summer nights, when the clubs and pubs had closed, there was always the old graveyard or, here and elsewhere, the ubiquitous 'cottages', though public toilets were never Jarman's style. He preferred his casual sex either in a club, in the open air, or on the street.

There was nothing more exciting than a stranger stopping
and looking back and the chase ending in front of a shop
window, mirrored in the glass; the long journey to his place or
yours; cocks throbbing and minds racing. Slipping him out of
his jeans and sucking his cock, the ecstatic kiss, the
discovered tattoo. Wild as a boy can be, sparkling eyes,
laughter, the taste of him, the sudden mad rush to orgasm
after hours on a tightrope of sensation.[13]

Moving west, there was the Yours or Mine on Kensington High
Street, and, in the centre of town, half a dozen watering holes of varying degrees of secrecy and sleaziness. Le Duce in D'Arblay Street,
which stayed open later than its rivals and played good music on its
indefatigable jukebox, was 'where the "hip" hung out', and 'bright
trousers and shirts swept away a grey past. Even Levis jeans were new –
all those lads sitting in tepid baths to shrink-wrap their arses and a
little sandpaper round the crotch to show off a packet; they shouldn't
be too tight, or your partner couldn't get his hand down the back and
dance with his fingers stroking your arse when no-one was looking.'[14]

After a night on the town Jarman either walked home, or, as he
grew more adventurous, repaired after breakfast in an all-night greasy
spoon to the Biograph Cinema, a fleapit in Victoria.

The Biograph showed 'dodgy' films like *The History of the
Body* or, now and again, a Pasolini film, and the most dreadful
German *Health and Efficiency* films with girls in leather pants,
topless, holding steins of beer.
  The straight mackintosh brigade hung out there. It was a
mix; you could make a real mistake if you put your hand on
the wrong crotch. He might be a drunken tramp who'd start
shouting and swearing – 'fooking queers!' – and then fall into
the aisle! By this time the whole cinema would be in uproar
and the old ushers would [be] staggering around with their
torches like searchlights at the height of a bombing raid.[15]

In writing about 'the thaw', Jarman sometimes gives the impression that his sexual awakening was both instantaneous and wholly

consuming. The truth was less simple. The thaw was gradual, and although it would one day claim him with an exclusivity that grieved some of his early friends, in the mid-sixties he still spent as much time at Gloucester Crescent as he did in any club or coffee bar and still travelled with his old circle to Northwood for the weekend. The thaw was also painful.

> The repression was difficult to confront – like finding your way down a foggy street. In the sixties, we were to be open but illegal. This did not make it easy to form relationships and led to fumbling, furtive sex. There was little or no celebration until the end of the decade . . . encounters took place in bedsits in an atmosphere of frustration. Long bus rides, and when you were there, shellshocked inability to love. Tortuous, stilted conversation until you got to the point. It was the Americans, at the end of the decade, who said 'Hi, let's fuck!'

The difficulties faced by this 'dazed first generation through the door',[16] and by young Jarman in particular, were legion. He worried what his parents might think; he fretted that he was not attractive. In searching for a 'regular lad',[17] he encountered more screaming queens than he knew how to cope with and was thrown into turmoil by his first visit to the clap clinic at UCH. Although declared 'clear', the experience of being directed to a basement directly opposite the Slade left him 'quaking'.[18]

Of course, as the middle-class son of a military father and the product of a public school, Jarman did his best to prevent his pain and confusion from showing. As with his trip to America, he preferred a positive gloss. 'Heterosexuality isn't normal, it's just common,' he would later proclaim, adding piquantly: 'It eventually dawned on me that heterosexuality is an abnormal psychopathic state composed of unhappy men and women whose arrested emotions, finding no natural outlet, condemned them to each other and lives lacking warmth and human compassion.'[19]

It is a telling ploy, to turn the tables in this manner, but it ducks the question as to why Jarman, who had pursued Ron Wright with such determination, should now decide he did not want to become half of a couple. Why did he opt instead to go around in a group, taking sex where he found it – within the group or outside it – casually, easily, without commitment, much in the way that a dog sniffs with a sort of companiable excitement at another? Was it because he was young? Because he was exploring himself? Because he liked being free? Because he found the idea of being part of a couple unutterably bourgeois? Or was it out of fear? Because for him sex and love had always been twinned with violence and rejection? Because, as a practising homosexual, he was now technically a criminal? Should we celebrate the thaw, as he himself was wont to do? Or should we scan it for clues as to why sex and love are invariably underscored by violence in much of his work; why his future compulsion to be promiscuous should have become so overwhelming; why he could, on the one hand, be so open, and on the other, so closed?

12

Becoming Derek

In late 1964, Jarman reworked some of the scribbles in his notebook into: 'Tentative ideas for a manifesto after 1⅓ year at an art school'. In part, this read:

> Theatre ballet and painting must be revived. This cannot be achieved separately. There must be intercommunication . . .
> There must be communal basis even if only from the artists themselves. Fragmentation and the perverted cult of personality at all cost is a force which has rendered the artist impotent . . .
> The painting school says you are not a painter. 'I'm proud.'
> . . . failures are to be desired as long as they are complete, stretched to their limits . . .
> . . . the audience must become participators. The creators the artist must abrogate his mystery.
> . . . turn Piccadilly into one vast shimmering glass funnel. 500 ft high. 6 skyscrapers . . . music all types from loud speakers sometimes Bach sometimes Beatles.[1]

The ideas are in fact far from tentative. Not only had they been gestating for some time, they were passionately held and would inform much of Jarman's future output – though not, it has to be said, in their entirety. The cult of personality was not later seen as a complete perversion, nor were failures always to be desired. Pride was not all Jarman felt at being told he was not a painter. At the start of his second year at the Slade, he still felt uncomfortable there and continued to take criticism of his abilities to heart.

It is no accident that architecture should figure so prominently in his manifesto. That November, he moved into a new flat in West Hampstead, where two of his three co-habitees were architectural students: Dugald Campbell, his old schoolfriend and flatmate from Witley Court, and a new acquaintance called Julian Harrap. With Campbell and Harrap the turning of Piccadilly 'into one vast shimmering glass funnel' was, as a topic of conversation, the rule rather than the exception.

The flat at 64 Priory Road, one of West Hampstead's quieter and more leafy streets, was on the bottom floor of a solid, handsome house, and unfurnished, allowing the new tenants to decorate their rooms to suit their separate tastes. Julian Harrap, nicknamed Pode, favoured a varnished floor, complemented by built-in cupboards; his space was shipshape. Lawrence Warwick-Evans who, with his girlfriend Pat, took the fourth room, was of a more romantic disposition; on one occasion he went so far as to cover his floor with autumn leaves in order to create a rural effect. Not surprisingly, the most conspicuously 'designed' of the quarters belonged to Jarman, whose room was at the front of the house, facing an oblong slope of garden and, above that, the street. His design constants – the antique reading chair, his candlesticks, easel, Güta Minton's 'friendship' plant, his books and the Georgian glass he was still collecting – were complemented by much that was new. Fabric, for a start. 'Saturated as he was with the romance of mediaeval Christianity',[2] once he had given the walls a coat of white ('White is the only colour for rooms,' he declared loftily),[3] he draped his room with fabric, principally a burgundy-coloured velvet. To heighten the mediaeval effect, he placed ecclesiastical-looking candles on the table he built specially for the room, burned endless joss-sticks and played appropriate music:

Gregorian chant and Albinoni. He acquired a tailor's dummy, which he dressed to suit his mood or the arrangement of the room. He installed a Pither stove, not because Priory Road could be cruelly cold – he never noticed the cold in any case – but for the look of the thing: its large circular base, its sheer iron sides, its stovepipe chimney. He made sure the scent of his joss-sticks was always offset by that of flowers: whatever he had seeded in the window-box plus at least a jam-jar's worth of Fritillaria.

In marked contrast to the care he lavished on such design minutiae, domestically speaking, he was slapdash. He lived on bread and cheese or scrambled eggs, frequently 'borrowed' from his long-suffering flatmates, left the washing-up and hogged the bathroom to go through his daily ritual of splashing his face with water forty times. Everything had to be done on his terms. When Campbell's girlfriend sneaked into his room to dry her knickers on the Pither, he was so outraged by this invasion of his privacy, he stuffed the offending garments into the stove and incinerated them. He would blithely keep the others awake with a Saturday-night gathering, then complain bitterly if kept awake in return. He cleared a space in the back garden where, alongside the jungle of weeds, Pode's boat and an old chicken coop, he gleefully grew a profusion of sunflowers. 'Just look at them!' he would jeer at Pode, who had taken responsibility for the sedate shrubs at the front, 'I've got rockets thrusting upwards, with their great faces following the sun!' Jarman saw Pode's pitiful shrubs as the horticultural equivalent of modern architecture, increasingly to be despised for lacking élan.

About the only event likely to galvanise Jarman into domestic frenzy was the arrival of someone important, usually his parents. Then, arms flapping, he would ensure everything in the flat was spotless – and that everyone was roped in to help, before *and* during the visit. Suddenly Pode was an asset. A sailor himself, he could entertain Lance with nautical chat. The others would be called upon to satisfy Betts' more landlocked concerns. Was her Derek eating properly? Sleeping sufficiently? Did he have a girlfriend?

Jarman's innate and touching vulnerability to such matters as parental opinion, Betts' as much as Lance's, meant that for all his flaws as a flatmate, the others could never remain cross with him for

long. Equally seductive was his undoubted charm, his sheer ebul-
lience. Despite a lingering shyness and his ability to keep his feet on
the ground, when not playing the part of dutiful son he loved to
dress flamboyantly, to attract attention and to shock. In Portobello
Road he had discovered 'an amazing second hand clothes stall with
the weirdest stuff which made me vow never to get anything new
again'.[4] Out went 'the fifties duffel coat and polo neck sweaters',[5] to
be replaced by an array of colourful waistcoats, hats, scarves and
shirts. He liked to affix a plastic fly to his face when setting out for
a party, especially if his journey involved a bus ride and the promise
of unsettling strangers. Wrongly but waggishly dubbing himself a
'screaming queen', he started to encourage men into his room and
his bed.

'Why don't *you* try it?' he would demand of Campbell and Pode.

'How do you know I haven't?' Pode would parry.

'You mean you have?' Jarman was, of course, instantly intrigued.

'That's my business,' Pode would reply.

Which would lead to an evangelical rant worthy of Michael
Harth. It's boring to be straight, Jarman would cry. The most interesting people are gay. He would then list his exploits in the pubs and
on the heath, pointing to the hugely influential people he met
there – judges sometimes, even peers.

In terms of dazzle and adventure, student life in and around 64
Priory Road was not dissimilar to a new play Jarman was hatching in
his notebook alongside the holiday poetry, the lists of things to do,
the manifesto and the jotted phrases that caught his ear at parties or
on the bus. The play was called *The Billboard Promised Land*, and
took the form of a picaresque and surreal adventure which, in differing versions and with differing casts, always unfolded along a
single superhighway that, like the Yellow Brick Road, led the traveller through a landscape known either as the Billboard Promised
Land or the Land of Cockaigne. The characters to tread the superhighway invariably included Topaz, either in the guise of the
Wandering Jew or Ludwig of Bavaria, the Begum of Flowered
Chintzes, and Borgia Ginz, whose name, if not aspect, was a reference to Jarman's former flatmate from Witley Court, Michael
Ginsborg.

In the real world, on that most super highway of all, public life, the folding of 1964 into 1965 was marked by two events which starkly symbolised the end of one era and the start of another: the state funeral of Winston Churchill and Harold Wilson's arrival in Downing Street. Spring 1965 also saw the making of a film that captured much of the spirit (and many of the pretensions) of London at the time: Michelangelo Antonioni's *Blow Up*. That same spring Ron Wright made a brief reappearance in Jarman's life: this time as friend and occasional lodger rather than lover. Together, he and Jarman sought employment as extras in Antonioni's film, though, owing to Jarman's vanity, only Wright appeared before the camera. Required to wear 'a hideous Swinging London T-shirt' and to dance to the Yardbirds, Jarman decided that: 'No way was I going to appear in this film in that T-shirt even in the background.'[6]

Cinema was starting to figure with some prominence on Jarman's cultural agenda. In part, this was due to his increasing tendency to go underground for entertainment and enlightenment. In this way, he encountered the films of Kenneth Anger, whom he adored for so gloriously addressing his own concerns, and began excitedly tracking down the work of other American film-makers of the avant garde: Bruce Baillie, Stan Brakhage, Maya Deren, Andy Warhol.[7] And, indeed, of the European avant garde: Cocteau and Genet. A second crucial influence was the film course which William Coldstream had started in 1960 and which provided those who took it with a comprehensive introduction to world cinema.

The course was run by Thorold Dickinson, who, in a long and distinguished career, had directed the original *Gaslight*, made documentaries, been programme director of the London Film Society and headed the film service of the United Nations. An approachable and immensely cultured man, Dickinson was passionate about cinema and would complement his carefully planned seasons and screenings with highly informative discussions and lectures. The discussions were held in the basement of the Slade, the screenings in the Physics Theatre at University College. Though not the most congenial of venues, thanks to Dickinson's and Coldstream's friendship with the curator of the National Film Archive, the theatre had been given a licence to show original nitrate film. This meant

Dickinson could screen films it was impossible to see anywhere else; films which were frequently flown into the country solely for a screening at the Slade.

Since leaving school, Jarman had made himself reasonably familiar with the cinema of the continent. Already he was enamoured of Fellini and Pasolini, plus such individual features as *La Dolce Vita*, *L'Avventura*, *Hiroshima Mon Amour* and *Last Year at Marienbad*. By not missing a single screening on the film course – or the chance to enthuse afterwards about what he had seen – he was now introduced to the work of Sergei Eisenstein, Carl Dreyer, Jean Renoir, Max Ophuls and the painter and documentary-maker Humphrey Jennings, a personal friend of Dickinson's.[8] He also attended talks by the likes of Edgar Ansty, Paul Rothko, Alberto Cavalcanti, Renoir and Grigori Alexandrov, who had worked so closely with Eisenstein. Although as yet Jarman had no inkling he might one day pick up a camera, he was receiving an invaluable theoretical training.

Sadly, these screenings did not take place every day. Dissatisfaction with the Slade was still Jarman's predominant emotion. Another year, and he would be able to throw himself into his subsidiary subject, which he was fairly sure would be stage design, but in the meantime he was more or less marking time and, because money was tight, exploring ways of supplementing his allowance from his father and his grant. Together with the teasingly handsome Lawrence Warwick-Evans, on whom he had developed a hopeless crush, he tried his hand at interior design. Decreeing with utter conviction that 'stripped pine is passé', he dragged Warwick-Evans to Chapel Street Market in Islington, where they invested in some Victorian sideboards, painted them in bold swirls of colour, then failed to sell a single one. More financially remunerative, though just as short-lived, was Jarman's involvement with Peter Docherty in the design of About Face, a small chain of boutiques in the suburbs of south London. The shops featured free-standing changing cubicles, the sides of which it was Jarman's task to decorate. This he did with a degree of eroticism that might have necessitated a rethink had any disquiet over his designs not been pre-empted by the ultimate failure of this attempt to bring Carnaby Street to the suburbs.

There was a brief stint of supply teaching in the East End, where Jarman was brought up short by the poverty of many of his pupils and sometimes obliged, in order to prevent hunger from completely undermining their powers of concentration, to share his lunchtime sandwiches with the more undernourished of them. Less traumatic was a stint teaching English as a foreign language for the Greater London Council which that summer paid for a visit to Greece.

In partnership with the young Stephen Hollis, another regular at the William IV, Jarman placed an ad in *The Times* seeking a lift to Athens. A few weeks later, the two youngsters packed themselves and their luggage into the car of a man who was so boring that when they reached Yugoslavia, rather than endure another word, they pretended they had travelled far enough and completed their journey alone.

In Athens, they spent a luxurious few days with Euphrosyne Doxiadis, a fellow student at the Slade, whose father, the well-known architect, owned a house overlooking the Acropolis. Then it was back to their budget and on to a ferry to the holy island of Patmos, where Jarman was drawn to the arid landscape, the ambience of mediaeval religiosity and timeless simplicity. He loved it that when the old woman on whose roof he was sleeping washed his clothes for him, she 'scented them with wild rosemary from the hillside'.[9] He and Hollis spent a contented couple of weeks experiencing this earthly paradise, until Jarman – tiring perhaps of the extreme monasticism of the island – took his leave of Hollis and headed for cosmopolitan Rhodes, where, thanks to some willing Greek sailors, he was able to counterbalance the divine with the carnal.

On his return home, he was finally able to start his subsidiary subject in earnest. In the prescient letter of recommendation written in support of Jarman's application to the Slade, Robin Noscoe had noted: 'He is not sure yet which branch of art he wants to take up, but his lively sense of colour and pattern could prove an asset in some sort of design career.' Earlier that year, as if straining at the leash, Jarman had started to incorporate three-dimensional design elements into his work. Of a trio of acrylla paintings done that February, his monthly report comments: 'In one of them a set square is fixed to the picture and represents a road in perspective. Another is of a pair of scissors drawn round and painted with grey on a white canvas.'[10] The restless student was ripe for what the theatre department had to offer.

The department had been started in the thirties by Vladimir Polunin, who, as a scene-painter, had worked for Diaghilev and therefore with the likes of Bakst, Benois, Braque, Matisse and Picasso. The tradition exemplified by Polunin of energetic interaction between the fine and the applied arts was continued by Robert Medley, who inherited the department in 1949. Himself a distinguished painter, Medley had, via his lover Rupert Doone, been closely involved with the Group Theatre and had designed some of their productions, including such Auden–Isherwood collaborations as *The Dog Beneath the Skin* and *The Ascent of F6*. By the time Jarman joined it, the department had passed to Peter Snow, an ex-student of Medley's, and Nicholas Georgiadis.

The course was centred on approximately three design projects per year – a play, a ballet and an opera – though since its aim was to encourage creativity rather than adhere to a methodology, if a student did not care for a particular project, he or she was free to tackle a design of his or her own devising. The Slade had no stage as such, so the students' designs were made to fit a miniature theatre which, with its elaborate lighting rig, was housed in the ground-floor room that comprised the department's somewhat cramped quarters. To round off the course, there were lectures by visiting designers, directors and choreographers, plus frequent visits to the theatre, the ballet, the opera, even to Stratford, where the chief scene-painter would arrange week-long sessions in which the students could familiarise themselves with the workings of the painting dock.

Over the next two years, under the relaxed aegis of Snow and Georgiadis, Jarman designed miniature sets for Stravinsky's ballet *Orpheus*, Shakespeare's *Timon of Athens*, Ben Jonson's *Volpone*, Sartre's *Huis Clos* and a second ballet, Prokofiev's *The Prodigal Son*.[11] Courtesy of Robby Nelson, now a student at the Drama Centre in Chalk Farm, he also joined forces in early 1967 with Michael Ginsborg to execute a full-scale, if rudimentary, design for Schnitzler's *La Ronde*.

Although Jarman chose to tackle *Timon of Athens* convention-ally – he 'feels it must be set in Ancient Greece, and dislikes Shakespeare in modern dress', notes his report – what distinguishes the majority of his designs is their imaginative flair and meticulous attention to detail. For the story of Orpheus' and Euridyce's journey from the underworld, Jarman turned again to Rauschenberg's *Dante Drawings*, though where Rauschenberg had used a technique of rub-bing his newsprint and photographs with a soft pencil to achieve a shaded effect, Jarman's college of male nudes and a Richard Avedon mental patient was sharper and more direct. Equally sharp, and of particular note in terms of his future work, was his distinctive use of geometric shapes – in this case steeply angled cones and a few spheres.

Orpheus is noteworthy in two other respects. First, it reflects Jarman's essentially conservative ambivalence about new trends in painting. As he himself explained: 'The gates of hell are the Brooklyn Bridge. This unconsciously delineated my attitude to "American" Popism, nicely. The Elysian Fields, on the other hand, are strewn with the perfect fragments of the classical world we were casually discarding.'[12] Secondly, the design reveals how, and with what results, Jarman's love of confrontation could bring him into conflict with forces of conservatism and authority he might other-wise have applauded, in this case his father and William Coldstream.

Lance somehow managed to ferret out the carefully hidden *Physique Pictorials* used as source material for the design's collage of male nudes. Though he never actually challenged his son with this discovery, for months afterwards 'his conversation was loaded with innuendo'.[13] Coldstream, by contrast, did nothing to beat about the bush. Sharply drawing Jarman's attention to the fact that there were 'acceptable limits of art',[14] he commented specifically and critically on the pornographic content of the design. Jarman was prompted by this doubly negative reaction to seek solace in his growing tendency to view the establishment as inimical, a force to be resisted and shocked. Cast in the role of *enfant terrible*, his response was to inhabit the role as vitally as possible.

Less controversial, though no less striking, was his set for *Huis*

Clos. Behind the closed doors of Sartre's title lay a room 'made entirely of red-hot velvet'[15] in which stood three equally vivid arm-chairs: one green, one blue, one black. For *Volpone*, he placed the protagonist's bed atop a mountain of richly realised treasure; a notion that was, for its time, as conceptually sophisticated as it was visually arresting. *The Prodigal Son*, by contrast, was spare in the extreme and, for someone against 'American Popism', pretty 'pop'. The road the prodigal must travel is indicated by a pylon, alongside which the different stages of his journey could be economically suggested: the orgy scene by nothing more than a free-standing pair of women's legs, a string of pearls, what looks like a lipstick and a scattering of white pills.

In his journals, Jarman gives the impression that because he did not like to work where he could be observed, he seldom painted within the confines of the Slade. 'I find it difficult to have people staring over my shoulder,' he wrote. 'At the Slade most of us have barricades for privacy and the place looks like a shanty town.'[16] In fact, for the first two years of his course he had signed in almost every day, which would indicate that he was frequently to be found behind his barricade. However, it is certainly true that by the time he started theatre design he was attending the school less often, not least because that term, through Michael Ginsborg, by now an art student himself, he was offered the shared use of a studio Ginsborg had rented at Landseer Studios in Cunningham Place, a stone's throw from Lord's Cricket Ground. The barricades were coming down, and so what if there was a tendency for the other Slade students to dis-dain the theatre department? So what if this prejudice was echoed at an executive level by the fact that Coldstream was less keen on theatre than he was on film? In the relative obscurity of his new studio, or the privacy of his room at Priory Road, liberated not only by the work he was doing, but by the fact that 'in the theatre room homosexuality was accepted quite openly',[17] Jarman was happier and freer than ever before. 'I'm working more and more in the the-atre room,' he wrote. 'I like working on shared projects. It breaks down the isolation of working as a painter . . . I can employ imagery I wouldn't dream or wish to use in my painting . . . The tutors . . . give me enough freedom to hang myself.'[18]

In time, that was precisely what he would do, and very publicly, too. What he did now was assert himself with sufficient confidence to close the gap that had sometimes existed between the professional and the personal. In early 1966, he exhibited a selection of his student work at the Rimmell Gallery, a small, newly opened establishment in the basement of an antique shop in St John's Wood, and did so under his own name. Although it would be several years before the change was permanent, Michael was finally giving way to Derek.

13

Father Figures

Thanks in part to the Slade, where Jarman was meeting an ever-increasing number of fellow artists, in part to his sexual openness, which had magicked an entirely new area of friendship into being, and in part to his discovery that the public and the personal sides of his life could be made to co-exist, festivities at Priory Road were becoming more frequent, more crowded, more colourful. As Jarman's social life took shape – becoming, in its way, as vivid a work of art as his designs or canvases – a desire to record it led to the appointment of the first in a line of unofficial 'court photographers': Ray Dean, a young Canadian he had met through Brenda Lukey. Other than with an occasional painting, Jarman was unable to pay for Dean's services, but so skilled was he as a social magician, and such good company, that Dean was perfectly happy to be at Jarman's beck and call, recording the faces that now surrounded him.

These included Ossie Clark, then a student at the Royal College of Art, and Richard Rowson, first met at King's, both of whom briefly shared Jarman's bed before becoming firm friends. Peter Logan, Nicholas Logsdail and Anya Sainsbury were all fellow students at the Slade. The flamboyant and witty Mario Dubsky, ex-Slade and in time a teacher at Camberwell, was introduced to Jarman by Geoffrey Rogers, who taught at the Central and was a regular of the William IV. Maggi Hambling and Keith Milow, who shared a house, were also at Camberwell, where the head of painting and sculpture until 1965 was Robert Medley. Medley still visited the Slade and soon became one of a handful of older men who during this period (and, in Medley's case, for the rest of Jarman's life) strongly influenced the younger man.

Medley had been instantly attracted to Jarman and had tried to seduce him in the back of a taxi. Although uninterested in reciprocating this advance – he pleaded toothache to deflect the patrician painter's ardour – Jarman nevertheless adored the range and depth of Medley's knowledge, especially in the fields of art, literature and history, plus the fact that, through friendship with such figures as W. H. Auden and Benjamin Britten, Medley provided an artistic and sexual link with a previous era.

Another painter to have a profound effect on Jarman was Patrick Procktor. Jarman spent a great deal of time at Procktor's flat in Manchester Street, where Procktor executed a watercolour entitled *Derek Telling Me about Orpheus*,[1] sketched a number of studies of Jarman's head and twice included Jarman's figure in the painting *Shades*, a pictorial 'diary' of some of the people then current in Procktor's life. The setting was a windowless bar in which, alongside the two versions of Jarman in his workaday costume of roll-necked sweater, jeans and donkey jacket, are the shadowy figures of a number of Jarman's friends, including Ossie Clark, Peter Docherty, Keith Milow, the publisher Nikos Stangos and Ole Glaesener. Through his friendship with another Dane, the sculptor Olaf Gravesen, who briefly shared the American's flat, Glaesener was the link to perhaps the most fabulous, certainly the most fabled, of Jarman's mentors: an American called Anthony Harwood.

In *Dancing Ledge*, where Harwood's picture first appears in the context of Jarman's life, Jarman has set his mentor alongside a still from *The Wizard of Oz*: Dorothy paling before the Wicked Witch of the West. The similarities between Harwood and the Witch are inescapable. Both are gaunt of feature, have exceptionally prominent noses and are dressed in black. In case we missed the point, in a later book Jarman would repeat the allusion in words: 'Anthony was a witch, he had a strong intuitive drive, he lived by intuition, this frightened other people, it made him suspect.'[2]

Then in his forties, the dazzlingly urbane – and often insufferable – Harwood was the maverick son of a prosperous East Coast businessman. Having been solidly schooled at Lawrenceville and Harvard, he had decamped to Europe, where he met his nemesis in the shape of the diminutive yet implacable Princesse Nina Mdivani, a White Russian with a background of breathtaking glamour and intrigue. Stout, silver-haired, shortsighted and at least a quarter of a century Harwood's senior, Nina Mdivani had, with her four siblings, made her way in the capitalist West by the only means she knew how: marrying money.[3]

When the 'marrying Mdivani' met Harwood, she was on her second marriage, to Denis Doyle, son of the creator of Sherlock Holmes. Sensing in Harwood a 'twin soul', Nina persuaded Doyle to employ her new passion as his secretary. The trio travelled to India, where Doyle died – so entirely to the convenience of his widow and his secretary that there were those who wondered whether his death had been natural. Apart from enabling the princess to make an honest man of Harwood, Doyle's death brought her a one-third share of the Conan Doyle estate. Imagining that the revenue from the estate would be enough to support her in the style to which she was accustomed, she raised a loan from the Royal Bank of Scotland and bought out the other beneficiaries. She soon discovered that not even the popularity of Sherlock Holmes could cover Mdivani extravagance.

Having little money of his own, Harwood was not much help on the financial front. His writing – privately printed editions of esoteric poetry and unperformed plays – would never find an audience beyond his immediate circle, while his skills as a business manager were, to say the least, questionable. But what distressed his wife most, causing her on one occasion to hire a private detective, was the fact that Harwood had a secret life.

In London, which he considered home, he kept a flat in the block above Sloane Square tube station, where he retired in the daytime to write his plays . . . You would find him sitting cross-legged on a silver cushion in front of his typewriter, with his work scattered across the floor . . . If you arrived hungry there was strong black coffee, fresh orange juice laced with rose water, and scrambled eggs which were scented.[4]

'Twin soul' to the princess he may have been, but where flesh was concerned, Harwood preferred the male of the species, the younger the better. Work was only part of the reason why he kept the flat, and Jarman only one of many young men to present himself at Harwood's door.

Harwood was a complex figure. The possessor of a fine mind, he introduced Jarman to *The Tale of Genji*, the work of Karen Blixen, Ouspensky and Jung.[5] On a less cerebral level, he was equally enthusiastic about the importance of knowing the right people, visiting the Biograph, or dressing in drag and draping himself and others with the absent Nina's many and fabulous jewels. Although a mystic by inclination, he was as heedful of the outer man as he was of the inner and something of a slave to style: 'He always dressed immaculately, if eccentrically, in silver wind jackets, black polo-necks, velvet breeches and court shoes with diamond buckles. His belt clasp was a snake in gun-metal with a diamond set in its head.' His flat, with its views of the London skyline, was a virtual temple to Harwood's taste. There was a minimum of furniture, just 'a bed, a glass table with three clear perspex cubes for seats, and one silver lustre vase with iris or scented narcissus'.[6] You took your shoes off on entering so as not to mark the cream carpet. Everywhere you turned, you saw your reflection in the grey glass of the mirrored walls.

While there is no evidence to suggest Harwood and Jarman were lovers, they could hardly have been closer, or more alike. Harwood was the greater poseur, and a dilettante, but in almost every other respect the similarities between the two men were remarkable, even down to the fact that at school both were famed for the size of their penises. Both were well read. Both favoured carefully designed environments. Both were susceptible to mysticism. Both were great talkers and given to monopolising the conversation. Both were generous to a fault. Both had a libertarian as well as an ascetic side. But perhaps what Jarman related to most was Harwood's sheer theatricality; the liberation inherent in the invention of a flamboyant persona.

Harwood was also a source of urgent verbal encouragement, possibly because he saw Jarman as someone who could avoid the mistakes he himself had made. 'You should not be paying attention to David Hockney or Patrick Procktor,' he told Jarman. 'You have far more resources, Derek; they are pygmies.'[7] Though in this particular area, certainly at this particular time, Harwood's words fell on stony ground. Artists like Hockney, Procktor or Andy Warhol loomed too excitingly if unnervingly large. As Jarman would later write: 'I was part of a second generation . . . The path seemed blocked. I didn't want to be a follower.'[8]

The sense of being bested by an older generation was to have a marked effect on Jarman's work. In the summer of 1966, he visited his parents in Seaview, where he did a series of drawings that were an early manifestation of the cool, abstracted approach to landscape that would dominate his painting over the coming decade. The often hectic energy of his earlier work was reined in and replaced by a series of stark and geometric canvases where people, if they figure at all, are mere squiggles. The angularity and emptiness of these canvases suggest a world that has no room, no time, certainly no use, for the confusions of humanity. Asceticism has won out over libertarianism, caution over boldness. It is a telling indication of the gulf that existed between the inner and the outer man; the taut, monochromatic insecurity of the one as opposed to the boundless and multicoloured confidence of the other.

Not that the spark had gone out of him completely. He had always painted as if for an audience – which he liked, where possible, to startle or shock – and no amount of insecurity could prevent him from trying to reach that audience. Just as 1966 had started with an exhibition, at the Rimmell Gallery, so it ended with some twenty of his works being hung by his old art master in the East Hall at Canford. And in January 1967 he took part in his most prestigious exhibition yet, the Young Contemporaries. Organised as a showcase for their talents by the students of the major London art schools, the Young Contemporaries had, from relatively humble beginnings, been growing in importance. In 1967, it was held in no less a venue than the Tate. From over 1,000 entries, work by just seventy-six artists was chosen for inclusion. Of these seventy-six, only three were invited to hang more than one canvas. Jarman was one of the three.

Ever since he had stuck a set square and a pair of scissors to two of his paintings, Jarman had been flirting with both three dimensionality and 'pop'. So for those who knew his work, it did not come as any surprise that the devices in the otherwise desert-like *Landscape with Various Devices* should be a pyramid of sponges and some circles of textured material, nor that the water in *Cool Waters* should drip from a real tap cheekily set alongside a real towel rail. 'You have to paint large at the Slade or nobody notices,'[9] he once said. *Landscape with Various Devices* was his largest canvas to date, and its combination of giganticism and sponge certainly did the trick: not only was it one of ten winners of the Peter Stuyvesant Foundation Prize for Landscape, but, together with *Cool Waters*, it was also included in the touring exhibition mounted by the Arts Council once the Young Contemporaries had closed.

Also showing at the Young Contemporaries were Keith Milow and Nicholas Logsdail, in whose company, along with that of Terrence Ibbot, Paul Martin and Paul Riley, Jarman would organise his next exhibition. For some time, Logsdail had bemoaned the fact that the Slade made little or no attempt to prepare its students for the practicalities of the outside world – how to apply paint painstakingly to the canvas, yes; how to sell that canvas, no. To rectify this state of affairs, Logsdail offered to turn his house in Bell Street, immediately to the north of the Marylebone Road, into a gallery. The others jumped at the idea, Jarman with such enthusiasm that it could sometimes seem he was the project's sole motivator. With the help of copious amounts of Polyfilla, white paint, cheap flooring and suitable lighting, they colonised three floors of the house and, in mid-April, as Jarman's last term at the Slade began, threw open the doors of the Lisson Gallery. Despite the location and relative inexperience of all concerned, the joint exhibition that followed, while not receiving a great deal of coverage or leading to significant sales, was nevertheless seen as a distinct success and the harbinger of many more to come.

As graduation loomed Jarman was feeling extremely apprehensive. Although he had found buyers for his work at the Rimmell Gallery and the Young Contemporaries, there remained an insidious chorus of often perceptive Slade reports to offset any recent successes. 'He does a lot of work and the cumulative effect is more convincing than the individual works seen separately.' 'He has to make a few pictures stronger rather than depending so much on quantity and experiment.' 'Much energy in a variety of directions, probably theatre design the most creative.'

In the event, Jarman's final submission of work was assessed most favourably. If he did not, as he later maintained, receive a first for draughtmanship, he was at least commended on both his drawing and his stage design. However, as far as keys to the future were concerned, his Diploma in Fine Art took second place to the compliment Anthony Harwood now paid him of giving him a key to Sloane Square and an open invitation to use the flat whenever he liked.

The flat would become, in Jarman's own words, 'a vital extension to my life'.[10] It signified an entrée into a world where, unlike the worlds he had inhabited to date – home, school, university, even art school – he could properly and finally come into his own.

14

Swinging Decayed

Across London from Sloane Square, in then unfashionable Islington ('Drizzlington', Jarman once termed it), stood 60 Liverpool Road, a decaying early Victorian house that dominated the corner with Bromfield Street, just north of Chapel Street Market.

Newly acquired by Michael Harth, the house had been purchased on the understanding that it was to be modernised by the friends to whom he offered rooms. Brenda Lukey and Roger Ford were to move with Harth from Gloucester Crescent and take the middle floor. Harth himself would occupy the ground floor. Richard Rowson would share the basement with the clutter of Harth's current hobbies: foul-smelling tanks of tropical fish interspersed with racks of equally pungent home-made wine. The top floor would go to Jarman, for whom the large front room would make an ideal studio, the smaller back one a more than adequate bedroom.

Thus it was that in early 1967, at the same time as he was helping to create the Lisson Gallery, Jarman was spending weekends at Liverpool Road mixing more Polyfilla and paint. As the gallery neared completion, so did number 60, and in March or April Jarman terminated his lease on the studio he had been sharing with Michael

Ginsborg, said goodbye to Priory Road and took up residence.

The house had the air of a commune. The bathroom – rather splendid and on the ground floor – also provided access to Harth's living quarters and therefore doubled as a passageway where, if the bath was not full of home-made wine, you might encounter the domestically maddening Jarman at his extended ablutions. On the middle floor, Lukey and Ford had knocked their rooms together and installed a mammoth table that seated over a dozen, making that the venue for any house party. The parties were innumerable, as were the visitors, a couple of whom even became semi-tenants. Keith Milow, who had a studio nearby, took to sharing Jarman's or Rowson's bed when he was in the area, which is why his pants feature in Jarman's own encapsulation of life in the house:

> Michael's tropical fish bubble away in the gloom of the
> basement. Stacked between the tanks are a thousand bottles
> of home-made wine. In the room above Michael plays piano
> selections from his musicals, which you never quite
> remember. Then he stops, and begins to type out one of his
> manuscripts. Brenda comes in from Chapel Market with
> volumes of the Arden Shakespeare sandwiched between
> cauliflowers, and trips over Keith Milow's pair of elephant-
> grey velvet pants, that lie in a hopeful and permanent heap of
> laundry outside her door. Roger is patiently stripping the
> wooden casements of the windows in their room. Upstairs on
> the top floor the record-player plays the Who, while the sun
> streams in through the window over my green landscape
> paintings and the rolls of used masking tape which cling to
> the floor.[1]

Given Jarman's flair for imparting information and generating enthusiasm, it would have been fitting if, on graduating, he had applied for a teaching post to fund his purchase of paint, canvas and all the masking tape needed for the straight lines that criss-crossed his landscapes. Instead, perhaps because his earlier forays into the world of education had not been altogether happy, he opted for the dole and spending every day in his eyrie of a studio, painting feverishly, pausing only to snatch lunch in a nearby café. 'I was impatient, wanted quick immaculate results, hated "the struggle", the time that it took physically to complete an idea – I envied Keith Milow's concentration.'[2]

His envy and the 'struggle' notwithstanding, within six months of graduating, Jarman saw his work selected for inclusion in no fewer than four exhibitions. He exhibited as both Derek and Michael – in one case as Michael-Derek: the transition was not yet complete.

First came the Edinburgh Open Hundred, organised by the recently opened Demarco Gallery in collaboration with the University of Edinburgh and held as part of the Edinburgh Festival in the university's David Hume Tower in George Square. Amid a flurry of controversy as to why, from 1,500 entries, the judges had chosen the hundred paintings they had as representative of the best in contemporary British art, Michael Jarman's *Landscape with Marble Mountain* failed to win a prize, though it was singled out for favourable mention in the press.

Next Jarman appeared alongside Raymond Gringhofer, Peter Joseph and Keith Milow in a second exhibition at the Lisson Gallery. Again there was a positive press response. Nigel Gosling, art critic of the *Observer*, elaborated on his earlier wish to award Jarman a 'silver thistle' in Edinburgh, commenting presciently: 'Derek Jarman shows a gentler variation of the canvas I admired at the Edinburgh Open 100, and a bunch of sensitively minuscule landscapes (these are best when toughest – English nostalgia is his danger).'[3]

This second Lisson exhibition was followed by the fifth Paris Biennale des Jeunes Artistes, held at the Musée d'Art Moderne de la Ville de Paris. Jarman was one of four young designers chosen by the British Council to exhibit work as part of the official British entry to the theatre decor section. He showed his designs for Prokofiev's *Prodigal Son*, which Guy Brett, writing in *The Times*, considered 'perhaps the best thing in its section'.[4] The designs did not win a prize, but they did add to the cuttings book. Under the heading 'TALENT', the *Evening News* gushed: 'He has big expressive eyes, an eager manner, a hair-raising taste in shirts. And talent . . . Five days after the prizes in all sections had been awarded, he wasn't at all sure who had won . . . "I've been busy doing the things I wanted to do," he said. "A museum a day and I still haven't visited the Louvre."[5]

Finally, there was John Moores' sixth biennial exhibition of modern British art at the Walker Gallery in Liverpool, where Jarman was again outflanked prize-wise: *Landscape with a Blue Pool* was pipped at the post by another, Californian pool – David Hockney's *Peter Getting Out of Nick's Pool*.

As has already been suggested, Hockney had long been a strong influence on the younger, more impressionable artist. By moving there, Hockney had helped point the way to America. By dyeing his hair blond, he had shown it was possible (and fun) to reinvent oneself. He had shown too, at a Slade ball, that one could dance openly with other men. Now, through Ossie Clark, Jarman met the man whose lifestyle he would characterise as 'the most enduring legacy of the 60's'.[6]

At the [Picasso sculpture] show we met David, who'd just arrived from California. He invited us back to Powis Terrace, which had been left unoccupied and was freezing. Ossie and I climbed fully clothed into the bed in the living-room while David made tea. David put on the TV and joined us. Ossie asked what he'd brought back with him, and David produced two suitcases, one full of physique mags featuring hunky American boys, and the other packed with fluorescent socks and brightly coloured underwear. I asked him if this was all he'd brought. He said he used to travel with luggage, but realised his mistake. One should travel as light as possible. Now he went in what he was wearing, and bought razors and even toothbrushes at the other end. This to me seemed the height of modernity.[7]

Although Jarman was capable of maintaining that he could not 'stomach the jokiness of the '60s, that complicity with rubbish',[8] he nevertheless found modernity increasingly attractive. While at Priory Road he had often passed the pedestrian crossing outside the Abbey Road Studios; and when walking back from the clubs or pubs in the dead of night, had even heard a blackbird singing – a blackbird he liked to think of as the one in the Beatles song. At Liverpool Road, the music that emanated from his record-player was no longer confined to Gregorian chants and the like. Now he also listened to the Who, Velvet Underground, the Rolling Stones, the Doors (Jim Morrison was a particular favourite) and Bob Dylan, who, like Morrison, was a source of visual as well as aural gratification. Permanent wall space was soon given to the portrait of Dylan that graced the cover of *Blonde on Blonde*.

In *Dancing Ledge*, Jarman called the sixties 'Swinging Decayed'[9] and provided a series of vivid verbal snapshots of some of its more appealing excesses and characters. His cast list of friends and acquaintances included artists, art dealers, theatre directors, fashion designers, models and minor film stars. Among them, to pluck just one from the hat, was the revered yet impish Pierre Sylvester Houédard – Benedictine monk, church historian, concrete poet and artist – like Jarman, Houédard exhibited at the Lisson Gallery, though it was the learned monk's personal appearance as much as his artworks that caught Jarman's eye. When he visited London from his Gloucestershire abbey, on the train Houédard would discard his habit in favour of an urban uniform of slightly satanic leathers complemented by a swirling cape.

Even 'Drizzlington' had its attractions. In Chapel Street Market one might catch a glimpse of Joe Orton, and at 99 Balls Pond Road, in a house co-owned by the artists David Medalla and Paul Keeler, there was the Exploding Galaxy, a commune's worth of dance and performance artists. Jarman went with the Exploding Galaxy to see Artaud's playlet *A Spurt of Blood* at the Royal College of Art. With its cow's head that dripped blood on to the audience, its rain of polystyrene rocks and the red balloon that was inflated and burst between the nurse's legs, Jarman thought this 'the best piece of experimental theatre that I've ever seen'.[10] He attended the Arts Lab in Covent Garden, where he saw a cut-down, single-screen version of Warhol's *Chelsea Girls*,[11] and, of course, the Roundhouse, the old turning shed in Chalk Farm which had become home to a string of sixties happenings.

Queuing for returned tickets for the Living Theatre at the Roundhouse, I bumped into Keith Milow with one of his millionaire friends. Keith has a passion for bankers, particularly if they are young and play squash. This latterday Maecenas had bought a dozen tickets which he was giving away at Keith's prompting to the young and promising with much ostentation. I managed to lay my hands on one. As we waited for the performance he managed to drop names like bricks – Andy, Jasper, Don, Dan, Claes – art bricks.

Then Julian Beck and his theatre commenced their performance with a dirge of 'can'ts' – you can't strip in public, smoke dope etc. They'd hardly begun when, immediately in front of us, Michael Chapman from the Exploding Galaxy, all six foot four of him, started to heckle in a loud voice. First he stripped, giving a loud commentary on the process and apologizing for his spotty torso, and then lit a joint, all the while shouting 'You can if you want to!' In this way the beginning of the performance was reduced to a shambles and the Living Theatre became the outraged guardians of their own negativity. 'Great – great – great,' said Keith's banker.

Later, when Michael passed by him in the interval he rushed up to him and said, 'You must have dinner with us.' But Michael, looking down from his great height, said, 'What the fuck do I need dinner for?' and spat at him right between the eyes.[12]

The sixties, then, were in full swing and Jarman was swinging with them. One should not lose sight, however, of the fact that throughout this period this most enthusiastic and social of people could also be compromised by his relative youth, lingering shyness and innate asceticism (that distaste for 'jokiness', his revealing use of the word 'decayed'). He was still emerging from a number of closets.

Sexually he was increasingly adventurous. With the possible exception of the puckish Keith Milow, with whom Jarman would have loved to share his bed more fully than Milow allowed, there was no shortage of willing partners with whom to experiment physically – and little hesitancy on Jarman's part, when he had tired of his current obsession, subtly and sweetly to palm the young man off on someone else. As he writes in *Modern Nature*: 'Tinker ✓, Tailor, ✓, Soldier ✓, Sailor ✓, Rich man ✓, Poor man ✓, Beggar man ✓, Thief ✓ – counting the tricks – Mass Murderer ✓ (that was later).'[13]

Yet when he visited his parents, it was invariably in the company of Lukey and Ford, and not simply because Fordy had the car. Equally important was the fact that, like Michael Ginsborg and Robby Nelson, Lukey and Ford were a stable, heterosexual couple who held down responsible jobs. And when, that July, it finally became legal in England and Wales for consenting males over the age of twenty-one to have sex in private, Jarman did not rush out and paint the town pink. 'I remember,' he wrote, 'the TV cameras coming down to Le Duce in 1967 when the law had been changed. Everyone afraid to be filmed and, at the same time, desperate the film should be made. I was one of those who didn't go out that night, worried that my parents might see me on the television.'[14] Although he was edged towards increased political awareness by the contrasting emotions he experienced that day – joy that, albeit with qualifications, the law had finally changed, and anger that such laws should exist in the first place – Jarman did not jump aboard the 19 bus to Soho or the King's Road, nor did a second pair of celebratory boots clump up the midnight stairs to his monastic bedroom beneath the eaves.

Socially, too, there were moments when Jarman, who usually stood at the centre of any gathering, would hold himself aloof or feel excluded. His later accounts of friendship with Hockney suggest greater intimacy than actually existed. Although Jarman certainly visited Hockney's flat in Powis Terrace, he never became a key member of the circle that gathered there. Nor was he ever an acolyte of the collector Bryan Montgomery, patron to many of Jarman's friends and contemporaries. Once a week it was Montgomery's practice to take a party of young friends to the Finnish Seamen's Mission in Rotherhithe for a sauna, followed by a Chinese meal in the East End. For a hungry artist, these evenings were a chance to stuff yourself with food at someone else's expense and maybe even sell a painting. Jarman was as hungry as the next person, and as in need of patronage, yet he was never to be found in Montgomery's van.

The issue of patronage – or, more accurately, where and how to find work – was one that exercised Jarman a good deal. Did his future lie in fine art, or would his design work pay the bills? He was practising both, plumping for the Roundhouse, that oasis of excess and anarchy, as the proposed venue for an imaginative production of *The Tempest* planned at around this time. He envisaged flooding the entire floor of the building, placing the audience on an island of inflatable silver rocks and trampolines, turning Prospero's cloak into a huge banner covered in magical signs, and having the actors perform in among the rigging of a sunken ship. The fates, however, had something else in store for the putative designer; something more grand and surprising. As Jarman would note in *Dancing Ledge*: 'The beginning of my career was to resemble the end of anyone else's.'[15]

At impossibly short notice, Frederick Ashton, director of the Royal Ballet, was looking for an appropriate designer to help create a new ballet he was choreographing to fill an unexpected gap in the programme at the Royal Opera House. Among those he consulted for suggestions was Nigel Gosling, who, in addition to being the *Observer*'s art critic, was also, with his wife, the dancer Maud Lloyd, 'Alexander Bland', the paper's ballet critic. Gosling had recently read Guy Brett's flattering mention of Jarman's contribution to the design section of the Paris Biennale. If he did not already know this from his friend Nicholas Georgiadis, Gosling now realised that the young painter whose work he had admired over the course of the summer was equally capable of design. Gosling promptly put Jarman in touch with Ashton, who explained that because of Jarman's inexperience, he could not commission him without seeing examples of his work. However, if Jarman was prepared to do some designs on spec., and providing Ashton liked them, the job would be his.

Shortly afterwards, on 21 November, the design subcommittee of the Royal Opera House was informed that Ashton had chosen Jarman over a number of other, more established painters. The subcommittee inspected the first batch of costume designs. William Coldstream, one of whose many committees this was, sounded a note of particular approval. Jarman, he said, had been 'a most talented student'.[16] The sketches were duly approved.

The scenario and music to which Jarman had been working was Richard Rodney Bennett's jazz setting of the rhyme

Monday's child is fair of face,
Tuesday's child is full of grace,
Wednesday's child is full of woe,
Thursday's child has far to go,
Friday's child is loving and giving,
Saturday's child works hard for his living,
And the child that is born on the Sabbath day
Is bonny and blithe, and good and gay.

In structure and tone, the piece was perfect for the divertissement Ashton had in mind – and in the few short weeks Jarman was given to complete his designs, he managed to capture the intended mood with a sharpness and delicacy which, to quote *The Times Educational Supplement*, 'is what one remembers most about the new ballet and offers a clue to its principal weakness. Through Derek Jarman's scenery and costumes Ashton has introduced real originality and a bright new look to ballet design of the "sixties".'[17]

A front cloth in the form of a calendar in dazzling dayglo colours deftly announced what was to follow: a jaunty and up-to-the-minute juxtaposition of varying geometric shapes and brightly coloured costumes. On the first night, Tuesday 9 January, the audience burst into spontaneous applause as the front cloth rose to reveal a stage dominated by two enormous circles, both brilliant red, between which preened 'fair' Monday, her costume – a leotard that went from white to pink, a red glove, a glittering skull-cap – dramatically complementing the colour and starkness of the circles, her narcissism emphasised by the cut-out mirror glinting at the side of the stage. Each succeeding scene centred on a similarly simple design motif: a pyramid of clear perspex balls for Tuesday; a blue and red love-knot for Friday; for Sunday, a roll-call of all the major design elements plus a towering figure 7 to denote the number of scenes. The costumes were equally striking, the most unusual being the matching tunics, blue on one side, red on the other, for Friday's bluesy lovers. In the words of the reviewer from *Queen*, as the two lovers 'turned and intertwined it was difficult to distinguish whose limb was which and what exactly it was doing – most effective and indeed proper for these permissive days'.[18]

Like *Queen*, and with very few exceptions (Richard Buckle in *The Times* considered the designs passé and dubbed them 'pop', causing a loyal Anthony Harwood to dash off a letter to Lord Thompson of Fleet in which he suggested with some asperity that 'Mr Buckle would do well to study trends in contemporary English art before speaking further'),[19] most reviewers had nothing but praise for the new ballet, sets and costumes included – although, as indicated by *The TES*, there were some who found the twinning of Ashton's classical steps with Bennett's jazz score decidedly disappointing. Audiences showed no such reservations. Jarman counted a total of seventeen curtain calls on the opening night, while on the final night of the season there was even an encore, almost unheard of in ballet.[20]

Jarman experienced Tuesday 9 January 1968 as a second Christmas Day. It was a white Christmas – London lay under a covering of snow – laden with presents. Betts had made her boy a silk shirt and jabot in cream, and trumped that gift with a pearl tie-pin. The designer Michael Fish had accepted a painting as payment for one of his 'frocks for fellas': the most sumptuous of brown velvet suits. Harwood produced 'a garland of silver bells held by a cascade of bows'.[21] Although, audience-wise, the thunder was stolen by the presence in the auditorium of Princess Margaret and Lord Snowdon, for Jarman what mattered was that so many of his friends braved the snow to show him support – and that one of their number, an admiring Robert Medley, then threw him a party.

When it was all over, what remained were the stories, which could be told and retold, gaining in fabulousness with each retelling. The headaches that, as a newcomer, Jarman had experienced in dealing with an institution as set in its ways as the Royal Opera House. Ashton's supportiveness. The legendary Nureyev, who partnered Antoinette Sibley in the Friday *pas de deux*[22] and led Jarman an equally intricate dance over his costume. As characterised by Jarman, theirs was a relationship of cat and defenceless mouse which, on the opening night – because Nureyev developed 'flu – resulted in a last-minute announcement that the star would not be able to dance. In the event, he did, *and* in Jarman's costume, *and* wearing a cap he had earlier scorned. Game, set and match to a rather shaken mouse. Later that month, Ashton wrote politely to Betts: 'Derek did a wonderful job and was very easy to work with and practical and sensible. He made a real contribution.'[23]

Jarman's career could not have started with greater éclat. And yet, just as in ballet there is usually a Carabosse to undermine the good work of the Lilac Fairy, so there was a troubling subtext to Jarman's stories about *Jazz Calendar*. Although the ballet had freed him from his easel and taken him among people, had he really been at ease in the Opera House? Why, despite the success of the designs, did Ashton not ask Jarman to work with him again? Was it that, in their heart of hearts, both Ashton and Jarman knew that what Jarman needed was to concentrate not on someone else's visions, but his own?

15

This Month in Vogue

As defined by Patrick Procktor, and with a fine disregard for the issue of student or political unrest, '1968 was the year when everybody wanted pink suede shoes, high heels, and to have what was This Month in Vogue.'[1] If anyone was in vogue, it was Derek Jarman. In the fortnight separating Robert Medley's party for *Jazz Calendar* and the party Anthony Harwood threw for Jarman's twenty-sixth birthday, the birthday boy was sufficiently in demand to receive a second design commission. Earlier that month, while *Jazz Calendar* was still in rehearsal, Dame Marie Rambert had been glimpsed by Jarman sitting 'quizzically in a box'. He noted despairingly that 'she made little comment about the sets' and that 'unlit, the Naples yellow cloths looked grey and the stage rather empty'.[2] Nonetheless, it was Dame Marie, galvanised by a further instance of Gosling patronage, who proffered the new commission.

A few years previously, a Romanian choreographer by the name of Stere Popescu had defected to the West following a Paris season with the Romanian State Ballet. The Goslings had seen and admired Popescu's work in Paris, and since they also had something of a reputation for helping political refugees – theirs was the house where

Nureyev lived when in London – Popescu turned to them for assistance. They brought him to the attention of Marie Rambert, in whose company Maud Gosling had earlier danced.

Willing to help, but only up to a point, Dame Marie cautiously offered Popescu the opportunity to create a short piece for *Collaboration Two*, the second of her company's annual workshops aimed at providing primarily younger choreographers, composers and designers with a stage upon which to mingle their talents and embody their ideas. The stage in question was that of the Jeanetta Cochrane Theatre. The young choreographers were drawn mostly from the Ballet Rambert, the student designers from the Central School of Art and Design. In the case of *Throughway*, however, the collaboration was between a man in his mid-forties, Popescu, and a designer who had been out of art school for almost a year.

As its title indicates, *Throughway* was about a journey; an anguished, autobiographical journey that, in the words of its displaced creator, moved through 'fear, threats, distraction and confusion to a kind of respite'.[3] Surrealistic in nature and set to a pre-recorded combination of sound and existing music, it involved a character called Hawk, a stylised tea party and what, for the dancers, was a puzzling sequence of robotic movements which, because Popescu spoke little English, he could not properly explain. Jarman's costumes did little to improve matters. Despite the slenderest of budgets, Jarman dreamed up a kaleidoscope of outfits for the twelve-strong cast, two of which were particularly eye-catching: bloated pink body costumes complete with pendulous breasts and dangling genitalia. Popescu was horrified. This grotesquerie was not at all what he wanted; and when, on the opening night, the audience greeted the piece – and the gargantuan breasts in particular – with audible titters, he was plunged into despair.

The notices did nothing to lift his spirits. Although Nigel Gosling, writing as Alexander Bland, spoke of the 'strange stammering integrity of this highly original piece',[4] his was the minority view. Jarman's designs garnered general praise, but the overall reaction was that of *The Times*, for whom the ballet was nothing but an 'insufferable muddle of second-rate, second-hand ideas'.[5]

On 5 March, the opening night, there had been another party, at

Anthony Harwood's flat, to celebrate Jarman's continuing ascent of the theatrical ladder. On the second night, Popescu begged the Ballet Rambert to withdraw his piece. He was refused. Distraught, the frustrated choreographer returned home and did something to make sure his wishes would be met: he took a fatal overdose of barbiturates. Jarman was stricken to the core. Like some of the ballet's more outspoken critics, who worried about the effect of their notices, he knew his costumes had played a part in the choreographer's unhappiness. Although *Throughway* appears by name in his cv, the sobering story of its two-night run and 'the lengths to which people can be driven by the failure of an event'[6] was something he seldom dwelled upon.

As traumatic, because it was closer to home, and in its way as final, was the day Roger Ford walked out on Brenda Lukey. This separation signalled the demise of an era, the passing of which, it suddenly seemed, was being marked by most of Jarman's older friends as they either changed partners, settled into jobs, or started to marry and raise children. Studenthood was most emphatically at an end, on the professional as well as the domestic front.

Within weeks of *Throughway*'s truncated run, Jarman had embarked on a third commission, one that, for all its potential glory, would test him sorely. Ashton, on hearing what it was, warned against it, at the same time conceding that of course Jarman had 'no choice'[7] but to accept. The approach had been made by letter:

> Dear Mr Jarman
>   Sir Frederick Ashton kindly gave me your address. I am a great admirer of your brilliant sets for *Jazz Calendar* and wonder if you would care to show me any photographs or designs for other work that you may have and have a talk with me about a possible project I have been asked to undertake in the summer.[8]

The letter was signed by Sir John Gielgud, and the 'possible project' was a production of *Don Giovanni* that the Sadler's Wells Opera Company[9] wanted Gielgud to direct when they moved into their new home, the London Coliseum.

In late 1967 the Wells, which had been planning for some time to move from its cramped quarters in Islington to the South Bank, had alighted on the Coliseum as a more central alternative. In April 1968, with just four months in hand until their opening night of 21 August, the company began the awesome task of converting the monumental Edwardian edifice in St Martin's Lane from its previous incarnation as a cinema back into a theatre. Jarman, meanwhile, was labouring as intensively on the sets and costumes. For someone who liked to work quickly, the amount of time and energy he expended on this was enormous. As he later explained:

> First I spent some weeks researching into past productions . . .
> I took patterns and motifs such as the obelisk and formal
> garden topiary as a starting point, and then attempted to
> synthesize these into a neoclassical twentieth century
> conception, but using traditional stage techniques . . . In
> designing the costumes . . . I tried to find symbolic
> equivalents for the various characters . . . Zerlina, the simple
> village girl, wears green, the colour of the countryside. For
> Elvira's clothes I have used shot colours so as to suggest the
> indecision of her attitude towards the Don . . . The sets . . .
> also follow a pattern of colour starting with an almost entirely
> monochromatic first scene . . . and reaching a climax at the
> end of the first act in the rich tones of the ballroom scene. In
> the second act the settings . . . become progressively darker.[10]

Fittingly, it was an earlier Sadler's Wells production – that of Charles Reading in 1938 – which suggested the way forward. 'Very simple architectural setting,' wrote Jarman in his notes, '. . . much the best of all productions owing to greater simplicity.' He hated what he called the 'fuzz' of 'unnecessary detail', the 'swags and dec-oration', the air of 'Chippendale reproduction', so often associated with Mozart. He was determined to avoid realism and particularisa-tion, which in his view would only undermine the work's metaphorical nuances. Both he and Gielgud were particularly keen that, unlike Zeffirelli's 1962 production, the opera should flow smoothly with no unwieldy changes of scene.

In conjunction with the conductor, Charles Mackerras, who had prepared a new performing edition for the occasion, the decision was taken to update the opera to the eighteenth century, roughly contemporary with Mozart, and to set it in Goya's Spain. Originally Jarman wanted 'a single all purpose set, and colour, masses of it, to combat the usual browns and greys of the theatre'.[11] In the event, although there was certainly colour – the myriad costumes ensured that – there was a different set for each scene and a series of drop cloths to demarcate the settings. Each cloth was a version of the scene it prefaced; a version, too, of Jarman's current style of painting. All displayed the same elements of two-dimensionality, sparseness and geometric form. As did the scenes themselves, for which Jarman revisited his student designs for *Orpheus*. Each set comprised a combination of geometric shapes, obelisks, cones, squares and circles, with only an occasional hint of realism: the banqueting table, for example, on which Jarman lavished the same attention to detail as he had on another of his Slade designs, that of Volpone's treasure.

Despite the care and thought that went into these designs, as Ashton had warned, Jarman's involvement with Mozart's masterpiece was doomed to ultimate failure. If it were not enough that builders and painters were everywhere in evidence, or that the company was unused to playing somewhere as vast as the Coliseum, or that Mackerras should fall ill a fortnight before the opening and have to be replaced, Gielgud, who had tackled opera on only three previous occasions, the last a decade earlier, was quite unable to provide a firm enough directorial hand. Both the inexperienced Jarman and the uncertain Gielgud changed their own and each other's minds so constantly, and to such mutually aggravating effect, that the general confusion soon reached epidemic proportions. At the dress rehearsal, the beleaguered director noticed that some of the chorus still did not know where to move and, as he struggled to instruct them against the wall of sound emanating from the orchestra pit, wailed exasperatedly: 'Oh, do stop that awful *music!*'[12]

Of course, the music could not be stopped. It had to be faced. And two days later it was. The snow that had blanketed London on the opening night of *Jazz Calendar* had been exchanged for the sticky heat of August, and in the papers there was dismaying news from

Prague, where Mozart's opera had first been performed: Soviet tanks
had rumbled into the city. The reviews for *Don Giovanni* did nothing
to relieve the gravity of that day's headlines. An example of their
waspishness is provided by the *Evening Standard*: 'The magnitude of
the disaster will long remain a cherished memory . . . Derek Jarman's
angular, abstract sets did not convey a thing and his Don Giovanni
palace looked like a cross between the Drug Store and the Swiss
Centre.'[13] *The Sunday Times* was more measured, but no less damn-
ing: 'Opinion varied as to whether Sir John's handling of the action
was too tame for Mr Jarman's fanciful sets, or whether (my own
view) the producer did his not very brilliant best against visual dis-
tractions that would have addled a genius. At all events the
combined result was disastrous.'[14] There were those whose criticism
was less harsh, even some who saw virtue in the designs,[15] but no one
who counted the production a success.

In the face of such critical hostility, one must assume the designs
left much to be desired. Indeed, Jarman himself would later accept
that his costumes had not been entirely successful. It is worth
remembering, though, that in the years that have elapsed since then,
opera design has undergone a revolution. In 1968, people expected
precisely what Jarman refused to give them: red plush, chandeliers,
curtains between the acts. Today abstraction is perfectly acceptable,
and audiences might have responded differently.[16]

Jarman's reaction to falling foul of the operatic establishment was
intense. In the margin of the *Evening Standard* review he sowed the
seeds of what was to become a lifelong battle with the media by writing jeeringly: 'example of high critical standard set by Eng press'. In
Dancing Ledge, where he adopted a more jocular but no less defiant
tone, his words were: 'A career that started in reverse has been
brought to an abrupt halt, not a moment too soon.'[17] With something of the ruthlessness with which he could set aside friends and
lovers when they had outlived their usefulness, he turned his back on
the establishment that had scorned him and pointed himself with
such determined cheerfulness in the opposite direction that many of
his circle were blinded to the fact that the débâcle had in any way
affected him. He also eschewed his circle, or those, at least, who
had 'deserted' him in favour of heterosexual (and therefore

establishment) domesticity. The time had come, he told himself, to 'slip quietly from the "scene" which for five years had been the centre of my life . . . and establish my own idiosyncratic mode of living'.[18]

The way forward was indicated by the brief tenure he enjoyed that summer of a house by the Thames which, because it was awaiting demolition, Anya Sainsbury's husband John was able to allow him, Peter Logan and the painter Tony Fry to use as a studio. After years of cramped terrace houses – with their equally cramping social expectations – Jarman found the South Bank of the Thames 'exhilarating. There was,' he wrote, 'space to spread out . . . Returning home late at night down . . . empty streets you felt the city belonged to you.'[19]

As demolition day drew near, the landlord of a pub in Upper Ground suggested that a warehouse next door might provide a longer-term solution. The ground floor was used for storage by a sweet manufacturer, but its upper two floors stood empty and perhaps waiting. Jarman left the business arrangements to Logan, who informed a young man from the letting agency that it was simply silly to stick to the figure they were asking: it would only mean falling behind with the rent. Miraculously, the young man acceded to Logan's logic and lowered the price. Thus did the warehouse at 51 Upper Ground, near the corner with Blackfriars Road, become in part an artist's studio.[20]

With Logan claiming the top floor, which he painted yellow, Jarman took the large, L-shaped room immediately below. He decorated sections of the floor by writing on the boards, hung the walls with works in progress and arranged the tools of his trade, altar-like, on his work table. He invested in a Baby Belling and an art deco sofa and walnut desk, at which he placed the Breuer chair given him in exchange for a painting by the model and actor Peter Hinwood. Behind the wooden partition that ran parallel to one wall of windows he created an occasional bedroom area out of carpets, cushions and a mattress; occasional because, although in his journals he gives the impression that he left Liverpool Road when he acquired Upper Ground, Jarman did not finally say goodbye to Islington for another year.

Since Upper Ground had no bath, visits to the public baths were part of the daily routine, as were meals at a neighbouring pub or café.

Celebrations might mean an oyster bar – oysters were a particular favourite of Jarman's – or the Boot and Flogger in Borough High Street, a mock eighteenth-century alehouse with a sawdust floor where champagne could be bought by the glass. At the studio, food and alcohol were kept to a minimum, tea being more or less the only beverage on offer. Although Jarman loved his friends to visit, he knew that if too many people felt at home in Upper Ground, and spent too much time there, his work would suffer. And in the aftermath of *Don Giovanni*, work – his own as opposed to outside commissions – became of paramount, consoling importance. Rather in the manner of a cook, or someone on a production line, he would arrange the 'ingredients' he needed on his work table, close the door and, working sometimes for days at a stretch, produce new pieces by the yard.

Three exhibitions followed in fairly quick succession. In August 1968, his designs for *Jazz Calendar* were included in a celebration of ballet at the Wright Hepburn Gallery in Belgravia. In January 1969, as part of the coming generation, he was part of *The English Landscape Tradition in the Twentieth Century*, a group exhibition at the Camden Arts Centre in Arkwright Road. The painting he showed was *Landscape with a Blue Pool*, which the Arts Council had just purchased – and which they supplemented almost immediately with a drawing: *Large Landscape Drawing Number Four*. Finally, in February 1969, he had his first solo show at the by now well-established Lisson Gallery. He exhibited fourteen landscapes, some ballet designs and in the basement what was termed an 'environmental and additative sculpture': 'three shallow aluminium troughs filled with that peculiar crushed green stone always associated with graves'.[21]

Nicholas Logsdail used the poster for the exhibition to juxtapose the worst of the *Don Giovanni* reviews with some rather more complimentary assessments of his artist's abilities. The debate thus engendered was one from which, judging by the sparse yet thoughtful coverage accorded the exhibition, Jarman emerged with honour. Writing in *Queen*, Elizabeth Glazebrook noted approvingly: 'Derek Jarman has two apparently distinct talents – one for stage and costume design, and one for painting. He seems exuberant and extrovert in the first case, using vivid colours and bold forms and sweeping lines. In the second case he seems quiet and thoughtful, painting with subtlety and exactitude, covering his canvases or panels very sparingly with paint.'[22]

What Jarman described as the 'static tension' between two- and three- dimensionality that existed as strongly in his cool, abstracted landscapes as it did in his character would, as his canvases became emptier and emptier, tug him towards the three-dimensional. To certain of his friends, this called into question his standing as an artist. Surely fine art was superior to the applied? To Jarman, such distinctions were meaningless. Besides, after *Don Giovanni* he tended to mistrust or ignore the opinions of others.

He started making sculptural pieces that relied heavily on his distinctive use of geometric form. He designed a garden for a cosmetics firm who wanted an unusual setting for a commercial. The design – sculptured fountains and fallen columns set in an area of endless green – was never used, but it served as a template for countless projects to come. As did Jarman's many suggestions to Anya and John Sainsbury for the layout of their garden at Ashden, their country home in Kent, to which Jarman was a regular visitor.

Geometric form featured just as strikingly in the designs, some of which Jarman included in the Lisson exhibition, for what was collectively called *Ballet for Small Spaces*. This was a group project devised and executed in the first instance by Jarman, Peter Logan and his wife Diane, Michael Ginsborg and Robby Nelson, Brenda Lukey, Richard Rowson, Keith Milow, a friend of Peter Logan's from Camberwell called Dilly McDermott and the actor Jonathan Kent. The idea was to combine music, art and performance in such a way as to express the unique vision of the group; in sixties-speak, to do their own thing; in Jarman's own, rather more revealing words: 'to enable a group of people to work freely unencumbered by an existing theatrical organisation. We hope the space we are working in precludes a theatrical success, in the conventional sense . . .'[23] The shadow cast by *Don Giovanni* is palpable and could clearly be dispelled only by its polar opposite, the group's first 'happening' at the Logans' house in Camden Town on Bonfire Night, 1968. Dressed in costumes that represented different artistic schools (cubism, surrealism), various of the group were encased in lightweight paper structures within which, to the acme of 'spaced-out' music – 'Thus Spake Zarathustra' – they inched across the Logans' living room before bursting free in a manner consistent with their differing disciplines and waving sparklers in the air. The many friends who had gathered on the stairs and gallery overlooking the performing area – or who spilled into the garden, so great was the crush – applauded vociferously. Vera Russell, founder of the Artists' Market in Earlham Street and doyenne of artistic endeavour everywhere, pronounced herself keen to help the group find funding. New horizons, it seemed, might be opening up.

An exhibition entitled *The Machine as Seen at the End of the Mechanical Age* happened to be on show at the Museum of Modern Art in New York. Jarman was given the catalogue for Christmas. Leafing through it, one can clearly see, in the collision between the mechanical and the human that characterises the work of artists like Giorgio de Chirico, Wyndham Lewis, El Lissitzky, Claes Oldenburg, Oskar Schlemmer and the Bauhaus, Kurt Schwitters, or that old favourite Robert Rauschenberg, many of the influences at work on Jarman, particularly with regard to the figures with geometric or abstract heads and hands that peopled his ballet designs. Equally under the sway of these influences, and that of Fernand Léger, was Peter Logan, who had been developing his own, purely mechanical ballet – coloured poles that dipped and turned in time to electronic music. Logan was offered an exhibition at the New Art Centre in Sloane Street, where – since his mechanical ballet would occupy only the ground floor – he suggested to Jarman they mount a further series of live ballets in the basement.

All might have been well (it certainly promised well: no fewer than five short ballets were planned) when a new person joined the group, one whose presence, now and for much of the coming decade, would frequently spell disruption where Jarman was concerned.

Patrik Steede was in many ways Jarman's twin. Also of middle-class origin, good-looking, brimming with laughter and exceptionally bright, he too had a father whose strictness he bemoaned; he too was both image-conscious and intent on kicking over the traces: 'blue jeans, cowboy boots, long straight sandy hair and [the] face . . . of Lorenzo di Medici'. Steede's, however, was an altogether less focused and more disturbing personality than Jarman's. Something of a gigolo in that he was invariably paid for by others, and of markedly unsettled sexuality, Steede had 'a gift or necessity for failure'.[24] As Jarman would later write in his diary, the realisation of any one of Steede's many dreams 'would have grounded him like a paragraph in this diary. Patrik lived in a Tabula Rasa, a blankness that allowed him a certain mystery.'[25] The darkness at the heart of Steede's personality could well have been caused by his horse-mad mother, who, Jarman always asserted, was a 'village sadist' who chained her son 'to the meathooks in the cottage kitchen and butchered him'.[26] If true, this would certainly explain the bizarreness of Steede's imagination. There is a tape-recording of Steede and Jarman together in the early seventies. Steede has a cat on his lap. 'Oh, this pussy's so warm,' he purrs at one point in precise, almost affected tones. 'I'd like to slit its tummy open and put my hands inside and carry it round as a muff.' To which Jarman responds sharply: 'Oh Patrik, what a horrible thought.'

Although Jarman loved nothing more than to engage with the sharpness of Steede's mind, Steede's 'horrible' thoughts were to unsettle his friend on more than one occasion. Steede was also close to Gervase Griffiths, to whom Patrick Procktor had lost his heart, and had travelled with Griffiths to Haiti, home of voodoo. On their return, it was agreed that Jarman and Steede would work together to devise the ballets for the small space in the basement in Sloane Street. Griffiths was co-opted to compose some music, as was the young Paul Buckmaster. What followed is poorly documented, and even more poorly remembered, but it would seem that Jarman and Steede fell out. Steede then worked on a piece of his own set to Griffiths' music, while Jarman devised something that involved the voodooistic decapitation of a chicken. Horrified, Logan vetoed its performance, whereupon Jarman accused him of the worst kind of censorship, that of one artist by another. For the duration of the exhibition Jarman stood tearfully at the door to the gallery handing out leaflets protesting at the manner in which he had been silenced.

Clearly, it was not only 'existing theatrical organisations' which were to be feared. Indeed, for all that Jarman had determined to turn his back on such organisations, there were still moments when they had their uses. Within a month of standing outside the New Art Centre handing out leaflets, he was sitting beside Sir Frederick Ashton in a box at the recently opened Metropolitan Opera House in New York for the American première of *Jazz Calendar*.

The ballet was not enthusiastically received, but that did not unduly upset the designer. His attention was elsewhere. On his first trip to America, San Francisco had beckoned; now it was Manhattan – and in particular Andy Warhol, whose lifestyle he was starting to ape.[27] Jarman did not manage to meet Warhol, but he did sit next to Candy Darling, one of Warhol's more outré stars, at Max's Kansas City, and she did at least invite him to visit the Factory, where Nicholas Ray was showing some of the films he had made with his students. Jarman found it 'incomprehensible' that the director of *Rebel without a Cause* should be making 'shaky, out of focus 16mm movies'.[28]

Five years had elapsed since Jarman's first trip to America. No longer in any sense a virgin, except perhaps cinematically, he indulged his fondness for American boys by visiting the bars as determinedly as he did the museums or the architectural wonders of Philip Johnson's glass house in New Canaan, where he and Anthony Harwood took tea with the house's owner. Because Harwood happened to be in New York, he had undertaken to arrange an apartment for Jarman. With equal generosity, Jarman played benefactor to Keith Milow, who had never visited the city and therefore qualified, in Jarman's eyes, for the gift of a plane ticket. Never mind that Milow was one of the people with whom Jarman did not always see eye to eye artistically, or that Milow should remain out of reach as a sexual target, it still gave Jarman the most enormous pleasure to be the means whereby a door, any door, could be opened. In all sorts of ways, some conscious, some not, he was establishing a pattern for the trips of the future.

Notwithstanding his generosity, money was tight. Although he had been decently paid for *Don Giovanni* and had subsequently sold a few paintings, between August 1968 and 1970 he managed pitifully little paid employment. From Robert Medley, who had been asked to caretake the theatre design course at the Slade in 1969, came a request to help structure the course and orchestrate another 'happening', this time with Yolanda Sonnabend, who had also studied at the Slade and had known Jarman since the Paris Biennale, where her designs had shown alongside his. That summer, when Robin Howard moved his company, the London Contemporary Dance Theatre,[29] into new premises at 17 Dukes Road, Jarman was among those asked to christen The Place by creating one of a range of staged events that took place throughout the building as evidence of the 'experimental ambience' Howard wished to foster. Bar some fragmentary notes for a piece called *Four Winds*, there is no record of what Jarman provided for the occasion, though we do know he helped Peter Logan, with whom he had long since buried the hatchet, with Logan's own event, an entire *Corridor and a Room for Robin Howard*.

His other design commission for 1969 was for the second half of a double bill by Peter Tegel which Nicholas Wright directed at the recently opened Theatre Upstairs at the Royal Court. Because theatre's abiding naturalism did not ordinarily allow for as free a use of colour as ballet or opera, it was a medium Jarman tended to belittle or avoid. The Royal Court, however, existed in a category all its own. Not only did it mean following in the footsteps of Procktor and Hockney, both of whom had designed there, but it was immediately downstairs from Harwood's flat, where Jarman spent so much of his time. When Geoffrey Rogers introduced Jarman to Tegel at the Lisson Gallery with a view to bringing the two of them together to work on Tegel's double bill, Jarman was happy to tackle *Poet of the Anemones*, the more surrealistic of Tegel's two plays. The first, *Blim at School*, he handed to Robin Hirtenstein, a friend from the Slade.[30]

The budget was derisory, but at least the surrealism of Tegel's play, in which the adult Blim underwent as many changes of costume as he did of persona, allowed Jarman a degree of visual inventiveness – and the opportunity to demonstrate that no matter what the theatrical organisation, his ideas were not to be trifled with. When one of the actresses objected to the wide-brimmed hat he insisted she wear, substituting a smaller, more manageable one of her own, Jarman filched her substitution and destroyed it, leaving Nicholas Wright to smooth matters over and find what was necessary from the budget to compensate the actress for the cost involved.

One of the more notable of Jarman's designs for *Poet of the Anemones* was a laminated cape of clear plastic in which was suspended a scattering of dollar bills. It was almost certainly Dom Sylvester Houédard, given to laminating his every poetic endeavour, who supplied Jarman with the idea, while as a shape and concept, the cape itself was something its creator had already discovered in his designs for *The Tempest*. Capes are both practical and sensual, especially when cloaking nakedness. They are geometric: if hung on the wall, they form a half circle. They have mythic overtones: by donning a cape, the wearer can effect a transformation. These qualities, particularly the latter, had considerable potency for Jarman, who now set about working and reworking this new possibility until the capes he produced – and began to hang on the walls of his studio – no longer resembled design, but approached the condition of painting or sculpture.

Being by the river had awakened in Jarman a passion for beachcombing. He began to incorporate rusted metal and gnarled driftwood into the capes, and to make sculptures from this flotsam and jetsam. The boy who had stared so fixedly at flowers had become a man who could stare with equal intensity at the detritus in his path and isolate its beauty. Both as a person and an artist, Jarman had experienced rejection. Now, by giving new life to the discarded and the decaying, he was questioning what should be valued, what rejected.

The undercurrent of repudiation and loss that had characterised so much of Jarman's life to date continued, albeit subtly, to make itself felt. That autumn his 'gardening soul mate' Güta Minton died.

> She leaves me the fine ebony writing table with the winged griffin mounts in brass. But it's too heavy and my parents fail to bring it over the garden wall. It's sold to an unscrupulous dealer. I try to get it back, but it's lost – in the window of a Bond Street dealer correctly priced and labelled 'French Directoire'.
>
> The garden is destroyed, bulldozers tear down the lime trees along the drive to make a 'close' of a dozen little houses. Not a brick remains of the old house.[31]

Jarman wrote this within four years of his own death, when his sense of impermanence was particularly acute. The loss he felt in 1969 was no less painful, his loneliness such that it was clearly noticed by Brenda Lukey, who was often to be found at the studio helping to sew capes.

Jarman dealt with his loneliness in typical fashion: by making a virtue of it. When Richard Rowson and his newly acquired partner, the writer Julian Mitchell, invited Jarman to their dinner parties, the latter accepted a couple of their invitations, then told them that dinner parties were not his scene. As he would later write:

> I soon got fed up . . . and returned to the wilds. It was much more fun being out alone, more unexpected . . . you could sit and chat for hours on a bench, and watch the cigarettes flare in the shadows, it was romantic and beautiful with the moon scudding between the clouds, the trees in winter silhouetted against the snow on the ground. I never frequented loos, but meeting people on the heath and lying in the grass under the stars with some stranger was ecstasy.[32]

Gradually, he let his old circle of friends fade away, and though he never completely lost touch with them, they were soon replaced by an entirely new set of people. In this he was greatly assisted by Peter Logan and his younger brother Andrew. Both the Logans – Andrew in particular – were consummate party-givers and helped make Upper Ground a Mecca for London's avant garde. Jarman was no longer overshadowed by Hockney or Procktor. He now had a stage of his own on which to star, plus a large supporting cast. There were the innumerable young men he met in bars or on the heath. There were fellow artists: Duggie Fields, Kevin Whitney, Luciana Martinez, John Dewe-Mathews. There were writers, models, musicians. And there were the Americans: young men who had come to London to experience all the old world could offer them and, as we have already heard Jarman note, to say: 'Hi, let's fuck!'[33]

Pre-eminent among these was the beautiful and charismatic Karl Bowen, a Botticelli angel with 'jet-black curls, grey-blue eyes, and a Texan slouch'.[34] Bowen hailed from Buffalo and had enough money – he was a member of the Kellogg family and the beneficiary of a trust fund – to underwrite his studies in architecture and painting. In time his money would help destroy him; at that time it only added to his allure. His was an irresistible mix of wealth, beauty, a slight nervous laugh and a dirty delight in sex. No matter where he lived, Bowen's room always featured a pile of pornographic magazines and 'a tideline of KY round the wall'.[35] His conversation was peppered with graphic accounts of his nightly adventures. It was his dream to bed 'an Italian football team – he collected postcards of all of them and jerked off so his spunk splashed across them'.[36]

Another was Herbert Muschamp, a friend of Bowen's and also a student of architecture. Knowing how empty the fridge at Upper Ground could be, how cold the studio could get, Muschamp invited Jarman to spend the Christmas of 1969 in Paris, where his boyfriend, Richard Blight, had a warm and well-stocked studio in the Boulevard Excelmans. By accepting this invitation, Jarman put himself in the way of a chance encounter that was radically to alter the course of his entire life.

16

The Devils

In helping to introduce Jarman to the writings of Carl Jung, Anthony Harwood had doubtless noticed the extent to which his protégé could seem to live in psychic rather than physical time; how, on occasion, Jarman's life could embody the more mystical precepts of the Swiss psychoanalyst. There can be few more striking examples of synchronicity – in this case combined with serendipity – than Jarman's return trip from Paris in January 1970. It was an example, too, of the way work would frequently come looking for Jarman rather than the other way around. To borrow his own account:

> On the train waiting to return home, I noticed a girl carrying two heavy suitcases. Something about the way she was dressed and her long hair told me she was English, so I shouted out of the window that there was a spare seat in our carriage, and she clambered in. Throughout the eight hour journey we chatted about the theatre and painting. Janet Deuter was teaching at Hornsey in the experimental light and sound department. She was a friend of Ken and Shirley Russell so she told me of their new film project, *The Devils*.

When we parted company she told me that she'd tell Ken
about me, as she was convinced we would get along.

I soon forgot about this. But a day later the phone rang and
Ken asked me if he could come over – 'tomorrow.' OK I said.
'I'll be there at eight in the morning,' and at eight he arrived
in the freezing empty warehouse at Upper Ground. He was
bowled over by the building, and while we huddled over mugs
of tea I pulled out the odd drawing from *Jazz Calendar* and the
Don, plus various other projects I had worked on. After
looking at them briefly he asked me to design *The Devils*. I
was quite taken aback by the suddenness of this offer, as I'd
promised myself that after *Don Giovanni* I would never design
again.[1] I asked him if I could think it over, and he gave me
twenty four hours. 'In the meantime can Shirley come to tea
to meet you?' In the evening I rushed out to see *Women in
Love*. On the strength of that, and conversations with a few
friends, I decided to plunge in.[2]

For the Ken Russell of 1970, the tag *enfant terrible* is one that fits
with peculiar neatness. In Russell, a baby-faced freshness and fondness for smocks were startlingly yoked to a mop of grey-white hair
and true terribleness of reputation. That February, *The Dance of the
Seven Veils*, his documentary on Richard Strauss, which featured,
among other things, a symphony orchestra in the composer's bedroom playing in time to the composer's orgasms, would signal the
end of a long association with the BBC and utterly horrify the era's
self-proclaimed defender of decency, Mary Whitehouse. Russell's
cinematic version of the D.H. Lawrence novel that Jarman had
dashed to see was proving equally controversial, as would *The Music
Lovers*, his soon-to-be-released take on the tortured Tchaikovsky.

Russell's new project, based on an Aldous Huxley book and a
John Whiting play,[3] was the true story of the religious and sexual
hysteria which, in the early seventeenth century, gripped the
Ursuline nuns of Loudun and led not only to the burning at the stake
of the unfortunate Father Grandier, the libertarian priest on whom
Sister Jeanne of the Angels had become fixated, but the demolition
of the walls of Loudun by a wily Cardinal Richelieu thus presented

Lancelot Elworthy Jarman as a young RAF officer. 'A very conscientious and hard worker colonial who has brains and power of application.' *Gaye Temple*

Elizabeth Evelyn Puttock, known as Betts, prior to attending the Viceroy's garden party, Calcutta, 1934.
Gaye Temple

Above: A wartime arrival. *Gaye Temple*
Right: Grandmother Moselle, or Mimosa, as Jarman always called her: perhaps his staunchest ally in the domestic war he was wont to wage with his father.
Estate of Derek Jarman

Betts with little Dekky and Gaye in the
overgrown garden of Manor Cottage, 1945.
'These spring flowers are my first memory.'
Gaye Temple

Villa Zuassa, Lake Maggiore, Italy,
August 1946.   *Gaye Temple*

Swanage, August 1950. Imagining oneself as a
smuggler.   *Gaye Temple*

Curry Mallet Manor, 1952. A place of
'honeyed memory'.
Estate of Derek Jarman

'Subcontinental suburbia'. Pakistan, early fifties.   *Gaye Temple*

In CCF uniform on the Northwood 'patch'.   *Gaye Temple*

Jarman, a dandified Casca, stands on the left of David Miller's De Gaulle-like Julius Caesar on the set of his first design for the stage. Canford, 1960.   *Desmond Vowles*

Jarman posing with his self-portrait on the occasion of his exhibition at the Watford Public Library, May 1961. 'I looked quite innocent,' was his comment on the photograph when he included it in *The Last of England*.
Estate of Derek Jarman

The innocent acquiring sophistication on a student holiday stop-over in Venice, summer 1961.
Estate of Derek Jarman

Further travels. Ron Wright, Canada, summer 1964.   *Estate of Derek Jarman*

Jarman relaxing in his antique reading chair at Priory Road. The larger of the two paintings is *After Poussin's Inspiration of a Poet*.
Ray Dean

Living in the Japanese manner. Anthony Harwood in his Sloane Square flat, at work on his version of *The Dreamers*.   *Ray Dean*

The reopening of the Coliseum as seen by Les Gibbard for the *Sunday Telegraph*, 2 June, 1968. Jarman is seated on the right of John Gielgud.   *Les Gibbard/Sunday Telegraph*

The group behind *Ballet for Small Spaces*, November 1968. 'We hope the space we are working in precludes a theatrical success, in the conventional sense.' Left to right: Jonathan Kent, Richard Rowson, Brenda Lukey, Jarman, Dilly McDermott, Keith Milow, Robby Nelson, Michael Ginsborg. Seated: Diane and Peter Logan.   *Ray Dean*

Jarman in the studio at Liverpool Road with some of the geometric shapes designed to be attached to the arms and head of a performer in *Ballet for Small Spaces*.   *Ray Dean*

The fine artist continues to embrace the performing arts. Mask made for a theatre design project, Upper Ground.   *Ray Dean*

Karl Bowen wrapped in Jarman's arms and in the dollar cape from *Poet of the Anemones*.   *Ray Dean*

Jarman admiring his multiple for the Lisson Gallery – the one that proved too expensive and fragile to mass-produce.   *John Dewe-Mathews*

The 'plastic fairies' say farewell to the sixties. Left to right: Herbert Muschamp, Michael Ginsborg, Karl Bowen. Upper Ground, June 1970.
John Dewe-Mathews

Above: Proud parents on the set of *The Devils*, 1970. *Gaye Temple*
Right: Flared trousers and a riverside balcony. Jarman, Peter Logan and Luciana Martinez at Bankside. *John Dewe-Mathews*

with a pretext for wresting power from a city that had become too independent; a story, to quote Russell, of the 'self-destruction of a citadel from within'.[4]

To design this citadel, the director was looking for someone as iconoclastic as himself. Though he liked what he saw of the drawings Jarman spread on his table with rather more care than the artlessness of his own account would suggest, it was probably Upper Ground that clinched the matter. To someone like Russell, who gloried in the most theatrical of images, the theatricality of the capes lining the walls of Jarman's studio indicated that here was a kindred spirit. The admiration was mutual, and although Russell was markedly the older and more experienced of the two, and although he and Jarman could and did cross artistic swords, from the start their relationship was essentially one of equals. If Jarman ever felt alarmed or cowed by the fact that he had never worked in film before, he did not show it.

What Russell wanted from the design was sufficient freshness to bring home the excesses of seventeenth-century Loudun to a contemporary audience. Early on he and Jarman watched Fritz Lang's *Metropolis*. Here, Russell felt, was a possible template for the cinematic city Jarman would have to build. Also in play was the work of other German directors of the Weimar period, such as Pabst and Von Stroheim; the films of Eisenstein, whose use of architecture to emphasise character was particularly relevant; *The Wizard of Oz*; even, perhaps, subliminal memories of the biblical epics of Jarman's cinemagoing childhood. There was Jarman's knowledge of architecture as derived from Pevsner and the years spent watching his flatmates at work at their drawing boards in Witley Court and Priory Road. There were the drawings of Piranesi, Esher and Ledoux. Finally, there was the obsession with geometric form to be found in Jarman's own paintings and his De Chirico-inspired sets for *Don Giovanni*.

Russell assigned Jarman an art director, the highly experienced George Lack, whose task it was to translate Jarman's drawings into precisely scaled elevations and models that could be set before Russell and his producers. Jarman and Lack would spend the day together at Jarman's studio before crossing the river in the evening to the Russells' house in Ladbroke Grove to assess the day's discoveries in excited exchanges that covered everything from Russell's script and his wife Shirley's costume designs to that day's drawings for the set and the fact – unearthed by Jarman – that fashionable Frenchwomen of the seventeenth century favoured mauve as a colour for lipstick.

Then, out of the blue, potential disaster struck. The film's backer, United Artists, who had been responsible for Russell's three previous features, unexpectedly bowed out and only after a suspenseful few months was a replacement found, in the form of Warner Brothers. Warner Brothers spelled change and compromise. The film would be shot at Pinewood, using the studio's extensive production facilities. Lack was replaced by Robert Cartwright. Jarman was assigned an office within the studio complex. The model of the set which he and Lack had built at Upper Ground with the help of students from the Central School of Art and Design met with a sudden and unexpected hostility as implacable as that of Richelieu himself. Out came a budgetary knife to amputate the gilded court and topiary garden of Louis XIII. More important than Jarman's original concept, as far as the new financiers were concerned, was how much cheaper it would be to use the garden at Pinewood. Many more compromises were to follow; compromises which, for Jarman, hit home most when the cameras at last started rolling in August. As he experienced it, not only were the extras who dressed his sets unpleasantly indifferent to their surroundings, but so was the director, who appeared to treat the designs as a backdrop instead of an integral part of the film. Jarman was learning the hard way that freedom of choice or movement on a feature film is often a contradiction in terms.

And yet, ironically, it was budgetary compromise which was responsible for the monumental city springing up on the back lot finally looking as arresting as it did. Because he could not afford both, Jarman had opted for size over detail, and because it would have been too expensive to build real walls, he had used mouldings which could be mass-produced and tacked on to flats. He and Russell decided that since the mouldings would in any case inevitably mean a uniformity of look, they might as well go for the easiest option, that of brick. When they tried painting the brick, it made the set look drab. Deciding that the original white of the mouldings was what worked best, Jarman abandoned any notion of colour (although, this being film, to get the bricks to look white on camera, he actually had to paint them beige). In his history of the hysteria that engulfed Loudun, Huxley likens Sister Jeanne's exorcism to 'a rape in a public lavatory'.[5] By trial and error rather than by design, Jarman had come up with an entire city that echoed the horror of that description.

There was victory, then, to be snatched from the jaws of cinematic compromise, and for all that his dungareed figure occasionally fell foul of the powers that be, Jarman's basic enthusiasm for the film never waned. In his role as 'the artist', which was what he came to be dubbed, there was immense satisfaction to be had in seeing his city take shape and in showing proud parents and awestruck friends around the dazzling expanse of it. There was the challenge of making props at his studio with the help of art students, or at Pinewood with the more experienced Christopher Hobbs, who soon became a close and valued friend. The challenge of accommodating the eccen-trically typed suggestions which Dom Sylvester Houédard, an expert on ecclesiastical history, fired at Jarman from his desk at Prinknash Abbey. The chance to ask Michael Ginsborg to produce a copy of Poussin's *Triumph of Pan* for Grandier's study and, as the study's other decorative feature, to rescue the classical statuary being discarded by the Slade in its efforts to modernise its life room – in particular a plaster cast of the head of Mausolus. The passing thrill of glimpsing a leathery Charlton Heston in a Pinewood projection room. The cachet of working with Oliver Reed, who played Grandier, Vanessa Redgrave (Sister Jeanne) and Peter Maxwell Davies, who wrote the music. The frisson of being on set during the orgies that were rumoured to have broken out among the nuns as Russell fuelled their hysteria by dispensing alcohol and playing Prokofiev's *The Fiery Angel*. Or of being present when, towards the end of filming, Russell mistakenly – and expensively – signalled for the walls of Loudun to be demolished when the camera was not rolling.

Despite the fact that for much of 1970, Jarman's existence centred on Pinewood, life by the Thames never ground to a complete stand-still. In June, time was found to mount a second one-man exhibition at the Lisson Gallery. Entitled *Upper Ground Works*, it was held in the Lisson Warehouse, a newly opened annex to the main gallery, and featured capes and banners plus *light*, a functional sculpture in which the word 'light' had been fashioned from a neon tube to stand,

six foot high, on an enamelled stand. This was Jarman's contribution
to a late-sixties, neo-Marxist attempt by the Lisson to democratise
fine art by producing 'multiples' that could be mass-produced and
sold cheaply to all comers. About half a dozen artists contributed to
the project, which never quite took off, in Jarman's case because his
prototype proved too expensive and fragile to mass-produce. Only
the élitist original ever saw, as it were, the light of day; even then, it
failed to dazzle. As an exhibition, *Upper Ground Works* passed almost
unnoticed.[6]

In return for the many ecclesiastical hints Dom Sylvester Houédard
had provided for *The Devils*, Jarman agreed to design a sculptural version of a Houédard poem which the mischievous monk wanted to
include in *Visual Poetries*, a loan exhibition of his work planned by the
circulation department of the Victoria and Albert Museum for the following year. The poem, written to be read vertically, ran:

H
as
H
is
H

The American satirist P. J. O'Rourke characterises the concrete
poetry of which Houédard was such a committed exponent in one
pithy sentence: 'The idea was to combine the visual arts with literature to make something that you can't read and isn't easy to look at
either.'[7] Jarman, by contrast, was all enthusiasm: 'What about a small
garden of H on fine steel stalks with brass flower letters so that the
whole thing vibrates gently at eye height?'[8] Houédard was delighted
with this conceit – a 'Kiff Garden', he called it – and before long
Jarman had roped in some colleagues from the film, including
Christopher Hobbs and Bryn Siddall, to help design the 'garden'
and find the necessary steel rods. Punningly entitled *Grass Poem*, the
piece was first shown over a year later at the V&A in late 1971, then
at various galleries and art colleges up and down the country.
Thereafter, it becomes the very opposite of concrete and mysteriously vanishes from sight.

Also that summer, Peter Logan and Jarman threw a party at Upper Ground to bid farewell to the sixties and to their studio, which was about to be demolished to make way for the IPC tower. Invitations – bearing a photograph of Jarman, Herbert Muschamp, Karl Bowen and Michael Ginsborg, waving wands and sporting clear plastic wings, cavorting as fairies on the studio rooftop – had been circulated with such very gay abandon that both floors of the studio swiftly became a heaving mass of friends both old and new. Mingling with unknown boys whose looks had netted them an invitation handed out on the King's Road were as many established faces including that of Ossie Clark, dispensing joints on the stairs, and no less a figure than Tennessee Williams, decanted from a reading at the Queen Elizabeth Hall. The plastic fairies had wrought real magic: not only was the noisy, all-night party not raided, it enjoyed virtual police protection. Lord Snowdon had recently visited the studio with a view to photographing Logan's work, and the local constabulary, alert to the royal connection and imagining perhaps that Snowdon might attend, accorded the partygoers at Upper Ground a degree of respect quite out of character with the times.

As it happened, the party took place on the first anniversary of a most memorable police raid: that defining moment in gay history when a group of wingless fairies, the drag queens from the Stonewall Inn in Greenwich Village, unexpectedly joined forces with other regulars from the bar to turn on their uniformed persecutors and answer back. A year later, in the autumn of 1970, a new political force was making itself felt in London. Calling itself the Gay Liberation Front, its aim was to consolidate the achievements of 1967 and beyond by making tangible the concept of gay pride.

Jarman had never joined any of the groups that shouldered the banner of law reform during the sixties. Like many gays who felt that after 1967 they could safely ignore politics and concentrate on having a good time, Jarman believed that 'life is to be lived first and proselytised after'.[9] So although he attended GLF meetings and readily absorbed its exhortations to step proudly from the closet; although he loved its jokiness – its use of 'radical' drag to question what is socially acceptable, its disruption of the Central Hall rally of the newly formed Festival of Light – and although he was

undoubtedly at one with 'its emphasis on the counterculture, its suspicion of hierarchies, its opposition to capitalism and its emphasis on
the individual',[10] he nevertheless tended to stand in uncharacteristic silence at the back of its meetings.

Older than many of the other members, he felt he 'had already
gone through the struggle and was already beyond it . . . [The GLF]
seemed so backward in its censoriousness . . . I disliked these well-
meaning rather lonely people laying down the law . . . there was an
element of joylessness about it.'[11] He also found that if you were not
full time with the GLF – which he, working on The Devils, could not
hope to be – you were viewed with suspicion. It was a period of pure
schizophrenia: the GLF as counterpoint to the homophobia of
Pinewood; being simultaneously in and out of the closet. The conflict might have caused Jarman to become aggressively political, and
in time it would, but then it simply made him wary of both the film
world and the GLF. Although he fervently believed that through the
transformation of the individual, society itself would be transformed,
his own focus remained personalised: either himself or a passing
fancy. That November, in what many regard as the first gay rights
demonstration in Britain, some 150 people marched across Highbury
Fields to protest at the prosecution of a gay man for allegedly impor-
tuning there. Jarman was not among their number. When he went
marching, it was in pursuit of the boys who conveniently caught his
eye at the rear of the GLF meetings.

He was also preoccupied with the move half a mile eastwards
from Upper Ground to Bankside, the third, and penultimate, of his
riverside studios and without doubt the most beautiful of them all;
even, according to its occupant, the most beautiful room in the
whole of London.

The studio was on the top floor of a riverside warehouse
alongside Southwark Bridge almost opposite St Pauls. Its
three arched windows overlooking the river had a spectacular
view, the room itself was slightly curved with a barn-like
wooden roof and white-washed walls. Beneath the windows I
built a platform so that people curled up on the cushions
could watch the water below. The aluminium greenhouse

which served as a warm bedroom also stood on the platform. At night the light reflecting off the water cast sinuous patterns all over the ceiling; at dawn the sun would come up over the iron railway bridge [into Cannon Street] and turn the river scarlet, reflecting in the facets of the greenhouse.[12]

Sharing 13 Bankside were Peter Logan and Michael Ginsborg – though it was only Jarman, who did not have alternative accommodation of any permanence, who made Bankside his home. This explains the effort he put into the building – and it did require effort. Although it had rarity value – for instance, a water-operated hoist and those lavishly raftered ceilings – it was extremely basic. Imagination was needed to realise its potential; imagination and money, which, in 1970, thanks to the reasonable rent and his handsome salary, Jarman had in unusual abundance. In the open area at the top of the stairs that linked the three studios, he installed a bath (without the protection of a partition, which made using it akin to taking part in the Living Theatre). Inside his studio, he attended first to the electrics, then added the two features which everyone who visited it will always remember: the platform and the greenhouse.

The platform stretched the whole width of the room, allowing one to lounge at any of the three windows and stare entranced as 'tugs with magical names like "Gypsy" and "Elegance", so low in the water they might sink, chugged past, their high chimneys belching dark smoke, towing strings of barges that dwarfed them; stacked with yesterday's rubbish in a swirl of screaming gulls'.[13] The greenhouse, which stood on the platform, is cited by many as the prime example of Jarman's uncanny ability to solve potentially complicated problems – in this instance, the cold – with solutions that were profoundly simple (or, one might add, to act on someone else's suggestion with a directness few could match). The suggestion came from Dugald Campbell, Jarman's old schoolfriend and flatmate, who, as an architect, had been asked to advise on how best to insulate the roof. Almost in passing, he remarked that if Jarman was cold at night, a small greenhouse would be about the same size as a double bed. Jarman pounced on the idea with such eagerness that once he had located a kit, lined up some friends to help assemble it and furnished his new 'bedroom' with a mattress, a scattering of cushions and a heater, he quite forgot how effectively the greenhouse would insulate him from the rest of the studio. The first time the phone rang while he was in bed asleep, he put his hand through the glass in the process of answering it.

Less remarkable, though equally an element of the design, was the enticing white hammock looped from the rafters. This effectively divided the long, narrow room in two, separating the platform and greenhouse from the small but colourful indoor garden Jarman planted by the window at the rear. Like its predecessors, Bankside was the harmonious sum of carefully chosen objects – including his staple pieces – which Jarman could stage-manage to suit the seasons or whatever arrangement of beautiful people he had collected to enhance his beautiful room.

Usually these were the young men who perched like birds on Jarman's platform before the nightly migration into town. On one starry occasion, it was Katharine Hepburn, in London to film Edward Albee's *A Delicate Balance* for Tony Richardson; on another, Richard Chamberlain. In the run-up to Christmas 1970, it was most of Jarman's, Logan's and Ginsborg's collective circle for a sumptuous dinner.

> We built a table the length of the room and sat forty people
> down to a three-course meal cooked by Peter on improvised
> calor stoves. The tables were banked with scented white
> narcissus from Covent Garden, and a 'walky-talky' telephone
> connected either end. At the end of the meal, joints wrapped
> in the American flag were served with the coffee, and then
> we played charades behind a beautiful collaged curtain, a
> Rousseau Garden of Eden that Andrew Logan had made on
> transparent polythene. Fred Ashton and I kicked off as
> Edward VIII and Wallis Simpson.[14]

John Dewe-Mathews, a photographer friend who had joined Ray Dean as a visual chronicler of Jarman's circle, played Desdemona to Herbert Muschamp's Othello, while John Sainsbury transformed himself into the serpent in Logan's Garden of Eden and Vera Russell became a majestic Britannia ruling some rather unruly waves.

A few months earlier, Jarman had picked up the tail end of a con-versation between his parents. 'I'm so glad our children haven't grown up normal,' he had heard Betts telling Lance as they did the washing up. 'They're so much more interesting than their friends.'[15] This gratified Jarman no end, though in actual fact, where Northwood was concerned, he still only ever hinted at his flamboy-ant lifestyle. True, that February, at his sister Gaye's wedding to David Temple, he had done his duty as an usher wearing a rather splendid but decidedly unconventional suit and without cutting his hair, his only concession to propriety being a tie. And when he proudly brought Karl Bowen home on a visit, he did not protest when Bowen lit a joint, prompting Betts to rush round opening the windows lest Lance return from sailing and notice the smell. But these were minor rebellions: at Northwood, Merryfield's male heir was still in thrall to parental discipline and expectations.

The Devils centres around a city under siege; Jarman's own life at the time was, as it always had been, similarly bedevilled: child versus adult, obedience versus rebellion, Metroland versus metropolis. No wonder there were two of him. The Jarman who worked, the Jarman who played. The Jarman who did not keep alcohol in the studio, the Jarman who seemed to choose his friends largely on the basis of their alcohol or drug intake. The Jarman who accepted his sexuality, the Jarman who could still keep quiet about it. The Jarman of unfailing politeness, and the colourfully dressed Jarman who, on being appre-hended by a policeman in Trafalgar Square as he kissed Karl Bowen goodbye, and as an object lesson on how to handle authority, emp-tied the contents of his Moroccan shoulder bag on to the pavement, put his hands in the air and cried, 'Don't shoot!', embarrassing the officer into beating a retreat. The Jarman who revelled in Ken Russell's outrageousness, the Jarman who later, and in private, called Russell 'the greatest rubbish artist of all'. The Jarman who had the surest sense of his own worth as an artist, and the Jarman who did not know where to go next.

17

Oasis at Bankside

Summing up 1970 from the vantage point of 1983, Jarman wrote: 'By the time I emerged from Pinewood in December, the easy life of the sixties – designing and painting – had gone for ever. It was now impossible to pick up all the threads.'[1] Although *The Devils* had paid well and had been stimulating to work on, and although the con- troversy aroused on its release in July 1971 was music to Jarman's ears, the film had demanded a year of his life without giving him much to show for it. His towering sets attracted a fraction of the comment accorded the film's director and subject matter. It was hardly a setback – not in the way *Don Giovanni* had been – but even so, it was not what an ambitious artist craved.[2]

During filming, Russell had ordered the destruction on camera of the statuary that decorated Grandier's study, an act of unexpected vandalism which horrified Jarman. Returning to a concept he had first explored at the Slade and in *Don Giovanni*, the outraged designer began to complement the increasingly empty landscapes he had been perfecting as the sixties drew to a close with a new set of paintings that featured 'dismembered marble torsos . . . piled one on top of another like used cars in a breaker's yard'. The paintings were, he said, emblematic of 'the graveyard of the old culture'.[3] On a more personal level, they could be said to represent the ruin of his hopes. He stood at a crossroads in his artistic life, and although the next four years would lay firm foundations for the future, it was not until January 1975 that a meeting as fortuitous as the one with Janet Deuter would unequivocally show the way forward.

In the meantime, work and play in the 'beautiful room' at Bankside continued unchecked and in exuberant unison.

The 'oasis'[4] that was 1971 kicked off with a first visit to Amsterdam, in the company of Karl Bowen, where Jarman visited the flea market to hunt for art deco and in the process discovered a new passion: old carpets, which he brought back to London by the bagful because they made such perfect covers for the cushions at Bankside. He had his ears pierced and acquainted himself with everything libertarian Amsterdam had to offer by way of bookshops, bars and saunas.

After Amsterdam, the two travellers went south to Venice. Thanks as always to Pevsner, whose lessons would never be forgotten, it was a trip 'awash with art and architecture',[5] as well as a subtle eroticism. The boys were befriended by a priest from San Servolo and invited on to the island where the priest worked, less because he thought they needed succour than in the hope that on being offered his priestly bed for a siesta Jarman and his Botticelli companion would divest themselves of their clothes. In the event, the priest was disappointed: the boys did not strip off for their afternoon nap, even though Jarman was clearly thrilled at becoming the centre of such very catholic attention.

Back home, in unintentional echo of Ken Russell, who was taking a holiday from controversy by making *The Boyfriend*, Jarman also used the plentiful time at his disposal to concentrate on the boyfriend – in his case, more than one of them. 'The greatest fun was bringing some unsuspecting boy back late at night, unpadlocking the old wooden doors of the derelict building, walking him through the cavernous spaces barely lit by dusty lightbulbs – until I opened my door on the top floor to reveal "The Studio".'[6] The boys thus escorted past the office furniture and up Jarman's industrial stairway to heaven were less and less likely to be English. They were variously Brazilian, Russian,

French; or, in one memorable instance, diabolically American.

Robert Mapplethorpe, then a young New Yorker who made jewellery, was on a visit to Europe to buy miniature skulls, bones or
glass dice to 'string together for his fetishistic jewels'. He and Jarman
made a beeline for bed, where – in between sorties to various street
markets – they spent much of the next few days. 'Two boys out on a
jewellery expedition, all sex and glitter,' was how Jarman would later
picture them, adding: 'He bought me two ivory skulls with diamanté
eyes that I mounted on a silver ring, which was a sort of premonition
of our future.'[7]

In 1971, this future (early death presaged by the most unexpected
and unfounded of put-downs: Mapplethorpe, now world famous as a
photographer, passing Jarman in a nightclub with the query, 'I've got
everything I ever wanted, Derek. What have you got?') was still so
distant as to be unimaginable. Neither could the Jarman of 1971
have guessed that in these affairs, albeit subconsciously, he was establishing patterns of emotional and sexual behaviour that would decide
a great deal of his as yet unimagined future.

At Odin's, the restaurant near where Patrick Procktor lived,
Jarman met a waiter by the name of Alasdair McGaw. Jarman's attraction to the young man was instantaneous and intense but, apart from
a bout of inconclusive horseplay, unreciprocated. The twenty-year-old
did not feel likewise about the older, hairier Jarman; he also noticed
that for all Jarman's warmth and openness, the older man was not
easy to approach. Physically and emotionally, Jarman was extremely
shy, allowing himself to be hugged only within the sexual act.

At the same time, partly because McGaw's background was similar to Jarman's and partly because McGaw was by nature rebellious (a
quality Jarman prized), the two men became the firmest of friends.
Far from abandoning McGaw for the next conquest, which is what
many a jilted man would have done, Jarman searched out his next
conquest with McGaw firmly tucked under his parental wing. He
fussed over and advised the younger man, warning him of the dangers of too unruly a life, while simultaneously – and paradoxically –
revelling in McGaw's escapades. It was not lost on McGaw that if he
took Jarman's advice too much to heart and became too settled,
Jarman could become quite anxious.

After a Saturday night spent dancing at the Yours or Mine in Kensington High Street, McGaw introduced his new friend to acid. Jarman made careful, colourful note of the event:

> I put on *Daphnis et Chloé* and the music runs through our
> heads in rivulets. Alasdair takes off his T-shirt and we lie in
> each other's arms as the sun comes up. The light dances
> across the river and streams through the mighty black Doric
> columns of Cannon Street Bridge. The sooty towers
> materialize out of the darkness, and the sun, catching the
> golden cross at the summit of St Paul's, gradually puts out the
> lights of the City. A fleet of barges is afloat on the Thames,
> seagulls screeching and diving around them . . . Tides of
> Ravel's music swell through the rafters and Alasdair floats in
> a rainbow geometry of carpets and cushions . . .[8]

The trip was interrupted by one to Northwood for Sunday lunch, the rainbow geometry continuing only when Jarman returned to London in the late afternoon to attend a screening of Fellini's *The Clowns* at the National Film Theatre. 'We all, a great party of us, our own Commedia dell'Arte, with our bright silks and satins walked down the river back to the studio . . . The garden at the end of the studio looked wonderful with the sun shining through the yellow flowers of the marrow plants. There is such peace here.'[9]

Through his environment, Jarman was attempting to establish a quite conscious alternative to his own family by conjuring up another kind of 'family' altogether: extended, and infinitely extendable, more relaxed, more colourful, more desirable. Yet while he might go dancing all night, might experiment with acid, might accept Mandrax from his mother when she worried he was not sleeping properly, he was not exaggerating when he wrote: 'I've got a strong element of self-preservation, I can be quite ruthless . . . I admire people who throw everything to the wind, but however close I sailed to the wind, I kept an orderly ship. If you look at photos of Bankside there is nothing out of place, it's more like a stage set than an artist's studio, it looks as though it's waiting to be filmed.'[10]

In 1971, it was still the films of others, not Jarman's own, that would disturb the peace of Bankside.

Through Frederick Ashton, Jarman had met the ballet critic Nicholas Dromgoole, who lent him a 16mm projector. Jarman arranged weekend showings of a surreal mixture of the Hollywood films Dromgoole was also able to supply, along with the more arcane alternatives brought from the London Film Makers' Co-Operative by the critic and film-maker John du Cane: 'The Wizard of Oz and A Midsummer Night's Dream crossed with Structuralism',[11] Michael Snow's Wavelength, perhaps, forty-five minutes' worth of a single zoom shot across a New York loft, zeroing in on a small photograph of waves on the far wall. Also shown were the films of Warhol, Genet, Cocteau. Nothing, with the possible exception of The Wizard of Oz, was treated with deference. Funny Face was played out of sequence, slowed down and without the sound. On one occasion, the artist and film-maker Malcolm Leigh, who frequently helped out as projectionist, smoked one joint too many and forgot the pick-up reel, with the result that a stream of celluloid snaked down to tangle with the hands that were always wandering surreptitiously in the gloom, seeking a responsive limb among those invitingly spread out on the cushions that comprised the metaphorical back row. An eccentric mirror image of the Yours or Mine, Bankside on these Saturday evenings resembled an unofficial gay club where what was mine might equally be yours.

In between the film showings and parties came a more or less constant stream of visitors and guests. Patrik Steede took refuge from temporary homelessness in a tent erected alongside the bath in the open area at the top of the stairs. In the bath itself, Dom Sylvester Houédard, in town on a visit, was on one occasion spied pouring a liberal amount of perfume into the water before washing himself. So well known did Bankside become in the course of 1971 that, in the summer, as part of the publicity surrounding the release of The Devils, it was featured in Italian Vogue. A year later, entirely on its own account, it appeared in the pages of Underground Interiors – Decorating for Alternate Life Styles.[12] Jarman was thrilled. Although, architecturally speaking, he tended towards conservatism (he was at the time alerting John Betjeman to at least one building he considered in need of protection), and although he took exception to some

of the 'underground interiors' between which Bankside was
bracketed ('Milanese moderne', he termed them),[13] to be publicly
acknowledged as alternate was, in Jarman's book, the ultimate recognition. Apart from anything else, it allowed him more fully to pit
himself against someone from whose shadow he had long wanted to
escape: the artist he privately renamed David Hackney. Visiting
Hockney's flat for that least favourite of social occasions, a dinner
party, Jarman noted with some satisfaction that 'the Art Deco Blight'
and the 'dollar dowagers' had taken over: 'Lemonade is served in precious Lalique glasses. There's a dining-table that would seat the
boardroom of the Chase Manhattan, and David has the food brought
in from Mr Chow's. The flat now parodies his painting.'[14]

What did it matter that Hockney was about to become the subject of A Bigger Splash, the Jack Hazan film devoted to his circle,
or that Jarman's brief appearance in the film would be predictably
tangential? Ray Dean and John Dewe-Mathews were both on
hand to continue to record his life, which was in many ways, certainly as it was lived on the Thames, much splashier than
Hockney's. When groups of earnest American tourists gathered in
Horseshoe Alley to pay their respects at the site of the Globe, it
was Jarman and his friends who accepted their homage. When
Jarman lifted his eyes to gaze smugly across the river to the commercial heart of London, he could and did view himself as its true
alternative.

His tongue was only half in his cheek when he provided Vogue
with this recipe for a floating party:

You will need one heavily ballasted Thames barge . . . a
stretch of calm blue water, and a perfect sunny June day . . .
you can decorate your barge in any way you like – with gold
trees and flowers like the Inca's golden gardens . . . like a
Channel Islands float, with all the flowers in your own
garden . . . you can invite your friends to sit on it, but if you
are more ambitious dress them as water nymphs, then of
course you decorate your barge with sea monsters . . . you
could commission a performance of The Tempest and play
Prospero yourself . . . p.s. if anyone wants me to build the

island of their dreams they can write to me at 13 Bankside
S.E.1.[15]

Neither was Jarman's offer of his services as a builder of dream
islands made entirely in jest. Despite 1971 being the year of the oasis,
a great deal of work, as necessary to him as breathing, was done.

Bankside operated like an arts centre. While Peter Logan per-
fected his mechanical sculptures and Michael Ginsborg his
paintings, Keith Milow, who rented Ginsborg's studio for a month in
the summer, experimented with paint and a plasterer's comb and
dreamed of moving to America. The moneyed Michael Pinney, met
through Robert Medley, organised readings of the poetry, mostly his
own, which he published through his own Bettiscombe Press. In
time, Gay Sweatshop, the nascent theatre group with which Jarman
came into contact through the Gay Liberation Front, would arrive to
rehearse their early plays. Meanwhile, Jarman resisted pressure from
the William Morris Agency, which had represented him on *The
Devils*, to move either into commercials or towards Hollywood,
where it promised to turn him into 'the world's leading film
designer'.[16] His experiences with Russell had made him wary of commercial cinema, not least because he had the sense that if he wanted
to preserve his life as a gay man, Hollywood was to be shunned.
Instead, he chose to concentrate on his capes, some of which he now
began to paint, in two main colours, black and blue, but mainly
blue: 'simple sky pieces to mirror the calm'.[17]

He was also writing. Returning to that favourite phrase of his, he
produced a substantial story entitled *Through the Billboard Promised
Land Without Ever Stopping*, in which he elaborated on the surreal yet
lyrical adventures to be had when travelling the superhighway. The
travellers are a blind prince and his valet, both disguised as beggars,
who set out in no particular direction and encounter such figures,
objects and places as the Begum of Flowered Chintzes; Michael
Ginsborg's almost anagrammatical alter-ego Borgia Ginz; the disembodied, godlike Topaz; an emperor who 'smiles with the art of
mirrors'; a sphinx with the words 'Silence is Golden' written in her
eyes; a swallow that darts through a film of net curtains; electric
pylons that have been 'gilded with pure gold leaf'; discarded statuary;

pyramids that burn with a cold blue flame; frozen waves that form a labyrinth in the sun's shadow; the strawberry beds of the eternal present; movietown; and the ruined city of Disc, where the archaeology is that of sound and the excavations are directed by poets 'silently sitting with expectant tape recorders and microphones, whilst students of literature quietly brush the earth with sable brushes to release the precious fragments of the past'. When, rather hesitantly, Jarman showed the story to Dom Sylvester Houédard for his opinion, the nervous author confided that 'this is by the way autobiographical although deeply buried'.[18] Indeed, to anyone familiar with Jarman's work, the literary acid trip he takes in *Through the Billboard Promised Land Without Ever Stopping* constitutes a virtual checklist of images and phrases central to his paintings and, later, his films. There is also a telling aimlessness about the journey, a sense that the sequence of its events is without true purpose.

That autumn he made his first film, a 16mm short, now lost, entitled *Electric Fairy*. The electric fairy was a young man with curly blond hair, a star on his forehead and stars on his tunic, headphones, jewels and carmine lips. The filming took place at Bankside, against a swirl of bubbles and a star-spangled backdrop of polythene designed by Andrew Logan. Also helping were Alasdair McGaw and Malcolm Leigh, who provided both the camera and a working knowledge of film. Leigh tried to explain to Jarman that a film needs a story, however simple, since without a story you have nothing concrete to cut together. Jarman could not have been less interested. Rather than having an end in view, he preferred simply to capture whatever chanced to unfold before the lens, attempting afterwards to give these arbitrary images a shape. It was, to a large extent, the approach he would favour all his life.

So excited was Jarman by the possibilities presented by this new venture that he immediately began talking about embarking on another project, though, as it happened, it was to be a full year before he managed a second film of his own. First would come more work for Ken Russell.

Although after *Don Giovanni* Jarman had announced his intention of shunning the opera establishment, and although, when asked by Nicholas Wright to undertake more design work for the Royal

Court, he had said the only play that would interest him was *The Tempest*, when Russell told Jarman he had been commissioned by the Royal Opera House to direct a piece for their 1972 season and invited him to tackle the designs, his response was an unequivocal yes. The piece Russell had settled on was a new work by Peter Maxwell Davies, the as yet unperformed *Taverner*. Not only did Jarman know and like Maxwell Davies from their joint involvement on *The Devils*, but the new opera chimed with many of his own obsessions. Set at the time of the Reformation, it charted the struggles between the composer John Taverner, his conscience and the Church. Its eight scenes of often bitter confrontation and acute dissection of religious and temporal hypocrisy and betrayal invited a design as feisty and as cutting as the opera itself.

The goal Jarman set himself was to create 'a modern opera in a style which belongs to the 1970s'. Drawing on sources as disparate as Cosmè Tura, Bruegel and James Ensor's *Entry of Christ into Brussels*, he toyed with the idea of either having the opera performed against a slow sunset on the cyclorama by a troupe of travelling players in the Gobi Desert, or else negating the opulence of the opera house itself by replacing the customary pink glow of the auditorium lights with blue ones and having the stage 'completely packaged as a Christo painting in pale blue material bathed in blue light'. In the second version, the stage would be as bare as possible, there would be no red tabs, the lighting grid would be visible and a vast wire cage would form a barrier between audience and singers. The scenery, which would be unpacked by costumed stage hands as needed, would make use of film clips and might be soft: the king's throne, for example, would be a Claes Oldenburg version of a design detail of Tura's. In addition, there would be Jarman's hallmark use of geometric shapes, in terms of both scenery and dress: God was envisaged as 'a great gold abstract shape, a nimbus'.[19] When not singing, the characters would wear masks and their costumes would jumble the ages: Taverner, as the story's anchor, would be dressed in period, but his mistress would hail from the thirties and the king would be attired in the style of Louis XIV. Ideally, the orchestra would also be costumed, with the conductor appearing as a mitred bishop. With Russell, Jarman then dreamed of festooning the roof of the opera house with dead oxen, wiring the seats for sound so that any whispered comments could be played back at full volume to the entire assembly, and lowering the doors so that the audience would be forced to enter the auditorium on their hands and knees.

Not surprisingly, these ideas for effectively transforming the hallowed precincts of Covent Garden into a rude approximation of the Roundhouse did not find favour. When the opera did receive its world première, in 1972, it was under the direction of Michael Geliot, with designs by Kalph Koltai.

Developments in the sphere of fine art were also tending to put Jarman beyond the pale – or, at the very least, on the sidelines. The Lisson Gallery was evolving in a direction that ran counter to Jarman's, and although, unlike some of his friends, Jarman did not seem to blame Nicholas Logsdail for this, or even to mind particularly, he was vociferous in his mistrust of the élitism and conservatism of the gallery scene in general. Indeed, in his more optimistic moments, he pronounced the gallery dead. The time was ripe, he proclaimed, for a new beginning. In support of this contention, and with the help of various friends, that November he, Logan and Ginsborg organised an exhibition of their own by throwing open their studios for two whole weeks.

The opening was a great success. Richard Chamberlain put in an appearance, as did Leslie Waddington. There were even some sales. Then, predictably, the visitors all but dried up, and over the following fortnight only a smattering of people came to see the drawings, paintings and capes hanging on Jarman's walls. The 'plush and hush of Bond Street seems far away',[20] noted Nigel Gosling approvingly in his review: precisely the point and, of course, the problem. The presence of an important gallery-owner like Waddington was gratifying, but if the numbers did not hold and sales were not made, then could the exhibition be counted a true success?

Not that Jarman lost a moment's sleep over such capitalistic considerations. His attention was already turning to a new Ken Russell film, a dramatisation of the obsessional relationship between the young French artist Henri Gaudier and Sophie Suzanne Brzeska, a highly strung Polish woman whose surname Gaudier would add to his own in order to mark the intense significance to him of their

relationship. Entitled *Savage Messiah* and scripted by Christopher
Logue, who had played Cardinal Richelieu in *The Devils*, the film
was based on a biography of Gaudier-Brzeska by the art historian and
collector H.S. Ede. The lead part was to be played by the unknown
Scott Antony, that of Sophie Brzeska by Dorothy Tutin. Also in the
cast were Lindsay Kemp, Michael Gough and a young Helen Mirren.

Russell, who thought of Jarman as 'the last true bohemian', was
confident his protégé would respond enthusiastically to Gaudier-
Brzeska's story. It did after all involve most of the standard bohemian
ingredients: penury, rebellion, an unshakeable belief in the primacy
of artistic genius and a pointlessly early death in the trenches of the
First World War. Russell knew, too, that Jarman was keen on the
painters of the period: Vanessa Bell, Bomberg and, in particular,
Wyndham Lewis, who spearheaded the Vorticist movement of which
Gaudier-Brzeska formed part.

One might also have thought that Jarman would take to Kettle's
Yard, Ede's Cambridge home, which housed his considerable collection of twentieth-century art. In its tranquillity and juxtaposition of
the artificial with the natural, of paintings and sculptures with stray
pieces of wood and stone and glass, Kettle's Yard chimes with
Jarman's own style of interior decoration. Perversely, however, when
Jarman visited Ede's museum home he felt like an intruder and was
instinctively mistrustful of Ede's desire, as he saw it, to deify Gaudier-
Brzeska, whom Jarman found 'equivocal'[21] as a character. In
particular, Jarman was struck by the fact that Gaudier-Brzeska had
been a friend of José Maria Sert y Badía, sometime husband of
Princesse Nina Mdivani's sister Roussie. 'Strange company for Ede's
rebel,' he noted caustically.[22]

Jarman was not the only member of the production team from *The
Devils* who had been asked to work on *Savage Messiah*. The presence
of, for example, Shirley Russell, George Lack, Christopher Hobbs
and Ian Whittaker, the set decorator on the earlier film, gave continuity and a cosy sense of family; the nearest, Jarman would later
remark, that Russell would ever come to making a home movie. But
this could not disguise the fact – in some ways it emphasised it – that,
in production terms, the two films were as different as it is possible
for films to be. Russell was funding *Savage Messiah* virtually single-

handed. The budget was minuscule. The design was largely a matter of choosing, and sometimes dressing, the locations needed to suggest early twentieth-century Paris and London; choices which, since Russell had firm ideas of his own on the subject, frequently did not involve Jarman at all, although he did persuade Russell to use the stairs at Bankside for at least one scene. There were some complicated props to make, but only a handful of sets, all built on next to nothing in a studio which, for all the pretensions of its name, was as cramped and basic as Pinewood had been extensive and well equipped. Lee International Studios, where Russell's co-producers, a Cockney duo by the name of John and Benny Lee, had their headquarters, was a far cry from Iver Heath. A disused factory on Kensal Road, it no more spelled feature film than Kensal Town spelled Hollywood.

To save both space and money, the sets were built inside huge wooden crates whose walls could be removed for shooting. The largest was the Gaudier-Brzeska London home, a dank and cheerless burrow beneath a railway arch. The most colourful were the Vortex, the nightclub run by the gallery-owner Shaw, and the equally Vorticist dining room of the art dealer, Gorki. The Vortex – a jagged configuration of abstract shapes in red, yellow and blue – was loosely based on the Cave of the Golden Calf, the legendary nightclub started by Strindberg's second wife, Frida Uhl, which had been partially decorated by Wyndham Lewis. Gorki's dining room gave Jarman another golden opportunity, that of creating objects that might have issued from Roger Fry's Omega Workshop, where, working anonymously, artists such as Gaudier-Brzeska and Wyndham Lewis could design anything from fabric to furniture in return for a basic fee and the certain knowledge that their contribution would be sold through the workshop. Jarman designed a room that was as colourful and as artificial as the conversation round its table. It contained a number of Omega chairs, an Omega screen, an Omega tray, even – with an attention to detail that would never register on screen – an entire set of Vorticist plates.

In order to produce these artifacts, Jarman turned Bankside into a modern version of the Omega Workshop and again enlisted the help of sundry students, this time from Wimbledon Art School. Paul

Dufficey was also on hand, teaching Scott Antony to wield an artistic pencil while himself providing the various drawings featured in the film. So convincingly could Dufficey transform 'any goose into a Gaudier swan'[23] that a visiting dealer whispered pointedly in the copyist's ear that should Dufficey happen to stumble across any 'original' drawings, he was to phone the dealer instantly. Later, much to Jarman's amusement, his Omega chairs achieved precisely what the dealer had hoped for Dufficey's drawings. Taken away to be sold after filming, they were snapped up by a man convinced of their pedigree.

Equally amusing was the way Jarman and Christopher Hobbs, in order to produce a marble torso for what Russell considered the central scene of the film – the sequence where, in a frenzy of artistic tenacity, passion and sweat, Gaudier-Brzeska works through the night to carve an audition piece for Shaw – had themselves to undergo similar and sometimes farcical extremes of tension, passion and sweat before the fruits of their labour would satisfy their demanding director. When Jarman later recounted the story in *Dancing Ledge*, he gently poked fun at Russell's assertion that: 'The central image of our movie is the titanic Struggle of the Sculptor to release his Genius from the intractable Marble.' Russell himself was termed 'Megalomanic'.[24]

Megalomanic or not, Russell had been correct in thinking Jarman would be drawn to the period and would – to an extent at least – identify with Gaudier-Brzeska. The film was also a happy one. Jarman rose with a mixture of alacrity and pleasure to the challenges posed by its budget, the smallness of its crew and the tightness of its ten-week shoot. However, it is hard not to come away from *Savage Messiah* – which, in design terms, is almost entirely naturalistic, and therefore not up Jarman's street – without wondering whether his two Vorticist set pieces were really reward enough.

Matters could not have been helped when, before sinking virtually without trace, the film opened later that year to a lukewarm critical response which made barely any mention of Jarman's work. The overlooked designer could have been forgiven for asking himself if being a film designer were not a form of artistic suicide.

18

Movietown

Now I am sailing on
this rocking chair
to where tomorrow washes
the pavilions of today
along a still straight treeless road.[1]

As a token of his friendship with Jarman, Michael Pinney of Bettiscombe Press had used a photograph of a gathering at Bankside on the front cover of *Nota Bene*, his most recent collection of poetry. On the back, in Jarman's own handwriting, was Jarman's phrase 'Thru the Billboard promised land'. Pinney now offered to publish a matching volume of the somewhat portentous poems Jarman had written in his early twenties. Like *Nota Bene*, *A Finger in the Fishes Mouth* would have a silver cover and feature Jarman's handwritten phrase on the back. On the front would be a Wilhelm von Gloeden photograph of a young boy with his finger in the mouth of a flying fish.

To plan the edition, Jarman and Pinney met at Bianchi's, one of Jarman's favourite Soho restaurants, where they decided which of

Jarman's poems were worthy of print: a total of thirty-two poems, each illustrated by a reproduction of a postcard from Jarman's own collection. Unfortunately, the printers chosen to print the collection were Christian and baulked at the postcard selected for 'Christmas 1964': that of a priest being pleasured by a nun. The offending image had to be put inside an envelope and inserted afterwards. Despite the opportunities thus offered for notoriety, the collection received no publicity. After a poorly attended reading and a valiant but doomed attempt by Pinney's niece to subscribe it in university bookshops up and down the country, it joined *Savage Messiah* in more or less vanishing from view.

The 'still straight treeless' road into tomorrow was proving anything but straight – although, to borrow from Jarman's most recent attempt at writing, neither was it without promise:

Movietown marked the frontier of the Billboard Promised Land, and as the Begum and her two guests drove along the super highway, it gradually grew darker, and the lights stretched out on all sides. Now everywhere were huge neon signs which winked messages at the traveller . . . In between the boards were great screens, held by fine silver wires, which showed movies for which, explained the Begum, shouting over the music, the City was famed, and from which it got its name.[2]

As soon as *Savage Messiah* was in the can Jarman, with Patrik Steede as driver, set off on a trip to Italy in a second-hand timber-framed Tudor Austin they nicknamed 'Hilton'. In Italy Steede's interest in all things masochistic was engaged by the many images he and Jarman saw of St Sebastian, the painfully martyred saint. Within days, he had 'dreamed up the idea of writing a film'[3] about Sebastian's life. While never going so far as to commit much to paper, he nevertheless began talking up a storm – and since homelessness had reduced him to living in a tent at Bankside, Jarman was the principal recipient of his enthusiasm.

Another enthusiast was Marc Balet, an American architectural student who owned and was adept at using a super-8 home-movie camera. Balet, in London for the summer, visited the 'Andy Warhol of London' at the suggestion of a mutual friend. As the two men sat talking in the summer sun, feet dangling out of the studio window to catch the breeze coming off the river, Balet described his camera to a spellbound Jarman.

Depending on the model, the super-8 camera of the seventies could vary considerably in terms of sophistication, but what all models had in common and what appealed to the penurious and technophobic Jarman was that, because the camera had been designed for home use by amateurs – super-8mm was a special amateur gauge which superseded the standard 8mm gauge – it was easy to deploy, portable and cheap to run. To make a film, you had simply to point the loaded camera in the right direction and press the button. As you moved from shot to shot, you would automatically build up a film that was effectively being edited in the camera, although you could also edit the film afterwards in the conventional manner if you wanted to alter the order of your shots. The film could be cranked through the camera at one of five speeds and, once processed, played back at any of these speeds, depending on what effect you wanted to achieve. Sometimes Jarman liked to film and project at three feet per second – a rate he said equalled that of the heart – though, in time, he also learned to shoot at six frames per second, then project at three. Not only was the result here swooningly dreamlike, it meant that a single roll of film could result in almost half an hour of screen time.

Jarman had grown up with home movies, his grandfather's and father's, and was keenly aware of their potency. 'In all home movies is a longing for paradise,' was how he put it.[4] Now, thanks to Balet, he had been shown a means of immortalising the paradise *he* had created, of making movies of *his* home, *his* friends, *his* extended family. He had been pointed towards a way of populating his empty canvases, of putting people where before there had only been either landscape, a sequence of geometric shapes or a set designed to dwarf its inhabitants. As a painter, Jarman had never shown much inclination towards portraiture; as a film-maker, this was to become one of his strongest impulses. Super-8 suggested how he might more fully expand his life into art, thereby closing the circle. It was a way of

further escaping Hockney's shadow and countering all those
Californian pools with a celebration of specifically London friends in
a specifically London milieu. A way of more truly becoming a
London Warhol. Of finding a visual voice.

Although Jarman had other friends with cameras of varying
degrees of sophistication, he opted to borrow Balet's basic model, and
when he bought a camera of his own, he chose the simplest Nizo he
could find. It was not the technology he wanted; it was what the
technology would allow.

He started, fittingly, with his home; a home movie in the purest
sense of the word. Using Balet's camera, he identified a series of
objects from photographs of the studio, then roamed the studio itself
until he had located the actual articles: his poster of Bob Dylan, his
paintbrushes, a skull used in *The Devils*, a teapot, a shirt. Again we
see the man who liked to rescue and rehabilitate junk from the river-
bank casting a characteristically egalitarian eye over his domain,
while at the same time giving expression to his sense of the magical
power inherent in the simplest of items.

Jarman is on record as saying of *Bankside* that it is 'very much a
painter's film. Bonnard comes to mind, little domestic details.'[5]
Elsewhere, and more frequently, he would dispute that his home
movies were in any way painterly, or that they constituted 'art'. They
were, he said, entirely ancillary to his painting, simply a means of
playing with and entertaining friends. *The Siren and the Sailor*,[6] a
staged piece that might marginally predate *Bankside*, is a perfect
example of the latter impulse.

That July, Jarman, Balet, Christopher Hobbs, Andrew Logan, a
boy called Ian and a Danish couple by the name of Ernst and Bente
Lohse all drove to Dorset to make a short film about a mermaid, a
drowned sailor and a masked god. The mermaid, or siren, was played
by Bente in a dress of black net. The sailor was Ian. The god was
Logan, splendidly arrayed in a multicoloured cloak and a mask of
silver and gold. The mask had been made by Hobbs, who also made
the only props: a flotilla of miniature boats fashioned from silver foil.
The soundtrack was to be the music that had accompanied Jarman's
first acid trip: Ravel's *Daphnis et Chloé*.

The scenario for *The Siren and the Sailor* was simple in the extreme. The first shot is of a boat at sea. Arms outstretched, the masked god stands on the clifftop at Winspit surveying the rocks below. The sailor lies drowned in a rockpool, a flotilla of tiny silver boats bobbing at his side. We see the mermaid making one of these boats. The god approaches and embraces the mermaid. The final shot is of waves lapping at the god's mask, which lies on top of the cloak he has been wearing.

It is not on record whose scenario this was, or what it signifies. Neither is it known for sure who wielded the camera, possibly Balet; it was, after all, his. The only account we have of the film is Jarman's, and he concentrates on the cussedness of the weather: the fact that at first attempt, after a cold and uncomfortable night spent trying to sleep in the caves at Winspit, rain stopped play, and that it was only the following weekend, when the sun finally shone, that the camera was able to roll.

Jarman ends his account as follows: 'By ten we've finished filming, and spend the rest of the day getting sunburnt . . . it is one of the very few fine days of summer.'[7] This enthusiasm for sunbathing should not prevent us appreciating that, in its way, *The Siren and the Sailor* served as serious a purpose for its maker, and is as much a 'home' movie – and celebration of home – as *Bankside*. By filming on the Isle of Purbeck, Jarman was reclaiming the landscape of his childhood and stamping it with the idiosyncrasy of his adult vision; keeping it a playground, but of an unmistakably grown-up nature. As Michael O'Pray remarks in *Dreams of England*, his probing and insightful analysis of Jarman's films, 'home' can denote not only that which is intimate and domestic, but also the countryside, certainly those parts of it that figure in Jarman's personal history.

It was one thing to have and celebrate a sense of home, another to be certain of its permanence. That September, Jarman's tenure of Bankside came to an end. Like Upper Ground, the building had been earmarked for demolition. Jarman filmed a final walk along Clink Street to Southwark Cathedral before returning for a similarly terminal inspection of his empty studio. *One Last Walk One Last Look* provided a fitting coda to his earlier footage of Bankside, giving the first film a new ending that was as dark and melancholy as the alleys that were about to be swept away. He further marked the occasion with one last film show, a dual homage to the power of the fairy tale at which he screened both *The Wizard of Oz* and the Max Reinhardt–William Dieterle *A Midsummer Night's Dream*. Then it was time to leave. 'When the films were over I didn't turn the lights on, so we all crept out of the building in the dark. Downstairs I shut the massive padlock. The demolition men, who have been tearing down the buildings all around us, will be in next week. Before winter there will be just a hole in the ground and Horseshoe Alley will be no more.'[8]

In its painful finality, the moment echoed what had befallen Anthony Harwood earlier that year. With the connivance of the porter, who had never cared for Harwood, and in order to settle some of Harwood's many unpaid bills, the bailiffs had gained surprise entry to the Sloane Square flat and brutally stripped it of most of its furnishings. Both events figured as harsh reminders that even the most beautiful of rooms was of necessity transient.

Thankfully, though, what the road into tomorrow removed on one stretch it replaced on another, even if Jarman was having difficulty seeing exactly where it was taking him. That November, he was in New York for the American première of *Savage Messiah*, held at the Museum of Modern Art. Using the trip to further acquaint himself with the New York avant garde, he also made himself increasingly familiar with another segment of the 'netherworld', the Continental Baths. Manhattan's Museum of Modern Art was not the only such museum with which he had contact that month. He had been invited to participate in a joint exhibition entitled *Drawing* at the Museum of Modern Art in Oxford, where, alongside forty-one other artists – including Barry Flanagan and Keith Milow – he was represented by one of his studies of shattered statuary, a chalk drawing wrily captioned *The Pleasures of Italy*. Then there were the pleasures of London, such as the occasion when Andrew Logan decided it would be fun to host an Alternative Miss World, a camp mirror image of the po-faced prototype in which each contestant would appear in the statutory three outfits – day, evening and swimwear – but on the clear understanding that anything would go. At the time Logan was living in a house in Downham Road in outer Islington which happened to have an old jigsaw factory in the back garden. As a building, the factory was unremarkable – single-storeyed, long, narrow and as drab as its surroundings – but Logan had tempered its austerity with some splendidly baroque furnishings, sheets of polythene to act as room-dividers and a pool that boasted a working fountain. It thus became part studio, part hostelry (Marc Balet lived there for a while, in one of the polythene sections) and a perfect setting for parties.

The secret of his success as a host, according to Logan, was 'Preparation – (24 hours) – thinking about [the parties] for a few weeks – decor has to be exotique and don't forget the people. Concentration and a joie de vivre – the right guests – surprises. The recipe for a swinging soiree.'⁹

Following his recipe to the letter for his first Alternative Miss World, Logan enlisted the help of his brothers and friends like Kevin Whitney and Luciana Martinez, and made sure there were changing rooms for the contestants, a rudimentary catwalk, music, lights, a compère and an impressive array of judges, including David Hockney, Diane Logan and Robert Medley.

Jarman had gone to great lengths to create Mrs Hippy (a latterday southern belle) as his alternative persona for the competition, only to see Patrik Steede, entering at the last minute as Miss Yorkshire, walk away with first prize. Distinctly put out to have to settle for third place and to find himself yet again playing second fiddle to Hockney (Jack Hazan was in attendance with his camera, and there is a scene in A Bigger Splash where, as one of many extras crammed into the heaving studio, the veiled figure of Mrs Hippy sashays all too briefly across the screen). Jarman nevertheless adored the evening, as did the rest of the participants. It set the pattern for an event that was to become, in Jarman's phrase, 'the Ascot of radical drag'.¹⁰

In 1972, radical drag was all the rage. Fostered by the Gay Liberation Front, it was an effective yet lighthearted way of questioning sexual stereotyping. A moustachioed man in a dress, with a handbag dangling from his hairy forearm, said more than a thousand slogans – and could have a laugh into the bargain. Or so thought Patrik Steede, whose position as the first Alternative Miss World inspired him to buy 'a Balenciaga evening dress, which he wore to the Queen Elizabeth Hall with a bead hat and cowboy boots, causing more stir than Pete Maxwell-Davies's songs for a mad king'.[11] It was a display of defiance Jarman heartily endorsed. In preparing his own ensemble for the contest, he had experienced enormous difficulty buying a woman's bathing cap at Derry and Toms. An outraged assistant had informed him he was in the 'wrong department'. It was only after demanding to see the manager and pretending to be a buyer for Ken Russell that the suspect shopper had managed to secure the cap and in the process rub the assistant's nose in her own bigotry. Steede in a Balenciaga gown helped even the score.

That July, on what was the nearest Saturday to the third anniversary of the Stonewall riots, London saw its first official Gay Pride March: a West End rally some 2,000 strong, followed by a picnic and party in Hyde Park. *Gay News*, Britain's first national gay newspaper, began to provide its readers with a much-needed sense of solidarity. Within three years, Gay Switchboard, another such institution, would also be founded. A sexual and social revolution was underway which would bring down the curtain on the sixties world of polari and coffee bars. In the not too distant future lay mammoth discos, a positive explosion of bars, restaurants and publications; an Americanisation and commercialisation of the British gay scene that led an entire generation, gay and straight, to gyrate to the words of what was effectively a hymn to homosexual love: the Village People's hit single, 'YMCA'. Heaven indeed.

Just as Jarman's filming in Winspit of *The Siren and the Sailor* had superimposed adult playfulness on childhood memory, now came the memorable moment when, as a fully functioning sexual being, he returned to another of his childhood Edens, the Borghese Gardens, with these theistic words: 'I returned to the Borghese gardens with a soldier I met in the Cinema Olympia. He had thrown his arms around me in the gods; later we made love under the stars of my Eden.'[12] Here lay the true pleasures of Italy, even if their fanciful author neglects to furnish this particular – and particularly innocent – account of the incident with the detail that, after fucking and giving a blow-job to his soldier, he developed a 'terrible sore throat'.[13] Capable of tempering his lust with sweeping romanticism, Jarman could also treat the question of sex with considerable lightness and hilarity, evidencing little hesitancy and none of the angry intensity with which, in his later journals, he would usually recount his sexual education. If it was true, as some thought, that he studied sexually at the feet of Karl Bowen and Mario Dubsky, both inveterate cruisers and connoisseurs of rough trade, he also learned how to fashion his escapades into anecdotes that reduced his listeners to helpless laughter.

And yet, although he was now thirty, to an extent he continued to tread somewhat carefully where sex was concerned. On his frequent visits to Amsterdam, when he went into an adult bookshop he would invariably make straight for the heterosexual section, wandering towards the gay section later, as if by accident. His nervousness in saunas was noticeable. He worried what people might think, once asking Malcolm Leigh: 'When people see me in the street, do you think they can tell I'm gay?'

Analysis of any psychological state can lead to oversimplification. Strands that are seamlessly interwoven have to be unpicked, sometimes giving a false impression. The truth lies not within a single strand, but in their interweaving. Uncertainty, boldness, hilarity, intensity, anger, defiance, romanticism, joy – all were present in Jarman's sexual make-up, as was a new compulsiveness. He took to dispensing with underpants, leaving potential partners in little doubt as to what awaited them, and began cruising so often, and with such singlemindedness, that it sometimes seemed as if his life depended on it.

He had rented the small and rather dismal back room in John Dewe-Mathews' first-floor flat at 5 St George's Terrace, NW3, overlooking Primrose Hill – a new hunting ground for the countless men Jarman brought back to the little room crammed with as much of his furniture and belongings as it would take. He also entertained on a less primal level. He took over Dewe-Mathews' large front room for the occasional film show and continued to supply the many friends who visited with endless cups of tea. For the rest, he worked. The most constant caller was Patrik Steede, with whom Jarman was now earnestly and urgently involved in planning a film of St Sebastian. Jarman badgered Dom Sylvester Houédard for advice on the history of the period, asked Andrew Logan if he would undertake the designs and, in between any number of heated exchanges with Steede as to

exactly how the script should be tackled, seriously discussed the feasibility of translating it into Latin once it had been finished to their
mutual satisfaction. Latin was, Jarman felt, the best way of guaranteeing historical verisimilitude on a low budget.

As a result of a chance meeting at Max's Kansas City in New
York with the manager of the Alice Cooper group, Jarman was asked
if he would like to design the staging for their forthcoming tour,
Billion Dollar Babies. He must have seemed the perfect find for a
group notorious not only for the sexual ambiguity of their epony-
mous lead singer but also for their interest in meticulously staged
shock theatrics: the rumoured dismemberment of live chickens, the
use of a boa constrictor as a prop, the regular onstage 'killing' of
Alice Cooper in an electric chair or on the gallows. Jarman joined
their current tour, *School's Out*, in Copenhagen, Berlin and Frankfurt
in order to familiarise himself with their style. It was a rock-and-roll
baptism by fire. So appalled was he by the group's excesses, narcotic,
alcoholic and sexual, that as soon as he decently could, he flew back
to England and simply sent them a letter explaining a staging for
Alice, whom he envisaged making his entrance 'on a huge articulated black widow spider. It would crawl out of a steely web on to the
Broadway stage with Alice at its helm holding a gold and leather
harness, dressed in rubies from head to foot, like Heliogabalus entering Rome.'[14] It would have made an impressive stage picture, one
that neatly echoed the dark, web-like circles which the singer liked
to paint around his eyes, but sadly Jarman's letter was not acknowledged, nor did he ever hear from the group again.

Not that he had either the time or the inclination to grieve over
this lost opportunity. Another Russell project had meanwhile presented itself. Earlier in the year, while still working on *Savage
Messiah*, Russell had asked Jarman if he would like to design *The
Angels*, a fantasy satire on modern times Russell was scripting for
MGM. Because of its fantastical nature, the script offered Jarman
much more scope than *Savage Messiah* and he indicated his interest.
MGM, however, pulled out, and the project floundered. This might
have angered Jarman greatly (in the interim he had been approached
by Stanley Kubrick, whom he felt obliged to tell he was not available), but Russell was able to save the day with a completely new

project offering equally dazzling design possibilities: a film version of Rabelais's *Gargantua and Pantagruel* being developed for Warner Brothers by Alberto Grimaldi, the Italian producer of Pasolini's *Decameron* and *The Canterbury Tales*.

John Baxter, Russell's biographer, who sat in on some of the session between Russell, his wife, Shirley, and Jarman, describes the working process thus: 'Russell supplies the motive force, the key structure, and draws on Jarman's visual flair to fill in the spaces. Not afraid to say "That's wrong" or "You've done that before", Jarman acts as a brake and anchor on Ken's ballooning imagination.'[15]

During the first two months of 1973, if Jarman was not in meetings with the Russells, he was in the back room at St George's Terrace, filling at least two notebooks with his brightly coloured designs for the hilarious, occasionally obscene adventures of the giant Gargantua. Russell had the notion to centre the film on a troupe of travelling players who start by acting out Gargantua's story, then end up being drawn into it. Jarman designed their caravan as a thatched house and, in an echo of the wooden 'O' that was the Globe, envisaged opening the film in a circular set of half-timbered Tudor houses. By March, both the script and the designs were well enough advanced for the team to move to Rome and start location-hunting.

19

Butler's Wharf and Beyond

It was not only *Gargantua* Jarman had in his sights when he travelled to Rome in March 1973. Because of their work together on St Sebastian, he paid for Patrik Steede to accompany him so that the latter could progress his script. While Steede researched – or, as Jarman suspected, concentrated on having fun – his paymaster set out every morning from their centrally located hotel to make the 'horrible daily journey through the snarling Roman traffic' to 'Grimaldi's steel and ferroconcrete palazzo at the edge of EUR',[1] the Roman film studios, where he was thrilled to discover that the production office for *Gargantua* was adjacent to that of Pasolini's *The Arabian Nights*. In the pantheon of European film-makers revered by Jarman, Pasolini ranked an undisputed first,[2] not least because it fascinated his disciple how closely the Italian's Marxist concern for the proletariat was linked to his sexual interest in working-class youth.

Youth held a similar fascination for Jarman – indeed, it was a particular youth, rather than *Gargantua*'s many production meetings and the search for possible locations and likely costumes, that was the central feature of his stay in Rome. The youth in question was

Gerald Incandela. Jarman wrote: 'Gerald lives in a tiny silver-painted basement near the walls of the Vatican. It is cluttered with objects: a treasured puppet, a large plastic apple-green ice bucket, and a small Art Nouveau table. He sits cross-legged on the bed with his friend Elizabeth. Both wear baggy white oriental trousers, are stripped to the waist, with masses of dark curly hair falling over their shoulders. They are playing in a scene from the *Satyricon*.'[3]

Ten years Jarman's junior, Incandela had been born in Tunis, where his father worked in a French bank, his mother as a dress-maker. In 1969 the family had moved to France, where Incandela finished his studies. After a brief period in Berlin, the twenty-year-old had gravitated to Rome to work in a boutique, frequent the fringes of the film world and now to mesmerise Jarman with his curls, his grace as a dancer, his cheeky sense of humour, even the eccentricity of his rather poor English. Jarman and Incandela became lovers and when, a few weeks later, the funding for *Gargantua* was unexpectedly withdrawn and the film collapsed, Jarman had no hesitation in bringing the younger man back to London with him.

Before leaving for Rome, Jarman had managed to secure himself a new riverside studio on the third floor of Block A1 of Butler's Wharf.[4] After marking time for a month in the tiny back room in St George's Terrace, he and his first live-in partner moved in. Located immediately to the east of Tower Bridge between Shad Thames and the river itself, Butler's Wharf is one of the larger and more imposing of the river's Victorian wharves. Now extensively renovated into a medley of luxury apartments, stylish shops and chic restaurants, then the warehouse was largely derelict and smelled strongly of its work-ing past as a grain store and of the Courage Brewery in the adjoining building, enhanced, if the wind was right, by a hint of something even more heady from a nearby spice warehouse.

Block A1 was at the eastern end of the warehouse, on the side adjoining a large plot of waste ground. Although the view north-wards across the river towards St Katharine's Dock and the city skyline was spectacular and the space afforded by the room itself in excess of anything on offer at Bankside, the studio's other two aspects (a narrow alleyway to the rear, the waste ground) were quite

Dickensian and the interior of the building had none of Bankside's quaintness or charm. Apart from two lines of wrought-iron columns dividing the centre of the room, mere concrete or brick abounded. All floors shared a toilet on the ground floor. The block was joined to its neighbour by a drab staircase. There was no bath.

Incandela was put into a pair of overalls and handed a brush to paint the wrought-iron columns green. The walls were whitewashed and hung with capes. In time, and in the style of Bankside, a toilet and bath were installed by the simple expedient of setting them down in the open room. Working areas were roughly divided from living ones; the greenhouse continued to do sterling service as a bedroom. Friends were encouraged to become neighbours. Peter Logan took the top two floors of Block A1, while his brother Andrew relinquished Downham Road in order to acquire the top floor in Block B. A thriving community was formed, including the artist Simon Read, the architect Max Gordon and, briefly, Christopher Hobbs.

The collapse of *Gargantua* had left Jarman more wary than ever of the machinations of the film world. In self-defence, he invested in a new Nizo and, over the next eighteen months or so, concentrated on generating a series of short films no one could ever take away from him. As before, what he shot was sometimes elaborately staged, sometimes simply what he happened upon. Some sequences were intended to stand alone, others were fragments. Some of the fragments were used to form a pool of images that could be used over and over again in ever-shifting combinations. There was a degree of technical experimentation – with the use of different-coloured gels, differing speeds, degrees of light, the effects that could be achieved through superimposition and/or the refilming of one section of film over another[5] – but in general Jarman was more drawn, sometimes consciously, sometimes not, to a painterly concern with a particular image or to exploring the many influences, cinematic and literary, which had helped shape his outlook on life than he was to the technicalities.[6]

In researching *The Devils*, he had hunted down drawings of sixteenth-century alchemists whose complicated experiments and cluttered shops provided him with some vivid visual ideas. They also introduced him to a line of thought that would increasingly come to fascinate him.[7] The alchemical tradition was one that tended towards the heretical, standing in opposition to the establishment, in particular the Church – something with which Jarman instantly identified. It was a way of exploring connections between the terrestrial and the celestial, between the four lower elements of earth, water, air and fire that exist beneath the moon, and the fifth element, the quintessence, of pure spirituality. According to alchemy, every object in the natural world signifies something metaphysical. The idea that the world is not simply materialistic, but is filled with spirits, with soul and intelligence, is an *anima mundi* where every object, albeit inanimate, has special properties, was one that gave Jarman a rich vocabulary for articulating the way he himself had always apprehended his environment. He liked the alchemical concept of the microcosm and macrocosm, of man as a miniature world reflecting the greater one; and of duality: that there are two sides to everything (light and dark, sun and moon, masculine and feminine, flesh and spirit), and that these opposites are found in all people, where they can be joined and made one – the alchemical conjunction. And, of course, he welcomed the fact that at the heart of all alchemy lay the attempt to transform base metal into gold. This provided Jarman, already a believer in transformation, with a potent symbol of the worth inherent in everything others might deem worthless. Finally, there were the secrecy and the magic. 'Part of my fascination with . . . the alchemists,' he later wrote, '. . . was their involvement in secrecy and closed structures. Why are so many gay filmmakers involved in closed structures? Surely because they reproduce their isolation in our society.'[8]

The word alchemy is derived from the Arabic *Al Kimiya*, or the Egyptian *khem*, the name given to the delta of the Nile. It was in Egypt that alchemy started with, most notably, a body of magical and philosophical writings attributed to Hermes Trismegistus (the Thrice Great Hermes), generally regarded as an Egyptian prophet from the time of Moses.[9] Links are also drawn to Thoth Hermes, the scribe of the gods, the Egyptian equivalent of the Greek Hermes and the Roman Mercury, and, later, to the Cabala, the great repository of Jewish occult, and therefore hidden, knowledge, a 'complete system of symbolism, angelology, demonology and magic'[10] imparted almost solely by word of mouth and only to highly learned initiates. All in all, it was a tradition and branch of knowledge that was, as the words 'hermetic' and 'occult' imply, sealed and difficult to comprehend.

At the time of the Renaissance, when divisions between science and magic were less rigid than they are today, and there was less stigma attached to the practice of magic, this hermetic tradition found vigorous and imaginative practitioners in such neo-Platonists and magi as Robert Fludd, Marsilio Ficino, Giordano Bruno, Paracelsus, Henricus Cornelius Agrippa von Nettesheim, St John of the Cross and John Dee, and in the strange and shadowy Rosicrucians. For philosophers and scientists such as these, the value of alchemy lay not least in its antiquity. The neo-Platonists had shown how much could be gained by returning to the past for knowledge; hence the Renaissance. After the Renaissance, however, there was a 'reaction away from the enlightened, inquiring liberalism of the neo-Platonists and Renaissance Magia and the mounting of a . . . drive against all suspected of witchcraft and magical practices'.[11] This drive was instigated largely by the Church, which feared that too much 'liberal inquiring' would undermine ecclesiastical authority. It forced an already secretive world into even deeper impenetrability, where it still languishes, except for the work of such people as the historian Frances Yates, who wrote many books attempting to exhume and understand this buried history, and Carl Jung, who plundered alchemy for some of his symbols of psychological and spiritual transformation.

Like Jung, whose work gave Jarman the confidence to let his dream images 'drift and collide at random',[12] Jarman also did some plundering, assembling for himself, out of the wide reading he was now doing into these and related figures, a catalogue of images and scenarios to embellish and enrich his films. It was a fitting match, for, as Jarman would note in Dancing Ledge, what is film but 'the wedding of light and matter – an alchemical conjunction'?[13] Nowhere is the 'alchemical' nature of Jarman's filming more apparent than when he slows down his super-8s to the point of dreaminess while simultaneously focusing on the tiniest of details. Here we have a visual metaphor for the way in which the microcosm reflects the macrocosm, the way in which the entire world, if one looks closely enough, is animate. Though what we must never forget is that Jarman was no dry theoretician of things alchemical; for him alchemy was simply a repository of ideas, scenarios and images upon which to draw at will, without always understanding or caring too much about their true significance. Although he claimed to speak Enochian, the language of angels, it is doubtful that he did.

Of far more importance to him always was a straightforward desire to have fun with his friends and, in an echo of what Ray Dean and John Dewe-Mathews had been doing for him, to act as their court cameraman. One of the first short films he produced during this period featured a young American called Gaby Longhi, a contestant in the first Alternative Miss World competition. Longhi had attended Logan's pageant wearing an emerald-green satin dress that had belonged to her mother. So struck was Jarman by the dress and its wearer that he asked if he might film her. The film was shot at Downham Road, with the help of Marc Balet and Andrew Logan. It was a case of erastz Hollywood meets Andy Warhol. There was a title card – an Andrew Logan mirror featuring two songbirds on a perch – announcing: 'Let Them Eat Cake Films Presents I'm Ready For My Closeup With Miss Gaby and Mr de Havilland'. A curtain rises. Miss Gaby is in her green dress, applying her make-up. She is watched by a young hustler, to whom, before putting some of her lipstick on his waiting lips and kissing him, she gives a rope of pearls. When he viewed the result, Jarman found the hustler too wooden, so there also exists a second version of the film which concentrates almost entirely – and with a swooning intensity, as if the camera were the eyes of a small boy watching his mother at her dressing table – on Miss Gaby as she applies her make-up. It is called *Miss Gaby Gets It Together*.

At Butler's Wharf, the budding film-maker held a picnic at which, in an unequivocally Warholian manner, Logan's friends were invited to be filmed kissing him: *Andrew Logan Kisses the Glitterati*.

He took both his camera and a young man he had recently picked up to the artist Duggie Fields' highly designed flat in Earl's Court, where, using extreme slow motion, he viewed Fields and the young man as if both were simply two additional artifacts in a room already stiff with them. Using a red gel, he filmed Incandela as a tourist being cruised through London by a photographer who ends up making love to him in the greenhouse: a red movie that becomes a blue one. In a short piece entitled *Stolen Apples for Karen Blixen*, he superimposed the face of one of Anthony Harwood's favourite writers over an image of Incandela in a cloak collecting apples being dropped from a tree.

Tarot, or *The Magician*, part of which he later incorporated into a longer film entitled *In the Shadow of the Sun*,[14] featured Christopher Hobbs in his bedsit in Islington. Looking like 'an extra from *Ivan the Terrible* in purple velvet with gold embroidery and a bulky fur collar',[15] Hobbs plays a magician who, by means of a key and a pack of tarot cards, conjures up Incandela. The latter wears a filmy black dress, a black nose and the rope of pearls first seen in the possession of Miss Gaby. The magician changes his garb. Now wearing a stylish top hat and tails, he uses the rope of pearls to strangle Incandela.

Also singled out for attention was one of the postcards Jarman had used in *A Finger in the Fishes Mouth*, that of a garden in Luxor. Eliding this image with various others, including one of the pyramids, which he then burned, he projected the consequent visual kaleidoscope on to the studio wall over images of Christopher Hobbs. Everything was then refilmed and the end result given the name of the initial postcard: *A Garden in Luxor*.

He filmed a Bill Gibb fashion show and one by Michael Fish choreographed by Frederick Ashton. In Denmark with Incandela, he filmed a walk taken on the island of Møn, then overlaid this footage with a static shot of the Milky Way, or some such galaxy, so that in one version this film becomes a 'space walk'. On an English excursion with his Danish friends Ernst and Bente Lohse, he leaped out of their blue Mercedes at Castle Howard to record fields of wheat and the Temple of the Four Winds, another piece of film he would later use for superimposition.

By coach from Victoria, with the Nizo running, he visited Andrew Davis, his old English teacher, now based at Marlborough. They went on a walk to that lesser Stonehenge, the standing stones at Avebury, with Jarman talking and filming all the way: the path, the fields, the trees, the sheep, the cows, the stones. This sequence shows Jarman's fascination with the past, how the past leaves traces of itself and how those traces – in this case, a circle of stones – have spiritual and mystical properties on a par with the landscape itself. We see too how closely Jarman's super-8 film-making could parallel his work as a painter. Later that year, he returned to the standing stones at Avebury as the subject of an extended series of drawings and paintings.[16]

Like *Tarot*, *Journey to Avebury* became part of *In the Shadow of the Sun* – hence the point of cataloguing Jarman's super-8 work in some detail. It gives a sense of how the work turned on itself, not unlike the figure of the serpent eating its own tail that is the symbol of alchemical fusion. Almost nothing in Jarman's life, no moment, no image, was without its place in the scheme of things. Put baldly, and with his post-war, middle-class upbringing in mind, he simply could not abide waste.

In *Dancing Ledge*, Jarman ends a description of Butler's Wharf by pointing out that, thanks to the neighbouring undeveloped plot, 'we have our own 1,000-feet terrace on the Thames where we can film undisturbed in the sun'.[17] Drawing on the help and involvement of whichever friends were on hand, he shot a number of staged tableaux there which he could then cut together in differing ways to form the basis of a whole studio's worth of titles: *In the Shadow of the Sun*, *The Art of Mirrors*, *Sulphur*, *Arabia*, *Green Glass Bead Game*, *Beyond the Valley of the Garden of Luxor Revisited*, *Death Dance*. The principal ingredients for these films were: fire; a fire maze, within the grid-like confines of which a number of shadowy figures went through a series of ritualistic motions; a burning rose; rows of burning candles; figures dancing, bowing, walking, cycling; figures whose features are obscured by paper bags, or else by the skull mask from *The Devils*; a mouth around which are clustered some flies; the mouth eating those flies; the head of Mausolus rescued from the antiques room at the Slade; the rope of pearls; St Sebastian; a figure with a camera; Narcissus admiring himself in a mirror; a figure flashing a mirror into the camera; dice being thrown across a mirrored grid; a finger typing: 'SLNC GLDN – tic tac – Ladies and Gentlemen Take your places for The Green Glass Bead Game –

Arabia'; a nude Jarman holding the glass bells given to him by Anthony Harwood on the first night of *Jazz Calendar*, plus a long, glinting rod – the wand, perhaps, with which he has conjured his dreams into such exotic life?

These sudden frenzies of filming were often spontaneous; what happened, and how it happened, tended to depend on who was there and the whim of the moment. In the filming of *Death Dance*, in which four naked men lie on the waste ground while the robed figure of Death, played by Christopher Hobbs, visits each of them in turn, cheerful improvisation seemed the order of the day. There was undoubtedly a degree of runic significance in the director's mind as to the positions adopted by the naked men, but when one of them jokingly asked him which way he wanted their genitals to point, Jarman did not seem in the least put out. 'Twelve o'clock. Twelve o'clock,' was his jaunty reply.

Afterwards, on the other hand, as Jarman's notebooks attest, he would put hours and hours of painstaking thought into how he might best assemble and contrast the sequences he had shot in order to build a film, and then another and another. The notebooks are also filled with jottings towards a wealth of films that never happened, or still lay in the future.[18]

There was a variation, for instance, on Yves Klein's anarchic notion of exchanging a 'zone of immaterial pictorial sensibility' for gold leaf, which Klein might – and indeed once did – scatter in the Seine while the purchaser of the painting burned his receipt. In Jarman's version, he planned to 'end tradition' by 'borrowing' the Goya etching that hung in Northwood, *The Disasters of War*, and burning it 'by the sun's rays'. The event would be filmed and the ashes 'framed between two sheets of glass and exhibited with the film. The resulting work to be exchanged for another work of art which will be similarly processed.' There would be a 'legally binding document to go with the work to prevent its resale unless an exchange is made and further work processed'.[19] Also, most intriguingly and tantalisingly of all, there is a note that reads simply: 'the blue film for Yves Klein'.[20] There were more images tumbling through Jarman's mind than there was time to capture them.

The notebooks also record how very cheap the process of filming in super-8 could be: £2 for paraffin and £4 for sawdust, plus £4.50 for candles, bought Jarman not only his fire maze, but an entire screen full of candles. It was just as well, because, in the absence of more conventional film work, money was in distinctly short supply and the super-8 film a long way from gaining credence as an art form, alternative or otherwise. True, there were tentative moves afoot to organise festivals of work in super-8, plus occasional symposia, some of which Jarman attended,[21] but in the seventies, 16mm reigned supreme. What is more, if you stood at the cutting edge, or formed part of the London Film Makers' Co-Op, what you did with your 16mm was destructure it, as in Michael Snow's *Wavelength*, that single zoom shot across a New York loft zeroing in on a small photograph of waves on the far wall. Although he was in essence an admirer of Snow, the structuralist stance was not one Jarman readily understood. To someone like him 'who had stumbled on film like a panacea this [destructuring] seemed a rather negative pursuit – like calling water H_2O'. Despite the fact that the prevailing orthodoxies forced him to concede privately, and with a degree of ruefulness, that he had 'failed to develop in the way that was expected',[22] he was fearfully proud that in a piece like *The Art of Mirrors* – in which a trio of figures move with hypnotic slowness across the screen while one of them flashes a mirror directly into the lens – he was doing something 'completely new'.

The footage for *The Art of Mirrors* came through the door this morning. It's some of the most unusual film I've ever seen. It will be impossible to edit as there is not a moment I'll want to lose – each reel is more surprising than the last. The mirrors flashing sunlight into the camera with the light meter set at automatic sends the whole film lurching into negative. Luciana Martinez and Kevin Whitney in black evening dress are excellent. There's one shot of Luciana where the light falls through her mesh hat on to the blue triangular make-up which is wonderful. Gerald [Incandela] looks sinister in his paper-bag mask . . . This is the first film we've made on Super 8 with which there is nothing to compare.[23]

To meet the bills, Jarman continued to do some sporadic teaching and accept commissions which, though they might not pay much, if anything at all, did at least put him vaguely in the public eye. For Andrew Logan's friend Michael Davis he designed a show of architectural drawings at the Architectural Association; somewhat cussedly, it has to be said. He blacked out the windows, put red bulbs in the light fittings and provided visitors with torches to inspect the work on view. For Hal Bromm, a visiting New York art dealer, he engraved a set of glasses in a manner reminiscent of his abstract landscapes. With Stephen Hollis, then running the Palace Theatre in Watford, he discussed designing Shelley's *The Cenci* as directed by Lindsay Kemp – a colourful combination of talents that never progressed beyond the talking stage.

For another new friend, and occasional participant in the super-8s, a young Canadian dancer with the London Festival Ballet by the name of Timothy Spain, he undertook the design of a ballet Spain was to choreograph under a scheme funded by the Calouste Gulbenkian Foundation to help professional dance organisations commission new works for public performance. Using as his score an electronic composition by Morton Subotnik, *Silver Apples of the Moon*, Spain choreographed a simple nine-minute piece for six dancers, three male, three female. The piece used only a third of Subotnik's score and was perhaps too slight for the design Jarman produced.

> The front cloth is painted from a black and white photograph
> of a galaxy – the set is simple, consisting of several hundred
> half-silvered bulbs in silver holders on transparent flex which
> hang from the bars in rows. Behind them is a second black
> and white cloth painted with arcs tracked by comets with
> small red, yellow and blue arrows. The costumes follow this
> through – the men are in black dinner-jackets with red,
> yellow and blue gloves and shoes, and silvered spectacles –
> the girls are in primary coloured tutus and the mirrored
> glasses. The opening is a *coup de théâtre* – no stage lighting is
> used, the curtain rises in darkness, and the hundreds of bulbs
> are suddenly switched on about six inches from the floor. The

dancers stand motionless against them; and as the music
starts they fly upwards, a thousand glittering stars.[24]

In this way, the silver apples of the moon were given splendid and
glittering shape while, with his front cloth, Jarman was again showing how he liked to recycle images: as we have just seen, a galaxy
featured in his films.

The ballet received its première at the New Theatre in Oxford
over two nights, 22 and 23 October, in a programme of four pieces
that formed part of the Festival Ballet's autumn tour. Jarman considered his designs 'probably the best'[25] he had ever done and was
delighted when, on the opening night, the audience greeted his *coup
de théâtre* with a round of applause. He was less thrilled by the
reviews. Although some gave his designs a complimentary mention,
The Times echoed the general view when it said that they 'overpow-
ered the ballet's modest interest'.[26]

Jarman was paid £600 for his work, hardly enough to keep the
wolf from the door, especially when one considers that, apart from
Gargantua, this was his only paid commission during 1973. He did,
however, manage to sell the occasional painting, and, in November,
in tandem with Peter Logan and Oliver Campion, he repeated the
exercise he had tried at Bankside and threw open the studio.[27]
Together with some earlier landscapes, including those painted on
the Isle of Wight in the mid-sixties, he showed the pictures he had
recently executed in the sudden and unexpected burst of painterly
activity triggered by his visit to Avebury.

Alongside his paintings, Jarman was also constantly showing his
films, sometimes spontaneously, sometimes by invitation, sometimes
as a prelude to a feature or as incidental entertainment at a party. On
occasion, pacing up and down as he did so and scratching his head,
he would attempt to explain the films, or at least the process by
which they had been made, while his audience sat on the floor, sipping wine or smoking joints, either on cushions or uncomfortably
negotiating the flotsam of empty bottles which, owing to the grain-
encrusted, cambered floor, always collected in the dip by the wall.

The journalist Duncan Fallowell attended one such film show in
May 1974:

Getting away from it all, over Tower Bridge, round and down
on to Butler's Wharf, Bermondsey, you are confronted by
astonishing views and a blood red sunset. Behind you a string
of warehouses from *Gormenghast*: Derek Jarman is at home
holding a private view of his films for about 150 people . . .
'The Arabian Trilogy' . . . Soubrettes, hustlers, coryphées,
transvestites jostle on stone landings – there is a party
upstairs round an enormous indoor pool filled with candles
and Bohemian jitterbugs to the Thunder Thighs. They want
to turn this part of the wharf into an off-beat drive-in cinema.
It would be astonishing.[28]

Others had less imaginative plans for the area: all along the river,
warehouses were mysteriously going up in flames, torched, some said,
by ruthless speculators set on redevelopment. Apart from producing
occasional leaflets drawing attention to this state of affairs, the occu-
pants of Butler's Wharf tended to turn a blind eye to the threat, as
when Jarman invited Nicholas Logsdail and his wife Fiona to the
studio to see some of his films. At the time Logsdail was using the
basement of the annex in Lisson Street to show films and stage performances and, while he no longer viewed the Lisson as his gallery,
Jarman had his eye on being included.

It was an eventful audition, with fire featuring dramatically both
on and off the screen. Jarman records it thus:

At about ten we heard a fire engine bell . . . 'I wonder where
the fire is,' I remarked, then walked out on the metal bridge
which crosses Shad Thames at the back of my room, to find
the building next door a sheet of flame. The firemen went wild
when they saw that what they'd thought were deserted
warehouses were in fact occupied. They shouted at us to come
down at once. I put the speakers out on the balcony and played
Roberta Flack's 'Sweet Bitter Love' as loud as possible over the
roar of the flames – I don't think they were amused – and went
back inside to save my films. Nicholas and Fiona took an
armful of drawings down with them. Thankfully by midnight
the fire was out, and I crept back upstairs to sleep fitfully.[29]

Thankfully, too, Logsdail agreed to show Jarman's films – though given the size of audience Logsdail could attract to Lisson Street, this hardly put Jarman on the film-making map.

Audience reaction was, in the main, bemused. Another word would be bored. During screenings at Butler's Wharf, hands wandered more determinedly than ever – particularly when Jarman discovered the trick of showing footage shot at six frames per second at a snail-like three, thus halving the speed with which his images crossed the screen. So very dreamlike, some felt, as to put one to sleep.

On paper, and in his journals, Jarman had little patience with audience incomprehension. Although he saw the super-8s as being structured around writing, to form a 'poetry of fire' where the pleasure is that 'of seeing language put through the magic lantern', he did not believe it necessary for an audience to articulate this: 'The first viewers wracked their brains for a meaning instead of relaxing into the ambient tapestry of *random* images.'[30] In reality, like most artists, he was extremely sensitive to criticism or indifference. He would have been horrified to learn that, on occasion, the joints being passed around had such an overpowering effect that his audiences relaxed way beyond the 'ambient tapestry' of his images. He hated being told that what he did lacked sense or value. He tended to discourage negative feedback, or deflect it with the argument that what he was doing was simply fun. Most determinedly of all, no matter what people might or might not say, he drew on his reserves of natural optimism to make sure he kept going, doing his best to ignore all disappointments and setbacks, of which, as 1973 turned into 1974, there were a number, some minor, some major.

In the first category was failure to secure the title in Andrew Logan's second Alternative Miss World. Jarman had taken along his own camera, later refilming his record of the evening through a pink gel to give it a suitably roseate glow. A nervous Gerald Incandela, Miss Synthetic, wore a frock of see-through plastic. Kevin Whitney was Miss St Germain Depraved, a Left Bank artist who managed to smear Karl Bowens' mink with his palette as he squeezed past 'Miss Manhattan' on the rickety catwalk. Andrew Logan was male down one side, female down the other, thus embodying the joke at the heart of the evening. *Tout le monde* was there to see the model and singer Eric Roberts carry off the crown – in the guise of someone who, to those in the know, was even more depraved than Kevin Whitney: Miss Holland Park Walk.

A month earlier, Jarman and Incandela – together with the perennially homeless Patrik Steede – had taken refuge from encroaching winter in Anthony Harwood's flat, recently vacated by its owner as part of a plan to relocate to New York. Sloane Square meant easier access to the King's Road and the gay life of the area; a welcome degree of cosiness obligingly allied to all things cosmopolitan. Christmas was even cosier, if less cosmopolitan. Jarman's sister Gaye and her husband David, now the parents of a young son and with a second baby on the way, had purchased a derelict farmhouse on the Hereford Road near Ledbury. The house, called the Verzons, would, thought the Temples, make an ideal pub and restaurant. Jarman was called upon to give advice. Together with Christopher Hobbs, he suggested colours and fabrics, persuaded Andrew Logan to provide a mirror, hung pictures and filled one room with stuffed animals bought at Hereford Market. He also made detailed plans for the garden – much more detailed than anything he had suggested to the Sainsburys for their property in Kent – envisaging an orchard, a meadow, an abstract and a Temple garden, a maze; though all Gaye and her husband ever had the time or money to achieve was the cutting back of the dead elms killed by the Dutch Elm disease that had recently ravaged the country, plus the planting of a yew, a pair of mulberry trees and some cypresses.

By Christmas the Verzons was sufficiently habitable for Jarman to bring Incandela and Steede to stay for a week. Recalling the visit afterwards, Steede wrote: 'I remember a fixation with Figaro and log fires at night. And dangerous games of Monopoly.'[31] Gaye remembers only that Incandela took endless photographs of her son, Sam.

Incandela's camera had been given him by Jarman, who was most keen that his young lover 'find' himself as an artist. To some, this was simply a measure of Jarman's generosity and skill at schooling those in need of support. To others, it was an indication that Jarman had tired of Incandela and was ready to move on, but needed Incandela to establish himself in his own right so that the moving on could be done with a clear conscience. Just as Steede and Gaye remember different aspects of that Christmas, so there are crucially conflicting memories concerning the import of what happened next.

Under the heading 'CRISIS', Jarman writes in Dancing Ledge: '31 January 1974, Sloane Square: My thirty second birthday, and Gerald left in tears. I've put him in a taxi to Thilo's.'[32] Jarman devotes just three sentences to Incandela's defection before briskly turning his attention to work and the parlous state of his finances. By contrast, in Incandela's version, it is Jarman who does the crying. Who do we believe? Was Jarman relieved that Incandela, who could be moody and demanding, had found another lover? Or was he devastated that yet again the object of his desire did not reciprocate that desire wholeheartedly? Was he piqued that an acolyte, a leading courtier in his ever-expanding court, had gone, as it were, republican? Or was he simply so very English, so intensely private behind that garrulous façade, that he could not begin to articulate his real feelings? Is that why, after just three sentences, the crisis becomes one of work and money rather than of the heart? Or was it, as Jarman would later maintain, that because of what he had witnessed of relationships as a child, and because he was in revolt against middle-class morés, he never even wanted to live with anyone? Or that if he did, and the person concerned was an artist, since the artist will always need freedom, any such relationship is bound to be transitory?

All we can say for certain is that behind Jarman's back, Incandela had been seeing a young art dealer, Thilo von Watzdorf. That it was to Von Watzdorf's house in Knightsbridge that Incandela's taxi took him. That Incandela had a forceful character and was an unwilling second fiddle. That he valued his creature comforts.

Of Jarman, we can say only that whatever his feelings for Incandela, emotional or sexual, he had never been faithful; that during their short experiment in domesticity, he had indulged in any number of one-night stands, anonymous encounters on the heath, even the occasional affair. That he was notorious for tiring quickly of his conquests. That his fondness for Incandela, and belief in his talent, were such that although relations between Jarman, Incandela and Von Watzdorf were understandably tense, the trio nevertheless managed to remain friends. Jarman would later visit

Incandela and Von Watzdorf in the country, where he filmed
Incandela with considerable affection,[33] and he never stopped promoting Incandela's career, eventually introducing him to the
influential American collector Sam Wagstaff, who had helped
launch Robert Mapplethorpe as a photographer and would do much
the same for Incandela.

During the course of 1973, Jarman had appeared with Michael
Davis in a short super-8 film entitled *High Noon*. The film was made
by Robin Wall, a young Canadian who had appeared in some of
Jarman's own super-8s, most revealingly as one of the four nude men
in *Death Dance*. For his own effort, Wall took as his starting point the
fact that how you make a film is by 'shooting' it. In a playful commentary on the violence inherent in film-making, he staged a shoot
out between Jarman and Davis in which their 'guns' were two Nizo
cameras.

Early in 1974, countrywide industrial unrest gave Britain a blitz-
like emergency in the shape of the three-day working week. For the
other two days, the lights were literally switched off across the country to conserve fuel stocks. Meanwhile, the IRA were stepping up
their campaign of violence against the British government and
people. Confrontation was in the air, providing the background
against which Jarman now duelled with his personal demons.

Although he never lost his extraordinary sweetness of temperament or generosity of spirit, he was perfectly capable of riding
roughshod over the people most loyal to him. For example,
Christopher Hobbs – who, to an almost slave-like extent, was forever
on hand to provide practical support for Jarman's flights of fancy –
was frequently the butt of derision. Without Hobbs, there is much in
Jarman's life that would not have been realised, a debt that Jarman
freely acknowledged with public praise. In private, however, he could
be ruthlessly dismissive of what he termed his helpmate's 'stuffiness'.
It was almost as if he could not bear to be beholden to another.

Yet neither could he truly bear to stand alone. For all the confidence and enthusiasm of his demeanour, beneath the surface he was
exceptionally vulnerable to anything that smacked of neglect or
criticism, even if only implied. When, a year earlier, Michael
Ginsborg and Robby Nelson had married, Jarman had been their

best man. After the marriage, and as children appeared, he seemed to lose interest in them. They had crossed into that heterosexual terrain on which Jarman had made it a point of honour never to linger for longer than necessary. And when the sexually dexterous Patrik Steede became seriously involved with a woman called Caroline, Jarman's hurt coloured his discussions with Steede about the script of their film on St Sebastian so forcefully on occasion that it was quite a relief when, early in 1974, Steede left for Italy to continue work on the script alone.

The year 1973 also saw Lance's retirement; seldom an easy moment for a man, especially an active one. Of course, he still had his sailing, which he pursued as ferociously as ever, plus some related teaching. He was able to turn his attention to studying the family genealogy. His finest hours, however, were over – a fact poignantly acknowledged when, a year earlier, he confirmed to the London Borough of Hillingdon that he was prepared to continue as the borough's 'Assistant Controller (Operations)' in the event of a 'war emergency'.[34] The title is splendidly militaristic; the reality pure *Dad's Army*.

In 1967, when Jarman had exhibited at the Young Contemporaries, Lance had marched excitedly through the Tate, rubbing his hands together in glee. 'Have you seen *our* painting?' he had demanded of visiting friends. The question betrays an uneasy mix of paternal pride and extreme vulnerability, that telling '*our*' highlighting the need to be included which lurked behind Lance's gruff, bluff exterior. The passing of youth and the inexorable advance of his wife's cancer increased this need to the point where it found its expression in the most extreme and secret behaviour. Lance had become a kleptomaniac.

Ever since those days in the sixties, from time to time personal possessions such as rings or paperweights had unaccountably gone missing at Merryfield. These isolated incidents now became more regular and more peculiar. Gaye and her husband had worked for a while in the Seychelles, and she had asked her father to look after the silver they had been given when they had married. On their return, she asked for the gifts back. Lance denied having had them. Betts suggested Gaye look in the loft, which, one afternoon when Lance was out sailing, she did, with some apprehension. She found the silver squirrelled away among a plethora of other treasures. Betts' sister Moyra visited from South Africa and was intrigued to notice that the car kept by Lance on blocks in the garage was brimful of groceries: toilet paper, tins of fruit and the like, which Betts explained away as Lance's spoils from a recent sideline, skippering a yacht in Southampton Water. The avoidance of too much truth in the Jarman household ran ominously deep and was closely allied to fear. As late as 1977, after Betts had been confronted by the obvious homosexuality of her son's first feature, she could still ask her sister what a homosexual was. And when, one afternoon, she inadvertently burned a saucepan full of milk, she buried the pan in the garden rather than confess to Lance that she had ruined it.

Only many years later, after his father's death was Jarman able to write with any candour about Lance's 'kamikaze mentality';[35] how the refined air commodore had felt 'cheated' by the country on whose behalf he had so valiantly fought; how perhaps his 'bombing missions through Tesco and Safeways'[36] were a way of recapturing the thrill of that war. Interestingly, though, of the fact that it was not until the week of Betts' death in 1978 that he and Gaye ever 'put two and two together' regarding Lance's kleptomania, Jarman remarks only that it 'seemed strange'.[37] Nor does he see any parallel between Lance's obsessive need to belong and his own. The family inability to confront its demons was itself a demon he could not easily face.

Instead Jarman was devoting his energies to his super-8s, breaking off only briefly to attend to two minor design projects, neither of which went altogether smoothly. Timothy Spain was expanding *Silver Apples of the Moon* for the London Festival Ballet's spring season – two performances that April at the Coliseum – by increasing the length of the ballet from nine to fifteen minutes through the creation of a new character, a creature of pure light, a moonbeam, who would appear as if nude before donning a tuxedo like the other male dancers. At the end of the piece, the moonbeam would divest one of the female dancers of her tutu so that, like him, she could escape her worldly being and join the realm of spirit and light. As expressed in the programme notes, the ballet was now about 'the birth, life and death of any civilisation or group of sentient beings'.

It was never envisaged that this new scenario would involve actual nudity. Spain, who was to dance the moonbeam, would – in addition to white body paint, silver hair and mirrored nails – wear a skin-coloured bathing suit, the woman a body stocking. Or so Spain would later maintain. At the time, the ballerina concerned appeared to be under the impression she might be required to appear nude and complained to the management, who shared her apprehension. Spain had used the word 'streaking' in rehearsal, thereby giving rise to a general fear that he might unexpectedly dispense with his bathing suit. With only one day to go before the opening, the decision was taken to withdraw his work. Apart from the critics, who were handed a slip of paper announcing that the ballet had 'failed to develop in the way that was expected', the first anyone knew of *Rose Variations* replacing *Silver Apples of the Moon* was when the audience took their seats.

The occasion should have marked Jarman's return to the theatre he had helped inaugurate. He was accordingly outraged – though more on Spain's account, it has to be said, than his own. He felt the management's stated reason for the cancellation left no one any the wiser as to whether the decision had been taken because the ballet was underdeveloped or for fear that the choreographer might be overexposed. This uncertainty, he argued, could fatally damage Spain's career. He insisted to Spain that they both visit the Calouste Gulbenkian Foundation to complain in person, and fired off a batch of letters taking the Festival Ballet to task for the high-handed manner in which, without 'open discussion', they had cancelled 'the one breath of fresh air that might have blown through a stagnant company'. In addition, he produced a limited edition of one hundred signed sheets of xeroxed paper which capitalised on the cancellation by means of a series of gnomic paragraphs, one of which gave both the title and the *raison d'être* of this most Kleinian piece of 'art terrorism': 'This work is titled "this work failed to develop in the way I expected, so I have cancelled it" – isn't it a pity that the world can't do the same with its bureaucracies.'[38]

Four days later, on Sunday 28 April, in response to a request from Anya Sainsbury to help with two of the contributions to a ballet gala she was organising with Petrus Bosman in aid of Friends of Fatherless Families, Jarman witnessed a second, albeit less distressing cancellation. His brief was to design costumes for the 'Esmeralda' pas de deux, to be danced by Lesley Collier and Wayne Eagling, plus costumes and set for 'Nocturne', a new pas de deux choreographed[39] by Peter Wright. When Lesley Collier injured herself in rehearsal, 'Esmeralda' had to be replaced by Wayne Sleep's popular send-up of Olga Korbut, the Russian gymnast, leaving only 'Nocturne' in the programme. Danced by Ann Jenner and David Ashmole, this flamboyantly romantic love duet was performed in the style of a Bolshoi *divertissement* and cried out – or so Jarman thought – for 'an outrageously romantic backcloth'.[40] Basing his design on a watercolour from *Beautiful Flowers and How to Grow Them*, the book he had been given as a child, he provided 'a spray of creamy pink butterfly orchids painted against the blue of a night sky with a crescent moon. The dancers have simple white costumes and dance in the moonlight under this enormous spray of flowers.'[41]

That year, 1974, held the promise of another, more challenging design project: for Ken Russell's film version of the rock opera *Tommy*. However, despite his financial situation and the blandishments of Russell and his producer, Jarman declined the offer. Having threatened as much ever since the days of *The Devils*, he was finally staying true to his own words: 'I've had enough of film design and the huge amount of energy and time it takes punches gaping holes in my own work.'[42] He was forcing himself into a position where he had no alternative, financial or aesthetic, but to take his super-8s ever more seriously. Setting painting aside, he planned film after film with footage shot and footage still to shoot; he held frequent shows of his work on the wall at Sloane Square; and although he had turned his back on Hollywood, he allowed himself to dream that if he followed Anthony Harwood and Patrik Steede, who had also recently moved to New York, maybe there, in the Billboard Promised Land, everything would come magically right.

The reverse proved to be the case, largely because in America, as Jarman quickly and brutally discovered when he flew there in early

June, his mentor had moved on. Harwood was spending as much time as he could with a young lawyer by the name of Robert Darling, either in the latter's apartment on West 9th Street or, when Nina was away, in a house he and Darling had taken together on Fire Island. It was here that Jarman found him, in the company of various new American friends, young males who did not particularly welcome a visiting Englishman with a prior claim on their host. Jarman met a boy on the beach and brought him back to the house, where they were observed horsing around naked in the pool by the visiting mother of one of the boys. According to her son, so horrified was she by Jarman's display of acrobatics that he was left with no alternative but to ask the interloper to leave. However, if Jarman's own account of the incident is to be believed, he was simply swimming and the mother had that morning, and without blinking an eyelid, watched a video featuring her son engaged in physical activities that were a good deal more suggestive than the crawl.

The real reason for Jarman's eviction was jealousy. He threatened to claim too much of Harwood's time. With his long hair and non-athletic body, he did not properly blend in with the American boys. 'Well tanned Ambre Solaire, work-out muscles, and faces wrinkled by over-exposure to the December sun-ray lamps,'[43] was how he waspishly described them. They in turn sniggered at the lamentable quality of his British dental work and lack of a tan. He would manage to visit Fire Island again that summer, but only by sleeping rough on the beach.

Money was a perennial problem. Before leaving London, Jarman had rented out his studio at Butler's Wharf and sold 'a decade's clutter',[44] to give himself a degree of financial ballast; for the rest – and how it must have irked him – he relied on 'the odd dollar'[45] from Harwood, who was in the process of doing up his new protégé's apartment on West 9th Street and paid Jarman to help.

The reluctant decorator took solace behind his Nizo. At Fire Island, either alone or with a couple of boys he had picked up, and using a variety of different-coloured gels, he filmed the waves, the beach, the plants, the jutting wooden posts. Also his companions: nude, in swimming costumes, or all in white and capped by a white paper bag; holding a starfish, with pearls on their eyes, playing a tambourine, pointing out to sea, or simply sitting next to a flashing mirror. With the tape-recorder he carried around with him as frequently as he did his Nizo, he made an ambient audiotape featuring the sound of gulls and waves. It was a rich seam of sound and images to hoard against his return to London, where they would go towards *In the Shadow of the Sun*, or be variously recycled in the other titles which complement that film: *Fire Island*, *My Very Beautiful Movie*, *The Sea of Storms* and *Kingdom of Outremer*.

He shot in the city too. Framing the footage with the famous 'Walk' or 'Don't Walk' pedestrian signs, he filmed his friend Herbert Muschamp striding through a canyon of skyscrapers and pointing out the architectural sights; a joke at Jarman's own expense, perhaps, since this was of course an activity for which he himself was famed. He filmed mannequins in shop windows and his favourite diner on the Lower West Side, where the waiter would always give him 'the biggest portions of french fries' to keep him going.[46] In a cinema called the Elgin, he filmed some of *The Devils* off the screen, later cutting the scenes together in such a way that he removed Grandier from the film and turned positive into negative, white into black and black into white, so that when, at the end, 'Madeleine escapes from the claustrophobic city of Loudun into the world outside . . . she walks into a blizzard of ashes'.[47]

He wrote to the art dealer Harold Bromm, whose SoHo apartment he was borrowing, 'Beach Street is wonderful and New York is living up to all expectations . . . I really would like to live here awhile.' Yet underlying his permanent public optimism was a more sombre reality. In the same letter he writes: 'I have seen very little of everyone as it is almost impossible to make connections here.' And in a postcard to Brenda Lukey he added that he was living on '$3 a day, next to starving . . . survival difficult'. Apart from his filming and the odd jobs he was doing for Harwood, work proved hopelessly elusive, as did acceptance. Even his old friend Patrik Steede seemed – according to Jarman, at least – oddly reluctant to discuss the St Sebastian project. This left only play. Fuelled by modest amounts of mescalin and acid, Jarman surrendered himself to the hedonistic excesses exemplified by New York in the mid-seventies. The derelict piers that stretched into the West River, where every night you would see 'young men often naked in the shafts of light which fell through the windows' – and where, at midday, you might find 'a guy in boxer shorts being blown as he leans against his bike'.[48] The 'heavily scented' bushes on Fire Island, equally alive with men, not to mention fireflies and 'silent floating will-o'-the-wisps'. The baths – the Everard, the St Marks or the Continental, where 'handsome drug dealers' would be 'sprawled out on their bunks gently masturbating, their doors slightly ajar to trap the unwary and, if you swallowed their bait, inhibitions cast aside, you'd be making love in that swimming pool packed with naked bodies'.[49]

It was a world that enticed, bedazzled and repelled. The anarchic hedonist welcomed it; the ascetic withdrew. Although Jarman cruised Fire Island with the best and worst of them, his filmic record is as austere as his painted landscapes. In his notebooks, the phrase 'the fight between love and chastity' constantly recurs. One senses that here, at the very edge of Jarman's known world in the Kingdom of Outremer, the land of 'cockaigne' across the sea, the fight was intensified. Among his books is a volume entitled *Eranos*, the third in a series of lectures delivered annually at the Eranos meetings. It includes such essays as Erich Neumann's 'Art and Time', Jung's 'On Synchronicity', Henry Corbin's 'Cyclical Time in Mazdaism and Ismailism'. The book is inscribed: 'St Marks Baths, NYC, Friday afternoon Sept 20'. That Jarman should visit the baths with this as his reading matter encapsulates the dichotomy.

The ascetic won the day. Quintessential Englishman that he was, Jarman found himself 'temperamentally unsuited to New York life',[50] especially without the protection of the figure who had drawn him there in the first place. As a wry sentence cut from the published version of *Dancing Ledge* has it: 'Time to go home, Princess, the ball is over.'

He returned to 'three months of dust and grease'[51] at Sloane Square, which he was soon sharing with two others: Malcolm Leigh and a young art student friend of Leigh's, Guy Ford. Attractive, blond, quick-witted, impulsive and gratifyingly enthusiastic about film, Ford quickly established himself at the very centre of Jarman's circle. It was a circle that continued to expand outwards as Jarman, perhaps to compensate for having lost a father figure of his own in Harwood, increasingly assumed the role himself.

Jarman continued to rent out his studio at Butler's Wharf to make ends meet and, when really desperate for money, would don a suit and go cap in hand to the richest of his friends. Leigh brought in what he could from a job as a gardener in Hyde Park. They did not have a phone, ate simply and, apart from late-night forays to one or other of Jarman's favourite haunts, or perhaps a weekend at the Verzons, did not go out much.

In essence, what Jarman was doing was once again marking time. Patrik Steede's letters to him during this period reveal how lonely and lost he was, especially when one remembers that they are written by someone successfully making the transition to New York that Jarman had so signally failed to achieve.

20 October. Please don't get too depressed – perhaps things are opening up for you again? . . . Enjoyed the Hockney film . . . yes we are both featured but the film is a good effort so have left well alone.[52]

13 November. Glad you are managing to muddle through somehow . . . the other day I bought a sale record of Edith S doing her thing in Façade. You once suggested it to Ken R for a film. I hereby suggest it to you . . . It would . . . seem the sort of project you could handle at this stage . . . Also do you know Rilke's Letters to a Young Poet? They would be very helpful in your present solitary existence.

22 January 1975. Thank you for your last letter, albeit a rather down one. almost bitter. it forced me to reanalyse my own feelings and to remind me of my feeling last year when I was in London just before leaving for Italy . . . your letter saddens me and makes me feel guilty because it is exactly the way I was talking and thinking . . . i don't want to return to that state because i can still feel how destructive it is . . . occasionally I get the feeling that if everyone is so poor in London maybe it is now time to start doing things without

looking for reward other than the fact of putting something together . . . i wish the world future looked more serene than it does.

Undated. Did you know that [Harwood] can't get back to England? Nina let this slip so it might not be all true – but it would explain a lot of things. Especially his virulent attitude towards England and everything English. If that really is the case watch out for the bailiffs because knowing him he won't have made any provision for the rent. And Nina certainly doesn't seem anxious to put any more of her money into a place she's never seen and he can't go back to. It's all so mad. I'm sure he will be in prison before he's done – the necklace that he gave Nina to appease her on her arrival cost $20,000. Unpaid for.[53]

Here the letters stop, brought to an abrupt halt by a sudden and unexpected development in the saga of the Roman martyr whose story Steede had recently seemed so reluctant to discuss.

20

Features

Ironically, given Jarman's antipathy to such gatherings, it was an encounter at a lunch party that breathed life into St Sebastian. James Whaley – young, handsome, charming, wealthy, a sometime student of the London Film School and keen to make his mark as a producer – asked Jarman if he had ever thought of making a feature. Jarman talked about *The Tempest* and his ideas for something on the heretical pharaoh Akhenaten. He also mentioned St Sebastian. Shortly afterwards, completely to Jarman's surprise, the young man with whom he thought he had been simply passing the time of day produced a synopsis and presented it to Jarman with the suggestion that they work together to realise their mutual dream.

Jarman had failed to mention that the idea was not exactly his; or, if he had, he had made light of the fact. His published account of the film's genesis is strangely imprecise on this question. Whereas his notebooks suggest that by now Patrik Steede had completed his script, and in a form suspiciously akin to that of the final film, in *Dancing Ledge* Jarman justifies his abandonment of his erstwhile collaborator by implying that Steede never did produce a finished script. Although Jarman would later take pains to put Steede's contribution to the project firmly on record, there was clearly 'an element of betrayal'[1] in the making of what became *Sebastiane*.

With Steede brushed conveniently under the carpet, pre-production on the film gathered momentum in a seemingly spontaneous, excited, frequently chaotic coming together of friends, friends of friends and, when necessary, the occasional indispensable professional – all contributing their tuppence-worth with no regard whatsoever for the hierarchies usually attendant on film production. In addition to his role as producer, Whaley helped write the script, on which any number of other friends and colleagues were consulted, including Robert Medley, Guy Ford and Dom Sylvester Houédard. Jarman had hoped that Houédard would also help with the Latin translation – still the only way he could see of guaranteeing historical verisimilitude on virtually no budget – but the monk was too busy. Instead, Houédard suggested Jack Welch, a young American classics scholar from Oxford. Meanwhile, since Jarman was such a novice, he and Whaley thought they had better approach a tried and tested professional to edit and provide directorial back-up. They chose Paul Humfress, who had been with the BBC for many years and who immediately became one more name in the roll-call of people who helped shape the script. Whaley then enlisted Howard Malin, a young friend just out of Leeds University, on the production side. The tongue-in-cheek name they took for their infant company was Megalovision.

Their progress may have seemed haphazard and flippant, little more than a simple extension of the super-8s, but there was a serious purpose to *Sebastiane*: to make a film that would validate the homosexual experience. Despite his claim at the time that he did not want to be a 'gay' film-maker, Jarman was extremely sensitive to the advances being made by gay liberation and to his own memories of how, as a child, he had read Wilde and Cocteau not because he found them particularly interesting, but simply because he was desperate for anything that would help him make sense of his sexuality. The figure of St Sebastian – subject of homoerotic art from Renaissance paintings to the novels of Mishima – fitted this purpose perfectly. Although Jarman would later acknowledge that the film had shortcomings,[2] he remained intensely proud that his first foray into professional direction produced 'perhaps the first film that depicts homosexuality in a completely matter of fact way, such as another film might depict heterosexuality'.[3] In *At Your Own Risk*, he writes: 'Years later, a young man in Glasgow said he had seen *Sebastian* [sic] on television; he had to turn the sound down because his parents were upstairs so he couldn't understand what was going on (despite the subtitles). He saw it later with the sound turned up but still didn't understand what the film was about; nevertheless he told me that it had changed his life.'[4] To have countered those watchful parents and helped direct a young life was, for Jarman, a crowning achievement.

In most versions of the Sebastian legend, Sebastian is a captain in the Palace Guard during the Emperor Diocletian's persecution of Christians. Because of his Christian sympathies, he is shot through with arrows, though such is his beauty that, in one rendering of the story, the soldiers can only bring themselves to fire at his arms and legs. Left for dead, he is rescued and given shelter by Irene, the widow of Castulus, another Christian martyr. He is later rearrested and either clubbed or stoned to death. With no more than a nod at this usual telling of the legend – a brief establishing scene set in Rome, during which the palace guard Sebastian is exiled by Diocletian for protesting at the execution of a Christian – Jarman set his version in the military outpost of Sebastian's exile. One of a small contingent of bored and isolated soldiers, Sebastian is set apart from the others by his Christianity. He is singled out, too, by the captain of the guard, Severus, whose violent lust he has unwittingly aroused. Sebastian has promised himself to Christ and will not submit to Severus, thus provoking a sadomasochistic relationship between soldier and captain that eventually leads to the death Sebastian has always subconsciously desired. He is tied to a stake on a rocky promontory and every soldier – including Justin, the only person to befriend Sebastian – is commanded by Severus to fire an arrow at their unfortunate brother-in-arms.

Interestingly, although the script posits and contrasts so many aspects of gay love (the sadism of Severus's lust for Sebastian; the masochism of Sebastian's love for Christ; unrequited love that is marred by guilt; the uncomplicated, guilt-free love shared by two other soldiers, Anthony and Adrian; even homophobia), and although the modest budget would keep costumes to a minimum, allowing the camera to linger over a great deal of nudity, ultimately *Sebastiane* is less about love and sex than about exile and the exercise of power; what it is to be an outsider.[5] This issue is explored in an intensely personal manner. Despite the number of people who were crucially involved in the production of the film, *Sebastiane*'s cinematic and visual debts are clearly to Jarman's own particular mentors. To Pasolini (one thinks especially of *The Gospel According to Matthew*) and, certainly in terms of historical playfulness, to Ken Russell: the film's first scene bears more than a passing resemblance to the masque that opens *The Devils*. To the photographs of Von Gloeden, for insouciant sexuality in a Mediterranean setting. To Jarman's own painted landscapes for the barrenness of that setting. To his adolescence for the mesmeric power of religion and perhaps a great deal else. As already noted, remove the Roman trappings, ignore the nudity, and the film's milieu becomes that of a boarding school, while Sebastian's brutalisation at the hands of Severus eerily echoes Jarman's own 'rape' by the Canford bullies. *Sebastiane* reminds us that despite its director's innate optimism and constant determination to make the best of things, his make-up contained more than a hint of the martyr. Underlying any celebration of the advances made by gay liberation during the seventies are the wounds inflicted by the repressions of the fifties and sixties. On the one hand, the film is a happy peopling of a landscape which, if Jarman had been painting it, would have remained empty. On the other, it teems with personal demons.

It was one thing to have a script, another to raise the money to film it. Lacking the resources to fund an entire feature, Whaley pooled his connections with Jarman's and, making the most of his own charm and looks, set out with Malin to persuade likely friends and passing acquaintances[6] to contribute anything from £500 to a few thousand. As a result *Sebastiane* is that rare cinematic creature, a feature funded solely from private resources. Of a final budget of some £30,000, about a third was raised in this way, enabling Whaley and Malin to buy film stock, make or hire costumes and props, offer a crew the industry rate, pay the actors, even guarantee their director a small fee.

The next task was to find a suitable location. Because his parents lived there and he was familiar with the island, Whaley suggested Ibiza. Jarman, however, was set on Italy. The two of them travelled to Rome, where they fortuitously happened upon the film designer Ferdinando Scarfiotti, who offered them the use of an isolated strip of coast his family owned in southern Sardinia.[7] Apart from a couple of ruined fishermen's cottages, two ancient fig trees and, on a nearby headland, an ancient but well-preserved watchtower, Cala Domestica consisted of just two small, rocky coves with sandy beaches, plus an endless sweep of sea and sky. It was perfect.

Back in London, Jarman started to compile one of the big black books in which he would always plan his films, pasting the script alongside sketches, cuttings and scribbled notes in such a way as to fashion not just a workbook, but an object of considerable fascination and beauty in its own right.[8] The design he undertook himself, with the statutory help of a student or two from Wimbledon. There was not a huge amount to do – the budget saw to that – but even so, such was Jarman's attention to detail that every object in the film had to be perfect, be it cloak, strigil, frisbee or the black leather nose which, in a notion borrowed from the super-8s, it had been decided that Maximus, the most loutish of the soldiers, would wear.

The cast, like the production crew, mixed amateur with professional, not least because it was proving difficult to persuade professionals to appear for such modest salaries in such an immodestly gay film. The leading man was Leo Treviglio, a friend of Scarfiotti's: a poet, dancer and performer with the Living Theatre.[9] The part of Severus was taken by Barney James, former drummer with the Rick Wakeman band. Richard Warwick, whom Lindsay Anderson had filmed to such sensuous effect in *If*, agreed to play Justin. With the lesser ranks of the garrison being filled principally by friends, Jarman turned for the part of Adrian to Ken Hicks, on whom he prevailed to do a mock screen test. Wearing only a pair of boots, the briefest of denim shorts and flaunting a well-oiled, tautly muscled body, Hicks stood before the mirrored wall in Sloane Square to demonstrate how a Roman might use the strigil to clean himself. His audition later became a short film in its own right.[10] Super-8 in hand, Jarman lovingly captured Hicks narcissistically scraping oil from his body before breaking the unwritten rule that a director should never sleep with a cast member by progressing with Hicks into the bedroom next door, where Hicks 'produced capsules of old-fashioned poppers in glass phials wrapped in cotton wool and had me fuck him on Anthony's enormous and ruined bed in the bright sun-light, lithe and glistening with sweat and his come all over the sheets and walls'. Recalling the afternoon many years later, the dying Jarman would write:

What a journey from the day I pushed my cock into Ron [Wright]'s arse ten years before when neither of us knew where we were going and the feeble strokes were stymied by guilt. Now fucking Ken . . . we rode back into an antiquity of fable, not an Eden but a Paradois Paradise and we were Alexander and Hadrian and every boy since then, power, conquest, surrender, my paradise was whole, balanced as the rhythm of the pendulum, back forth, pleasure pain, but none of the guilt.[11]

Jarman's need to belong and to claim a rightful place in the world frequently led him to view his actions in the context of the past. In an echo of the classical torsos which littered his canvases, a frequent fantasy of his when having sex was that looming over the bed would be the figure of a homosexual from history: Alexander the Great, say, or Caravaggio, or Edward II. So vivid could these figures seem that on occasion Jarman would go so far as to imagine it was the histori-cal figure and not the contemporary boy with whom he was consummating his lust. Sebastiane (and, in time, Caravaggio and Edward II) was an extension of such private fantasies into the public realm. In these films, Jarman's concept of a gay lineage was given shimmering embodiment on the screen.

During February and early March, returning with Paul Humfress and Luciana Martinez to one of the landmarks of his childhood, Jarman also found time for a more complex, though never fully realised, piece of super-8 filming. For the Corfe Castle film, or Troubadour, as it is sometimes known, Christopher Hobbs came up with two mediaeval costumes: one a white calico gown and pearl-encrusted headdress, the other a suit of armour with double-headed axe fashioned from silvered cardboard.[12]

In late March these items provided Jarman with two of his three costumes for the increasingly popular Alternative Miss World, held in 1975 at Butler's Wharf. He went as Miss Crêpe Suzette, a fading film star – though not so faded that she did not possess a personal dress designer: Christopher Hobbs in the guise of 'Choufleur de Paris'. Gloria Swanson was the inspiration for Jarman's make-up, while for his coiffure he turned to Keith of Smiles, who had cut his hair for many years. Pressing some blonde dye into service, Keith gave Jarman a crew-cut into which, at the back, he cut a coloured triangle. The suit of armour enabled Miss Crêpe Suzette to appear as Joan of Arc and to conceal a tape-recorder behind the breastplate. On being questioned by Molly Parkin, taking a break from writing to be a rather belligerent compère, Jarman surreptitiously switched on the tape-recorder and, as if by magic, began miming to the strains of Josephine Baker singing 'J'ai Deux Amours'. The calico gown was also utilised, though the *pièce de resistance* was undoubtedly a silver diamanté dress Jarman had first used in *In the Shadow of the Sun*. This he accessorised with swimming flippers and 'a headdress made from a green rubber frog, with pearls and lashings of ruby and diamanté drops'.[13]

The glamorous, glittering crowd that squeezed into the top-floor studio included all the usual suspects, plus a real-life film star in the person of Carrol Baker, who, for added glamour, dressed as yet another film star, Jean Harlow, in a dazzling silver sheath and a swirl of white fur. Miss Crêpe Suzette was up against some two dozen other competitors, many of them just as eye-catching, though such was Jarman's flair and determination to win that this time the judges finally awarded him the crown. The throne was somewhat insecurely placed on a small platform high above an indoor pool constructed below the stage. The orb and sceptre were presented to the vertiginous winner by a none-too-confident tightrope walker who wobbled towards her on a rope stretched from the back of the room on to the stage itself.[14] Then came the *coup de théâtre*: the winner's cloak, an old parachute dyed puce, dropped from the ceiling to envelop Miss Crêpe Suzette in its brightly coloured folds.

The evening had been another feather in Andrew Logan's party-throwing cap, though not even his exceptional organisational skills could prevent an element of mayhem. Moments after Jarman had been crowned by the previous title-holder, Eric Roberts, the former Miss Holland Park Walk, the outgoing Alternative Miss World had pushed Molly Parkin into the pool because Miss Parkin, smiling sweetly, had unwisely voiced the opinion that Miss Holland Park Walk had done well to make a success of her life for someone not of 'our' colour. Earlier Miss Statue of Liberty had come perilously close to setting the building alight when she spilled burning petrol from her flaming torch. If someone had not been deft with the fire extinguisher, London's demimonde might have been reduced to a quart du monde. Then, at the end of the evening, everyone had to feel their way out of the building because the lights on the stairs had failed. A poignant postscript was provided by the sight of Carrol Baker, rather the worse for wear, throwing her ruined shoes into the Thames from Tower Bridge. By contrast, that other film star, Miss Crêpe Suzette, was clicking her heels in delight.

Within two months of his coronation, Jarman had again joined James Whaley in Sardinia, where the two of them nervously awaited the arrival of their cast and crew. Since no permission to work in Italy had been arranged, everyone was required to smuggle the necessary equipment into the country by distributing it between their luggage. Once cast, crew and gear had been safely accounted for and billeted in a spartan hotel in the small town of Iglesias, almost an hour's drive from Cala Domestica along a ruinous road, they were ready to begin.

From the photographs taken by Gerald Incandela – stills photographer and bit-part player – and from the short films shot by Jarman and Hugh Smith, the sound assistant, what followed looks like pure holiday: suntanned bodies frolicking against a backdrop of sea and sky. Yet paradoxically, although filming with Jarman usually felt more like fun than work, on *Sebastiane*, because it was his first film and there was so much to learn, the process proved far from easy.

We're up at six; a quick cup of black coffee and a dry roll are provided by the hotel. This has been supplemented by boiled eggs after complaints about the meagre breakfast. Then we're off over the rock-strewn dirt track to the location, where those who've stayed the night have brewed tea on a camp fire. We are filming by about 10.30, and carry on with a short break for lunch – wine, mineral water, fruit and rolls, which Luciana buys at 5.30 in the morning at the market. Then work until six, before trekking back over the mountain to a proper meal in the hotel. It's a long day, and with temperatures soaring into the nineties, exhausting. After four weeks of this the idyllic cove and desert landscape shimmer with a subtle malevolence – trudging through the sand dunes with heavy equipment across razor-sharp rocks and through thorn bushes parallels the isolation of the group of Roman soldiers in their remote outpost, and has given the film an edge. If any of us thought we were making 'boys in the sand' when we arrived that illusion is now dispelled.[15]

In fact, the realisation that the jaunt would involve more work than play had come on the very first day, when the disbelieving cast discovered that the film really was to be made in Latin. There was some hasty rearrangement of lines, and a demand for Jack Welch to give extra tuition to those most in need of it. Money never ceased to be a worry. Despite the tightness of the budget and the meagreness of the food, on more than one occasion it ran out entirely, forcing Whaley to Rome, from whence he would miraculously return with sufficient lire for the film to continue. Luciana Martinez fell seriously ill and had to go into hospital, leaving an ill-prepared Howard Malin to take over the catering until another friend could step into the breach. One assistant found 'trudging through the sand dunes' too arduous and quit, thereby reducing the crew to three. For the final scene – Sebastian's martyrdom – a sizeable portion of the budget had been spent on an expert in special effects from Cinecitta, the inefficiency of whose arrows made filming the scene literally a torture. Earlier, in the love scene between Adrian (Ken Hicks) and Antony (Janusz Romanov), there had been technical difficulties of a different order. Hicks insisted on sporting an erection, but did not fancy Romanov enough to produce one. Eventually Gerald

Incandela came to the rescue, hurrying Hicks behind a rock to achieve the desired effect, which caused Paul Humfress to accuse Jarman of being a pornographer. It was an accusation Jarman hotly denied, though there can be no doubting how thrilled he was to have had a hand, so to speak, in the first hard-on ever to appear in a British feature.[16]

As filming progressed and Jarman grew in confidence, tension between himself and Humfress increased. Although there were many things he could never have done without Humfress' help, he came to find his collaborator's presence increasingly irksome. It was not Jarman's way to throw tantrums (a mild 'Oh, Lordy' was the most he could muster when things went wrong) and he never confronted Humfress with his feelings, but he would later say of *Sebastiane*: 'This is the only really unhappy film I've ever worked on.'[17]

On the other hand, for almost every problem that arose on location there was an answering wit and ingenuity to solve it. For light, professional cameraman Peter Middleton, who shot the film with a single 16mm camera and just two lenses, depended on sheets of tinfoil and the local shepherd boys to hold them in place. For night scenes, he covered the roofless cottages with strategically ripped black polythene to create the effect of moonlight. Although the script was adhered to more closely than is sometimes maintained, the nature of the location and the strengths and weaknesses of the actors necessarily dictated changes, which had to be improvised on the spot. In the original script there is a scene where Sebastian's peacock is killed by Max. This was cut because no one could bring themselves to do the deed. Instead, a last-minute pig hunt was substituted, plus a mock battle in the sand using the beetles found 'clinging to the poisonous plants which live in the sand dunes'.[18] One of the beetles was named after one of Jarman's most hated adversaries: Maria Domus Alba, or Mary Whitehouse.[19]

Throughout filming, there were rumbles of disapproval from Iglesias' chief of police. The presence of the youthful cast and crew in such a small town had not gone unnoticed; nor had the antics of those who stayed overnight at the beach to guard the equipment. They befriended the local shepherds and threw constant parties – despite dire warnings from Neil Robinson, the film's assistant in

Rome, about the Sardinian shepherd's fondness for his sheep and the consequent risk of anthrax. Eventually the police chief demanded that Whaley give an account of himself. Whaley told him that they were university students making a documentary about Roman soldiers, and when the chief visited the location, invented endless ways of keeping him looking the other way during scenes involving nudity.

Finally, after six arduous weeks, the filming was complete and, by the end of July, everyone and everything was safely back in England. Now began the slow, often painful, process of assembling a finished film; a process that would last the length of a pregnancy. The footage had been shot in colour, but as there was insufficient money to edit in colour, the rushes were developed in black and white and, since it had not been possible to organise standard daily viewings of the rushes in Sardinia, only when Jarman sat down with Humfress in the latter's cutting room in Westbourne Grove did they see what they had to work with.

Their first discovery was that they did not have enough material for a feature. It was therefore decided that the original opening scene – in which, against a backdrop of a Jean-Léon Gérôme's painting of the Coliseum, Sebastian finds himself unable to countenance a Christian execution – should be expanded into a 'lavish party' at Diocletian's palace 'to celebrate the birth of the sun'. Christopher Hobbs was asked to make Sebastian a golden breastplate and wreath; Berman and Nathan's was scoured for further gold or silver costumes; Andrew Logan's studio was earmarked as the location and Logan persuaded to cover the floor with a wash of pink marble, Ian Cairnie to paint a Pompeiian frieze.

Dom Sylvester Houédard was asked to find a new translator for the extra dialogue (Jack Welch having vanished to Lesbos) and invited to play Diocletian. Regretfully, he had to decline: 'Sept 13 we shall be just ending the curious renaissance institution of the so-called retreat and that afternoon the abbot's cousin is bringing 50 pious ladies so I just can't get away.'[20] Instead, the role went to Robert Medley.

The emperor's guests were culled from the usual faces seen at an Andrew Logan gathering, all dressed as outrageously as possible.

Recycling decadent London was, Jarman declared, the only sure way of doing 'ancient Rome cheaply'.[21] Logan himself wore a bright yellow felt toga and, as a medallion, a large plate surmounted by a three-dimensional Eiffel Tower. The photographer Johnny Rozsa 'dyed himself pure gold and carried a lyre'.[22] Kevin Whitney was the court painter, Luciana Martinez the wealthy Roman matron supposed later to have buried Sebastian, Eric Roberts the executioner whose vampiric dispatch of the emperor's favourite (he bites his neck) causes a horrified Sebastian to voice an objection and face consequent banishment. As Diocletian's entertainment, Jarman persuaded Lindsay Kemp, met on *Savage Messiah*, to devise a dance with the troupe from his acclaimed show *Flowers*.

Sadly, Jarman's hope for a 'cruel cocktail party where the glitterati met oriental Rome'[23] was frustrated by the problems that frequently attend a shoot. It rained, and the noise of the rain on the roof repeatedly interrupted filming. Those who could got stoned, slowing the day even further. Nor had there been enough rehearsal. The filming of a scantily clad Kemp being circled by his troupe, who dramatically waved giant phalluses and eventually splattered Kemp with a mixture of yoghurt and wallpaper paste ('a condensed milk orgasm'[24] was how Jarman termed it), took so much time that there was pitifully little left to concentrate properly on the party to which Kemp's dance should have been a mere prelude.

With the film completely in the can, but the money needed to finish the editing coming in only fitfully, the wearisome process of eking out the footage so that it could become a full-length feature continued. Between September 1975 and April 1976, Jarman spent two or three days of every week closeted with Humfress in his cutting room. Meanwhile, although as yet he had no idea what the final result would resemble, his essential confidence encouraged him to start developing something else for the giant screen.

In addition to some vague talk of a follow-up to *Sebastiane*, using the more usual version of the legend, the one where the martyr is rescued by Irene, Jarman turned to *Akenaten*,[25] an incestuous and bloody dynastic saga centring on Egypt's one heretical pharaoh.

Jarman's papers contain a jumble of ideas as to how he might have tackled the film, plus more than one rendering of the script.

Shortly before he died, when he decided to publish five of his unrealised films in *Up in the Air*, he went through his papers and chose a
'definitive' draft for his publishers.

Jarman's story, not always historically accurate, is narrated by the
Sphinx. The place is Egypt, the time about 1400BC – though, lest we
feel too removed from this distant past, as the Sphinx starts its nar-
ration, some tourists 'pass by taking a photo or two'.[26] Akenaten,
who as a child was banished from Thebes by his father to grow up in
the desert in the shadow of the sun, returns there as an adult, marries
his sister Nefretiti and, in the desert between Thebes and Memphis,
builds a new city to honour what he thinks of as his true father, the
sun's disc Aten. The city is called Akhetaten, and with it is created
a new religious and social order. The old gods are overthrown; Aten
becomes the new and, more crucially, only god and the only truth –
a god and truth worshipped in the form of his son, Akenaten, he who
is 'devoted to Aten'. With this introduction of monotheism into
what had previously been a society of many religions, worship is
simplified, but not family relations. Akenaten has slept with his
mother Tiye, who has given birth to twins, Smenkhare and
Tutankhamun.[27] When the twins grow to manhood, Akenaten
deserts his wife for Smenkhare, to whom he becomes betrothed.
Nefretiti kills herself, whereupon Tutankhamun, plotting with his
mother Tiye to overthrow Akenaten, kills Smenkhare and wrests the
throne from his father, who kills Tiye and retreats into the desert,
taking the corpse of his beloved Smenkhare with him. 'He stares
motionless into the sun. We see that he is blinded by the sun.
Slowly, as he is blinded, the light goes out.'[28]

Jarman had long been fascinated by ancient Egypt. A 'desktop
Howard Carter cursed with curiosity, a dream of immortality, the
Mummy's Curse' was how he lightly described himself in *Up in the
Air*.[29] The truth was more subtle. For someone who had turned his
back on the Church but still had a strong spiritual sense, Egyptian
religion and history were a rich source of sustenance. Equally, Egypt
was an empire – and empires, like families, since both provide such
sharp examples of the exercise of power, were a subject dear to
Jarman's heart; they feature in virtually all his films. Finally, and
perhaps most crucially, there were the attractions of Akenaten

himself: a Blakean leveller, someone who thought man could be as radiant as a god, and who smashed the old gods, putting himself in their place; who, as he reinvented and transformed himself, supplanted his father and followed his heart's desire; whose sexuality, in its vexing variety, meant both freedom and challenge. This potent family saga provided Jarman with the means both of exploring and transcending the tensions and love that can exist between father and son, son and mother.[30]

The script is not an easy one to grasp. It is written in an elliptical and poetic style that forbids easy analysis – which is, of course, partly the point. The emotions that exist between people and within families do not lend themselves to easy encapsulation. If the story has an extractable message, it lies in the scene where Akenaten sails down the Nile with Smenkhare in a golden barge. He is escaping the oppressive strictures of the old Thebes and travelling towards the site of his newly created city. His words run: 'I answered the riddle of life in the eyes of the Sphinx that afternoon. The answer was life. The blush on a cheek, the blossom opening on the lily pond, a moment without shadows, and I built this truth here in Akhetaten and vowed I would never leave it.'[31] Not only to accept, but positively to glory in who you are; that, and to celebrate the diversity of life. Here, Jarman suggests, rests the 'truth'.

In developing the script, Jarman again turned to the ever-knowledgeable Dom Sylvester Houédard for historical advice. For the design, he consulted closely with Christopher Hobbs. Placing the script and his own sketches alongside Hobbs' watercolours, he compiled another of his workbooks: a lovingly illustrated version of the script and story that sets flashes of historical richness and camp excess against a basic austerity, much in the way these elements co-existed within Jarman's own character. He decided there would be 'no HOLLY-WOODRAZZMATAZZ'. The design would be 'as simple as butter muslin with fine white limestone walls, sand and perhaps a gold bracelet or a scarlet ribbon'.[32] The film would be low-budget and shot entirely on abstract sets that would not imprison the viewer in any one time or place. In this way, Jarman hoped, the imagination would be set free.[33]

Or that, at least, was one idea. There was also talk of making the film in Italy, and of travelling to Egypt, though whether this was for research or to explore filming there is not recorded. As to potential casting, Guy Ford suggested David Bowie for Akenaten. It was a penetrating idea and, exalted though it was, Jarman readily embraced it. He and Ford would return to it in the future.

Equally careful thought went into *The Angelic Conversation of John Dee*,[34] though since none of the various versions of this unrealised and incomplete script was included in *Up in the Air*, it is even harder than with *Akenaten* to judge the film that might have resulted. What is clear, however, is that with this film, Jarman was gathering together many of the strands, imagistic and thematic, that had underpinned his super-8s, while at the same time forming a template for many of his future efforts. To an extent, the same can be said of *Akenaten*; but with *The Angelic Conversation of John Dee* the process is even more noticeable. The script is a virtual dictionary of Jarman's interests and influences.

John Dee was an eminent Elizabethan scientist: a mathematician, geographer, astrologer and alchemist. He was a confidant of Queen Elizabeth I, whose horoscope he famously drew, and for whom he acted as a secret agent, signing his letters $\overline{007}$. Dee claimed to be able to converse with angels in Enochian and published detailed accounts of these angelic conversations. He was, many maintain, the figure Shakespeare had in mind when he created Prospero. Then, when Dee was an old man and might have expected to rest on his laurels, he fell victim to that general 'reaction away from the enlightened, inquiring liberalism of the neo-Platonists and Renaissance Magia' that has already been noted. Caught up in the 'nation-wide drive against all suspected of witchcraft and magical practices',[35] he was suddenly seen as a charlatan and sorcerer and effectively banished to Manchester.

Being muffled and marginalised by institutions more powerful than oneself and having one's reputation questioned was an experience Jarman, particularly as a gay man, knew all too well. It was why he identified as strongly as he did with outsiders; identified with, and took delight, where possible, in rehabilitating them. It was what he hoped to do for Dee.

Jarman described *The Angelic Conversation of John Dee* as a 'dialogue between Queen Elizabeth I and Dr John Dee in which Dr

Dee unfolds the mechanics of the universe with the aid of his scrying mirror and the intervention of the Angel Ariel'.[36] The film was to have two elements. On one hand, there would be conversations between the historical figures of the Queen and Dee in the winter of 1600. These would take place either at Dee's house in Mortlake, or in a series of different locations, and would be filmed in 16mm with the help of Guy Ford. For the locations, Jarman was torn between using the brutal anonymity of a handful of heavy industrial sites, or else a scattering of the more personal of his 'sacred' places: Portland Quarries, Tilly Whim, Avebury, Chesil Beach, the caves at Winspit. Then would come seven sections of film in which the universal order was unfolded; the actual visions of the angel Ariel, who, as an angel, was nothing less than 'the sun's true shadowe . . . by which thou mayest turn all metals into the most pure gold'. This spirit of fire and air, this pearl of fire, this fiery rose, this phoenix was, as envisaged by Jarman, clad entirely in black with 'a diamond crash helmet and diamond winged boots in the mercurial tradition, mirrored sunglasses and one diamond earring'. His visions would be shot in super-8, using colour and the slow-motion style to which, in that gauge, Jarman was increasingly tending.[37]

The lyrical, mystical, incantantory and often impenetrable journey Dee offers his sovereign has its antecedents in Through the Billboard Promised Land — the city of Disc makes a reappearance — though it was to a clutch of more recent and sophisticated sources that Jarman turned for the poetically charged dialogue: Jung's Sermones, Mysterium Coniunctionis and Psychology and Alchemy; Dee's Monas Hieroglyphica ad Mortuos; Kelley's Alchemical Writings; The Tempest ('out of which the project grew'); and, finally, the three Rosicrucian manifestos: FamaFraternitatis (1614), Confessio Fraternitatis (1615) and Johann Valentin Andreae's The Chymical Wedding of Christian Rosenkreutz Anno 1459, in his own copy of which Jarman wrote: 'It's very dangerous to be a man and few survive it.'

Contrary to what one might expect, given Jarman's description of the script, it is the essentially private arena of the psychic and spiritual condition of man, rather than the more public one of the 'mechanics of the universe', that seems to lie at the heart of the piece. As the sphinx encountered by Dee and the Queen on their travels puts it in a speech that echoes that of Akenaten in his barge:

> *Hear me in the Great Silence*
> *woe to the man who replaces the many by the single*
> *for he shall give birth to torment.*
> *Consider the world's diversity and worship it*
> *for the lesser gods are many and the world is*
> *mirrored in their image.*
> *By denying these gods their multiplicity*
> *you deny your own true nature.*[38]

In late 1975 and early 1976, while still editing *Sebastiane*, Jarman began exploring practical ways in which to make *The Angelic Conversation of John Dee*. He applied for money from the Arts Council[39] and, although he affected to despise television, even approached the arts producer Humphrey Burton at the BBC, saying sweetly: 'I wondered if in any way television and I could cooperate and produce something.'[40] It was, however, to be over a year before anything concrete would come of the forty-minute script, and when it did, it was in the guise of another film altogether.

Meanwhile, Jarman was still considering *The Tempest*, the project particularly close to his heart. A year earlier, in 1974, he had mapped out a version of the play set during the course of 'one stormy afternoon' in the cell-cum-alchemist's laboratory ('furniture of crushed mirror . . . golden globes . . . a maze let into the floor') to which Prospero has been confined – and where, observed by those who have banished him, he has further isolated himself through his 'cabalistic studies'. Prospero is in his mid-thirties – 'haggard and withdrawn', though with traces of 'a great and charismatic beauty' – and he takes all the parts. Jarman's contention was that too many people approached *The Tempest* as an 'external masque play', whereas in fact – written as it was at a time when the new king, James I, was fearful of magic and 'the great Elizabethan dream was in retreat, with Raleigh in the tower and Dee banished to Manchester' – it was Shakespeare's *Salo*; his 'most personal and internalised comment on his condition'; a 'final testament, an alchemical cypher with all the old mediaeval cosmogency at war with the future'; 'a final effort to knit his world together'. In line with the historian Frances Yates, Jarman believed that in the play Shakespeare was using secret texts 'to liberate himself from the known limits of man and to attempt a reconciliation'. If all the parts were played by Prospero, the 'loneliness of the old poet at odds with the society in which he lives' would be properly emphasised, as would the 'introspective nature of the work'.[41]

Jarman also wanted to weave some of his own favourite images into the tale. With Villa Zuassa in mind, he decided that the first scene between Prospero and Miranda, in which Prospero plays both parts, would be enacted in a mirror. In the mirror would appear 'a young girl dreaming in a high white room, swallows are building nests in the rafters, a maid tries to dislodge them'. Caliban would be Prospero 'distorted out of recognition, a mediaeval monster out of the Isenheim altarpiece'. The film would be in black and white 'and filmed with the greatest effect of chiaroscuro' – until the point when Prospero 'calls down the gods' for the masque. Then, à la *Wizard of Oz*, everything would dissolve into colour and a golden circle, 'a golden Avebury of stones in a shimmering green field', would replace the cell.[42]

While travelling to Italy to set up *Sebastiane*, Jarman and Whaley had worked on a more conventional cut-up of the play; one that adheres quite closely to the final form the film would take. This version was set in a large country house containing a succession of empty rooms. The parts were no longer all played by Prospero. Ariel, who at first is nothing but a voice, materialises halfway through the film wearing mirrored glasses and dressed entirely in white: plimsolls, trousers, T-shirt. Caliban is young, black and beautiful. In an attempt to set the film 'in no time at any particular moment' – because, Jarman argued, 'the Tempest is a continually changing mirror in which we can see ourselves reflected and would be diminished by any attempt at a literal explanation' – Prospero performs his magic with a calculator; the house is lit by 'perpetually glowing light-bulbs'; and at one point the suggested background music is 'Stormy Weather'.[42]

At the same time, Jarman was collaborating with Ken Russell on a script entitled *The Space Gospel*.[43] This was an idea of Russell's, and he did most of the writing. The earth is a zoo, on which, as a scientific experiment, Gabriel and Michael, a pair of good astronauts from another galaxy, have placed Adam and Eve. A rival astronaut (the Devil) introduces evil. Gabriel and Michael counter by introducing Christ. Thereafter the film is a fairly straightforward retelling of Christ's story, but with Christ as a pawn in the battle between the astronauts. Until, that is, his resurrection – a twist that neither side has planned. The astronauts are left 'staring dumbly at each other unable to accept the fact that they have been used by a power greater than theirs; a power which transcends science and becomes the ultimate mystery, the mystery men call: GOD.' It was an amusing conceit, but not exceptional – nor one likely to find favour in cautious Hollywood, where Russell was pitching it. Not surprisingly, it failed to go into production.

It was almost a year since the lunch party at which James Whaley had appeared, and yet another would elapse before *Sebastiane* finally opened. Even so, although Jarman had complained bitterly of *The Devils* that it had swallowed a year of his life, as he and Paul Humfress laboured on *Sebastiane* in the cutting room, he remained remarkably sanguine. He was, or so he thought, in control.

21

Jubilee

In the course of making *Sebastiane*, Jarman had his palm read by Umberto Tirelli, the Italian costumier. Tirelli unsettled his subject by pronouncing sombrely: 'You are an alien, Derek . . . You will die violently.'[1] Jarman took this prediction very much to heart. Some years later, returning from a party in Bath, he was on the motorway with a group of friends when their car broke down. So terrified was Jarman that someone would drive into them from the rear, thus fulfilling Tirelli's prophecy, that he hysterically forced everyone to vacate the car until help arrived.

Death was in the air. Also in 1975, Pasolini, with whom Jarman had always identified, met a brutal end in Ostia at the hands of a rent boy. And in January 1976, Jarman's friend and mentor Anthony Harwood departed the world – as dramatically and mysteriously as he had inhabited it.

Harwood's nemesis had been New York. The move there had been a liberation, but accompanying that liberation had been stresses that would have taxed anyone, never mind a man in advancing middle age: the frenetic company of younger men, the bath houses, the drugs. Then, as if this were not strain enough, Harwood and

Nina had defaulted on the loan taken out with the Royal Bank of
Scotland to buy up the Conan Doyle Estate and the receivers had
been called in. A heart attack was perhaps inevitable, though so
hurried was Harwood's funeral that more fanciful stories immediately
started to circulate. It was a drug overdose; sadomasochism was
involved; he had been murdered by a rent boy. Or, most quaintly of
all, he had expired midway through a meal and Nina, famously shortsighted, had not noticed until a waiter had come to pull back his
chair. Given Harwood's garrulousness, this last theory is most
unlikely but, whatever the truth, it is entirely fitting that even in
death this most fabulous of showmen should continue to prove the
stuff of legend.

Although Harwood had moved on from Jarman and Jarman was
now old enough to survive without the help of a father figure, his
demise still left the world an emptier place – and, in the short term
at least, with the rent on the Sloane Square flat conspicuous among
Harwood's many unpaid bills, a less hospitable one. Jarman had been
involved in some earlier skirmishes with both the bailiffs and the
porter, a man called Bob, who had never approved of his presence in
the block. Now it was all-out war. Two attempts were made to evict
Jarman. The first court case, amazingly, he won. As a result of the
second, however, not only was he ordered to leave the flat within the
month, but he was forced to settle the back rent, something he could
ill afford to do.

He took his revenge by throwing a 'removal party' which, of
course, he filmed, thus creating a colour coda to earlier black and
white footage of life in the flat. The floors were stripped of carpet,
the walls of their mirrors. Every available surface was 'redecorated'
with multicoloured graffiti: 'Owing to interest tomorrow has not
been cancelled'. Jarman invited his friends to help themselves to
whatever he had been unable to sell and urged them to make as
much mayhem as was physically possible. He wanted a real 'fuck you'
affair.

The following morning, when he finally came to take his leave of
the trashed flat, he came across a pile of newspaper cuttings in a cupboard. Noticing one that featured the curse of the Hope Diamond,
he pasted it carefully to one of the windows, all of which bore 'neat

little crosses' engraved with the diamond he used to score his antique glass. The combination of crosses and curse would, he hoped, strike fear into the hearts of the landlords. The rest of the cuttings he scattered in a blizzard over the floor. As he handed the keys to the malevolent Bob, which he did with the politest of notes 'saying the late Anthony Harwood and I couldn't thank him enough for his kindness',[2] Jarman's only regret was that he was unable to add one last sequence to his film: Bob's face when he opened the door to Harwood's flat and saw the devastation.[3]

That summer Jarman took his Nizo to a fête organised by Andrew Logan and Luciana Martinez to help Ulla Larson-Styles, the friend who had introduced him to Robert Mapplethorpe, pay a fine for shoplifting from Harrods. When he later came to record the afternoon in *Dancing Ledge*, he referred to it as 'a wake'. 'This sunny party with its long-haired musicians was,' he wrote, 'the last ghost of the sixties.'[4] Harwood's death and the departure from Sloane Square had marked the end of an era.[5]

In 1976, the Arts Council launched a Film-Makers on Tour scheme, the aim of which was to encourage wider distribution of experimental film. Jarman was one of the eight film-makers chosen to participate[6] and, as a newly enrolled member of the recognised avant garde, was given another opportunity to screen his work at the ICA. Using three projectors, plus a turntable and cassette-player for musical accompaniment, he showed a mini epic: a three-screen version of the footage which made up *The Art of Mirrors* and *In the Shadow of the Sun*. Further 'official' recognition came in 1977, when he was invited to take part in *Perspectives on British Avant-Garde Film* at the Hayward Gallery. Here his work was included in the section on Expanded Cinema. He screened some reels of what he called *It Happened by Chance*, footage haphazardly pieced together from the surplus material stored in his 'rubbish bin'.[7]

As for *Sebastiane*, the snail-like editing process was doing little to reconcile initially good-humoured artistic differences between Jarman, Whaley and Humfress, and would ultimately lead to real rancour when Humfress insisted upon (and was granted) an equal credit with Jarman as co-director. Although it had always been understood that, as the more experienced of the two, Humfress should hold Jarman's hand directorially, and although Jarman never denied the significance of Humfress's contribution to the finished film, he did not consider Humfress's demand justified. The credit as director should, Jarman believed, have belonged to him alone.

In early April, when all Jarman and Humfress had to show for their Herculean labours was a rough, unsubtitled black and white cutting copy – and despite the fact that Jarman was fond of maintaining bashfully that he never imagined the film would achieve more than a handful of screenings at the ICA – he and Whaley took this copy to Paris to show to the selectors for the Cannes Film Festival. It was not accepted. On a more positive note, and at the behest of Guy Ford, who was able to effect an introduction, Brian Eno, formerly of Roxy Music, had agreed to do the music.[8] By now the film had been blown up from 16mm to 35mm and had emerged from its monochrome chrysalis into glorious colour. It had also, though not entirely to Jarman's liking (he preferred the Latin unmediated), been definitively titled and subtitled. For much of its early existence, it had been called *Sebastianus*; now, in line with one of Jack Welch's many suggestions, the simple vocative case was chosen: O Sebastian, to give it its English translation.

In June, the director of the Locarno Film Festival came to London looking for British films – and miraculously settled on *Sebastiane*. Accordingly, that August, alongside such offerings as Oshima's *The Empire of the Senses* and Pasolini's final film, *Salo or the 120 Days of Sodom*, Jarman's first feature received its première at the Swiss end of Lake Maggiore, where it caused something of a sensation. At the statutory news conference after the screening, Jarman and Humfress faced a barrage of largely hostile questions dealing as much with the patent amateurishness of the film as with its content. It was a potentially explosive situation which Howard Malin, quick to see the public-relations value of any controversy, did everything in his power to inflame.

Despite this most promising of starts publicity-wise, Whaley and Malin were unable to find a distributor. In the mid-seventies, with British cinema at an all-time low, the odds were formidably stacked against a film in Latin by an unknown director. In the end, it was one of Jarman's early supporters – the film-maker and critic Tony Rayns –

who came to the rescue by delivering David and Barbara Stone, the owners of the Gate Cinema in Notting Hill, to Humfress's cutting room. The Stones liked what they saw of *Sebastiane*, and of Howard Malin, and agreed with Malin and Whaley that they and Megalovision would jointly exhibit and distribute the film. It finally opened at the Gate in late October, where, thanks to continuing publicity,[9] the queue for the first afternoon performance broke all house records.

What the more doubtful distributors should have realised was that a film like *Sebastiane*, cresting as it did the wave of gay liberation and featuring such an unfettered display of male nudity, would be essential viewing for a great many people. Apart from those who, like the singer Holly Johnson, found it 'an affirmation that Homosexuality could be beautiful, shameless and out in the open',[10] there were countless others who may have attended for less noble reasons. At the opening night, Johnny Rozsa arrived without under-garments and sporting a transparent plastic mac. His was not the only mac to be sighted at the Gate in the months to come.

Equally noticeable at the opening night were Jarman's parents. A starker contrast to the majority of Jarman's friends than the upright figure of the air commodore and his frail wife would be hard to imag-ine. It is quite possible Jarman had been secretly banking on his film only ever surfacing for a few nights at the ICA; at least then he would not have had to expose himself quite so publicly to parental scrutiny. Though in the event, just as the reviews concentrated more on *Sebastiane*'s exceptional power[11] than they did on its shortcom-ings, so Lance and Betts valiantly subsumed any shock they might have felt at what they saw on screen into simple pride at what, against enormous odds, their son had achieved.

When required, Jarman's first feature proved it could do service as an impeccable calling card not only where parents were concerned, but with authority in general. On one occasion, albeit in a manner that would later anger rather than amuse its victim, it even saved him from possible arrest and the sort of publicity his parents would most certainly never have welcomed. After revisiting his film one evening to gauge audience reaction – a habit to which he would become increasingly addicted – he was walking home through

Holland Park when he allowed himself to be lured into a corner by a handsome young man who turned out to be a policeman, and who only released his quarry on being told he was a film director. Recalling the incident many years later, Jarman bitterly encapsulated its moral as: 'Only the fact that I was middle-class, white and had a film on at The Gate stopped a verbal assault – "You fucking Queer" – becoming physical . . . Heterosoc fuck in public on any hot day in Hyde Park near-naked without an eyebrow raised. It is important to reclaim our sexuality from those who seek to sanitise its expression and weave it into the fabric of bourgeois British morality.'[12]

After sixteen successful weeks at the Gate, *Sebastiane* transferred to the Scene 2 in Leicester Square, in a programme with Kenneth Anger's *Scorpio Rising*. It also moved to the Screen on the Green, Islington and played widely outside London, involving Jarman in a wearying round of provincial publicity. Internationally, its fate varied from country to country. In Spain and Italy it fared well, benefiting in Spain from the liberalisation following the death of Franco, and in Italy prompting Jarman to record: 'Alberto Moravia came to the first press show and praised the film in the foyer saying that it was a film that Pier Paolo [Pasolini] would have loved.'[13] It was received less enthusiastically in France and Germany, while in America – where it did not open until March 1978, having taken eighteen months to find a distributor – it sank virtually without trace.

Among the few New Yorkers to see the film was Patrik Steede, who later delightedly told Jarman, 'I took my lawyer, but at the end of it he said: "It's so terrible it's not worth suing."'[14] It seemed that, for all its success, Jarman's film was doomed to trail rancour in its wake. In Britain, the avant garde, whose ranks had been slowly opening to its maker, took the view that he had sold out: it was not on to have your work exhibited in Leicester Square when there was the Film Makers' Co-Op. More unpleasantly, Jarman gradually became convinced Megalovision were cheating him of his share of the profits. So successfully had Whaley and Malin talked up the film that he had difficulty believing it had not done twice the business the company accounts suggested.

The months immediately before and after the opening of *Sebastiane* were not easy ones for Jarman. With his studio at Butler's

Wharf still rented out, the second court case over Sloane Square had left him both penniless and homeless. Home became wherever someone could provide a bed; even, for a while, a rooming house in Drayton Gardens, presided over by an eagle-eyed proprietress who banned visitors after eight o'clock. He then moved into a shared first-floor flat at 76 Redcliffe Gardens which, though far from perfect, was a distinct improvement on the rooming house. His two principal flat-mates were (or had been) boyfriends of Luciana Martinez: the very American Donald Dunham, who had appeared in *Sebastiane*, and the very English Rufus Barnes, a bookseller. Best of all, he had his nocturnal freedom back.

One night while drinking in the Coleherne with Kevin Whitney, he whispered: 'Look behind you. There's the most beautiful boy in the world.' So entranced was Jarman by the faun-like creature he had spotted that he seemed almost paralysed, and it was Whitney who approached the vision, whose name was Jean-Marc Prouveur. A recent graduate from art school, he had left his home town of Lille to find his way in London and spoke hardly any English – though this did not deter Jarman, once introduced, from bombarding the bewildered youth with a positive torrent of words.

Prouveur was dark, slim, sultry-looking, possessed of an impish sense of humour and fiercely ambitious. In the words of one observer, he was a veritable *garçon fatale*; according to another, he had an aura of 'Genet-like illicitness'. He painted, but had plans to be a photographer. The similarities to Incandela were so absolute that it is not surprising Jarman should have fallen for Prouveur and would embark on a relationship with a familiar ring. Like Incandela, Prouveur was given a nickname. Incandela's had been 'Cat'; Prouveur became 'Chaton', or 'Cat Two'.[15] Like Incandela, Prouveur figured as a sexual partner for only the briefest of moments, after which the relationship became purely paternal, revolving largely around Jarman's determination to devote himself to Prouveur's education. But this is to look into the future; at the time all Jarman could see was the sheer desirability of his new companion. Before long, since he knew his room in Redcliffe Gardens would be empty for a week in November, he had invited Prouveur to move into it.

To help America celebrate 200 years of independence, Jarman

had been asked by the collector Bryan Montgomery to join five other British artists – Michael Ginsborg, Mario Dubsky, Keith Milow, Michael Craig-Martin and Bill Jacklin – in a shared exhibition at the DuBose Gallery in Houston, Texas. What Jarman would later term Montgomery's 'bicentennial art junket'[16] was hardly crucial to the success of America's birthday party, nor was it likely to enhance reputations – the DuBose Gallery specialised in modern art of a distinctly unremarkable nature and was located some way out of the centre of Houston – but he was among friends and would not have dreamed of turning down what was effectively a paid holiday to the States. In recent years, absorption with film and lack of studio space had made painting difficult, doubtless the reason why he had taken to engraving glass and working on small pieces of slate, into which he would etch geometric arrangements of pyramids and tiny figures; miniature, monochrome echoes of the starkness of his earlier landscapes. It was a sequence of these slate drawings he exhibited in Houston.

The group had only a matter of hours to hang their work before the first of many parties. They were taken on an art tour of the Exxon skyscraper and to the home of a Nieman-Marcus; though what Jarman cherished most was the quiet trip he made to the Rothko chapel, where he was mesmerised by the sombre panels the painter had hung on all the available walls, creating an effect akin to that of the religious muralists of the seventeenth century. He found the visit as profoundly moving as the one he had made as a student to the Issenheim altarpiece in Colmar.

In *Dancing Ledge*, Jarman characterises 1976 as the last year of concentrating 'almost exclusively'[17] on his super-8 films. Yet, while he certainly took his Nizo to America, filming wherever he went – a short film succinctly entitled *Houston, Texas* was the predictable result – 1976 did not see anything like the home-movie activity that had characterised 1973 and 1974. That degree of concentration on the super-8s would not be repeated, and although he would never entirely forsake his super-8 roots, neither would he ever again devote to his home-movie making – or, until the very end of his life, his painting – the intense application he had at the start. The making of feature films was fast becoming his *raison d'être*.

On Jarman's return from America, it immediately became apparent that his relationship with Prouveur – even if already more paternal than sexual – would not survive the confines of Redcliffe Gardens. There was nowhere in the flat for them to escape one another. They started to row volcanically – so volcanically, in fact, that certain of their friends took to muttering darkly about Orton and Halliwell, and indeed might have seen their fears made bloody reality had not two things intervened: a return to Butler's Wharf and the advent of a second all-consuming film.

Although the rent on Butler's Wharf had for three years been a vital means of keeping some very persistent wolves from the door, for Jarman the prospect of having sufficient space to cohabit more peaceably with Prouveur overcame considerations of money. For Prouveur, who was concentrating more and more on photography, Butler's Wharf meant a chance to pursue his art as well as continuing to enjoy the benefit not only of Jarman's generosity – it was Jarman who paid the bills – but, just as importantly for a young man making his way in a foreign city, his mentor's many contacts.

By partitioning the studio into separate zones, giving each a bedroom and an area to work, the warring pair immediately improved relations, though without ever dispelling all acrimony. The rows and sulks continued, with Prouveur complaining bitterly about such things as Jarman's shameless use of the very public toilet, or of amyl nitrate, the cloying smell of which could permeate the entire building. Murder, however, became less of a possibility, while Prouveur's gripe about Jarman's poppers indicates also that the non-sexual nature of their relationship was not precluding sex per se – for either of them, as it happens. In the months to follow, Butler's Wharf witnessed something of a sexual merry-go-round as both Prouveur and Jarman entertained their separate partners and, when the occasion permitted, poached what the other had claimed, or hoped to claim, for himself.

Then there was the film which, by throwing its maker back into the arms of Megalovision, left very little time for domestic dispute of any description. As early as 1974 or 1975, Jarman had caught sight of a young woman he would not easily forget: 'She stepped off the Brighton Belle at Victoria. White patent boots clattering down the platform, transparent plastic mini skirt revealing a hazy pudenda. Venus T shirt. Smudged black eye paint, covered with a flaming blonde beehive . . . the face that launched a thousand tabloids . . . art history as make up.'[18] This living art object went by the name of Jordan[19] and worked in the King's Road boutique run by Vivienne Westwood and Malcolm McLaren, known variously over the years as Let it Rock, SEX and Seditionaries. She was, to borrow the phraseology of the social historian Jon Savage, 'the first Sex Pistol'; her life 'a *pas de deux* with outrage'.[20]

Jordan was also a regular at the Masquerade Club and the Yours or Mine, where Jarman got to know her. Flaunting her signature make-up, she was among the partygoers who appeared in the first scene of *Sebastiane*, and on Valentine's Day 1976 Jarman filmed her at a party of Andrew Logan's which provided the recently formed Sex Pistols, the archetyepal punk-rock band, with one of their very first gigs. As Jarman later recalled:

> The Sex Pistols were playing on Andrew's stage for a slightly bemused audience of glitterati while Jordan and [Vivienne] threw themselves about with bacchic abandon, hurling insults at the band and the audience. John Rotten turned his back on us and sang to the Roman frescoes, while the drummer, Paul, picked his nose. Christopher [Hobbs], who guarded me and the camera from the pushing and shoving, said when it was all over – 'Thank God that's finished and we'll never hear of them again.'[21]

Nothing could have been further from the truth. The music press were at the party and Malcolm McLaren, who was managing the band and knew how to engineer a photo opportunity when one was needed, persuaded Jordan to get onstage with John Lydon (Rotten) and start stripping. It was the start of a crazed collision with notoriety that would bring the Sex Pistols national headlines for swearing on television, see their raucous and controversial rendition of 'God Save the Queen' top the charts in Jubilee year and find Jarman's super-8 footage of Logan's 'Valentine's Ball'[22] eventually making its (uncredited) way into *The Great Rock and Roll*

Swindle, Julien Temple's operatic take on the band's short but spectacular career.

There is considerable irony in the fact that Jarman should have
first heard the Sex Pistols in Logan's studio. Where once Jarman had
said of Logan that he 'ought to be the most revered of artists . . . Fly
away with him on Pegasus, over the rainbow',[23] now what he said
was:

> The Andrew Logan all-stars have dominated the social life of
> London since the beginning of the decade, since David
> Hockney went into tax exile with the other working-class
> heroes of the sixties. They missed the sixties, but inherited
> the daydream which they tried to make a reality for a second
> generation. But they were the flash of the Super Novae before
> darkness. Now the seventies have caught up, and been pulled
> from under their feet by a gang of King's Road fashion
> anarchists who call themselves punks.[24]

Where once Jarman had celebrated Logan's camp, his lightness of
touch, now he found those qualities superficial rather than magical.
Logan was being supplanted in Jarman's imagination by the band
who had played at Logan's party, the *soigné* glitterati by a new milieu
that was rougher, tougher and more energetically youthful.[25]

Jarman was always acutely sensitive to changes in the fabric of
society. On many levels, his life is a litmus paper which reflects the
major stages of Britain's social history in the second half of the
twentieth century, from postwar austerity to the dying days of
Thatcherism. The despairing and angry mood of the mid-seventies, of a country facing economic recession, virtual war with the
IRA and an uncertain post-imperial future – a mood epitomised by
punk – awakened Jarman's passion and instinct for keeping abreast
of the times. It also resonated powerfully with his personal demons,
his deep-seated restlessness, his fear of ageing and of not holding
centre stage. The fact that Logan and his 'all-stars' had, in Jarman's
view, inherited Hockney's mantle and 'dominated' the social life of
London in the seventies was cause enough to turn away from them.
It did not sit well with Jarman that Logan's fabulously decorated

studio should be the river's prime location for parties – and since he could never hope to usurp Logan's crown, he was forced to look elsewhere. He would never stop attending Logan's parties, particularly on New Year's Eve, but, as he confided in more than one ear, Logan and his côterie were getting older and more staid, whereas he – Peter Pan that he was – was not yet ready to grow up. Jarman desired youth, preferably of the male variety, with the result that it was not only the Logan all-stars who found themselves spurned. Many of Jarman's female friends began to feel less at ease in his company – never ostracised exactly, but definitely less welcome. Precisely as he had done in the late sixties, when he had first started running with the glitterati, Jarman was in the process of reinventing himself.

The change seemed to highlight the differences between the two sides of his character. The rebel in him was becoming more active, more demanding, as was the daredevil. The boys to whom he was often most deeply attracted tended more than ever to be hellraisers. Their allure, however, was not solely one of danger, for with the danger went emotional scarring – and here Jarman's role was preeminently that of mentor and parent; someone who could, in healing the boy's wounds, perhaps make good his own. The gentle and gentlemanly side of him – the middle-class, establishment side – would never disappear.

So, although one can see why Jarman should be attracted to the subversive, ebullient energy and anger that was punk, one must not forget that the classicist in him, the conservationist and cynic, harboured severe reservations. As he himself said: 'The music business has conspired with [the punks] to create another working class myth as the dole queues grow longer to fuel the flames. But in reality the instigators of punk are the same petit bourgeois art students, who a few months ago were David Bowie and Bryan Ferry look-alikes – who've read a little art history and adopted Dadaist typography and bad manners, and are now in the business of reproducing a fake street credibility.'[26] The final irony – that as punk was gathering momentum, Margaret Thatcher was assuming leadership of the Conservative Party – was one which, when it hit home in the following decade, made absolute sense to Jarman. Just such a political progression was what he foresaw in *Jubilee*, the film he was about to make. Beneath the work's undoubted 'jubilance' lies a chilling cocktail of political cynicism and mistrust of the media.

The impetus for *Jubilee* was provided by Jordan. Jarman's original idea was to record her milieu on super-8, in more or less documentary fashion, though when he spoke to Whaley and Malin about the idea they immediately saw that the burgeoning punk movement might mean box office and suggested a feature instead.[27] With Whaley dipping into the profits from *Sebastiane* to develop the film, Jarman picked up his pen and completed the script so swiftly that he was ready to shoot before any real thought had been given as to where the rest of the money might be found.[28] Feeling that he could not approach the same people who had invested in *Sebastiane*, Whaley gambled what little money remained in Megalovision's coffers on flying to Teheran to solicit the help of an old schoolfriend. By the time he returned – amazingly, with sufficient funds virtually to complete the film – the first sequences were already in the can. Having seen a street he wanted to use and hearing that it was about to be demolished, Jarman had taken advantage of the Whit weekend to film there, not caring that the money was not yet in place, or that he had neglected to seek the necessary permission.

Working closely with Whaley and discussing each stage of *Jubilee* (a 'New Wave Movie' from 'R.I.P. Off Films') with regular arbiters like Robert Medley, plus whoever happened to be passing through Redcliffe Gardens at the time, Jarman strove to give the film verisimilitude by immersing himself in the fanzines that had sprung up around punk, complemented by a suitably anarchic range of subsidiary source material: Valerie Solanus' *Scum Manifesto*, Erich Fromm's *The Fear of Freedom*, William Burrough's *The Wild Boys*. Then, to set his vision of the age within an historical perspective, he cannibalised his script of *The Angelic Conversation of John Dee*. The result, as Keith Howes noted perceptively in *Gay News*, is 'a Seventies' equivalent of an Ealing comedy'.[29] Dee calls on the angel Ariel ('the sun's true shadow') to show Elizabeth I the future of her kingdom. This future (our present and the core of the film) provides a stark contrast to the Arcadian serenity of the Elizabethan framework. It is topsy-turvy and centres on a gang of wild girls and the episodic, haphazard forays they make from their chaotic headquarters in Southwark into the equally chaotic urban wasteland that surrounds them. Their leader is Boadicea, or Bod for short, queen of the new disorder; a 'black' antithesis to the white that is Elizabeth I.[30] Her five gang members are: Crabs, a sexually voracious 'casualty of true romance';[31] Mad, a revolutionary pyromaniac, named for Madimi, one of the angels with whom Dee conversed;[32] Amyl Nitrate, a twin-set-and-pearled 'historian of the void';[33] Viv, a boiler-suited lesbian artist[34] and Chaos, their mute au pair. Attached to the group are twin gay brothers, Sphinx and Angel, who live, love and die in unison, meeting their end in a tatty bingo hall at the hands of two trigger-happy policemen.[35]

As we follow the gang's adventures in and around their Southwark headquarters, we see Bod kill Queen Elizabeth II and steal her crown. Crabs and Mad suffocate Happy Days, one of Crabs' less fortunate one-night stands, then dump his corpse in the Thames. Bod strangles the number one singer Lounge Lizard. The policemen kill Kid, a young musician befriended by Crabs. Amyl and Mad avenge Kid's death by killing the two policemen. In the background, pulling the strings and laughing insanely at the extent of his power, is the media mogul and 'sinister impresario of mediocrity',[36] Borgia Ginz. Ginz has the whole of this splintered and violent world in the palm of his hand. He has turned Buckingham Palace into a recording studio and Westminster Cathedral into a throbbing discotheque in which Christ and the twelve apostles perform orgiastically before a gyrating audience. Sleepy Dorset has become a separate country where blacks, homosexuals and Jews are banned and Ginz can retreat to the splendid seclusion of the home he shares with the retired Hitler to pronounce with cynical satisfaction: 'They all sign up in the end one way or another.'[37]

In an early note, Jarman wrote that the film was dedicated to 'all those who secretly work against the tyranny of Marxists fascists trade unionists maoists capitalists socialists etc . . . who have conspired together to destroy the diversity and holiness of each life in the name of materialism . . . For William Blake.'[38] It follows, he later said, 'the structure of the Dream Allegory, in which the hero or heroine dream themselves in a transfigured landscape where they meet figures who embody psychic states, like Anger and Jealousy, Hope or Despair'.[39] Apart from minor compromises, the finished film adheres closely to this vision. There is less extreme and explicit sex and violence in it than in some early drafts, but these omissions do not alter the essence of what happens on screen any more than the title changes: *Honi Swar Key Maly Ponce* and/or *HƎGH FAꟻLION*. True, the film does not unite super-8 footage with found footage and fabricated film to the extent that 'documentary and fictional form are confused' – also Jarman's initial intention – though even in this regard, 'art and life' in *Jubilee* are still very largely 'synonymous'.[40]

As with *Sebastiane*, with which it shares a number of names and faces, the cast and crew were a blend of friend and stranger, amateur and professional. On the production side, the most obvious and important newcomers were Tom Priestley as supervising editor and Mordecai Schreiber as production manager. As to the cast, Jordan played Amyl Nitrate; a scantily clad Little Nell of *Rocky Horror Show* fame was Crabs; Hermine Demoriane, who had walked the tightrope to crown Jarman as the third Alternative Miss World – and who would walk it again in the film – was Chaos, the mute au pair. From the troupe of Lindsay Kemp came David Haughton as Ariel and The Great Orlando (the blind Jack Birkett) as Borgia Ginz. Jenny Runacre, whom Jarman had already filmed at a lunch given by the fashion designer Rae Spencer-Cullen (otherwise known as Miss Mouse) and who had worked with Pasolini, took the dual role of Elizabeth I and Bod. Richard O'Brien, best known as the creator of *The Rocky Horror Show*, played a measured Dee. Ian Charleson and Karl Johnson linked arms and limbs as the twin brothers, Angel and Sphinx. Toyah Willcox gave violent voice to Mad, Linda Spurrier was Viv and, thanks to an introduction from Jordan (after she had cut the word 'fuck' into his back and Jarman had caught sight of her handiwork in the King's Road), a painfully young Adam Ant appeared as the would-be singer Kid.

In the months before filming, Jarman had made endless rounds of punk concerts looking for likely faces to put before his camera. In this way, he settled on Wayne County to play Lounge Lizard,[41] Gene October to play Happy Days[42] and the Slits to play a gang of disaffected street girls. For the soundtrack, songs by these and a handful of other groups and arrangers were integrated into a film score provided by Brian Eno.

The production was based at Butler's Wharf. There was some distant location work – John Dee's house in Mortlake was actually in Northamptonshire, the exterior of Borgia Ginz's country retreat was that of Longleat, the final sequence in which Elizabeth I and Dee dematerialise was filmed on the cliffs at Dancing Ledge – but otherwise the film was shot entirely in London, principally around Southwark, Rotherhithe and Victoria Docks. All along the river, the property developers were as active as ever, and throughout 1977 the empty warehouses continued to go up in flames. The apocalyptic desolation of the area, fringed as it was with 'rotting estates, closed shops and boarded windows',[43] mirrored to perfection the desolation Jarman was dissecting, while at the same time allowing him to rescue on celluloid that which the developers were intent on destroying. In this way – and most fittingly, given that punk shared a similar impulse – *Jubilee* stands as yet another example of the way Jarman liked to rehabilitate what would otherwise be discarded.

The most obvious design work, particularly in costume terms, was to be found in the film's Elizabethan sections, the province of Christopher Hobbs, though it was no small task to achieve a similarly accurate look for modern London. John Maybury, a film student of just eighteen whom Jarman had met at a Siouxsie and the Banshees concert, was given the responsibility of designing some of the punk costumes, plus the rubbish-strewn, graffiti-covered Southwark HQ. In this he was helped by his friend Kenny Morris, drummer with the Banshees. As general dogsbody and guardian of the Southwark set, Jarman roped in another, even younger lad by the name of Lee Drysdale. Drysdale hailed from the East End, possessed a body that could cause palpitations among more elderly admirers and was film-mad – 'the Artful Dodger of Cine-History,' Jarman dubbed him, 'more energetic than a night at the Roxy'.[44]

Drysdale it was who, early in the shooting, had the youthful effrontery to tell Jenny Runacre that she sounded as if she were reading her lines, a breach of etiquette so potentially damaging to Runacre's confidence that Jarman uncharacteristically lashed out and hit his otherwise invaluable young Man Friday. Although

Jarman's calm generally kept hysteria to a minimum, the relative speed with which the film was made (late June to mid-August), plus the fact that the technical resources, while an improvement on *Sebastiane*, were nonetheless sparse, led to more than one such fracas. Matters were not helped by the real fear throughout filming that the authorities might halt proceedings. Not only was it evident that local residents viewed this 'punk invasion' of their surroundings with some suspicion, but proper permission to film had never been obtained – not even from the film unions, whose power in those pre-Thatcher days was awesome.[45] Light relief was supplied by the orgiastic party scene in which Christ (Lindsay Kemp) 'performs' in the bowels of Westminster Cathedral. This was actually filmed in the Catacombs club and was, in its way, a rerun of the party that opened *Sebastiane*. Again peopled almost exclusively by friends, it lasted all day and involved such quantities of drink and drugs that by the time a wrap was called, some of the participants were so comprehensively unwrapped it would take them a day or two to recover – a veritable case of art becoming synonymous with life.

Although Jarman was not able to combine documentary with fabricated footage to quite the extent he originally planned, it is still true of *Jubilee* that it does inextricably mix the real with the fictional – and, more particularly, the autobiographical with everything. The film is full of transformations and inversions: a cathedral that is a discotheque; a Dorset that represents the very worst of Little England, a place whose inhabitants are so dozy that Hitler can retire there unnoticed; wild gangs that are feminine rather than masculine. These inversions are a metaphor for gay life, itself an inversion of what Little England would regard as the norm – an attitude, since it marginalised him, that Jarman had always hated. He would later say of both *Sebastiane* and *Jubilee* that they were fuelled by anger, and of the punk revolt that it 'somehow got under my skin . . . it opened up all sorts of wounds which go back of course to the schooling . . . the actual venom poured out . . . it was made more aggravating by being gay and having one's life bottled up'.[46]

There are also more playful elements of autobiography in the film. The name Borgia Ginz is taken from that earlier picaresque adventure *Through the Billboard Promised Land*, while the way the character

is conceived and played carries more than a whiff of Louis XIII from
The Devils. There are a number of coded references to Jarman's childhood, among them that Dorset was his childhood county and that
Viv starts painting by copying dinosaurs from a picture book. There
is the use made of *The Angelic Conversation of John Dee* and, in particular, Ariel's speech begging us to 'consider the world's diversity
and worship it'. The glimpse we are given of the head of Mausolus in
the scene with Lounge Lizard. The presence in the film of so many
of Jarman's friends and its setting, the streets and warehouses where
he lived. The way Ariel lies on the rocks at Dancing Ledge at the
very end of the film, a direct echo of *The Siren and the Sailor*. The fact
that – exactly as one of Jarman's heroes, Werner Herzog, had done in
The Enigma of Kaspar Hauser – Jarman managed to include a section
of super-8 in the finished film.

For this, Jarman hit on the idea of filming Jordan dancing round
a fire in a disused dock in Deptford while Steve Treatment, a young
man he had recently met, tossed books on to the fire, then hacked at
his hair with a pair of scissors. In the background stood three masked
figures, two of which represented Michelangelo's David and Death
respectively. The plan was also to burn a note, which is against the
law, and to capture this criminal act on camera, though in the event
all that was burned, apart from the books, was a Union Jack. It was
a fragment of the resulting film that found its way into *Jubilee* as the
most dreamlike, disembodied, and perhaps most beautiful of its
sequences.[47]

In supreme contrast to *Sebastiane*, post-production on *Jubilee* was
quick and painless. Once shooting was completed, Whaley and
Malin found an Australian distributor who stumped up an advance
of some £17,000, then did a deal with EG Records for the soundtrack. The film was cut in cameraman Peter Middleton's house in
Ealing and was ready to open in February 1978 – exactly a year after
Jarman had first put pen to paper. There was a last-minute panic
when it looked as if the censor might not grant the necessary certificate, though, after meeting him, Jarman agreed to shave a few
seconds from the suffocation of Happy Days so that the murder
would not seem to be happening in real time. It was not a compromise he was particularly happy to make, but at least it was minimal

and meant the première could go ahead. So, on 22 February 1978 – not within Jubilee year, the original plan, but not far out of it – Derek Jarman's second feature christened Gate 2, the Stones' new cinema to the east of Russell Square.

At the screening, the proceedings were interrupted by shouts of 'This isn't punk!' from the audience, while the man in front of Jarman and his parents fainted and some of the extras stormed out in disgust because, it transpired, they were Christians. It must have looked as if another *succès de scandale* was in the bag. Then came the reviews. Some were complimentary, a couple raved, but in the main they gave the film a firm thumbs-down. *Jubilee*'s intensely private core and somewhat uneasy mix of exuberance and bleakness – as Jarman himself put it, 'Just as it seems that it is settling down it's off in another direction, like a yacht in a squall'[48] – was simply too puzzling for all but the most entranced of viewers. Vivienne Westwood even went as far as to have a T-shirt printed on which, at some length, she detailed why she despised the film. It was, she said, 'the most boring and therefore disgusting film' she had ever seen. She could not 'get off watching a gay boy jerk off through the titillation of his masochistic tremblings. You pointed your nose in the right direction then you wanked.'[49]

Jarman would later joke what an honour it was to have a Westwood T-shirt devoted entirely to him. It put him on a par with that other queen, the one with the safety pin through her lip. But at the time it distressed him deeply that those in the know should shun the film – some of the worst reviews came from the music press – and that almost no one seemed to appreciate the political point he was making. So out of tune was he with the traditional left, so not of the prevailing school of social realism, that few could discern what it was left to him to articulate in *Dancing Ledge*: 'Afterwards, the film turned prophetic. Dr Dee's vision came true – the streets burned in Brixton and Toxteth, Adam [Ant] was on Top of the Pops and signed up with Margaret Thatcher to sing at the Falklands Ball. They all sign up in one way or another.'[50]

22

Stormy Weather

Jubilee helped delineate the shape – that of being primarily a film-maker – into which Jarman's life was beginning to form. Whereas before 1977 his activities had revolved around any number of arenas, now they tended to be tied to the film of the moment. The net effect was that while Jarman's daily existence became steadily busier and more demanding, it also became simpler and more focused.

Apart from some teaching, some unrealised, unfinished film projects and the return to Butler's Wharf, 1977 had belonged entirely to *Jubilee*. Almost the only trip Jarman took that year was in late October, when he and Prouveur paid a short visit to Gerald Incandela, who had recently moved to New York.[1] The following year also revolved around film: even Jarman's first London exhibition in over four years was film-related. Timed to coincide with the opening of *Jubilee*, it was held at Sarah Bradley's newly opened World's End Art Gallery at 390 King's Road, a stone's throw from Seditionaries. It ran for a month and included some display cases of the source material, jewellery and assorted small props from the film, plus a couple of stills taken by Prouveur in his capacity as one of the film's two official photographers (the other was Johnny Rozsa), some photographs of Jarman's early super-8s, two capes, a series of eight small paintings entitled *Burning the Pyramids* and a series of eight drawings on slate entitled *Archaeologies*. A modest exhibition, it passed unnoticed by the art world.

1978 also saw a revival of *Jazz Calendar*, for which there was a modicum of touching up to do. *Sebastiane* finally, and briefly, opened in New York, followed soon afterwards by the equally fleeting appearance of *Jubilee*. Both films were also shown in London, prompting *Time Out* to pigeonhole their director as the creator of 'a double dose of Jarmanesque decadence'. Jarman made an evanescent appearance of his own on celluloid, in the non-speaking, walk-on part of a cruiser in Ron Peck's *Nighthawks*. Because of the brave, open way Peck used his film to explore the necessarily schizophrenic existence of a gay geography teacher in a London comprehensive school, Jarman warmly identified with *Nighthawks* – and with the part he played. He made, he declared, 'a very creditable cruiser, so lost in myself I burnt my fingers instead of the cigarette'.[2]

He had sufficient leisure for more film evenings at Butler's Wharf and, on Sunday afternoons, a statutory 'at home', where there might be an impromptu cabaret in the form of one of Jarman's conquests taking a bath. There were daily expeditions to Soho for sustenance, both gastronomic and sexual. Such favourites as Jimmy's, Pollo, Presto or Pâtisserie Valerie for food; for pick-ups, the Salisbury, Global Village, Heaven or perhaps the latter's more decadent neighbour, the Sanctuary.

Another massive warehouse party, this time to celebrate Prouveur's twenty-first birthday, illustrated just how comprehensively Jarman's milieu had changed in the eight years since the Upper Ground extravaganza bidding farewell to the sixties. In 1970, the height of daring had been a hugely inebriated Tennessee Williams, or Ossie Clark sitting on the stairs rolling joints. 'For Jean-Marc's party,' by contrast, 'everything was boarded up and from midnight Adam and the Ants played, beer and whiskey . . . replaced marijuana and the pace was noisy and frenetic. People swam in the bath, fucked in the darkened bedrooms, the next morning it looked as if more people had danced on the walls than the floor. It took three days to get back to normal.'[3]

Exemplifying the rowdiness of 1978 was a new, and extremely troublesome, young man called Andy Marshall. Just nineteen, Marshall was the product of fiercely religious parents who, on learning he was gay, had disowned him. Jarman had met him at Bang, the discotheque on Tottenham Court Road, where, in the course of a brief conversation, he had scribbled his name and number on a piece of paper for Marshall. Shortly afterwards, Marshall was sent to prison in Ashford for stealing and crashing a car. When asked if he knew anyone who would stand him bail, he gave Jarman's name. Although considerably taken aback to receive a call requesting bail for someone he hardly remembered, Jarman instantly complied and, in the months that followed, provided Marshall with shelter at Butler's Wharf whenever he needed it. On the first such occasion, Jarman put the teenager in his own bed and joined him there. Marshall did not care for this arrangement, and told him so, whereupon Jarman rang another young friend and invited him round to make up a threesome. Still not interested, Marshall moved into Prouveur's bed before seeking the relative safety of the sofa.

As described by Jarman, Marshall possessed 'a GBH manner which he wears under a black peaked Japanese schoolboy's cap and combat jacket, accentuating his black sunken eyes. His moth-eaten haircut, his fingernails, bitten to the bone on scarred hands, suggest menace.'[4] Having accepted that sex was out of the question, Jarman saw behind Marshall's air of menace – and his prodigious appetite for drink and drugs – to the intelligence and talent underscoring the youngster's allergy to authority. By soliciting the help of friends like Christopher Hobbs, Jarman was soon intent on helping Marshall realise his potential. As he wrote in *Dancing Ledge*: 'The opposition seem determined to turn Andy into a criminal; and we are just as determined they are not going to win.'[5]

Marshall became the latest and most electrifying of the chorus line of young men who provided Jarman with the opportunity to act out a scenario which was coming to obsess him: the dialogue that could take place between the artist, often older, always gentler, and the rebel. A dialogue that was on one level sexual, on another paternal, on another adolescent; a Blakean fusing of innocence and experience – except that the innocence did not always lie with youth, nor the experience with age.

Amid the kaleidoscope of projects gestating in Jarman's imagination (some marked merely by a note in the margin of a diary; others in varying stages of synopsis form, all constituting a palimpsest of the films that would become completed screenplays or emerge on to the screen itself) was *Aeon*. Aeon, or X, is an artist who pursues a young boy called Amor, whom he meets in the plaster-cast room of the Victoria and Albert Museum, and with whom he later travels through a desert landscape on the boy's motorbike. Then there was *Archaeologies*, a 'journey in inner space' to be made in a mixture of 16mm and super-8, in which an artist who is painting a young nude man by candlelight strikes a series of matches when the candle goes out. As each match flares, we see a sequence of visions. Appearing in the film is a character called Topaz. There was *The Bees of Infinity*, a film about Anthony and 'Kleopatra' and the end of a 'dream of a classical and civilised world ruled from the east'. This was to be set either in a baron's villa in Capri, or in the queen's tomb, where Charmian, Cleopatra's handmaiden, is remembering her mistress's past. The resulting flashbacks would be shot in dreamlike super-8, with music by Brian Eno.[6] And there was *Pure Heaven*, an unfinished and excessively camp stage musical about the jealousy of Venus and Gain (Mother Earth) for Psyche, whose transcendent beauty threatens their security.

Overshadowing all these jottings as tyrannically as it would come to dominate the next seven years of Jarman's life was a project which its creator would eventually term his personal Sword of Damocles. Triggered by an earlier chance meeting with an art dealer called Nicholas Ward-Jackson, the project was *Caravaggio*.

Ward-Jackson had long nurtured the idea that there was a splendid film to be made about Michelangelo Merisi da Caravaggio (1573–1610), a significant but in those days frequently neglected figure, most famous (some would say notorious) for the violence of his temper, his dramatic chiaroscuro and unconventional, revolutionary use of ordinary people as models for the religious figures in his art. Until the film-maker's tragic death, Ward-Jackson had thought Pasolini would make the perfect director for his imagined film; or, failing that, Roman Polanski: someone at least who was either gay or prepared to tackle the subject of homosexuality head-on so that the homoerotic aspects of Caravaggio's arresting canvases could be fully explored. Then Ward-Jackson had seen *Sebastiane* and, at an exhibition of work by Maggi Hambling at Vera Russell's Artists' Market in Earlham Street, had chanced to mention to Robert Medley that perhaps this Derek Jarman, whoever he was, might be the person to get to grips with Caravaggio. Medley replied that not only was this Derek Jarman a friend of his, but he happened to be at the exhibition. Ward-Jackson and Jarman were introduced and immediately repaired to a nearby pub to discuss the proposition.

The rapport between the two men was instantaneous, but as Jarman was still filming *Jubilee* and Ward-Jackson was then living in Quito, it could not be acted upon straight away. However, the next day Ward-Jackson sent Jarman a copy of Walter Friedlaender's *Caravaggio Studies*, and within the year, as soon as *Jubilee* was in the can and Ward-Jackson had returned from Ecudor to live in London, Jarman introduced his new friend to James Whaley and Howard Malin.

Jarman's relationship with his first producers was at a crossroads. Although he was talking to them about a number of possible projects, including a sequel to *Jubilee*, and although he had come to rely on them as a source of reasonably regular income, if only of the petty-cash variety, he had never overcome his suspicion that they had cheated him of his share of the *Sebastiane* profits. Nor did he welcome the fact that Malin had become as friendly as he had with David and Barbara Stone who, for all their commitment to avant-garde film, enjoyed a lifestyle of relative opulence instinctively mistrusted by Jarman. For their part, Whaley and Malin were harbouring doubts of their own about their director, whose singularity of purpose they were beginning to find restrictive. When, in the course of Whaley and Malin's lunch with Ward-Jackson, it became apparent that despite being well-heeled, this Ward-Jackson did not possess the kind of money that would ensure the funding of a new film, Megalovision dropped out of the picture, leaving the newcomer with little alternative but to develop *Caravaggio* alone. In May 1978, under the auspices of Associated Art Advisors, Ward-Jackson's own company, and for an initial fee of £2,500, Jarman's new producer commissioned his new director to write the first script of a film that took its original title from the motto on Caravaggio's knife: *Nec Spec Nec Metu* – no hope no fear.[7]

Jarman's plan was to travel to Italy to work on the script there. He would again let Butler's Wharf to help cover expenses and, since *Jubilee* had been selected for La Semaine de la Critique,[8] take in the Cannes Film Festival en route. Jenny Runacre drove Jordan, Tony Rayns and – thanks no doubt to the continuing potency of Umberto Tirelli's prophecy – a very nervous Jarman to France. Stopping in Paris to drop Rayns and collect Jean-Marc Prouveur, they visited the Louvre, where Jarman wanted Runacre to see Caravaggio's *The Death of the Virgin*. He made a short film, *Every Woman for Herself and All for Art*, of Jordan standing alongside the Venus de Milo as the chara-banc parties flocked through the gallery to be photographed with the statue. The film-maker and his own party then went in search of the Louvre's most famous painting, inadvertently causing 'the inconceivable' to happen: 'The tourists in this immense gallery forgot themselves and life became more important than art. Groups of Japanese turned their backs on the *Mona Lisa* and their cameras on Jordan. The hidden video recorded this for the guards and suddenly the walls of the gallery parted and we were arrested and hustled into a secret lift which whizzed us down to the basement, where an angry curator expelled us.'[9]

The incident both excited and outraged Jarman. He would, if he could, have made an issue of it by summoning the press. But the film festival beckoned and, as it happened, there would be enough press attention and drama there to satisfy them all.

As they approached Cannes Runacre's car broke down, and they had to be towed the final few kilometres. On reaching their humble hotel on the outskirts of the city, Runacre's luggage was stolen, leaving her nothing to wear. The thieves disdained the peculiarities in Jordan's suitcase, though she did not entirely escape wardrobe problems: she rose from dinner one hot night to find that her rubber skirt was melting clean away.

Also in Cannes were Whaley and Malin, Christopher Hobbs, Hermine Demoriane and Lee Drysdale. Jarman relished being able to share with them the furore that seemed to accompany the exotically dressed Jordan wherever she went. He was thrilled that she was photographed with David Bowie, and when he, Runacre and Jordan took the stage at the Five Nation Televised Opening in the gilded casino with festival director Louis Malle and a riot broke out among the audience of invited punks, his delight knew no bounds. As a film, *Jubilee* was failing to set the world alight, but as a photo opportunity it was proving a sell-out.

Jarman and Prouveur proceeded to Rome by train, quietly settling into a hotel near the Spanish Steps, where they were briefly joined by Ward-Jackson, Hobbs and Whaley. To an outsider, it might have looked as if they were on holiday. Visiting Capri, where they swam in the blue grotto, and neighbouring Ischia, Jarman took his Nizo wherever they went, recording a sequence of short films to commemorate their excursions: pedestrians in Rome, Prouveur and Hobbs by the fountains in the gardens at Tivoli, Prouveur and Hobbs in the Pantheon, Hobbs at some ruins in the country. Such activities did not, however, distract Jarman from the matter at hand, and by July he had achieved the purpose of the trip: a first-draft script.

Using such biography and art history as was available, much of it supplied by his friend Simon Watney, who had written a dissertation on the subject as an undergraduate, Jarman dovetailed a selection of the known facts about Michelangelo Merisi da Caravaggio with supposition and a reading of certain paintings to arrive at an impressionistic, imagistic account of the life that is equally an elucidation of the work. His script opens with a sequence in super-8: Caravaggio dying more or less as he is known to have died, from a heart attack in Porto Ercole, but actually on the beach, as Jarman has it, and after attacking the waves with his sword and crying: 'The blue is poison.' Then, in flashback, we are treated to a series of vignettes which encapsulate the major events and paintings of the artist's life. He meets a brother and sister called Ranuccio and Lena at the Termi di Satourno and later makes love to Ranuccio, whom he includes in his painting *The Martyrdom of St Matthew*. He is taken up by Cardinal Del Monte. He uses the bricklayer Cavalino, lover of Del Monte's banker friend Giustiniani, as the model for his

Profane Love (*Amor Vincit Omnia*). He and Ranuccio are imprisoned after a brawl with the critic Baglione. Cardinal Scipione falls in love with Lena and has Caravaggio paint her as the Madonna as a cover for their assignations. Caravaggio meets and is fucked by a shepherd boy called Jerusalem, whom he paints as St John. Lena, who has fallen pregnant by Scipione, is found dead in the Tiber, presumably on the orders of her lover. Ranuccio is arrested for her murder. Caravaggio uses her corpse as the model for the Virgin Mary, and his influence with Scipione and the Pope, whom he also paints, to have Ranuccio released. Ranuccio attacks Caravaggio for painting Lena's murderers and is himself killed by Caravaggio in the ensuing fight.

The fevered but strangely disjointed script – Jarman was more interested in the texture of each moment than in how the moments hung together in a narrative sense – ends with Del Monte recounting the final months of Caravaggio's life to Giustiniani and the painter Rubens.

In real life, although there is mention of a Lena as 'Michelangelo's girl' and a four-a-side brawl with a certain Ranuccio of Terni, who died immediately afterwards, there is no evidence to suggest that Ranuccio even knew Lena, or that Caravaggio loved Ranuccio. That Caravaggio was, if not homosexual, then certainly bisexual, was an inference Jarman drew almost entirely from the way the painter tackled the male nude. It was from the paintings too that he deduced Caravaggio's ultimate responsibility for Ranuccio's death. Unusually for him, Caravaggio signed his painting *The Beheading of St John the Baptist* (done in Malta after the brawl) with the words 'I Caravaggio did this', which Jarman somewhat fancifully posited as a coded confession to murder.[10]

His draft complete, Jarman was ready and anxious to return home. First, however, he made a brief detour south to Taormina for his second film festival of the year, where he was expected 'to help with the Italian pre-publicity for *Jubilee*'. It was an altogether lonelier and more dispiriting experience than Cannes. 'The film was shown on the last night of the festival at 2.30 a.m.; I left an hour into the film, leaving an audience of nine in the cinema, of whom at least four were asleep.'[11] Matters at home turned out to be no less disquieting.

In February, when Jarman's mother had attended the premiere of *Jubilee* (remarking brightly to her son how very 'accurate' she had found the film), it had been in a wheelchair. By the summer, Betts' cancer was, in the words of her doctor, 'beginning to overwhelm her'.[12] She could no longer use the automatic car Lance had bought her, nor manage the recently installed stairlift. She and Lance decided to have a bungalow built in their garden, with the kitchen and bathroom geared to Betts' restricted mobility. It was hoped the house would be ready by November. Betts was hugely relieved and wrote with unintentional pathos to Jarman in Rome: 'I am pleased it came from him, and not from any further pushing on my part.'

Prior to this overdue decision to vacate unmanageable Merryfield, Lance had invested in another small bungalow in a modern close in Pennington, on the outskirts of Lymington in Hampshire. It was tiny – he had to install a caravan in the garden for when Gaye and her family came to stay – but at least it provided him and Betts with the prospect of escape from Metroland.

The thought of two new homes excited and exhausted Betts, in and out of hospital in Wendover, as the doctors tried to control her escalating pain. To her sister Moyra she wrote: 'It is no use pretending I have not been desperately depressed, mostly frustration – & I know this will pass and was bound to be – but it is so unlike me & as soon as we are organised house wise and I can get around I will be OK.' The letter was written on 15 July. Within a fortnight, her doctors were telling Lance that the situation was hopeless. At the end of the month, Betts entered hospital for the last time.

On Friday 4 August, Jarman went with Gaye to visit their mother. Betts was alert and could talk. Jarman told her about his Italian trip. On the Saturday, she was barely conscious, her speech little more than a whisper. Jarman and Gaye felt it only right to leave their mother and father alone together – yet in doing so they unwittingly allowed Betts to die alone. Whether because he was unable to face what was happening, or whether because he had simply popped out for a cup of tea, he was not at his wife's side when the fight finally went out of her.

In *Dancing Ledge*, Jarman grants his mother a less abandoned final moment. 'My sister and I took one fragile hand each as her life fluttered away like the proverbial swallows. It was difficult to know whether to speak or not – neither Gaye nor I could believe that after all these years of attentive listening she wouldn't hear. I asked her if she was comfortable – "Are you all right?" – and she whispered so quietly that maybe I imagined the response: "Of course not, silly, but you are."[13]

In the original manuscript, he then adds the sound of swallows: 'Itys. Itys. Itys.' Ever since his stay at the Villa Zuassa, this had been a special sound for him. Now it became a mantra to mark Betts' departure from the world.

A week later, Elizabeth Evelyn Jarman was cremated at Chilterns Crematorium in Amersham. She had not wanted any fuss, but because the law demanded one, however short, there was a service. Only Jarman and his father were present. The entire family did, however, attend a memorial gathering in the hospital chapel, along with the many nurses and doctors who had come to know and love their exceptional patient over the eighteen years of her illness. As a mark of respect Jarman removed his earring and, although he had not forgiven his father for not being with Betts at the end, and never would, he still grasped Lance's arm as they left the service.

Air Commodore Jarman was ill-equipped to deal with the devastation he felt at the loss of his wife. When he took charge of her ashes, beyond saying vaguely that he had scattered them 'a little bit here, a little bit there', he refused to tell either of his children what he had done with them. His kleptomania became uncontrollable. On 27 July, around the time he had first been told Betts did not have long to live, he was caught shoplifting two bottles of whisky. He never attempted to deny that he had taken them, merely saying he had intended to buy them as a gift for the nurses looking after Betts, but because he was not sleeping properly and was therefore not in full control of his faculties, he had neglected to pay for them. He pleaded guilty before the magistrate on 2 August, just three days before Betts died, making no mention of his wife's illness as a mitigating circumstance.

Later he told Yana Spence, his sailing companion, that by pleading guilty he had hoped to keep the incident out of the newspapers.

If this was true (he might have pleaded guilty simply because he knew he *was* guilty), the ploy signally failed to achieve its desired effect. 'EX-AIR CHIEF FINED FOR WHISKY THEFT', announced the *Daily Telegraph*,[14] the paper most likely to be read by Lance's peers. A distraught Gaye had to ask the hospital to vet the newspapers before passing them to the dying Betts.

Certain of Lance's friends took a most condemnatory view of the incident. Others could not imagine so upstanding a man being guilty of such a tawdry offence. The cause, they felt, was emotional distress. Led by his doctor, who wrote a statement in Lance's defence, they insisted on a second hearing. The stipulation of English law that, having pleaded guilty in a magistrates' court, a plaintiff cannot then change his plea, made it impossible for the second court to find Lance not guilty. What it could do, though, was pronounce that the circumstances surrounding the alleged offence merited an absolute discharge.[15] In this way Lance was effectively exonerated. Both his barrister and his solicitor waived their fees.

In *The Last of England*, when Jarman says it was on Betts' death that he and his sister finally put two and two together regarding their father's kleptomania, he is not being altogether accurate. In fact, the process was far from instantaneous. That Christmas, Lance stayed with Gaye and her family, now living in Oxford. Some money went missing from the dresser. Immediately accusing his six-year-old grandson of taking it, Lance announced that he knew exactly where it could be found – in an upstairs drawer. What had actually happened was that Sam had seen his grandfather take the money, forcing Lance, in a desperate attempt to cover his tracks, to accuse the one person capable of revealing his guilt. Sam duly protested the truth, but because of his age he was not believed until much later – by which time the child had almost started to wonder whether he might indeed have been the culprit, so fiercely and constantly did Lance hector him to take responsibility for his actions.[16]

'If our society condoned patricide, I think both my sister and I would have attempted it,' wrote Jarman in *The Last of England*. 'We discussed it half-jokingly over the telephone often enough.'[17] With the passing of the years, Lance's kleptomania became so reckless that on his visits to Gaye, he would sometimes help himself to such items as the lawnmower, or a bicycle belonging to his granddaughter Kate. On these occasions, it would be Jarman's job to distract the thief, usually by means of embarking on an instalment of an ongoing argument over the South African situation, while Gaye and her husband David stealthily emptied Lance's car boot of its illicit hoard.

If kleptomania is a symptom of emotional loss, of wanting to take back that which has been stolen from one, the way it now dominated Lance's existence is painful evidence of the awful extent of his loneliness. His future did not look bright; nor would it be. In the eight years of life still left to him, he would see his horizons inexorably narrow. Since work had already begun on the bungalow in Northwood, he had the building completed, then moved into it. Merryfield, the dream house he had so lovingly designed, was put up for sale. Later Lance sold both the Northwood and Pennington bungalows, moving into a nondescript house in Lymington. Ever faithful to the memory of happier times, he named it Merryfield.

Lance had always planned to sail home to New Zealand when he retired. Betts' illness had forced him to put this dream on hold. Now he was seventy-one, and felt it was too late. He was reduced to the Welsh Harp, to Southampton Water, to his researches into his family tree and, when he moved permanently to Lymington, to cultivating a circle of old ladies – his 'girls', he called them – for whom he mowed lawns, cleared gutters, replaced fuses. Despite a minor stroke in 1980 and the onset of diabetes, he remained remarkably fit and energetic: 'tanned, athletic, in shorts and running vest'.[18] Nevertheless, one has the sense that the fire had gone out of him. Nor could he, at this late stage, seek much solace in his children. Although he made fairly regular trips to Oxford to stay with Gaye, he almost never visited his son – and when Jarman went to see him, the lack of real warmth on both sides was unmistakable. Tea, accompanied by 'very stale biscuits',[19] would be taken on the lawn, followed by lunch in the local pub. Every visit would begin with the words: 'When are you going back?'

Betts' death gave rise to an equal maelstrom of emotions in her son. In his memory, she remained forever smiling, warm, open, serene. The way she had hidden her difficulties with Lance; the pride she had taken in Jarman's achievements, the concern she had felt for his welfare; the comic flourishes her final, drug-induced forgetfulness had produced (at a rather important dinner party she had covered the strawberries with mayonnaise instead of cream): all this, and more, Jarman remembered, cherished, mourned. But he sensed also that perhaps her 'smile and charm was the disaster of her time and class'.[20] At last he could admit to himself that her perfection had been a daunting standard against which to measure himself. For the first time ever, he was free of this particular parental obligation. He felt a sense of elation and release. Later, after Lance's death, he would say of both parents that while he could 'write of them with sympathy', he could just as easily 'forget to tell you that my heart danced on their last breath'.[21]

Meanwhile, he had the extreme good fortune, in the very month of Betts' death, of a third feature dropping unexpectedly into his lap. When it was finished, he would dedicate it to the memory of his mother.

Because he was learning that as a film-maker you must have more than one project in development and flirt with as many producers as possible, at the same time as he had been talking to Ward-Jackson about *Caravaggio*, Jarman had formed a notional company (the Storm Film Company) with Guy Ford and Mordecai Schreiber. They wanted to see if they could find a way of realising *The Tempest*. Whereupon, as if by a wave of Prospero's wand, a new producer appeared on the scene: the twenty-nine-year-old Don Boyd. Such was Boyd's ability to conjure films out of thin air that the critic Alexander Walker would call this director-cum-producer the 'Boyd Wonder'. In Boyd's own terminology, he was a 'fake Brit' – half Russian, half Scottish – and every bit as ebullient as Jarman in his enthusiasms.

Through a business colleague, a financial adviser called Roy Tucker, Boyd had discovered a decidedly unconventional source of funding for his films. If a number of individuals paid money into a limited partnership from which, because of the structure of that partnership, they were never going to see much of a return, the money thus invested could, for the individuals concerned, be set against their tax as a loss; quite a substantial loss, in fact, since the way such investments were assessed meant that the paper loss was about four times the original investment. Thereafter, the individuals left the partnership, taking their losses with them, along with the very small hope that one day, after everyone else had taken a cut of any profits, they might see a small return on their investment. It was this 'small hope' that transformed what might sound like tax evasion, which is illegal, into tax deferral, which is not – a technical nicety not greatly appreciated by the tax authorities, who eventually ensured that this loophole in the system was closed. In 1978, however, the money set aside through these partnerships was enough to fund the making of a whole package of features, provided each was made for exactly the amount designated and completed before April 1979, the end of the tax year. Boyd already had two such films in hand, and was searching for a third when it was suggested he talk to Jarman, who, with a flourish, produced his script of The Tempest.[22]

Having established that Ford and Schreiber could stay involved with the project, Jarman and Boyd quickly agreed terms: a budget of some £150,000, including, for once, a decent fee for Jarman himself.[23] Next, because Boyd knew he would be in America for much of the shooting, he assigned Jarman his young assistant, Sarah Radclyffe, as associate producer. By the end of August, Jarman knew he had precisely seven months in which to make the first-ever screen version of Shakespeare's play.

Between August and December, the delighted director put his earlier versions of the play through a series of brisk rewrites. While remaining true to his intrinsically Jungian reading of the text and to the fact that, in the play, he saw Shakespeare both celebrating and bidding farewell to a Renaissance world of magic which, in the person of John Dee and others, had become discredited under the new materialism exemplified by James I, Jarman also made every effort to avoid what he saw as a weakness of Jubilee: that he had written too much dialogue. Taking full advantage of the narrative freedom allowed him by the structure he had settled on, that of the film being Prospero's dream, he pared away as many of Shakespeare's speeches as possible, including the one in which Prospero abjures his 'rough magic' and promises to break his staff and drown his books. In line with Frances Yates, Jarman felt that here Shakespeare was simply pandering to the politics of his time, throwing away the magical past to make his contemporary audience feel comfortable. Besides, Jarman himself was too young to abjure his own magic and not yet ready to break his staff or close his books.

He also added a new finale, a modern-day reworking of the original masque suggested to him by the story he had heard of Cocteau taking twenty-one sailors to his friend Francis Rose's twenty-first birthday party.[24] The sailors from the shipwreck would dance a joyous and impromptu hornpipe to celebrate the play's many reconciliations: in particular, the union of Miranda with Ferdinand. A golden goddess would appear, singing Cole Porter's 'Stormy Weather'. 'I don't want to bless the union as Shakespeare did,' Jarman told the *International Herald Tribune*, 'because the world doesn't see the heterosexual union any more as a solution. Miranda and Ferdinand may go into stormy weather.'[25] He then added a framing device to help explain his reading of the text – an older Prospero, now retired, reminiscing on the beach of a tropical or Mediterranean island – though at the last minute this had to be axed for reasons of budget and time. He still saw the film unfolding within the confines of a house and relying on 'atmosphere rather than directional narrative'. He imagined it being shot in black and white, or 'colour drained to monochrome',[26] rather in the manner of a German expressionist horror film, with only Prospero's visions and the finale in full colour.

While doing the rewrites – and, as always, canvassing every passing person for his or her reaction – Jarman was actively casting and hunting for locations. For the older Prospero, he first approached John Gielgud, with whom he had discussed the play as far back as 1968, when they had been working on *Don Giovanni*. Gielgud politely but firmly declined.[27] Jarman next approached Terry-Thomas, who was living on Ibiza, which could have provided an ideal location for Prospero's retirement beach. Terry-Thomas accepted, writing eagerly from Sandy's Bar with a barrage of questions. 'A Thought has just occurred to me and mine. I am to play Old Prospero, but what about the younger Prospero? Does the actor look like Terry-Thomas and sound like Terry-Thomas, and have a gap in his teeth? Otherwise how will the audience know? . . . By the way, what sort of voice do you want? My own natural voice, or a very old throaty one, or what?' By the time this letter was written, the older Prospero had been cut, leaving only his younger self. Spurning tradition, Jarman had always seen his Prospero as being in his mid-thirties ('haggard and withdrawn', he had written, with traces of 'a great and charismatic beauty'),[28] and he pursued the likes of Ian Holm and Terence Stamp before settling on the anarchic writer, sometime magician and champion of squatters' rights, Heathcote Williams. For the rest, Jarman managed an unusual, often inspired, mix of the known (his own repertory company, as it were) and the unknown, but with a firmer ballast of professional actors than ever before. Alongside such regulars as Karl Johnson (Ariel), Toyah Willcox (Miranda), Jack Birkett (Caliban), Claire Davenport (Sycorax – though at one stage he thought of her as the King of Naples), Richard Warwick (Antonio) and Helen Wallington-Lloyd (A Spirit), he included David Meyer (Ferdinand), Peter Ball (Alonso), Ken Campbell (Gonzalo), Neil Cunningham (Sebastian), Christopher Biggins (Stephano) and Peter Turner (Trinculo). His four-year-old niece Kate played the young Miranda and, as all three goddesses rolled into one, there was the singer Elisabeth Welch, whose first revue appearance on the London stage in 1933 had featured the Cole Porter number with which, in a blaze of alchemical gold, she crowns the film.

With crew stalwarts Peter Middleton as director of photography and John Hayes taking responsibility for sound, Ian Whittaker from *The Devils* and *Savage Messiah* was asked to be art director, Yolanda Sonnabend the designer. Among the old friends roped in on the production side, Stuart Hopps, who had been at King's with Jarman, was persuaded to choreograph the final hornpipe.

For the film's exteriors, the location chosen was the one Russell had used for Loudun in *The Devils*: Bamburgh Castle and its adjacent stretch of remote Northumberland beach. For the interiors – the twilight hinterland of Prospero's isle – they settled on Stoneleigh Abbey, near Coventry, part of which, having been damaged by fire, was uninhabited. In addition to such Miss Havisham-like touches as the richly brocaded curtains that still hung at some of the windows, and would have fallen apart if touched, the once splendid eighteenth-century rooms boasted 'phosphorescent greying mirrors, and chandeliers, which, when we later lit them with a hundred or more candles, animated the plaster ceilings in an unexpected way: the gods and goddesses, encrusted on them amongst fruit and flowers, danced in the flickering light'.[29]

Not only was this the perfect 'House of Dreams',[30] an undisputed 'island of the mind' and a sufficiently abstract setting to ensure 'the delicate description in the poetry' could not be 'destroyed by any Martini lagoons',[31] that its entrance hall should also chance to contain a portrait of Elizabeth, daughter of James I, was a piece of synchronicity which, Jungian that he was, Jarman pounced on as a significant blessing. One of the earliest recorded performances of *The Tempest* was at the court of James, as part of the festivities for the marriage of Elizabeth, later known as the 'Winter Queen', to the Elector Palatine. Absolutely every god and goddess, or so it seemed, was smiling on the film.

Although always emphatic that film design was not about 'dressing' the film 'in a kind of wrapping, like a doily around a birthday cake',[32] thanks to the furniture and other artifacts to be found at Stoneleigh, not to mention the generosity of its owners, the Leigh family, Jarman, Yolanda Sonnabend, her assistant Steven Meaha and Ian Whittaker were able, when necessary, to dress the rooms they used quite magnificently, transforming them into a series of truly magical spaces. Magic is, of course, central to the play, and the design of the film also proliferated with subtle pointers to the 'pre-Scientific approach to the physical world'[33] that Jarman so admired in the work of the Renaissance magi whose quasi-mystical thinking underpinned his reading of the text.[34]

For the costumes, a sense of timelessness was aimed at, thereby creating a sartorial 'chronology of the 350 years of the play's existence'.[35] There might be echoes, for example, of the New Romantics, which in turn would cause the film to reflect, however glancingly, 'the deep insecurity of our time and the conservatism it has engendered'.[36] Jarman was equally keen that the costumes reinforce character. The way Miranda's dress is festooned with shells and feathers, so that it looks as if she carries the island about her person, is a precise indication of her upbringing, just as Prospero's rumpled but once magnificent velvet waistcoat and breeches hint at a richer, more cosmopolitan past.

Timothy Hyman, interviewing the film's director after its release, applauded the result thus:

> In *Jubilee*, the magician John Dee conjured up an Ariel who was essentially pastiche: but in *The Tempest* the magic is real . . . The contemporary world through which Shakespeare's play has been filtered – (so that the Island becomes a drop-out's squat, covered in Cabbalistic chalk graffiti; Miranda has an Afro hairstyle; Prospero is embodied by the playwright and Ladbroke Grove Anarch, Heathcote Williams; and Caliban's given to Jack 'Orlando' Birkett, lecherous veteran from the Circuses of Lindsay Kemp) – is certainly peripheral to me, yet I'm forced through Jarman's vision to recognize it as a creative present . . . even the lurking narcissism in Jarman's aesthetic is here, on this barren island, put to good use.[37]

Jarman once remarked that whereas *Sebastiane* had taken place in sunlight, and *Jubilee* in a stormy twilight, *The Tempest* was a film of the night. 'By the time filming was commenced, on 14 February, we were living in another world. The cameras began to turn with the house in darkness, its shutters closed against the blizzards outside.'[38] The lighting was kept as low as possible,[39] the camera as static, so that not only would the action seem to emerge, dreamlike, from the shadows, it would also unfold within each shot 'as within a proscenium arch'.[40]

It is very possible that, in his mind's eye, Jarman was 'rehearsing' *Caravaggio*; he certainly talked a great deal to Peter Middleton about chiaroscuro and the use of flickering light.[41] He was also exploring a notion articulated best in his brief and fragmentary notes for *Night – a Film of the Dark*, never made, unless *The Tempest* is it. 'The western world,' he wrote, had 'hardly ever contemplated darkness as a positive nourishing source of renewal. We strive towards the light but what of darkness? Is it not there that our sickness might be cured?'[42] It was an idea he would revisit more than once in the years to come, in his films, his painting, even his private life, much of which he chose to act out under the cover of darkness.

The Tempest was an intense, and intensely enjoyable, shoot. Jubilee had been too shambolic to be entirely enjoyable; Sebastiane, for all the holiday-like perfection of its locale, too riven by internal tensions and insecurities. On The Tempest, by contrast, despite the stormy weather, there was only serenity and laughter. Kitted out against the cold in coat, overalls, thick socks and combat boots, Jarman presided over his filmic family which a cheerfulness and calm that isolated them from anything untoward just as surely as the banks of snow were isolating Stoneleigh from the rest of the country. He was still a novice to many aspects of film-making and relied heavily on Middleton's experience and expertise, but this much he had learned: that 'with small resources you allow the work to take its own course'. He tried, in Heathcote Williams' phrase, to 'flow with the glue'[43] – and, whenever necessary, to improvise. John Scarlett-Davis, whom Jarman had met through Andrew Logan and whose job as assistant director could encompass anything from scrubbing Jarman's back in the bath to keeping company with the director's previous night's pick-up, remembers driving with Jarman to Stoneleigh in a very old Citroën Deux Chevaux whose windscreen-wipers had broken. When they encountered a snowstorm, Jarman, without pausing in his conversation, extended a hand through the window and operated the wipers manually so that their journey could continue without interruption. It is an image that wonderfully encapsulates both his method and his determination.

The other image that captures what it was like to work on the film is that of the cast and crew at their evening meal in Stoneleigh's long, narrow, arched refectory. After dinner and the nightly viewing of the rushes, if those billeted at the house itself wanted entertainment they were obliged to provide it themselves. One of the runners on the film, an ex-child-actor and aspiring musician by the name of Simon Turner,[44] played his guitar and provided backing music on his tape-recorder. Karl Johnson wielded a second guitar. Jack Birkett sang, as did Elisabeth Welch on the day of her shoot. Birkett also danced. There were readings-cum-stagings from Heathcote Williams' play *The Immortalist* and a whole sequence of *divertissements* from Williams himself, who lived and slept in costume. He displayed his skills at fire-eating, performed magic tricks and, on one notable occasion, having drunk particularly deeply of the cider supplied by Simon Turner, leaped on to the table declaring ominously: 'I've been entertaining you lot far too long – if no one entertains me within one minute I'm going to piss all over you.' Nobody responded quickly enough and, within moments, Williams was peeing 'a cider torrent'[45] over the assembled company.

Of the filming, Jarman would later say: 'I realised with *The Tempest* that you could do anything; up to then I had felt rather constricted.'[46] He was especially thrilled when Neil Cunningham likened the shoot to 'a party given by a great eighteenth-century magnate like Beckford'.[47] As Jarman explained in *Dancing Ledge*, 'In all my work I've tried to make the working experience enjoyable. For me that is more important than the end-product. The only audience I worry about is my collaborators on the film; everything, and everyone else, is outside the circle.'[48]

From Stoneleigh, the team drove north through further blizzards to Bamburgh, the roads round Coventry seeming like a hallucination after the intensity of the twilit shoot. Once the snow had been brushed off the dunes and blue filters placed before the lens, David Meyer walked naked from the waves while Stephano, Trinculo and Caliban danced along the sands as if, Jarman later realised, following the Yellow Brick Road. It was an anxious few days. The weather could easily have caused them to run disastrously over schedule. As it was, they managed to wrap by the end of March: only days before Jack Birkett was due in Italy for his next job, never mind the end of the tax year.

Post-production took place in London, where the final collaborative strand, the soundtrack, was added. Jarman had originally earmarked Brian Eno to do the music, with perhaps David Bowie to sing Ariel's songs; by now he knew what marketing sense it made to have an LP to accompany a film. In the end, because he was familiar with Hodgson's work from past collaborations with Peter Logan, he settled on Wavemaker, the musical partnership of Brian Hodgson, organiser of the BBC Radiophonic Workshop, and John Lewis. Their electronic score, created in part from the recorded vowel sounds of the cast, was extremely atmospheric but hardly album material. For this, a new friend of Jarman's, a young Scotsman by the name of James Mackay then working at the Film Makers' Co-Op, helped arrange the release of the obvious single: Elisabeth Welch singing 'Stormy Weather'.

By July the film was ready. Blown up from 16mm to 35mm, it was premiered in late August at the Edinburgh Film Festival, alongside another of Don Boyd's similarly financed features, the more aggressively titled *Scum*, and to general enthusiasm. In November it was shown at the London Film Festival, where again it was applauded. A month later, it was included in the first-ever NFT season to be devoted to Jarman's films.[49] In February 1980 it travelled to the Berlin Film Festival,[50] then to Hong Kong and Cannes before finally opening in London in May at the Screen on the Hill in Hampstead. With barely an exception, the reviews were excellent. Of Jarman's 'latest bric-a-brac brainstorm', Nigel Andrews in *The Financial Times* enthused: 'though there will be much shaking of heads at Jarman's way with the text . . . it's the Bard's rebirth in cinema'.[51] David Robinson in *The Times* maintained that 'in a British cinema that has rarely much to boast about', the film 'reveals a talent that shines bright and cuts deep; and, if the British film establishment does not make use of it, it is an industry more sunk in folly even than one had thought'.[52] Alan Brien in *The Sunday Times* went so far as to call it 'one of the most original and masterly films ever made in Britain'.[53]

Jarman was overwhelmed, even alarmed. 'It's the first of my films that people all seem to like,' he told Brian Hodgson in a programme note for the NFT. 'And that worries me slightly, because in a sense I think it's better to be *disliked*, to be slightly more dangerous as an artist than THE TEMPEST allows.' He need not have worried. In September 1980, as part of a British Film Week, and in the presence of its maker, the film received its New York première. Overall, the reviews, if more cautious than in Britain, were far from negative; yet there was one so implacable in its hostility that it completely upstaged all others. Written by Vincent Canby, it appeared in no less a newspaper than *The New York Times* and stated baldly that the film 'would be funny if it weren't unbearable. It's a fingernail scratched along a blackboard, sand in spinach, a 33-r.p.m. recording of "Don Giovanni" played at 78 r.p.m. Watching it is like driving a car whose windscreen has shattered but not broken . . . There are no poetry, no ideas, no characterizations, no narrative, no fun.'[54]

To a man obsessed by car crashes, and whose most painful previous critical mauling had been in connection with Mozart's opera, the references to a shattered windscreen and *Don Giovanni* suggested that, in order to inflict maximum hurt, Canby had meticulously researched Jarman's past; either that, or the gods had suddenly stopped smiling. Either way, the review effectively killed the film's chances in America.

This second of the two major setbacks suffered by Jarman at crucial stages of his career was particularly shaming in that it was witnessed by such old friends as Karl Bowen, Keith Milow, Robert Mapplethorpe – and, of course, Patrik Steede. Steede invited Jarman to his apartment to admire a new recording of the *Ring Cycle* and was heard to murmur that he found Canby's review 'charitable'. Then came the small matter of Jarman's current *affaire*, the twenty-year-old Shaun Allen. Allen, who was taking a year out from an English degree at Oxford, had been persuaded by Jarman to accompany him to New York, but was not yet ready for the level of commitment Jarman seemed to want of him, with the result that the impact of Canby's review was exacerbated by the minor yet nonetheless unwanted tensions of an imploding relationship. It is hardly surprising that during the course of Jarman's stay his always ambivalent relationship with the Big Apple should visibly sour. It was, he said, 'a city of glittering towers built on deep foundations of alienation and misery'.[55] Even the sexual liberation it represented and championed had become questionable. Looking about him at the 'desert of ageing lawyers and execs with hangdog moustaches and work-out muscles', he asked acerbically: 'Did the young men who waged the battle of Christopher Street in the sixties know where they would lead us?'[56]

Back in London, fate had one final, if also minor, ignominy in store for the director of 'one of the most original and masterly films ever made in Britain'. In the first of their annual film awards, the

Evening Standard had included Jarman in the category of most promising newcomer.[57] Duly donning a dinner jacket and setting off in
hope for the ceremony with some of the cast and crew who had
shared the horrors of New York, Jarman was very dispirited not to be
called to the stage to collect an award. When David Meyer said
something consoling along the lines of 'Maybe next time,' Jarman
replied with absolute certainty that no, this was the nearest any of
them were going to get.

23

Montage Years

Although Jarman maintained that what had always interested him about *The Tempest* was that 'no one can pinpoint the meaning',[1] his own reading of the play was fairly unequivocal and deeply pessimistic. Jarman's Prospero is, in the words of Michael O'Pray, 'sinister, intense, secretive and cruel'. Such reparation as Jarman's arrangements of the action allows is arrived at only through magic and in a 'fantasy world', not through any 'real political or personal understanding'.[2] The film deals despairingly with the chilly horror of imprisonment and enslavement, of being subservient to the whim of another; the unbearable sadness of banishment and exile, of being denied one's rightful place in the world – themes that thread themselves through most of Jarman's films, often more powerfully than the more obvious theme of sexuality.

It is in keeping with the pessimism at the core of the film that it should be *The Tempest* for which Jarman experienced the most painful public rejection in his career as a film-maker. Fitting, too, that the bitter winter of its creation was also Britain's 'Winter of Discontent', of strikes by lorry-drivers and grave-diggers, of rubbish and rats in London's West End and a dissatisfaction with Jim

Callaghan's Labour government so deep and rancid that it poisoned the entire country. As the film was being edited, there was a general election in which the Conservative Party, led by Margaret Thatcher, swept triumphantly to power with a far-reaching political and social agenda that would notoriously banish the concept of society, certainly as understood by someone like Jarman.

Later he wrote that although he 'would hate to equate *The Tempest*, full of forgiveness and maturity, with the politics of Thatcher's infantile regime',[3] with hindsight he could see clear parallels between the way John Dee was discredited by James I and the brutal manner whereby, under Margaret Thatcher, the Conservatives severed Britain's links with what Jarman saw as the essence of his country's heritage. Although at the time of Thatcher's first campaign, he tended to admire rather than fear the Iron Lady, he soon came to regard her with intense loathing. 'A wild anger bubbles away like magma below the surface,' he wrote in *Dancing Ledge*. 'I check it. Burroughs said that sometimes he was possessed by the evil spirit – I understand the feeling: a dizzy surge in the blood, the heart beats faster, the eyes turn inwards. The rarer action is in virtue than in vengeance.'[4] In *The Last of England*, he visualised his anger thus: 'Elizabeth II's boarding Britannia . . . The ship sails over the horizon with its geriatric cast. Hell-bent for a rendezvous with their assets in Laguna, far in the jammy West where the Imperial sun has not yet set. Leaving the rotting shires to rot. After they have gone, in the deathly silence a small boy dances on the quay, throwing a last stone for England and St George.'[5] Meanwhile, Jarman's body found its own, non-verbal way of substantiating the anger bubbling below the surface: around now he began to suffer from irritable bowel syndrome, a classic symptom of stress.[6]

Not for the first time in Jarman's life, a shift in the fortunes of his country coincided with a shift in his own fortunes, making his empathy with the times in which he lived that much more acute; making the individual – from his public pronouncements to the private spasms of his colon – that much more of a mirror to his world.

For a number of reasons (problems with the developers, a wish to reflect his growing distance from the Logans and their circle, a desire for a more central base) he decided that the time had come to stop running a 'gay Butlins' and to quit Butler's Wharf. In July 1979, immediately work on *The Tempest* was finished, he ceded the studio to Jean-Marc Prouveur and, through Christopher Biggins, took a lease on a studio flat in Phoenix House, above the Phoenix Theatre. At £620 per annum, the rent was well within his means and the flat, although minuscule, perfectly adequate for his needs.[7] The street entrance was an anonymous door just off Charing Cross Road. A noisy, semi-industrial lift ascended to the fourth floor and the flat itself, where a galley kitchen and tiny bathroom overlooked the courtyard and vertigo-inducing rear walkway, along which Jarman soon established a line of greenery in a cluster of pots wired to the railings. The single front room, as square and functional as the building itself, overlooked the constant noise of Charing Cross Road and the multiple windows of the St Martin's School of Art.

Here Jarman set about creating a monastic cell that was, as ever, a vindication of his aesthetic sense. The simple mantelpiece above the basic electric fire and the uncompromising grid of the uncurtained window were offset by a shifting collection of carefully arranged objects: 'a fold-up bed, two chairs, a metal office desk, and some carpenters' stools from the old studio';[8] Jarman's own paintings, a photographic portrait of a young man by Angus McBean, a handful of books, shells, stones, Anthony Harwood's Japanese tea bowl, the head of Mausolus, a singing saw (a new acquisition), a pair of ivory swords, Güta Minton's 'friendship' plant, a gold clock in the shape of a fanciful sun.

At the same time, because he knew he would need additional studio space, he rented a small room from Christopher Hobbs at 20 Hanway Works, just a stone's throw from Phoenix House in a narrow, Dickensian alley behind Tottenham Court Road. Here he dedicated an entire wall to his books and the overflow of his drawings, paintings and less treasured *objets d'art*.

A month after making the move to Phoenix House, Jarman was found at Blitz, the weekly club run by Steve Strange and Rusty Egan, by an ashen-faced Alasdair McGaw, who had recently moved into Butler's Wharf with Prouveur. A fire had broken out at the studio.[9] Jarman rushed with McGaw to the river. 'It was a rather extraordinary experience,' he said afterwards.

Wonderful, I thought, I won't have to worry about moving all that stuff. Everything was in there, it all burnt except the films, fortunately they were somewhere else. I felt very strange. Like sitting up all night on a film shoot because you were on the edge of your seat all the time. Things like the roof collapsed then another floor went and everyone plied me with tea and whisky. And I sat and of course hundreds of people were coming to watch so you sat watching your house burn down with all these onlookers.[10]

It is a vivid account and, to an extent, accurate. Where it differs from the truth is in the assertion that the studio was still his and that the fire destroyed his belongings. These were already at Phoenix House and Hanway Works; it was Prouveur and Peter Logan who lost their possessions. But because Jarman was beginning a new chapter in life – and given the name of the building to which he had moved – the image of himself as a phoenix rising from his own ashes was too apt to be ignored; true in the psychic, if not the literal sense. Thus was born one of the more potent of his personal myths.

If only the phoenix, once risen, could have faced a less fractured and frustrating future. It was not in Jarman's nature to mope (to get angry, yes, but never to despair, certainly not in public) any more than it was to twiddle his thumbs. Yet between 1979, when he finished *The Tempest*, and late 1985, when *Caravaggio* finally went into production, he had excuse enough to do both. His life, public and private, was paralysingly on hold: a montage of disparate, disjointed moments awaiting a major twist in the plot to catapult it into its final narrative rush.

Because Phoenix House was so central, it attracted a constant stream of visitors. While the minute kitchen spewed forth endless cups of tea, Jarman paced the main room, an urban lion in an urban cage, scratching his head, clicking his fingers, smoking the occasional cigarette or sampling a joint, expounding on the possibilities inherent in some current project, the difficulties of finding finance, vividly dissecting a pet hate, laughing, gossiping, or showing a sample of his super-8s. The audience for these impromptu film shows and verbal riffs comprised as spontaneous yet complex a selection of friends both old and new, work colleagues, plus a hard core of extremely good-looking young men.

There was the intricately tattooed Dave Baby, one of the 'punk faces' Jarman had chosen for *Jubilee*. Having overslept and missed being in the film, now he was everywhere in evidence. There was Chris Barnes, also known as Judy Blame, who worked in Heaven, made jewellery and turned many heads with the outrageousness of his dress. There was Derek Dunbar, lead singer of the group Jimmy the Hoover, and Adam Nankervis, a young Australian artist passing through London, on to whose naked body Jarman projected *In the Shadow of the Sun*, then, while Nankervis masturbated, filmed the result. There was the half-English, half-Dutch Gerard Raimond, who had graduated from a single session of fumbled sex – initiated by means of a standard Jarman ploy, the perusal of a copy of *The Best of Physique Pictorial* – to becoming Jarman's unofficial chauffeur and one of his most frequent companions on his weekly visits to Camden Lock Market.

On Saturday afternoons, John Scarlett-Davis and his companion Volker Stox were generally 'at home' for tea in their flat in Chelsea's Stadium Street, which often afforded the opportunity for a pick-up in the nearby King's Road. Saturday nights might mean Heaven, where Jarman met the alluringly beautiful, inquisitive and impish Ken Butler, a student of English and American literature at Sussex University. Recalling the meeting a year later, Jarman wrote: 'All the difficulty of 1983, the uncertainty about *Caravaggio*, the considerable financial chaos and the frustration of three years without work were offset by my meeting Ken, who smiled at me across a crowded bar in Heaven last March, bought me a vodka on the rocks by semaphore and then appeared and disappeared all through the year like a will o' the wisp. My first memory of him was laughing as if he had no cares in the world amongst all those earnest boys in crocodile T-shirts – we haven't stopped laughing since.'[11]

The passionate friendship that developed between Jarman and Butler would outlast most of his others. Over the next few years, Butler was a frequent visitor to Phoenix House, even lived there at times. The communication that had started in silence, with sign language, soon expanded into every area of Jarman's life, from the personal to the professional – accompanied always by doses of healing laughter. It is no coincidence that of all Jarman's attachments from these years, Butler was the one Robert Medley chose to pair with Jarman in his painting *Sunday Morning*.[12]

With the passing years, Jarman's sense of responsibility towards those younger than himself had grown ever stronger. Obsessed as he could be by his own affairs, he was constantly mindful of the needs of others. His generosity knew no bounds and he displayed a positive genius for knowing exactly when a person needed to be treated to a meal. His diary for 5 March 1981 contains a characteristic *aidemémoire*: 'Ring Lichfield about Jean-Marc's article. Ring Romaine [Hart] for Lee [Drysdale] job.' He continued to support Andy Marshall, for whom he had stood bail, encouraging him in his newfound project, furniture-making. He introduced Marshall to anyone he thought might buy his pieces and began to acquire a selection of them himself, starting with the 'Falklands throne', a substantial, virtually mediaeval chair fashioned, like all Marshall's pieces, out of wood collected from skips or builders' yards.[13]

Although his affair with Shaun Allen had wound down, he still played the part of Allen's mentor, sternly nudging the younger man in the directions he thought he should be following, introducing him to people who might be of value, offering him work. Allen repaid this interest by effecting an introduction of his own: to the work of Heraclitus, the gnomic Greek philosopher whose handful of fragmentary utterances Jarman soon began to weave into his work.[14]

Because Jarman's financial situation in the early eighties was often parlous, apart from various trips to Italy to further the cause of *Caravaggio* there were few excursions abroad, certainly for holidays. In September 1981, he accepted an invitation to be a judge at the Cork Film Festival, and in late 1982 there was a visit to Ken Butler in San Francisco where, as part of his degree, Butler was spending a year at Berkeley, and where he was able to help organise some showings of Jarman's films, plus a talk that paid Jarman enough to fund the trip. For the rest life revolved around Soho.

Apart from the endless cups of tea, Jarman's kitchen saw little in the way of domestic activity; at most, the supplementing of tinned lentil soup with slices of sausages – made virtually inedible by the fact that he always neglected to remove their plastic skins – enthusiastic jam-making and the boiling of sheets, a washday ritual of insanely Victorian proportions to which he was inexplicably attached. Come mealtimes, he was most likely to be found at one or other of his favourite restaurants, usually tucking into the same dish he had been eating for at least the past month. With food as with sex, Jarman was a creature of ritual and habit.

His was a low-key Soho, running parallel to the one inhabited by Francis Bacon, Daniel Farson and Jeffrey Bernard. The pubs Jarman frequented were not theirs. His were the Salisbury, Global Village or Brief Encounter, though he was just as likely to venture further afield, notably to the Bell beside King's Cross, which provided good hunting for 'psychobillies', the young boys whose 1950s rockabilly look (hair cut flat on top with a small quiff, jeans, plaid shirts) he particularly fancied, even if they differed from their rockabilly counterparts in that they were generally on speed.

For nightclubs, he still visited old haunts like the Catacombs, or Traffic, just to the north of the Bell, where, if he was travelling from Soho, he might go by cab – and if he did, would always ask the driver to drop him a few streets short of his destination because it was not 'the sort of place to arrive at in a taxi'.[15] Otherwise, since by the early eighties the focus of gay life had decisively shifted from west London to the West End, he had little need to wander beyond Bang, immediately across the road. Almost as close were the Pink Panther, Flamingo, Heaven and the Sanctuary. For slumming it, there was London's answer to New York's Mineshaft, the secretive, 'word-of-mouth' basement club in an alley behind Heaven, where, if this took your fancy, you could be pissed upon by the young roughs drawn to this stygian locale.

Also word-of-mouth – and every bit as sleazy – were the parties held in a ground-floor council flat in Vauxhall, at one of which Jarman was sighted taking full advantage of the dimensions of his 'snake' by standing by the window while someone outside the flat gave him a blow-job across the sill. What he liked best of all, though, was the Subway in Leicester Square, home to the first of London's official and fully functioning 'back rooms'. Here, fuelled by his statutory vodka and ice, or by the very occasional flirtation with a tab of

Ecstasy or acid, even opium, and by an increasing number of cigarettes, Jarman explored and celebrated exactly the kind of sexuality
he had so bitterly criticised on his last visit to New York.

Jarman's sexuality had always been extraordinarily complex. In
At Your Own Risk, he wrote simply, if a touch defiantly, of himself at
the end of the seventies: 'I cut my hair short, took off my earrings,
put on a leather jacket and, armed with KY and poppers, took off
into the night . . . I was happy.'[16] In *Dancing Ledge*, he celebrated a
charged encounter at the Subway: 'His body is hard, like marble,
and flawless. His face is tough, utterly nondescript, chipped like an
old statue – a lip damaged from a punch. He's wearing jeans and a
black vest. There is a home-made tattoo on his right shoulder. He
puts his beer on the space invaders machine and plays it till two,
then walks into the back-room, unzips, and produces the biggest,
thickest cock I've ever seen.'[17] In the unpublished original, he then
gives an equally heightened, almost ritualistic and possibly apoc-
ryphal account of the likelihood that it was this boy, this latterday
Adonis, who first fucked him. 'I'm totally infatuated by him . . . The
Temple whore who serves the initiates. The healer in the Abaton.
Tonight I put myself in the way of the boy. He enters me carefully.
He knows he is tearing me apart. The pleasure is so intense I come
with tears of relief after a score of deep firm thrusts.'[18] Of his initiation into anally receptive sex, Jarman would then write: 'Now I
know that until I'd begun to enjoy it I had not reached balanced
manhood. You must make the sacrifice to bury the centuries. When
you overcome yourself you understand that gender is its own prison.
When I meet heterosexual men I know they have experienced only
half of love.'[19]

Later, in an interview about why he had discovered love so late in
life, he probed even deeper:

> I just found . . . the whole sexual act at that stage seemed to
> be very violent and have that element of violation in it. I
> quite liked that . . . we were performing this act as a sort of
> revenge. I think it was very prevalent in the seventies, you
> know? . . . I was quite happy . . . to have sex publicly . . .
> putting it on like it was a display . . . I mean the sixties were

an isolated fragment . . . by the seventies you could go to a
club where there might be two or three thousand people . . .
where everyone was having sex . . . compared with the
past . . . it was extraordinary . . . that element of violence
which was based on all the repressions that one . . .
suffered . . . how do you get to love oneself if everything
you've been told about you is negative? . . . it takes a long
time.[20]

At the same time, the young man who had walked home from the
coffee bars of the sixties through the streets of West Hampstead listening for the blackbird along Abbey Road was still listening for –
and, perhaps more significantly, still hearing – its song. 'It's very
cold. I've just come in slightly drunk from Heaven at 4 a.m.
Somewhere in the rooftops of Phoenix House my blackbird has
started to sing . . . he creates the purest notes like the violin that
dreams with itself alone at the end of Scheherazade.'[21]

In part, it was scarcity of work that sent Jarman out on the town
so frequently. As he confided to his diary: 'Frustration leads to sexual
activity.'[22] And the years 1979 to 1985 were certainly remarkable for
how few of his projects got off the ground; how little 'alchemical
conjunction' there was between matter and light.

Although as a rule he tended to scorn cinematic adaptations and
was not partial to novels, his papers for these years list a number of
mooted adaptations, novelistic and theatrical. In the aftermath of
The Tempest, he talked to Heathcote Williams about working on
two or three projects, including a version of *The Rake's Progress*. He
considered Ronald Firbank's *Prancing Nigger*, Thornton Wilder's *The
Bridge of San Luís Rey*, the Auden–Isherwood collaboration *The
Ascent of F6*, Goethe's *Faust*,[23] *Beowulf*,[24] Thomas Mann's *The Holy
Sinner*[25] and Wyndham Lewis's *The Human Age*.

He talked to Toyah Willcox about *Camberwell Beauty*, a short
film concerning 'the death of a real punk rocker'. He returned time
and again to Egypt as a setting and continued to toy with the idea of
something based on Cleopatra. He read extensively around the life
of Joan of Arc. He hoped to work again with Elisabeth Welch and
Jack Birkett; for the latter, he earmarked the story of Aubrey

Beardsley. He dreamed of starting a film magazine called *City Lights* and of writing about a Soho prostitute.

Together with the young Julian Sands, then undecided whether to be an actor, a director, or a writer – and whom he saw a good deal in the early eighties – Jarman wrote *B Movie*, a lighthearted take on his usually vitriolic views of how Britain was being sold down the river. Subtitled *Little England/A Time of Hope*, *B Movie* is, in every sense of the phrase, a 'Carry On'[26] of *Jubilee* – and, like the earlier film, a remarkably prescient portrait of what would happen to the country in the coming decade.[27]

Borgia Ginz, Lord Protector and dictator of all England, is lying in state in Westminster Hall prior to his funeral service, to be conducted by the Archbishop of Canterbury in the refrigerated vaults of the Churchill Centre for Suspended Animation, where Ginz's body is preserved in ice.

Meanwhile, at Sotheby's, England is being auctioned off. The entire country is bought by C.T. Slicker – except, that is, for Lot 44, the Isle of Dogs, which the busker Adam[28] purchases with 50p handed to him by a passerby.

Adam, who lives on the Battle of Britain Estate, gives his mother, a Marilyn Monroe look-alike, and his father, a teddy boy, his unexpected acquisition as a silver wedding present. With a paper crown taken from a cracker, he proclaims his father King Rocker the First of the Isle of Dogs.

After playing with his band at a nightclub called the Krieg,[29] Adam is summoned to Dorset, Ginz's old country estate, ostensibly to play for C.T. Slicker, Slicker's daughter Veronica[30] and various generals, including Genocide. The occasion is that of Slicker's coronation as King Charles the Last of all England except the Isle of Dogs. On arrival Adam is thrown into prison, where he meets Red Flag, a trade-unionist. Veronica, who has the hots for Adam, persuades her father to let Adam play at the coronation ball after all, then puts a sleeping drug into everyone's drinks so that she can elope with Adam – and, incidentally, Red Flag.

In the Churchill Centre, the body of Borgia Ginz in its ice cube has been wired up to a computer. The screen illuminates briefly with a 'message' from Ginz: 'To be or not to be that is the answer.'

Adam, Veronica and Red Flag cross the Dorset border, where they are stopped by a female customs officer. Forsaking Veronica, Adam and Red Flag flee towards London. The spurned Veronica, King Charles and Genocide set out to wage war on Adam. Back at the Isle of Dogs, where King Rocker and his wife Mary Lou are now living in a caravan, Adam rallies his troops to defend his and his father's little patch of England.

On the 'cryogenic' computer screen, the words '. . . England that was wont to conquer others, hath made a shameful conquest of itself' are appearing.

On her determined march towards the Isle of Dogs, Veronica, crazed by bloodlust, poisons her father and crowns herself. She takes Genocide as her lover. With Veronica's tank crushing everything in its path, Adam's girlfriend, Monique, suggests 'Operation Mantrap'. She and the other girls strip and seduce the Dorset forces. Genocide dies masturbating at the sight.

King Rocker announces he would rather be living in his old home, the Villa Blue Hawaii, so he abdicates and declares England a republic. Veronica is auctioned at Sotheby's. In the Churchill Centre, the computer short-circuits and explodes, burying the Archbishop of Canterbury with it. Adam and Monique toss the crown of England into the sea.

The last line of the script reads: '[Adam] and Monique kiss and the camera pulls away and away and away. Red Flag is the pilot of the helicopter which films this ravishing aerial shot.'[31]

Or that is how it reads in the published version. In the original, the shot is 'ariel'. This could be little more than one of its author's spelling mistakes, but if so, it is a telling slip, Jungian rather than Freudian; a subtle allusion to *The Tempest*, to the importance of not letting magic be eroded.

At around this time, Jarman happened to be talking to the actor and writer Steven Berkoff about the possibility of Berkoff appearing in another of his scripts. Hugely attracted to what he called Berkoff's 'Tom Cat'[32] aura, Jarman was all enthusiasm when it was suggested that he join Berkoff in dashing off a draft screenplay of Berkoff's current stage success, *Decadence*. Seemingly tailor-made for Jarman in terms of invective and a sweeping disregard for the niceties of naturalism, this splenetic study of the English class system and the war between the sexes in fact proved less than ideal as a subject. Unable to bypass its 'torrent of language',[33] Jarman produced a script that was little more than a 'paste up [of] the play with rough indications of the shots'.[34] With supreme self-confidence, Berkoff thought that 'in view of the response from audience and critics, and the great power of the play, it should be simple to raise a miserable £300,000'.[35] As Jarman was fast discovering, however, 'a miserable £300,000' was far from simple to raise, especially given a script as wordy (and therefore uncinematic) as theirs.[36]

There were rough notes for *The Bees of Infinity*,[37] a recycling of an earlier and (for Jarman) immensely evocative title meant to invoke the nature of angels, who, with their honeyed thoughts, are like bees who traverse infinity, carrying wisdom from dead soul to dead soul; wisdom that can only be discovered on earth by an archaeology of soul.[38] On this occasion, the title covered an impressionistic montage of images loosely derived from the work of the French theorist and dramatist Antonin Artaud, whose *A Spurt of Blood* had so impressed Jarman in the mid-sixties.[39] This is not to be confused with *Night Life, The Bees of Infinity, Commonplace Book*, eleven typed pages of single-spaced, equally dreamlike images, many lifted directly from Jarman's past and past writings: the swallows at the Villa Zuassa, a lunch at Stoneleigh Abbey, the Subway 'Fuck Bar'. Others are truly from the realm of dream or nightmare: hacked limbs in an Edwardian office building, a fragment from World War Three in which a nuclear bomb lays waste to Britain, a flower-filled summer field. The piece opens at a desert customs post in Iran. 'A child – myself? – sits at a typewriter or computer on a simple wooden table. On closer inspection the keys of this exquisite machine turn out to be solid silver tablets . . . I watch myself warily.' Although the images that follow are more often distressing than they are peaceful, the piece ends in 'silvery sunlight', in Lombardy, at the 'perfectly comfortable villa from *Through the Billboard Promised Land*, which contains all known knowledge in its perfect geometry'.[40]

There was *Egypt, Egypt, Egypt*, a video project developed with John Maybury and James Mackay who, since helping in their different ways with *Jubilee*, had both become stars in Jarman's filmic firmament. It was intended that *Egypt, Egypt, Egypt*, comprising ten sequences that would result in a film some forty minutes in length, should be shot entirely in a studio and filmed on super-8. The super-8 would then be transferred to video in a new process Jarman, Maybury and Mackay had recently started to explore. As we shall shortly see, in technical terms this was a highly significant development in Jarman's film-making; in terms of ambience and setting, however, the project harked backwards rather than forwards. Besides its obvious dependence on the religious beliefs and practices of ancient Egypt, it recalls *Akenaten* and dips into that relatively small pool of images on which Jarman was constantly drawing, recycling them as continuously – and resourcefully – as his character names and titles.

We are in an empty black room that contains a coffin on a black dais draped with a black silk pall. The pall floats away to reveal the actor, who will be known as Soul, lying in the coffin. Soul is wearing a formal black suit. At his feet is a triangular wreath of red roses. In his hands he holds a skull. On his eyelids are two gold coins.[41] There is a close up of Soul's mouth, from which curls a plume of smoke.

Soul leaves his body and is transformed into a ghostly figure swathed in mummy-like bandages. He floats down a corridor of naked human souls, all wearing the mask of Soul himself, all carrying a mirror that flashes blinding white light into his eyes as he passes. Soul enters an inferno and fragments into a silver snowstorm. We see Anubis, the jackal-headed god, standing alone in the empty black chamber with his exquisite black and gold scales. The scales are six foot high. On them Anubis weighs the souls of the dead. Soul reaches into his bandages and rips out his heart. The bandages turn red. Soul holds his heart above the scales. A drop of blood falls into them and transforms into a ruby. Nepthys, the black-winged goddess of night, appears. Anubis plucks a single feather from her wings and places it on the scales. In a series of superimposed and slow-motion images of sunsets, sunrises and other natural phenomena such as waterfalls and rainbows, the life of Soul flashes past. This cascade of images is held together by the image of Soul, wrapped in a shimmering sheet of gold, dancing his life in reverse. The final image is of

Soul smashing a mirror that reflects the sun. Next, Thoth, the ibis-headed scribe of the gods, enters Soul's life into the Golden Book. Meanwhile, Soul sits cross-legged on the floor in his shimmering scarlet bandages playing a board game for his immortality with the Great Devourer. There is a close up of the board. On a gauze screen, we see, in the form of a stylised shadow play, Soul's body being dis-membered by the Great Devourer, who gorges himself on Soul's flesh and blood. A group of women tear their hair and clothes in a classi-cal show of grief. Soul is then baptised. In reverse motion, and covered in gold, he erupts from the blue waters of paradise. Against a great gold wall, he confronts Osiris, Isis and Horus, who sit enthroned in flames. A storm of golden confetti almost obliterates him as Isis returns his ruby heart. He reaches the fields of the blessed, where, in a great gold chamber, a huge golden ball is passed around as exquisite youths and maidens make love to him. The sequence solarises into the sun.[42]

Originally, the plan had been to film partly on location in Egypt, but the prohibitive expense dictated a studio. The music was to be provided by Brian Eno, possibly from existing but previously unre-leased material, which would be licensed through E.G. Records. The film would be shot in the first half of 1982 for release in September and, if successful, would form the first of a trilogy of tapes co-produced with E.G. Records.

In the event, since none of this came to pass, a year later Jarman and Maybury refashioned Soul's journey for *The Archeology of Soul*, a 'television piece using dance, mime and montage'. Still set to music by Eno, but minus any references to ancient Egypt, this new piece was given its underlying structure by Rilke's *Duino Elegies*.[43]

Using the method he was bringing to bear on *Caravaggio* – the study of the artist's life 'through his pictures' – Jarman then wrote a proposal for a documentary on Robert Medley.[44] The proposal was tied to the 1983 publication of Medley's autobiography and the related retrospective of his work at the Museum of Modern Art in Oxford in the spring of 1984. It was circulated under the auspices of Aldabra, the film production company recently formed by Sarah Radclyffe and Tim Bevan. Their principal area of activity was the pop promo, though solely as a means of gaining the expertise, contacts and money to make features – an ambition which, starting with *My Beautiful Laundrette* and a new company name, Working Title, they were soon to achieve.

Again with Aldabra, and with the dancer Michael Clark in mind, Jarman's next proposal was for:

SLNC

GLDN

SILENCE IS GOLDEN

NIJINSKY'S LAST DANCE

The idea here was to make a twenty-minute film about the final, impromptu dance famously performed by Nijinsky before a group of some 200 people in a room in the Suvretta House Hotel in St Moritz in 1919.[45] Chopin's Prelude 20 in C Minor – part of the music to which Nijinsky danced – would form the basis of a soundtrack that would also include electronic music from the group COIL plus quotations from Nijinsky's diary. The film would integrate archive with staged, hallucinatory footage in a style similar to *In the Shadow of the Sun*. In terms of structure, it would follow *The Archeology of Soul*, with which it shares a constant theme in Jarman's work: a burning desire to escape the confines of the body.[46]

Then came *Lossiemouth*,[47] in essence little more than a simple home movie 'based on film taken by my father during 1940, and telescoping several incidents from his and my mother's life during the early months of world war II'. Not only telescoping, but playing fast and loose with the facts, the film was

> to open with marriage and the picture of Lance and Betts in the lych gate . . . One telegram opened amongst the others at the wedding is an order for Lance to return within 48 hours to Lossiemouth, where he was stationed . . . [He] has to fly on the first operation from Lossiemouth – to bomb the oil installations in Norway to stop them falling into enemy hands. It's a day raid, and it's thought it will be a push over – so when [the] men fly off the wives gather in the mess to prepare tea for their return. The raid isn't a push over,

though, and the planes do not return when expected. Some never return. The wives wait and wait. Eventually, luckily for Betts, Lance's plane is one of those that do return.[48]

Alan Bennett – who had met Jarman on a couple of occasions, once to pick his brains about Morocco for *Prick Up Your Ears*, the film about Joe Orton and Kenneth Halliwell Bennett was scripting for Stephen Frears – was asked by Jarman if he would like to co-write the film. He declined.

More fully realised was *PPP*, or, to give it its full title, *The Assassination of PPP in the Garden of Earthly Delights*, a film in six sequences dealing with the brutal murder of Pasolini.[49] The first sequence is of the filming of *Salo*, Pasolini's final film, in 'a torture yard which resembles the garden of earthly delights of Jerome Bosch in the Prado'. In the second, Pasolini and a young man eat in an expensive restaurant. In the third and fourth, Pasolini picks up a young hustler at the railway station and feeds him in a cheap café. In the background, Christ and his twelve disciples are enjoying a banquet. At a petrol station, a young attendant puts the money Pasolini pays him into his mouth. In the last sequence, as in real life, Pasolini is attacked and killed by the young hustler – though the realism of the scene is compromised when a film star arrives to meet Pasolini and 'CUT' is called.

Jarman also started a script about another of his idols, Jean Cocteau, and his relationship with the young Creole writer Raymond Radiguet.[50] It is 1963. The elderly Cocteau is in a lift. He stares at his reflection in the mirror. 'Mirrors are the doors through which death comes and goes. Watch yourself all your life in a mirror and you will see death at work like bees in a glass hive.' He opens the door to his apartment to find 'a snow blizzard taking place in his room'. His furniture is buried under drifts of snow. Giant icicles hang from the chandeliers. We are taken back in time to Cocteau's childhood and a dialogue between himself and Radiguet. Where Cocteau is hesitant and conservative, Radiguet is an utter rebel. Yet again, Jarman was probing one of his favourite dichotomies.

Another artist to claim Jarman's attention was Vladimir Tatlin, the Russian constructivist. Together with John Chesworth and

Robert Cohan, both of whom Jarman knew from the ballet world, he wrote a treatment on Tatlin in which the artist shows his work to a panel who subject him to an interrogation quite Stalinist in its ferocity. Afterwards, when Tatlin steps outside, we see him walking into Piccadilly and discover that the board he has been facing is none other than the Arts Council, to whom he has been applying for a grant. It is a neat and deeply felt joke – though not one Channel 4, to which the proposal was submitted, thought worthy of committing to the screen.

Of the many unrealised projects that date from the early eighties,[51] there are two full-scale features which, from late 1979 to 1985, though most actively between 1979 and 1981, Jarman tirelessly worked and reworked. They are *Neutron*[52] and *Bob-up-a-Down*.

Artistic as opposed to social and political responsibility, the 'conflict between the active and contemplative life',[53] was a dynamic that had exercised Jarman for many years. In *Neutron*, he placed it at the centre of the film. With *Dr Dee*, the conversation had been with angels; now Jarman wanted it to be between the artist and the revolutionary, the respective characters of Aeon and Topaz.

Like *Night Life*, *The Bees of Infinity*, *Commonplace Book*, *Neutron* starts with a typewriter – in this case Aeon's. It types the opening lines of Rilke's *Duino Elegies*:

> *Who if I cried would hear me*
> *Among the angelic orders*

Simultaneously, a radio is broadcasting jumbled fragments from the Book of Revelations. In combination with 'the muzak of the spheres' and a great deal of static, this religious mumbo-jumbo will continue to be heard throughout the film.

We are in a post-nuclear, apocalyptic world run from an underground bunker. It is all in the starkest contrast to the pre-lapsarian perfection of the world previously inhabited by Aeon and his girlfriend Sophia. He dreams of her and their vanished Arcadia throughout the film.

Aeon is on the run: from the feral children who roam the ruined streets, the ruthless patrols of paramilitary outriders and uniformed orderlies, the crazed religious acolytes who at one point capture him. He is rescued by Topaz, a young revolutionary he once saved, in thanks for which Topaz gave Aeon a gun and two bullets. It is by the gun that Topaz lives. As he says to Aeon: 'While you sang about the end of the world we fought to save it.'

Aeon eventually surrenders to the orderlies and is taken into the bowels of the earth, where he makes two cataclysmic discoveries. The first is that the person in charge is none other than a transformed Topaz, a bizarre Christ figure complete with stigmata and twelve apostles. The second is that Sophia has also been captured and is due for elimination. There is a hint (made gruesomely explicit in the earliest drafts of the script) that the red wine being drunk by the followers of Topaz is actually the blood of other unfortunates who have already been rounded up and eliminated.

Aeon dresses in a white suit, pockets the gun that Topaz gave him and shoots Topaz in the huge central hall. The stigmata transfer to Aeon. Aeon and Topaz are, it is suggested, ultimately the same person; two sides of a single coin.

What Jarman seems to be tracking in the character of Aeon is nothing less than the aeon, or age, of Christ, whose message has been fatally corrupted, not least by the Church. The 'new Jerusalem' of Blake has become a police state run by angels. The only hope of redemption is to wipe the slate clean and begin the journey again.

The literary and filmic origins of *Neutron* are various. There was Jarman's extensive reading of Jung, whose *Aion* gave the artist–Christ figure his name. There were the revelations of St John the Divine; Blake; *1984*; *Heroes and Villains*, Angela Carter's postapocalyptic novel of a world divided between town and jungle. There was all of science fiction, plus any number of Jarman's own earlier writings.

The script sprang equally (and arguably more pressingly) from contemporary politics and Jarman's Blakean vision of the Conservative Party as greedy despoilers and belittlers of his beloved Albion. The most telling symbol he could envisage for this new barbarism was the recently developed neutron bomb, which was popularly held to have the chilling capacity to destroy people without damaging property.[54] As important was Lee Drysdale, 'the Artful

Dodger of Cine-History,' who partnered Jarman in writing the initial script. The dialogue between Topaz and Aeon was largely the dialogue that East End, working-class Drysdale, a member of the Worker's Revolutionary Party, enjoyed with Metroland, middle-class Jarman.

As this political and verbal sparring match moved between Phoenix House and end-of-the-round breaks in Soho for lunch or tea, so the possibilities in store for the emerging script started to escalate. Kendon Films, the name under which Don Boyd was then operating, offered Jarman script-development money and to produce the film, while Guy Ford made a casting suggestion that prompted Jarman to jettison any ideas he may have harboured to shoot on super-8 for next to nothing.[55] Dusting down an idea he had first suggested when Jarman was working on *Akenaten*, Ford ventured David Bowie as the perfect Aeon. Jarman leaped at the idea and flew with Ford to Switzerland to meet Bowie and discuss the script. To their delight, Bowie seemed interested. Christopher Hobbs was asked to draw an elaborate storyboard. Locations such as Battersea Power Station and/or the Berlin Wall were enthusiastically mooted. Steven Berkoff, then appearing in *Hamlet*, was asked if he would bring his 'Tom Cat' aura to the part of the revolutionary Topaz. Bowie was taken to see Berkoff perform and to watch a screening of *Jubilee*.

Jarman was in film heaven. For all that he liked to rubbish the mainstream, he was far from impervious to the benefits of having someone of Bowie's stature attached to his script – even if the singer had said his name could not be used to raise the money. But as quickly as it had come together, it all fell apart. Boyd was in America and, in Jarman's view, thus unable to move the project along with the speed needed to ensure Bowie's continued commitment. Then an incident in London further discouraged *Neutron*'s prospective leading man. After the screening of *Jubilee*, Bowie asked Jarman if he was a magician, an imputation Jarman rightly – and hotly – denied. There the matter might have rested, had not Bowie, after a visit to Phoenix House, left behind an empty Marlboro packet. Jarman, never immune to celebrity, put the packet on the mantelpiece, where he knew it would provide an impressive talking point. Bowie paid the flat a further visit and – as perceived by Jarman – was so

horrified to see the trophy so prominently displayed that he immediately bowed out and went to New York to play *The Elephant Man*,
taking with him the chances not only of *Neutron* being made as a
big-budget film, but, as things turned out, of it being realised at all.
Afterwards Jarman would laugh at how susceptible Bowie must have
been to see the cigarette packet as a talisman, a means of subduing
him to Jarman's wishes, though of course Bowie might simply have
been disturbed to find such fan-like behaviour in a putative director – or perhaps he was having second thoughts about the script.
After all, in its early drafts it was uncomfortably uncompromising: in
addition to cannibalism, there was the graphic rape and murder by
Topaz of a young girl.

For someone who, at least until *The Tempest*, was accustomed to
work and money coming in search of him rather than the other way
around, the early collapse of *Neutron*, allied as it was to an ongoing
difficulty with the funding of *Caravaggio*, came as a body blow, a blow
exacerbated by the behaviour of Guy Ford. Over the years, Ford had
become invaluable to Jarman as a general factotum and Man Friday,
but, as a result of falling victim to heroin, had developed an alarming propensity to 'lose' or be 'robbed' of money he was given. Finally
he was caught forging Don Boyd's signature on a cheque. At first,
Jarman did everything in his power to protect his friend. He persuaded Boyd not to pursue the matter of the cheque. He gave Ford
money. He asked Nicholas Ward-Jackson to provide Ford with a
room during a period of homelessness. But as the heroin took over
and Ford spiralled out of control, heading towards a spell in
Wormwood Scrubs, Jarman began to distance himself from his
former collaborator.

At the same time, he was casting around for another way of taking
Neutron forward, using the summer of 1980 to rework the script with
a second collaborator, Tim Sullivan. Fresh out of university, where he
had read law, but keen to make films, Sullivan had met Jarman
through a mutual friend, been invited to Phoenix House to see the
super-8s and, on the basis of that one meeting, received a call asking
if he was willing to help knock *Neutron* into better shape. He most
certainly was, and worked extensively on the script with Jarman,
putting it through a number of drafts.[56]

Meanwhile, Jarman was reacquainting himself with Vanessa Redgrave, an even more ardent member of the Worker's Revolutionary Party than Lee Drysdale. Although he did not 'agree with Vanessa's theories for the solution of the problems', he did applaud 'her analysis of what the problems are' and in his ongoing research for his script was fascinated to observe at first hand 'what an artist with great passion was doing'.[57] The observation was short-lived, but while it lasted, Jarman accompanied Redgrave to political meetings and on more than one march. That New Year's Eve, instead of going to the Logans' party as usual, he even helped spread her gospel:

> We drove up to the flats in Marchmont Street, near where I had lived in 1963, and worked our way down the dimly lit corridors in the freezing cold . . . The reception at each flat was unexpected – a small bald man cautiously peered round one door, and when he recognised Vanessa his eyes popped. He quickly disappeared, and we heard an excited whispered conversation. He reappeared with the words – 'Go away Vanessa, we don't want your type round here. We vote Conservative.' And closed the door firmly. I couldn't help smiling, and I think Vanessa caught me.[58]

Sadly, the changes to *Neutron* failed to improve its prospects. At the end of 1980, Jarman put the script aside to sleep 'between its covers like a Cruise or Pershing in its silo'.[59] In the summer of 1983, he gave it a final revision, this time with the help of the social historian Jon Savage, who had become a close friend,[60] though by then events had overtaken the project. Films like *Escape from New York* (1981) and *Blade Runner* (1982) had covered similar ground. Soon *Brazil* (1985) would be added to their number and Jarman would be siphoning much of the atmosphere of *Neutron* into another film entirely. It must also be acknowledged that for all the vividness of its setting, because *Neutron*'s public and political aspects interested Jarman only in terms of quite personal concerns – the limits of his own spirituality, for instance, and what was essentially a private dialogue between the two sides of his nature – it has a hermetic quality that mitigates against narrative clarity. Later he would admit ruefully: 'I never really worked it out properly.'[61]

Neutron's final image, that of Aeon as a mediaeval pilgrim with 'a palmer's wide-brimmed hat and a shepherd's staff', setting out on 'a brilliant sunny day'[62] to start his journey anew could as easily have come from the other feature over which Jarman was labouring at much the same time: *Bob-up-a-Down*. The period here is resolutely mediaeval, the setting agreeably rural: the Isle of Purbeck, in fact. The story is one of Jarman's most straightforward, certainly most heterosexual. Prophesy, a young girl from a small village above Dancing Ledge, is claimed in marriage by the blacksmith, Rollo, but has set her heart on the coal-black figure of Bob-up-a-Down, the charcoal-burner who lives in a hut on the outskirts of the village and clambers through the trees wild as a monkey, playing his hurdy-gurdy. Gytha, Prophesy's grandmother, plots with Rauf, a blind priest, to ensure Prophesy's marriage to Rollo. In desperation, Prophesy visits the Anchoress, a seer who lives nearby immured in a stone cairn. The Anchoress gives Prophesy two amulets which she promises will set her free. Although the amulets do not in the short term protect her from the plans laid by Rollo, Gytha and Rauf – against her will she is married to Rollo – on their wedding night, Prophesy's ring falls into the fire and in attempting to retrieve it Rollo is burned alive. Meanwhile, in fury, Bob has set fire to the Anchoress in her cairn. Later he will also kill Rauf, the blind priest. The men of the village go hunting for Bob, who manages to outwit and kill them all. Prophesy goes to sit on the seashore. Bob finds her. She turns away. The women of the village approach and force Bob into the sea, where he drowns. They then build a cairn around Prophesy, who begins to sing with the voice of the old Anchoress.

The sources for this story, originally titled *The Spring under a Thorn*, were principally Jarman's and were culled from as far back as Canford and King's, where he had first read Chaucer and *Piers Plowman*, plus a plethora of more recent but similarly mediaeval influences: *The Book of Margery Kempe*, for example, and the York cycle of miracle plays. The script itself, however, was written almost entirely by Tim Sullivan who, because he was on the dole at the time and had nothing to lose, said yes when, on finishing work on

Neutron, Jarman asked him whether he would care to write an original script. He was given Jarman's source books, allotted the room in Hanway Works and supplied with the simplest of briefs. Jarman wanted an anchoress who was walled up in a cairn, a charcoal-burner, a part for blind Jack Birkett, for the dialogue to be in mediaeval English and the script to play like a mediaeval Japanese horror story.

Sullivan had barely started work when Jarman flew to New York for the opening of *The Tempest*. Not surprisingly, his state of mind on his return somewhat interfered with the progress on the script, which was further hampered when Sullivan landed a job with Granada Television. But they persevered, producing an early draft in August 1980, another in February 1981 and a third that October. Thereafter, Jarman continued for some years to tinker with the script, though more or less on his own.

Bob-up-a-Down's production history, such as it was, was decidedly less star-struck than *Neutron*'s and considerably shorter-lived. Jarman gave Don Boyd first refusal to provide development finance, an offer Boyd declined. Backing was then obtained from the National Film Development Fund (NFDF), the fund administered by the government-instituted National Film Finance Corporation (NFFC) to help develop scripts the corporation believed stood a reasonable chance of commercial success. The money hardly represented riches, but it did at least mean that Sullivan and Jarman were not longer working for nothing. Various submissions of the script followed, none successful, until, like *Neutron*, *Bob-up-a-Down* was overtaken by other films, and by Jarman's eventual indifference. Though he would remain fond of the story, his final word on the subject, as included in his introduction to the script, published alongside *Neutron* in *Up in the Air*, was that circumstances had 'liberated' him from 'a worthy film'.[63]

In *Dancing Ledge*, in an entry dated 4 February 1983, Jarman writes: 'Nicholas [Ward-Jackson] rang from Rome last night and . . . swore he'd serve writs on the producers . . . if they thought of producing my script of *Bob-up-a-Down*, which the British Film Institute might finance, which he added was hardly a film script at all.'[64] Desperate to protect the interests of the other script on which Jarman was labouring throughout these years – the convoluted story of Michelangelo Merisi from Caravaggio – Ward-Jackson had become increasingly dismayed by Jarman's professional promiscuity. He had been particularly upset by *Neutron* and *The Tempest*, especially as the latter had come so hard on the heels of the very first draft of *Caravaggio*. Indeed, he and Jarman might easily have fallen out over the Shakespeare if, once he had expressed his disapproval, Ward-Jackson had not decided that the better course of action was to embark on a second draft of the Caravaggio script with another writer.

The person he commissioned was Simon Raven, who swiftly produced a second, substantially longer version of the Caravaggio story. Raven used many of the elements of Jarman's first script, and faithfully followed Ward-Jackson's brief to be as sexually explicit as he wished. The result, however, was much more conventional, less fevered and playful, than Jarman's original. Ward-Jackson sent it to Jarman with the scribbled note: 'For Derek who will now proceed to run another mile, with love from Nicholas.'

Which is precisely what Jarman did – but in the opposite direction, as if only then could he reclaim ownership of his material. As soon as *The Tempest* was complete, and under a new title, *Penny Dreadful*, he sketched a simplified version of Caravaggio's story 'to be realised in a large empty sound stage painted grey . . . ideally everything should be constructed to have the scarcity of one of Caravaggio's paintings – absolutely no props except for those called for in the action – all the costumes to be faithful reproductions of those in the paintings with the exception of the baroque extravaganza dinner party – the lighting to be that of Caravaggio's own paintings, abstract and not realistic, so that the figures are etched like jewels against the void'.[65]

In essence, this is how the film was finally made: in a studio, against the sparsest of settings, using a combination of costume, light and sound to create richness and historical detail. But this was not how Ward-Jackson envisaged his pet project, not at that stage. In 1980, between working on *Neutron* and *Bob-up-a-Down*, Jarman was urged to 'unsimplify' the story and take it out of the studio. In one draft he added a contemporary element by starting the film with a group of tourists being shown *The Beheading of St John the Baptist*, then flashing back to 1595 and the young Caravaggio. In another, subtly different version of a similar vintage, this modern framing device was jettisoned in favour of one somewhat closer to that used in the finished film: the three days Caravaggio spent in jail in Porto Ercole shortly before his death. This version was entitled *Blue is Poison*, a title taken from Caravaggio's choice of red rather than blue paint for the Virgin Mary's dress because, he said, 'blue is poison'. Ultramarine blue was also, of course, the most expensive of colours, which was one of the reasons why it was generally reserved for the Virgin.[66]

In March 1981, this framing device was edged towards its final form. The script was now bracketed not by Caravaggio in jail, but by Caravaggio on his deathbed. Jarman's aim had always been to tell the artist's story through his paintings, with the paintings themselves providing the narrative. By structuring the film as the delirium of the dying protagonist, he was able to bind it indivisibly to the process of creation he was intent on dissecting. 'The alchemist and painter reduce and restrain the burning action of light. They separate the sky from the earth, the ash from the sublimate, the outside from the inside, and when the hour of happiness is over carefully gather the heaped up ashes.'[67]

Next, as if fearing that the project might be escaping him and to remind himself of its personal relevance, its author reintroduced a modern element.[68] Now the story is 'framed' by Jarman himself being phoned by Chase Manhattan III, an American film producer who asks if Jarman will make a sexploitation film of Caravaggio for the video market. By literally writing himself into the script, Jarman makes explicit the links and similarities between himself and his subject.

A voice-over by Baglione, Caravaggio's rival, is intercut with Vincent Canby's verdict on *The Tempest*. Caravaggio speaks the opening lines from Ginsberg's *Howl* ('I saw the best minds of my generation destroyed by madness . . .') and 'dreams' of Alexander the Great making love: 'Imagine the chain of lust which separates my bed from Alexander the conqueror of the world. The emperor and the soldier the soldier and the philosopher the philosopher and the waiter the waiter and the gypsy the gypsy and the artist a great arc of semen spurting across the centuries.'[69] While studying the painting

The Martyrdom of St Matthew, the character of Jarman says: 'God I hate priests . . . the pernicious self-hatred they've fostered amongst homosexuals themselves, which is the key to Caravaggio's life and destruction – it's written all over the painting.' And when Caravaggio paints the Pope, Borghese touches on the debate Jarman was having with himself in *Neutron*: 'Revolutionary gestures in art are a great help to us; keeps the quo in the status. Never hear of a revolution made with paintbrushes, hadn't thought of that, had you?'[70] The character of Pasqualone, the village idiot, is introduced. The young Caravaggio and a childhood friend inspect Pasqualone's penis, an escapade echoing Jarman's childhood infatuation with Davide at Villa Zuassa. The version ends with Jarman walking along the beach at Porto Ercole. A boy – the young Caravaggio – is mending a fishing net. He puts out his hand. Jarman takes it. We freeze on the two, linked hands.

In his partial account of the making of *Caravaggio* in *Dancing Ledge*, Jarman writes: 'Had Caravaggio been reincarnated in this century it would have been as a film-maker, Pasolini.'[71] By identifying Caravaggio with perhaps his favourite film-maker and giving his latest version of the script such a clear autobiographical element, Jarman was spelling out the ways in which he saw himself reflected in his subject. Apart from his homosexuality, which Jarman could only guess at, there was the defiant use Caravaggio made in his work of the young men with whom he consorted; the fact that as an innovator – most notably for his startling use of ordinary people as models for the saints – he was both derided and misunderstood; the struggle to balance the turbulence of his social life with his need, as a painter, for contemplation and quiet. These similarities between author and subject provided Jarman with a powerful means of examining the artist as he exists in relation to society and, in particular, the intriguing tension between the violence of Caravaggio's life and the restrained, classical nature of his work.

For many of these versions of the script – including the one that followed a year later, in July 1982, when the autobiographical element was removed and such references as there were to the twentieth century were expressed more subtly, through props and sound effects – Jarman had been using outside help.[72] Now came a truly major outside influence. She came at the insistence of Ward-Jackson and in the formidable form of Suso Cecchi D'Amico, the Italian scriptwriter who, in a long and notable career, had worked extensively with Luchino Visconti on such films as *Bellissima*, *Senso* and *Le Notti Bianche* (White Nights).

In early 1983 Jarman flew to Rome to meet D'Amico at her flat in the Via Paisiello, just across the road from the block where he had lived as a child – and where, he now noticed, there was a mimosa tree, 'a cloud of yellow set off against an ochre palazzo'.[73] Speaking 'rapidly in Italian with a deep bass', D'Amico told Jarman that 'Caravaggio has to be more forceful, the script more violent'. They must, she said, 'concentrate on the murder of Ranuccio'.[74]

Jarman was tongue-tied and, when he left the apartment after that first meeting, dropped his pen, smashing the nib. If the sight of mimosa – his grandmother's favourite flower – had been a good omen, this he took as quite the reverse. Yet in a manner of speaking, to smash his pen was precisely what was needed. As he and D'Amico continued to meet through the following week to sip tea, discuss art as a form of theft, gossip about Visconti and watch an Italian film on St Filippo Neri for period detail, she helped him to jettison anything that stood in the way of reassessing character motivation and distilling the story into a more coherent whole. The central character of the mute assistant was introduced, as were a couple of major plot points concerning Ranuccio and Lena, the young couple with whom Caravaggio becomes so obsessively and disastrously involved. We see Lena consciously planning to fall pregnant by the Pope's nephew, Scipione Borghese, to ensure her place in his affections. As before, it is a course of action that backfires – she is drowned in the Tiber and Ranuccio is accused of her murder. As before, it seems likely that Scipione has engineered her death and Caravaggio pleads unsuccessfully, first with Scipione, then the Pope, for Ranuccio's release from prison. The new development is that on his release, Ranuccio confesses to Caravaggio that he did kill Lena, because she stood in their way. It is this unexpected and chilling confession that provokes Caravaggio into killing Ranuccio. 'We build a house very strong,' D'Amico told Jarman. 'After we furnish. Then the film will be small masterpiece.'[75]

Ever since the moment in 1980 when Jarman had been required to 'unsimplify' the script, Ward-Jackson had wanted a big-budget film. As we shall shortly see, this ambition was horribly thwarted, with the result that in December 1984 Jarman reverted to his earlier title, *Blue is Poison*, and started to reduce the script to the level of his 1979 *Penny Dreadful* treatment. 'This script is the 13th rewrite of the story of Caravaggio,' he wrote in a preface to the new version. 'The film is intended to be made against simple black drapes in one studio set with props, with a very low budget . . . It would be shot in 16mm, transferred to video, and edited with video effects before being blown up to 35mm . . . The characters would not attempt to look like their originals in the paintings – the paintings would be filmed from slides.'[76]

Just how difficult and draining the process of arriving at a '13th rewrite' had been is reflected in the words Jarman chose to introduce the final scripts. They belong to Picasso: 'Nothing can come about without loneliness. I have created a loneliness for myself which no-one can imagine.'

Standing behind these many rewrites, holding the hoops through which the scripts were required to jump, was ringmaster Ward-Jackson, blessed in equal measure by drive, enthusiasm and naïveté, certainly where film was concerned. In 1978, at the start of the process, Ward-Jackson had taken delivery of Jarman's first draft, the one written in Rome, and shown it to Melvyn Bragg at London Weekend Television. Bragg suggested doing a mini-version of the story for the *South Bank Show*. Such a programme would, it was argued, provide an effective 'trailer' for the feature to follow. Ward-Jackson worried that this might have the contrary effect of stealing the feature's thunder. Jarman agreed and they did not pursue the idea.

Then came *The Tempest*. After Ward-Jackson had overcome his anger at Jarman for allowing himself to be distracted, he went to visit his errant director at Stoneleigh Abbey to suggest they hire another writer. At the back of Ward-Jackson's mind was the worry that they were losing time and that Jarman's first draft might lack narrative clarity. By now he had discussed the draft both with Bragg and with Mamoun Hassan of the NFFC. Hassan had told Ward-Jackson he could only fund projects with a proper script, admitting to some doubts regarding Jarman's scriptwriting ability.

Jarman did not particularly relish the idea of another writer laying hands on his material, but he could hardly object, so he gave his nominal blessing to Simon Raven. Then, when he had finished *The Tempest*, he promptly reclaimed the script for himself, citing the fact – with which Ward-Jackson could scarcely disagree – that Raven's version, albeit competent, lacked originality. The exercise had been misguided, and although it did not adversely affect Ward-Jackson's relationship with Jarman, it did sow the seeds of a certain disillusion and doubt.

Ward-Jackson continued to maintain a dialogue with Hassan and Bragg, and to proclaim the project as being in firm pre-production. The truth of the matter, however, was that *Caravaggio* had hit a wall, leaving the fledgling producer unsure where to turn next. Nor was his position helped by *The Tempest*'s disastrous American première. Such an impasse might have caused some people to temper their ambitions or give up entirely. Ward-Jackson merely raised his sights, becoming convinced that Jarman's past failures stemmed primarily from a shortage of resources. Jarman himself was ambivalent on this point: part of him welcomed the thought of a big budget, part of him hated the idea. But he was happy to let Ward-Jackson follow his nose. Who knew where it might lead? So, with Ward-Jackson still footing all the bills and slipping Jarman what pennies he could to help keep the wolf from the door, Jarman continued to rework the script – and to hedge his bets with *Neutron* and *Bob-up-a-Down*.

In May 1981, Ward-Jackson flew with Jarman to the Cannes Film Festival. The Croisette, it was hoped, would be teeming with co-production partners. Back in London, he had Jarman approach and interview potential actors – including Nigel Terry for the title role. The thinking was that by attaching the right names to the project, the money would be easier to find. At the same time, since Italy was, after all, where they planned to shoot the film, and Ward-Jackson was a frequent visitor there in his capacity as an art dealer, the indefatigable producer concentrated on exploring possibilities within the Italian film industry.

This avenue of approach led first to Giuliani de Negri, producer of the Taviani brothers. Jarman greatly admired De Negri's work and was delighted to be flown to Tuscany to meet the man, as were Christopher Hobbs and Yolanda Sonnabend, both slated at different points to design the film. Then, in early 1982, attentions switched to Giacomo Pezzali, a tycoon with fingers in many pies, business and political.[77]

From the outset, Pezzali's apparent enthusiasm for *Caravaggio* as a big-budget Italian feature allowed Ward-Jackson to renew his dialogue with the NFFC, who were happy to join forces with Pezzali as long as there was at least one further co-production partner. Ward-Jackson turned to the newly formed Channel 4. Not yet on air, but everywhere evident, Britain's first new television station since the inception of BBC2 had, as part of their remit, a very real commitment to the funding and screening of British films. Not only had they already purchased a considerable catalogue of such films, including Jarman's, they were also actively commissioning new work from independent film-makers on a co-production basis. They entered willingly into discussion with Ward-Jackson, and although no contract was signed, their commitment seemed as solid as was necessary.

There were further casting sessions at Phoenix House. Jarman began studying Italian. A new lawyer was put in charge of matters contractual. And at a timely exhibition that was running at the Royal Academy – *Painting in Naples 1606–1705: from Caravaggio to Giordano* – a grand party was thrown to announce the film. That December, Jarman flew once more to Rome with Ward-Jackson, this time in the hope of signing contracts with the Italian co-producers. Significantly, no such contracts were signed, though the co-producers did slip Jarman '£1,000 on Christmas eve'.[78] Christmas was spent with Ward-Jackson in Tuscany, where news reached them of a controversy designed to dent Jarman's marketability.

According to the *Daily Star* of 30 December 1982, Britain faced the danger of 'MORE CHANNEL 4 SHOCKERS. They buy two gay films for showing uncut.' The films specified were *Nighthawks* and *Sebastiane*. In a diatribe that stretched across two pages, the paper fulminated against Channel 4 for buying a film in which, it claimed, 'the Latin dialogue is used to disguise a script packed with pornographic language'. It quoted one 'TV insider' as saying: 'I know Channel 4 is keen to cater for minorities, but homosexual gladiators must be the smallest minority of the year.' A Tory MP called for the withdrawal of the station's right to broadcast, while in an accompanying article, Patrick Hill – who had seen the film 'at an extremely private showing' – had a burning question for the channel's chief executive, Jeremy Isaacs: 'Will you let your teenage son and daughter watch this film?'

In their defence, Channel 4 issued a reply to the effect that the films had been bought as part of a package. They had no intention of actually showing them. Later, Isaacs would explain that of course this was not the case. They had every intention of showing the films and had said what they had simply to throw the tabloids off the scent. Jarman might also have taken comfort from the fact that the newspapers' target was less obviously himself than the new television station, which had been coming in for a great deal of tabloid flak since going on air that November. But he had never had to face such public hostility before. The experience left him and his confidence in the new channel, severely shaken.

He put on a brave face. 'New Years Resolutions – Get on with it,' he wrote in his appointments diary on 1 January. But the furore over *Sebastiane* could not have come at a more sensitive time. Behind the scenes, discussions with Channel 4 over *Caravaggio* had not been progressing smoothly. There were reservations about the script – which, it suddenly transpired, were shared by Pezzali. Enter Suso Cecchi D'Amico, whose pedigree impressed everyone, not just her collaborator, and whose work on the script seemed to do the trick. There were further recces to Italy and excited talk of filming at the Villa d'Este. To ensure that 'Thumper' (as Ward-Jackson's assistant, Francesca Moffat, had nicknamed Jarman) did not bounce off elsewhere, Ward-Jackson finally insisted that his director abandon *Neutron* and *Bob-up-a-Down*. It was high time, he said, that Jarman 'rationalise a career that had been continuously without focus'.[79]

Then, out of the blue, came the bombshell: Channel 4 withdrew. The official reason given was a conflict of interest with the NFFC, which wanted a three-year 'window' in which to exhibit the film theatrically before it appeared on television, while Channel 4 demanded the right to show it sooner. Unofficial sources whispered that the new channel had overextended itself financially and was technically bankrupt.

Jarman confided to his diary that *Caravaggio* had changed 'from a positive to a negative force in my life . . . the centre of the project has gradually shifted from a film I would make to a film at any cost and my life and friends have been sacrificed to his obsessions as Nicholas declared them inadequate to fulfil his dreams . . . an enormous lethargy set in as the project foundered'.[80]

With hindsight, it can be argued that Ward-Jackson and Jarman showed undue naïveté in pinning their hopes on Channel 4 without a contract. In addition, if they had been more canny, they might have waited to see if the whispers about bankruptcy were true – and if, when the money came on stream again, they could resurrect the deal. As it was, they felt too let down. They fired off a letter to the station's board of directors, accusing the channel of dishonest behaviour and of jeopardising a major British production by a major British director. And at that year's Edinburgh Film Festival, at a conference on independent production, Ward-Jackson made an impassioned speech that reiterated the charges levelled in the letter.

If there had been any chance of reviving Channel 4's interest at a later date, this had been well and truly scuppered. Now Pezzali, whom Jarman had never quite trusted, announced that without Channel 4, he too was withdrawing. Before long, the NFFC had done the same. Hopes for *Caravaggio* as a big-budget feature lay in shreds.

Jarman interpreted Channel 4's rejection of *Caravaggio* as a rejection of his entire modus operandi. He even saw it as a rejection of a whole swathe of independent film-makers – and by the very people who should have been supporting such independence. Hurt and angry, he hankered after the 'wild west' of the seventies when, for all the difficulties that the British film industry had faced, a maverick like Don Boyd could fund a handful of films without reference to too many orthodoxies. Channel 4, compromised by a necessary alliance with advertisers, had 'put barbed wire across our prairie'.[81] Jarman wished

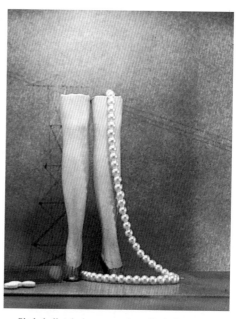

We Wait, c. 1960.
Private Collection/photograph: Fraser Marr

Slade ballet design: scene from Prokofiev's *The Prodigal Son*, 1967.
Present whereabouts unknown/photograph: Ray Dean

Cool Waters, oil on canvas with tap and rail, c. 1966.
Collection/photograph: Ray Dean

Dress rehearsal, *Don Giovanni*. Sadler's Wells Opera Company, Coliseum, London, August 1968. *Ray Dean*

Dress rehearsal, *Silver Apples of the Moon*.
New Theatre, Oxford, October 1973.
Estate of Derek Jarman

Kevin Whitney and Luciana Martinez on super-8 in
The Art of Mirrors, 1973.
James Mackay

Two of the *GBH* series and Andy Marshall's grandfather clock, ICA, London, 1984. *Estate of Derek Jarman*

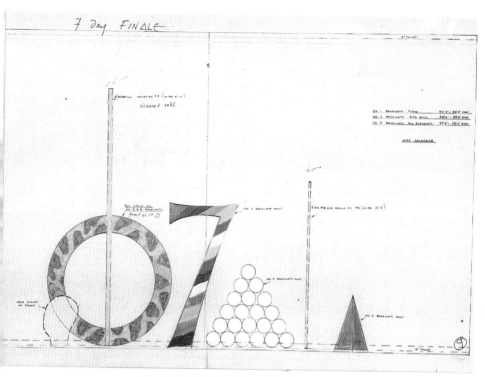

Design for the finale of *Jazz Calendar*, 1967.
Royal Opera House

Jarman hanging *Sculpture Garden*, c. 1967.
resent whereabouts unknown/photograph: Ray Dean

Jarman holding *Construction*, c. 1968.
Present whereabouts unknown/photograph: Ray Dean

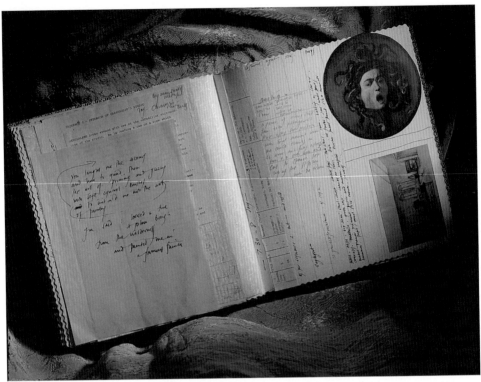

Workbook for *Caravaggio*, 1985. *Estate of Derek Jarman*

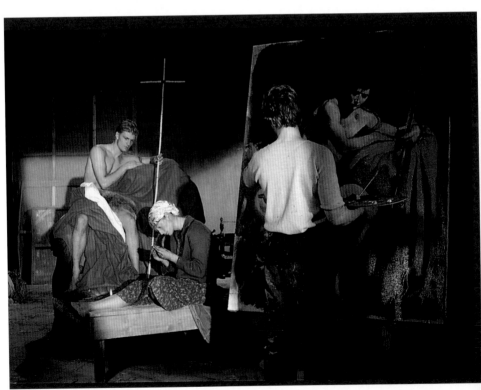

Lena (Tilda Swinton) sits at her lover's feet while Caravaggio *Nigel Terry* paints
Ranuccio (Sean Bean) as St John the Baptist, *Caravaggio*, 1985. *Mike Laye*

Tilda Swinton
in *The Last of England*, 1986.
Mike Laye

Prospect Cottage.
Howard Sooley

The interior of Prospect Cottage.
Howard Sooley

The garden at Prospect Cottage.
Howard Sooley

Silence, mixed media, 1986.
Estate of Derek Jarman/photograph:
Prudence Cummings Associates

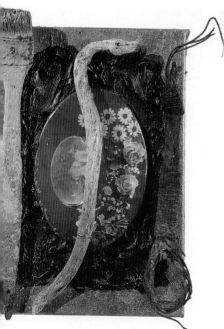

The Serpent, mixed media, 1989.
*Private collection/photograph: Prudence
Cummings Associates*

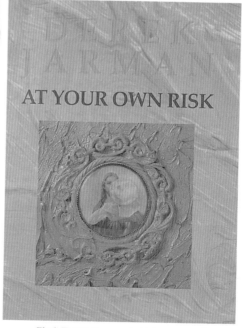

Flesh Tint as incorporated into an unused
cover design for *At Your Own Risk,* 1992.
Chris Mackenzie/Random House

Clancy Chassay as the young Wittgenstein is harangued by his tutors, played by Anna Campeau, Roger Cook, Michael O'Pray, Tony Peake, Michelle Wade and Tania Wade. *Wittgenstein*, 1993. *Howard Sooley*

Fuck Me Blind, oil on canvas, 1993.
Estate of Derek Jarman/photograph: Prudence Cummings Associates

Jarman painting *Dead Sexy*, 1993.
Howard Sooley

for Warhol, another figure from the 'wild west': 'an absolute icon. Because one of the things that Andy did was say "yes" to everyone . . . Suddenly all the people who are saying "no no no" are in power.'[82]

As we have seen, money during the montage years of the early eighties was in uncomfortably short supply. To supplement what little came in from his films and scripts, or from Ward-Jackson in hand-outs, Jarman borrowed from friends, did a fair amount of teaching, sold the occasional painting and undertook some design work,[83] notably in a new collaboration with Ken Russell, who had been asked by the Florentine company Teatro Comunale to direct a production of Stravinsky's *The Rake's Progress* as part of the city's 1982 annual musical festival, the forty-fifth such Maggio Musicale Fiorentino. The venue was the ravishingly pretty Teatro della Pergola; the conductor Riccardo Chailly. Jarman had not been Russell's first choice as designer (that had been Mike Annals), but Russell was confident Jarman would give him what he wanted: an updating of the Auden–Kallman libretto from eighteenth-century London to the present day.

And indeed he did. Jarman's visualisation of Tom Rakewell's journey from innocence to depravity and thence to Bedlam, in the course of which he moves from the country to London and falls prey to the temptations of the plausible but sinister Nick Shadow, could hardly have been more up to the minute. For his arrival on to the London 'scene', Rakewell sported a gold suit, sailor cap and T-shirt 'depicting Mrs Thatcher as a vampire holding a skull'. Shadow finally became 'a drug dealer in a heavy black leather coat . . . with his heroin death-kit'. The brothel-keeper, Mother Goose, wore 'Queen Mother drag'[84] – a white ballgown, blue satin sash and tiara – and was accompanied by a chorus in army camouflage gear suggestive of the Falklands War. Anne Trulove, Rakewell's girlfriend, bore a distinct resemblance to Lady Di. The street outside Rakewell's London home was peopled by punks and piled high with black plastic refuse bags from the Winter of Discontent. Among many other such 'art objects', the house's interior boasted an enormous Hockney on the rear wall. One of the artifacts in the scene in which Rakewell's belongings are auctioned was a blow-up plastic woman wearing black knickers. The graveyard in which the hero's nemesis arrives to collect his payment became an underground platform at Angel. A large overhead clock hinted that time was running out, an exit sign indicated the direction Rakewell would be taking, a series of Hogarth portraits slyly replaced the usual adverts on the white tiled walls as a reminder of the opera's genesis. The same walls, nicely reminiscent of Jarman's and Russell's first collaboration, *The Devils*, doubled for the institutional bleakness of Bedlam. For this final scene, the principals wore eighteenth-century costume. The drop cloth provided another link between the opera's past and present: on it Jarman placed a period swain and his paramour against the background of an illuminated Piccadilly Circus.

It was a rushed and eventful job. Russell first approached Jarman in mid-March, just two months short of the opening night; no time at all to design sets and costumes for a full-length opera in three acts plus an epilogue. But Jarman had good reasons to accept. He was broke, had always enjoyed working with Russell, and he saw the commission as 'a kind of revenge.'[85] It allowed him to make the demonic Shadow's 'home' a television set, to criticise Thatcher, to mock the indiscriminate consumerism of the art world by visualising Rakewell's London residence as a mad museum.

After a frantic few days in London, 'collecting magazines and books that throw up ideas – punk, "new romantic", the Royal Family, horse racing' – he flew out to Florence to show the management his notebooks and explain that he was 'never going to be able to make finished drawings for an opera with nine separate sets and about one hundred costumes in ten days'.[86]

In mid-April, he was moving between Florence and Rome, where some of the costumes were being made. In Rome, in the course of his own rakish progress through the city, he was attacked one night on the Capitoline Hill. 'Cruising the parks brings an immense exhilaration,' he wrote. 'You leave the everyday world behind, with all the repressions you have acquired to adjust to straight society.'[87] That particular evening it was drizzling and the usually busy park was deserted. Jarman was set upon by a gang of youths and relieved of everything he carried, 'about 50p and a bottle of poppers'. The only blessing was that as his assailants were wearing Italian shoes – 'soft Gucci numbers' as opposed to the heavy 'bovver boots' that would have been the chosen footwear of their British counterparts[88] – the bruising they inflicted was superficial. All the same: 'The whole experience and the aftermath was like the motorcycle crash I had several years ago when we wrote off Alasdair's Laverda. I know now that when an animal is killed it feels nothing. In extremity the senses are scrambled.'[89] And when he confided the experience to the rehearsal pianist back in Florence, the pianist showed him a sobering item from the next day's paper: 'That night a businessman from Turin had been murdered in exactly the same spot.'[90]

Less life-threatening were the confrontations in rehearsal. Jarman endowed the angels with gargantuan phalluses, which led to a battle with the management over what was acceptable, length-wise, on the stage of the Pergola. When one chorus member was supplied with a scarf bearing the logo of Solidarity, the Polish trade union, the communist stage-hands came out on strike. Rakewell's inflatable plastic woman, which had to be smuggled into the country in the first place, was given its black knickers only because of further management misgivings: they insisted that such a salacious prop could not be allowed onstage nude.

These were contretemps which Jarman rather enjoyed, even when he lost, and when, at its première in mid-May, the opera was enthusiastically received, he professed himself well pleased with the result: 'Modern London is perfectly at home in the Pergola Theatre. My operatic punks and new romantics have a flamboyance which mirrors the eighteenth century.'[91]

Nicholas Ward-Jackson flew to Florence for the opening. So did Jarman's new friend Ken Butler. Rather than attend the first-night party, Jarman and Butler escaped to a gay bar, where Jarman promptly vanished into the shadows with a Florentine youth: uncompromising behaviour for someone who was ostensibly courting Butler and had little reason to trust young Italian men. But then, Jarman always was a creature of contradictory responses.

For instance, he had been staying in a *pensione* abutting Giotto's belltower, in a humble attic room that reverberated to the sound of the bell but had a classic view of the 'multi-coloured marble geometry' of the tower and the jackdaws circling it. 'At night,' he wrote, 'the geometry fades to a chalky white, while the golden ball on the dome glows in the moonlight.' As his description shows, he was anything but indifferent to the beauty of this setting – and yet, possibly as a result of his disillusion with *Caravaggio*, he was as acutely aware of the city's other side. 'It rains and the granitic streets are like dead prisons. The Arno runs vomit-coloured through the middle. The Renaissance: camouflage for rapacity.'[92] He filmed a group of punks in Santa Croce, watched from his plinth by a disapproving Dante,[93] and while celebrating their energy and the vibrant juxtaposition they provided of new with old, he also wrote: 'Florence is a grey, dull city, invaded by hippy drug-addicts who have crawled out of another era.'[94]

Jarman's next significant design commission was for a ballet: *Mouth of the Night*, staged by the Mantis Dance Company and choreographed by the company's leader, Micha Bergese.[95] Involving seven dancers and divided into five sections for five different times of night, the ballet had evolved through Bergese's and Jarman's design discussions from a purely philosophical piece to one with a definite political edge. The *Mouth of the Night* was the black hole – Thatcherism in Jarman's book – currently devouring Britain's creativity. The designs were arrived at solely by discussion, without any ideas being committed to paper, and were executed by a number of helpers allowed by the designer to realise his vision as they saw fit. The costumes were the province of Anne Gruenberg, acting like everyone else in response to Jarman's overall conception. The piece was danced to an electronic score specially composed by the group Psychic TV, whom Jarman had introduced to Bergese when the original choice of composer fell through.

The critics were in the main baffled when, in February 1985, the ballet opened at the ICA prior to an extensive tour. 'A disco at the end of the world, crossed with a Midwinter Night's Dream', was the closest the *Observer* could come to pinpointing its meaning.[96] In general, it was only the design that garnered any praise. This had ended up as a highly theatrical and nightmarish mix of the ancient and the modern: a painted backcloth of nude figures suggestive of purgatory or the Last Judgement, which Jarman had fronted with an altar-cum-wreath and bracketed on one side by the cut-out, semi-sculpted body of a falling man, on the other by an enormous skull. The Blakean figure of the falling man represented the arts turned upside down and plummeting towards the black hole of night. The skull represented the death inherent in this scenario. It was another example of Jarman's 'revenge' on the forces he regarded as standing in his way.

If not always challenging, these design commissions were at least diverting, and as beneficial in keeping Jarman's artistic muscles in trim as the many film scripts he wrote during the montage years; both allowed him to rehearse images and ideas he would use in future films. What they were not was particularly well paid. However, on the earnings front Jarman had discovered an alternative form of employment which was just as much fun and considerably more remunerative: the pop promo or music video.

This invaluable new string was added to his bow in September 1979, when Jarman was asked by her record company to make three videos to promote Marianne Faithfull's new album, *Broken English*. The songs he was asked to cover were the title track, 'Witches' Song' and 'The Ballad of Lucy Jordan'.

Undaunted by the fact that he had never before worked in this genre, Jarman decided the only way to achieve a desirable effect was to use a mixture of 16mm and super-8. For the 16mm footage, he enlisted the services of Peter Middleton and his assistant, Bob McShane. For the super-8, he turned to Guy Ford and Julian Sands. Christopher Hobbs was roped in to help with the design, John Scarlett-Davis to act as Jarman's assistant.

The video for 'Witches' Song' – an ode to the wild, pagan women Faithfull had known – starts in black and white, with the singer alone outside St Paul's Cathedral. She is confronted by a sinister figure wearing a mask made out of a brown paper bag. The film switches into colour and moves to a bonfire in Docklands, where 'Marilyn', the feminine alter ego of the young nightclubber Peter Robinson, who passed himself off as a reincarnation of Marilyn Monroe, 'marries' the naked and heavily tattooed Dave Baby. Baby then makes love to her while a group of masked men and women dance around the fire. The video features many of Jarman's friends and an even greater number of his trademark super-8 'tricks': the masks, flashing mirrors, a bonfire, the derelict docks.

The film for 'The Ballad of Lucy Jordan' – who, at thirty-seven, knows despairingly she will 'never ride through Paris in a sports car with the warm wind in her hair' – follows Faithfull wandering in black and white through central London. Across her face, in colour, are superimposed images of the domestic drudgery that tyrannises her.

'Broken English' had been inspired by the German activist Ulrike Meinhof and written in response to the rise of fascism in Britain in the late seventies. Jarman's accompanying film echoes the lyric's central question – 'What are we fighting for?' – by placing Faithfull in an amusement arcade, where she puts a coin in a slot machine and watches as on the screen, in parody of a video game, film footage flashes past: the Bikini Island H-bomb explosion, the Blitz, Hitler and Mussolini, fascist soldiers on the march, troops at war, refugees, Oswald Mosley, anti-fascist demonstrations from the 1930s, National Front demonstrations from the late seventies. In the background, face hidden behind a skull mask, stands the arcade's sardonic, watchful owner, Julian Sands.

Within two years the satellite channel MTV had begun to revolutionise the entertainment industry by broadcasting music videos twenty-four hours a day. A further two years on, Sarah Radclyffe and Tim Bevan had set up Aldabra to cash in on this sudden and insatiable market. Radclyffe knew Jarman could be relied upon to work imaginatively with the rawest of raw materials and within the tightest of budgets and schedules – precisely what was required when a record company asked for a video of one of its bands to be put together in a matter of days. Moreover, in the world of the pop promo, evolving as it did out of the club and fashion scene to which he was no stranger, Jarman's name had cachet.

The prospect of earning in the region of £1,000 for a few days' work was not one Jarman could afford to ignore, however much working to order for money was something he 'would dearly have wished to avoid'.[97] Accordingly, from 1983, and in fairly swift succession, he made videos of Steve Hale's 'Touch the Radio, Dance!', Lords of the New Church singing 'Dance with Me', Carmel's 'Willow Weep for Me', Wang Chung's 'Dance Hall Days', Billy Hyena's 'Wide Boy Awake', Jordi Valls' 'Catalan', 'What Presence' for Orange Juice and 'Tenderness is a Weakness' for Marc Almond.[98]

In general, although Jarman would come to think of the music video as the only contemporary 'extension of the cinematic language',[99] and although some of his work in this area was highly regarded and not without influence, it is more valid to categorise his work on these videos as merely serviceable – a fact Jarman himself acknowledged in a 1984 interview with Michael O'Pray, when he admitted to being 'not very good' at making them.[100] Their importance was to give him the chance to experiment further with his stock imagery, to keep abreast of new technology and to work with people he could earmark for future features.

In his introduction to *Bob-up-a-Down* in *Up in the Air*, Jarman characterised the montage years as 'a strange moment, the odd pop promo, autobiography, painting again, leather jackets sweaty with vaseline and come, and a mediaeval anchoress'.[101] It is a summation that perfectly captures the linked haphazardness of the early eighties.

24

Angelic and Other Conversations

Of the many strands forming the montage years, four stand out: painting, writing, a new direction in home-movie making and a new disease, first classified in 1981.

The painterly aspects of Jarman's work on *The Rake's Progress* and *Mouth of the Night* reflect his return to the easel in the early eighties. With no film in production, painting provided the perfect way of filling time and soothing frustration while maintaining contact with an artistic self. Since he no longer possessed a studio – apart, that is, from the room at Hanway Works – the paintings were unusually small; unusual, too, in their style and subject matter. For inspiration, he turned to the iconography of the alchemical tradition, 'the technical drawings of Robert Fludd, Athanasius Kircher',[1] to Elizabethan and Jacobean poetry and drama, especially the metaphysicals; to Jung and the Jungian analyst James Hillman, whom Jarman was reading voraciously at the time; and to the fragmentary sayings of Heraclitus: 'Death is all things we see awake, all we see asleep is sleep . . . What awaits men at death they do not expect or even imagine . . . The fairest order in the world is a heap of random sweepings.'

'I have broken the stranglehold of my landscapes,' Jarman crowed.[2]

He had also stopped being 'victim to acrylic and masking tape'.[3] He was working in oils again, which he found a complete liberation, as he did this new emphasis on myth and the figure instead of geometric emptiness. In clear contrast to his earlier landscapes, as cool and resolutely superficial as they are devoid of figures, the new paintings – small, black squares in which shadowy figures and symbols were etched or suggested by streaks of red or gold – were more intimate not only in scale, but in the manner in which they probed the most private of Jarman's concerns. Although seldom without elegance, and therefore a certain reserve, they were darker, in every sense of the word, than their predecessors, more passionate, angry, fearful, more personal. The shadow of Hockney has gone for good; in its place, Jarman's own shadow falls across canvases whose darkness suggests the nightlife to which he was so partial: the gloomy back rooms, the boys, the alchemical gold to be panned in such chance encounters.

In December 1981, at the invitation of David Dawson, who ran the B2 Gallery in a large warehouse at Wapping's Metropolitan Wharf, Jarman had his first exhibition in three years: a joint affair with Cerith Wyn Evans, Duggie Fields, Michael Kostiff, Andrew Logan, Luciana Martinez and John Maybury. The B2 specialised in experimentation; it was where James Mackay, after leaving the Film Makers' Co-Op, was programming super-8 seasons – and where Jarman, now that he no longer had Butler's Wharf, occasionally showed his films. For the opening of the exhibition, which involved film as well as painting, the Neo-Naturists (a group of female performance artists whose speciality was to paint and then disport their naked bodies) colourfully supplemented the works. In addition, the exhibiting trio's many friends turned out in force to provide their own less sensational support. Sadly, neither exhibitionism nor loyalty greatly helped sales or coverage. What the event did provide, however, was a much-needed spur. As 1982 dawned, Jarman found himself painting with more determination than ever.

'It is therapeutic,' he wrote, 'the smell of oil paint in Phoenix House gives me an old high.'[4] He painted through 'January, stopped for The Rake, and worked again through September.' The paintings were 'altering significantly'. Whereas the first group were 'austere' and 'emblematic', the second group used 'gold as a ground, and were based on nineteenth-century photographs of the male nude mixed with sexual and religious iconography, back-room paintings, which culminated in a large painting based on El Greco's "Pietá". Caravaggio deeply affected these paintings.'[5] Crucial to the function served by Jarman's paintings in the early eighties was the chance it offered of researching *Caravaggio*, of exploring the ambience and imagery of that painter's oeuvre, of establishing quite how solitary was the life of a painter.

Month by month, the new work accreted on the walls of Phoenix House, itself a mini-gallery, until, by the end of the year, Jarman had enough for an entirely new exhibition. In November, he hung twenty-two of the new paintings, framed and behind glass, in a show he entitled *After the Final Academy*. His first one-man effort in twelve years, the show was held at Edward Totah's Gallery at 39 Floral Street.[6]

Although to a large extent the paintings had been made to serve another medium and purpose, that of *Caravaggio*, and although Jarman must have been aware that he was working in a style not then in vogue, it was nevertheless important to him that the show should be well received; not least because, as a film-maker, all he seemed to be experiencing at the time was rejection. But if he thought a move from Wapping to Covent Garden would make a difference, he was in for a double disappointment. Again, a great many friends turned out for the opening, but again there were no sales and virtually no coverage, unless one counts a single paragraph in *City Limits* ('stylish and striking') and a passing mention in *The Times*, where he 'shared the honours with Van Dyck' and was 'damned on [Van Dyck's] reputation'. He was visibly wounded: 'Many of the misgivings I felt about painting in the early seventies resurface . . . No one has paid the least attention to the films and their relation to the work. The art world exists in a vacuum . . . At my private view, swilling drink, after one hour the Tate "buyer" was asked by Norman Rosenthal of the Royal Academy [an old friend] whether that institution would ever buy a Derek Jarman. "Who is Derek Jarman?" was the response.' It led the supposed hero of the hour to conclude darkly: 'Britain isn't working any more.'[7]

It was Jarman's vision of a Britain that wasn't working any more that fired his next significant assault on the art world. In early 1984, the ICA mounted a reasonably comprehensive retrospective of his paintings, timed to coincide with another piece of general stocktaking, the publication of *Dancing Ledge*, his first stab at autobiography. To complement the assortment of pre-existing work he had gathered for the exhibition, Jarman provided half a dozen new paintings, the GBH series: less *Grievous Bodily Harm* than *Great British Horror*, or *Great Britain Holocaust*, even *Gargantuan Bloody H-Bomb*.

The seeds of this retrospective were sown in mid 1983, in discussions between Sandy Nairne, exhibitions director at the ICA, and the journalist Mog Johnstone, who was planning a book on Jarman entitled *Megalovision*. Ever since the mid-seventies, when Jarman had first shown his super-8s at the ICA, the gallery had retained its links with him and held further screenings of his films. The fact that Johnstone was now planning a book, and that Jarman himself, impelled by Ward-Jackson's concern to promote both his forthcoming film and its director, was writing a volume of autobiography made him, in Nairne's eyes, an ideal candidate for retrospective assessment.

The original idea for the exhibition was as a *Walk Through the Seventies*: a selection of photographic stills from Jarman's films, and of his design work, with a written guide encouraging 'a discussion of a period when film, design and painting were all worked together in the same spaces and how they influenced each other'.[8] Hoping to redress the injustices of the Totah exhibition, Jarman wanted to show that the various strands of his work should be viewed as a whole, not in uninformed isolation. Nairne then insisted that the angle of the retrospective be altered to include paintings rather than photographs, some of them new, and that the cinema and cinematheque run a comprehensive season of Jarman's films. The net result was that when the exhibition eventually opened – on 3 February 1984, in the ICA's Upper Gallery – the idea of photographs had been supplanted by a representative selection of Jarman's paintings, stretching all the way from three 1962 landscapes produced at Kilve, through his seventies cape for Dom Sylvester Houédard, to a handful of more recent capes[9] and the brand-new offerings Nairne had requested, the six paintings that comprised the GBH series, which were hung in a separate room. The accompanying season of films included features, those Jarman had designed as well as those he had directed, super-8s, many enjoying their first public airing, and pop promos. Also included was Andy Marshall, who, as well as figuring as a model in some of the paintings, exhibited some of his furniture – chairs, beds, a table and a grandfather clock – in a section named *In Sheer Luxury*.

In contrast to the privacy of the paintings at Edward Totah's, the GBH series – large (ten feet by eight)[10] and produced on specially prepared, canvas-backed newspaper – added up to the most determinedly public of statements. Having originally thought of doing 'a picture of Mrs Thatcher on a slashed through canvas entitled *Blood on her hands*', then discarding this idea as 'too obvious',[11] Jarman settled on the map of Britain, inspired by the Jasper Johns paintings of the American flag. The shape of the country, when he opened an atlas to study it, struck him as resembling an H-bomb explosion, so that was how he painted it: viewed through a circle, amid swirls of gold and fiery red, as a target area, an apocalyptic explosion, a wreath. And just as you could take your pick as to what the letters GBH signified, so you could of the meaning of the paintings themselves. John Roberts, writing in *Art Monthly*,[12] saw them operating on three levels: 'as a visionary projection of Britain under a nuclear fall-out cloud . . . on a retrospective level as a picture of Britain in the grips of the fires of Toxteth, Brixton and Bristol, and as a glorious act of expulsion and exorcism: the ritual burning of Little England.'

Yet even in this most public of works, there was also a private element. The fire was the purging fire of Heraclitus, the gold alchemical – making the series as much to do with regeneration and transformation as it was with political anger – while the circles were not only military, but referred equally to the Kircher who had helped inspire the Totah paintings and whose belief in a world where 'all levels are joined by a chain of similarity'[13] matched Jarman's own view of the universe.

Roberts commented too that the room where the paintings were hung, containing as it did 'two imitation baroque clocks (stopped at 12 and smeared over their faces with flecks of red)', comprised 'the best painting installation I have seen in ages'. This was not by chance. Two of the painters who most impressed Jarman were Rothko and Klein, and what he particularly valued in their work was 'the fact that they create an atmosphere to be entered by the viewer, rather than imposing on us a particular preconceived experience or meaning'.[14] His intention, once he had completed the GBH paintings, was to have them create a space and an ambience, a masque almost, not unlike Rothko's chapel in Houston. He imagined the paintings being viewed to the sound of the chiming clocks; or, perhaps, to Mozart's Requiem.

Media coverage of the exhibition, although not on the level that would have been accorded an established – and establishment – artist (Jarman was too much a minority taste and figure for that), and although not always complimentary,[15] was nonetheless substantial. There were a number of magazine features, a lunchtime talk at the ICA chaired by Ken Campbell and a documentary by John Scarlett-Davis broadcast on South of Watford.[16] Most gratifying of all, The Times, when it came to cover the show on 7 February, seemingly saw the error of its ways and not only gave Jarman top billing in its art round-up for the day but treated him in precisely the all-embracing manner he craved. 'So many younger artists these days have such limitingly neat, orderly careers,' enthused John Russell-Taylor, 'that it comes as something of a relief, and certainly a breath of fresh air, to encounter Derek Jarman at the ICA . . . defending, as it seems, the artist's right to be untidy.'[17]

Coinciding as planned with the retrospective came the publication of Dancing Ledge. Jarman was, of course, far from being a novice with the pen; apart from his many scripts and outlines, there had been his earlier fiction and his book of poems. None of the above, however, despite their pervasively personal nature, count as pure autobiography. Dancing Ledge does, and, as such, is highly significant. Autobiography splendidly complemented Jarman's film and other work, providing an ideal outlet for his distinctive voice. It allowed him to reminisce, gossip, joke, muse, explain, teach and rant. It let him be himself in a way he had never found easy in, say, his painting. It gave him a solid platform from which to examine his private self and assume the mantle of his public persona: the prophet, the spokesman, the cultural irritant he would increasingly become. He had once told Dom Sylvester Houédard that he considered the writing of painters to be 'peripheral', except for the 'marvellous journals' of Delacroix.[18] Now he had written a journal all his own and, in the ensuing years, his writings would become anything but peripheral. Indeed, there are those who rate him more highly as a writer than they do as a painter or film-maker. In another life, it might even have been the path he followed. In one of his notebooks he once scribbled: 'I never really meant to be a filmmaker, it just presented itself as a medium; it could have been writing, perhaps it should have been; a piece of paper and pencil costs little – celluloid strangles you in pounds and dollars – like painting, whose economies are haywire and its connection to any real necessity tangential – one ends up another piece of junk in a rich living room.'[19]

Jarman started *Dancing Ledge* because, with the failure of his 1982 exhibition still in mind, he wanted to 'tie up' the 'connections between painting and film' and between his features and the super-8s, which were 'as much a centre of my life as the feature films and painting'. He believed too that there were not enough autobiographies 'where the gay aspect is put fairly to the fore'.[20] He wanted to write about his sexuality not as one of a 'they', but as an 'I'. To take stock, in fact, an activity he hoped would counter the depression induced by *Caravaggio* and allow him 'to move on without the millstone of his past': 'Writing the book closes the period and leaves me completely free either to do nothing – retire like Marcel Duchamp and play chess – or to carry on and do something quite different.'[21]

The idea for the book had been suggested by Nicholas Ward-Jackson as part of his campaign to keep *Caravaggio* on the road and its director's profile and spirits sufficiently high to make this a real possibility. Indeed, it was while staying with Ward-Jackson in Tuscany that Jarman first picked up his pen.

26 DECEMBER 1982. MONTEVERDE, TUSCANIA
All through Christmas, spent in this old farmhouse high on a
windy hill in Tuscany, I have told myself I must begin
recording the labyrinthine saga of the Caravaggio film.

From January to April 1983, he wrote furiously, at the kind of speed he liked to paint, and with equal ease, treating the major events and people in his life section by section until he had amassed a vast jumble of pieces. These he then had typed. He called this 'diary after the event' *Jigsaw*, a reference to the haphazard nature of the material and the fact that frequently the pieces fitted together in a synchronistic fashion suggestive of the most Jungian of jigsaws. As he wrote, he showed the results to Ward-Jackson, who was sufficiently impressed to introduce Jarman to Naim Attallah, the owner of Quartet Books.[22] They had lunch, and a contract was signed. In July, Jarman asked Shaun Allen, then leaving Oxford, if he would help edit and shape the material. Taking as their keynote the idea that Jarman was explaining himself in terms of the difficulties he had been experiencing with the funding of *Caravaggio*, he and Allen initially tried to group the material by theme. When this proved impossible, they fell back on a vague chronology, though still allowing synchronicity to determine the order of certain passages and always giving the impression from the way the entries were dated that they had been lifted from a diary written at the time, rather than compiled at a later date.

By November the text was finished. After some last-minute changes, the book was renamed after the stretch of Dorset coast that loomed so large in Jarman's life and dedicated, in hope, 'to the British cinema'. At the same time, Jarman was gathering together his photographs and placing them in chronological order in very large and beautiful black photo albums. These he would continue to keep until he died, by which time they would number fifteen and provide a parallel autobiography to the one he supplied in words. The many illustrations for *Dancing Ledge* were selected from these albums.

On 28 February 1984, Quartet threw a party to celebrate publication. The venue chosen was the entirely appropriate Diorama, built by Pugin as a showcase for the earliest form of moving pictures. To fill it, Quartet allowed the author to invite as many of his friends as he liked. The prodigious guest list was colourfully bolstered by the unique talents of the Neo-Naturists and Elisabeth Welch, who, when she started to sing, did so through a blizzard of pink petals that fluttered from the ceiling on to the assembled throng. In Charing Cross

Road, within a few hundred yards of Phoenix House, Rufus Barnes, one of Jarman's old flatmates from Redcliffe Gardens, helped Christopher Hobbs to transform a window in Shipley's, the bookshop where Barnes worked, into a highly theatrical tableau that positively demanded the attention of passersby.

Then came silence. Although *Dancing Ledge* was more widely reviewed than Jarman later remembered, it hardly made headlines. In particular, it was paid scant attention by the film world at which it had largely been aimed. In 1985, writing in *National Heroes: British Cinema in the Seventies and Eighties*, Alexander Walker would speak for the ayes when he described it as 'a brilliantly evocative book . . . that reads as if it had been constructed by a jewelled magpie of more than usually eclectic tastes. Intensely personal, infuriatingly discursive and riveting voyeuristic.'[23] For the nays, the *TLS* described reading it as 'a maddening experience, akin to watching a set of muddled rushes in a viewing room double-booked by the British Film Institute and *Gay News*'.[24] Not words designed to raise the spirits of a writer desperate for his message to be both heard and understood.

In the book's final chapter, alongside the inventory Jarman made there of his possessions, he offered another: of gay nightclubs and his own sexual education across the years.

Now, from out of the blue comes the Antidote that has thrown all of this into confusion. AIDS. Everyone has an opinion. It casts a shadow, if even for a moment, across any encounter. Some have retired; others, with uncertain bravado, refuse to change. Some say it's from Haiti, or the darkest Amazon, and some say the disease has been endemic in North America for centuries, that the Puritans called it the Wrath of God. Others advance conspiracy theories, of mad Anita Bryant, secret viral laboratories and the CIA. All this is fuelled by the Media, who sell copy and make MONEY out of disaster . . . I decide I'm in the firing-line and make an adjustment – prepare myself for the worst – decide on decent caution rather than celibacy, and worry a little about my friends. Times change. I refuse to moralize, as some do, about the past. That plays too easily into the hands of those who wish to eradicate freedom, the jealous and the repressed who are always with us.[25]

AIDS was the Jungian shadow, the black thread in an otherwise golden design; a nightmare scenario which, as it impinged ever more fatally on the world's consciousness, would rewrite the history of everyone it affected. In July 1981, in the same month that Britain indulged in an orgy of celebration over the wedding of Prince Charles to his fairytale princess, an article entitled 'Rare Cancer Seen in 41 Homosexual men' appeared in The New York Times. Initially, there was no mention of this 'gay cancer' in the British press – though Jarman did have a warning system all his own, if only he had known how to read the signs. Not long afterwards, Karl Bowen was writing from New York, where he had moved: 'I haven't been feeling too well because I have ulcers in my rectum and I haven't been able to be fucked in 5 months . . . But I just found out I have Amoebia [sic] – which half the gay population in New York has – brought I believe from Vietnam . . . I'm running around too much trying to keep up with [a] 19 year old who takes 3 tabs of acid to get gently high (don't worry, I stay away from that – grass is quite good enough . . .).'[26] But Jarman did not know how to read the signs. Years of repression, and of resisting repression, meant that although he might lecture Bowen on the use of drugs, he would never have dreamed of suggesting Bowen stop sleeping around; or of himself looking for unwonted dangers in the activity. The 'right' to sex had been too hard won for it to be abandoned, especially at the prompting of the so-called moral majority. Later, he would tell an interviewer he did not think it was 'the freewheeling sexuality of the sixties that led to AIDS'. In Jarman's view: 'AIDS was something that came into the situation, it wasn't because everyone was having a wild sexual life. If you say that sort of thing you have to say that cancer was invented by smokers.'[27]

Because the syndrome first surfaced in America, it was seen as purely American: Bowen's problem rather than Jarman's. Even when Capital Gay, the recently established London paper, reported the death of four men in November 1982, it did so under the headline:

'US DISEASE HITS LONDON'. This was the month Jarman visited Ken Butler in San Francisco, where he had one of his first serious talks about the new disease with Ron Wright. 'Ron told me how serious the problem had become in San Francisco and he recommended that I stayed away from the bathhouses.'[28] In the spring of 1983, *Panorama* and *Horizon* broadcast documentaries about AIDS, giving rise to much fevered speculation in the gay bars and press as to its likely causes, whether it would mushroom in Britain, whether the government was doing enough to combat it.

That April, there were six reported cases of AIDS in Britain. By July, the number had risen to fourteen; by October, it stood at twenty-four. The tabloids began to zero in on the 'killer disease', fuelling a nationwide hysteria. Was it safe to kiss someone who might be infected, drink out of the same cup, use the same toilet, be in the same room? Then, in April 1984, came the announcement that the HIV retrovirus had been isolated as the syndrome's cause.

As a sexually adventurous gay man, Jarman had always known and accepted that his lifestyle carried risks. He had been a regular visitor to the clap clinic since his mid-twenties, had witnessed or experienced more than his fair share of muggings and police activity, was even the occasional lover of a serial killer, one Michele Lupo, who dispatched a total of four male victims before he was convicted in 1987. But, as he said, 'none of us had ever imagined this violent virus'.[29] Nor, to begin with, could he wholly absorb its many implications. He was still going out most nights and, during 1983 at least, the 'decent caution' to which he referred in *Dancing Ledge* did not preclude unprotected sex. 'The plague, though present, is still far away in my mind,' he wrote. 'I can't see it really taking hold, and sex is so sweet to abandon for a threat.'[30] As his 'middle-aged cock' began to flag, he played the passive partner with more and more frequency, thus putting himself at even greater risk.

Like many of his peers, Jarman was in a Catch 22. Even after the cause of the disease had been pinpointed, there were so many conflicting theories about the behaviour of the virus, and such a low level of reliable medical information, that it was not unreasonable to shrug one's shoulders and surrender oneself to fate. Besides, as the gay community began to come under threat from those who saw AIDS as a sure sign of the long overdue wrath of God, the fighter in Jarman, the man who had struggled painfully for years to come to terms with his sexuality, went on the offensive. The last thing he intended was for any figure of authority to tell him how to behave.

In an odd way, he seemed almost to embrace the disease. At a dinner party, when a friend commented on how awful AIDS was, Jarman replied challengingly that it was now part of everyone's life. Schooled in stoicism as the son of an air commodore, one of the positions in which he had always felt comfortable was with his back to the wall. It is a fitting coincidence that Christopher Hobbs now made what looked like a death mask of Jarman's face; and that Jarman chose this mask – albeit with the cheeky addition of an ear-ring, a golden sphere and some loops of celluloid – as the cover design for *Dancing Ledge*.

The fourth important strand threading through the early eighties was a re-examination, and consequent regeneration and ramifica-tion, of Jarman's work in super-8. In a 1985 interview, he is quoted as saying:

> The feature films were an attempt to make a rapprochement between [the world of super-8] and the more formal world of film-making . . . when *The Tempest* was finished, I thought perhaps I would be able to carry on making bigger films and somehow keep my subject matter . . . [but] it turned out to be quite impossible if I wasn't to just do what most people do, which is adapt a script and say, this will be commercial. I could have easily done that at that point . . . But somehow it was too late. I was already middle-aged and I knew what I really wanted to do, and it became a sort of crisis of middle-age, like 'Okay, so if I sell out and do the sort of films that they want, what sort of life am I going to have for the next 20 years?' . . . There was no home to go to. There was no consistent funding in this country for the smaller feature film. The Gay element made it even more difficult . . . I went back to doing super-8s . . . and last year I finally had the courage of my convictions to say right, that sort of film-making, my own peculiar sort of film-making, is really my film-making.[31]

He had found that 'narrative is the first trap of commercial cinema', scripts the first form of censorship[32] – 'because when a script lands on the desk of a commissioning editor, from that moment they're mucking about with it'.[33] The script, with all the inherent limitations it places on spontaneity, becomes joint property and therefore wrests control from the film-maker; in this case, a film-maker with clear ideas about the sort of free-floating films he wanted to make. If one thinks of narrative as a straight line drawn through a script, Jarman's abhorrence of it calls to mind the boy who used to stare so intently at the flowers, absorbing their every texture; the adult who preferred poetry to the novel. He once said, 'in my films it's important to look into the corners'.[34] His obsession with texture, shape and light was why, in his work, each design element, each object, is so charged with significance; and why his interest lay with the objects rather than in the demands of story. His was cinema as an extension of our ability to study our surroundings; cinema as a way of reminding us, even teaching us, how better to see. 'I don't make films,' he would explain, 'I make moving pictures.'[35]

Because he still carried his camera with him wherever he went, much of his super-8 work in the early eighties was a simple record of his travels, friends and home. There is the footage he shot in Italy when designing The Rake's Progress, or in Oxford visiting Robert Medley's retrospective. There are shots of an assortment of young men in Phoenix House, and of the guests at Jordan's wedding to the musician Kevin Mooney in July 1981, on the steps of Marylebone Town Hall. There were, too, a handful of more carefully constructed pieces.

He once took his camera to one of the regular teas held by John Scarlett-Davis and Volker Stox in Stadium Street.[36] He filmed the gathering, then built an entire film around the young men dancing on the roof terrace. Dreamily introduced by the image of a crystal ball on the windowsill at Phoenix House, the scenes of the informal thé-dansant are intercut by Scarlett, one of the more striking figures on the club scene, sipping champagne; Dave Baby and Judy Blame in bed together; Dave Baby displaying his intricately tattooed torso on Hampstead Heath; Jordan dancing with Keith Hodiak in The Secret of the Universe, a one-act play by Jonathan Gems for which Jarman had supplied the designs. Coinciding as it does with the moment when Jarman was beginning to introduce his sexuality more markedly into his paintings, *B2 Movie* is the first of his home movies to be explicitly gay.[37]

The subject of *Waiting for Waiting for Godot*[38] is the technical rehearsal of a RADA production of the Beckett play designed by John Maybury, who asked Jarman to film it. It involved, among others, Sean Bean, Gerrard McArthur and, on the technical side, Johnny Phillips, all later to appear in at least one Jarman feature. Maybury's set included a number of TV monitors and was very harshly lit by projectors. Jarman's super-8 footage resulted in a film of extreme graininess, while his title reflects the fact that what he was capturing on camera was not the play itself, merely an extended rehearsal.

In September 1982 William Burroughs came to London for *The Final Academy*, a three-day event of readings, performances, films and an exhibition-cum-video installation at the Ritzy in Brixton[39] that would in part suggest to Jarman the title of his 1982 exhibition. Because he knew some of the organisers, Jarman was included in the party who drove to collect Burroughs from Heathrow and take him to breakfast at the Chelsea Arts Club. Over the next few days – at the Ritzy, the B2 Gallery, Heaven, a pub and a shop in Tottenham Court Road – Jarman remained safely behind his camera and trained it on his long-time icon. He was transfixed by Burroughs' patrician mid-western twang, by the humour of his readings and by the dichotomy between the rather frail and pukka-looking gentleman on view – cap, glasses, tie and jacket – and the constant scramble for drugs to keep the writer functioning. Jarman shot a number of reels, almost all of which he gave away. The one he kept, of Burroughs in the shop in Tottenham Court Road and then in a pub, was given a soundtrack by Psychic TV and became *Pirate Tape*.

Shortly after the Brixton event, Jarman sent the Arts Council *The Dream Machine at the Final Academy*, a proposal for 'a short film consisting of footage taken during the recent visit of William Burroughs and Brion Gysin to London'.[40] The dream machine was a rotating cylinder, full of slits and lit from within, built many years previously by Burroughs, his then lover Ian Sommerville and Brion Gysin.

When placed on a turntable, it 'produced rays of light at thirteen flashes per second' and was, its makers believed, possessed of magical properties and 'capable of inducing visions'.[41] Tim Burke had filmed Gysin gazing raptly at the machine. Jarman's idea was to incorporate this footage with his own film of Burroughs reading from his work,[42] images of other Ritzy performers and new footage he would shoot specially to reflect certain passages from Burroughs' reading. The soundtrack, provided by 23 Skidoo, would be a mix of music and Burroughs' thoughts on immortality.

In January 1983, the Arts Council awarded Jarman £2,500 towards making a 16mm short based on this super-8 footage. By then, Jarman had discovered that there were various projects planned around the Burroughs visit, so he changed tack and encouraged the idea of a portmanteau film inspired by Burroughs' dream machine. Burke's footage of the machine would link the 'dreams' of four other film-makers: Michael Kostiff, John Maybury, Cerith Wyn Evans and Jarman himself.[43]

It is not, however, to these relatively straightforward examples of his craft that Jarman was referring in that 1985 interview when he said he 'went back to doing super-8s'. Nor did 'going back' mean a simple return to the beginning. In middle age, given his ambitions and what he had learned from his features, this would have been impossible. In youth, as he wrote in his diary, not only do you have the energy to avoid 'the formal structures', but your art-school friends are by and large 'on the magic carpet with you'. Now those friends had been 'blown to the four corners', or were 'embalmed as books on coffee tables'. As he had rethought painting, so it was necessary to 'rethink super-8s for the over forties'.[44]

Luckily, he had met the perfect person with whom to realise this challenge: the young James Mackay. Not unlike Don Boyd, whose rhetoric about creating alternatives to the conventional film industry Jarman particularly loved, Mackay had an even more extreme agenda: to find more widespread distribution for the sort of experimental films usually consigned to the margins. This made him, for Jarman, the 'most faithful to an idea of cinema'[45] of all the producers with whom he worked. They formed a relationship which, since it is in the nature of directors to mistrust their producers, and for producers to want to control and own their directors, had its ups and downs, often explosively so, but which was nonetheless central to Jarman's continued career in film.

Since showing a super-8 film invariably meant running the actual film itself, and was, therefore, a dangerous business (the film could easily be damaged), Jarman proposed to Mackay that if a way could be found to preserve his super-8s on 16mm, they could share the cost, and, since 16mm could be more easily copied and projected, the profit. The film with which they started was *In the Shadow of the Sun*, perhaps the most complex of Jarman's super-8s. During 1980, from a source at the Berlin Film Festival,[46] Mackay found the money needed to blow this footage up to 16mm and, for the soundtrack, suggested Throbbing Gristle, the band on whose Industrial Records label he had arranged the release of 'Stormy Weather'.

The band's leader was Genesis P-Orridge, a self-styled art guerrilla who had started life in Solihull as plain Neil Megson. P-Orridge was the founder of COUM Transmissions, a performance art group dedicated to the shattering of society's taboos (the group had created a furore with their 1976 *Prostitution* show at the ICA, which included a cast of the Venus de Milo 'with a used tampon on each arm').[47] By 1980, COUM Transmissions had long since evolved into Throbbing Gristle,[48] whose emphasis was on music, though without for an instant neglecting their mission to subvert. Jarman immediately took to P-Orridge and, in much the same way as he admired Vanessa Redgrave for her commitment and energy, if not always her solutions, he quickly came to applaud P-Orridge's enthusiasms, even if he did not always endorse his new friend's every utterance or action. There was both naïveté and disingenuousness in Jarman's attitude, but to give wholehearted support to someone whose work you respect had always been more important to him than to nit-pick over the nuances of that person's stance. Besides which, he very much liked the group's 'attempt to develop' Burroughs' 'literary cut-up theory into sound'[49] and saw their style of electronic music as the perfect complement to what he was attempting with film.

Working quickly, and for no money, Throbbing Gristle provided Jarman and Mackay with precisely the blast of music they were after.[50] In return, Jarman offered to film the group's forthcoming

December concert in Heaven. Wearing wax earplugs – 'because for half an hour I had to lean into the speakers to get the best possible angles' – he captured the band playing 'Slug Baig-Brighton', 'Maggot Death Studio' and 'Maggot Death-Rat Club' from their album *Second Annual Report*, then 'refilmed the result, cutting it together with old black and white footage from the film of Dante's *Inferno*'.[51] *Throbbing Gristle: Psychic Rally in Heaven* comprises a hazy P-Orridge as seen through the black and white swirls of the superimposed film and against a pulsing strobe light. Operating as Dark Pictures, his newly formed production-cum-distribution company, Mackay then raised money from the Arts Council to blow this electrifying eight or nine minutes' worth of footage up to 16mm – though, since the Arts Council funding was minimal, he had to ask a friend at RCA to take a wax impression of the key to the rostrum room so they could let themselves in after hours and film the titles themselves.

The Berlin Film Festival screened the 16mm version of *In the Shadow of the Sun* in the Forum Section in 1981. Without telling the authorities, Mackay managed to slip in *Throbbing Gristle: Psychic Rally in Heaven*, thereby creating an unexpected and unscheduled double bill. For Jarman, on only his second visit to the festival, the experience was electrifying, Damascan even; he found the impact of his footage and its 'blaze of impressionistic colour' truly awe-inspiring when played before a 'large audience on an enormous screen'.[52] Together with the audience's palpable enthusiasm, it gave him a much-needed fillip at a time when his more formal film-making seemed hopelessly mired. It showed him that what he came to call his 'cinema of small gestures' could be thrillingly expanded into a public statement. If one can pinpoint any one source, it was this experience of sitting in that auditorium in Berlin that ensured there would henceforth be two strands to Jarman's feature film-making, the public (like *Caravaggio*) and the private (such as *The Angelic Conversation*).

Shortly afterwards, *In the Shadow of the Sun* opened in London at the newly refurbished ICA cinema – to a distinctly less enthusiastic response and much smaller audiences. *Time Out* unflatteringly described the film's principal images as 'slow cavortings by would-be mythopoetic figures (i.e. naked folks)', before concluding that

Jarman's 'genuine imagination as a designer appears totally in abeyance' and that 'with a running time of 54 minutes, it's just not possible to keep your mind from wandering out to make a baloney sandwich'.[53] Jarman was livid, for himself and the ICA. He saw their innovative programming being crucified with him and laid the entire blame for the poor audiences at the door of what he dubbed 'Tired Out': 'I wish I could write a trite one hundred word review, destroy two years of hard work, and sink this magazine of powerful dilet-tantes.'[54] In his zeal for what he had achieved, he could not comprehend that a non-narrative, avowedly experimental film might not be greeted in the same way as *The Tempest*; he simply did not see a difference between the two strains of his work. He wrote acidly: 'The Germans are much more excited by my work. The English remain suspicious; they want prose, socially committed stuff to bore their pants off so they can leave the cinema and believe they have seen "reality".'[55]

Meanwhile, certain crucial technological developments were rad-ically altering the face of the cinematic avant garde. In the old days, news programming had been shot exclusively on 16mm, making that the cheapest and most plentiful of the gauges. Now video was in fashion, making 16mm far less commonplace. Then came the pop promo, which gave rise to an even faster expansion of video tech-nology. Suddenly, super-8 was no longer the poor relation; it and video became the medium of choice for the younger film-maker. In 1981, a group of German super-8 film-makers came to London to show their work, giving their season a wonderfully uncompromis-ing (and assonant) title: *Alle Macht der Super Acht* – 'All power to super-8'.[56]

Already bolstered by Berlin, a festival that would continue to champion him in the coming decade, and by the many other festi-vals which began to show his work,[57] Jarman's profile switched from filmic pariah to trail-blazing prophet. He was taken up as a figure-head by such young directors as John Maybury, Cerith Wyn Evans, Michael Kostiff, Anna Thew, Constantine Giannaris, Isaac Julien – and, in 1983, at the urging of friends who warned him of the risk of being left behind by technology, he acquired his first video camera. He wrote cautiously: 'With the invasion of video, the Super 8 camera is becoming a thing of the past. This saddens me as the video image is still a poor second. However, that will soon change. What worries me is that each advance in technology reinforces the grip of central control and emasculates opposition – though this can work both ways, and it is for us to ensure that technology will promote greater independence and mobility.'[58] He began to explore the possibilities of video as assiduously as he had those of super-8, even going so far as to purchase a television set, purveyor of his most hated medium, so that he had a monitor on which to view his new footage.[59]

Television, albeit of an unusual kind, featured rather strongly at this point in Jarman's life. In the wake of *In the Shadow of the Sun*, he was keen to work further with Genesis P-Orridge, who once said that this initial collaboration 'was always intended as a first move towards a genre of Ambient videos, watchable many times, in much the same way as Ambient music is used to enhance or complete an environment'.[60] In 1981 Throbbing Gristle disbanded, resurfacing a year later as Psychic TV,[61] still a group with a mission.

'Thee Temple Ov Psychick Youth,' proclaimed an early manifesto, 'has been convened in order to act as a catalyst and focus for the Individual development of all those who wish to reach inwards and strike out . . . The world is full of institutions that would be delighted if you thought and did exactly what they told you. Thee Temple Ov Psychick Youth is not and NEVER WILL BE one of them . . . We are not seeking followers, we are seeking collaborators, Individuals for a visionary psychick alliance.'

Archaic spelling apart, this sounds admirably straightforward, its intention as old-fashioned, in its way, as the spelling. However, the methods chosen by Psychic TV to liberate its 'collaborators' in Thee Temple Ov Psychick Youth were anything but old-fashioned – and fatally open to misinterpretation. There was the sound, on their album *Force the Hand of Chance*, of being buried alive; a pamphlet containing images of mass suicide at Jonestown, Guyana; an openly acknowledged fascination with body piercing. In addition, there were plans for a television series 'to be viewed in the night, between the hours of Midnight and six am'. The aim here was 'to cause things hidden in the dark to appear and to take the dark away from them'; and if, the manifesto continued, the programmes 'seem to be emphasising those aspects of life normally suppressed or censored as subversive, contentious, disturbing or too sexual, it is because that suppression is a deliberate attempt to limit the knowledge of the individual'. Freedom to be yourself was the thinking behind footage of voodoo-style ceremonies involving the throwing of chicken bones, or of what looked shockingly like on-camera killing.

Psychic TV never did broadcast any programmes – albums, pamphlets and word of mouth remained their principal means of expression – but they did ask Jarman if he would be their 'spokesman'. He readily agreed and was filmed in a dark suit, white shirt and tie against a plain backdrop, at a sheet-covered desk or altar on which stood the Ptv logo and a skull; then at a lectern, where he held aloft the triple 'cross' of the Temple. This footage was never used as intended – on television – though some years later, with a voice-over provided by someone else it was included in a video compiled and circulated privately by P-Orridge. The video contained staged scenes of ritual magic, apparent child abuse and what looked like the abortion of a five-month-old foetus. When it fell into non-Temple hands and was featured in a documentary on Channel 4 dealing with the emotive subject of Satanic ritual abuse, an avalanche of moral indignation was unleashed. P-Orridge, who happened to be out of the country at the time, decided not to return. Meanwhile, Jarman's image as spokesman appeared in the tabloid press, and for a day or two he was besieged by reporters over his very peripheral part in the matter.[62]

Unexpected and unwelcome notoriety apart, the real significance of Psychic TV to Jarman lay in the way P-Orridge helped close a door on the seventies and in the experiments which, as a direct result of the 16mm blow-ups of In the Shadow of the Sun and Throbbing Gristle: Psychic Rally in Heaven, Jarman now began to conduct with a view towards further expanding his super-8 film-making. In 1982, when Jarman, Maybury and Mackay were planning Egypt, Egypt, Egypt, they had discussed filming on super-8, then transferring the super-8 to video. In 1983, one of the first things Jarman tried with his newly acquired video camera was to project In the Shadow of the Sun on to a naked Adam Nankervis and capture this superimposition on video, which he could then replay and study on the monitor. In 1984, for the retrospective that accompanied the ICA exhibition, he needed to catalogue all his old super-8 footage. To do this, he and Mackay projected the footage on to the wall of the cinema at the ICA, videoed it, then – after adding music and an explanatory commentary by Jarman – used the video as their 'show print'. For fun, they also projected film Jarman had shot of the Pantheon in Rome on to Steve Radnall, the ICA projectionist, and videoed that. The technology was in place for Jarman to embark on another conversation with angels.

Following the ICA show, his diary is awash with notes and meetings for a number of projects. After the many frustrations of *Caravaggio*, and with Mackay so firmly at his elbow, it seemed as if the effect of reappraising the achievements and direction of his working life had been to galvanise him, particularly into taking the new technology one step further. Thinking of shooting on super-8, then transferring the super-8 to video and the video to film, Jarman began to dream a non-narrative work originally titled *Psychic Billy's Angelic Conversation*.

Although jumbled, his notes for *Psychic Billy* are crystal clear in their intent:

> Form: The reasons for super-8 and how the medium dictates the form – e.g. non-narrative/sound rebuilt afterwards, the 'quality' of the image, the limited palette of 16mm, 35mm
> Various concepts: The cinema of noise, a film which does not dictate to the audience, allows the mind to wander and draws its own conclusions
>> reclaiming small gestures
>> the passion of a head turning
>> transforming a landscape
>> the connections are with painting and not the novel
>> the doors of perception, perhaps quote this is an 'ideal'
> manual on Film – the harpies of advertising, the method of Filming akin to a heartbeat . . . the whole problem with the so called gay cinema of realism presented to ghettoise a whole section of the population, social realism, the enemy of 'the people'.[63]

This time the 'conversation' was not between John Dee and the angels; it was more personal than that. It was between Jarman's film-making and his sexuality; between his cinema of small gestures and the 'psychobillies', whose look he so liked; more specifically, it was between Jarman and Paul Reynolds, a young man who happened to epitomise everything to be lusted after in a psychobilly.

Jarman thought Reynolds, then twenty-six and studying for a PhD in archaeology, the possessor of 'an amazing face, moody with great sadness, he seemed set apart'.[64] One evening at Heaven, slightly drunk, Jarman 'mugged up the courage' to approach Reynolds and ask him if he might film him. Soon afterwards, in the Bell with Jarman, Reynolds noticed an attractive, slightly younger stranger, Philip Williamson, and suggested they involve him. Keen to film the affair he assumed would result, Jarman later said: 'It was a platonic affair with Paul, which became a love affair when we discovered Philip.'[65] In fact the affair between Reynolds and Williamson was very short-lived, but Jarman was blithely unaware of this and, over the coming months, sometimes shooting alone, sometimes in the company of James Mackay, but always allowing the images to accrete spontaneously, he trained his camera on his two actors, either jointly or in isolation, tracking the love he imagined to be blossoming between them.

In *The Last of England*, Jarman describes *The Angelic Conversation* as: 'A SERIES OF SLOW-MOVING SEQUENCES THROUGH A LANDSCAPE SEEN FROM THE WINDOWS OF AN ELIZABETHAN HOUSE. TWO YOUNG MEN FIND AND LOSE EACH OTHER. THE FILM ENDS IN A GARDEN.'[66] On the soundtrack, he later added Judi Dench reading from Shakespeare's sonnets. This helped give shape to the sequences; though, in the final analysis, such 'story' as there is resides almost entirely in the images.

The film opens with a quote:

> Love is too young to know what conscience is.
> Yet who knows not conscience is born of love.

Williamson sits at his Elizabethan window, an image to which the film returns more than once. On one level, what follows is his reverie. As Jarman says, it is slow-moving – some would say self-indulgently so. In the charged and sensual way it dwells on the texture of its landscape, the 'small gestures' of its actors, it is also highly impressionistic, almost hallucinatory. There is a flashing mirror, glimpses of a rotating radar, a burning car. Jointly or separately, Williamson and Reynolds carry a barrel, a wooden yoke or cross, a fan, a golden ball, a flame in a cup, a flare. They walk along the fence that surrounds the radar, along the coast, through fog, through a cave, through a garden. They swim. They wash and crown the figure of an emperor, they fight their own shadow, they wrestle. Tenderly, they kiss. Flowers obliterate the radar and, in the final image, Reynolds buries his face in a bank of blossom.

Jarman later explained:

> I came to the ideas after I made the film, as we cut it
> together . . . The beginning had symbols of industrialism –
> the burning car. The cross [or yoke] related to industrialism –
> a sort of Buñuel moment. The weight of received thought.
> The fog and night journey is the idea of a journey which is so
> important in Jung . . . the caves were places where analysis
> began . . . the place where the world might be put to right . . .
> The descent into darkness – that is like Rimbaud – the
> descent into the other side is necessary. Then I saw the
> swimming sections as absolution, the ritual washing of the
> world . . . and the sunlight comes out and one is in the fresh
> air. I saw the section with the emperor as service for others.
> It's based on the first poetic elements of our culture – the
> wanderer, the giver of dreams – The psychotic wrestling
> match is with oneself . . . and there is a sort of restitution, a
> sort of homoerotic scene . . . The signal – the radar thing –
> which at first is so menacing . . . is eradicated by the flowers.
> This is almost back to the beginning and this time the
> sunlight is there.[67]

Equally important to the film was an intensely personal conversation Jarman was having with himself: with his friends, some of whom appear in the film, his past, his influences and private myths. He filmed in Phoenix House and at the ICA, on the Isle of Grain in the Thames Estuary and – most tellingly of all – at Dancing Ledge, on the wild and lonely cliffs where Elizabeth and Dee had walked, in the bare, ascetic caves of Winspit, where he had shot *The Siren and the Sailor*, and at Montacute House near Curry Mallet, the Elizabethan manor of his childhood, whose garden, with its topiary and yew obelisks, echoes so many elements of Jarman's painting and design.[68]

As well as powerfully celebrating English landscape, the film draws clear distinctions between a brutal present and an ideal past. It is in the pastoral tradition of film-makers like Powell and Pressburger and Humphrey Jennings, and of Jarman's school and university studies into *The Wanderer*, the Anglo-Saxon poem which deals with a solitary man's bitter-sweet journey towards spiritual wisdom. It acknowledges, too, other more recent filmic influences. The glimpse we have of the ICA projectionist on to whose body Jarman had superimposed footage of the Pantheon in Rome was a means of smuggling a hint of Italy, and therefore of *Caravaggio*, into the film. The shimmer of alchemical gold from the same sequence came from Cerith Wyn Evans, who used it in his *Epiphany*.

Jarman wanted to make a film without self-hatred, without the violence and imprisonment implicit in so many gay or homoerotic films, even his own *Sebastiane*. Although destruction 'hovers in the background' – the radar, the surveillance, 'the feeling one is under psychic attack' – at the end 'the blossom takes over'.[69] As he wrote in his diary, 'There had never been a good screen kiss in a gay film. I wanted to right that . . . it is a gentle film . . . the other side of the coin.'[70] It was not everyone's cup of ambrosia (Tony Rayns considered it close to 'a homosexual version of heterosexual kitsch'),[71] but for Jarman it remained the film of which he was always the most proud, the one he felt most truly represented him.

As crucial to the finished film as the artistic and thematic conversations Jarman was having with himself were the more pragmatic conversations he and Mackay were having with Peter Sainsbury, head of production at the BFI and a man determined to foster the interests of alternative cinema. Before joining the BFI, Sainsbury had founded The Other Cinema, 'a counter-mainstream distributor and exhibitor', and (with Simon Field) the magazine *Afterimage*, the journal of 'avant-garde and radical film'. He had first seen Jarman's super-8 work in the mid-seventies, when he had found it 'aimless and portentous'.[72] On seeing *The Tempest* in New York, he had set aside his reservations, though by this time he regarded Jarman as too successful, and possibly too commercial, for the BFI, which, after all, had only limited resources for helping film production and therefore worked with people unable to find funding elsewhere. Jarman had managed to raise the money for not one but three features from independent sources, while his current project, *Caravaggio*, was being touted in big-budget terms.

Now, however, Sainsbury could see that the frustrated director was desperately in need of assistance, certainly if he wanted to pursue his cinema of small gestures. They discussed *Bob-up-a-Down*, which Sainsbury was keen for his production board to take on, and when that proved impossible, Sainsbury went to Phoenix House and, over a couple of sessions, saw what could be achieved if the footage Jarman and Mackay had jointly shot that summer, at the rate of three or six frames per second, was projected more slowly on to the wall, then refilmed off the wall by a video camera connected to a video deck whose buttons, when twiddled, could affect the texture and colours of the slowed-down, blurry image.

Sainsbury was intrigued and, 'in a spirit of experimentation, for the sake of technical research and out of a desire to establish a working relationship with Jarman by supporting the creative process that interested him',[73] decided that rather than commission a new project, they should see what could be done with this existing material. As a first step, the production board agreed a modest provision to enable Jarman to edit and transfer his material from three-quarter to one-inch videotape. The successful result of this transfer, and the discovery of an equally successful new system for transferring one-inch videotape to 35mm at two-thirds the cost of other systems, led the board to 'commit sufficient finance to complete the process'. It was the first time the BFI had funded anything on the basis of rushes, rather than a script, and it had cost them only around £50,000: 'about one-fifth of what would normally have been spent on a very low budget feature'.[74]

The initial edit, undertaken at Phoenix House with the help of various film-making colleagues, was finished by September. For music, Jarman turned to Peter Christopherson and Geff Rushton of Coil, who supplied an atmospheric electronic score incorporating an array of sound effects, plus the sea interlude from Benjamin Britten's *Peter Grimes*. At about the same time, Jarman had the belated idea of having Judi Dench read fourteen of Shakespeare's sonnets as an oblique commentary. This was a fusion of a quite separate notion – to film the sonnets – with the material to hand. It was also, as far as Jarman was concerned, a perfect way to proclaim the homosexual bias of Shakespeare's verse while providing himself with a spoken soundtrack that was tough rather than sentimental, for, as he said: 'It's tough being in love.'[75]

In February 1985, within a month of finishing the final mix and just a week after *The Mouth of the Night* opened at the ICA, *The Angelic Conversation* received its world première at the Berlin Film Festival. It was shown out of competition, in the Information Section, where it was accorded a generally warm reception. *The Times*, tempering its praise with a caveat that would later be more widely taken up, pronounced: 'Ultimately the film seems like an excellent short that spun out of control, yet there is ample evidence in its dream-like images of Jarman's singular poetic gift – a rare commodity in British cinema.'[76] It was given its British premiere that summer, at a late-night screening at the Camden Plaza, where it was shown as part of London's annual Gay Pride celebrations. The proceeds went to the AIDS charity named after one of the four men whose deaths had been reported by *Capital Gay* in November 1982: the Terrence Higgins Trust.[77]

Because *The Angelic Conversation* had to an extent supplanted *Caravaggio*, Jarman was wont to call it 'my *Caravaggio*'. Others, too, sometimes spoke of it as a version of the later film. Yet only in a metaphorical sense: in a literal sense, *Caravaggio* was still a separate entity – and, thanks to Jarman's collaboration with Peter Sainsbury, it was about to become a reality. First, though, came *Imagining October*.

The BFI had been invited by the (USSR) Union of Cinematographers, at the time tentatively encouraging the liberalisation that would lead to glasnost, to show the work of five independent British feature-film-makers in Moscow and in Baku on the Caspian Sea.[78] Although, since *The Angelic Conversation* was not yet completed, Jarman was not then a film-maker with a BFI-funded feature to his credit, he was included in the group which flew to Moscow on 1 October 1984. The film he took was *The Tempest*.

The Nizo was particularly important on this trip. Earlier in the year, as part of a programme that would also feature John Maybury's *Big Love* and Cerith Wyn Evans' *Epiphany*, the London Film Festival had asked Jarman to screen a new work during November's festival. Thinking he would be able to show something from *The Angelic Conversation* as work in progress, Jarman had blithely accepted this invitation – only to discover that the BFI was unwilling to have the film shown publicly until it was finished. He was suddenly left with a mere six weeks in which to produce a new film to keep his promise to the festival.

In Moscow, the British film-makers were shown the city, found seats at the Bolshoi and the State Circus, taken to drinks at the home of the British ambassador (all 'Knightsbridge twee' and 'braying Oxbridge lads and lasses').[79] For the rest, their time was spent in the headquarters of the cinematographers' union, where they took their meals, watched Soviet films[80] and attended seminars. At one of these seminars, one of the assembled experts described *The Tempest* as 'camp'. In a country where homosexuality was illegal, use of this English word was as close as anyone dared come to mentioning, or criticising, the film's homosexual overtones. Although Jarman had privately resolved not to raise the subject of his sexual orientation unless someone else did, this remark was a challenge he felt impelled to meet. 'Perhaps you're referring to my homosexuality,' he said. 'I'm glad you've raised this, it's important to me, many artists are gay.'[81] He cited Shakespeare, whose sonnets he was on the point of appropriating for *The Angelic Conversation*, then proceeded to list a number of others, including Eisenstein and Tchaikovsky. He felt the audience 'move uncomfortably'.[82]

Fascinated by Russia as the flip side of the American capitalist coin, Jarman kept a detailed diary, painstakingly noting encounters such as the above, as well as any oddities in his surroundings, no matter how trivial. The constantly running Nizo captured images of everything from the graves in Novodevichy Cemetery – where, from Khrushchev's tomb, he pocketed a pair of conkers that would later yield two small trees for the pots outside Phoenix House – to a particularly bleak landscape of beach crossed with oilfields in Baku, where he filmed the house a mason had constructed to the memory of his drowned daughter: 'an extraordinary construction of concrete and tiles with sculptures of deer, dolphin and mermaids around a great ramp spiralling like the remains of a shell'.[83] What provoked him were testaments to the indestructibility and quirkiness of the human spirit, either that or evidence of attempts to crush that spirit.

As part of the group's tour of Moscow, they were taken to visit Eisenstein's tiny, book-filled flat, where Naum Kleiman, the keeper of the flame, gave them tea in the great director's cups. Overawed to be in the home of one of his mentors, Jarman was particularly intrigued by Eisenstein's extensive library, much of it ordered from Zwemmers in Charing Cross Road, a stone's throw from Phoenix House. He took down Eisenstein's original copy of John Reed's *Ten Days That Shook the World* – the seminal account of the October Revolution on which, in part at least, Eisenstein had based *October*, his film of the uprising – and was astounded to see that wherever it occurred, Trotsky's name had been inked out. This had obviously been done after Eisenstein had made the film, certainly after Trotsky had been discredited by Stalin and erased from public memory: presumably, either by Eisenstein himself, fearful in the wake of Stalin's purges to be found in possession of a book featuring such a compromising name; or else, after his death, by someone supremely protective of the director's memory. Whatever the case, Jarman found such blatant censorship irresistibly fascinating. Asking one of the other British film-makers, Peter Wollen, to sit in Eisenstein's chair and turn the pages of the book, he stood at Wollen's shoulder and shot his troubling discovery. He then had himself filmed in the chair.

Jarman later said that with the single exception of his first trip to America in 1964, his visit to Russia 'had more effect on me than any other journey I've made out of this country'.[84] Not only did it provide him with a focus for the strong sense of marginalisation the eighties had instilled in him, but thanks to Eisenstein's study it gave him the idea for his new film, *Imagining October*. Immediately on his return to London, with just a month to go before the film's appointed opening, he set about placing his footage from Moscow and Baku within what he felt to be its appropriate political context.

As someone who, politically, had always related best to whatever affected him most personally, Jarman's direct experience of the sometimes puzzling mixture of friendliness and repression he had encountered in Russia found a powerful echo in his complicated feelings about Britain. At the drinks reception at the British ambassador's home in Moscow, a diplomat had, with jaunty upper-middle-class superiority, joshed: 'The Sovs don't allow us to wander, ha ha, it's ghastly isn't it?' Yet in London, in 1984, the bookshop *Gay's the Word* was being raided, as was the Bell pub; striking miners were being charged by police, and in the background droned 'Margaret Thatcher's monotone, inciting violent action, misquoting Saint Francis'.[85]

On an even more personal level, Thatcher was also dealing the beleaguered film industry a double whammy. As the government prepared effectively to privatise the industry by removing state support, it was announcing 1985 as 'British Film Year'. What British Film Year – under the aegis of its president, Richard Attenborough, its chairman, Gary Darknall, and a body of five vice-chairmen that included the producer David Puttnam, in charge of national events – was designed to celebrate was the so-called 'renaissance' of the British film; an entirely spurious renaissance as far as many informed observers could see, given that not only was the government dismantling its support for the industry, but cinema admissions had fallen to an all-time low. Jarman had a further quibble: the 'renaissance' was fatally partisan. He took particular exception to the fact that its flagship – possibly even its *raison d'être* – appeared to be Puttnam's own *Chariots of Fire*, the film which, on winning its clutch of Oscars in 1982, had famously prompted Colin Welland, its scriptwriter, to crow: 'Look out, the British are coming!' Even more distasteful to Jarman was the fact that the film had bagged its Academy Awards just as Britain was springing to the defence of a cluster of remote islands in the south Atlantic, and that the films minister was soon to boast that Puttnam's and Hugh Hudson's feature had helped boost morale. If British cinema was to be fêted, Jarman believed it should be without reference to jingoism and American Oscars. He also thought the list of films singled out for praise should include a significant number of non-mainstream directors. The more conventional path being followed would, he declared, do British film no ultimate favours. He quoted darkly the example of a more recent Hudson epic, the ill-fated *Revolution*, which, in its attempt to rival Hollywood, was costing the equivalent of dozens of low-budget features, crippling its producers in the process.[86]

Underlying Jarman's anger was, of course, hurt and outrage at his exclusion from this film 'renaissance', a hurt exacerbated by the fact that Puttnam had come to films from, of all worlds, advertising, and was a friend of Charles Saatchi, then responsible for marketing the Conservative Party; that it was a quote from, of all people, William Blake that had given Puttnam's chauvinistic film its title; and that when the film was being promoted, actor Ian Charleson had been persuaded to drop the decadent and disreputable *Jubilee* from his cv.

All this conspired to make Puttnam Mammon incarnate in Jarman's eyes, and *Jubilee*'s erasure from Charlson's biography the capitalist equivalent of Trotsky's removal from Eisenstein's book: censorship by means of market forces.

Jarman's vitriol flowed into *Imagining October*, which starts with the caption: 'Sitting on Eisenstein's chair – Moscow 1984 – October.' We see Jarman on the chair. What follows is, as it were, his dream.[87] There are slow-motion images of fire, shots of the architectural titanism of Moscow, heart of the empire, and the footage of Peter Wollen holding the censored book. 'Eisenstein censored! Trotsky erased!' There follows a string of captions designed to drive home the point of the film by mixing Blakean poetry with political sloganeering in a 'scenario of Repressions' that lists the 'Politics of regression through economic idolatry'. Finally we read:

PRIVATE SOLUTION
Sitting in Eisenstein's study with a home movie camera
    imagining October
A cinema of small gestures

Jarman had originally written the captions as a continuous rant, to be spoken as a voice-over. Shaun Allen dropped by for tea and suggested they be broken up as slogans and printed on screen. This had the effect of preventing the film from becoming too fluid and dream-like, as well as providing a possibly unconscious homage to Eisenstein's great work, which, of course, also uses captions.

Now comes a close up of a paintbrush. On the soundtrack we hear Benjamin Britten's setting of Blake's 'O Rose, Thou Art Sick'. In order to make a whole film, not to mention his point, Jarman needed to supplement his Russian material, which he did with video footage shot in London of the painter John Watkiss. In a sequence designed by Christopher Hobbs, Jarman filmed Watkiss painting five of Jarman's young friends, all dressed in 'British military uniform' and 'carrying the red flag'. While Watkiss paints them in a style 'resembling Soviet Realism',[88] the young soldiers form various tableaux. They embrace, eat a mock last supper at a long table under two huge portraits of Lenin, discard their uniforms and dress in civilian clothes.[89] There are images of the Red Flag, of flowers, more footage of Moscow and the small gestures to be found on the freer fringes of the empire – the innocence of children playing in Baku, a young lad with a mouthful of golden teeth who dazzles the camera with his smile.[90] Then the paintbrush is cleaned and laid aside. Peter Wollen's finger points to Trotsky's erased name. There is the Red Flag, there is fire. Jarman sits in Eisenstein's chair, smiling seraphically.

Jarman was once again investigating the divide between art and politics. In particular, he was hinting at the power of the paintbrush to cauterise aggression. *Neutron* collides with *Caravaggio*, but in a cinema of small gestures. And lest we pigeonhole the film, or its politics, too neatly, we are shown the palpable eroticism inherent in a military uniform.

Up until the moment when the film's twenty-seven minutes were cut together, the funding had come entirely from Jarman's friends.[91] Now Peter Sainsbury was able to slip the film-maker the few thousand pounds it took to transfer the footage via video to 16mm. Jarman then asked Genesis P-Orridge and David Ball of Soft Cell to provide a score. With barely a day in hand, the film was ready for its festival screening. Shown late at night at the Lumière in St Martin's Lane in London, it received a generally warm reception.

It also provided a bizarre coda to decades of misapprehension between East and West. Since *The Angelic Conversation* was in line for the forthcoming Berlin Film Festival, James Mackay, who produced *Imagining October* for Jarman, thought it would make sense for the festival to screen the new film as well, and took it to Berlin to show the selectors. They were horrified. Even though no one had forbidden Jarman to use his camera, to film in this manner behind the Iron Curtain was, they said, utterly irresponsible; a deliberate provocation and an act which could put a great many jobs at risk: those of the people in the Union of Cinematographers, the group's guides, even Naum Kleiman.[92] A member of the Communist Party was dispatched to view the film at Phoenix House. His reaction echoed that of the Berlin selectors. 'This film,' he announced, 'must never be shown.'

Jarman was so appalled to think he might harm the people who had entertained him in the USSR that, although it went against the grain to condone censorship, he readily agreed that if the film were to be widely distributed, the offending footage of Peter Wollen's finger pointing at Eisenstein's book should be cut. He accepted, too, that the slogan 'Eisenstein censored! Trotsky erased!' could be inked over, and that it was perhaps best if the film were shown only at relatively minor festivals and retrospectives, certainly as little as possible on the continent.[93]

As well as illustrating Jarman's essential kindness – the welfare of the Russians was of far more concern to him than the fact that his film would effectively disappear – the incident points up his political naïveté. He appeared not to see how he was being subjected to the very process he had been criticising, and never questioned the motives of those who advised him to do what he did. Though the sting in this particular tail lies not with communism, but with capitalism. As long as Jarman made the suggested changes to the film, in time the BFI were prepared (even keen) to distribute it commercially. What prevented them from doing so was not fear of Soviet retribution, but the censorship of capital: the cost of clearing rights with the musicians' union for Britten's setting of 'O Rose, Thou Art Sick'. Indeed a song of experience.

Alongside the first screening of *Imagining October* came publication of a book which further inflamed Jarman against 'the ad man'
Puttnam and his cinema 'of the new right, shallow, opportunist,
ugly, and a betrayal of care for the weak'.[94] This was James Parks'
Learning to Dream, a survey of the British film industry launched at
an ICA seminar in the run-up to British Film Year. If he had not
been so exercised over this misplaced jamboree, Jarman might have
realised that Parks' survey did its creditable best to be even-handed
and was far from unsympathetic to the problems facing independent
film-makers. But at the time, all he could see was that whereas Julien
Temple's *Absolute Beginners*, as yet unmade, received more than one
mention, of *The Tempest*, a virtual manual of how to dream cinematically, there were none. Jarman dashed off a manifesto of some
dozen pages, and then, just as he had stood outside the Arts Centre
in 1969 handing out leaflets to protest at the exclusion of his ballet,
distributed his manifesto in the foyer of the ICA (suddenly dubbed
'The Institute of Cupidity and Avarice') immediately before the
seminar to launch Parks' book.

Although Jarman's stance suggests a degree of petulance at not
being included, his thinking went deeper than that. As he would
later write: 'My reaction to being called a camp filmmaker is one of
passionate anger, which the simple translate as bitterness. This is
quite mistaken as I do not want to be part of their renaissance. It has
nothing to offer except glossy emptiness. I wouldn't give a frame
of ... "Angelic Conversation" for all their phoney production values
and I'm not prepared to be measured in $ bills.' What he desired was
a return to the humanist and conservative (with a small 'c') values of
a world represented by a figure like Sir John Betjeman, who died that
year: 'not a change of policy, but a change of heart'.[95]

Among the list of 'things to be done' at the start of Jarman's diary
for 1985 are the words: 'Shake up British Film Year but chiefly make
85 the year of *Caravaggio*.' He knew a film of his own would be his
best revenge – more telling, more satisfying than any number of
manifestos. And, at last, seven long years after his first encounter
with Nicholas Ward-Jackson, the saga of *Caravaggio* was heading
towards its conclusion.

During the making of *Imagining October*, Peter Sainsbury and

Jarman discussed an entirely new possibility for *Caravaggio*, that of the BFI funding the film at the greatly reduced level of around half a million pounds. A few years earlier, the BFI had won an increase in its government grant, which went specifically to the production board. At much the same time, it embarked on a successful partnership with Channel 4, which agreed to part-fund certain films in return for the right to show them on television. This meant the BFI could back its projects to a previously unheard-of level – and just at the time when a big-budget *Caravaggio* seemed finally to have fallen by the wayside.

Because Jarman was then revising the script to be shot in video and 16mm (the scaled-down '13th rewrite' he called *Blue is Poison*) 'against simple black drapes in one studio set with props, with a very low budget', he was completely open to Sainsbury's suggested solution. Ward-Jackson was less receptive, but pragmatic enough – and tired enough – to see the sense of accepting what the BFI could offer. The production board gave their blessing, as did Channel 4. Indeed, Jeremy Isaacs declared himself 'tickled pink' that after the earlier, much-publicised furore over the film at Edinburgh, the channel should again be involved. The budget was set at £475,000. The already full opening months of 1985 – finishing *The Angelic Conversation* and taking it to Berlin, designing *Mouth of the Night* – led briskly into the equally busy, much more focused task of putting *Caravaggio* into production. And to a much more cheerful Jarman. When the journalist Jane Solanus asked him if, in the light of the BFI and Channel 4's ultimate support, he was embarrassed about his criticism of British Film Year, he 'just laughed: "When I couldn't work I was very angry. Now I can work, obviously, I'm not quite so angry."'96

Between March and September, when the film started shooting, *Blue is Poison* was put through a number of final rewrites. The budget enabled Jarman to spread his wings a little. He still wrote with a single studio in mind, but where in the thirteenth rewrite he felt he could not recreate the paintings forming the spine of the story and would have to work from either slides or contemporary approximations, now he had the money to recreate them more faithfully, in period and in costume, and for Christopher Hobbs to execute a number of copies. Elsewhere, he subtracted rather than added. The many explanatory voice-overs he had given Caravaggio's assistant, the dumb Jerusaleme, were reduced and transferred to Caravaggio himself. A great deal of sexual explicitness was excised.[97] Ignoring its lack of a clear narrative, the resulting script is Jarman's most conventional and measured to date; much like the medium in which, for the first time ever, he was about to work: 35mm. A far cry from the heady confluence of Genet and Pasolini that Ward-Jackson had first imagined he might produce. Perhaps Jarman shared his erstwhile producer's exhaustion – he certainly seemed reluctant to risk anything that might jeopardise the film's chances.

During pre-production, Jarman worked mainly out of Phoenix House, where he had his first answerphone installed. Apart from Dom Sylvester Houédard, as usual supplying page upon page of eccentrically typed historical information, his principal workmate in the early stages was designer Christopher Hobbs. Because they had both been thinking about the film for so long – and because, in design terms, it had come full circle, from small to big budget and back again – it was possible to arrive at the design remarkably quickly. Since all they could afford was a series of flats, from which streets as well as entire Roman rooms had to be constructed, they wisely adopted the slogan 'less is more' and rang the changes by locating the look of the film across what Jarman termed the 'classical' period between the Renaissance and the Italy of the 1940s and 1950s, 'the last time the world was intact before modern consumerism and Americanism swamped it'.[98] Just as the design for *The Tempest* had incorporated elements from all 350 years of the play's existence, the props and costumes for *Caravaggio* would range from those of the sixteenth and seventeenth centuries to those of the 1940s, and occasionally beyond. The paintings would be recreated in period, as would the extravagant party thrown by the banker Giustiniani to unveil *Profane Love*. Ranuccio, however, would own a motorbike and Giustiniani would do his sums on a small pocket calculator. Jarman was 'obsessed by the interpretation of the past';[99] not an 'archaeological' portrayal, as in the work of a painter like Poussin, but a more Caravaggio-like mingling of past with present that would elucidate as well as recreate. So, while Hobbs tackled his copies of the required Caravaggio paintings, Jarman arranged screenings of such seminal post-war Italian films as *Bicycle Thieves*, *Ossessione* and *Rome, Open City*. Equally influential were Dreyer's *La Passion de Jeanne d'Arc*, Godard's *Passion* and Koudelka's *Gypsies*, a photographic record of the Romanies of Middle Europe.

In May, there was a sudden change of production head at the BFI, Peter Sainsbury yielding to the academic Colin MacCabe. MacCabe took over the somewhat sensitive finalising of matters contractual: the settling of accounts with Ward-Jackson and the NFFC; the paying off of James Mackay, who up to then had been helping Jarman on the production front; the worry over whether, given the prior involvement of Simon Raven and Suso Cecchi D'Amico, copyright in the script was clear; the hiring of Sarah Radclyffe as the film's producer. The western half of Limehouse Studios, relic of an old order among the stirrings of redevelopment on the Isle of Dogs, was settled on as the ideal studio. Cameraman Gabriel Beristain joined the discussions about which colours to use for the sets and how best to light them. On costumes, Sandy Powell, with whom Jarman had worked on a number of pop promos, made her first foray into features. Casting proceeded apace. As his hero, Jarman had long wanted – and now secured – Nigel Terry, who bore an 'uncanny resemblance' to the only existing portrait of Caravaggio.[100] Friends and acquaintances slated to appear in less important roles were either conveniently ignored or speedily recontacted. John Gielgud was approached, only to give Jarman his most unequivocal refusal yet: 'I'm afraid my experience in Caligula some years ago has led me to be very wary of indulging my advanced years in semi-pornographic films.'[101] Hours were spent on the phone to the casting director and with the 'dreaded Spotlight'. The putative candidates were interviewed and videotaped at Phoenix House, or jotted down in the margins of Jarman's diary: Paul Reynolds or Simon Turner for the dumb Jerusaleme; Annie Lennox for Lena; Alec Guinness for Del Monte. In the end, Jarman arrived at a considered mix of adept and novice, known and unknown, among them Michael Gough, whom he knew from *Savage Messiah*, as Cardinal Del Monte, Caravaggio's elderly patron; Jack Birkett as the Pope; Robbie Coltrane as his venal nephew; Nigel Davenport as

Giustiniani; a cheeky Dexter Fletcher as the young Caravaggio. For the film's young lovers, he chose two virtual unknowns. As Ranuccio, the lithely limbed Sean Bean, last glimpsed as a shadowy participant in *Waiting for Waiting for Godot*; as Lena, Tilda Swinton, a young stage actress fresh from her first seasons at the RSC and the Traverse in Edinburgh. Swinton had only been in front of a camera once before, and then only in a student film, but Jarman did not see this as a problem. On the contrary, not only was he instantly struck by Swinton's similarity to Caravaggio's Magdalen, he loved the fact that whereas many of the other actresses he had interviewed had arrived wearing Renaissance-style earrings and the like, she had turned up without even make-up. 'I tried to find people who didn't have many preconceptions', he later said.[102] He may also have been struck by a further similarity Swinton bore, certainly on camera: to Betts, Jarman's dead mother. Although there were other newcomers to the cast and crew with whom he would work again – for example, Spencer Leigh (whose 'face like a cornfield with clouds scudding across the sunlight, melancholy and laughing'[103] became that of Jerusaleme), or Nigel Terry, Lucy Morahan, Annie Symons, Annie Lapaz, the official stills photographer Mike Laye – none would equal the intense importance to him of Tilda Swinton, both on and off screen. She became his dearest friend, surrogate wife, confidante, muse: a blank sheet on which he could scrawl his distinctive, cinematic signature.

For extras, the all-important forms and faces that would populate the broader canvas of the film, Jarman and Simon Turner, who also played Fra Angelica, trawled Soho, street, bar and restaurant; Brick Lane; the Circolo Gramsci, London Society of Italian Communists; the Cypriot Centre in Wood Green. At the same time, Jarman and Powell were as carefully haunting the costume houses and second-hand markets for clothes, while Jarman and Hobbs did likewise at Brick Lane and Camden Lock, searching for props. Given the sparseness of the design, each prop was of prime importance. Indeed, Jarman was fond of remarking that where the narrative most truly lay was in the objects. 'Behind each detail of the film,' he commented, 'lies another reality.'[104] The pots on Caravaggio's working table were the pots Jarman had used to mix his own colours at eighteen.

Jerusaleme's whistle, carved from a bone Hobbs had found on a Roman site in southern Spain and bearing the words 'Veni Voco' ('Come when I call'), was the whistle Ariel had used in *The Tempest*. The gold teeth given certain of the characters – which, said Jarman, fulfilled the same function as the Latin in *Sebastiane*, helping 'more than anything to give our English actors a touch of the south'[105] – were fresh in his mind from his recent visit to Baku. Del Monte's fabulous art collection was suggested by its absence rather than its presence. Objects shrouded in sheets indicate the bulk of it; all one actually sees with any clarity are a gold wreath and a black dish. Less was in every way more.

At this point in Jarman's history a future biographer – myself – makes a first appearance. In January 1985, I was a fledgling literary agent looking for clients. A friend called Una Hurding, who worked for the British Council and was in constant contact with Jarman promoting and arranging tours of his films, suggested we meet. I invited him to lunch, in the course of which – seemingly without hesitation and brimming with his usual enthusiasm – he decided I should represent him. Our first project was the book Ward-Jackson had always planned would accompany *Caravaggio*. By August this had taken final shape and had been contracted to Thames and Hudson, where Jarman's editor was an old friend, Nikos Stangos. Part script, part explicatory diary, *Derek Jarman's Caravaggio* included over a hundred specially commissioned photographs by Gerald Incandela, asked to leave New York specially to follow the shoot. Without a moment's delay, Jarman began to keep the diary. On 26 August, amidst a flurry of final preparations, he wrote:

> I experimented with nail varnish and gold leaf and managed to make a perfect gold tooth which I sported all day, it was extraordinary how no one remarked on it . . . I'm smoking much too much, wake up exhausted, it's particularly lethal with vodka, really I lead such an extraordinary life . . . a very handsome lad said to me last night, why are you propping the bar up every night Derek? I said to him what alternative was there? Either I sit alone at home a total recluse or change my lifestyle and sit around unbelievably dull dinner tables with

my contemporaries like so many paintings at a private view or hang out in the bars. I really feel for Francis Bacon when I pass him in Compton Street. I hope I'm wearing a leather jacket in my 70s. I see no reason to return to the middle class respectability that it has taken me so long to shed.

The day before filming began, after some last-minute screen tests and a final night at Heaven, Jarman woke with a positively final hangover – 'no more late nights' – and suffering from

that odd disassociation one experiences before a long journey sets in . . . one never lives so completely for the moment. Filming is once and for all, there is no going back for a replay. Perhaps that luxury comes with a large budget but I doubt it. I'm certain my upbringing on RAF stations helps with the organisation: planning a military campaign must be similar. The here and now once and for all; we all know we're pouring a pint into a half measure but it must be possible to create at least the illusion of being relaxed. Though I doubt I'll take in those who know me well . . . such a lot seems to hang on the success of this project . . . I've truly set myself up for a come uppance . . . I'm not trying for reproduction but rather seeing through to the spirit of our fictional subject; after all what do we know about Caravaggio . . . the paintings themselves form the most complete document . . . such a desperate struggle for redemption in the work and such acceptance of the dark and brooding shadows . . . by expressing his baffled rage with his world he triumphed over it . . . sitting here . . . thinking of past, present and seven years work scattered like a jigsaw all over the place which has to be put together between now and the end of January.

When filming started on Monday 2 September, the pattern of the next six weeks was set. The phone in Phoenix House would ring at 7 am. The car would arrive at 7.30. Jarman would drive with Sarah Radclyffe in the autumn dark along the river to the Isle of Dogs, using this time alone with his producer to solve any problems;

he was absolutely determined not to go a day over schedule or a pound over budget. At the Isle of Dogs, the car would sweep through the newly cleaned gates and along the brick road laid through the half-reclaimed, half-built industrial wasteland; a case, as Jarman noted happily, of following 'the red brick road'. Inside the studio, he worked very quietly, occasionally asking Beristain: 'Do you think it's time to lose my temper?' He still did not 'understand all the technicalities of filmmaking' – though this, as he said, 'can be a great advantage as you have to trust those who are working for you.' Neither was he sure of being good with his actors and was worried enough on this score to ask the opinion of Michael Gough, who assured him his fears were groundless.

With few exceptions, it was a happy set and a remarkably straight-forward shoot; as hoped, the film came in on time and on budget. On Friday 11 October, after an afternoon spent filming Ranuccio's murder at the hands of Caravaggio, it was a wrap. There was a lavish banquet on set for the cast and crew, followed by a 'Caravaggio Ball' which Jarman left at 4.30 am, considerably earlier than the most indefatigable of the revellers, some of whom were found asleep among the crumpled costumes the following morning.

Returning to Phoenix House, Jarman encountered 'unswept dust, the crockery unwashed in the basin, walls that need painting. The neglect the film has created. A thick pall of grime covers everything. I fall into unwashed sheets exhausted . . . I am now a chain smoker and I have lost nearly a stone in weight.'[106]

In November he flew to Italy with Tilda Swinton, Spencer Leigh and Budge Tremlett, the dubbing editor, to capture Italian sounds for the soundtrack as a corrective to the artificiality of the studio. They recorded the noise of traffic, a storm at Porto Ercole, Piero Donati playing a Frescobaldi toccata on the actual organ the composer had used. On their return, Jarman asked Simon Turner if he would provide the score. Using instruments from the period and mixing his music with the sounds recorded in Italy, Turner happily and swiftly obliged. Less satisfactory was progress on the Thames and Hudson book, the December deadline for which was rapidly approaching. Incandela had become suspicious that his contribution to the project was not being accorded the attention or honour it deserved and was threatening to withhold his services. Only at the last minute did he release the stylish photographs used to illustrate Jarman's final corrections to the script and diary.[107]

In between these shenanigans, which effectively spelled the end of a friendship, Jarman found time to dash off a pop promo for Bryan Ferry's *Windswept*, made under the auspices of Sarah Radclyffe's Aldabra. It was the first promo he had embarked upon without being in desperate need of the money. Thanks principally to *Caravaggio*, his income for 1986 looked set to double that of 1985, rising to a comfortable £25,000 or so. Not since *The Devils* had he been so flush – or able, as he was now, to rid himself of debt.

In February 1986, with post-production complete and following a clutch of private screenings in London, Gerard Raimond and Ken Butler drove Jarman to Berlin, a city in the grip of the fiercest cold in living memory. It was Jarman's fourth festival and he handled it like a pro, charming the press and, with his boundless energy and charm, his apparent ability to have fun while he worked, and his 'entourage' of production associates and attractive young men, radiating a glamour that went a long way towards dispelling the cold. The screening was packed, the film (showing in competition) respectfully received. Then, when it came to the awards, it horribly and significantly failed to win a major prize. There was no golden bear for *Caravaggio*, only the somewhat faint praise of a silver one for Beristain's photography;[108] which is not to underestimate the worth of the silver bear, simply to note that, for a film with so much riding on it, nothing less than first prize was ever going to be sufficient.

Jarman's finished version of the troubled story of a remarkable artist and his doomed relationship with the young Ranuccio and Lena was imaginative, accomplished, meticulously designed and, as Berlin acknowledged, beautifully shot. It was also highly revealing of its maker and of the artistic and commercial processes by which all art, including the film itself, comes into being. With quiet yet unsettling intensity, it explores the artist's essential passivity; how his prime concern is to look, record and, if his art demands it, steal from those around him. It looks, too, at how his art can steal from him. It studies the requisite stillness of the artist's studio and how that stillness is always at war with the boisterousness of life itself. It calls to mind one of Jarman's favourite sayings: SLNCE is GLDN. The silence in the film, of Caravaggio working and of Jerusaleme, his dumb assistant, is indeed golden, as golden as the coins Caravaggio gives Ranuccio to model for him and which Ranuccio then stuffs suggestively into his mouth. As golden as the teeth of the guests at Giustiniani's party for the unveiling of *Profane Love*, or the two coins which, when he dies, are placed upon Caravaggio's eyes. Here the film moves from an exploration of the personal into an exploration of the public. The artist's eyes, his means of seeing, are sealed by gold. Gold spells patronage, for, without gold, there can be no surviving, and, without surviving, no seeing. Jarman is skilfully tracing the complex, often bitter 'interconnections between art, power and sexuality';[109] how art is funded, how that funding invariably involves power, how that power is frequently expressed in sexual terms. He traces, too, the supremacy of politics, both private and personal. When Pope Paul Borghese declares: 'Revolutionary gestures in art are a great help to us,' a Hitchcockian Jarman stands in the background of the shot, dressed as a priest, quietly sprinkling holy water, as if giving sly benediction to the Pope's cynical 'message'.

And yet, for all its many fine and subtle qualities, *Caravaggio* exudes a whiff of staleness, even flatness. Perhaps, as we have already speculated, Jarman, like Ward-Jackson, was somehow exhausted by the film before the camera started rolling. If so, the exhaustion shows and would have unwelcome consequences: faint praise in Berlin was a chill indication of more lukewarm responses to follow.

It is a cruel paradox that *Caravaggio* should have met with an uninspired reception, for during 1985 and into 1986, despite Jarman's acute sense of being marginalised by British Film Year, his star was in small-scale but very definite ascendance. Between October and December 1985, Michael O'Pray mounted a touring retrospective of his films (and of some of the films that had influenced him) from a programme originally put together for the Metro in Derby. Entitled *Of Angels and Apocalypse*, the retrospective ran over a three-month period and toured some half-dozen venues, including Edinburgh, where it coincided with that year's festival screening of *The Angelic Conversation*, *Imagining October* and *The Dream Machine*, as well as the talk Jarman gave in which he once again laid into British Film

Year.[110] As an accompaniment to the retrospective, *Afterimage* devoted virtually an entire issue to Jarman's work. There was a lengthy interview, conducted by Simon Field and O'Pray, a filmography, outlines for two unmade projects and an array of articles by O'Pray, Mark Nash, John Roberts and Tony Rayns.[111]

Albeit safely packaged under the umbrella of a critic's choice rather than at the channel's own, unambiguous instigation, hard on the heels of this retrospective Jarman's three features were finally aired on Channel 4, in a season presented by the film critic David Robinson. These screenings were a coda to the furore that had erupted around Channel 4 and *Sebastiane* in December 1982. That furore and Ward-Jackson's subsequent attack on Channel 4 at Edinburgh had had the paradoxical and beneficial long-term effect of forcing the company's commissioning editors to sit down and watch all of Jarman's films; something, it became apparent, they had not done before.

A long-time champion of Jarman's work, David Robinson was the person who, in 1980, had said (with remarkable prescience, given how lopsidedly British Film Year would develop): '[*The Tempest*] arrives in a British cinema that has rarely much to boast about. Derek Jarman, with his third film, reveals a talent that shines bright and cuts deep; and, if the British film establishment does not make use of it, it is an industry more sunk in folly even than one had thought.'[112] Now, at the fag end of British Film Year, Robinson was giving the British public the chance to see what they might have been missing; though, just to be on the safe side, his choices were broadcast late at night and in reverse order, the safety of Shakespeare preceding the punk violence of *Jubilee*, which in turn preceded the nude homoeroticism of *Sebastiane*.

'Robinson's Choice', as it was called, had two distinct consequences. On one hand, in that it forced Jarman to link his monitor with 'central control' to see his work and, more particularly, the reaction it generated, the season brought about a grudging accommodation with his most despised medium – even if he could still write rancorously (and with a touch of hyperbole): 'Of British independent film-makers I had the honour to be the last to have my work shown. The Channel's monopoly had stopped me in my tracks for five years.'[113] Then, as a final slap in the face, the films – with the exception of *The Tempest* – began to generate the same bitter controversy as they had on their original purchase.

In early December, Jarman's *bête noire* Mary Whitehouse wrote to the chairman of the Independent Broadcasting Authority:[114] 'I am enclosing with this letter copies of the National VALA's [Viewers and Listeners Association] monitory reports of [*Jubilee* and *Sebastiane*]. In doing so I am well aware that I may be committing an offence against the Post Office Act but the situation created by these two programmes is so serious that the risk has to be taken.'[115] She then asked the director of public prosecutions to bring charges against the IBA for allowing Channel 4 to show the films. Simultaneously the MP Winston Churchill was launching his campaign to extend the Obscene Publications Bill to cover not only print media, but television and radio as well. In the ultimately unsuccessful but highly publicised journey through Parliament of this bill, dubbed the Video Nasties Bill because its main focus was the potentially harmful effect of 'video nasties' on children, *Jubilee* and *Sebastiane* were cited time and again as prime examples of the sort of pernicious filth the amended bill was struggling to guard against. Making reference to the scene from *Jubilee* in which the policeman is killed, Churchill wrote in outrage to *The Times* to criticise the IBA for its 'tactlessness and effrontery' in screening such a film 'within 5 months of the murder of a Tottenham mob of PC Keith Blakelock'.[116] Feelings were running high, battle lines being drawn. While Jeremy Isaacs appeared on television to defend the films, the director Michael Winner used the occasion of a seminar at BAFTA to accuse Jarman of making pornography.

The lack of universal acceptance that seemed to be dogging his work could lead Jarman to see himself as the victim of a homophobic conspiracy when possibly what he was suffering from was sheer indifference and incomprehension. But he was nevertheless very clear and vocal in pinpointing the unfairness of being pilloried in this manner. Setting aside a hint of disingenuousness (of course he wanted to reach as wide an audience as possible), we can take him at blazing face value when he wrote in angry capitals 'I NEVER WANTED, OR MADE MY FILMS FOR, THIS TELEVISION AUDIENCE, OR THEIR BLOODY CHILDREN.'[117] He was so angry that he almost seemed to forget adverse reviews he had suffered in the past. Soon after this, he told a friend that on the whole his films had received a favourable press until they went on television. He was equally clear and vocal about the partisan nature of the controversy. Why was the violence in a police series like *Starsky and Hutch* acceptable, but not that in *Jubilee*, which at least attempted to deal with the issue? Or, even more infuriatingly, why, during a commercial break in the controversial screening of *Jubilee*, could the morally outrageous fact that Hitachi used Caravaggio's *Calling of St Matthew* for their commercial, symbolically replacing Christ with their latest television pass completely unnoticed and uncensored? It left Jarman wondering if he could ever win. When *Jubilee* had first appeared, it had been attacked by the left. Now it was being attacked by the right. He began to feel like a latterday Wyndham Lewis: a true 'enemy', unable to do 'anything correctly'.[118]

Additional criticism came from another even less welcome source. To assess the impact (if any) of British Film Year, ITV screened three programmes in which three film-makers offered their personal reflections on the state of British cinema. In Alan Parker's *A Turnip-Head's Guide to the British Cinema*, Parker and one of his contributors, David Puttnam, 'took the opportunity to launch' powerful 'personal attacks' on Jarman.[119] Among other things, Puttnam derided his adversary for criticising the Oscars when he would never win one himself. 'Happily, the Oscar,' crowed Puttnam, 'is nothing that Derek Jarman will ever have to worry about.'[120]

Although, where Puttnam was concerned, Jarman could never pretend he had not provoked a response, he still found the controversy he aroused profoundly hurtful, not least because it was often so intensely personal and vindictive. His despair at the contempt in which he was held in some quarters, allied to a very real fear that the bad publicity might lead to an attack on his person, made the cracking of private jokes at Puttnam's expense about the only way he had of defusing the situation. As he noted in his diary: 'Someone rang me up at four in the morning last night and said: "I'm 22, incredibly beautiful, I know where you live and I want to come round and suck your cock." I suggested that as it was rather late, why didn't he come round tomorrow, but then he started getting abusive and said he wanted to murder me. For a moment I was sure it was David Puttnam up to his old tricks again.'[121]

He was certainly in no mood to enjoy the irony that one positive effect of all this controversy was his heightened profile in the count-down to the launch of *Caravaggio*; even a degree of increased sympathy and support. What he does seem to have enjoyed, how-ever, apart from the opportunity for some good-natured grumbling, was the treadmill of interviews to which he was subjected in the weeks immediately preceding the opening. He sometimes found himself speaking to as many as four journalists a day; small beer, per-haps, by Hollywood standards, but not by his own.

On 23 April, he gave a *Guardian* interview at the NFT. The fol-lowing night, the long-awaited film was given a charity première at the Lumière in St Martin's Lane, with the proceeds going to Action Against Aids. *Derek Jarman's Caravaggio*, with special photography by Gerald Incandela, appeared in the bookshops.

The film did respectable business, though on the critical front, despite attracting the occasional rave and/or pasting,[122] the reaction was oddly muted. There was a general consensus that the use of anachronism did not always achieve its purpose, that perhaps Jarman knew 'the tale too well to sense the need to tell it clearly',[123] that somehow the film lacked life. John Russell Taylor, writing in *Sight & Sound*, spoke for many when he said: 'By the standards normal in British cinema, *Caravaggio* is an enterprise of extraordinary daring and resonance, carried out with a single mindedness – and sheer efficiency – which cannot be faulted. By the standard of Bresson or Pasolini, unfortunately, it remains all too suggestive of love amongst the waxworks. The breath of life is somehow missing.'[124] In time, Jarman too harboured doubts. Watching the film a year later in Rome, he found it 'too assured' and could hardly believe it was his.

Still, the film had been made, and it allowed its maker to refute accusations that he had a butterfly mind and lacked staying power. It raised his profile in a way that could not be reversed and, although he must have been disappointed that the reaction was not more enthusiastic, there was much of which he could be proud, as when the writer John Berger wrote to him personally to say what a fine study of an artist it made. Best of all, it freed Jarman from the driving force of Ward-Jackson's ambitions. As he would later confess, not only had these been more than he had bargained for, they had not always brought enough reward: 'I see myself at this stage as essentially having failed as a film-maker. Making *Caravaggio* exhausted me emotionally and mentally . . . I was really a happy-go-lucky person until the beginning of the Eighties.'[125] The question now was whether or not, with the Damoclean sword of *Caravaggio* lifted, Jarman could somehow reclaim 'his own centre'.[126]

In one of his many interviews for the film, he summed up his position in the following terms:

> The whole drift of my film-making since *The Tempest* has been much less aggressive . . . in a strange way, the recent controversy over *Jubilee* and *Sebastiane* has unbalanced everything and focused everything back about eight years . . . there is a whiff of sulphur about me. Which seems to leave me with two choices: either playing to the gallery and being the man you love to hate or sidestepping the whole issue. I know what I want to do next . . . I want to make a film called Xenophobia, which will be St Joan in Britannia, a film of Britannia on trial . . . if Channel 4 won't fund me, I'll go straight to Germany this time. I've done the battle with *Caravaggio* and don't want to wait another seven years. It was never my intention to get into this confrontation over everything. I'd like to have a gentler relationship to my audience and to my own mind . . . It's odd to find that one is such a pariah.[127]

What he may have feared by then, but did not yet know for certain, was that as one Damoclean sword was removed, another, far more terrible, was already hanging in the flies, ready to take its place.

25

The Last of England

Although he knew much of 1986 would be devoted to the launching of *Caravaggio*, Jarman's diary note to himself on 1 January was about the need to get other projects 'underway'. 'Get about a little more' was another instruction; be less of a 'prisoner at Phoenix'.

The projects he had in mind included the resuscitation of certain existing plans – the Pasolini outline, for instance, *Lossiemouth*, *Neutron* – as well as the idea of paying *Jubilee* the same compliment as *Caravaggio* and preserving its script in a book. Sadly, none of these possibilities would be realised, unless one counts that fact that some of the thinking behind *Neutron* did resurface in *The Last of England*, and that within a few months of instructing himself to 'get about a little more', Jarman was playing Pasolini in a short student film by Julian Cole. Called *Ostia*, this was an imagined account of Pasolini's last night. For Jarman, it involved a 'gruelling' trip to Camber Sands to be 'murdered and buried in freezing mud at 4 am as an uncertain sun came up'.[1]

Other, more fortunate, ideas would see the light of day, though only in the future and not necessarily as first envisaged. In a review of *Caravaggio* for the *Literary Review*,[2] Edmund White wrote that the film put him 'in mind of Marlowe – the glowing intensity, the ramshackle structure, the pagan sensuality and violence, the high-flown rhetoric, the meaty fascination with men and the rather abstract admiration of women. Jarman really should do an Edward II one of these days.' Marlowe's tragedy was promptly added to Jarman's list, where it joined some notes entitled *Bliss* that would one day become a film called *Blue*. There were also plans for another book, this one on cinema and theatre, to be published by Macmillan in their Dramatic Medium series. Between February and April, Jarman did a burst of interviews for this with the academic David Hirst.

More immediately – and more ambitiously – he was invited by Don Boyd to contribute a segment to *Aria*, a feature-length selection of operatic excerpts Boyd was assembling for the screen. Originally conceived for television, the project had become a feature when Boyd's powers of persuasion had delivered him a line-up of contributing directors that a producer might kill for: Nicolas Roeg, Charles Sturridge, Jean-Luc Godard, Julien Temple, Bruce Beresford, Robert Altman, Franc Roddam, Ken Russell, Bill Bryden – and, of course, Derek Jarman. Only two strictures were placed on the ten directors, that of the budget, and that the music be taken from the RCA catalogue. Otherwise, they were free to interpret their chosen piece however they saw fit.

After flirting with the idea of doing 'The Queen of the Night' as massacred by the coloratura screech of Florence Foster Jenkins, Jarman plumped for Leontyne Price singing 'Depuis le Jour' from Charpentier's *Louise*. Then, through what he termed 'an act of defenestration' – jumping out of the window into the unknown, but with a safety net of trusted friends and colleagues, including James Mackay as producer of the segment – he swiftly devised and shot the very simplest of scenarios.[3]

Beneath a shower of petals, an old woman[4] stands alone on a stage. She wears an elaborate dress and brandishes a large fan. She bows to an imaginary audience. She is remembering the love of her youth. Her memories are shot in super-8, as if filched from a home movie and with all the apparent simplicity and aching nostalgia that implies. Her younger self is played by Tilda Swinton, her lover by Spencer Leigh. As she remembers them, they spend time together by the sea. Alone, Swinton runs elusively between the box hedges in the garden of her family home.

Although Jarman was never under any illusions about the worth of his contribution to *Aria*, the segment was not without personal significance. Ever since the cameras had stopped rolling on *Caravaggio*, he had been training his Nizo on Swinton. 'Depuis le Jour' was the first fruit of this cinematic love affair; the first hard evidence, too, of Swinton's screen resemblance to Betts. On a more public level, it was extremely flattering for Jarman to have been asked to keep such illustrious directorial company – and, for all his misgivings about this junket, not a little fun, a year later, to be given an excuse, with Swinton on his arm, to revisit the Cannes Film Festival, where the finished feature had been chosen for the closing-night gala.

'Ten Go Mad on the Riviera' was how Jarman titled his diary reminiscences of the festival when they were eventually published. The title could equally apply to the ten segments of *Aria* – including a moustachioed Theresa Russell as King Zog of Albania; a gymful of bodybuilders; marital infidelity in a motel; a nude Elizabeth Hurley; Wagner in Las Vegas; John Hurt wandering enigmatically through the entire piece in preparation for his finale as the clown in *I Pagliacci*. Not surprisingly, the film won no prizes (unless one counts Nigel Andrews of *The Financial Times* awarding it his 'Potty Palm' for 'filmic folly beyond the bounds of credibility'),[5] and at its gala screening there were boos among the cheers. Jarman thought Ken Russell the only director to have paid real attention to the music; the others, himself included, he saw as using the film simply 'as a backdrop for a series of rather arbitrary individual fantasies, none of which had the depth or complexity of the original work'. He agreed with Nicolas Roeg, who unsettled the film's distributors at a promotional dinner by raising a glass and saying: 'To this dreadful film we've all enjoyed making so much with Don Boyd.'[6]

Albeit of a classical kind, 'Depuis le Jour' was in effect a pop promo. It was not the only promo Jarman made that spring. For Rick Rogers, manager of the singer Matt Fretton, he made a short film of Fretton for Rogers to use as a calling card when approaching record companies. Next, he helped the label Rough Trade solve a pressing problem with the Smiths, one of their headline bands. Rough Trade were keen to promote and develop the band visually, but were stymied by the band's insistence on not appearing in videos. The label therefore asked Jarman if he would make some short films which, without featuring the camera-shy Morrissey, or any other members of the band, could nevertheless be used for promotional purposes. Jarman proposed the model of *Broken English*, three films of three of the band's new songs, two from their forthcoming album ('The Queen is Dead', 'There is a Light that Never Goes Out') and a third, 'Panic', that was to be released a month later as a single.

Jarman was constantly adding to the circle of young film-makers with whom he socialised and worked, and this now included Chris Hughes (who helped on *Aria*) and Richard Heslop, two recent graduates of film school. For his new commission, which Mackay was again to produce, Jarman gathered many of these talents around him, and in a more collaborative manner than ever before. Although he remained overall director, he asked Heslop to take principal responsibility for 'The Queen is Dead' and John Maybury for 'There is a Light that Never Goes Out', keeping 'Panic' for himself.

'Panic' allegedly came to Morrissey and Marr after they heard a radio announcement of the Chernobyl nuclear disaster followed by a DJ playing 'the upbeat vacuity' of Wham!'s 'I'm Your Man'.[7] By means of the sort of fast, aggressive cutting often favoured by his young film-making friends, Jarman expertly echoed the song's mood of apocalypse and despair. His images of urban decay, of a begging hand extended immediately in front of the camera, of children innocently chanting, 'Hang the DJ, Hang the DJ', and of a man turning dizzyingly on a bridge across the Thames, judder and flash across the screen with all the intensity of the song's spitting anger.[8]

Rough Trade and their band were sufficiently pleased with all three songs to agree to Mackay's suggestion that the resulting fifteen-minute short be blown up via the now familiar route of transferring super-8 to video to film and given a cinematic release alongside Alex Cox's *Sid and Nancy*, where it helped establish Jarman's name with an entirely new and much more youthful audience, one which could readily relate to the vertiginous speed of his editing. Later the same year he made a second video for the Smiths, this time entirely on his own, for 'Ask', a song about the crippling shyness of adolescent love. It proved a less happy match of director and subject, certainly as far as Morrissey was concerned. Jarman's decision to illustrate the lines 'If it's not love, then it's the Bomb that will bring us together' by means of a ball with the word 'bomb' written on it being tossed from person to person, as if in play, was not seen as suiting the song's essentially tragic tone.

Jarman's Nizo, by no means cast aside on his attainment of cinematic 'adulthood' with *Caravaggio*, also fuelled the year's major undertaking: a gradual accumulation of super-8 footage under a clutch of titles and with no clear narrative in sight until the very end; a sort of haphazard diary that could be codified only after the event.[9] In this way, he had been filming his shadow racing across the seemingly limitless expanse of Camber Sands while playing Pasolini for Julian Cole when he became aware of 'a thin plume of black smoke'[10] on the horizon: the nuclear power station at Dungeness. Then, while making the promo for Matt Fretton, he had ended up filming for an afternoon at Dungenesss, and had briefly toyed with the idea of buying one of the old railway carriages converted into cottages on the shingle near the power station. Ever since visiting the Sainsburys at Ashden in the early seventies, when he had scanned Romney Marsh from the ridge on which their house was built and had seen the power station at the marsh's furthest tip, 'brooding under storm clouds, patches of sunlight blowing in from the west',[11] he had felt a certain affinity with the area. Now, since he had recently given up his studio at Hanway Works and was being slowly squeezed out of Phoenix House, currently something of a museum for the hulking pieces of furniture he had acquired from Andy Marshall, 'Westward Ho!', as the railway carriage was enticingly called, seemed to present an agreeable and unusual solution to the problem of urban overcrowding. But although cheap, and despite Jarman's improved income, the carriage was, sadly, beyond his means.

However, what Dungeness did offer was the perfect landscape for the film taking shape in Jarman's mind. Not only did the power station provide the best visual metaphor he had yet encountered for his own anger, the personal 'magma bubbling away beneath the surface', but the area's haunting bleakness was equivalent to the barren landscapes he had been painting in the late sixties – a place crying out for habitation and imaginative transformation.

Known technically as an 'apposition shingle beach', one of only four such sites in the world, Dungeness is a vast shingle bank which, 'like the ivory fang of a prehistoric shark',[12] bites into the sea twenty miles south of the white cliffs of Dover. Wind-whipped and desolate, a stony full-stop to the flat poetry of Romney Marsh, and as different from the marsh as the marsh is from the rest of Kent, lying so lush and lyrical on the other side of the Royal Military Canal, Dungeness equals the edge of the world. 'Toto, I have a feeling we're not in Kansas any more,' says Dorothy – and one could well be in America (with pieces of polythene for tumbleweed, Jarman likened the Ness to the badlands of Montana), or somewhere over the rainbow, for don't the scattering of wooden fishermen's shacks lining the single road look as if they have been dropped from the sky, and doesn't the power station resemble the Emerald City? Parallel to the road and the shacks is the miniature Romney, Hythe and Dymchurch Railway, where tiny tank engines puff their Thomas-like way all summer from Hythe to the old lighthouse. The old lighthouse is now a museum, the old barracks, a pub: the Britannia, known for its fish and chips. Here, at the head of the shingle bank, there stands a new lighthouse that sweeps its cold beam across the shingle and out to sea. Around it cluster the converted railway carriages, though what draws the eye, no matter where one stands on the Ness, are the towering, humming hulks of the two power plants, the squarish, older Magnox and the newer, curvilinear Advanced Gas-Cooled Reactor. Down the steeply angled shingle to the sea itself, past the fishing boats, there is a lifeboat station, a second pub, then you are on your way out again, towards the flooded gravel pits, the land that belongs to the Ministry of Defence and – in the distance, towards Ashford – Lydd, with its single spire and unexpected airport. Nowhere, except around the power station and the MoD land, are there any fences; every inch of Dungeness lies equally exposed to wind, sea and sky. There is nowhere to hide; and yet, paradoxically, as Jarman noted, even in sunlight, the place 'has a secrecy about it'.[13] On his first visits there, it reminded him strongly of the 'eternal note of sadness' that sounded for Matthew Arnold in 'Dover Beach'.

The fractured notes Jarman was keeping towards the film slowly taking shape in his mind explain that he wanted 'to explore through metaphor and dream imagery the deep seated malaise in current Britain . . . to explore in particular the roots of current right wing philosophies and their necessity to find scapegoats . . . to explore the structure in which the image is controlled by emphasis on "quality", and therefore expense leading to the deliberate creation of rarity and monopoly.' In part, he was reacting to his old bugbear, the film industry – to the censorship of capital he had delineated in *Imagining October* – and giving voice to the frustration he felt at not being able to work more easily. In equal measure, he was spelling out the anger and despair he felt at the state of his beloved country after the desecration, as he saw it, of seven years of Conservative misrule. The film would be an antidote to *The Chariots of Fire*, his own *Caravaggio* and the Toryism of Margaret Thatcher.

It would possibly centre on 'a girl called Britannia, a modern day Joan of Arc, who befriends a spider in her cell. The spider tells her story to cheer Britannia up, and when she is finally squashed by Britannia's inquisitor, turns into goddess Kali and sets Britannia free.' Or it would involve 'Prophesy (Tilda Swinton), another Joan of Arc figure who leads an armed attack on a cruise missile base in the Fenlands, is captured and killed, though not before a young guard falls in love with her whilst she tells him of a vision she had of St George in a bluebell wood who tells her to take up arms for the sound of bells for England and St George.'[14] Less heroically, he also saw it in terms of 'the sinking of the Titanic, the Titanic being Great Britain';[15] a film about 'dreams that go wrong'.[16]

The title most commonly attached to the evolving film was *The Dead Sea* – the Dead Sea of Victorian values (a particularly loaded phrase taken from one of Thatcher's many hectoring speeches to the nation), and of 'post industrial decline, whose stagnant waters erode the crumbling cities'.[17] And *The Dead Sea* it more or less remained until the film was virtually complete, when Swinton said to Jarman: 'You can't call it that. It's the most vibrant film I've ever seen.' It thus became *The Last of England*, after the Ford Madox Brown painting of a Victorian couple aboard an overcrowded ship bound for a new life abroad, faces sombre as they contemplate a future far removed from the rapidly receding white cliffs of Dover. Exile – political, aesthetic and sexual – was one of the major themes of the film, as was the idea that the only sensible thing to do with the not-so-good ship Britannia was abandon her for a smaller craft. Although this spelled the sadness of exile, at least it meant the faint hope that one might sail through the night to an as yet unspoiled Arcadia.

With all these ideas jostling inside his head, but without any script, in the same haphazard fashion he had made *The Angelic Conversation*, but on a more ambitious scale, Jarman now started to dog someone other than Swinton with his Nizo: Rupert Adley, most commonly called Spring, the son of an MP and a former public schoolboy. Spring was in the post-adolescent process of kicking over the traces, as violently and with as many drugs as he could. After a brief affair with Jarman, he spent much of 1986 living at Phoenix House, though with frequent absences in search of rather more high-octane amusement than his avuncular friend was always able to provide.

Apart from drugs, Spring's passions included the American soap operas *Dynasty* and *Dallas*, his *bêtes noires Caravaggio*. In a word, he found Jarman's film-making 'pointless'.[18] Jarman borrowed the version of *Profane Love* that Christopher Hobbs had painted for *Caravaggio* and filmed Spring attacking, then masturbating over this portrait of a twelve-year-old cupid with 'his finger up his arse'.[19] The last, not just of England, but of seven arduous years, this was a way for Jarman to kick over his own traces and reclaim the screen entirely for himself.

The film gathered momentum and structure. *Aria* had introduced James Mackay to Don Boyd, who allowed Mackay and Jarman to use his offices in Great Newport Street as their base. A small production unit began to form, at its head a director determined that, when actually filming, he would work in his most extensively collaborative manner yet. As he had explained in *Dancing Ledge*:

I have a very low opinion of art and an even lower opinion of what is accepted as art, put high on a pedestal, high as it is possible to make it without rendering it totally invisible . . . Unobtainable, it has a negative function in the education process. Culture begins at school and is completed at university, by which time all aspiration to selfhood is stifled, and the mind is colonized by dead wood . . . Only when art is demoted to the ranks again, treated as nothing remarkable, will our culture start to breathe. The spurious individualism of the Renaissance, which both engendered and was born of capital, is dying. An art which began by collaborating with the banks of the Medici ends in bankruptcy on Wall St. On the way, it destroyed the sublime anonymity of the Middle Ages and replaced it with stolen goods.[20]

Caravaggio had brought this home most forcibly. What Jarman craved more desperately than ever – as desperately as he craved it in the sexual arena – was a form of 'sublime anonymity'.

By midsummer, to the footage he already had of Tilda Swinton (and of Spencer Leigh) and Spring were added the sounds Simon Turner recorded around the wedding of the Duke and Duchess of York, and footage shot in Liverpool by Chris Hughes and Leigh, plus a good deal of London footage, taken principally in a ruined factory at Beckton, to the east of the Isle of Dogs, where Jarman and his small crew braved barbed wire and guard dogs to get inside. There was still no script, but Jarman had long since realised he would be using Dungeness much less than originally intended: 'somehow it wasn't right for the film'.[21]

In August Jarman flew to America and Canada to launch *Caravaggio* there, accompanied by Spring and the Nizo. After a decade of rejection, Manhattan seemed to be accepting him. As the film enjoyed perhaps its most positive reception yet, there were stylish parties for him and his extensive entourage; sympathetic interviews; flying visits to various cities; the news that the Walker Art Center in Minneapolis would be mounting an exhibition of his paintings and a retrospective of his films, which they planned to tour.

The purchase of the American rights to *Caravaggio* by the distributors had been underwritten by Mark McCormick, a wealthy descendant of the Chicago industrialist who had invented the reaper. McCormick and his companion, Leland Wheeler, invited Jarman and Spring to stay in their luxurious Upper East Side apartment. It was, Jarman told David Hirst, like stepping into *The Garden of the Finzi-Continis*. Virtually the only fly in the ointment was Spring, whose torn jeans and aggressive manner raised eyebrows in the elegant lobby of the apartment block and who, after a number of evenings spent AWOL in the New York clubs, unexpectedly elected to remain in America when Jarman returned to London.

To lose a central figure midway through shooting might have caused a less certain director to abandon his film entirely, or at least to radically alter tack. Not Jarman. Never for an instant did he allow Spring's disappearance to dent his determination to amass the footage needed for a feature. In this, he was backed by an equally tenacious producer. During the early, ambient stages of the film, relatively little backing had been needed: the cost of petrol, food, the odd prop and the super-8 stock. For the next stage, which was to include a fortnight's location shoot (the only formal set-up for the film), costs would escalate. There was no point in approaching the BFI – Jarman had already had his share of their limited funds. Instead Mackay spoke to ZDF, the German television station, who had seen and admired Jarman's work in Berlin, to British Screen, the reincarnation of the National Film Finance Corporation, and to Channel 4. All gave reassuring indications they were prepared to support Jarman in whatever his next venture might be. There was, however, still a dearth of hard cash, so Mackay underwrote the location shoot with money loaned by Ward-Jackson or set aside from *Aria* and the most recent pop promos. He used it sparingly, paying everyone the bare minimum and, where possible, getting people to accept deferred payments.

Meanwhile, Jarman was faced with the sudden need to put his ramshackle feature marginally on hold and concentrate on his painting. With the exception of *Charting Time*, an exhibition featuring the drawings and notes of a dozen avant-garde film-makers which had opened earlier that year at the Hatton Gallery in Newcastle Upon

Tyne before transferring to the Serpentine Gallery in August, and in which Jarman had shown the wonderfully detailed and eclectic note-books he kept to accompany his films, it had been two years since his last involvement with a gallery, and as long since he had devoted much time to his painting. Then came the surprise announcement that he had been shortlisted for that year's Turner Prize, the arts equivalent of the Booker. Worth at that time £10,000, the prize was awarded by the Tate Gallery for 'the greatest contribution to art in Britain' during the previous year. Jarman had been nominated 'in recognition of the outstanding visual quality of his films'.[22]

The Tate was a prime example of the sort of institution Jarman had in the past criticised and would normally be expected to shun. All the same, it did not take him long to decide that if he accepted the nomination and won the prize, he could always donate the money to AIDS research. For someone who had started life as a painter, but had always been forced to operate on the fringes of the art world, to be singled out like this was too great an honour to be refused.

So that August, spurred by both the Turner Prize and the impend-ing exhibition in America, now planned for Cornell University, he began to paint again, and with an intensity bordering on the fever-ish. Although the paintings he churned out were still small, still predominantly black, still flecked with gold, they differed quite sig-nificantly from his work of the early eighties. He was now pressing gilded glass into the black pigment, and engraving the glass with a fragment of Heraclitus or some other gnomic utterance before smashing it with a hammer, thus fracturing the piece at the point of final creation. 'As I do this,' he told his diary, 'I have to shut my eyes from the splinters.' He wondered whether this made him unique: the only artist to close rather than open his eyes at the 'crucial moment'.[23] His diaries hinted too at the profound despair that informed these paintings. Although by nature the most resolute of optimists and a firm believer that, through art, sense could be made of any existence, in a piece entitled 'THE SOUND OF BREAKING GLASS' he wrote: 'My world is in fragments, smashed in pieces so fine I doubt I will ever re-assemble them. The God that rules over the debris is SILENCE: you'll hear him in the wind that chases through the ruins. In the silence I'm impelled to speak, to remind myself of my existence, violating the God.'[24]

He also pressed small objects into the pigment, creating assemblages which displayed 'a three dimensional, sculptural effect'.[25] In *Panic*, the item used was a duplicate of the small set of Pan-pipes Spring had played on film. Apart from a possible nod at the video made for the Smiths, the title of this work derives from the story of Pan who, with his pipes, gave the travellers in Arcadia a fright, causing what we term 'panic'. The painting is a perfect example of how Jarman had found a style that wholly embraced his aims. Not only could he work quickly, something he had always valued, but he could have the objects in the painting ricochet into words, thus accommodating his learning. He could even amalgamate what he was doing in paint with what he was doing on film. As he explained: 'I always look for props which are charged, that have resonance. After they've been used on the film, something is lost, but by using them on the painting, they're given a new life.'[26]

For the Turner Prize, Jarman produced nine new paintings, all incorporating fractured glass, four featuring the word 'night', two candles, one the words 'blue is poison', one the gold outline of a skull, one a crucifix, one a remote-control for a television, one Caravaggio's knife with its motto, 'Nec Spe, Nec Metu'. He called these small, dark works *Caravaggio Suite*.[27] On 24 October they were collected from Phoenix House to be hung by the Tate alongside the pair of huge and colourful canvases submitted by Gilbert and George, who had also been shortlisted for the prize.

Almost immediately Jarman's attention was cruelly claimed by the sudden death of his father, who had that summer suffered a second stroke. More serious than the one he had suffered in the early eighties, it resulted in a spell of almost a month in Southampton General Hospital. He lost mobility and all speech, and underwent what was, for his son at least, a startling and welcome change of character. 'When I arrived at his bedside . . .' wrote Jarman, 'he broke into a radiant smile . . . He seemed happier than I ever remembered. Perhaps he was always a child who wished to be looked after.'[28]

While he was in hospital, it fell to Jarman and Gaye to sort through Lance's house and find what their father had been hiding from them. What they discovered exceeded their wildest imaginings. It was, to quote Jarman, 'the maddest inheritance. 90 bottles of whisky (he never drank), enough baked beans to fill a kitchen cupboard, 100 stolen cartons of lavatory paper, on and on, drawer after drawer, pens by the gross, envelopes by the thousands.'[29] There were supplies of toothpaste, hundreds of toothbrushes, a good deal of silver, a pile of girlie magazines, mountains of food and what seemed like a museum's worth of artifacts relating to the Second World War, including three loaded pistols. There were files containing typed copies of the hundreds of letters Lance had written to New Zealand as a young man, exact details of the cost of his children's education and evidence of his obsessive search to locate his roots.

Taking 'two presentation photo mounts in leather', embossed with, of all things, the royal coat of arms, Jarman and Gaye put a photograph of Betts in one of them and took it to the hospital to place by Lance's bedside. Jarman instantly regretted his action: 'I have never seen such distress . . . It was as if all his secrets had been discovered.'[30] Lance might have undergone a change of character, but the past had not been eradicated. When Gaye put photos of the rest of the family by his bedside, the picture of Sam, who when younger had threatened his grandfather's secret, was mysteriously removed.

Although Lance never regained the power of speech, he did reclaim a degree of mobility, enabling him to be moved to a convalescent home on the Isle of Wight, where his mobility continued to improve. In every other respect, however, he was too ill for the home to cope with, and he was soon dispatched to a nursing home in the New Forest, where he suffered another stroke. Visiting him that evening, Gaye and Jarman found their father unconscious and strapped to the bed. When Gaye put out a hand to touch him, he let out a growl which made her jump across the room. Jarman wondered if he should perhaps speak, then decided that as he and his father had never shared a language for emotions, it was 'too late to invent one'.[31] By the same token, he and Gaye agreed that as Lance was barely conscious, there was little point in staying by his bedside. Taking their leave, they returned home. A few hours later, with only a few photographs to witness the moment, Air Commodore Lancelot Elworthy Jarman breathed his last.

Gaye and Jarman finished emptying his house as quickly, painlessly and discreetly as possible. They asked the women for whom he had done odd jobs if anything of theirs was missing, and returned whatever items they could to their rightful owners. In the shed, Jarman found some of the garden tools he had used as a boy and put them aside to take to London, where he would clean and oil them. Beyond the family, he and Gaye told hardly anyone about Lance's death and decided against putting a notice in the newspaper in case it encouraged renewed coverage of Lance's kleptomania. Of the cremation, attended by only immediate family, Jarman wrote: 'As the kindly priest talked well of him, I thought: how sad that none of us can shed a tear.'[32]

Lance had never told either of his children what he had done with their mother's ashes. They knew precisely what to do with his. Gaye parcelled them up and posted them to New Zealand. There, the vicar of St James's church in Riccarton held a second service and the ashes were scattered in the graveyard under the same rose bush as those of Lance's father. The man who, fifty-eight years previously and brimming with hope, had set sail for Southampton on the SS *Ionic* had finally returned home, having seen the last of England. When his mother had died, Jarman had dedicated his forthcoming film – *The Tempest* – to her memory. He made no such gesture towards his father. All the same, it feels as if his next film could stand as an implicit and not untender paternal memorial.

As one influential figure departed from Jarman's life, another arrived. That October, he attended a gay film-makers' workshop in Newcastle Upon Tyne. In the audience for the screening of *Imagining October* was Keith Collins, then working as a writer of software for the Ministry of Defence. With his green eyes and dark hair, the twenty-three-year-old Collins possessed the looks of a matinée idol and a restless intelligence to match. Captivated, Jarman quietly obtained Collins' address and, on his return to London, began writing to him in terms that left the intensity of his feelings in little doubt: 'I wish I had been able to abduct you when I came to Newcastle but perhaps one shouldn't say this, particularly on paper, but there we are, perhaps it's better to be straightforward . . .' There was a ps: 'I still don't know your surname.'[33]

The second half of November found Jarman and his crew for *The Last of England* based in a cluster of vans and Nissen huts at Victoria Docks, where, in a derelict and hellishly cold flour mill adjoining the apocalyptically named Millennium Mills,[34] they undertook the for-malised shoot that wrapped up an entire year of ambient filming. The schedule was steady (as many as eight hours of improvised camera-work a day) and extremely demanding, more so even than *Caravaggio*. With *Caravaggio*, Jarman had at least known 'whether the film was working'. With *The Last of England*, although he sensed – and quite rightly, whatever one thinks of the final result – that the film would always be 'more alive'[35] than its predecessor, as there were no daily rushes, only the photographic stills brought to the set each morning by Mike Laye, however promising these looked, only at the very end of the shoot would Jarman know for sure that the film had come out as intended. All he had to go on during their allotted time at Victoria Docks was the excited and voluble support generated by the highly collaborative way in which he had chosen to work.[36]

To help fund the shoot, before leaving Victoria Docks, Jarman quickly executed two pop videos for the soon to be dissolved Easterhouse: '1969' and 'Whistling in the Dark'. Then, in late November, he had himself filmed writing at his desk in Phoenix House. This last-minute footage would give him a structure for the finished film, that of its maker writing and dreaming it into being – the same structure he had used for *The Tempest, Imagining October* and, to an extent, *The Angelic Conversation*.

Meanwhile, the Turner Prize was being awarded in a ceremony at the Tate. Jarman was prepared for the worst. The critic Waldemar Januszczak had written waspishly in the *Guardian* that if Jarman won, it would be like 'giving the prize for Michelangelo studies to Irving Stone'.[37] The bookmakers William Hill had listed the odds against this dire prediction coming true as 7–1. By contrast, Gilbert and George, the eventual winners, stood at a commanding 6–4. Even so, and although he had so little respect for the art world, Jarman's diary entry for the evening cannot hide his disappointment. 'The sound system was so bad that no one could hear a word. Melvyn

Bragg gave up entirely and just handed out the prize to Gilbert and George. Gilbert grabbed the cheque without so much as a thank you and the whole sorry thing was over . . . their calculated bad manners and art crafty slyness truly complements the brutish art scene.'[38]

However badly Jarman felt about this outcome, it paled into insignificance when, a month later, he received another, infinitely more devastating result; one that had been anticipated for far longer and with far greater dread. Since its insinuation into his conscious-ness in the early eighties, the spectre of AIDS had grown yearly more terrifying and had begun to impact with increasing ferocity on Jarman's life. In August 1985, immediately before shooting began on *Caravaggio*, his old friend Mario Dubsky had become the first of his immediate circle to be claimed by the disease. 'Mario had been extremely troubled in the years before,' Jarman later recalled. 'In a pub one evening he shouted at me that I had not spent enough time with him at his exhibition in Camberwell. I said I had thought he was busy and had better people to talk to than old friends. He said I'd betrayed him – we'd all betrayed him . . . That was the last I saw of him. There was no sign he was ill.'[39] As if the fact that Dubsky had suffered an ugly and premature death were not distressing enough, his unexpected loss was followed by ghoulish telephone calls. 'The phone didn't stop ringing,' Jarman noted in his diary, 'people seemed to take pleasure in the telling. None of these people ring except at times like this.'[40] A second death in 1985, that of the actor Rock Hudson, the first internationally famous celebrity to be carried off by AIDS, brought the disease to the attention of a much wider public. To an extent, this greater awareness was welcome, yet it also inten-sified the virtual witch hunt to which many gay men, characterised as plague-bearers, were being subjected. The tabloids, disseminators of scare stories since 1983, continued their campaign of vilification. To their clamour was added the homophobia of such figures as James Anderton, Greater Manchester's chief constable, who preached thunderously that homosexuals were 'swirling about in a human cesspit of their own making'.[41] Various countries refused admittance to anyone suspected of having come into contact with the HIV virus. Insurance companies took a broadly similar stance. There was talk of AIDS being made a notifiable disease. Jarman wrote: 'We're on the defensive . . . all the advances of the last few years could be removed in the twinkling of an eye.'[42] Added to which there was, of course, the secret, sickening fear that he himself stood in the firing line – in more ways than one.

Setting this alongside the many ways Jarman had felt himself to be under psychic attack in the eighties, most crucially as a film-maker, one can understand why he should now start to link the virus that might be threatening his body with the 'virus' of Thatcherism he saw attacking the body politic. To many, himself included, the government seemed to have taken too long to respond to AIDS, and when it did, to have done so with insufficient commitment and money, too much of which went on campaigns to advertise the dangers posed by the disease as opposed to urgently needed research and medical facilities. Did the Tory administration truly care what happened to gay people? The question – and its inevitable answer – enraged Jarman.

In early 1986, during the course of a regular check-up at the VD clinic, the doctor had suggested Jarman take a test to see if he was HIV positive. At the time, he was coping with Mary Whitehouse, Winston Churchill and the furore created by the television broadcast of his films. Already subject to late-night telephone death threats, he felt too 'insecure' to follow the doctor's advice. 'I saw the news leaked to the *Sun* and the *Star* with visions of ending up as part of the daily diet of terror that sells these malevolent and jaundiced newspapers.'[43] But the doctor had planted a seed and, despite considerable uncertainty about the advisability of being tested (in the absence of any cure, did it help to know you had a fatal disease?), as more and more of Jarman's friends took the test and discovered they were HIV positive, so it began to feel inevitable that he would have to follow suit, if only out of solidarity. It is here, in the growing trepidation he must have felt as 1986 slipped by, that clues abound as to why his paintings that year were so despairing. That he had more or less convinced himself of the outcome of any test we can deduce from something he said in one of his last interviews of that interview-filled year. He told the *Observer* he would be making his next film 'in a hurry'. 'I can't afford another six years. No metropolitan gay man can be sure he will be alive in six years' time.'[44]

As he said, this, he knew that his appointments diary contained two

entries for the morning of 22 December: '9.30 Appointment. 11.30
Don Boyd.' The appointment was to hear the result of his AIDS test.
It was exactly as he had feared.

> The young doctor who told me this morning I was a carrier of
> the AIDS virus was visibly distressed. I smiled and told her
> not to worry, I had never liked Christmas. I had put on my
> dark black overcoat I love so much to walk to the hospital.
> Wearing it at my father's funeral a few weeks ago I looked
> more sombre than the undertakers. It gave me confidence for
> this meeting . . . It was almost with relief that I listened to the
> doctor's catalogue of do's and dont's – shaving, hairdressing,
> all the little details . . . I stopped at the stationers and bought
> a daybook for 1987 and a scarlet form to write out a will.[45]

The orderliness of his actions – 'I thought how fortunate to be
forewarned,' he added, 'so that one can wind one's life up in an
orderly fashion' – calls to mind his military father and leads one to
wonder whether it was Lance's death that had finally freed Jarman to
thus confront the possibility of his own.

Whatever the case, it would take a while for the news to sink in.
One of the ways he ensured that it did was utterly to disregard the
doctor's advice not to tell anyone.[46] At his second appointment on
the morning of 22 December, he immediately shared the news of his
diagnosis with Don Boyd. That other people knew helped 'stabilise
the uncertainty' – and, in those early days of the disease, the uncertainty was perhaps its most distressing aspect.

'What does that mean?' asked Boyd.

'I've got to get as much out of life as possible,' replied Jarman.

He also turned for consolation to his diary, where, in the torrent of
words which poured out of him, one can glimpse the fear and distress
that shadowed the sunny face he kept turned towards his friends.

> At lunch Christopher [Hobbs] arrived unexpectedly and . . . I
> broke the news to him. At first he expressed sympathy which
> I told him I didn't really need as I could see many advantages;
> one had perhaps avoided a gruelling old age, cheated the

bomb. Chris said . . . I might live so long that I would regret these words. I told him that my work only really preoccupied me and I experienced the world with mounting despair. The bomb had dropped in my mind years ago. Life in Phoenix House had changed subtly so I often felt imprisoned there. I had 2 problems [those] who commissioned and insured the films and the dream of a wild love affair with a lad I met briefly in Newcastle last September. Now this could never happen unless he was willing to sit around the fireside. In the market I bought him a pair of gold cufflinks. It seemed a sensible gift. Something you might have got from a solid uncle. And a mirror for Tilda.

Later:

mirror mirror please god I don't get the awful disfiguring blemishes of Kaposi . . . in the 'Jungle' this evening . . . two of the . . . lads . . . had said how do you look so young Derek?, and then how old are you? 45 in a month. Tell us the secret, they said. I have no secrets, I lied, I inherited my father's constitution and I have had the most privileged life. I went in search of myself and never did a day's work that I regret. However bleak my films might seem the gold shone through. At that moment Johnny [Maybury] passed by and said something that took my breath away. 'You seem to have changed, Derek.' 'I can't have, it's only two months since we met, perhaps it's my hair cut.' No he said, something's different, and then he was off into the shadows. I wanted to chase after him but stopped myself.

And later still:

> *his flashing eyes his floating hair*
> *weave a circle round him thrice*
> *and close your eyes with holy dread*
> *for he on honeydew hath fed*
> *and drunk the milk of paradise*

Coleridge's ecstatic poem conveys more than I could ever hope on the empty white page in the dawn. I shut my eyes and conjure the exhausted calm in the dawn, not this grey winter dawn but a dawn in which the rising sun transfigures the loved one sung in by the blackbird who sits on the flower pots of my city garden. We must fight the fears that threaten our garden, for make no mistake ours is the garden of the poets of Will Shakespeare's sonnets, of Marlowe, Catullus, of Plato and Wilde, all those who have worked and suffered to keep it watered. Perhaps he left before dawn to join the daily grind, perhaps he will play truant and feign a bad cold. Perhaps he will throw his life to the winds and say I never liked that job and stay for the rest of a lazy day. Perhaps it will be forever. Perhaps a tear falls and splashes the page. Pull yourself together and put on the best of your masks to face the new day.[47]

On the night of 23 December he went to Heaven with Alasdair McGaw.

We were in immense high spirits as we walked to Charing Cross. He remarked that I was crossing the road with a reckless disregard for the traffic. 'Not like the old days when you crept about so cautiously.' I noticed immediately he told me. As the evening wore on a great calm descended. I'd crossed over and was untouchable. For the first time in months I was free from the tangle of fear that had grown up like poison ivy.[48]

Early the next morning, Jarman left for Shropshire and the Welsh borders, where he, Christopher Hobbs and Rick Rogers were to spend Christmas at a country-house hotel. The hotel turned out to be 'ghastly',[49] overrun by elderly women intent on involving the trio of men in their games, which they spent much of their time gloomily avoiding. Jarman found midnight mass on Christmas Eve no more enlivening. 'Perhaps this is what the C of E is all about,' he mused, 'a tedium that would send the living quite dead into the afterlife; and if, after all, heaven is like this, it should be no more difficult to cheat oneself in than fiddle the DHSS.' Not that he had any desire to enter heaven, unless of the discotheque variety. 'If heaven is conducted like this,' he wrote, 'half-threat, half-chat-show, thank God I'm never going to get there.'[50]

Two days later, he was back in London.

The first of the cards I opened . . . informed me in a postscript that Arthur Bressan, the filmmaker I had met in Newcastle last autumn, was very ill with pneumonia brought on by the AIDS virus. He was a brilliant vivacious man who kept us all entertained during the three days of the festival . . . Arthur told us of how he had made porno feature films through the seventies as this was the only alternative by bright openly gay filmmakers to the numbed cinema in Hollywood . . . We had to bear witness to this time [said Bressan] and hope that others in the future would be able to speak their desires clear and remember the few brief years since Stonewall as a time of hope.

. . . I've a fund of stories as rich as anything in Boswell and Orton that have happened to me and my friends, encounters not unlike Boswell's on Westminster Bridge or Orton in the gents in Islington.[51]

Jarman saw these stories as brave, wonderful and defiant. He also used them to speculate as to where he might have caught the virus: 'I picked up a very handsome leather boy from NYC, 23, he was on the rampage, he fucked me rotten in a cubicle and then we went home where the performance was repeated . . . I never felt the panic that some have related, just a dull resignation.'[52] On 28 December he wrote that his diary had 'filled in a long Sunday in which I could have felt sorry for myself. Perhaps it's the first hysterical reaction but it's impossible to stop thinking of the virus.'

As a way of keeping his sanity, he turned towards the work that might lie beyond his immediate task of knocking the disparate footage for *The Last of England* into coherent shape.

Reread both Marlowe and Brecht's versions of *Edward II*. Both would be difficult to adapt for the screen . . . the

advantages of Brecht are the possibility of a German
production. Manfred[53] is already in touch with his daughter
and she is interested in a meeting. But Brecht is hallowed
ground and I don't dare to think of the consequences of
tampering with him. I don't want to make Edward weak or
vacillatory . . . I want to be on his side, make the love affair
noble. This has never been attempted with a homosexual
love affair.

He was also painting. He once acknowledged that in all painting
there is 'a certain hopeless quest for immortality'.[54] Yet it was less
immortality than practicality that now led him to it. Although he
realised that painting could never become a full-time occupation, it
was one of his current ambitions 'to end up like Monet, at the age of
80, splashing paint all over a canvas in a sunlit garden'.[55] If he
became ill, he knew that painting would at least provide 'a way of
working, quick and gentle. I often think of Matisse, bedridden, cutting out "Jazz". If necessary, you can work in bed. I see painting as a
lifeline.'[56] He saw, too, that even if he did not fall ill, film could no
longer be relied upon. There was no saying whether he would be
allowed to travel as easily as he once had, or if he would be insurable.
That alone could spell the end of his career as a director.

On New Year's Day, he painted a total of eight canvases. One of
the paintings from this time was a 'self-portrait' for his forty-fifth
birthday. Set into the black paint was the whistle used by Ariel in
The Tempest and by the dumb Jerusaleme in Caravaggio. 'Veni Voco' –
'Come when I call.'

26

A Fifth Continent

O Rose, thou art sick!
The invisible worm
That flies in the night,
In the howling storm,

Has found out thy bed
Of crimson joy,
And his dark secret love
Does thy life destroy.[1]

For someone as sensitive to signs as Jarman, 1987 did not start promisingly. On 6 January, he and Tilda Swinton had their photographs taken by Angus McBean, one of whose photographic portraits had long been the only piece by any artist other than himself to hang on the walls of Jarman's flat. When the session ended, McBean announced: 'You are going to be my last sitter.' As he 'pressed the button for the last time "Stormy Weather" was playing on the stereo'.[2]

There could have been few clearer ways of signalling the end of an era, unless it was another appearance Jarman made in front of the camera, to play his old friend Patrick Procktor in *Prick Up Your Ears*, Stephen Frears' film about Joe Orton and Kenneth Halliwell. In 1967, when Peter Gill had commissioned Procktor to draw Orton for a programme insert for his Royal Court production of Orton's *Crimes of Passion*,[3] Jarman had been twenty-five, living in Islington, catching glimpses of Orton in Chapel Street Market and visiting Procktor in his Manchester Street flat, where he himself had featured in more than one of Procktor's paintings. Now, in his mid-forties and feeling 'like mutton dressed as lamb',[4] Jarman was required to stand in front of an easel and roll back the years by pretending to be Procktor while Gary Oldman, lying naked on a rug, pretended to be Orton.

Doors were closing. With private panic, uncertainty and despair came a crippling caution. Jarman's libido, once as unflagging a constituent of his daily life as fun and laughter, went on temporary hold, as did certain gestures of affection. Because there was still so little clear information about AIDS, he stopped kissing people when he met them, or else made sure he kissed only air. He worried about touching the children of friends, about sharing cups and glasses.

His fears were magnified by the fact that his diagnosis coincided with the government's as yet most determined attempt to educate the public about the disease. A leaflet on AIDS was put through the letterbox of every household in the country.[5] There were newspaper advertisements, posters, a campaign on radio and television and in the cinema, public discussion and articles in the written media. Such a widespread raising of public awareness should have been wholly to the good, only the method chosen by the government to convey their message was hardly designed to calm the fears of a person recently diagnosed as HIV positive. Intent on shocking the public into immediate awareness, the campaign favoured apocalyptic images of danger and death: an exploding mountain, an iceberg, a giant tombstone. Nor did the subsequent newspaper coverage, with its hair-raising predictions of how this terrible plague might decimate the country, make matters any easier. 'AIDS: THE NEW HOLOCAUST'[6] ran a not atypical headline.

In the circumstances, the public face of confidence and determination Jarman put on his private fears is all the more remarkable. Perhaps it was simply his background. He knew he had a war to fight and that if he wanted to outwit or hinder his enemy, what was needed – more as a matter of self-preservation than a conscious crusade – were meticulous planning, tactics, courage. Still intent on not allowing his diagnosis to imprison him in secrecy, he resolved also that it must never lead to any outward display of self-pity. If there was comforting to be done after he had broken his news to anyone, invariably it was the bearer comforting the recipient. More interested in moving forward than in talking about how he felt, he discouraged discussion of his emotions.

He armed himself with as much information on the disease as he could, bemoaned its scarcity and plotted how best to rectify this state of affairs. Ever the expert at replenishing himself with new faces, he began to change the composition of his court, finding new friends to suit his new situation. He forced himself to count his blessings and to see blessings where others might have thought they could not exist. He rejoiced that HIV had given him back his isolation and the privilege of being an outsider; that he was unlikely to become an old man, a consideration which particularly delighted the Peter Pan in him; that early death, as he had once noted caustically of Orton, was almost always good box office. The possibility that people might stop showing his films caused a degree of alarm, but he saw that the virus could also provide him with a most effective soapbox, that it might in fact secure his position as not only a film-maker but a public figure.

The key to his entire campaign was work. He had always worked hard; now he would work even harder, frenetically almost, using work as a means of riding his despair and combating loss. Starting with *The Last of England*, he would use the time he had left to produce a quantity of films, paintings and books commensurate with the very longest of lives.

As with *The Angelic Conversation*, and, to a lesser extent, *Imagining October*, in post-production the principal problem posed by *The Last of England* was to find a structure for footage shot so randomly. Because he could not assess exactly what he had to work with until the footage was cleaned and transferred to video, it was only by tirelessly viewing and reviewing the material, writing a belated description of the film for ZDF and using another workbook (a whirlpool of notes, pictures, newspaper clippings and memos) that he started to map out the film. He divided it into some fifteen sequences, dipping into his bag of titles for their names: 'Bliss', 'The World's End', 'Deathwatch', 'Night Life', 'The Art of Mirrors', 'The Archeology of Soul', 'A Dance at the Edge of Time', 'The Pandemonium of Images', 'Art of Memory'. He also watched his family home movies: a Sunday lunch in the twenties, Arcadian images of himself and Gaye as young children playing in the garden with Betts, glimpses of imperial India and his father's Wellington bomber at Lossiemouth – footage which provided a poignant and unsettling counterpoint to his own images of contemporary desolation and decay.

Working with his usual gang and seeking the opinion of anyone who happened by, Jarman spent January on a rough edit of this material at Don Boyd's office in Great Newport Street. Although the overriding rhythm to which he cut the footage together echoed the relentless pace of the music video, the music to which he normally worked was Benjamin Britten's *War Requiem*: 'the perfect foil to my more intuitive film-making'.[7] Once this stage was complete, Peter Cartwright, who had similarly tidied up *The Angelic Conversation* and *Imagining October*, arrived to do a final edit and, in the process, establish an even clearer map of the filmic terrain. By March, the film was ready for transfer to 35mm.

At this point, it was still silent. For a 'sound' map that would give it added shape, Jarman now turned to another old colleague, Simon Turner. Much as he might have liked to use the music of Britten, or, come to that, a track or two by Psychedelic Furs, *Imagining October* had taught him how prohibitively expensive and therefore counter-productive this could be. So, working around four admonitory passages of voice-over written by Jarman and read by Nigel Terry, Turner set about composing some original electronic music, organising and adding sound effects, then commissioning a number of other musicians either to write or perform pieces specially for the film – including Marianne Faithfull, who, because it was a song Betts used to sing at bedtime, was asked to record 'The Skye Boat Song'.

Jarman described the finished film as a dream allegory: 'The poet wakes in a visionary landscape where he encounters personifications of psychic states.'[8] In this way, he linked it to both *Jubilee* and the unrealised *Neutron*. Although there are elements of hope in the film – besides the fact that, at the end, a group of refugees sails into the darkness towards an eventual sunrise, Jarman always maintained that the act of filming was in itself an act of hope – the overall ambience is one of anger and despair. 'The easiest way to communicate the atmosphere of the film,' he wrote, 'is to suggest that it will be made to . . . the pattern of the requiem Mass.'[9] He also pointed a finger at Christmas in Charing Cross Road; in particular, the Christmas he had just lived through, when, during the 'long, bleak, empty days' separating Shropshire from the New Year, he had stood at his window in the grip of a panic that could ravage him 'like a bomb blast' and stared dully at the street below, 'charged with the mindless energy of the dispossessed, shouting, smashing bottles, blowing whistles and kicking empty beer cans'.[10]

There is a great deal of loutish destruction in the fevered and fractured flow of images that constitute *The Last of England*. While the 'poet' Jarman sits at his desk, alternatively dreaming, writing, or assembling one of his paintings, we see Spring stamping on, then masturbating over, Caravaggio's *Profane Love*. He shoots up in the corner of a derelict factory, wanders through a wasteland playing the pipes of Pan. A flare[11] leads us through this landscape of urban desolation. Spencer Leigh is taken on to a rooftop and cold bloodedly shot by a group of soldiers in balaclavas. On a raised platform draped with the Union Jack, a naked man grapples drunkenly with another figure in military garb, face similarly hidden. Soldiers round up a group of refugees on the banks of the Thames. A naked tramp (Christopher Hughes) gnaws at a cauliflower.[12] A crippled businessman (Gerrard McArthur) pours grain from his bowler hat. A devilish creature in a tutu (Mathew Hawkins) twirls in a maniacal dance. A Buddha-like figure(Gill Beckett) spins a globe. An archaeologist (Paul Reynolds) goes quietly about the business of disinterring and inspecting the past. James Mackay pushes a pram containing a baby smothered by pages of the *Sun*. Three women in black (Jo Comino, Jordan and Joan de Vere Hunt) carry a wreath of red poppies. There is a grotesque wedding. Whirling like a dervish, an impassioned Tilda Swinton takes a pair of enormous scissors to her dress. In heart-wrenchingly vivid colour, we glimpse Jarman and his sister as children, playing in a succession of gardens, see the flashes of imperial India and Lance's Wellington bomber, New York, Liverpool and the Albert Memorial. We hear music, sounds, advertisements, the voices of Nigel Terry and Hitler. We see a final flare. The refugees are aboard a small and fragile craft, sailing into the night.

To some, it is a nightmare vision of Great Britain; to others, a vision of the nightmare that is Great Britain. For Jarman it was almost certainly the latter, as well as being a haunting and elegiac account of an entirely internal voyage, through despair and desecration into the welcoming arms of night. By choosing to work as he did (cheaply and on his own terms, rather than following the *Caravaggio* route), he was reclaiming control of his life at a most critical moment – and in as extreme and flagrant a manner as possible, as if pinching himself violently to make sure he was awake.

Jarman liked to hold up his modus operandi – simply pick up a super-8 camera and film your friends – as the ideal template for any film-maker desperate to escape the constraints of fund-raising and the film and television industry in general; as one in the eye, in fact, for the David Puttnams of his world. Yet peering behind the scenes at how his original super-8 footage reached the screen, one realises that although his method was cheap to start with, the process of post-production was actually very expensive and involved a number of rows, wrangles and manoeuvres which, while not earth-shattering or unusual, do show that, even standing outside the mainstream, Jarman was never immune to many of the unavoidable strictures inherent in the film-making process. Spontaneity came at a price.

In December, as the super-8 footage was being viewed and transferred to video, ZDF confirmed that they would contribute DM120,000 (about £40,000) to the new film. In return, the station would acquire the German television rights. Over £200,000 was still needed towards a final budget of some £260,000. Don Boyd suggested to Mackay that the perfect distributors would be Tartan Films, a company Boyd himself had helped found. Tartan, no doubt thinking they would have another *Caravaggio* on their hands, were immensely keen. Mackay entered into negotiation with them, but with little intention of quickly finalising a deal – he had fingers in other pies. Meanwhile, British Screen made a handsome contribution towards the production costs and Channel 4 offered the same as ZDF. Not wanting Channel 4 to handle the British television rights, Tartan demanded that Mackay turn down their offer, and only after the threat of legal action did they and Mackay finally agree terms under which, in the United Kingdom only, and excluding television, Tartan could distribute the film. Distribution rights for the rest of the world went to the Sales Company.

Nor was that all. Clearance had to be obtained from Equity, the actors' union, and ACTT, the technicians' union, both of which wanted reassurance that the film had been made in accordance with union practice and with union members, which, of course, it had not. Parliamentary permission for the use of excerpts from members' speeches in the voice-overs[13] was, after some correspondence, refused. The film was invited to the forthcoming Tokyo Film Festival in October, though in order to qualify, it needed not to have been screened on television first. Mackay therefore had to beg ZDF – unsuccessfully, as it turned out – to alter their schedules.

As these problems were being sorted out, Jarman was also laying determined siege to Keith Collins, the young man who had so entranced him in Newcastle. He had written more than once to Collins before Christmas, enclosing with one letter the cufflinks he had bought with Christopher Hobbs in Covent Garden on the day of his diagnosis. The letters continued in the New Year.

the best present I could have would be to see you for my birthday at the end of the month. I'm sending you a ticket which if you want to use you're welcome. My dad was a kleptomaniac, promise. A really great thief, only the best silver, and since during the last years of his life he refused to eat anything but baked beans, salting away his 'slag', 'loot' or whatever, I'm suddenly able to do a few mad things, as he forgot to hide the money, knocking both me and my sister sideways as it's rather an indecent sum. So we all have skeletons in the cupboard. This relationship had a silver lining you might say; please accept the ticket on his

behalf . . . I was going to ask you if you are still free late
March–early April if you would like to help me take some
pictures to the States. Cornell University is paying for two
tickets so the pictures could be carried over in the hand
luggage . . . the trip should only be 8 or 9 days, three in
Cornell and a week in N.Y.C. . . .[14]

In February, after Collins had visited Phoenix House and been
given a copy of Roland Barthes' A *Lover's Discourse*, Jarman wrote:
'Dear Green Eyes . . . I think the idea of becoming a student is a good
one. I was at college until I was 27 and I don't think it did harm. I'd
organise bed and board. I'd make a good old fashioned landlady . . .
I don't think you need to be a poor mature student and what's
poverty after all? I'm not too worried about feeding you, after all, if
you can bear the dependence, which I know would be difficult for a
boy with wild green eyes.' The letter ends with a story which, to the
alchemist in Jarman, would have put paid to any negativity inferred
from his photographic session with McBean. On Collins' first visit to
London, Jarman had wanted to buy the young man an antique ring
from a shop in Burlington Arcade specialising in old jewellery
dredged from the Thames. The ring did not fit, so Jarman bought one
for himself instead: an old but unremarkable-looking black ring inset
with a small black stone. There followed a miraculous discovery.
'And guess what,' he wrote, 'there's gold. I wore my medieval ring all
last week and gradually the base metal turned to gold before my eyes
as the muck wore off it. I couldn't quite believe it but neither the
prospector/the museum he showed it to/or the shop in Burlington
Arcade noticed it. Don't you think that's extraordinary? So extravagance can pay!' The stone turned out to be an emerald, as green as
the eyes which had Jarman in thrall.

    In one of Collins' replies, sent after a week in London and the gift
of another book, he wrote: 'I've just got back – drunken – from the
club, after reading most of *Dancing Ledge* on the coach. Please don't
let what we have be reduced to a paragraph of autobiography.' There
was little chance of that.

    Asked around this time if he had regrets about how his sexuality
had determined his friends, Jarman answered revealingly: 'If I hoped

to find orgies, they weren't orgiastic; if I hoped to find permanence, it wasn't permanent. Deep down it was unsatisfactory, neurotic, but this was forgotten in the excitement.'[15] He had never wanted permanence, not in the conventional sense, though when he now wrote about Phoenix House, and how it had 'imposed isolation' on him and 'somehow outlived its purpose', it was not merely his clothes cupboard being 'jammed with paintings'[16] that bothered him; he was worried too that there was not enough space for cohabitation. In the wake of his diagnosis, and with the advent of middle age, the possibility of permanence was no longer so rigorously scorned. And in the person of Collins, it acquired irresistible allure.

The child of staunchly religious parents (his father was a Methodist lay preacher, his mother played the organ in church), Collins had been brought up with his elder sister in a small mining village on the outskirts of Durham, where his father was employed as a manual labourer. He attended the village school followed by the local grammar, emerging with the A-Levels and the parental backing – but not the money – to go to university. His parents wanted him to study medicine. Instead, he took a degree in applied computing at Newcastle, helping to pay his way by writing software for the defence industry.

On his first visit to Phoenix House, Collins had barely got through the door and begun to greet Jarman with a kiss before Jarman pulled back and said quietly: 'There's something you should know. I'm HIV.'

In many ways, the announcement was a blessing in disguise. As usual, Jarman had fallen for someone who did not find him in the least sexually attractive. In any other circumstances, this might have created considerable tension; as it was, though obviously Jarman felt a degree of disappointment, with the pressure lifted, he and Collins found they could enjoy each other's company in almost every other way. A new passionate friendship was born; the most passionate and enduring of them all.

By April, Collins was accompanying Jarman to America for his exhibition, *Night Life and Other Recent Paintings*. Held at the Herbert F. Johnson Museum of Art, Cornell University, Ithaca, it comprised the nine pieces from the *Caravaggio Suite* together with twenty-three of the 'private and devotional'[17] paintings Jarman had been working on in recent years, and was linked to *Of Angels and Apocalypse*, the touring retrospective of Jarman's films brought across from Britain by the film and video programme of the Walker Art Centre in Minneapolis. The two of them travelled sufficiently well together for Collins to decide, on their return to London, to succumb to Jarman's blandishments and move permanently into Phoenix House.

Onlookers wondered whether the relationship would last. Setting aside the obvious depth of Jarman's passion for Collins, how could two people live in so small and crowded a space, particularly when they were so different? Jarman was forty-five, a southerner, middle class and ex-public school. Collins was two decades his junior and from the poorest of northern backgrounds. He worked in computers, not the arts, and, like Spring, did not share Jarman's taste in films. He was similar to Spring in other respects, too. Whether or not consciously and in rebellion from his parents makes no matter, but the fact remains that the young Collins was, in the eyes of many, little more than a lager lout – or, in his case, a Newcastle Brown Ale lout. He drank, smoked, generally raised hell and made no secret of the fact that his involvement with Jarman did not preclude him from having sex with other people of either gender. There were those of Jarman's old friends who regarded him as little more than a cheap hustler, a gold-digger – and their worst suspicions seemed to be confirmed when, with something approaching mathematical thoroughness, Collins began to oust some of them from Jarman's life. Why, they wondered, did Jarman put up with this? Was he blinded by lust? How long before the scales would fall from his eyes?

What these observers failed to put into the equation was that if Collins was jealous of them, this jealousy might indicate that Jarman mattered to Collins as much as Collins did to Jarman. They were also ignoring the fact that while in private Jarman might occasionally shake his head over Collins' excesses, he was nevertheless complicit in his companion's behaviour. To be taken over in this manner and cut off from certain old friends was something Jarman seemed, if not always to welcome, certainly to tolerate. Given his diagnosis, perhaps he needed a dragon guarding the lair. It undoubtedly suited him to have someone as willing as Collins to fetch and carry for him.

Jarman nicknamed Collins 'Hinney Beast',[18] soon shortened to

HB – a Geordie term of affection which did not always find favour with Collins, whose only form of retaliation was to call Jarman 'Fur Beast', as their notes to each other reflect:

Hinney Beast you are the best fun in the world, wasn't I lucky to find you? yours, senior citizen.

> Oh Hinney Beast
> Ware hav u gon
> I hope to Johnny Mills
> I am missing u
> this morning
> and did not wak up
> to find you there
> being furry. I was
> mad and sad all morning
> thinking you were
> som wer else
> and did not hav you to
> lok at in the Bath
>
> Oh Hinney Beastie shining brite
> in the Forest of the nite
> your favourite thing has gone a huntin
> in the glades and woods of Hampstead
> do not worry ill be back
> put your head upon the sack.

To which Collins might reply: 'Oh furry beast, What a funny day and finding out the red-haired boy fancied me, what a shock! Anyway, you are my favourite, and I don't think he could live up to my expectations (or yours). Hope you had fun and fur on the Heath. You are my favourite and I do love you lots and lots. Geordie beast. (ps) If Johnny is at the LA I might stay with him. Otherwise I'll be home drunk and furry later.'

The likely permanence of the relationship galvanised Jarman into carrying out a plan that had for some time been forming in his mind:

to find a second home. Although *The Last of England* was not yet out of post-production, already he was thinking of a new film, to be made in a similar fashion, by shadowing Tilda Swinton with his Nizo. In May, he, Swinton and Collins again ended up in Dungeness, in search of fish and chips and the chance to film Swinton on the shingle, pursuing the ceaseless beam of the lighthouse. Spotting a 'For Sale' sign outside one of the fishermen's cottages, they asked the owner if they might look around. Enchanted, and undeterred by the wind whipping across the Ness – or by the owner's confirmation that no, it never stopped – Jarman instructed Swinton to drive immediately to the estate agents. Within days, his offer of £32,000 was accepted, and the Dungeness estate had agreed to his purchase of some extra land for the bargain price of £700.

Built at the turn of the century, the cottage had at one stage, or so it seemed from old photographs, boasted a pink roof, a detail which delighted Jarman, though when he bought it, the roof, like the walls, was entirely black, the building's only colour the 'cheery'[19] yellow of its windows and doors. It was the simplest of dwellings. Four small, square rooms led off a central corridor that ran from the front door to the narrow kitchen at the rear. Also at the back, in a shorter passage off the main one, was a shower and toilet. The kitchen overlooked the miniature railway and the power station. The two front rooms faced the road and the sea. These Jarman planned to use as his living room and study-cum-bedroom. One of the back rooms would be a spare bedroom, the other his studio. The loft, reached by an outside staircase and running the entire length of the eaves, would be given over to storage.

Equally representative of the angelic and the apocalyptic, the cottage was on the one hand the 'perfectly comfortable villa' Jarman had first written about in *Through the Billboard Promised Land*. On the other, it was a version of the 'little lead-lined house' he had dreamed up when filming *Ostia* with Julian Cole, 'The Villa Chernobyl', which had 'a Geiger-counter ticking in the hall where the grandfather clock used to chime away the hours', and was visited only by 'foolhardy adventurers who braved the desert landscape for tea and scones'.[20] It fitted its new owner like a glove and came with a name that could not have been bettered: Prospect Cottage.

Equally fitting was Dungeness itself. Ever since Canford, where he had been drawn to the art shack that stood on the edge of the school grounds, Jarman had loved places that were interzonal, that stood between other worlds, or on the fringes of them. Nowhere could have been more interzonal, more on the edge than Dungeness. He had always enjoyed beachcombing, and here he could beachcomb to his heart's content. He had always liked pylons, and here they were, marching away from the power station across the marsh towards the interior of Kent. He relished openness; starkness; rigour; to be in the teeth of the wind; he hated things snug, smug, too comfortable, too pretty. And when he discovered that because the marsh was a rela-tively recent reclamation from the sea, and therefore new land, it was known in some quarters as the fifth continent,[21] this description, like the name of the cottage, put the seal on things. For the alchemist, the fifth element, the element that resides above the moon and beyond those of earth, air, fire and water, is the element that endures, has permanence, embodies man's goal: the quintes-sence. Dungeness, the fifth continent, was Jarman's quintessence. One is tempted to suggest that there is no other place on earth he could possibly have ended up.

It was around now that he performed what was for him a highly symbolic act: he broke the wand used by Prospero in *The Tempest*. Writing about the moment in *The Last of England*, he states simply: 'Last week I broke Prospero's wand, Dee's hieroglyphic nomad. I took hold of it silently, shut my eyes for a moment, then smashed it.'[22] In his original diary, he prefaces this with: 'Prospero, the magi-cian of magicians, who left the world like a monk to retire to his cell, in the magic isle (prison) to bring his own conflicting passions to completion (stasis). At which point the task performed (reconcilia-tion, forgiveness) he breaks his magic wand and goes back, he retires.'[23] Did Jarman think of Dungeness as retirement? In the same passage, also not included in the published version, he wonders how far into the future he can look; wonders, too, since he is feeling 'liv-erish today', whether he wished his illness on himself. 'Why this obnoxious hankering after martyrdom?' he asks. Such were his pri-vate musings. On the surface, meanwhile, notions of retirement seemed laughable.

No sooner had he bought Prospect Cottage than he was off to Cannes with Swinton to help promote *Aria*, then back to London to put the finishing touches to *The Last of England* and to undertake his fourth, and most elaborate, pop promo of the year. The first had been 'Out of Hand' for the Mighty Lemon Drops, the second and third, a pair for Bob Geldof: 'I Cry Too' and 'In the Pouring Rain'. All had been customarily simple in terms of image and storyline and shot as cheaply and quickly as possible. The new promo, for the Pet Shop Boys' hit single, 'It's a Sin', was altogether more lavish.

To begin with, it was shot on 35mm – the first time since *Caravaggio* Jarman had worked in this gauge. It was *Caravaggio*, in fact, that had suggested him to the Pet Shop Boys, who had known immediately on seeing the film that here was the 'look' they wanted for their video. Their confidence was not misplaced. With Mackay again acting as producer, the backing of much of the usual team, now bolstered by Keith Collins, and the unexpected luxury of a substantial budget, Jarman slickly and stylishly evoked the seven sins appearing in sequence to the jailed Neil Tennant, as, under the guard of Chris Lowe, he awaits a mediaeval trial for his wrongdoing.

The moment he had finished shooting the video, Jarman left the editing in the capable hands of Peter Cartwright to fly with Collins, Swinton and Mary Davies from the BFI to Rome, where he attended the Italian première of *Caravaggio*.

The first screening of *Caravaggio* was in the Sala d'Ercole in the Capitoline museum . . . the evening was at first very uncomfortable as a group of dour art historians read esoteric papers [in Italian] on [Caravaggio's] influence . . . after the talks . . . we were released into the floodlit gardens along balconies and staircases to a reception, after which the film was projected. Tilda, Keith and I sat beneath the enormous screen staring up almost vertically. The film now dubbed into Italian began . . . The design, the draughtsmanship, the detailing of the picture is carried through with such precision . . . after eighteen months absence I could 'see' our film for the first time, *Caravaggio* is now an Italian movie. At the end of the screening I held my breath, the audience of historians applauded. Walking back through the streets I felt released from the task, like Ariel. It was nine years to the day since I had started on the first script. On a terrace high above the city . . . the view looked eternal but we were changing. One of the lights flickered out, the swallows disappeared into the eves, the new moon climbed into the indigo sky. All the ghosts were out in the empty piazzas cooling themselves at the fountains . . . I love the night. Rome is a city for the night.[24]

He was keeping his diary on a more regular basis than ever before, had also accepted a commission to write a brief, congratulatory preface for *Lindsay Kemp and Company*, a photographic celebration by the German photographer Anno Wilms of his old friend's life and work, and was making copious notes for his new film with Swinton, then called *Borrowed Time*.[25]

The notes open with the words of Prospero: 'Now my charms are all o'erthrown . . . let your indulgence set me free.' They are for a feature film, ninety minutes long, to be shot in 35mm, set in Dungeness and Romney Marsh. There would be 'a series of interlocking stories held together by Tilda at Dungeness. These stories almost like daydreams but they include documentary style such as the Falklands. They explore the past, what we have lost (like landscape) and the present future.' The past was represented by such images as a dressing-up box in an attic; the future by the idea that 'we could build the cairn from Bob-up-a-Down into this project so Tilda becomes Prophesy'.[26]

In addition, and despite a brief bout of 'bloody bronchitis',[27] he was also tackling a commission for Robin Baird-Smith of Constable, who earlier that year had expressed interest in publishing a book of Jarman's thoughts and opinions, interlaced with autobiography. Seeing this as a new and exciting way to use some of the material he had taped with interviewer David Hirst in 1986 for their proposed book on cinema and theatre, for which his enthusiasm had waned, Jarman merged this with excerpts from his diary, the voice-overs from his new film and further interviews with Michael O'Pray and others. On the insistence of his publisher, the result was given the same title as his forthcoming film – *The Last of England* – even though the book in fact covers a range of films, including, in some detail, *The Angelic Conversation* and *Imagining October*.[28] Its 'central dynamo'[29] is unequivocally Jarman's relationship with his father. Lance's death allowed Jarman to write about his formative years, and Lance's role in them, with a frankness which had not been possible in *Dancing Ledge*, and which surprised and distressed a number of family friends. There are undoubted similarities between the two books – both dart between the professional and the personal in a seemingly haphazard fashion, both cover many of the same events (to the extent, on occasion, of self-plagiarisation) – but as Jarman wrote in an abandoned 'preword', 'The passing of four years creates a different view.' The later book is much darker, more angry and despairing than its predecessor.

The other project of substance to occupy 1987, in note form at least, was *International Blue*,[30] originally called *Bliss*,

> a fictional film exploring the world of the painter Yves Klein, inventor of the void, International Blue, the symphony monotone. A film without compunction or narrative existing only for an idea. In the cacophony of voices Yves found the silence of the immaterial, expressed in a series of symbolic gestures performed in six short working years before his early death at 32 [in 1962]. Yves is mercurial, enigmatic. A westerner who held the highest stage of his time in Judo 'Kodokan', a Knight of St Sebastian . . . a devotee of St Rita, the patron saint of lost causes . . . The proposal is to develop a feature length film in 35mm exploring further the juxtaposition of sound and image that exists in *The Last of England*, but unlike this film to produce an atmosphere of calm and joy. A world to which refugees from that dark space might journey.[31]

Yin to the yang of *The Last of England*, *International Blue* is a clear indication of how, as he rode the emotional rollercoaster of HIV, Jarman was desperately seeking an oasis of peace within himself; somewhere without the pandemonium of images, without voices, where the SLNC was indeed GLDN. In the figure of Yves Klein, whom he had long admired for his experimentation, flamboyant show-manship and for being a follower of the patron saint of lost causes, he had found the ideal focus for such a search: an artist who had died young, but whose life and art had been so inextricably linked that he had nevertheless realised an artistic and spiritual journey of consid-erable note.

Klein's monochrome paintings, simple expanses of a single colour, had led to a series of works executed in the vibrant, ultramarine blue that became his trademark: International Klein Blue, or IKB, as he called it. Klein believed in the power of this colour to vivify and sensitise not only the viewer, but the object it covered, especially when that object or canvas was without the trammels of form and line. His search for immateriality continued with *The Void*, an empty white gallery permeated with the aura of blue, at the opening of which visitors drank a blue cocktail in the courtyard. He also devel-oped the idea of selling zones of space for pure gold, which Jarman had himself aped in the early seventies. Then came panels covered with gold leaf; fire paintings, executed by means of a giant fire torch; drawings for an *Architecture of Air*, of fire fountains and fire walls, air furniture and air roofs; and the symphony monotone, consisting of a single, endlessly repeated note.

Jarman hoped his homage to Klein might take the form of an imageless screen in IKB, complemented only by a 'sophisticated Dolby stereo soundtrack which would tell the Yves Klein story in sound and jazzy be-bop'. Then, because he realised such blue blank-ness would make the film almost impossible to fund, he planned that it should take the form of a masque set in a blue room. A series of poems and dialogues concerning the evolution of Klein's art towards the immaterial would be spoken, sung or chanted liturgically by the dramatis personae. These comprised Klein himself, St Rita, the Knights of St Sebastian and IKB, a blue, mercurial messenger of the gods. Over the years, as the project took surer shape in Jarman's mind, these poems and dialogues were added to and elaborated upon. They referred to all the aspects of Klein's work and included quotes from Heraclitus, *Piers Plowman* and various Rosicrucian texts. They even plundered images from *Through the Billboard Promised Land*.

Certain of them survive into *Blue*, the film this proposal eventually became. Others do not. They all give insight into Jarman's frame of mind.

> *Sunday*
> *I want to share this emptiness with you*
> *Not fill the silence with false notes*
> *Or put tracks through the void*
> *I want to share the wilderness*
> *Without fences*
> *The others have built you a highway*
> *Fast lanes in both directions*
> *I offer you a journey without direction*
> *Where our paths cross for a moment*
> *Like the swallow that flies through*
> *Our ancestors mead hall*
> *Arm yourself like a Beowolf*
> *For a journey into the unknown*
> *I offer you uncertainty*
> *No sweet conclusions*
> *When the light gives out*
> *There are many paths and many destinations*
> *I went in search of myself*[32]

> *Silence is Golden*
> *Silence falls on the pandemonium of images*
> *An infinity of silence*
> *Without compunction*
> *At the worlds end*
> *I pick up a paintbrush*
> *And demonstrate the evolution*
> *Of the immaterial*
> *For the astronauts of the void*
> *Lost in time and space*
> *I dream of a blue heaven*
> *Where dead souls whisper*
> *Silence is Golden*

The second half of 1987 was largely taken up with the launch of *The Last of England*. The film was premièred in mid-August at the Edinburgh Film Festival, where it played alongside *Aria*. In the main, it was well received by its audience and there were some excellent reviews. '[A] piece of dynamic cinematic poetry that sees Jarman breaking out of the poised historical languor of *Caravaggio*,' declared Trevor Johnston in *The List*.[33] 'I suspect and I hope that this is a great film,' wrote Ian Bell in the *Scotsman*.[34] Then, in a sour foretaste of the reservations which would swamp the film when it opened in London, William Russell disparaged it in the *Glasgow Herald* as containing 'the biggest ragbag of secondhand, exhausted images ever collected together in one film'.[35] Its maker confided in his diary: 'Came out of the screening in a cold sweat. Did I really make this film? Am I the decaying necromancer of the review in the Glasgow Herald? . . . I'm certainly not the pessimist many think. Things are hard enough this year but I can still raise a faint smile. Although I feel I'm growing apart as [if] I were hovering above all this, an intense disassociation from the daily apocalypse.'[36]

Not that Jarman let this torment show. Instead, he took every opportunity offered by the festival to talk excitedly about *International Blue* and *Borrowed Time* as his next projects; and when he returned south, it was to throw himself into a second video for the Pet Shop Boys, 'Rent', and into the stamping of his personality on Prospect Cottage.

With the help of Collins and whoever could be persuaded to act as his driver, Jarman stripped the cottage of all previous 'home improvements', all traces of carpet and wallpaper, uncovering its original wooden floors and tongue-and-groove walls, which he either repainted or wax-polished over the original varnish. He scoured local shops for furniture and reclaimed certain prized possessions, in particular his old Pither stove, from the friends with whom he had stored them. He also cleared the surrounding shingle of rubbish, noting sadly in his diary: 'The shingles preclude a garden.'[37]

To some, despite the care Jarman lavished on it, because he never worried about whether there were enough chairs, or whether you had a side table on which to put your drink, the villa would always remain too austere; a perfectly *un*comfortable one. For its owner, however, it spelled only peace. He began to spend more and more time there, reading, walking, painting, writing his film proposals and in his diary: 'All alone, what a luxury. Something I have completely forgotten about in the years at Phoenix House. To find such quiet I would have to go back twenty years to the early days of my studio at Upper Ground when I worked through days of quiet as this; no phone, no films, book interviews, articles, demands, requests, no callers at all . . . It's so perfect down here, I think I'll delay my return to London, surely no one will miss me.'[38]

Although to himself he fretted continually about his health (Kaposi's sarcoma, blindness, dementia), 'all in all', despite some early-morning coughing and spluttering, what he termed his 'phantom illness' was not on the rampage. More worrying were the occasional difficulties he and Collins were experiencing as they settled into their relationship.

Spring had returned from America and briefly reappeared in Jarman's life. Inevitably, there came an evening when Collins returned to Phoenix House to discover Spring there, liberally covered with baby oil and nothing else. Collins was well aware – how could he not have been? – that Jarman's libido, although suppressed, was not entirely quiescent, but he did believe they had an agreement: that Jarman was free to go hunting in the bars and on the heath provided he did not bring anyone home. Here was not merely a naked young man, but an ex-lover. Seeing red, Collins physically attacked Jarman while the well-oiled Spring made good his escape. Thereafter, if Spring wanted to see Jarman, he did so in Dungeness, where Collins was less in evidence.

Gradually, a modus vivendi established itself. Collins affected not to care for Dungeness and, once he had helped Jarman move in, became a less and less frequent visitor, enabling Jarman's older friends and lovers to call there in peace. A form of domestic schizophrenia took hold. Phoenix House became primarily the domain of Collins, Prospect Cottage that of Jarman. In time, almost all of Jarman's most treasured possessions, including Andy Marshall's bed, chair, clock and chest, were moved from London to Dungeness, where the dour heaviness of Marshall's pieces perfectly complemented their new surroundings. Meanwhile, Phoenix House was stripped to the bone and kept that way – a gleaming example of immaculate minimalism.

In spite of James Mackay's failure to persuade ZDF to delay their screening of *The Last of England*, the film's invitation to the Tokyo Film Festival had not been rescinded and, in the last week of September, Jarman went to Japan in the company of Mackay, Tilda Swinton and Simon Turner. On one level the experience was positively Kleinian: 'Here is the immaterial and the void in the blue incense smoke [of the temple],' he wrote in his diary, 'so far from the heavy Holy waters of christianity.'[39] On another, it was agreeably non-spiritual. Taken by Takashi Asai, his Japanese distributor, to a screening of *The Angelic Conversation*, he was stunned – and delighted – to find queues of young girls waiting to get into the film. He was not used to such sizeable, or such young, enthusiastic and predominantly female audiences, and he was doubly flattered by many requests to sign copies of the small book Asai had published to coincide with the release of the film because, he felt, Japan needed a proper introduction to Jarman. Equally successful was the festival screening of *The Last of England* – so successful, in fact, that Jarman did not seem to mind unduly that Japan's strict anti-nudity laws would require it to be censored for the remainder of its run.[40]

Beneath the surface, however, all was not well. Jarman's inner worries about his health, the future of his relationship with Collins, what his next film might be, whether it would be possible for him to make it, took sudden and alarming form in an explosive row with Mackay, in the course of which Jarman informed his producer that not only was he never going to make another pop promo, but he never wanted to work with him again. Personal anxieties aside, there were a number of ostensible reasons for this. Filming on 'Rent' not having gone according to plan, Jarman had been ordered to reshoot the second half of the video on his return from Japan. Being beholden in this manner to a mere video was not something he appreciated. Added to which, between 'It's a Sin' and 'Rent', Mackay had stepped from under the umbrella provided by Don Boyd and formed his own company, Basilisk. The young distributor who had started his professional life by simply sharing Jarman's passion for super-8 was becoming too much the producer, and therefore no longer to be entirely trusted, for wasn't it in the nature of all producers to cheat their directors whenever possible?

Having discharged his extra night's filming on 'Rent', Jarman retreated to Dungeness with Collins. A gale struck the country, laying waste to swathes of southern Britain, an event Jarman took as the most dire of omens.

Friday 16 October: 'The whole building shaking with protest as the wind whistled in an ever increasing pitch, the lights had gone and in the pitch black a single candle hardly gave hope for safety. I lay awake in a fearful sweat.'

Saturday:

I'm not seeing eye to eye with Keith and everything I do seems to make it worse. I'm feeling like a prisoner – everything seems to have come to roost with the storm – which has stirred all the black thoughts up that had settled . . . we picked up a few groceries but had hardly gone 100 yards before I rose to Keith's constant nagging and told him he bored me – I meant the nagging not him – he handed me the groceries and took off . . . then packed two bags and left saying he would find a car to hire in Folkestone . . . he's not to blame, I'm just not in the right state to cope with temperament.

Sunday:

I was so exhausted I slept well for the first time in a week. In some ways I'm happier alone, perhaps that's why I came here in the first place. I don't think it's wise to share the pain of it all and a trouble shared is a trouble halved seems selfish. I hope he's happy in Phoenix. This hovering illness with its psychosomatic aches and pains takes better care of itself without others around . . . I worried all day about the yew tree next door to St Clement's . . . if it's gone I'm going to be heartbroken.

That in the midst of his distress Jarman should be worrying about the ancient yew in the churchyard in Old Romney says a great deal about him. The tree, which he could see from the road every time he entered or left Dungeness, was unscathed; not so himself, as the next day's entry, written in an unusually jagged hand, makes painfully clear.

It's almost impossible for me to write about the nub of the matter. Out of sight is out of mind and vanity mixed with uncertainty keeps thoughts of the virus in some distant fenced off part of my being. You could call it a concentration camp . . . even the day to day account of this diary glosses over, leaves everything between the lines unwritten. The summer and autumn has been a time of waiting, perhaps all my time now will be spent in this waiting room . . . waiting for a change. Like this old house in the gale. I'm waiting also for the film, the book, and my painting show which will pass me by as if in a dream in the next few days . . . now the storm has passed and I'm alone . . . I've smoked the last cigarette Keith hid to protect me. Hidden with anguish because I am surrounded by anguish, I can feel it and it frightens me . . . At seven this morning I put out the rubbish and then methodically placed the ladder against the front of the house to paint the roof, but the task defeated me . . . the angle was as sharp as Keith warned and it frightened me. Why should I still be frightened by heights? Behind the facade I've been in turmoil . . . the waiting is characterised by indecision. My mind darts this way and that, is full of non sequiturs . . . I toyed with the idea of a last film. Need it be a last film? and thought of the wanderer and the dream of the rood filmed here very simply in the landscape. Possibly even a landscape film . . . what's happening? What's happening? I skate across the surface. The depths are too deep to plumb. A pandemonium of images floated past through the summer and every idea bought its own doom. Scotched by a lack of enthusiasm by those I have grown into working with who have now acquired confidence and identity and with them aspirations that are no longer my own. The paths have

diverged. I'm addicted to my own small footpaths. They
sought me out as an ally, put down roots and grew up like a
copse around an old tree threatening light and air. It was
right, of course . . . I need others to hold the ladder. Who? In
my own strange way I'm in love with both Keith and Tilda,
though love is perhaps not the right word. Perhaps a
camaraderie, something more military. A friendship and
partnership. The gaps are enormous. Keith quite rightly
demands physical affection, he's twenty two, but in flight
from the physical, the body, I can hardly get a hard on, the
virus has sapped the will and put up signs DANGEROUS
KEEP OUT. Do not touch. Keith is hurt by this and goes into
the attack. Turns his need for attention into aggression. A
whole side of me masochistic and dependent wells up, let
someone else take the strain, retire, become a gardener . . .
BE HAPPY but then was that my lot? Should I not go down
fighting – and then of course the battle might not be
joined . . . the problem with Derek is he has never fulfilled his
promise. But then that's nonsense, if they made the frame
miniature I was forced to be a miniaturist, there was no grand
design in my time, just a mediocrity that the peace would not
disturb and a war that could not be joined . . . Should I halt
all this? Can I live alone? Can he? He's in love with me. Like
any 22 year old, love at 22 is physical and I'm a cold fish. I've
run off twice in the night and been unfaithful. Anonymous
encounter with someone who knows you are positive . . . he
hates that they are getting closer to me. Punches. But how
can I ever explain it wasn't that, no he wasn't being
displaced. It was an old adventuring spirit, part of my time,
something that has gone, it was: am I still attractive even
with this double hurdle and forgotten in the morning.
Forgotten? Well but us not him. I feel my work is in ruins – or
rather should I say which way to go? The bills have to be
paid . . . I've ended up with a view of a storm tossed sea and a
nuclear power station. Which lights up at night like the
emerald city in the land of Oz . . . it's as if my life was going
full circle from the cinema in which a distant five year old

bolted as the dust clouds blew us into the air . . . is life not repeating art . . . the best of me says Stop Stop Stop look around, communicating a few perhaps poor ideas I convinced myself was the life blood which ran into foul streams. The media turned me from a merry old wizard at the time of The Tempest to a black hearted devil . . . of course I know the problem, I didn't deal with day to day life. The films are removed from a recognisable social milieu. Like the RAF camps in which I grew up. Grew up? . . . the clouds are blowing in from the west, I'm drifting with them far away from what I had intended to write. Am I getting beneath the surface or is this just maudlin self-obsession? . . . what to do . . . well there's good works to lose yourself in (selflessness) or the bad old selfish ways . . . so is it Edward II . . . a huge crew, unions . . . and in the hands of my own homespun friends catastrophe . . . or Yves Klein the great blue film of the immaterial no image a cop out? or the fifth quarter of the globe, the wanderer and the dream of the rood made here in Kent quite simply . . . what would you do?[41]

If the gale had not been omen enough, he was now writing on 'Black Monday', the day the London stockmarket collapsed. And indeed one collapse did prefigure another: that of his hopes for *The Last of England*, which opened later that week at the Prince Charles Cinema off Leicester Square. As at Edinburgh, the opening brought forth a few voices who championed the film, but in London these were hopelessly outweighed by those who hated it. Writing in the *Monthly Film Bulletin*, Steve Jenkins summed up the general view when he said: 'Nothing is said or shown here about paranoia and beauty in a declining landscape that was not said more succinctly and defiantly in, for example, Jarman's short promo films for The Smiths.'[42] The film closed within a week.

The book, sharing as it did a title with a failed film, sank with its namesake, even though it was more widely reviewed than *Dancing Ledge* and, in the main, most flatteringly – *Time Out* saluted its author as 'the sort of troublemaking visionary who one day may be compared with Blake'.[43]

In the last week of October, coinciding with the release of the film and the publication of the book, a new dealer by the name of Richard Salmon had arranged a comprehensive London exhibition of Jarman's most recent work. Although he co-owned the Karsten Schubert Gallery in Charlotte Street, Salmon also exhibited in his large and airy two-roomed studio at 59 South Edwardes Square, and it was there, under the title *Paintings from a Year*, that he offered Jarman the opportunity to cover whitewashed walls with work, in this instance 132 canvases painted in the course of the previous fourteen months.[44]

Featuring Jarman's by now trademark use of shattered, occasionally golden glass, as well as broken lightbulbs, bullets, old Coke tins, condoms, calipers and rusty nails, plus a liberal sprinkling of carefully chosen words to underline the messages inherent in the arrangement of these objects in the thick, black[45] swirls of paint ('God Bless American Express', 'Eyes are surer witnesses than ears', 'The fairest order in the world is a heap of random sweepings'), these paintings were 'hung in the manner of a Victorian salon, with the small dark canvases banked in rows on the walls and arranged in eight symmetrical groups'.[46] Less Victorian were their concerns: AIDS, the destruction of the landscape, consumerism, American culture and private reverie. Sadly, there were few sales, nor was the coverage accorded the exhibition extensive, but at least what little there was was well considered. Simon Watney noted perceptively that the images traced a 'cultural catastrophe in modern Britain of which most people seem completely unaware'.

In November, Jarman collected his thoughts on the super-8 film which, for much of the year, he had been planning with Tilda Swinton and showed them, together with a sample tape, to Channel 4. The film outlined in Jarman's dictated notes would never be made, or not as originally envisaged, but because the notes give such a clear idea of how Jarman's more spontaneous film-making evolved, they are worth quoting from at length:

Notes towards a new film . . . as yet undefined, to emerge from the landscape which surrounds the Ness . . .
It started really early in April, when a decision was made

to attempt to follow *The Last of England,* which, because of the method of working was in effect a shot into the dark. With a second film made possibly or probably in the same manner, that is through video transfer from super-8 and 16mm, but with the possibility of synch sound and also the possibility of filming in 35mm.

The film started off initially as a situation to make a film in and around the very end of *The Tempest* with Miranda left behind in the magic island . . . So initially I thought of characters of Caliban and Ariel, who transformed into a pixie called Twinkle-in-the-Eye after I found a pixie in the market at Camden one Sunday afternoon, for which I made a series of notes which are the following:

Various ideas in July 1987

These started off from a series of props I discovered.

Use a ship in a bottle for a series of dissolves for travelling through time and space in the film.

Film the sea and the fishing boats from Dungeness, the low horizons, the dark waves, such as I shot in the section of *Aria.*

Tilda weeding a walled garden in a period costume based on a nineteenth-century fisherwoman with a headdress, perhaps . . . ancillary to some action that was happening independently of the film, so her emotions might be different to what was happening in an idyllic day.

Building a table: ask for a young furniture-maker to construct a table during September which would be made from railway sleepers and timber boards, and which would be constructed in the garden of Prospect Cottage with the nuclear power station in the background, the backdrop being the nuclear power station at the end of the Ness.

A dressing-up box: perhaps a chest in the attic, which could transport us like the ship in the bottle through space and time, in other words a series of costumes like charades into which Tilda might get.

An introduction of a messenger, perhaps an Ariel, perhaps Dawn Archibald or Spring on a motorbike, bringing a message across the Ness.

Hang-gliders across the field, low shots across the marshes.

There were other ideas; I found three African cloths which I thought could actually be the costumes of perhaps three goddesses, and at that point I met Liz Ranken, the dancer–choreographer from DV8 [a dance troupe], and I thought she could possibly be one of the three figures, and possibly Barbara Stone, who would be walking across the Ness, they would be rather like the chorus, a Greek chorus.

Then I thought of refugees along the roads of Kent, prams, suitcases etc., filmed in super-8 from a passing car.

Maybe a voice-over from an older lady, perhaps in her eighties. At one point we thought of using Tilda's grandmother who is in her late eighties to reminisce about her childhood.

Another idea was to introduce a Caliban figure, perhaps Nigel Terry as a fisherman, a sort of figure who might also be like Bob-up-a-Down in a film that I wrote. He was a man of the woods, a charcoal-burner, and I still rather like the idea of the charcoal-burner.

We could build a cairn for Bob-up-a-Down, and introduce certain of the ideas in that particular film in which there was an anchoress who lived in a cairn who gave advice to the villagers who came to her.

At one point Tilda said she would like to be a witch, so we discussed that . . .

We thought at one moment of dancing all of history in a set that could be built in a studio.

. . . Perhaps we could use nuclear explosions from archive film to change between scenes, and the whole film could spin each time, rather like the newspapers in the thirties films, and introduce us to a new section.

. . . I found two red flags – they're flags used on a landing strip – and I thought of the cargo cults in the South Sea Islands and that mystical runway, galactical construction that has been found in Peru.

. . . Then we thought of more humorous things . . . when the Wright case[47] came up, of a roomful of ladies with steam kettles doing the mail, so a sort of sequence of thirty women all steaming letters open.

At that point came the idea of biblical references, sort of washing feet, Jacob and the angel wrestling in the shingle at Dungeness.

At Covent Garden I saw an immaculate roadsweeper and thought of the designer future in which even the pneumatic drills were being used in full evening dress.

. . . I thought how shall I alter Tilda, and thought of making her wear a moustache all through this film and otherwise be dressed as a woman. It seemed a very strange addition and harked back to the black nose of Max Wall and of Sebastian.[48]

We developed the idea, at least I developed the idea, of roadsweepers, dustmen, butchers, all going to work in Visconti like evening dress and when we came to the miniature railway I thought perhaps this may be a way of certain people arriving. At that point I stopped and we went to Edinburgh for the opening of *The Last of England* and thought of making a film which would be the four seasons in the nineteenth-century walled garden at Kimmergen,[49] in which one could follow the seasons with the planting of the flowers, collecting eggs, and weeding the garden, digging, picking apples, potting up cuttings, all garden pursuits. At that point I picked up some clogs from the market and asked Sandy [Powell] if she could make a dress, still at the same time thinking of a dress like the photographs of nineteenth-century fisherwomen.[50]

Three things emerge from the notes. One is that Jarman was most keen to release Swinton from the usual 'parameters' within which actresses were expected to work, thereby ensuring she was never 'trapped into becoming a sex object'. Another is that he hoped to extend and deepen the range of his images. 'I wanted to make deeply serious images, much more serious than the images that I have been actually able to make, and much more moody, and slower and longer and much less brittle.' Finally, he wanted the film to concentrate on

the landscape. 'I'm really interested in the landscape as a protagonist . . . in an animate landscape which you could call "Rule
Britannia" . . . the landscape is indissolubly linked to who we are and
who we might be, if the landscape is destroyed we will destroy ourselves.' He planned to move through this landscape by means of the
'winding paths' rather than the highway ('the film itself should be
meandering and it shouldn't have a highway story with a destination
because there isn't a destination really') and for the film to 'lead
into the garden, the whole idea of a hortus conclusus, the garden of
Eden if you like . . . the symbol of the garden should be strong in our
lives, and after all, Kent is called the garden of England, if you want
to make the film link up with *The Last of England* that would be a
very fine title for it.'[51] And *The Garden* is what it would eventually
become.

The two other projects to be claiming Jarman's attention at this
time were both non-filmic. The first was *L'ispirazione*, a new opera
which the Teatro Comunale, remembering the success of his collaboration with Ken Russell on *The Rake's Progress*, had invited him to
direct for the fifty-first Maggio Musicale Fiorentina. He had never
directed an opera before, but this was of no consequence to the
Teatro Comunale, who saw in him the perfect match for Sylvano
Bussotti, the opera's multi-talented composer and lyricist. Intrigued
and flattered, Jarman had accepted the invitation. Bussotti, who
spoke barely a word of English, came to London to sing his opera in
person for its putative director at Phoenix House, while Jarman
returned the compliment by flying to Italy for further discussions.

The second project, never to see the light of day,[52] was a book
about sex and death he was hoping to write with the help of
Matthew Helbert, a young doctor he had initially met at Traffic,
the club in York Way. Helbert worked in the AIDS unit at St Mary's,
Paddington, where he was now visited in a professional capacity by
a frightened and reluctant Jarman who, on his return from Tokyo,
had woken one morning to find his sheets covered in something
that was either blood or the beetroot-stained remains of his previous
night's dinner. Fearing the former, he imagined that during the night
he had bled from his rectum. Although his GP ascribed the episode
to stress, Jarman decided to consult Helbert at St Mary's.

Allaying Jarman's fears by giving him, aside from his irritable bowel syndrome and a degree of weight loss, a clean bill of health, Helbert told his patient that he was keeping a journal of musings on homosexuality and AIDS which, together with some taped conversations with Jarman – joined, on occasion, by Swinton and Collins – formed the basis for their proposed book.

For Jarman, who was extremely shaken by this first visit to hospital since his diagnosis, and his first real sight of people with AIDS, the 'sex and death' tapes were a form of therapy and stock-taking. They helped him assess how he had arrived where he had and how best to move forward. They also enabled the teacher in him to pass on advice to other, younger men who might be facing the hurdles he had faced. Like his diary, they gave a crucial insight into his state of mind as he approached the first anniversary of his diagnosis.

Despite maintaining that AIDS had 'still in some ways not caught up with me', he admitted to 'running this year with an excess of work which I deliberately undertook as perhaps a way of coping with the situation initially'. Although he classified the reaction as 'superficial', he confided that 'the idea of being disfigured by the illness seems more horrendous than the illness itself'. He was still worrying in particular about blindness and 'degeneration of the mental faculties'. He was not afraid of dying; on the contrary, all artists were 'death-obsessed' and dying young had 'its own mythology. I feel I'm part of history in that sense because a lot of gay artists died young.' Besides which, another thirty years of life would be onerous. 'It's hard work carrying the weight of oneself around.'

What did frighten him about death were 'the steps leading to it'. Already he was finding social situations 'very unnerving'. He never went to parties, could not easily cope with new people. He was more self-contained than previously. He did not 'resent the fact that I've virtually chosen a life of celibacy . . . That's a certain relief', then he rather contradicted himself by saying that although, since becoming HIV positive, he had 'slept with someone' only twice, and safely on both occasions, he hated it that sexually he now felt constrained; he preferred sex to be something he could lose himself in. It was a vital part of his life, fuelling his work, and providing a way of meeting friends.

During the year he had been 'intensely aware of the physical world', feeling both closer to it and further away. He had always liked being alone sometimes and had always been 'absolutely a stickler for the aesthetics of my environment'. In hospital, he knew he would miss both his solitude and his own room. Just as he had always feared film or painting 'as an institution', he feared 'the institutionalisation of the illness', though he also predicted that he would be 'a good patient because I'm in awe of authority'. That was the contradiction: he was in flight from authority because he was in awe of it. The 'moment of behaving oneself' would be 'the moment one became one of the fathers'.

On a more general note, he was hugely exercised by how society reacted to sexuality, and angry that the sixties were being 'reinterpreted'; that their 'promiscuity' was being blamed for AIDS. Likening AIDS to being in the trenches, he maintained that repression was what allowed the disease to travel. What was needed was openness. He was assessing articles of faith like articles of clothing, to see what fitted best, both as an individual and as a spokesman for the constituency he was beginning to realise he represented.

A month later, on 21 December, at 'Prospect Cottage at the fifth quarter of ye globe', he made *Sleep has the House*. It marked his first year of living with HIV. He wrote bitterly:

> First anniversary. I've been married to the virus for one year. It's a dull moral little marriage of monogamous closed horizons girt round with floppy condoms. The virus has clamped me with fidelity, blinded my happily wandering eyes . . . I make a wish both terrible and silent for a day when we're all equal, a day when a boy and a girl can only kiss in privacy behind the blinkered family doors and the family becomes even for you the prison you invented. Virus for a virus.[53]

In order to escape his own imprisonment, earlier in the year he had taken a decision which would crucially shape the rest of his life: he had publicly announced that he was HIV positive. From the beginning, rather than follow his doctor's advice, he had chosen to tell his friends. Then, in writing *The Last of England*, he had found he could no more keep it secret on the page. So, in the run-up to publication, in an interview he gave his close and trusted friend Nicholas de Jongh for the *Guardian*, he arranged for the diagnosis to be mentioned, almost in passing, halfway through the piece, where de Jongh explained that Jarman 'reveals in his new book that he has been diagnosed as HIV positive. This does not mean he will contract Aids in the future, but it does show that he has been exposed to the virus. And this fact must and does frame his life with question marks.'[54]

Since the mid-eighties the public response to AIDS has significantly altered, making it difficult to remember how brave and unusual this declaration then was. A gloveless Princess Diana might recently have touched the hand of an AIDS patient, but the very fact that this incident had the impact it did is an indication of the fear and stigma then attached to the disease. Little wonder so many of Jarman's friends thought he was making a dreadful mistake by being so open.

Yet that was his nature and, although the announcement did bring some of the flak of which he had been warned, more importantly, this step towards 'politics in the first person'[55] provided him with a platform and a *raison d'être* that would help him make considerable sense of the situation in which he found himself.

27

Sod 'Em

Having attended one of its first London performances as a student, and having edited *The Last of England* to its strains, Jarman had 'often thought of the possibility of visualizing Britten's *War Requiem* without fixing it like a butterfly on a setting board and thereby diminishing it'.[1] Thanks to Don Boyd, whose *Aria* had given the producer access to the powers that be at Decca, this now looked a real possibility – as long as they used the Decca recording of the original performance without tampering in any way with the music, and as long as Jarman's script met with the approval of the Britten estate.

Arriving at an appropriate scenario was not easy. In effect, what Jarman (who worked on his various drafts of the script with, among others, Boyd and Tilda Swinton) was having to do was make a feature-length silent film; either that, or a very long music video. The storyline had to be self-evident, mirroring not only the music, but the eight Wilfred Owen poems which, together with the words of the Latin mass, formed an integral part of the requiem. Deciding to film in a mixture of 35mm, super-8 and video that incorporated 'found (or documentary) footage', and to focus on soldiers and nurses, since everyone knows what it is that soldiers and nurses do, Jarman and his cohorts fashioned a 'loose story' around 'Owen, a Nurse, and the Unknown Soldier'.[2]

The nurse wheels an elderly veteran along a path. The veteran shows the nurse 'an Edwardian miniature hidden in his wallet of a young nurse whom she resembles'.[3] We hear the veteran's voice reading part of Owen's 'Strange Meeting', the poem with which the requiem concludes:

> the truth untold,
> The pity of war, the pity of war distilled.

What follows is, as it were, the veteran's memories sieved through Owen's poetry. In a tableau consciously echoing the composition of Charles Sargeant Jagger's Royal Artillery memorial at Hyde Park Corner, the nurse grieves over the body of Owen, which lies on a stone altar. Super-8 returns us to the tranquil past. Owen and his mother hang out the washing. The nurse 'plants a garden by the light of a lantern in the dusk'.[4] The film then alternates between further glimpses of simple domesticity enshrined in an Arcadian past and a series of tableaux from the First World War: soldiers being drilled, digging trenches, preparing for battle, returning from battle, sleeping; a vaudeville Britannia beckoning a young, drum-beating Owen to war; a group of nurses playing blind-man's-buff in an empty hospital ward; a surreal snow-filled room in which a German soldier kills the unknown soldier and Owen the German soldier; the burial of the unknown soldier; a re-enactment of 'The Parable of the Old Man and the Young', Owen's savage retelling of the story of Abraham slaying his son, used by Jarman to symbolise Owen's own death in the trenches at the hands of all the fathers and overfed captains of industry who send their young sons to do battle on their behalf; the unknown soldier, now in the form of Christ, wearing a crown of thorns and carrying Owen's body; a recreation of Piero della Francesca's *Resurrection*; wreaths of red poppies that become a basket of white poppies in the closing moments of the film. Punctuating these tableaux is found footage of war throughout the century, from 1914 until the present day.

Boyd, for his part, was walking the producer's treadmill. In conjunction with Liberty Film Sales, a distributor, the BBC, in the guise of their new Independent Planning Unit, whose first feature this would be, were persuaded to put up a budget of £670,000, barely enough to make the film, or so Boyd maintained, unless Jarman agreed to a deferred payment. Against a percentage of eventual profits (never to transpire), the acquiescent director was given a token ten-pound note, which he pasted into a draft of the script, writing alongside it: 'This is my fee for the script.'[5]

Meanwhile, in his role as citizen, Jarman was anything but acquiescent in the face of certain developments on the political front. In 1987, the Conservatives enjoyed their third consecutive victory at the polls. A year previously, they had successfully abolished an archenemy, the Greater London Council (GLC), and felt in a position to embarrass – and with luck weaken – other Labour-led local councils with similar sympathies towards 'minority groups' such as gays and lesbians. Given impetus by an AIDS-related and tabloid-driven public antipathy towards homosexuality, family values of Victorian virulence were high on the government's agenda. A new clause was added to the Local Government Bill then passing through Parliament. It read: 'A local authority shall not a) intentionally promote homosexuality or publish material with the intention of promoting homosexuality and b) promote the teaching in any maintained school of the acceptability of homosexuality as a pretended family relationship.' The numbering of the clause would change as it progressed towards the statute book, but to its supporters and opponents alike it was known as Clause 28.

To be told that your relationships are, by their very nature, 'pretended' is bad enough, as is the assumption that your sexual proclivities can be promoted and are, by implication, matters of simple choice. But even more frightening to many was how imprecisely the clause was worded. What was to stop a library being prosecuted for stocking the works of Oscar Wilde? Or a grant-aided theatre being shut down if it mounted one of his plays? Or gay bars and bookshops, which required a licence from the local council, being permanently closed? No amount of denial by the government that this was not their intention could placate those who felt themselves under threat from the clause, especially at a time when AIDS was making such devastating inroads into the gay community that many gay men felt besieged to begin with.

In much the same way that a raid on the Stonewall Inn had been the spark igniting American gay liberation in the late sixties, Clause 28 mobilised the British gay and lesbian communities in an unprecedented fashion. New political groupings were formed or strengthened, individuals who had never spoken out on political issues or admitted publically to their sexuality now did so, and an old term of abuse – 'queer' – began to be adopted as an ironic badge of pride. For Jarman, already outraged by what he saw as the inadequacy of the government's response to the crisis of AIDS, Clause 28, the final denial of his rights, the final exclusion, was the spur towards a positive ferment of fury and protest which would continue for the rest of his life. As he wrote of an interview on *The Media Show*:

A sudden white fury, bullish and truculent, bubbled up when I was in front of the camera. I felt I was face to face with the enemy . . . I said my sole intention was to promote homosexuality and the pretended relationships I so much enjoy . . . said I knew a thing or two about pretended relationships as I was the child of one . . . After it was over I felt tired and a little guilty . . . Then I got up and decided that years of discretion should be thrown to the winds . . . let's pick up the gauntlet.[6]

If his earlier tirades against British Film Year were a first flexing of his vocal muscles and his decision to speak openly about his diagnosis a first merging of the personal with the political, his reaction to Clause 28 was, to borrow from Yves Klein, an architecture of fire that rested on these foundations. From now on, Jarman would always term himself queer, never gay; he would jubilantly champion his right to be so; and he would openly celebrate the fact that the clause had brought people together in the way it had. 'What had begun to look like a moribund movement,' he wrote, 'full of political diehards, bitter infighting and bar banter, woke up. The kiss of death became the kiss of life – a new lesbian and gay movement emerged, stronger than ever, more angry, more focused.'[7]

In late January, as Clause 28 entered its committee stage in the House of Lords, Jarman joined a couple of London marches and was present at a packed meeting at the Playhouse Theatre where leading figures from the arts protested against the bill. He spoke at a conference in the Central Hall, Westminster organised by the newly formed UK Aids Vigil Organisation, where it distressed him that the speeches by the journalist Duncan Campbell and Peter Tatchell, the political activist and founder of the new organisation, could not have been more widely heard. In the pub afterwards, Campbell – then under considerable fire for his controversial and provocative journalism – told Jarman that 'it was great meeting the other most hated Englishman'. Jarman mused: 'It was something that had never occurred to me. Hated? I sat on the bus and thought about it. I suppose it's true but I'd always thought of myself defended by impregnable bastions of love.'[8]

Sadly, Campbell's assessment appeared accurate, certainly if Jarman's next public engagement was anything to go by. In early March, he spoke in a University of London Union debate on censorship and the arts, with particular reference to Clause 28, now going through its final reading in the House of Commons. Sharing the stage were Duncan Campbell; Gerald Howarth MP, recent proponent of an attempt to introduce a variation on the Obscene Publications Bill; and, standing in for Mary Whitehouse, who had a migraine, a member of the National Viewers and Listeners Association by the name of Jamie Bogle.

Discussion from the floor was opened by a woman who stood up to give a two-word definition of filth: 'Derek Jarman'. Howarth said: 'I perfectly accept the right of people who have a different chemical make-up to be homosexual if they want to . . . but I believe that it is a deviation.' Jarman had his supporters, both on stage and in the audience, but to be challenged in this way rather proved the point he had made in his speech – that the clause could function as a 'Trojan horse' – and when, as the exchanges became more heated, Howarth further 'clarified' his position by saying that Jarman's homosexuality was 'an abhorrent practice and I've told you so, and I think that it revolts me',[9] the relative silence in which Jarman sat for the rest of the debate suggests even more vividly than his articulateness how very distressing he found it to be vilified in this manner.

To anyone puzzled as to why Jarman should have become so angry and vituperative as the years passed, the answer lies in occasions like this; though because he was genuinely someone who had always thought of himself as 'defended by impregnable bastions of love' – and because he was the product of a middle-class upbringing prizing politeness above all else – his anger could have a contradictory sweetness to it; he was seldom less than a gentleman.

Despite widespread demonstrations, which included the startling sight of a group of lesbians abseiling into the House of Lords from the public gallery as the venerable peers voted in support of the bill, within a fortnight of the London Union debate, Clause 28 became law. That the battle had been lost in no way discouraged Jarman from continuing to speak out against the clause, or on the subject of AIDS. Having a platform from which to discuss these issues became a kind of therapy; one of the principal means of holding at bay the terrible insecurity that underscored his public anger. As part of 'the long slow haul to change people's perceptions',[10] he even ventured into what, for him, was enemy territory by agreeing to an interview with a tabloid, the *Sunday Mirror*.[11] Beneath the headline, 'HOW TO COPE WITH LIFE AFTER AIDS (AND EVEN HAVE A LAUGH SOMETIMES)', he explained how he thought others could benefit from his tragedy. Criticising the government's 'tombstone philosophy' for merely ticking 'everyone off in a school-mistressy way', he tried to put across some practical advice for safe sex. To avoid alienating his readership, he also told an uncharacteristic lie: he 'was never that promiscuous'. *Mirror* readers were not to know that, when reading *The Swimming Pool Library*, a novel by another old Canfordian, Alan Hollinghurst, which is in large part an explicit celebration of homosexual life before AIDS, it would bring 'a lifetime flooding back. I went to sleep counting sexual adventures like sheep in this cold and empty room, all the warmth and adventure gone in several short and catastrophic years.'[12]

In January, while developing the script for *War Requiem*, Jarman had gone to Budapest for an opening. In February, he was in Berlin for *The Last of England*. The film was shown (out of competition) in the Forum Section. Its three screenings were packed and it won two

prizes: a Teddy Bear (the festival's recently created award for gay
and lesbian film-makers) and the annual award of the Confédération
Internationale des Cinémas d'Art et d'Essai, given in recognition of
the film's 'artistic qualities as well as its inspired originality and freedom of creation'. During the festival, Jarman was bolstered by the
presence of a number of those who had worked with him on the film,
as well as by friends and wellwishers. Julian Cole's *Ostia*, in which of
course he featured, was also showing. As had been the case a year
earlier, the visit provided a much-needed fillip. 'To bring a film to
Berlin is a sweet relief,' he told his diary, 'the audience is strong,
opinionated, intelligent. They send back serious echoes.'[13] As did
fresh audiences a month later, when the film walked off with a prize
at a Madrid Film Festival.

However, in neither Berlin nor Madrid could he escape Clause 28,
or being HIV positive. Most of the interviews he gave concentrated
on the clause – and in Berlin, after the film's packed second screening, 'A middle-aged Italian lady asked if she could see me alone . . .
she told me she had had the virus for nearly four years, and had told
no one. She came from a small town . . . where she felt the reaction
would be terrible. We sat and held hands for two hours, and swapped
stories. When . . . she had left I was suddenly overwhelmed with
tears, the first time the virus had touched me. For up to now it has
frozen every emotion.'[14]

On his return from Berlin, Jarman felt utterly exhausted and considered asking Lorraine Hamilton, his agent, to release him from his
commitment to direct *L'ispirazione*. Quite apart from the creative
challenge posed by directing an opera for the first time, the project
threatened to involve an alarming degree of subsidiary difficulty and
unpleasantness: Jarman spoke hardly any Italian and had to obtain a
doctor's certificate from Teatro Comunale in case the 'very conservative chorus' complained about working with a director who was
HIV positive. In the end, he ignored his instincts and carried on.
With hindsight, he should have obeyed his inner voice.

L'ispirazione is based on *Die Gutmachende Muse*, a fable by Ernst
Bloch, in which a neglected eighteenth-century composer,
Wolfgango, is rescued from oblivion by his daughter, Serena, who
copies out and stages his opera, casting herself in the leading role.

Sylvano Bussotti, who was also designing the work, updated this simple story to a point so far in the future that eighteenth-century fashions and conventions have found favour again. He also added a number of new characters to further complicate and comment upon the action. For one of these, the non-singing part of Futura, the Mistress of Theatre and Space, Jarman hit on the idea of importing Tilda Swinton, who would deliver her monologues in English. His other innovation was to open the opera with a short film featuring Swinton in footage culled largely from *The Last of England*. This he decided to blaze across the stage during the opening moments of the opera.

It was a bold concept and an undeniable *coup de théâtre*. Thereafter, however, at least according to *The Times*, the staging was 'flat, static and symmetrical';[15] no match at all for Bussotti's futuristic design excesses. Like Gielgud with the ill-fated *Don Giovanni*, Jarman had bitten off more than he could chew. Not even the fact that Teatro Comunale paid him the honour of mounting a comprehensive retrospective of his films to accompany the production could alleviate the mix of creative and personal misery the occasion engendered. Because he spoke so little Italian, practically the only way he had of controlling people was to shout at them, making rehearsals an uncharacteristic and noisy hell. He was missing Collins and hating the weather: 'foul – cold and wet and mildewy'.[16] He also fell out with his beloved Tilda.

For some time, there had been tensions in their relationship. The sheer intensity of their involvement, personal and professional, inevitably brought moments when they chafed at the ties that bound them. And then there was Collins, who threatened Swinton's centrality to Jarman, causing a degree of mutual jealousy. Although this was usually concealed – and, when not, something Jarman was known to relish – in the main it was discomfiting and could lead him to turn away from both of them. Once, when talking to Swinton about 'all our emotional entanglements', he told her: 'I'm married to the house, like Stanley Spencer in Cookham, and my painting, and I wouldn't have it any other way, love for me is folly . . . I'd go for friendship any day, as for sex it's best anonymous.'[17]

In the stressful atmosphere of Florence things became so bad that the two of them stopped speaking to each other. With 'La Swinton' driving him 'round the twist'[18] and the production ditto, Jarman felt 'overwhelmed by isolation'.[19] Retiring to his small and simple room, he turned for consolation to his pen and began to dash off *Sod 'Em*.

Consulting Marlowe's *Edward II* and writing 'fast and furiously' in his distinctive longhand in a large notebook into which he also pasted pictures of beautiful young men, Jarman finished the script within days of his return to London. A vitriolic version of *B Movie: Little England/A Time of Hope*, without any of the latter's humour and precious little hope, the result was a sour mix of 'the early nineteenth-century cartoons of Gillray, Cruikshank, Goya's *Disasters of War*, and the Carry On Films'. Jarman imagined it would 'define the limits'[20] of his anger.

It is 19XX. The police and security forces have been privatised and 'have established themselves as private fiefdoms with the government as an advisory body'. The chief of police, Cesspit Charlie, is blind. The SAS '(Straight and Sexist)' are commanded by our old friend General Genocide. The government is headed by Margaret Reaper, whose every accessory is Tory blue. When she gives her 'Xmas message to the nation', she is 'all in blue sitting in front of a blue Union Jack, a large bunch of blue roses on the table, sipping a blue drink'. A true case, one could say, of blue being poison. The royal family 'appear weekly on prime time Saturday TV in *The Family*, a soap opera, whose scripts are vetted by Central Office'. The death penalty has been reintroduced and homosexuality recriminalised with wide-ranging penalties. There are orders to proscribe the works and identities of Shakespeare, Newton, Byron, Wilde, Marlowe – and a certain Derek Jarman. 'The homophobia generated by the AIDS crisis has reached a new dimension, everyone carries identity cards (with HIV status), mass quarantining has been introduced, and holiday camps like Butlins have been requisitioned as detention centres.'

There is a warrant out for the arrest of Edward, a young actor, for playing the title role in Marlowe's tragic history of the young king hounded from the throne and tortured to death for his attachment to Piers Gaveston; a role he plays as a defiant way of showing where homophobia can lead. Edward and his lover Johnny Gaveston, either as themselves or as Edward II and his favourite Piers, are on the run. The script follows their pursuit by the forces of repression.

Jarman envisaged the film with 'a complex soundtrack which like that in *The Last of England* will tell much of the story'. The voice-over that accompanies, complements and explains much of the action comprises fragments of Oscar Wilde, Marlowe, T.S. Eliot, *Neutron*-like snatches of the Book of Revelations and Jarman's own diaries; oblique references, too, to Phoenix House and Prospect Cottage, the fifth quarter of the globe, even Jarman's University of London Union debate with Gerald Howarth. In an early scene ('All Our Dads'), Edward I, an 'austere military' father, announces to Edward and Johnny: 'No son of mine is fucking queer, I'd be quite prepared to kill both of you.' Edward's voice-over traces his and Johnny's persecution back to 'Section 28, which was the first of many similar acts of legislation restricting human rights . . . It was pivotal, like Kristallnacht, or the burning of the Reichstag, it fixed itself in the imagination'. The repression of gays is linked to the government's plan to eradicate all 'opposition and plurality' and create a 'monotonous monoculture'. Young Edward spells out the danger in this: 'Do you know where all of this might end? Full circle with pink triangles in concentration camps, certainly in their minds if not in reality.' Young Johnny then links repression with the HIV virus:

> *The virus is stupid and ruthless*
> *A good Catholic*
> *It hates condoms*
> *It's the silent majority*
> *The silent consensus*
> *The Pope*
> *The Prime Minister*
> *The family*
> THE ENEMIES OF OUR LIFE.

Help is at hand. God ('a bearded lady in an enormous scarlet ball-gown') has come to the conclusion that Reaper's Britain is a 'fucking mess', and is therefore susceptible to a petition to 'protect Edward and Johnny' presented by Wilde, Shakespeare, Marlowe and Byron, all dressed in drag. Meanwhile, Edward and Johnny have taken the law into their own hands. Picking up guns, they mow down Cesspit Charlie in mid-oration on the *Wogan* show. 'WAKE UP BRITAIN,' shouts Edward, 'BEFORE THEY SWITCH OFF THE LIFE-SUPPORT MACHINE, OR ARE YOU ALREADY DEAD?' Margaret Reaper convenes her Cabinet. In a parody of the Last Supper, she sits among them and issues her retort to the British people: 'Are you with us? Or against us?' General Genocide has Johnny tortured and shot. Eventually, Edward too is caught and killed. Margaret Reaper, all her enemies dispatched, axes *The Family* as a soap opera and prepares to crown herself 'Margaret the First of England Queen, Dictator and Defender of the Faith'. The good God intervenes. 'Betsy Battenberg', who was about to be burned alive, is rescued at the last minute, while Reaper and Genocide are cast into a bottomless pit, 'falling in a flaming vortex through their own past, a video nasty of the Falklands, the miners' strike and Toxteth'. Johnny kisses Edward and is blessed by God. There is a great drag ball in heaven, filmed by Visconti. Then God says: 'Wake up, wake up Edward, wake up Johnny.'

It has all been a dream. Edward and Johnny are in bed. Johnny gets up to make tea. Edward says: 'This morning, etched bright with sunlight, precise as the shadows cast by my life, I emptied my pockets of time, the eternal that neither endures or passes, lay in my hand, world without beginning or end, always and now.'[21] Johnny brings in the tea. They kiss.

It is impossible, in a few paragraphs, to do justice to this script; it is too angry, too nightmarish, too packed with image and incident. To an extent it defines the limits of Jarman's anger, though it is perhaps truer to say that the anger it displays is limitless. It also ends on a note of peace and hope. The good God has waved her fairy wand, there is tea in bed for Edward and Johnny. This scene comprises one of the first images of homosexual love in Jarman's work to be domestically rather than romantically, sexually or violently defined. As such, it forms part of the oblique love poem to Collins running like a vein of gold through Jarman's final films.

At much the same time, in addition to *War Requiem*, he was continuing to give a great deal of thought to *Borrowed Time* and writing a second version of *International Blue*, which he had begun to discuss as a potential project with James Mackay. There was the vague possibility of resuscitating *Bob-up-a-Down* and talk of filming *Man to Man*, the one-woman play by Manfred Karge in which Tilda Swinton had recently appeared at the Royal Court.[22] There was the ongoing idea to make a film about Dungeness and its community.[23] With a young photographer called Matthew Lewis, he discussed producing a book of photographs (half his, half Lewis') called *Narkao*. For another Lewis, David, he appeared as a hermit-like medicine man in *Dead Cat*, a short student film also featuring Genesis P-Orridge. And then there was his diary which, under various titles (principally *Borrowed Time* and *The Fifth Quarter of the Globe*), he had been keeping fairly constantly ever since his diagnosis.

In late summer, he showed *The Fifth Quarter of the Globe* to Robin Baird-Smith at Constable, who was of the opinion that it failed to cohere as a book. He suggested that instead it be cast as a novel; not a proposal, given what Jarman thought about the novel, that was ever likely to bear fruit.

Another focus of activity was painting. This Jarman did mostly at Dungeness, where he now had a proper studio, and where, owing to this new location, the paintings began to change. Still predominantly black, still occasionally flecked with gold, they were otherwise becoming much more sculptural, more three-dimensional as they began to accommodate the flotsam collected by Jarman on his walks along the beach: stones with holes through them, weathered driftwood, rusty metal, old tin cans, gloves, pieces of plastic. Just as his studio room in the cottage harked back, in its peacefulness, to his studio at Upper Ground, so were his paintings returning, in their use of found objects, to the work done alongside the Thames in the late sixties and early seventies – but in a more aggressive manner. As one critic put it, these new works struck 'an indignant chord with God, or time itself'.[24]

Increasingly, Dungeness stood at the still centre of Jarman's embattled world. He was consciously splitting his time between London and Kent, business and quietude, a polarity captured to perfection in his diaries, where vitriol is tempered by serene descriptions of the Ness. He would travel there with whoever was driving him, buying supplies along the way. From the cottage, he might mount further expeditions to familiarise himself with the area, to visit Rye, or one of the nearby churches, especially St Clement at Old Romney. For food, the company might trek up the coast to the Greek restaurant on the road to Little Greatstone, or to the Britannia for fish and chips. Failing that, they stayed home for tea and some of Jarman's home-made jam, maybe the marmalade which, each year at the appointed season, he lovingly made with Seville oranges. By day they would comb the beach for stones and driftwood; by night they might go walking through a darkness cut at regular intervals by the sweeping beam of the lighthouse. If it was cold, they might snuggle under the duvet to watch *Blind Date*. There would always be a great deal of fun and laughter. The diary entries can suggest only gloom, yet despite Jarman's manifest anger and private fears, on the surface he was still as ebullient as ever, as fizzing with restless, infectious energy.

Then the company might depart, leaving him on his own. Now, experiencing the occasional twinge of loneliness, he would paint, sculpt from driftwood, write, continue his struggle to stop smoking, 'start the grandfather clock for company',[25] or practise the mandola, an instrument he had happened upon in Edinburgh as a prop for *Caravaggio*, and which had supplanted the musical saw in his affections. Most healingly and absorbingly of all, he would tend what was rapidly becoming a garden.

After Lance's death, when Jarman had reclaimed his childhood gardening tools from Lymington, he told the *Observer*: 'I sometimes wonder whether I should be doing all this [film]. I always wanted to be a gardener; I love growing things.'[26] In those days all he had been able to grow were flowers and small shrubs, in pots on the balcony at Phoenix House. In the wake of his diagnosis, gardening seemed more of an impossibility than ever. 'Of course it's too late for me to build a garden now', he wrote. 'You need years and friends to swap the cuttings and exchange little recipes.'[27] When he moved to Dungeness, he had not for an instant considered that the terrain might allow for gardening. Yet, like 'all true gardeners',[28] he was an optimist, and it was not long before he was proving his more pessimistic assessments of himself and the Ness gloriously wrong.

The process started with a combination of beachcombing and tidying up around the cottage. In replacing an old rockery of broken bricks and concrete with a collection of flints, some grey, some white, a few red, which he set into the beige shingle separating the cottage from the road in a series of symmetrical circles and squares, Jarman created a stone garden of mini henges ('dragon's teeth',[29] he called them) that gradually segued into horticulture. He planted a dog rose behind the house, staked with a piece of driftwood adorned with a necklace of holed stones. He started to care for and replant the indigenous sea kale, *Crambe maritima*; again, driftwood sticks topped by stones or sea shells marked the location of the plants. Other poles would provide support for the indigenous yellow poppies. Then, step by tentative step, he began introducing new plants, though always within the limits of what the shingle and the biting salt winds – indeed, the Dungeness estate – would permit.[30] Manure was dug in, plants proliferated, so too the manner of their support. Suddenly it was not only driftwood stakes that sprouted so becomingly from the shingle: there were shafts of rusting, twisted metal, fragments of chain, old railway sleepers. He and Steve Farrer, one of his film-making gang, restored the eighteenth-century bench he had rescued from the garden of Güta Minton in Northwood. His planting became more adventurous, stretching to vegetables as well as flowers: gorse, mullein, sea pinks, roses, fennel, curry plants, santolinas, lavender, cornflower, iris. The shingle surrounding the cottage was now indisputably a garden, formal at the front, where it adhered to the outlines of the original flint garden, informal at the back; though, since everything had been planted and placed with such delicacy, at a distance the whole blended so seamlessly into its bleak surroundings that it seemed the work of nature.

Given this new sphere of activity, it is not surprising that the film Jarman was then calling *Borrowed Time* should eventually become *The Garden*. His own 'borrowed time' became this garden, a place of great aesthetic beauty and startling singularity, an 'avant garden' and area of magic, where its alchemist of a creator could take sanctuary from the outside world and heal himself.

By the summer of 1988, the outside world had coughed up the money for *War Requiem* and preproduction was underway. At

£670,000, the budget, although an improvement on *Caravaggio*'s, was as already noted, still barely enough on which to shoot an entire feature, let alone one set in period. Finding somewhere to film that would properly enhance the piece's war tableaux would be crucial to its success. The serendipity of a newspaper article about the imminent closure of a Victorian hospital led to the perfect site. Within the Gothic embrace of Darenth Park, set on a hill overlooking Dartford, there huddled an abundance of suitably atmospheric spaces – 'underground tunnels, vaulted cellars, ruined wards, a mortuary, stables and extensive grounds'.[31] These spaces would provide not only the sets but a plethora of production offices. They were also within easy and affordable reach of central London.

As with all Jarman's films, both cast and crew featured old friends, among them Tilda Swinton (back in favour as the nurse), Nigel Terry, Sean Bean, Spencer Leigh, Claire Davenport, Keith Collins (to help with the editing and making a brief screen debut shaving in the trenches) and, as designer, Lucy Morahan, who had been an assistant on *Caravaggio*. Jarman's original choice for Wilfred Owen had been Daniel Day-Lewis who, that spring, had been a visitor to Prospect Cottage with Tilda Swinton, but when he announced that he could not undertake the role it went instead to Nathaniel Parker.

For the veteran whose reading of 'Strange Meeting' opens proceedings, Boyd and a somewhat overawed Jarman secured the services of eighty-one-year-old Laurence Olivier, whose final film this would be. Other newcomers included Patricia Hayes as Owen's mother, Owen Teale as the unknown soldier, Clancy Chassay as the young Owen, Richard Greatrex as director of photography and Rick Elgood as editor.

That September *The Last of England* was shown at the Venice Film Festival. Neither the film, nor Jarman's geographically driven comments at an accompanying seminar on the future of video – he spoke of television as 'the black algae poisoning the lagoon' – met with much enthusiasm. One woman said in reply, 'We think *you* are the algae.'[32]

As equivocal was the film's reception in the States when, later that month, it was included in the New York Film Festival.[33] Although it afterwards enjoyed a short but not unsuccessful run at the Film Forum and subsequently won the Los Angeles Film Critics' 1988 'Achievement Award in Independent Experimental Film', during the festival itself the reviews it gathered were far from glowing ('the longest and gloomiest rock video ever made,' griped *The New York Times*),[34] and people walked out in droves. However, it did give Jarman another excellent opportunity to mount his soapbox. Describing him as 'dark and vigorous', 'exuding an intense physical energy', 'incredibly smart and funny and entirely assured', the *Village Voice* noted approvingly of his press conference that 'this charming man [was] clearly pleased as punch to be at the podium'. His presence 'was almost more compelling than his film'.[35]

While he had the energy for unlimited public speaking and criticism of Margaret Thatcher, he was not up to hitting the town. He was again enjoying the lavish hospitality of Mark McCormick and Leland Wheeler in McCormick's Upper East Side apartment, where there was much exuberant youthfulness on hand in the form of Collins and Gerard Raimond, both of whom had accompanied Jarman on the trip, as had Tilda Swinton. But much more evident was the chill omniscience of death. For anyone gay, New York in the late eighties was a significantly more sombre city than it had been in the seventies. When Jarman saw the film-maker Howard Brookner, whom he had first met during *The Final Academy* in 1982 and who had since become one of his dearest friends, he found him tragically confined to a wheelchair.

In early October, *War Requiem* began its three-week shoot with a morning spent capturing Olivier on film, then on audiotape as he read 'Strange Meeting'. Despite the actor's age and the director's apprehension at working with so exalted a thespian as 'Sir Lazzers', the morning passed without incident, as indeed did the rest of the shoot. The fact that Jarman had not worked with Greatrex before did nothing to prevent the two of them collaborating as closely and in as relaxed a manner as Jarman always did with his cameramen. With more 35mm footage in the can than they had ever thought possible, on 4 November they finished the shoot bang on schedule and comfortably within budget.

Meanwhile, Lynn Hanke, an American art historian and publicist with a passion for film, who, through Don Boyd, had met Jarman that September in New York, was brought over by Boyd to help research the archive war footage that would supplement what had been shot on 35mm and super-8. Now began the task of cutting the three strands together, in time to the music, but without losing narrative coherence. It was not easy. 'The combinations' were 'inexhaustible', making it 'very difficult to fix and finalize a sequence'.[36] There was always another, equally valid alternative, which was perhaps why Jarman seemed unusually remote from the post-production and editing process; he simply could not engage as intensely with the material as he had on The Last of England. Still, ever mindful that he was working to a deadline (because of the BBC's involvement, the film had to open in January if it was to enjoy a cinematic release before its television première at Easter), he never let this uncertainty slow him down. Allowing Rick Elgood his head and leaving the editing of the violent war footage entirely to John Maybury and Keith Collins, he ensured that the first answer print was ready by mid-December. On New Year's Eve, there was a private screening of the film at the Cannon Cinema in Shaftesbury Avenue, where it would officially open a week later, in tandem with an exhibition of seventy-six new paintings at Richard Salmon's studio in South Edwardes Square.

When, in the spring of 1989, the script was published by Faber and Faber, Jarman wrote: 'In my heart, I dedicate my film of War Requiem to all those cast out, like myself, from Christendom. To my friends who are dying in a moral climate created by a church with no compassion.'[37] The words sound a note of defiance missing from the finished film. Although not without anger and indignation, or echoes of Jarman's most personal concerns, War Requiem is oddly restrained. Powerful, certainly, but not as powerful – or, with the possible exception of Maybury's sequences, as unsettling – as might have been expected. Nowhere does the film explore the irony that Britten's essentially conventional music should have co-opted Owen's angry and anti-establishment poetry. Perhaps this is why it was never a film Jarman particularly valued. He later said it was made 'too fast'[38] and frequently forgot to mention it in round-ups of his work.

By contrast, most reviewers were distinctly impressed. For Tim Clark of Time Out, it was 'a major artwork . . . Jarman's finest to date'.[39] For *Variety* it was similarly 'Jarman's most mature effort . . . a moving and highly original cinematic visualization of Britten's impressive choral work'.[40] And the *Daily Telegraph*, not known for its espousal of the Jarman oeuvre, trumpeted that 'never can a musical piece of such magnitude have been translated so powerfully into another medium . . . It is hard to know which is the more devastating – the vivid clarity of the director's vision, or the horrific actuality.'[41] Only in Berlin, where the film was shown in competition at the same time as *Imagining October* received a long overdue screening as part of the Panorama Section, did the reaction match that of the film's maker. Here, although Jarman himself was, as ever, warmly received, the film was not. 'The silence at the end was a total . . . 30 seconds that seemed two minutes; then the audience crept out in silence, passed by me as if I was a ghost come to haunt them, chill their blood.'[42]

Paradoxically, at this moment being a ghost was the furthest thing from Jarman's agenda, even if he did frequently fret about the state of his stomach and chest. Although the coming year would bring major illness closer, and although an in-depth television profile of Jarman, broadcast in the spring of 1989, had a definite whiff of the obituary about it,[43] the only requiem Jarman was considering was Britten's. To the two features, two books and three exhibitions which had appeared since his diagnosis, he still had four features to add, plus an even greater number of books and exhibitions. He was far from ready for the closing credits.

28

I Walk in this Garden

On the second anniversary of his diagnosis, Jarman told an inter-viewer: 'December 22 . . . becomes a kind of key day in my life now, and I think: "Ah, that's another year over." On that day and over Christmas I think, what shall I do next year? I've concentrated so hard on Requiem it's kept all that at bay in a way . . . I'm going to make a film about gardens next. I want *out* from hard-hitting . . . Why should I be on the frontline all the time?'[1] Although he did strive for peace where he could (his hatred of David Puttnam was now 'all in the past'),[2] Clause 28 had put Jarman too firmly in the front line to make retreat a possibility – and when he did come to make the 'film about gardens', it was far from idyllic.

As Jarman's producer, James Mackay had had his differences with Jarman, but neither these nor the fact that he not been involved with *War Requiem* had in any way lessened his commitment to Jarman as a director. However, since it was proving difficult to manoeuvre *The Garden*, still called *Borrowed Time*, towards realisa-tion, 1989 was to have a somewhat fragmentary feel to it. Its spine is supplied not by film, but by Dungeness and the most consistent diary Jarman had yet attempted. Starting on 1 January and continuing until the September of 1990, this diary, published in 1991 as *Modern Nature*, unfolds on an almost daily basis, allowing careful study of the small print of Jarman's bipartite existence. It details the yin of London, with its endless meetings, the incessant phone, the surging traffic and press of people in Charing Cross Road, Soho meals and drinks, the odd afternoon of teaching, weekend visits to the market at Camden Lock, the annual march to celebrate Gay Pride. It also encapsulates the yang of Dungeness: sea, sky, shingle and solitude; regular waves of visiting friends, in between which Jarman frequently had only Jet, his neighbour's crow, for company; his painting, the ever-expanding garden. 'The gardener digs in another time, without past or future, beginning or end. A time that does not cleave the day with rush hours, lunch breaks, the last bus home. As you walk in the garden you pass into this time – the moment of entering can never be remembered. Around you the landscape lies transfigured. Here is the Amen beyond the prayer.' The diary also revisits and lingers over the past, and is the most carefully wrought of all Jarman's published works: the most sustained, poetic and thoughtful.

Pre-eminent among the many work projects occupying Jarman's mind while Mackay battled to raise money for both it and *The Garden*, was *International Blue* – or, since it underwent as many changes of title as it did of script, *A Blueprint for Bliss* or *Blueprint*.[3] Jarman dreamed of recording the actor Matt Dillon's heartbeat for the soundtrack: 'it would be a great first credit'.[4] Sounds were crucial to his thinking for the film. After gilding 'a small pocket book for *Blueprint*', he walked along the beach and 'thought the film might follow the sound of footsteps, a journey with the continuous murmur of lazy waves, sea breezes, thunder, and stormy growlers. In the swell: dreams and recollections, the gemstone city of *Revelations*, brazen trumpets, the *Song of Solomon* – could all this be resolved with the *Tai Te Ching: great fullness seems empty?*'[5] In this version, the film was a dialogue between Yves Klein and St Rita of Cascia: '80 minutes of film in I.K.B. ending with a breath of GOLD.'[6]

Apart from the super-8 footage he was continually shooting for his own pleasure, or to add to *The Garden*, the only filming he did until *The Garden* came to fruition was for the Pet Shop Boys.

The duo were scheduled to tour Hong Kong and Japan, followed by three venues in Britain: Birmingham, Glasgow and Wembley Arena. They wanted the show, their first-ever full-length live concert, to be highly theatrical and to involve an element of film. They saw in Jarman someone capable not only of staging the event, but of providing the requisite number of back projections. The money on offer was substantial and much needed, and since Jarman had in the main worked well with the group in the past, his answer was an unhesitating yes.

With Mackay producing and the technical support of as many of the gang as he could muster, among them Keith Collins, Jarman lost no time in tackling his new brief. Working in both super-8 and 16mm and mixing footage from his own and other 'libraries' with an equal amount of new material, some shot on location, some in the course of two brief studio sessions in south London, by the end of May he had assembled back projections for eight of the concert's songs: 'Opportunities', 'Heart', 'Paninaro', 'Nothing Has Been Proved', 'It's a Sin', 'Domino Dancing', 'King's Cross' and 'Always on my Mind'. This impressionistic multiformity of material was swiftly edited, then blown up to 70mm, the gauge in which it would be projected on to an enormous screen at the back of the stage.

In its flamboyant theatricality, the end result was very like the effect Jarman had achieved at the start of *L'ispirazione*, and hugely to its creator's liking: 'It's a medley that cavorts through the styles of the underground . . . Effects like these will never have been seen on film before.' Because he had done too little filming that year, his enthusiasm knew no bounds, particularly where his new version of 'It's a Sin' was concerned. In the eyes of its maker, this lurid vision of Dionysian excess approached 'Grunewald or Bosch'.[7]

Now came stage two of the project: directing the show itself. Jarman had been 'dreading these days for weeks'.[8] In the event, they proved far less onerous than expected. Not only had the various departments (dance, costume, lighting) been subcontracted to highly professional parties, but the ubiquitous computer technology involved in a concert of this scale meant that, however theatrical the show needed to be, the director never had 'much leeway for anything creative'.[9] The entire show was put together in a matter of days, with Jarman directing the proceedings as 'unobtrusively as possible'.[10]

Or, as he later put it: 'Neil [Tennant] staged us all and I helped him.'[11]

The rehearsals were held at the Academy in Brixton. After ensuring that the lights changed on cue, the six dancers knew where to place themselves for their dazzling routines, the backing singers ditto; that Courtney Pine, who accompanied Tennant and Lowe on the saxophone, was comfortable and that there was time for the Pet Shop Boys to effect their many (and, in Tennant's case, extremely elaborate) costume changes, the nominal director pronounced himself pleased with what had been achieved – 'a song and dance show of considerable sophistication'[12] – and waved the company off to the Far East with an easy heart.

Jarman was then asked if he would film the concert at Wembley in late July. He, Mackay and Collins were able to fly to Glasgow to see the performance there, but this was all the preparation they managed. It made filming the event, which had to be done in the course of the three actual concerts, with just one extra afternoon for close ups and special angles, even more nerve-wracking than directing the show itself. There was also not enough money to shoot on film, so they had to use video. It was, Jarman said, like sitting on the edge of a cliff.

'Filming,' he wrote, 'is a contradiction as there are five cameras mounted in fixed positions to interfere with the sight lines of the least number of seats. Loss of contact with the cameramen is almost complete, the music so loud you can barely make yourself heard.'[13] For much of the time he was communicating via headphones and a bank of monitors from a van outside the stadium, worrying that his inability to move his cameras would mean he would never cover the show successfully, fretting that he had no control over such details as Tennant's make-up, effective on stage, less so on video. On the Friday afternoon, he sat in the empty auditorium in his trademark boilersuit, 'eyes bulging like an over-anxious headmaster',[14] issuing frantic instructions through a handheld microphone as he lost his battle with time to cover all the songs before that evening's performance. At the end of the afternoon, apologising through his microphone if he had been irritable, he looked as though he had experienced 'some of the worst hours of his life'.[15]

The horror was not over. The finished film, entitled *Highlights*,

ends with a shot of the crowd outside Wembley and a snatch of
Jarman's voice saying: 'Hey, well done everyone. That was wonderful.' Nothing could have been further from the truth. If the filming
had been nightmarish, so was the editing. There was barely enough
usable material. 'Could this be hell?' Jarman wondered, adding
mournfully: 'I had a sudden flash of it going on relentlessly, through
hundreds of years.'[16] Although every attempt was made to echo the
show's triumphant theatricality, no one could pretend the film was a
success. Nor was it greeted as one. Chris Lowe 'hated' it, saying it
looked like *Top of the Pops*. Jarman's only defence was the conditions
in which they had been working. 'It was as if,' he wrote, 'I were to
hand Chris five notes, inferior recording equipment, and two hours
with people shouting to get it over – and expected to get a number
1 hit.'[17]

The Pet Shop Boys had wanted Jarman to accompany the concert
to Hong Kong and Japan. He had declined. Although he did some
travelling that year, he needed to conserve his energy for what was
fast beginning to rival almost all his other activities: his champi-
oning of gay and AIDS-related issues. 'I had foolishly wished my film
to be home, to contain all the intimacies,' he wrote. 'But in order to
do this I had to open to the public. At first a few genuine enthusiasts
took up the offer, then coachloads arrived.'[18] Almost every time he
visited London, he would find the door to the flat blocked by
'another enormous pile of letters'.[19] He noted: 'Reaction to me has
changed. There is an element of worship, which worries me.' He
worried too that he had perhaps 'courted' the worship.[20] It was complicated. On one hand, this was what he had always craved: to have
a voice, to be worshipped. Yet the responsibilities involved were irksome and time-consuming, his pre-eminence possibly the result of all
the wrong things: 'My sense of confusion has come to a head, catal-
ysed by my public announcement of the HIV infection.'[21]

Thanks to the rate at which he had been painting since his diagnosis, he had accumulated sufficient work to field seven separate
exhibitions in the course of the year. There was the one in January at
Richard Salmon's. Then, in March, he was in Paris for an exhibition
and film retrospective at the Accatone Gallery. In July, to coincide
with a festival of cinema, there was a show entitled *Pintures de*

l'Apocalipsi at the Galeria Ambit in Barcelona. Next came a group effort at Lydd Airport and the Martello Tower at Dymchurch as part of the Romney Marsh Arts Festival. Entitled *The Marsh in War and Peace*, the show included work by Marion Bataille, Peter Fillingham and Luke Oxley as well as Jarman. Another group exhibition of small, tarred collage pieces at the Lyth Arts Centre, Caithness was followed by a solo show at the Richard Demarco Gallery in Edinburgh. At much the same time, in Glasgow, at the Third Eye Centre in Sauchiehall Street, there was a new and angry installation.

The National Review of Live Art, which showcased new work 'from less well-known artists' and encouraged 'more established artists to make work for new contexts', was in its ninth year.[22] On being invited to contribute to this celebration of live performance art, Jarman decided to make an installation that would confront homosexuality and homophobia head on. His first thoughts were for

> a tomb/cenotaph, 'Et in Arcadia Ego': two young men
> entwined in Rodin's *Kiss*, a shepherd with a staff and drapes
> from Poussin's painting. Near the tomb is a bed with two boys
> asleep – a scarlet counterpane painted with the number 28.
> There is a virus painting – crucifix, KY, and condom –
> brightly lit. A pornographic video-tape, or a recording of
> telephone sex broadcast in the gallery – the visitors use their
> own money to pay for the service. A large painting, almost
> monochromatic, of condoms.[23]

The idea of the bed with two boys asleep in it would remain the lynchpin of the installation, as would the vitriol; the medium, however, would change. The fact that the houses at Dungeness were covered in black tar varnish had given Jarman the idea of using melted tar as the fixative for his collages. That summer, with the help of David Lewis, in whose student film he had recently appeared, and who was often on hand when Jarman was filming the Ness, he covered a variety of objects in the substance, or in a mixture of pitch and feathers. He found the process wonderfully satisfying, like 'building sand-and-water pinnacles and spires on the beach as a child',[24] and decided to use it to tackle the installation.

The walls of the gallery will have several beds, mattresses, sheets, discarded clothes, all tarred and feathered. In the beds could be bibles, condoms, the clothes – jeans and sweatshirts, sports clothes; uniforms – a fireman's or policeman's.
Quotations from the newspapers, photos of loved ones and families, found photos, alarm clocks, a telephone, a tarred and feathered TV.
    In the centre of the gallery an oasis: a bed with two young men surrounded by barbed wire; on the wire, press cuttings, as if blown by the wind; and a tarred and feathered skeleton wearing a concentration camp uniform, spreadeagled as if shot trying to enter the space.[25]

On 1 October, he drove to Glasgow with his two young men, Gerard Raimond and Collins, stopping on the way at Tilda Swinton's family home to deliver the two horsechestnuts he had brought back from Moscow, both of which had, for some years, been in desperate need of a garden. He had always maintained that one came from the grave of Khrushchev, the other from that of Chekhov. As he left the trees (labelled 'October 1984 Novdevechy cemetery') by the Swintons' door, he noted with wry satisfaction: 'Politics: 4 feet 3 inches – poetry: 6 feet 6 inches.'[26]
    In Glasgow, he was lent space at the workshop of the Citizens' Theatre. With the assistance of two of the theatre staff, the designer Stewart Laing and his assistant, John Harkins, he began the gloriously mucky business of tarring and feathering seven mattresses, which he then strapped to the walls of the gallery and scattered with the belongings of the bed's supposed occupant, be he footballer, policeman or something more anonymous. In the words of a contemporary witness: 'One, for instance, has copies of a 1950s *Physique* magazine and a book open at Freud's analysis of Leonardo da Vinci's homosexuality: another has a copy of Plato's Symposium open at the page where he says that young men must love each other, below it is a photo of two young men doing just that.'[27] The pages of tabloid homophobia (supplied by Simon Watney) were plastered to the walls and pillars of the gallery. In a clip frame, Jarman put the Scottish pound note he had received in his change when buying a newspaper

on the day the exhibition opened. He had circled in red the picture of Edinburgh Castle and written underneath it: 'Aids Hospice Edinburgh'. He fervently hoped visitors would add press cuttings of their own, or photographs of loved ones, which they could attach to the pillars and the barbed wire around the bed.

Seemingly naked, Collins and Raimond lay side by side under the sheets of the central bed, reading, daydreaming, on occasion sleeping. Jarman, meanwhile, was in the background, hopping from foot to foot as he observed the reaction of the people who passed through the gallery every day. The responses were mixed.

Sunday 15
The talk at the gallery was difficult. Someone objected to the obviousness of the installation, and then complained it was bad art. Others sprang to its defence. I talked of the barbed wire that had hemmed me in, quite literally, in the RAF camps – the fenced-in boarding school, the proscribed sexuality, the virus. During the discussion those who did not like the show caused me great sadness. Could they not see beyond art?[28]

Yet in many ways Jarman's fortnight in Glasgow had been the high point of his year. 'I've hardly slept,' he wrote, 'swept off my feet in a torrent of conversation. Even if the installation is bad art it has led to good ends, provoked but not trapped the audience.' The 'intense work' had 'obliterated the garden' and suggested an alternative reality: 'I can live in a hotel room with a change of blue overalls, toothpaste, a razor, and this diary.'[29] Much as he needed the peace and quiet of Dungeness, it was good to feel alive again and in the thick of things.

He returned home to news of the death of film-maker Paul Bettell, whom he had first met in Newcastle along with Keith Collins, and who had worked on *War Requiem*. It was not the first death the year had thrown at him, or the most painful. In April, he had spoken for the last time to 'dearest Howard Brookner, so far away in New York. He can only groan now, his bright mind slowly invaded by a terrible infection that is depriving him gradually of his faculties . . . I didn't know if he understood a word – long silences and the low wounded moaning. No words now. The echoing emptiness of those groans encircling the world by satellite. It left me confused, fearful and terribly sad.' Within a month, Brookner was dead. 'April,' wrote Jarman, 'is much crueller than ever Eliot imagined'.[30] He produced a poem:

> I walk in this garden
> Holding the hands of dead friends
> Old age came quickly for my frosted generation
> Cold, cold, cold they died so silently
> Did the forgotten generations scream?
> Or go full of resignation
> Quietly protesting innocence
> Cold, cold, cold they died so silently . . .[31]

Because Brookner had kept his illness secret from his Hollywood bosses for fear they would scupper his final film,[32] Jarman dreamed him the most public – and de Mille-like – of obsequies: 'a grand procession, like the Parthenon frieze, of naked young men with wands and torches, trumpets and banners, a triumph over death for dear Howard, figures draped in diaphanous silks with golden crowns and oiled torsos, naked youths on elephants, leading white oxen with gilded horns bearing all the heroes of history, Alexander, Hadrian, Michelangelo, Whitman . . .'[33]

A further reminder that to an extent we all live on borrowed time came in mid-June. Collins had taken up boxing and, while sparring at his gym, had been hit on the head and had suffered a minor stroke. The twenty-four-year-old was partially paralysed down his left side. Worst affected were his face and speech. Jarman was devastated: 'Three days blur in anguish. The sky fell in leaving a blank page filled with tears. Then, clenching his hands and staring skywards behind dark glasses, HB started to turn the dark back, and a chink of light appeared. A twitch in the eye became a miracle. At the lowest moment he sat under a towel in the bathroom and said "Please don't look at me" . . . A sense of our fragility on this sunny afternoon.'[34]

Luckily, the paralysis proved temporary and the outward effects of the stroke soon became virtually undetectable. More far-reaching were its less tangible ramifications; the way it reminded both Collins and Jarman of what they meant to each other: 'Every cell in my body wills his regeneration. HB's arrival in my life has saved me from collapse in the past two years. I wish to do the same for him.'[35]

They were anything but a conventional couple. They spent as much time apart as they did together, even at Christmas, with Collins still tending to gravitate towards an increasingly minimalistic Phoenix House, Jarman to Dungeness. Their many differences were as marked as ever, their separate sexual adventuring as flagrant. But there could be no doubting the maturation of their mutual affection. Although Collins could still seem intent on driving a wedge between Jarman and certain of his friends (within a year, Gerard Raimond would join Andy Marshall and Spring on the periphery of Jarman's circle),[36] he no longer asserted primacy in physical terms; they might still argue, but assault was a thing of the past. Collins was growing older, becoming less wild, and had been so securely drawn into Jarman's orbit – working with Peter Cartwright as an editor, appearing in *War Requiem*, typing up Jarman's manuscripts – that to leave his companion would have been an almighty wrench.

Meanwhile, a new and final title had been selected for the film which would round off the year. *Borrowed Time*, still sometimes referred to by Jarman in his notes as *The Wanderer* or *The Dream of the Rood*, briefly became *The Garden of England*, then simply *The Garden*. Although the film still lacked a script as such and would be made in much the same way as *The Last of England* – 'home-movie making really gone sort of slightly grand'[37] – it had developed considerably in Jarman's mind since the notes and related short tape of late 1987. Then the starting point had been the end of *The Tempest*, with 'Miranda left behind in the magic island for which I would use the landscape in and around the Ness'.[38] This landscape, especially Jarman's garden, remained the heart of the film; but how it was treated, approached and walked through had undergone a number of transformations.

A second starting point was the final image from *The Last of England*. Where had the refugees from that film sailed? Perhaps to Dungeness? Here the idea was to pick up on Tilda Swinton and a lover and film their Dungeness love story. In its simplicity and sweetness, this would provide an antidote to the earlier film.

Or, inspired by a painting of the crucifixion that hung in Prospect Cottage, and borrowing heavily from those two favourite Anglo-Saxon poems, 'The Dream of the Rood' and 'The Wanderer', he considered structuring the film around the crucifixion and the question of who merits or receives God's grace. 'The Wanderer', being a poem about divine grace, gave Jarman ample material for that, while 'The Dream of the Rood', being both a vision and a poetic history of the actual cross, or rood, on which Christ died, led towards the crucifixion and the question, for whom *had* Christ died?

Next, the narrative device became that of a spaceman descending to earth at Dungeness, where he encounters a landscape

> *All laid low by the pestilence*
> *Desolate now, the courts, the steeples*
> *and domes discoloured*
> *Where once a bold nation gleaming with gold,*
> *wanton with wine,*
> *Splendid and shining stood proud,*
> *And inviolate.*

He digs in the shingle and 'uncovers a golden time capsule bearing the legend "ROSETTA", which he takes back to his spaceship, a Kleinian 'luminous blue oval'. Inside the capsule are a collection of videotapes and film, 'all that remains of our vanished world'. The spaceman studies this 'Pandemonium of Images' by casting them on to the luminous blue. They recreate a past and a topography. There is a simple village, a city where it is 'always Christmas', a power station that fuels the city. A mad minstrel crosses this landscape 'telling of the city and its insatiable appetite'. Mary Magdalen finds a young black man washed up on the shore. The black man leads a donkey into the city of perpetual Christmas. He is set upon by the police, thrown into a cell, given 'electrical shock therapy, which weaves round him like a crown of thorns'. Finally, the 'crucified youth is swallowed by the cross, which is resurrected as a beautiful oak tree in an icy field'.[39] We hear 'The Dream of the Rood' being sung.

In 1989, a number of substantial changes were made to this central theme of crucifixion and Christ being set upon by an uncaring community. The characters of the black man and the spaceman vanished. The framing device became that of the dream allegory: as the film's maker, Jarman himself would dream his film into being. The garden would be the gardens of both Eden and Gethsemane, while the landscape of Dungeness, with its boats and fishermen, would be a Sea of Galilee. There would be an actual Christ, whose appearance and passion would be mirrored and intercut by that of two gay lovers who, at moments, would share his torments. This enabled Jarman to focus more powerfully and bitterly than in previous versions on the attitudes of the Church to gay men and its role in the AIDS crisis. He hoped to show that, thanks to St Paul's proscriptions against homosexuality, the Church had lost sight of Christ's original message of love. He also wanted to draw attention to the fact, as he saw it, that papal decrees against the use of condoms were homicidal. 'We are,' he wrote, 'dealing with people who are actually morally reprobate.'[40]

During the course of the year, as Mackay had become involved with the Pet Shop Boys, Jarman had briefly feared his producer might neglect The Garden. Mackay, however, had the bit between his teeth and, despite having already spent two fairly unsuccessful years struggling to raise the money, never for a moment wavered. By early 1989, he had a promise of some £50,000 from Channel 4 – a minuscule sum when set against the level at which he hoped to budget the film. In an attempt to reduce the budget while still persuading Channel 4 to part with more money, Mackay told them the film could be made purely as a landscape film, with music by Simon Turner and Vaughan Williams; or, if made with actors and as a romance between Tilda Swinton and a lover, that the lover might be played by Daniel Day-Lewis. At the same time, he was in touch with Takashi Asai, Jarman's Japanese distributor, whom he hoped would help fund both The Garden and International Blue, or Blueprint as it was now known. In Germany, he was pursuing ZDF, enthusiastic contributors towards The Last of England. He was talking to Sony, Mute Records and the BFI.

By late summer, the deal was still not properly in place and Jarman was beginning to worry about the 'usual Basilisk chaos'.[41] 'The Garden creaks on in typical "Jamesian" manner,' he wrote, 'nothing, as ever, foreseen. No meeting equals no money. He [Mackay] has acquired a ghastly video of the Pets' show to pay his phone bills, and lost my film, for the time being.'[42] As things turned out, it was this 'ghastly video' that would save the day. Mackay had decided that since the work he had done for the Pet Shop Boys had put him in profit, some of this money could help pay for two short shoots that would at least start the ball rolling.

The shoots were planned for September, leaving the fractious director little time to finalise his cast. There had never been any doubt that the film would feature Tilda Swinton, now given the dual role of the Madonna and the unnamed woman who watches the film unfold. The other principal female character, Mary Magdalen, went to Spencer Leigh. Christ was to be the artist Roger Cook, whom Jarman had known at the Slade. Jody Graber, the 'enemy child' from War Requiem, was both a young Christ and a young Jarman. For that triumvirate of evil – Devil, Judas, serpent – Jarman chose one established actor, Pete Lee-Wilson, and two unknowns: Philip MacDonald (Judas) and the exotically tattooed Mr Drako (serpent). A number of old friends and stalwarts were also called upon, as were most of the usual technicians.

Come September, Jarman was not in the best of health. He had been suffering night sweats and had recently caught a chill. 'I don't feel ill, but weak, and my temperature fluctuates. When I stoop in the garden I feel giddy and take a minute to recover.'[43] Giddiness notwithstanding, the first day of the new month was the inescapable first day of 'official' filming at Dungeness. The film was still taking shape in his mind.

> Tilda, Roger Cook, Spring and David here at lunch time.
>   We went on a recce up beyond the power station, and came to these decisions: that The Garden should have menacing terrorist newsmen; that at moments the film should be theatrical, that naked angels should light scenes with flares; that Drako and Spring will be the devil and his disciple; that the week after next we should film Christ walking along the great empty road into the sunset beneath pylons crackling and buzzing with electricity, that he should

be confronted by a jogger – Graham – who is swearing about the state of things.

Other sequences: we will place the bed on the sands and light it with flares as the tide comes in. We should have a sequence in the studio – writing. That we will film the childhood of Christ outside the railway carriage, and Mary Magdalen at the Listening Wall.[44]

In the last week of September, the cast and crew once again descended on Dungeness, this time for a couple of days. Backed by a generator and a bank of lights, they filmed with a single 16mm camera, supplemented by ambient work in super-8. It was far from easy manoeuvring the heavy equipment and cables across the shingle and they were further hindered by the wet and windy weather, but, nevertheless, they did manage successfully to capture the sequences Jarman had outlined.

Given the film's subject matter, there was some speculation among the crew as to whether their difficulties in moving equipment across the shingle were some sort of omen. The fear that what they were doing was blasphemous and might incur the wrath of God was subtly present, even in the director, who was also wrestling with the demon of his illness. After everyone had gone, he noted in his diary: 'The two days have passed in a delirium. The violation of the house, the chaos and extreme fatigue leave me lurching backwards and forwards. I feel as tangled as the sheets which move through the hurricane of my dreams.' And when he drove with David Lewis to London to prepare for his trip to Glasgow, he encountered a portent of his own. Stopping in Dungeness to deliver a cheque, he opened the car door and 'almost stepped on a large grass snake writhing at my feet – it opened its mouth in agony. The car had run over it. An ill omen. We hadn't seen it – the snake of wisdom who brought the knowledge of good and evil, man's best friend, serpent of memory, great figure of eight, lying with its back broken and its mouth open, crying in silence.'[45]

With Jarman in Glasgow erecting his installation at the Third Eye Centre, Mackay continued his struggle to finalise funding for what was now a semi-completed film. He faced some unexpected and last-minute disappointments (the BFI, on whom he had pinned great hopes, declined to be involved), but by dint of conjuring certainty from thin air and encouraging the various partners to sign on the dotted line by leading them to believe that more money was pledged than was always strictly the case, at the end of October, with the budget now standing at some £450,000, he secured cast-iron commitments from Channel 4, ZDF and Takashi Asai's Uplink. Shortly thereafter, British Screen joined the roster. Mackay was still fractionally short of his final goal, but there was now sufficient money lined up to embark on the last stage of filming: a studio shoot in December at James Electric, off the Old Kent Road.

Jarman was still far from well. The night sweats and giddiness were continuing. 'Stomach destroyed again, and teeth on edge; at sixes and sevens. My centre is knocked sideways, I've fallen off the edge of hope.'[46] Neither the excitement of Glasgow, nor the funding for *The Garden* greatly improved matters. As October drew to a close, the film's director was

> plagued with misgivings about *The Garden*. Looking at the rushes over the past six days, I discovered not one sequence that worked. Glaring faults everywhere: no close ups, camera faults, out-of-focus shots, shots that fall like confetti. 16mm deadly, with no resonance. There is not a shot that is not ugly.
>
> Why should this happen?
>
> No more the coherence of shared projects – this has become too big to manage. Shackled with dozens of hangers-on I cannot improvise. The shoot is a hydra – I cannot hear anything for all the voices asking questions.
>
> We have no organisation. James, the producer, makes arbitrary decisions about cameras, accuses me of being 'absent', foists 16mm on me – a truly hideous experience.[47]

Not even on the heath, where, in 'a separate and parallel world, under the stars' he could usually find solace by fading 'away into the dark',[48] was he able to escape unease.

The good-looking jogger, who I've seen dancing alone on the street outside Comptons . . . skirts round the few groups of men and disappears only to reappear again half an hour later. After ignoring me he suddenly passes by, and turning a corner I find him standing, facing me.

I knew before I touched him that this encounter was doomed. I was freezing cold and all he wanted was attention that he could reject. The fact that I had turned my back on him earlier was the reason for his provocative stance. He kissed me very reticently and said 'Suck it mate'; but before we made contact disappeared, this time for good.[49]

November found Jarman at Dungeness with Simon Turner, viewing the tapes of what he had filmed so far and working out 'a credible beginning to The Garden'.[50] Mackay flew to Turkey to film background landscape for the footage to be shot in the studio. Collins turned twenty-five. The Berlin Wall came down. Jarman tiled the kitchen at Prospect Cottage, put in an extra window and replaced the outside steps to the loft. In his diary, he was remembering his past and recounting it in particularly vivid detail.

He continued to worry. 'Behind the facade my life is at sixes and sevens. I water the roses and wonder whether I will see them bloom. I plant my herbal garden as a panacea, read up on all the aches and pains that plants will cure – and know they are not going to help. The garden as pharmacopoeia has failed.'[51] He was scared that Dungeness had also failed him professionally. Because the new film was about the garden, that was where he had been shooting it and where, all along, he had tried to base himself; but, despite a fax machine enabling him to communicate ideas to the production office in London, he feared that his absence from Phoenix House was starting to impede the film's progress.

He had two and a half weeks to finalise preparations and decide on additional casting for December's eight-day shoot, when he would film the gay lovers whose torments mirror those of Christ. While Simon Turner took care of the extras, Jarman lined up an array of regulars, including Dawn Archibald, Michael Gough, Jack Birkett and Vernon Dobtcheff. He asked Jessica Martin, then appearing in

Me and My Girl, to mime the 'Think Pink' number from *Funny Face* for the sequence in which the gay lovers are married. For the lovers themselves, he was hoping for Sean Bean and Rupert Graves. When this proved impossible, he turned at the last minute to Collins and one of Collins' friends and former lovers by the name of Johnny Mills. Collins had only ever played an extra in *War Requiem*, while Mills, who worked for Islington Council, had never appeared on screen at all. Undaunted, on the basis of a quick 'audition on video',[52] Jarman declared himself satisfied that they could carry the day. Collins, already engaged to help edit the film, promptly adopted the screen name of Kevin, thereby creating a mythical 'twin brother' as his acting persona.

Then came a 'frightful bust up'[53] with James Mackay over the use Mackay was proposing to make of the back projections for the Pet Shop Boys' concert. Hoping to set up a deal with Japan for the video release of *The Garden*, Mackay had realised that if he tacked the projections on to the feature, he could get three to four times the money he would get for *The Garden* on its own, which would solve, at a stroke, all his funding problems. To Jarman, the very idea was a travesty. 'The elegiac garden film that has hung like an albatross – to be sold on the back of video wallpaper made for the Pet Shop Boys.'[54] Although he had once said how proud he was of his concert version of 'It's a Sin', now he shrieked that the only film of any worth was the one for 'Nothing Has Been Proved' – and that, anyway, he had never wanted the films to be shown on their own, that he had only made them 'to bail Mackay out', and why was Mackay going behind his back? He was beside himself with fury. After a 'five minute slanging match', he was scribbling furiously in his diary: 'This is the parting of the ways!' Over the course of the next day, however, his anger gradually abated, and two days later, on 3 December, the studio shoot began.

Everything was filmed, in both 16mm and super-8, on a pile of shingle laid on the studio floor to replicate the conditions of Dungeness, and against a blue background on to which a variety of landscape and other shots could later be added. Though differing widely in tone, the dozen or so sequences Jarman had planned for his parallel version of Christ's passion all shared a degree of surrealistic theatricality. There was the idyllic innocence of young love: Collins and Mills in a bath together, asleep in bed, discovering the Madonna's crown buried in the shingle. There was Jessica Martin energetically miming 'Think Pink' against a backdrop of Gay Pride marches and the two young lovers in matching pink suits cradling a baby; what one might term a post-nuclear family. There were elements of repression and horror. Jody Graber as a schoolboy being menaced by his masters, who beat a long table with their canes. Pete Lee-Wilson as the Devil, dancing with a handful of credit cards, while in the background, dangling from a noose, swung the body of Philip MacDonald as Judas. The lovers being taunted and later flogged by a group of 'skinheads dressed in Father Christmas robes'.[55] The lovers being covered with treacle, kapok and feathers by a group of malevolent policemen. The lovers carrying a cross. The lovers dead. There was the strangeness of twelve women in black sitting, apostle-like, at the long table and running their fingers along the rims of their glasses to make them sing. There was the sweetness of a final meal at the same table, to which Tilda Swinton brings a basketful of Italian *biscotti*. The wrapping papers from the biscuits are lit and, as they spiral upwards, turn from flame to invisible ash.

Because some of the filming had been done on super-8, there had been no daily rushes. Only on returning alone to Dungeness for Christmas could Jarman start viewing the material that had been transferred on to video in preparation for post-production in January. He was far from convinced the second shoot had given him the wherewithal to weave the film of which he dreamed. 'So many fleeting moments lost to the camera,' he wrote, 'which seems destined to point in the wrong direction.'[56]

His state of mind was not improved by passing the third anniversary of his diagnosis in what was still an extremely parlous state of health. His nights were an endless 'treadmill of unease, hour after hour of tossing and turning'.[57] He frequently woke 'shivering and damp with sweat, my eyes glued together'.[58]

The fact that Working Title had, with the BBC, suddenly come up with the money for him to write a script of *Edward II* gave him something wonderfully complex and concrete to focus on, yet even that, come New Year's Eve, was not enough to give him the confidence to articulate any wishes for the year ahead.

29

Blue Prints

Although *Modern Nature* contains references to how unwell Jarman was starting to feel in the final months of 1989, it never conveys the full extent of his developing illness, or the despair it engendered. To appreciate how critical the situation was becoming, one has to read between the lines. That *The Garden* was troubling him as much as it was speaks volumes; usually he sailed through his films with consummate ease. Then there were ill omens like the snake, or lonely visits to the heath; the painful matter-of-factness with which he recorded the death, almost always AIDS-related, of friend after friend after friend.

By the beginning of 1990, illness had come to the fore. On 1 January, he was in Dungeness viewing the rushes for *The Garden*: 'so appallingly inept no wonder I am ill'. The next day was little better: 'A very slow start – hardly slept. Brewed myself porridge, so painful to swallow I had to talk to myself as a diversion. I have never had such an unpleasant cold . . . It has made this Christmas, never a good time for me, the most depressed I can remember.'[1]

A further affliction was itchiness. This had started much earlier, while he was scripting *War Requiem*, when sometimes his scalp had become so uncomfortable that he could not concentrate without continual scratching from Collins. Now the itchiness was more widespread and frequently so acute he could hardly bear to be inside his skin.

Itchiness, aching limbs and hacking cough notwithstanding, there was much work to be done. Together with Peter Cartwright and Collins, he was viewing the rushes of The Garden preparatory to a rough edit that would impose some shape and narrative on their disparate raw material. There were meetings with Mackay and the distributors about publicity and with Simon Turner to map the soundtrack. The poems that would form the voice-over were written and their recording by Michael Gough arranged.

The BBC had asked him to present a ten-minute tour of a favourite building for their series Building Sights. He chose Garden House, the home his old art teacher Robin Noscoe had built for himself in the fifties. To clarify certain details of family history for Modern Nature, he was corresponding with his Aunt Moyra. He was approached by Annie Lennox to direct a video for 'Every Time We Say Goodbye', which she had been asked to perform for Red Hot and Blue, a charity concert of Cole Porter songs.[2] In addition to his own painting, he was making 'a series of gouaches', ultimately unused, for the cover of Jon Savage's history of punk rock, England's Dreaming. He was giving considerable and constant thought to Edward II. He was being interviewed for the release of War Requiem and monitoring its reception in New York, where it was savaged by his old foe Vincent Canby.[3]

In February, he was dealing yet again with the tabloid press, which had been alerted to the potentially blasphemous nature of The Garden. He appeared on The Late Show to pay tribute to the recently deceased Michael Powell. He was asked to comment on the AIDS-related death of actor Ian Charleson. While others praised Charleson for his 'strength and honesty', his 'courage in coming clean in death', Jarman could remember only that Charleson had unwittingly been running 'for the opposition'; that he had accepted the removal of Jubilee from his cv to 'protect his reputation' and concealed his HIV status until the very end. A number of Jarman's friends found his attitude too harsh and begged him to 'let sleeping dogs lie'.[4] He resolutely refused. For him, the issues were too important and wide-ranging.

February ended with a visit to Warsaw, where he had been invited by a group of young Polish film-makers to lecture and show his films. It was a punishing week: over and above the daily screenings and lectures, he agreed to take part in an impromptu film recording his impressions of the country.

On his return he found himself entering a 'twilight' zone of mounting fever, monumental night sweats, nausea, continual aches, lethargy and disorientation. Forced to subsist almost entirely on peppermint tea, he was literally wasting away. 'The razor bumps over the bones of my face. Even the bones themselves have shrunk. My hands seem half their normal size. My raw stomach aches and aches.'

He was in and out of St Mary's for check-ups, worrying whether the illness was 'HIV-related or just a bloody infection'.[5] At the same time, in a desperate attempt to minimise what was happening, he was laying everything at the door of either exhaustion or psychology. When not blaming 'the hectic days' in Warsaw, where he had been acutely affected by the ubiquitous poverty and the scant support or recognition afforded to gay people and their organisation, he was citing a recent letter from his Aunt Moyra, which had, he claimed, reawakened buried memories of childhood clashes with his father over food. These, he said, tearfully, were why his stomach was playing up. 'I know I'm not *ill*,' he wrote, 'but I'm very depressed.'[6]

On 19 March, after a particularly sleepless and feverish night, he took a taxi to St Mary's. 'Each bump and jolt on the road and the traffic lights an eternity. The doctor takes me into his small consulting room – prods, taps, and shines bright lights into my eyes. I feel weak and helpless. He says he is putting me into hospital; immense feeling of relief.'[7] His doctors suspected he might have TB of the liver, but could not start proper treatment until they knew for certain. To delirium, pain and diarrhoea was added the discomfort of a battery of invasive tests. Still unable to eat, Jarman saw his weight plummet even further. It seemed he might not survive. The Polish trip fresh in his mind, he named his bug General Jaruzelski and fought it on two flanks: with citizen antibiotic and a regimen of debilitating and stupendous sweats which left the countless pairs of colourful pyjamas Collins had bought him sopping wet. The nightmarish days were brightened only by the constant attendance of Collins and Raimond, by visits from Gaye and his countless friends, or by the evening when, alone, he heard a cleaning lady singing a negro spiritual.

> I opened the curtains a fraction to hear better. When she passed by I called out to her and she came in; I said 'Your song is wonderful' and she smiled. She said the spiritual was called *Spirit of the Living God*; she placed her hands on me and very quietly, with a voice of great beauty, sang to me. It was the most moving moment, I couldn't hold back the tears. She smiled, blessed me and carried on with her round.[8]

On 2 April, he was moved to a ward designed specifically for the treatment of patients with AIDS and finally given a scan, which confirmed that he did have TB of the liver. Treatment could at last begin in earnest: a bewildering array of pills, some needing to be taken for a matter of months; others for the rest of his life. He responded more or less immediately and, although still painfully thin and weak, began to emerge from the dark, disorientating nightmare of the preceding three weeks. By Easter, he was well enough to be discharged.

It had been a close call, but he had survived – and with the horrors had come a great outpouring of love from friends and colleagues, doctors and nurses. The previous year he had committed himself to the care of Collins when Collins had suffered his stroke; now it was Collins' turn to make an equal commitment to him, a contract of care on which the younger man would never renege. In the pages of his diary, Jarman summed this up in just two words: 'HB, love'.[9]

His brush with death had galvanised him into sudden activity. 'Everything is going to change – clear the flat, send papers to the National Film Archive. Give paintings to AIDS charities, rearrange Prospect's filled bookshelves. Clear Phoenix House entirely – get rid of everything, no more clutter, start painting, get *Edward II* underway. Plant the garden.'[10] He was as good as his word. No sooner had he left St Mary's than he was emptying Phoenix House, sending

certain of his papers to the BFI, rushing to check on the garden at
Dungeness and see how extensive the damage was from that winter's
harsh storms. He lodged his paintings with Richard Salmon, made
secret alterations to the will he had drawn up earlier in the year.
Only with *The Garden* was he perhaps less than diligent, possibly
because the film had already somewhat slipped from his grasp. As
they persevered with the edit, Cartwright and Collins had always
tried to bring what they could to the ward to show their director,
only to find him too ill to react with any clarity. Earlier in the year,
when the film's funding bodies had been shown a first cut, their
reaction had been positive, but Jarman had seen that two of the
sequences needed refilming. In the end it was Christopher Hobbs
who directed the extra day's filming, and Simon Turner was laying
down the sound and music without much directorial supervision. It
was just as well Jarman believed as fiercely as he did in the 'sublime
anonymity' of the Middle Ages. On *The Garden*, this communal
approach to the making of a film was reaching its apogee.

As illness forced Jarman to become more of an orchestrator of the
efforts of others, sometimes simply a benign presence in the background, the fact that he had always encouraged an entourage ensured
a constant army of young workers to carry out his wishes – providing,
of course, that its members did not fall foul of Collins. One such
helper was Stephen McBride, an extra in *War Requiem* and a voice in
The Garden, whom Jarman now asked to help with *Edward II*.[11]
Since this would inevitably involve acting as nursemaid as well as
scribe, that May McBride took a house of his own in Dungeness,
where Jarman was spending as much time as possible.

Jarman's diary reveals the extent to which he was in need of someone to assist him through the day:

Tuesday 8
I'm knitting together, except for the terrible itching brought
about by the steroids . . . Derek B. has brought both myrrh
and, last night, frankincense to put in almond oil; but apart
from smelling like an old church I'm afraid it hasn't done the
trick. When he came with the frankincense yesterday, he
said, 'Gold next.'[12]

Friday 11
I feel better today, I've been poorly all week. My liver aches, all my nerve endings are inflamed by the pills, which heat me like a furnace and turn my pee barley sugar orange. My hair . . . has turned silky and grows at silly angles. I itch and itch, under my chin and down the sides of my legs . . . A hot bath burns, an orgasm overwhelms with pain.[13]

Thursday 24
I've not enough flesh to keep the chill from catching me by the neck, and the cold, like the sun, burns my irritated skin . . . I sit down like a constipated dowager. My balls hurt when they hit the sofa, so I perch on the edge of the chair.[14]

Three days later, only five weeks after his first discharge from St Mary's, he was back on Almroth Wright Ward with pneumocystis carinii, or PCP, a form of pneumonia usually deemed an early manifestation of AIDS. Barely able to breathe, he was put on oxygen: 'The shadowy black bats of breathlessness swarm through the evening, roost in my lungs. The oxygen whistles up my nose like water gurgling at the dentist's. There is nothing quite as frightening as losing your breath in a fit of coughing . . . TB below, pneumonia above, the line of pills has grown again. Chemical wedding.'[15]

The moment had come when Jarman knew he could no longer hope to conjure himself out of his predicament. The pneumonia was indisputably AIDS-related, not the result of visits to Poland or childhood clashes with his father. It could easily prove fatal. He contemplated his funeral: 'I wonder if I'll end up with tacky white marble – or a slab of black Purbeck, like the old tombs in Romney church, with fine freehand lettering.'[16]

Later he wrote: 'I make plans for my convalescence. I don't want to die yet.'[17] Accepting the fact that he had crossed a critical threshold in no way lessened his resolve to resist defeat with all the resources at his disposal. Although forced to lie flat on his back for two weeks, he continued working on the script for Edward II with Collins. 'HB sits here each afternoon typing, bouncing about, tickling my feet, flashing his green eyes, flexing his new muscles so his lizard tattoo crawls about. He kept me laughing for three hours. Without him I wouldn't have got this far, he's so naughty.'[18]

As *The Garden* finished its long journey through post-production Jarman was discharged from hospital. In Dungeness he primed some new canvases and managed some surreptitious watering in contravention of a hosepipe ban. With the help of Stephen McBride, with whom he continued working on *Edward II*, he collected white pebbles from the beach for the central bed at the front of the cottage. He was thrilled and flattered when, among the flow of people who had begun stopping to investigate the garden as they drove through Dungeness, there were two gardeners of distinction, Beth Chatto and Christopher Lloyd.

At the end of the month he was in London for the annual Gay Pride march. He delivered the first draft script for *Edward II* and attended a preview of *The Garden*. 'I think people liked it,' he wrote cautiously in his diary.[19] What he did not record was how, on introducing the film, he had blamed his obvious weakness on the cocktail of drugs he was being forced to take. 'Anything good?' came a crass cry from the back.

One of the side-effects of his treatment for TB had been that his eyes hurt terribly and were unbelievably sensitive to bright light. After an appalling migraine one Saturday night in mid-July, he discovered he could not read the Sunday newspapers. An emergency scan revealed toxoplasmosis, toxo for short – lesions or abscesses on the brain which cripple the part of the body controlled by the affected section of brain. In Jarman's case, it was his eyes – both eyes, too, and not, as is more usual, only one. He found himself back in hospital, unable to read or even watch television.

No books to read, no newspapers. So, what did I think about during the long hours?
I watched the clock.
On the first day its face was a fuzzy halo, the digits telescoped and disappeared.
On the second day I could see the red second hand move in a jumble of black.
On the third day I paused, looked and looked again and read the time.

Bankside: the most beautiful room in London. *Ray Dean*

Jarman and Patrik Steede in 1972 before travelling together to Italy, where Steede would hit upon the idea of writing a film about St Sebastian.
John Dewe-Mathews

Mrs Hippy interviews Andrew Logan at his studio in Downham Road for the April 1973 issue of Andy Warhol's *Interview*.
John Dewe-Mathews

Jarman moves with Gerald Incandela into
Butler's Wharf, May 1973.
John Dewe-Mathews

Cat Two: Jean-Marc Prouveur.
Estate of Derek Jarman

Filming 'undisturbed by the sun' on the
undeveloped plot adjoining Butler's Wharf.
The film is *Death Dance*. Shown are Kevin
Whitney (with paper mask) and Robin Wall.
John Dewe-Mathews

Home movies in super-8. A nude Jarman
holding a glinting rod and the glass bells given
to him by Anthony Harwood, as he appears in
In the Shadow of the Sun.
Estate of Derek Jarman

Sebastiane: the 'cruel cocktail party' where the 'glitterati' meet 'Oriental Rome'. Among those featured are Robert Medley as Diocletian and Eric Roberts as the executioner. September 1975.
Kobal Collection

Part of the 'gang' from *Jubilee*, 1977. Left to right: Jenny Runacre, Little Nell, Jordan and Toyah Willcox.　*Estate of Derek Jarman*

While the sailors rest from their hornpipe, the director of *The Tempest* consults his director of photography, Peter Middleton. February 1979.   *Bridget Holm*

Above: Jarman in his role as designer confers with Ken Russell over *The Rake's Progress,* Florence, May 1982.
Foto Marchiori, Florence
Left: Ken Butler sits for Robert Medley.
Estate of Derek Jarman

The Rake's Progress. Nick Shadow as a drug dealer with his 'heroin death kit' on the platform of Angel tube station.   *Foto Marchiori, Florence*

Elisabeth Welch entertains Jarman and friends at Quartet's party at the Diorama in London to celebrate the publication of *Dancing Ledge* in 1984.   *Estate of Derek Jarman*

Jarman on the set of *Caravaggio*, with Tilda Swinton in the background as Lena, September 1985.
Mike Laye

'Home movie-making really gone sort of slightly grand.' Jarman filming the refugees from *The Last of England*, November 1986. Among those featured are Alasdair McGaw, on the left of the picture, and Michael O'Pray, centre. *Mike Laye*

James Mackay, producing and supervising continuity on *The Garden*, Dungeness, late 1989.   *Estate of Derek Jarman*

Hospital as office.   *Howard Sooley*

Watched by Christopher Hobbs, Jarman dons the crown of England. *Edward II*, Bray Film Studios, March 1991.   *Liam Longman*

The Sisters of Perpetual Indulgence honour the 'first Kentish saint since Queer Thomas of Canterbury', Dungeness, September 1991.
Howard Sooley

Pansy: 'a true story'. Jarman with Jimmy Somerville and Isaac Julien at a demonstration to mark the twenty-fifth anniversary of the 1967 Sexual Offences Act, 25 July 1992.
Bill Short

Above: HB and Fur Beast in Venice for the showing of *Blue* at the Biennale, June 1993. Jarman is wearing the linen suit made for him by Nick Knightly.   *Howard Sooley*
Right: 'So we are left with documentaries and diaries like mine and even they cannot tell you . . .'   *Howard Sooley*

On the fourth day I could read the numbers round the
dial – people appeared out of the gloom, some younger, others
older; their outlines filled in like pieces of a fancy jigsaw.[20]

'How many aftershocks,' he wondered, 'must I endure till my
body, broken, desiccated and drained of colour, fails to respond? I live
in a permanent hangover, after years of good health.'[21] He worried
what would become of Collins if his companion had to become his
'guide dog'. As worrying was the thought of what he would do without Collins, for only when Collins was there could Jarman 'cope
with blindness'.[22]

Eventually he was discharged, in time to travel to Edinburgh for
the world première of *The Garden*.

'I want to share this emptiness with you.' So begins the soundtrack. 'I went in search of myself,' continues the voice of Michael
Gough. 'There were many paths and many directions.' His tones are
sonorous. 'That was a brilliant rehearsal.' Now the voice is Jarman's,
recorded during the actual shoot. *The Garden* is a strange, disjointed
film, not easy to make sense of. Even though Jarman, as the person
dreaming the film, was largely absent during the editing, the result is
nevertheless highly personal, almost impenetrably so. It is also very
revealing. At its core is a parable about the cruel and unnecessary
perversion of innocence. Tilda Swinton plucks a chicken, an act
redolent of a simple and warm domesticity. There is a pillow fight.
Feathers fly, but again the act is innocent. Then the gay lovers are
tarred and feathered. Now the feathers represent repression: innocence has been perverted. Throughout, footage of Dungeness – and
of the garden in particular – is intercut with other, more violent
and sinister images, all conspiring to put the garden under threat.
Meanwhile, Jarman's manifest anger is accompanied – and mud-
died – by the film's marked ambivalence to the ways of the world, a
striking disgust with the excesses of the flesh. The serpent in his
leather harness is an overtly sexual – and nightmarish – figure. You
wonder whether Jarman is asking himself if his own sexual appetite
was not perhaps to blame for his illness. If sexual spontaneity is not
as dangerous a force as repression. If the garden is not under threat,
albeit subconsciously, even from the gardener. The film flagellates its

maker alongside his supposed enemies. Then it suddenly turns its back on such troubling complexities. Purifying water flows across the screen. Ariel-like, fire transforms lifeless matter into air. Last but not least, the film is a love poem to Collins. As it traces, celebrates, even romanticises HB's love for another man, the very camera seems to fall in love with its subject. He supplies the film's final image.[23]

In general, the film was enthusiastically received. *The Financial Times* even went as far as to call it 'the revelation of the Festival', trumpeting that 'after the Doomsday hectoring of *The Last of England* and the dutiful pieties of *War Requiem*', here was 'a work in which passion and control miraculously come together'.[24] There were dissenting voices, but not many. To all concerned, it seemed as if the film's arduous and fractured journey towards completion had been worth every tortured step.

On the train home, Jarman found himself 'frozen with pain'.[25] Within days, he was back in St Mary's to face what he later called the year's 'final indignity'.[26] The focus of pain was his stomach. His doctors decided they had no alternative but to open him up to see what was causing it. They found a dangerously inflamed appendix, which they immediately removed.

Ever since his pneumonia, Jarman had been told that the moment might have come for him to try AZT, the drug then most favoured for impeding replication of the virus and, if not halting, then at least slowing down the progress of the disease. At the time there was considerable controversy and disquiet over the drug's efficacy. It was said that it had been rushed through its clinical trials and that Wellcome Burroughs, who had developed it, were chemical profiteers. AZT could also have severe and toxic side-effects. Jarman was in two minds. Was it wise to commit himself so wholeheartedly to the chemical route? Would the good effects outweigh the bad? It was an issue he debated at length with friends at home and in America, where experience of the drug was more comprehensive. It was the toxo that decided him; that, and the fact that, at this point in the drug's history, it was possible to be put on a lower dose than had been the case when it was first introduced, thereby reducing the risk of toxicity. Starting in September, he began taking a medium-to-low dosage, 'another pill to swallow twice daily'.[27] The only side-effects seemed to be a change in his colour – he soon acquired the ruddy, tanned appearance associated with some patients on AZT – and a 'sustained manic high',[28] which, given all that he still intended to achieve, was not entirely unwelcome.

Although by no means frail, Jarman was no longer anywhere near as strong as he had been. He had become somewhat forgetful and his sight was slightly blurred, making it difficult for him to read small print. He was becoming prematurely old. And yet, thanks in large measure to AZT, or so we must assume, after 1990's series of seismic attacks on his health he was granted a respite of almost two years, in the course of which, though enfeebled, he was able to pick up the threads of his life. He did this with such determination that when you were with him, you could easily forget how poorly he actually was. Looking now at photographs from 1991 and 1992, one is struck by how ill he sometimes looks. Yet at the time, and in the flesh, his vitality seemed to banish ill health to the wings.

Despite – or, more likely, because of – the depredations of illness, he was seldom out of the limelight. Since he had publicly admitted to being HIV positive and set himself up as a spokesperson for gay politics, the fact that he was now terminally ill made him a positive magnet for the media. A prime example of the Orton effect: death as good box office. In the course of reviews of his work, or when interviewing him about a new project, virtually everyone wanted to discuss what it was like to be 'living with AIDS'. Jarman's reaction to this intrusive, almost salacious attention was double-edged. In part, he hated it – 'I've become the object of necrophilia,' he would wail, adding sombrely that there was no such thing as 'living' with AIDS; you only died with it – but he also welcomed the opportunity of being heard and having such a sure platform for his views. There was a great deal in society's reaction to sexuality, and to AIDS, which he passionately believed needed addressing and altering.

When in Edinburgh for the film festival, he took part in a one-day seminar entitled 'Aids and the Media'. With the help of Collins, who directed the film, he made his short homage to Robin Noscoe's Garden House. He was interviewed by TVS for their series *The Human Factor*. At greater length, and in greater depth, the BBC devoted an entire *Arena* programme to his life and work. For Radio

4, he agreed to sit in the psychiatrist's chair and be probed by Dr Anthony Clare,[29] his disarming openness winning him the admiration of many listeners. At the BFI, Colin MacCabe commissioned Michael O'Pray to write a study of the films and himself visited Dungeness to interview Jarman. At the fourth Leeds International Film Festival in October there was the presentation of the 'Le Prince' award for innovation. In a ceremony at the NFT, alongside Krzysztof Kieslowski, Jeanne Moreau and Fred Zinneman, he was made a fellow of the BFI. In Japan he was honoured with a comprehensive painting exhibition and film retrospective, to which he would have flown had he not just come out of hospital.

As his strength gradually returned, so he resumed work; perhaps a trifle more slowly than was customary, but no less determinedly. Given how difficult it had been to make *The Garden*, and how ill he had been in the interim, he knew he would never have the energy to make another unscripted and improvised film. What he needed was the tightest of narratives and the safety of a script: *Edward II*, in fact, which had the added advantage of the involvement of Working Title, a company whose size and efficiency would keep any production problems at bay.

As 1990 drew to a close, the script for *Edward II* was doing the rounds of various funding bodies; filming would start, or so it was hoped, in early 1991. Jarman contacted his old friend Dom Sylvester Houédard for advice on his final revisions, and started to discuss the design with Christopher Hobbs. Following the pattern set by *Caravaggio* and their unrealised *Akenaten*, Jarman had determined that what they came up with should be 'as pure and simple as the Noh or a temple garden'.[30] He was playing the casting game. He knew he wanted Collins as the jailer, Lightborn; for the rest, it was out with the fishing rod. Perhaps Daniel Day-Lewis for the King? Matt Dillon for Gaveston? The possibilities were as endless as they were tantalising.

Painting, still perhaps his surest way of addressing his condition, remained a constant solace. His assemblages now incorporated stark evidence of his illness. Into the pitch were pressed pills, pill bottles and boxes, syringes, thermometers: the chimera of a chemical existence. Equally important was his diary which, in early 1990, had been accepted for publication by Mark Booth of Century.

Between September, when he made a final entry, and the end of the year, Jarman shaped the raw material into the book it would become. Instrumental in this process were Collins, who had taken down some entries when Jarman had been too weak to pick up a pen, and who typed them all up, and Shaun Allen, who had so ably assisted the author with *Dancing Ledge* and *The Last of England*. Because the diary format imposed an automatic chronology, unlike with *Dancing Ledge* no major reordering was necessary. It was more a matter of ensuring that everything made sense and arguing about whether or not to delete or tone down the passages describing Jarman's nocturnal visits to Hampstead Heath. The title, which chimed perfectly with the way society viewed homosexuality as a deviance, something unnatural, was supplied by an old friend.

'I was describing the garden to Maggi Hambling at a gallery opening. And said I intended to write a book about it.

'She said: "Oh, you've finally discovered nature, Derek."

'"I don't think it's really quite like that," I said, thinking of Constable and Samuel Palmer's Kent.

'"Ah, I understand completely. You've discovered modern nature."'[31]

During 1990, a new force had entered gay politics. In the past, gay issues had tended to be the preserve of the left, which was inclined to view gay activists as recruits to the general revolutionary cause, thereby marginalising them. The new group, called OutRage!, aimed to create a specifically 'queer' activism answerable only to its own concerns. As the name suggests, this was an activism which, in its fight against homophobia, would tackle oppression in a radical way, using civil disobedience where necessary. There was to be no violence, but no politeness, either – certainly no assimilation into mainstream society. For someone like Jarman who, ever since his fitful involvement with the GLF in the early seventies, had always been mistrustful of the 'dour left', and whose year of illness had hardened rather than softened his political stance, OutRage! signalled a welcome development. Not only was he familiar with its founder members – Simon Watney, Keith Alcorn and Chris Woods – but, as already noted, he particularly liked the idea of being queer rather than gay. This recycling of an old insult properly encompassed, or so he thought, the complexity of his sexual and political life. Unlike 'gay', 'queer' announced that homosexuality was difficult, different and far from anodyne; sometimes gay, but at other times sad and furious. Jarman unhesitatingly became one of OutRage!'s most ardent and active supporters.

Within a year of its formation, the group – and Jarman as an individual – were given a very specific target for their anger. Any joy experienced over Margaret Thatcher's recent resignation in the wake of countrywide demonstrations against the poll tax did not detract from the chill brought by the new Criminal Justice Bill, Clause 25 of which classified certain 'gay activities' as serious sex crimes, thus empowering judges to pass longer deterrent sentences when considering them. The five gay 'offences' listed were: indecency between men in public, solicitation by a man in public, procuring others to commit homosexual acts, living on the earnings of a male prostitute and indecent assault on a man. Although defenders of the bill argued that it was not intended to penalise consenting, victimless homosexual behaviour, to others the first three 'offences' suggested that the bill might criminalise something as innocent as kissing in public, or introducing two men at a party, and were scandalised that such harmless behaviour could be put on a par with indecent assault.

Meanwhile, Jarman was about to provoke considerable controversy on a separate, if allied issue: the announcement in the New Year's honours list for 1991 that the actor Ian McKellen was to receive a knighthood. It horrified Jarman that the openly gay McKellen should have accepted an honour from a government whose attitude to gay causes was so unsupportive. Not only that, but on the same list, being awarded an identical honour, was James Anderton, the homophobic police chief from Manchester. Jarman vented his outrage in an open letter to the *Guardian*, the excitable and angry first draft of which Simon Watney and Nicholas de Jongh helped him to tone down. The letter was published on 4 January 1991, the day *The Garden* began its short but reasonably successful run at the Camden Plaza.

While having 'no quarrel with the designation' and without wishing to belittle McKellen's achievements as an actor or champion of gay causes, Jarman wrote: 'As a queer artist I find it impossible to react with anything but dismay to his acceptance of this honour from a government which has stigmatised homosexuality through Section 28 of the Local Government Act, signalling that gay relationships are to be regarded as just pretence, and which is poised by means of Clause 25 of the Criminal Justice Bill to take important steps towards recriminalising homosexuality.' He took issue, too, with the recently formed Stonewall group, of which McKellen was a leading member: 'This has set itself up as a gay lobby and campaigning group, without any consultation from the gay community and which refuses to hold open meetings. Unlike the riot which could be open to anyone, it's a very closed shop.' He ended with a question for the putative knight: 'Why did you accept this award, Ian? It has diminished you.'

Choosing to maintain a dignified silence, McKellen made no answer. There was, however, no shortage of people prepared to reply on his behalf. A flurry of correspondence and articles ensued. Some commentators took Jarman's side; many more did not. The most comprehensive rebuttal came on 9 January when a group of eighteen luminaries stated that 'as Gay and Lesbian artists' they regarded the knighthood as 'a significant landmark in the history of the British Gay Movement. Never again will public figures be able to claim that they have to keep secret their homosexuality in fear of it damaging their careers.'[32] The eighteen who wished thus to 'respectfully distance ourselves' from Derek Jarman's letter, were Simon Callow, Michael Cashman, Nancy Diuguid, Simon Fanshawe, Stephen Fry, Philip Hedley, David Lan, Bryony Lavery, Michael Leonard, Tim Luscombe, Alec McCowen, Cameron Mackintosh, Pam St Clement, John Schlesinger, Antony Sher, Martin Sherman, Ned Sherrin and Nicholas Wright.

Jarman replied that 'the McKellen 18 seem, sad to say, to see no further than the end of the artistic arena'. What, he wondered, of 'gay footballers or cricketers, lesbian tennis players and athletes, gay miners or lesbian diplomats, gay building labourers or lesbian doctors?' Did the supporters of the McKellen knighthood 'seriously say to these people, "Come out! Sir Ian has shown that you're safe. It won't damage your career." Of course not.'[33] If there was any suspicion that an element of pique or smallmindedness lay at the root of

Jarman's reaction – a bitter cry of 'What about Sir Derek?' – his clear-sighted and passionate concentration on what he believed to be the very real and harmful issues at stake allayed it. Whatever his private emotions, there can be no doubting the fierceness and clarity with which he was prepared to pursue the fight for public justice.

Two days later, Jarman and Collins boarded a plane for New York, where *The Garden* was being shown at the Film Forum as part of *The Cutting Edge*, a season of six films being premièred there before going on a nationwide tour. The papers carried news of war. In the Gulf, because Saddam Hussein refused to withdraw from neighbouring Kuwait, the United Nations were orchestrating an attack on Iraq. Safe in the hushed luxury of Mark McCormick's apartment on East 62nd Street, Jarman paid as scant attention to these military strikes as he did to the relatively low-key opening of his film; what concerned him was the fight on his own doorstep. On 13 January, the day after he arrived in New York, the *Observer* carried a robust defence of McKellen by the Labour MP Chris Smith, the country's only avowedly gay MP. Over the next few days the faxes flew fast and furious as Jarman, helped from home by Nicholas de Jongh and Alan Beck of the Sisters of Perpetual Indulgence, drafted a reply for publication, or so he hoped, later in the month.[34]

On his return from New York, he and the singer Jimmy Somerville joined a march organised by OutRage! to protest against Clause 25, which ended up at Bow Street Police Station, notorious as the station where Oscar Wilde had been taken on his arrest. The country had recently been hit by severe snowstorms and it was a bitterly cold evening. Even so, over 200 people joined the march. When they reached Bow Street the sight of curious audience members entering the opera house across the road for a performance of *Tosca* gave rise to a rare chant: 'We're here, we're queer, and we're not going to the opera.'[35] A dozen of the protestors came forward to give themselves up as 'criminals'. Jarman turned himself in for procuring two young men to kiss on the pavement.[36]

Throughout much of December and January, Jarman had been casting, selecting a crew and making adjustments to the script for *Edward II*. Since accepting it, Working Title had taken only six months to confirm final funding for the film. A budget of some

£750,000 was raised from the BBC, British Screen and Takashi Asai in Japan. It was Jarman's largest budget to date, but that did not mean he could be profligate: costs had likewise escalated, a further reason to make the film in a studio, within the simplest of sets. During his recent stay in New York, he had visited the Cloisters with his friend Lynn Hanke. Walking through the serene environs of this uptown oasis of monastery and chapel, he had cited the transported European building as a perfect example of what he wanted for *Edward II*. It was exactly what Hobbs would supply: a series of timeless rooms and corridors that never detract from the force of the story. Or from Sandy Powell's costumes, which in true Jarman fashion bridged the ages, mingling the vaguely mediaeval with the utterly modern day: camouflage gear for military Mortimer, courturier crispness for icy Queen Isabella.

By February, Jarman was so deeply into pre-production at Working Title's Camden headquarters he had neither the time nor the energy for the Berlin Film Festival, where *The Garden* was showing in the Forum Section – and where, lending credence to his contention that it was at heart a thoroughly Christian film (he used to liken it to Pasolini's *The Gospel According to St Matthew*), it received a special mention from the jury of the OCIC (International Catholic Organisation for Cinema and Audiovisual Media).

Because of his uncertain health, the producers of *Edward II* required Jarman to work alongside someone who could step into his shoes should he fall ill. He chose Ken Butler. Together, Jarman and his 'ghost' put the script (now pasted into one of two workbooks Jarman was assembling for the film) through its final changes.

Comprising some 2,600 lines of blank verse, Marlowe's play falls into five acts and twenty-three scenes. It records Edward's infatuation with his favourite, Gaveston, whom Edward rescues from exile on his father's death. The presence at court of the loud and obnoxious Gaveston riles the archbishops and barons, in particular the uncle-and-nephew team of Mortimers senior and junior. Edward's scorned wife Isabella, despairing of ever enjoying her husband's affections, joins forces with the Mortimers in plotting Gaveston's removal. Gaveston is forced to flee, then killed. Isabella and the younger Mortimer become lovers. The King is made to resign his crown and thrown into prison, where he is handed to a hired killer, Lightborn. 'See that in the next room I have a fire,' instructs Lightborn. 'And get me a spit and let it be red-hot.'[37] This is the only explicit reference Marlowe makes to the manner of Edward's death, popularly held to have been the insertion of a red-hot poker into his anus. The play ends with the young Edward III avenging his father's death by ordering the execution of Mortimer.

In the hands of Jarman and his collaborators, Marlowe's epic was stripped to essentials and divided into eighty-two short sequences; only the core of the verse was retained. There were some simplifications, plus a few minor flourishes. The two Mortimers were conflated into a single character. The action is viewed in flashback by an already imprisoned Edward, allowing the scenes between the King and Lightborn to be spread across the entire length of the film. When Kent, Edward's loyal brother, dies, it is at the hands of Isabella, who bites him in the neck. Most daringly of all, Jarman supplied a surprise happy ending. Edward's supposed death is treated as a nightmare, from which the King awakes to find his young son dancing on the cage containing a chastened Isabella and Mortimer.[38]

Although the opposite might easily have proved the case, working within the confines of an existing script – one he once confessed to disliking[39] – did not make the resulting film impersonal or divorce it from Jarman's most pressing concerns. Aside from cracking a rather feeble joke that the introduction of as much sex and violence as the script could contain would help him achieve his aim of an 'Elizabethan lay' rather than an 'Elizabethan play',[40] he saw *Edward II* as one more skirmish in the battle he had joined on the pavement outside Bow Street. As an avowedly queer director, he wanted to make an unequivocally queer film, one which celebrated rather than avoided Mortimer's famous speech about the sexual lineage of the mightiest kings and their minions. Interestingly, he also resisted the obvious temptation to make Gaveston sympathetic. After all, Gaveston 'had lived with Edward for ten years before the marriage to Isabella. The clowning could be a bid for attention.'[41] Instead, the object of Edward's undoubted and deep affection remained the hustler from history. 'Not all gay men are attractive,' wrote Jarman. 'I am not going to make this an easy ride. Marlowe didn't.'[42]

In accordance with his designs on Marlowe's play, Jarman peppered the blank verse with the word 'fuck'. There is much flaunting of male flesh: a pair of rent boys fucking in Gaveston's bed, a man dancing with a snake, a naked rugby scrum, a scene set in a gym. The posse of hostile nobles is preceded at one point by a pack of baying hounds; at another, they resemble Parliament. Mortimer's troops include riot police, while Edward's supporters are envisaged as rioters against the poll tax and culled from the placard-waving ranks of OutRage! and the Sisters of Perpetual Indulgence: the 'inheritors of Edward's story'.[43] And when Edward (Steven Waddington) bids adieu to Gaveston (Andrew Tiernan) prior to his final banishment, the two men dance to the anachronistic accompaniment of Annie Lennox singing 'Every Time We Say Goodbye'.

On another level, *Edward II* is a re-enactment-cum-reinvention of Jarman's familial past. Isabella (Tilda Swinton) and Mortimer (Nigel Terry) bear a strong resemblance to Betts and Lance, and Jarman's niece, Kate, last seen on screen in *The Tempest*, makes a brief appearance as a seamstress. The film centres on a nuclear family and its bloody struggle to tame a wayward member. It dwells in some detail on how the young prince (Jody Graber) observes the behaviour of his elders. This, the film suggests, is how children learn to be adults. At one stage, we see the prince playing with guns. Eventually he eschews such barbaric masculinity. When we see him dancing on his mother's and Mortimer's cage, we realise he will not be following in Mortimer's footsteps: he is wearing lipstick, heavy earrings and a pair of high-heeled silver shoes. The queer future, one feels, is safe in his hands. Young Edward posits an alternative. If he clicks those heels together, the home to which he will be transported will not be nuclear; rather, it will include everyone from Gaveston to the Sisters of Perpetual Indulgence. In the version of the script published to coincide with the release of the film, there is a picture of Jarman with the cast and crew. The caption opposite reads: 'nuclear family free ZONE'.[44]

Shooting started on Monday 18 February at Bray, near Windsor, in the old complex that had once been home to the Hammer House of Horror and was currently used both for film and as a recording studio. The building allotted to *Edward II* was as basic as the film's two sets, the steel-plated, semi-industrial prison and the series of blank walls and cubes designed by Hobbs in such a way that they could be moved and rearranged to suggest an unlimited number of different spaces. The shoot lasted just five weeks and went like clockwork, with the satisfactory result that although it did not prove possible to film everything as scripted, the production did not over-run and, on Saturday 23 March, exactly on schedule, the words 'It's a wrap' were called, champagne was poured into plastic cups, and a 'beaming' Jarman presented with 'a sturdily built, old-fashioned Raleigh Chiltern bicycle, complete with sensible wicker basket'. 'It's from Norman Tebbit,' shouted a wag.[45]

Champagne and timing notwithstanding, the six-day weeks proved arduous and, despite being energised by the act of filming, Jarman was not always well enough to attempt the early-morning trip to Bray; there were days when his 'ghost' had to deputise. There were also arguments with the production office over the fact that Jarman wanted the special stationery he had arranged for the film (the letterhead featured a faint background of militant queer slogans) to be used even for invoices and letters to the bank. And there were a couple of potentially lethal encounters with a band and a singing star from a neighbouring studio.

The band was Status Quo, the star Cliff Richard, and the encounters occurred on the day the Sisters of Perpetual Indulgence joined forces with thirty-odd members of OutRage! to play Edward's supporters. Having registered Richard's presence on site, the cocky activists took advantage of a break in filming to invade his studio and 'out' its occupant, whose sexuality had long been a matter of speculation in gay circles. The singer was not amused by this chanting, whistling invasion, nor that the sign outside his studio was changed from 'closed set' to 'closet set', nor by the Mirror's subsequent headline: 'CLIFF GAY JIBE FURY – STAR TAUNTED BY MOB'.[46] This threat to the status quo spread to the band of that name. The noise from their rehearsals had for some time been bothering everyone on the poorly soundproofed set of Edward II. In retaliation a 'nun' pissed in the doorway to their studio and OutRage! put 'Cool to be Queer' stickers on their cars. There was heated talk of 'Edward II Limited' being sued and a real, if momentary, risk of the film being closed down, averted only after a series of profuse apologies.

By contrast, post-production unfolded almost entirely without mishap, so that between the end of March and mid-August, when the film premièred at the Edinburgh Film Festival, Jarman was easily able to turn his attention to rushing out the accompanying book. Initial attempts to interest a publisher in a combination of the original play script and the film script, plus a commentary and a plethora of illustrations in the form of design sketches and stills, had failed. Meanwhile, Jarman had been speaking to a new collaborator, a young man called Malcolm Sutherland who was well versed in desktop publishing. Sutherland and Jarman decided to produce the book themselves, whereupon the BFI came to their rescue. Colin MacCabe put an office in Soho at their disposal and, on the understanding that the two authors would take responsibility for the design and compilation of the book, agreed to cover their basic costs, then print and distribute the finished article.

Queer Edward II made no attempt to include the text of Marlowe's play. Instead, the meat of the book was simply the film script: 'Edward II improved by Derek Jarman', as the running head had it. To the script was added a brief commentary on the process of filming by Jarman, Ken Butler and Tilda Swinton. Each page also featured a queer slogan: 'Gender is apartheid', 'Our orientation is not your decision', 'God was a confirmed bachelor', 'Out, proud and livid'.

The book carried an angry and defiant dedication, devoid of the leavening of humour that could soften the anger in the man himself, leading some to wonder whether Jarman was not being used by OutRage! and the like simply as a cipher to further the queer cause. There could after all be no doubting his effectiveness as a figurehead. But although he was critically ill and therefore perhaps particularly susceptible to persuasion, he knew what he was doing. For all his personal charm and sweetness, his political anger was real. Out, proud and livid: if the slogan applied to anyone, it applied to Jarman.

He was doing a great deal of writing, either on his own account or, as it were, under licence. He was readying *Modern Nature* for the printer, a process not without drama as the various parties continued hotly to debate whether or not to cut parts of it or make additions. He was starting a new journal, his most sustained ever; he would stop writing it only when literally no longer able to hold a pen.[47] He was agreeing that he should perhaps be the subject of a biography; giving his blessing to Glitterbug, [48] a proposal put together by Jon Savage in which it was first mooted that the early super-8 films might make a perfect documentary; actively encouraging his friend John Furse to write a film script centring on his complex relationship with his father.[49] He also gave Takashi Asai permission to produce a book of images from the films together with Asai's own photographs of Dungeness. Anxious that Jarman should live to see the end result, Asai lost no time in getting down to work. Enlisting the help of Malcolm Sutherland, he marshalled the film images he wanted, then commissioned Howard Sooley to photograph the chosen images off the video monitor.

Sooley had met Jarman during the filming of Edward II. Discovering a shared interest in plants, Jarman had added the lanky photographer to his fleet of drivers and Sooley was soon ferrying his new friend between London and Dungeness, making detours along the way to visit favourite nurseries. At Dungeness, he spent hours with Jarman in the garden itself, helping to expand and develop it.

Jarman acknowledged Sooley at some length in the last book he would ever write, the short but vivid account of his garden illustrated by Sooley's photographs and published only after his death.

Howard Sooley is like a giraffe, a giraffe that has stared a long time at a photo of Virginia Woolf; he possesses the calm and sweetness of that miraculous beast. When he takes a photo he stands like a T that has lost half an arm; he smiles, clicks, mutters little words of encouragement – more to himself or to the garden – 'Oooh,' he says, 'that's nice' . . . It is he who has informed the second phase of building our paradise, brought me to Elizabeth Strangman's Hellebore Heaven, to Sempervivum Sam, and to the most charming nursery in England – Madrona, up the road in Lydd . . . He is one of the most distinguished Englishmen that I have met and his portraits of me have changed the way I look. They are flattering but also revealing and have replaced the photos of 'Derek the black magician' that photographers caught like measles in the early 1980s.[50]

Sooley's photographic record of Jarman's final years is in fact incomparable: a visual equivalent of the journal Sooley's subject was himself so religiously keeping.

What these ventures indicate is the imminence of death; loose ends are being tied up, an archive made ready. And yet, paradoxically, whereas 1990 had been overshadowed by illness, 1991 was a year of constant activity. Although Jarman was considerably frailer, tiring easily and needing frequent rest, and although he suffered from memory lapses, headaches, a troublesome stomach, sore throats, sleeplessness, breathlessness and constant itching, he showed no intention of taking life easy. There was simply too much to be done.

He was discussing a second attempt at desktop publishing, this time of Shakespeare's sonnets illustrated by stills from *The Angelic Conversation*. He was toying with a number of films. Something, perhaps, on the mediaeval mystic Margery Kempe? Or a contemporary version of *The Picture of Dorian Gray*, in which a sculpture would replace the fabled painting and Collins would play the eternally youthful Dorian?[51] Then there was *Raft of the Medusa*, an American play by Joe Pintauro about a group of patients with AIDS. This, it was felt, would translate powerfully to the screen. And, of course, there was *International Blue*, currently called *Bliss*.[52]

The previous January, two days after the London première of *The Garden*, there had been a charity screening of the new film at the Lumière in St Martin's Lane, in aid of St Mary's Hospital. The event was prefaced by a live performance of an hour-long *Symphonie Monotone*, a complementary step towards *Blue*.

The screen was suffused in IKB, the Yves Klein blue, on which, at intervals, was projected a series of slides: images from Jarman's super-8s and of passages from an essay on blue.[53] Dressed entirely in the colour of the moment, Jarman and Tilda Swinton sat at a table to the side of the screen and recited the poetry and dialogues Jarman had been writing for the film. Because these related to the 'passion, psychology and nature of blue',[54] the word itself was endlessly repeated in a variety of different guises: blue rinse, blue mood, singing the blues. The two readers ran their fingers around the rims of wine-glasses to make the singing sound used in one of the sequences from *The Garden*. Jarman had hoped to place a naked and blue devil under the table and have him frequently interrupt proceedings by cursing both the readers and the audience. He had also hoped to distribute blue fruit and have a cannon fire blue confetti into the auditorium. In the event, he made do with Jody Graber (the young prince in *Edward II*), who handed pebbles painted blue and gold to various audience members, plus a couple of dancers. On the floor in front of the screen sat eight musicians who, under Simon Turner's leadership, improvised some purposefully monotonous music, thus providing a meditative ambience in which the minds of the listeners could drift into the blue in pursuit of Jarman's evanescent poetry.

It was the first of a number of such concerts mounted in advance of the film. On 3 February, the second was held at the Electric Cinema in Portobello Road. This time the concert was followed by a screening of *Jubilee* and the proceeds went to OutRage! Then, over the eighteen months that followed, there was a series of similar concerts in Bari, Ghent, Rome, Berlin and Tokyo.[55]

In the late eighties, when Mackay had embarked on his struggle to raise the money for *International Blue*, there had been moments when it seemed to Jarman as if the film he envisioned would never withstand the funding process. At one point, money might have been forthcoming from Sony in Japan, but only if the film adopted a more conventional biographical approach. This Jarman refused to countenance – and it had probably come as something of a relief to him to be diverted by *The Garden* and *Edward II*. Now, though, he was ready to return to the fray.

He had spoken to Working Title about the project and, under their aegis, had even experimented with producing a strip of purely blue film. Working Title had, however, been unable to raise any money. Jarman then asked Takashi Asai if he would take over the production. Asai was more than willing, but immediately found he could not feasibly control the process from Tokyo. Besides which, although at moments Mackay might have wished he could throw in the towel – and although he certainly hoped to steer Jarman away from the idea of a film without narrative – he had become too involved to pull out. And anyway, it now looked as if there might be light at the end of the tunnel. After *Edward II*, Channel 4 offered to fund development of a script.

Working principally with David Lewis, Jarman set to work mapping out a number of proposals for the new script. In these, Klein's art, his pursuit of the immaterial and the colour blue remained central, as did Jarman's poetry and Klein's own *Symphonie Monotone*. The film was still feature-length and would be shot on 35mm to form a notional trilogy with *The Last of England* and *The Garden*. The first film represented the underworld, the second the real world, *Bliss* paradise. For the rest, Jarman completely abandoned his original concept, that of a purely blue screen, and considerably modified its successor, the masque dedicated to Klein and acted out against a blue background.

In one outline, the film became 'a startling vision of heaven' and a 'history of passion through myth and reality'. A circus floats in a blue void. 'Giant blue velvet curtains' sweep aside to reveal 'a spinning carousel' whose gilt horses carry the viewer into history. The ringmaster conjures up 'a menagerie of fabulous beasts' – a Minotour, a Sphinx, a Gryphon – plus a sequence of visions that drift through the blue void. There are dancers, jugglers, tightrope walkers and acrobats. They perform a number of classic love affairs: Aphrodite and Mars, Antony and Cleopatra, Lancelot and Guinevere, Tristan and Isolde. The ringmaster then 'leads us through a gallery of the greatest works of art, customised to become testaments to our fading millennium while a celestial orchestra performs the finest music'. To this would be added a more personal past evoked by footage from Jarman's home movies.[56]

In another version, the central theme was London. 'The city will be revealed in documentary form as it is journeyed through by our hero, a voyager named Bliss, who will be played by three different actors: young, middle-aged and old. Observed only at dawn, the city is eternal and timeless, while the duration of the film encompasses Bliss's whole lifetime.' The voice-over would come not from Jarman's poetry, but from Bliss's diary, and would recall Bliss's life growing up in the city. Each sequence would 'illuminate the difference between subjective memory and documentary reality'. The only remnant of 'the original Klein idea' would be a 'sea of time, presented as a blue void' in which the images of London, plus further echoes of Jarman's work in super-8, would float.[57]

Slowly but surely, Jarman was inching the film away from Klein and the immaterial towards something more social and more personal. Intersecting with the idea of a voyage through history, and of tracing a London life from cradle to grave before floating into the blue, was Jarman's newfound passion, queer politics, which took the film in a new direction. In *Edward II*, he had touched on the way the young prince observed his elders and then reacted to them. He wanted to take this process one step further, moving it from the margins of the film to the centre of the screen. He was soon to turn fifty. For the first twenty-five years of his life, his sexuality had made him a criminal. For the second twenty-five, it had made him a second-class citizen. Now, some would have added, it was killing him. He himself would have disputed such a crude analysis, but, even so, the thought must at times have crossed his mind. Little wonder he should want to make sense of his life by writing his own queer history; that he should wish to assess a lifetime's worth of sexual struggle. How secure were the advances made in the sixties and seventies? Did the repressions of the eighties mirror those of the fifties? Could they be resisted? What about the future? The character of Bliss was dropped. In his place came Pansy. Plus a new co-writer, Malcolm Sutherland.

Subtitled 'a true story'[58] and written in very free verse, *Pansy* was conceived as a screen musical made in 'bright as a button vision'. The first half, dealing with London in the fifties and sixties, was written as 'a satirical pantomime'. The second half, revolving around the idea of '1984' and reflecting Britain in the eighties and early nineties, was structured as a night of TV entertainment. It was envisaged that both halves would be intercut with news footage, flashes of soap opera and commercials. In its totality, the film would 'recall and examine British attitudes to homosexuality over the past forty years'.

The purpose was deadly serious; the style less so. Jarman drew on such influences as the satirical cartoons of Gillray and Cruikshank, but used 'as if they had been working in the 60s for Walt Disney'; *The Rake's Progress*; *Spitting Image*; the Carry On films; *An American in Paris*; *One from the Heart*; *Oh! What a Lovely War*. In addition, he plundered his scripts for B Movie: *Little England/A Time of Hope* and, to a greater extent, *Sod 'Em*, also influenced by Gillray and

Cruikshank. To allow himself the necessary stylistic freedom, he and Sutherland wrote the film to be shot in a studio against painted panels and a blue screen.

The story is narrated by Dick Trace It, a female detective, and follows the fortunes of an orphan called Pansy as he is rescued from the clutches of his adoptive parents, Lord Kinky Kincorra and Lady Homophobia, by Stormin' Norma, his clippie fairy godmother, and a lover called Homobonus, or homo for short, a historical figure who was burned at the stake during the Middle Ages for being a faggot. Featuring such cartoon grotesques as Archbishop Deeply Caring, Justice Blind Justice, Betsy Battenburg, Sir Thespian Knight and our old friends Cesspit Charlie and Margaret Reaper, it culminates in outright war between a repressive status quo and the forces of Queer Nation and the eventual establishment of a new millennium of hope, the Rosenreich. The film's final two images are divided between revenge and love. First we see 'Margaret Reaper in the jaws of Hell'. A 'horrible mush of masticated blue blood runs down the screen'. Then Pansy and Homobonus are married in a storm of confetti.[59]

It is a strange script: angry yet ebullient, childish yet poignant, intensely personal. In charting what is essentially Jarman's own story, it even manages to suggest his earliest cinematic memory. In addition to the many influences on the script which he acknowledged, there is an added whiff of *The Wizard of Oz*: like Dorothy, Pansy is in search of home, has the help of a fairy godmother, the unshakeable belief that there *is* somewhere over the rainbow.

By early October, Jarman and Sutherland had completed a reasonably polished first draft. Dubbing it 'a musical film covering anti-queer legislation from the 60s to the 80s', and explaining that Simon Turner would undertake the music and Dean Broderick the arrangements, and that Lionel Bart was being approached as a potential lyricist, Mackay sent the script to Channel 4. Blanket rejection lay ahead. Aggrieved that the piece's only relation to *Bliss* and the colour blue – which was what they had agreed to develop – was perhaps the blue blood of the penultimate image, Channel 4 replied sharply that they considered the script better suited to the stage than to celluloid. Bart was similarly unenthusiastic, even though, as someone who had written so widely about London, he seemed the ideal lyricist. He did not like the way the character of Sir Thespian Night made fun of Ian McKellen, nor that the script was so virulently anti-heterosexual.

By changing *Bliss* into *Pansy*, it seemed that Jarman had frightened off his only source of funding. In November, the indefatigable Mackay wrote again to Channel 4 with a 'new' idea: to merge *Sod 'Em*, *Bliss* and *Pansy* into a single project. The bait was ignored, though, as it happened, it would not be long before another department within the company would help realise the project – not as *Pansy*, but in the simple, ostensibly unfundable manner in which Jarman had first envisaged it: as a blue screen devoid of image.[60]

That Channel 4 should turn down a script so close to his heart and history did little to soften Jarman's perception of the film and television establishment as essentially homophobic – or, if not homophobic, then hugely indifferent to the gay experience. However, any frustration he felt over the fate of his latest script was offset by the rewards and demands of his position as an increasingly public figure. At the end of June, he was in Berlin to take part in the city's annual celebrations for Gay and Lesbian Pride. In July, he paid a second visit to Moscow, where *The Garden* was being shown in the city's film festival: 'the first official performance of a gay movie in the Soviet Union', as he would boast.[61]

Back at home, he embarked on one of the most exhaustive rounds of newspaper interviews he had ever given. Arranged by his publishers, its aim was to promote *Modern Nature*, publication of which was celebrated by a party at Richard Salmon's studio on 7 August. 'So much attention,' Jarman chuckled happily, 'I'm obviously fruit of the month.'[62]

The next morning, he opened the *Guardian* to find a solus and complimentary review of the book. 'The first,' he noted, '. . . that we've had for a book in a national newspaper'.[63] Other reviews were not all as positive – the *Sunday Telegraph* found the book 'unreadable' and took its author to task in a most hostile fashion – but what counted more with Jarman was the fact that, if not reviewed as widely as he might have been, he was still being given serious consideration in the pages of no fewer than six national newspapers.[64] It was a far cry from 1984 and the scant attention paid *Dancing Ledge* – which, incidentally, had continued to sell quietly but so steadily over the years that Quartet now reissued it in hardback, with a new photograph by Howard Sooley for the cover and a proselytising preface from Jarman: 'On 22 December, finding I was body positive, I set myself a target: I would disclose my secret and survive Margaret Thatcher. I did. Now I have my sights set on the millennium and a world where we are all equal before the law.'

Although *Modern Nature* was by no stretch of the imagination a bestseller, between the book, his films, the garden and his public pronouncements, Jarman's persona and message were starting to reach a much wider circle – not least because the extraordinary sweetness and charm with which he could coat the bitter pill of his anger meant that he always gave the sense of a man dealing with illness and repression in the most exemplary of manners: bravely, openly and with consummate grace.[65]

The letters he received were rarely negative. The person who wrote to say Jarman had given him AIDS and to demand a cash settlement was a real exception. Even the committed Christians wrote more in sorrow than in anger, assuring Jarman that whatever he might believe, God still loved him.[66] For the rest, Jarman's correspondents (as frequently female as they were male, as often straight as they were gay) stood testament to the incredible way his work and example had touched a multiplicity of lives. Many letters obviously came from young gay men, but they came also from gardeners who would send seeds and advice; from students writing theses on his films, or wanting to know how to enter film; from fellow HIV sufferers; even from the occasional lunatic, including a thirty-year-old 'male, monosexual earthman' who, by his own description, was 'as varied as Leonardo, but lacking a certain genius'. The film director Bryan Forbes wrote to say how much he and his wife Nanette Newman admired Jarman. Holly Johnson of Frankie Goes to Hollywood revealed that ever since getting an erection at the age of fourteen watching *Sebastiane* 'at an adult cinema in Liverpool', Jarman had been a source of inspiration to him. People who had never met Jarman, and were never likely to, whose relationship to the arts was often remote, would write to say they felt he was talking directly to them, and to thank him.

There was the man who had met Satyajit Ray and simply had to pass on the information that Ray had spoken about Jarman's work with 'great interest and admiration'. There was the married couple spurred by Jarman's films and his battle with HIV 'to think seriously about the issues and ultimately to support those organisations campaigning for the recognition of gay rights and the proper treatment by all society of victims of HIV and AIDS'. The 'longstanding anti-gay' who wrote that Jarman had provided him 'with sufficient insights' to make him feel 'truly contrite'. Or the thirty-five-year-old who had gone to Paris to come to terms with his 'sexuality and terrible feelings of fear and disorientation' and who took *Modern Nature* with him, read it and found the courage 'to move forward'.

If Jarman ever felt like quitting the limelight – and at times he did – these unbidden letters always gave him pause. Besides which, as he confided in an interview to the American film director Gus Van Sant, being briefed by friends like Nicholas de Jongh, Alan Beck, Simon Watney or Sarah Graham before appearing on television was pleasingly like playing 'the president', and being 'a political activist'[67] a new career; a most viable alternative to film.

On 12 June 1991, wearing a T-shirt that proclaimed him 'Queer as Fuck', he attended a mass wedding in Trafalgar Square where women swore fidelity to women, men to men. A bouquet was thrown, which Jarman caught. In late July,[68] he and Malcolm Sutherland wrote jointly to the *Guardian* to defend the practice of outing, then claiming headlines in the wake of threats from an offshoot of OutRage! to make public the sexuality of certain gay politicians and other leaders of society. On 13 September, he joined a number of other protestors on the pavement outside the *Guardian*'s offices to dissociate himself from an article the paper had run the week before. Entitled 'Gay Abandon' and written by Rupert Haselden, himself an AIDS sufferer, the piece had argued that in the face of AIDS, most gay men 'were living for today because we have no tomorrow' and were increasingly accepting 'what, terrifyingly, we are coming to see as our fate'.[69] The despairing fatalism of the article was, in Jarman's eyes, as in those of many others, not only inaccurate but extremely dangerous. He supported a call for gays to boycott the newspaper. Later in the month, he further lambasted its editor, Peter Preston, for failing to cover the occasion when Sir Ian McKellen, as a founder member of Stonewall, took tea with the prime minister, John Major. Jarman felt Preston should have pointed out that for those gays who were not members of Stonewall, this meeting represented their exclusion from a partisan and assimilationist group. However, as Preston responded, if gays were indeed boycotting his paper, to denounce the meeting would perhaps have been 'somewhat redundant'.[70]

Lying down without a fight was something the compulsive Jarman did only under duress, when too ill to get out of bed or leave the house. In 1991, such moments were rare. In his garden, he started to keep bees, a new source of wonder and experiment. He revelled in the ceaseless company of what Collins termed the 'Dungenettes': the young men, many of them newcomers to his circle, who flocked to Prospect Cottage to spend time with its owner. He partook of the usual Soho outings and meals, including a visit to see the Chippendales, where he and his party turned out to be the only men in the audience. He continued to make night-time visits to Hampstead Heath, frequently in the teeth of miserable weather and health.

The role played by Collins in his life was rapidly extending beyond that of green-eyed boy, all-important jester, typist and tickler of feet and scalp. The erstwhile wildcat was now a surrogate parent, worried that by spending so many nights roaming the heath his charge was jeopardising his health. One night in July, Jarman was forced to note in his diary: 'HB had sabotaged my armoury – KY disappeared, and my bottle of poppers filled with perfume.'[71] It did not stop him, of course, any more than the fact that what he found under the midnight trees was not always worth the trouble. 'A dull voyeuristic sort of night,' he wrote in early August, 'two short-haired lads with fine physiques put on a public display, snapped on condoms like surgeons with rubber gloves.'[72] But then his trips to the heath were no longer about sex, or very rarely, and most certainly not about being sensible. They were a way of seeking companionship and validating a queer existence; of celebrating his differences from straight society. Where other people chose to stay at home, or in the light, he went in purposeful search of the dark. He wanted an arena beyond the reach of respectability; to kick over the traces; to be his own person; to meet his own kind; to prove to himself that he was still alive.

Against the background of such driven behaviour, the other work he managed to squeeze into the year ceases to seem like work at all – reminding us that he had never drawn a distinction between work and play, particularly if the work involved a brush and canvas.

Whereas his paintings from the early eighties onwards had usually been black and frequently took three-dimensional form, he suddenly made a switch to abstract but conventional landscape, bursting into surprising technicolour in the process. The new works showed as much fascination with impasto as the old, though where before the thickly applied whorls of paint had at the most contained the occasional streak of red, now the colours positively duelled for space on the canvas. Linking them in his mind to 'the Van Gogh cornfields',[73] Jarman created these dazzling landscapes not with a brush, but with a screwdriver, and described them as 'ecstatic'. 'The swelling in my heart,' he wrote, 'throws itself into the reds and gold, floats in Caerulean, drowns in the cobalt and hides in the deep sage green of sadness.'[74] Although it was the simple suggestion of Richard Salmon that some colour in his work would not come amiss that had caused Jarman to tackle these canvases, they are also undoubtedly a celebration of his passage from darkness into light as he rode out the illness of the year before. Equally, they indicate failing eyesight; it was easier to paint in vivid colour than in black.

With the help of Peter Fillingham, whom he had first met when they exhibited together in 1989, and a friend of Fillingham's, Karl Lydon – two of the most supportive of the young men to have entered Jarman's life – he found time earlier in the year to create an installation for an exhibition at the Design Museum exploring the relationship between designers and consumers. The exhibition homed in on four areas of creativity – home-making, dress, eating and gardening – and the installation, a recreation of the garden at Dungeness placed before a huge photograph of Prospect Cottage and its windswept surroundings, was included in the latter section.

Jarman found it 'strange to be back at Butler's Wharf. The money has gilded the heart of it though the old iron gates that I unpadlocked each evening are there and the graffiti that says John Dale Stalag is still on the door of the furniture warehouse, everything else is scrubbed, all the fun vanished.'[75]

Reminders of an Arcadian past were hard to bear; as tormenting as they were sweet. They came in many guises. In tandem with Madeleine Morris, recently graduated from the Slade, he undertook the design of Les Blair's West End production of *Waiting for Godot*, London's largely unsuccessful attempt to echo the New York production of the play, in which Robin Williams and Steve Martin played the two clowns for comedy rather than pathos. At the Queen's Theatre, the same trick was entrusted to Adrian Edmondson and Rik Mayall. Jarman and Morris chose to accentuate the artificiality of the piece, and of theatre itself, by placing a patently artificial tree stump atop a rocky knoll. Their backdrop was a paint-smeared wall, possibly a skyscape, and they enclosed the entire set within a box featuring cut-out doors on each side. As a concept, it was admirably and 'suitably bleak',[76] even ugly, but its 'aggressive artificiality'[77] did not find any more favour with critics and audiences than the somewhat heavy-handed production – and judging by the glancing diary references Jarman makes to the experience, which he oversaw rather than shouldered, he does not seem to have enjoyed it; probably because it only served to remind him of happier, more energetic productions.

Waiting for Godot opened on 30 September, midway through an almost unbroken avalanche of activity. August had brought the Edinburgh Film Festival and a gala screening of *Edward II*, for which Jarman invested in a special tweed suit, 'tailored long ago in Shanghai and never worn'.[78] In it, he felt lordly, and witnessed his film's lordly reception. The cinema was packed, the audience appreciative. In early September, he was in Venice at the head of an entire party of family and friends, staying on the lido at the Hotel des Bains, lunching in Torcello, indulging his passion for Italian ice-cream and watching Swinton scoop the Venice Festival's Coppa Volte Best Actress award for her portrayal of the icy Isabella. Again the film was well received.

Sunday 22 September brought what Jarman would often refer to as the happiest day of his life. For this, he was in Dungeness where, after a week spent enjoying 'his first free days' all year, he was canonised by the Sisters of Perpetual Indulgence.[79]

During the making of *Edward II*, Systah Frigidity of the Nocturnal Emission OPI (also known as Ian) had written to thank Jarman for their day's filming. The letter confirmed a proposition put by the sisters to their director between takes.

> The Sisters of Perpetual Indulgence wanted to confirm that we will be canonising you, if you agree to the sainthood. The London Order – the Mary Emission to St Julie of the Brown Paper Packages Tied Up With Bits Of String – hasn't canonised anyone before, and we're very pleased that you will be our first saint. The honour goes to anyone who we feel has made an extraordinary contribution to the Lesbian and Gay Community and is a sign of our respect. We're not sure of your title – whether you should be St Derek of Dungeness, or of the celluloid Image, or something else. Any ideas would be gratefully received.[80]

The service, conducted in High Polari, was held in the garden and led by Mother Fecundity of the Mass Uprising. It opened with 'the baying of Derek': the sisters and 'gathered faithful' (about fifty in all) clustered around his 'bijou lattie' and called him forth. After some dithering – should he be 'plain ordinary Joe Saint or something a little more glittering?' – Jarman had opted for glittering. When he emerged from the house, he was dressed in the 'sparkling golden robe'[81] worn in the film by Edward II. His face was covered with a veil, which helped hide the fact that, although determined to relish all of the silliness and underlying seriousness of the ceremony, somewhere he felt less than comfortable about the canonisation.

He was presented to the sisters by 'the Best Man (or nearest available thing)',[82] twice rejected, then accepted and led in hymn-singing processional to an altar, made out of a simple plank of wood, at the far end of the garden. On it stood various objects, including an

enormous inflatable banana and a toy dog. Jarman, now seated on
the throne set before the altar, was treated to the 'well-cum':

Sister Celebrant: How bona to vada your dolly old eeks.
Sisters: Bona to vada you.
Gathered Faithful: To vada you bona.

There were some readings, one from *Miss Manners' Guide to
Excruciatingly Correct Behaviour*, the hymn 'All Nuns Bright and
Beautiful' and a sermon from Mother Fecundity. Then the heart of
the service, a laying on of hands, after which the saint was crowned
with a 'bona helmet' and 'presented with a chain made up of plant
bulbs, cock rings and pornographic pictures'.[83] He was hailed three
times as Derek of Dungeness of the Order of Celluloid Knights, an
honorific suited to both where he lived and what he did, which at
the same time slyly mocked a certain knighthood. There was a closing hymn:

Amazing Pride, how sweet the sound
That saved a wretch like me.
I once was lost, but now am found,
'Twas afeared, but now am free.

Robe flapping in the afternoon breeze, the 'first Kentish saint
since Queer Thomas of Canterbury'[84] went with the sisters for a
lighthearted paddle in the sea, then took tea in the garden. He
thought he might make a business of the holey stones he liked to collect on the beach: 'I'm into the holy amulet business.'[85]

His photographs of the canonisation are the last pictures to be
pasted in what would be his final album. No more images, graven or
otherwise, would be enshrined there. After this, St Derek was aimed
at the void, off into the blue to confront the awfully big adventure
that had been stalking him ever since the day in 1986 when he had
first heard he was HIV positive.

30

Do Not Go Gentle

Tired of being 'spread all over the breakfast table like toast and marmalade each morning',[1] Jarman asked his agent to stop all interviews. Only 'seventy per cent healthy', he was suffering the effects of a post-canonisation 'autumn depression'.[2] Of course, the interviews did not stop, quite the contrary, and it is questionable whether he would have welcomed it if they had; but with his health deteriorating, his energies did of necessity turn inward.

In mid-October he travelled to Leeds and Newcastle for previews of *Edward II*. These were followed by a charity première in London.[4] At the same time, the NFT – borrowing a phrase of Ken Russell's and dubbing the newly canonised saint 'The Last Bohemian' – mounted a season of his features, now nine in number, plus three shorter films.[5] A trio of publications made their appearance: *Queer Edward II*, the reissue of *Dancing Ledge* and *Today and Tomorrow*,[6] a perpetual calendar handsomely illustrated by seventeen colour plates of Jarman's paintings and assemblages.

Despite the tightness of its focus and control, the manner in which *Edward II* mixes contemporary politics with ancient history, calculated crudity with relative sophistication, meant it did not meet with universal approval. Some criticised it for being too strident, and, in its portrayal of Isabella, plain misogynistic. Writing in the *Evening Standard*, Alexander Walker carried the debate into the realm of the personal: 'Like the director himself, these days, the movie possesses a strong streak of wishful martyrdom. I think it's getting on people's nerves to hear Jarman advertising himself – or being advertised – in every branch of the media as the most famous living HIV positive victim.' Although Walker did go on to say that 'the dying fall that the unfortunately stricken film-maker deliberately emphasises in his version of Marlowe's play gives it a terminal power',[7] his review was seen by Jarman's friends as 'unfair', 'negative' and 'gratuitously hurtful'. The words are those of Jarman's consultant Tony Pinching, who sprang to his patient's defence. Citing Jarman's openness about his medical status as evidence of 'his honesty and willingness to help foster more sensible attitudes to HIV', Pinching pointed out that it was unfair to blame Jarman for 'voyeurism in the media'. 'Like any artist in the public eye, of course he must advertise his work,' wrote Pinching, 'and it is by his work he should be assessed, not by his virus.'[8]

There the matter might have rested, had not Walker decided to respond. Picking up on Pinching's praise for Jarman's 'willingness to help foster more sensible attitudes to HIV', Walker struck back with: 'I did not detect much of this willingness when I read Jarman's recent diary, *Modern Nature*, where he gives the promiscuously gay "and brave" encouragement for a night's revelry on Hampstead Heath between 10.30pm and 3am.'[9] Jonathan Coe, reviewing *Modern Nature* for the *Guardian*, had said that 'the pages which dwell in rapturous, magical detail on the pleasures (and dangers) of cruising after dark on Hampstead Heath are surely enough to make all but the most rabid homophobes feel a pang of excitement and, yes, even envy.'[10] By contrast, Walker viewed Jarman's ardent advocacy of promiscuity as highly irresponsible.

The cause of this controversy now replied on his own behalf.[11] Suggesting that Walker 'give up film reviewing for a week or so and research the HIV epidemic if he wants to be involved', Jarman stated flatly that as long as safer sex practices were adhered to, 'the first lesson he will learn is that HIV is not linked to promiscuity'. In a passage cut from his letter as published, he continued angrily: 'Who is he, who neither states his HIV status nor sexual preference, to criticise the right of myself or any PWA [person with AIDS] to have sex. The precautions we take are our affair. Moral censure will not solve the problem.' He made the point that he could easily have removed the offending passages from *Modern Nature* and had indeed been under some pressure to do so. He had left them in so as not to 'close doors'. If Walker thought that being open about one's HIV status was a 'peccadillo', then 'he should think harder'.

To be battling illness against a background of such remarks only served to intensify Jarman's 'overwhelming anger'. Colin MacCabe had loaned him another small Soho office where, 'fizzing with fury', he picked up his silver pen and 'took the first stab at AYOR'.[12] Between October and Christmas, apart from visits to Dungeness, the occasional demonstration and a trip to Amsterdam to receive an award for *Edward II*,[13] he concentrated on assembling the book whose title had been suggested by Collins.

'At Your Own Risk' – AYOR for short – is the designation given in gay guides to the more dangerous places to cruise or search for casual sex. As a phrase, it perfectly described Jarman's contention that how one had sex was a private matter; something handled purely and necessarily at one's own risk. It also neatly yet defiantly encompassed the book's purpose, which was a continuation of *Pansy*'s: to pen a queer history, thus rectifying the lack of autobiography and example Jarman himself had suffered as a young man. Writing specifically for the young men of the nineties, he wanted to detail the sort of pressures to which he had been subjected in living a queer life, to trace the homophobia of his time. Again he wanted to replace 'they', 'them' or 'one' with 'I' or 'me' – to tell his own and other people's stories, with anger and outrage where necessary, but also with defiance, humour and in celebration.

In order to achieve the required mix of memoir, history and agit-prop, of personal reminiscence, newspaper reportage and hard fact, Jarman dedicated the entire Soho office to the matter in hand. The doorbell said AYOR and the walls were plastered with homophobic articles and headlines taken from the archives of Simon Watney and Peter Tatchell. Tatchell, together with such politically engaged people as Sarah Graham, one of Jarman's few female associates from this era, or Alan Beck of the Sisters of Perpetual Indulgence, was becoming an increasingly important part of his life. Because Jarman was writing primarily for those younger than himself, and because his health made collaboration with others more pressing than ever, he worked on the book with a handful of young men who could help with the research, interviewing him at length on his life and opinions, then shaping and typing up the end result.[14]

The finished book was subtitled 'A Saint's Testament' and divided into six sections, one for each decade from the 1940s to the 1990s. From the very first page it made its agenda clear. '*At Your Own Risk* recalls the landscapes you were warned off: Private Property, Trespassers will be Prosecuted; the fence you jumped, the wall you scaled, fear and elation, the guard dogs and police in the shrubbery, the byways, bylaws, do's and don'ts. Keep Out, Danger, get lost, shadowland, pretty boys, pretty police who shoved their cocks in your face and arrested you in fear.'[15]

Anger at injustice underpinned almost every paragraph, as did a bitter humour:

Deviant heterosexuals are the product of sympathetic, warm and overprotective fathers, and cold distant mothers.
Whatever the cause, aversion therapy was probably their only chance. Like all compassionate Queers, I knew heterosexuals needed help desperately. How could they be saved from themselves? Perhaps a nice clerical counsellor sponsored by the Church of England.[16]

With the book only days from completion, Jarman spent New Year at Dungeness: 'curious that I had survived another year'. He was not sleeping well and his skin was a constant irritation, leading him to write dispiritedly in his diary: 'I know I'll not keep this diary up.' In fact, he would. He also wrote: 'I've been hoovering my mind all through the holiday for a project for this year but found nothing except an enormous lethargy.'[17] Again, the words do not reflect reality. The year 1992 would be rich in plans for various projects, some realised, some not.[18] And when he visited St Mary's for a check-up on 20 January, everything was judged to be 'in order'. Using liquid nitrogen, the doctor burned off the molluscum contagiosum, the small, white, viral spots now dotting his face, and complimented him on his 'excellent' AZT-induced 'suntan'. He was then advised to remove his AZT from its identifying packets when he and Collins attended the Sundance Film Festival for a screening of *Edward II* because it was illegal to enter the United States with an HIV-related infection without obtaining special dispensation beforehand.

Held annually in the mountain ski resort of Park City in northern Utah, the Sundance Film Festival, the brainchild of Robert Redford, is dedicated to independent film-making, though, because this year's low-budget director or non-mainstream actor might be next year's Hollywood sensation, there are always plenty of first-division players in evidence and the festival is gift-wrapped in a degree of luxury not usually associated with the avant garde. There were personal drivers to ferry Jarman and Collins through the snow-filled streets and they were billeted in a 'condominium four times the size of Prospect Cottage with a jacuzzi that would have swallowed a football team'.[19] Unfortunately, this turned out to be so heavily chlorinated that Jarman could not use it; it seared his sensitive skin.

Edward II was not the only 'queer' film being screened at Sundance. Others included Tom Kalin's *Swoon*, Greg Araki's *The Living End*, Christopher Munch's *The Hours and Times* and Phillip R. Ford's *Vegas in Space*. This slew of same-sex film-making led to much trumpeting in the press over what was termed the 'new queer cinema' and during the festival there was a discussion panel called 'Barbed Wire Kisses' on the subject. Naturally, Jarman participated and was introduced as a 'cultural icon'.[20] To some he may have seemed too old to form part of this new wave, but to most he was a vital father figure. The press debate about the new queer cinema – did it really exist? Did it have a future? – helped the maker of *Edward II* reach his largest American audience to date.

Moving on to Mark McCormick's New York apartment, Jarman caught up with friends, among them Malcolm Leigh, now living at the Chelsea Hotel, where he threw a party to celebrate Jarman's fiftieth birthday and imparted some bitter news. Patrik Steede had recently died. Before leaving London, Jarman had learned of the death of Dom Sylvester Houédard. Later in the year he would hear of the suicide of Karl Bowen. The passing of this trio, particularly of Steede and Bowen, both so vital to the optimism associated with youth and the early seventies, affected Jarman deeply. As he wrote of Steede: 'all that hustle turned to ash in New Jersey, and I hear about it second hand'.[21]

His eyesight was starting to fail. He began to harp constantly on the darkness of McCormick's apartment and could not wait to get into the street, where he walked on whatever pavement afforded the most sunlight. Soon he would be unable to manage without glasses and they would need to be repeatedly replaced in ever-increasing strengths.

He returned to as much gardening, beachcombing and caring for his bees as his strength would permit – and, although he still felt like avoiding the limelight, more politicking and controversy. Before Sundance, he had learned that the *Evening Standard* intended to offer him a special award for cinematic achievement. Citing as his reason the paper's palpable homophobia, he declined the award and, even though he knew he would be in America at the time of the ceremony, attended a meeting to plan a disruptive 'zap' in which members of OutRage! would line the pavement outside the Savoy Hotel to offer the paper an award of their own for 'Outstanding Contribution to Homophobia'. Even in his absence Jarman's name became a feature of the evening when Sandy Powell, collecting a prize for her costume designs for *Edward II*, *The Miracle* and *The Pope Must Die*, used her acceptance speech to echo the sentiments of the protesters outside and to salute Jarman for refusing his award.

In the run-up to the 1992 general election, OutRage! were demanding 'equality now' and arranging a series of demonstrations to 'expose and challenge state homophobia'.[22] On 6 February there was a march from Bow Street to the Houses of Parliament in calculated defiance of the law forbidding demonstrations in the immediate vicinity of Parliament while it was in session. Wearing his 'sober banker's coat,'[23] Jarman made a short speech in Bow Street, then joined Peter Tatchell, Jimmy Somerville and a sizeable crowd as it moved towards Whitehall. Leicester Square tube station marked the point where the demonstrators entered the prohibited area. As they turned into Charing Cross Road, a pink ribbon strung across the street was cut by a Margaret Thatcher lookalike. 'She who must be obeyed' informed the assembled throng that she washed her hands of them; they were now John Major's problem. Tatchell warned those who did not want to be arrested to stay off the road. Watched by a phalanx of photographers, the police attempted to force the protesters on to the pavement. At this point some of their number, among them Jarman, Somerville and Sarah Graham, lay down in the road. Arrests were made and those detained taken to a police station near the Oval, photographed, searched, put for a short while in cells, then cautioned and released. 'I think,' wrote Jarman, 'I had rehearsed this moment in my mind ever since I came to London as a student . . . here I was finally arrested for being myself in this disgraceful society.'[24]

In the middle of February he was in Glasgow for an exhibition of his assemblages and recent landscapes at the Art Gallery and Museum, Kelvingrove. The landscapes were receiving their first public airing, though it was less for them than for the AIDS-related assemblages with their condoms, pill boxes and crucifixes that Jarman named the exhibition *At Your Own Risk*. The notion of risk lay at the very heart of this selection of his work: the risk inherent in being alive, in being queer, in facing death. One of the assemblages was of a single thermometer and a clutch of crumpled and empty bags of the kind used for administering intravenous drips. Below the bags was a small plaque which, with a wit as black as the paint holding the assemblage together, asked the question: 'TB or not TB?' The work on display provided its own inevitable and not always palatable answer: to be, of course, even at the risk of TB.

Next he was in Berlin for the city's forty-second film festival and the opening there of *Edward II*. The screening was packed and the film well received, its director surrounded and supported by his usual entourage of friends and admirers. Yet there were signs that this second festival of the year was a festival too far. Suffering as he was from an 'appalling cold', he found the endless interviews terribly draining, and seemed to derive little comfort either from the two awards the film picked up, or from the fact that it was shown in the Forum Section, for films that were youthful and innovative. In fact, he fretted that his Berlin audience was too old, too 'cosily West'.[25]

Back in London, he continued to 'hoover his mind' for a new film project. In addition to *The Picture of Dorian Gray* and *Blue*, around which he was constantly thinking, ideas he considered included the play *Angels in America* and another film about a garden: Monet's this time, not his own. Then there was *Narrow Rooms*. This James Purdy novel of sexual obsession in remote West Virginia had long been at the back of Jarman's mind as a potential project. Now the fact that at Sundance he had met and been welcomed by a new circle of independent American film-makers made filming something American – possibly even in America – suddenly seem feasible.

In between considering these possibilities, he helped Takashi Asai with his book of images from the films, and clashed with Century over the cover for *At Your Own Risk*. He was keen to use *Flesh Tint*, one of his own assemblages of a condom partially obscuring a picture of Christ. Century, however, had last-minute qualms about the advisability of featuring this image and, without properly consulting Jarman, substituted one of a truncated and naked male torso on a ground of messy blue paint. The author was not best pleased.[26]

He was still feeling low: depleted of energy and tormented – especially in the early hours of the morning – by his aggravated skin. News came of yet another AIDS-related death, that of Graham Cracker, Alasdair McGaw's partner. With Collins away in Newcastle on a visit, a lonely Jarman felt overwhelmingly 'sad and foolish to be ill and in love'. Yet he was determined not to succumb to his ailments and resolved to 'fight this gloomy lethargy that puts me to sleep on the sofa each afternoon'.[27]

Like writing, painting was an activity that could banish lethargy without exhausting him – and, as luck would have it, the Manchester City Art Gallery had invited him to provide them with a one-man exhibition. Because of the size of the gallery, Jarman realised that his small assemblages would not be appropriate. He needed to tackle the kind of public works last attempted in the GBH series for his ICA retrospective in 1984. Turning to the homophobic headlines he had plastered all over the AYOR office, he decided that if he photocopied these and pasted them in repeated rows on to

canvases measuring some 250cm by 150cm, the Warholesque result
would provide the perfect background for raging against the mean-
ness of the tabloid mind.

First, he needed a big enough studio and a pair of hands to help
stretch and prepare the canvases, as well as mix the paint. Richard
Salmon supplied both: a lofty room at South Edwardes Square, plus
the services of Piers Clemmet, one of his assistants. Earlier in the
year, Jarman had asked a doctor about the feasibility of painting
with his own infected blood, only to be told he could never produce
enough for his needs and that the complications of sterilising the
blood would be well-nigh insurmountable. The way he now planned
to cover the tabloid headlines in a wash of colour – red in the case
of the painting called *Blood* – and then scrawl a message of his own
in the wet paint graphically recalled his original impulse. Starting in
early March and working with a headline from the *People* – 'SEX
BOYS FOR SALE AT QUEEN'S GROCER' – he had Clemmet mix the paint,
then splashed the canvas with an angry combination of red and
black on which he scrawled 'EIIR', adding for good measure: 'cocks'
and 'arse'.

Aside from some initial problems encountered in stretching such
large canvases, he had hit upon a style of painting that was wonderfully quick to effect, and the work soon mounted up. Not all the
paintings made use of photocopied headlines. *Queer* simply featured
the word itself written across the shape of a heart. It was, if you like,
a love letter to its creator's new identity: not proud to be gay, but I
love being queer. The triptych *Love Sex Death* – in which, one word
to a canvas, the three words were etched into a vivid impasto of
paint that graduated in colour from dark blue to fiery red – spelled a
less definable message; quite how each word related to its neighbour
and colour was left for the viewer to decide.

Creating these new paintings was not without its difficulties.
Their subject matter was anger-inducing, Jarman's health a constant
handicap. He was now suffering from 'a dizziness behind the eyes'
and an intermittent headache that made concentration difficult.
Yet he was content. The paintings 'burnt back the years' and the
'heady' smell of turpentine, despite aggravating his headache, had a
Proustian potency. It reminded him of the art shack at Canford and

'youthful optimism'.[28] The bus journeys to and from South Edwardes Square gave the days structure, while the square's garden provided welcome visual ravishment as it burst into blossom.

In mid-March, after another check-up at St Mary's and a further burning of the molluscum, Jarman once again travelled to New York, this time for the official opening of *Edward II*. In the two months since his last visit, Mark McCormick, a manic depressive, had been taken ill and into residential care, so Jarman and Collins stayed at the Mayflower Hotel. Continuity was provided by Malcolm Leigh, who threw another party at the Chelsea Hotel before the screening. Here Jarman met James Purdy, who gave his blessing to the development of *Narrow Rooms*.

New York was followed by a wet Los Angeles and another hotel, the legendary Château Marmont. *Edward II* was in the Los Angeles Gay and Lesbian Film Festival. Despite its charms, Jarman found the festival dishearteningly like that year's Berlin: 'thoroughly middle-aged and middle income and respectable'.[29] He was feeling decidedly sorry for himself. He wondered why almost no one called. Where was Steven Waddington, for instance, who was filming there? Why no Lee Drysdale, no Julian Sands, no David Hockney? One could be forgiven for imagining that the entire film establishment had turned its back on him, which could not have been further from the truth. As part of a satellite link to London, where the main ceremony was taking place, Jarman attended a BAFTA lunch where he was placed next to Jodie Foster and presented with the Michael Balcon award for his outstanding contribution to British cinema.

Back home, as the American screenings, interviews and parties, the visit to a gay rodeo and the stretch limos 'receded into dreams',[30] Jarman experienced an immense weariness. Life had become akin to walking a tightrope. If he defaulted for an instant on the intense concentration his work required, he would fatally lose his balance. It was as if he feared that, by stopping, he might stop for good. So, much as he hated his multiplicity of pills and longed to escape their ceaseless tyranny, he continued to swallow them. He tackled his itches with enough garlic to empty the room and cheered himself up by measuring his own infirmities against those of his contemporaries. A chance encounter with David Hockney, whose deafness 'gave him a stoop as if he was taking a curtain call', left Jarman feeling 'alive and rather well'.[31]

He joined Marina Warner and Guy Brett in selecting the entries for that year's New Contemporaries, the show in which he himself had featured so successfully as a student. As a result of his meeting with James Purdy, he thought more seriously about adapting *Narrow Rooms*. Despite being far from certain that his finances could properly stretch to it, he drew on what remained of his father's money to start construction on a back extension to Prospect Cottage, so that at last he would enjoy a proper, sizeable bathroom and an extra room, which, he decided, should have windows on two sides to give an uninterrupted view of the rear garden. With his Manchester exhibition only six weeks away, he returned to South Edwardes Square where the gardens were 'ablaze with camellias, japonica, and spring bulbs'.[32] With the continued help of Piers Clemmet, he painted furiously, joking that if he did not work fast enough he would end up as a sort of artist in residence at the City Art Gallery, finishing the work in situ.[33]

The days spent painting in Salmon's studio were an urban idyll. Apart from the glory of the gardens, there was satisfaction at seeing the large new canvases accrete, there were talkative lunches at a nearby Lebanese restaurant, regular visits to Rassells nursery. A casual observer would have noticed only Jarman's cheerful determination – though because he was walking a tightrope, the abyss, like his dizziness and turpentine-induced headache, was ever-present. 'At moments,' he wrote, 'I wish my physical self would evaporate, cease. No more aches and pains. HB tells me to hold on . . . Monet paints his garden, I paint the wilderness of illness, my sad subject, no *Jazz*.'[34]

A clue to his private despair was the irritation he felt at the way his time could be claimed by total strangers clamouring to interview him, have him sign his photograph, or visit the garden. He found such intrusions increasingly irksome, 'particularly the demands for photographic sessions that will take over a day and leave a record of wrinkles'.[35]

The imminent publication of *At Your Own Risk*, coming as it did hard on the heels of the appearance in paperback of *Modern Nature*, gave the media a focus for their interest. They descended on Jarman in droves and not always in a spirit of co-operation. Catherine Bennett from the *Guardian* conducted an interview which its subject found so aggressive that he was not in the least surprised to be told by friends that the paper had actively intended to publish something hostile.

'Lesson of the Gay Guru' appeared on 9 April and was illustrated by a picture every bit as 'horrible' as the accompanying text. Jarman's head had been grafted on to the body of Michelangelo's David and the image duplicated. In version one, the resulting freak carried a camera. In version two, a megaphone. The message was clear: the 'gay' artist as agitator. 'The last time Derek Jarman met the *Guardian*,' began the article, 'he came with a few friends. Civil, but cross, they stood outside the door last September shouting "We're here! We're queer, We don't read the Guardian!", and accusing the paper of liberal homophobia.' Whether or not the paper consciously intended to avenge Jarman's anger over Haselden's 'Gay Abandon' piece, the tone of Bennett's interview was certainly as hostile as he had feared it would be. Peppered with phrases like 'the grand old man of inversion' and 'the authority of the sickbed rather than the artist', it dismissed *At Your Own Risk* as Jarman's 'most disjointed autobiographical hodge-podge to date'. Some – perhaps many – doubtless concurred; to Jarman, the comments evidenced mere vindictiveness. He was hurt, angry and undermined. Self-critical enough to see his reaction as paranoid and self-pitying, he still felt locked in a battle that would never end. Could anyone outside his immediate circle comprehend the pressures which, as a queer man, he was forced to endure? For a moment he dreaded his forthcoming publication. 'Take a deep breath,' he instructed himself, 'and get ready for the AYOR onslaught, there is going to be no good press – I can feel it, I've had more than my fifteen minutes.'[36]

His prophecy proved false. More representative was the interview by Clement Freud that appeared in *The Times*.[37] Freud had travelled to Dungeness to meet his subject and concluded his account of their meeting as follows: 'On the 25-mile journey to the station, the driver, who is a woman from Cork, tells me what a joy it is to drive Mr Jarman, "who is such fun and so very interesting and polite and modest". I tell her she is preaching to the converted.' As the interviews got underway, Jarman hit his stride and found himself enjoying them. Commenting in his diary on how everyone assumed him to be on 'permanent holiday' because of his ruddy colour, he added: 'I am maybe, I can only thrive on this attention.'[38]

Had this truly been the case, the exhibition in Manchester would have restored him to full and instant health. Since its inception, the exhibition had enjoyed many potential titles, including *Shipwrecked*. Eventually these evolved into the simple but incontrovertible *Queer* – with the startling result that the enormous banner covering the Victorian exterior of the gallery, which could be seen up and down Princess Street, was something of a 'world first for civic gay pride'.[39] 'QUEER DEREK JARMAN', it proclaimed.

The gallery produced a substantial catalogue that included four short essays on Jarman's work. There was a gallery guide containing a lengthy interview and a number of postcards. The media speculated luridly and inaccurately as to whether Jarman had painted his new canvases with his own blood. A video recording was made of the proceedings.[40] Jarman read from and signed copies of *At Your Own Risk*. There was a screening of *The Queen is Dead* and *Edward II* at Cornerhouse, where Jarman gave a talk. Making further use of the back projections from their 1989 tour, the Pet Shop Boys played at a concert to celebrate the tenth anniversary of the Hacienda, one of Manchester's most popular nightclubs. Jarman appeared on stage to introduce the band.

Despite his jokes about having to finish the paintings in situ, Jarman had been able to complete more canvases than he actually needed. He judged the overall effect of the twenty-eight new pieces he chose to complement the sixteen smaller works included from the Kelvingrove exhibition as 'splendid'. He was not the only one. The reception accorded this, his first exhibition in a major municipal gallery, was extremely positive. There were even sales, including the purchase by Manchester itself of *Queer*.

Meanwhile, *At Your Own Risk* was proving itself a magnet for further plaudits. Praise was invariably tempered with a degree of criticism – and, in the case of *Gay Times*, what Jarman considered naked hostility – but the coverage was far from unsatisfying. *The*

Times caught the general tone: 'a dog's dinner of a book, passionately, incomprehensibly, often lazily thrown together, but somehow very memorable'.[41]

When the hero of the hour returned from the intoxication of Manchester to the calm of Dungeness, it was with a nasty cough, an extremely sore mouth and a temperature. He was still stalked by amnesia, an acute sensitivity to sunlight and the incessant itching. His consultant, Tony Pinching, had transferred from St Mary's to Bart's. Jarman did the same. On his first visit to Andrewes Ward, he was told he had a chest infection and that the soreness in his mouth was the result of 'a vicious HIV-induced attack of gingivitis'.[42] The additional medication he was prescribed included hydrocortisone, which at least had the positive side-effect of giving him the energy to be up at five, ready for the day.

June, spent largely in Dungeness, was remarkable serene. 'I am so in love with the place,' he wrote, 'please God I see another year.'[43] When the days were at their calmest and he had managed a reasonable night's rest, there was much good humour. Anya Sainsbury, whom Jarman had not seen for several years, was due to pay a visit. On the appointed day, the phone rang. Collins answered it, then came into the garden to 'say the Palace was ringing. Lady Di was coming down with Anya, and would there be space for her and two bodyguards to spend the night'. Lord Sainsbury had recently been made a Knight of the Garter, so 'this was not so far fetched that I did not believe him. "Oh God Del, what do we call her?" he asked. "Ma'am," I replied. When I got to the phone it turned out to be Karen from Penguin. HB went wild with squeaks of laughter. For the rest of the day he was going round saying, "So much for your republicanism, Derek: MA'AM." "I was well brought up," I said, "and whatever I might think there's no need to be impolite."'[44]

Penguin had called because Jarman was among a handful of well-known figures chosen to participate in a poster campaign to promote the imprint. After another assault by liquid nitrogen on his facial spots, he was photographed reading one of their titles. In return, he was given a complete set of Penguin Classics which he asked to be sent to Bart's.

The extension, or west wing as Jarman termed it, reached completion. While Brian the builder lined the corridor leading to it with bookshelves from floor to ceiling, Jarman put the new rooms in order. He bought two 'grand' chairs, wielded a paintbrush and oversaw the installation of a door to the bathroom which boasted a specially inscribed glass panel, 'HB Paradise', though the rooms were of course paradise to both of them. To be able to take a bath or listen to music while contemplating the back garden was more than ample compensation for the inconvenience of the building works.

Jarman next looked out his unproduced film scripts and sent them to Vintage, his paperback publishers, with the proposal that they publish a collection of them to accompany a reissue of *The Last of England*, retitled *Kicking the Pricks*.[45] He gave a less arresting title – *More of the Same* – to his current journal, which he was equally keen to see between covers. He talked about directing a play for the Citizens' Theatre in Glasgow and turning *Modern Nature* into an opera with Simon Turner. Failing that, he considered creating a cycle of songs based on the journal which could then be incorporated into the Blue concerts Turner was still mounting. Maria St Just, who controlled the estate of Tennessee Williams, asked if he would be interested in filming the rarely performed *Outcry* with Paul Scofield and Vanessa Redgrave.[46] He visited London frequently, sometimes to see his doctor, more often to see friends or attend meetings. In late June, he joined the annual march for Gay Pride. On 25 July, he was prominent at an OutRage! demonstration to mark the twenty-fifth anniversary of the 1967 Sexual Offences Act. The demonstration began in the shadow of the statue of Eros in Piccadilly, where, with the aid of a megaphone, Jarman read Sonnet 116: 'Let me not to the marriage of true minds admit impediment.' Around his neck hung a placard which made a simpler statement: 'STILL WAITING AND F*CKING FURIOUS'.

Jarman's principal focus, however, was on a trio of very particular projects: *Narrow Rooms*, *Chroma* and *Wittgenstein*.

Set in a small mountain town and viewed largely through the eyes of Vance De Lakes, brother to one of the protagonists, *Narrow Rooms* traces the links in a fevered and obsessive chain of gay love. Because of the way each link in the chain leads to its neighbour and each story is shadowed by another, the novel as a whole is less about its protagonists than it is about all men; the archetypal violence and intensity inherent in every gay relationship. Towards the end of the book, Vance's brother Sidney says of himself and Roy Sturtevant, also known as the renderer: 'There was no renderer . . . and there never had been any Sidney De Lakes . . . for he felt he was back thousands of years ago with his "eternal" lover or husband or sweetheart, whatever name, on whom he now poured out his love.'[47] To play the part of the renderer, 'the "eternal" lover or husband or sweetheart', Jarman chose Collins, whom he also asked to help write the screenplay. If it had been made, the film would have stood as one more testament to Jarman's abiding love for HB.

In consultation with Jarman, Collins spent part of the summer working on a first draft, later handed to Ken Butler for revision. Meanwhile, Jarman entered into discussions with Working Title, who, in the person of Antony Root, approached the American independent producer Christine Vachon. Vachon had close links with the 'new queer cinema' and knew Jarman from Sundance and Berlin. Root then left Working Title, who dropped the project. Jarman quickly put Vachon in touch with Steve Clark-Hall, who, with Root, had co-produced *Edward II*.

On 31 May, Jarman had written: 'I dreamt all night of writing a book on colour, not scientific or in any way academic, free floating through the spectrum. Maybe the *Tractatus* unlocked it.'[48] It would be a long time before, again thanks to Collins, he hit on a satisfactory title for the book he eventually called *Chroma*, but the notion of a non-scientific, non-academic amble through the colours was crystal clear from the outset. Century reacted with enthusiasm, a contract was signed and, spectacles at the ready, Jarman was soon plunged into a keen round of reading into his new subject. He began to 'free-float through the spectrum', starting with white then progressing to red, 'a difficult colour'.[49] Writing in longhand on whatever sheets of paper he had to hand, he jotted down ideas, anecdotes and autobiography in the order they came to him. His only focus was the colour under consideration, to which end he often wore an appropriately coloured article of clothing: a red T-shirt for the chapter on red, yellow pyjamas for yellow, and so on. Finally, with the assistance of several helpers, the sheets of paper were typed up, ordered and shaped.[50]

Jarman's reference to the *Tractatus* relates to what was perhaps his most pressing project of the summer, an entirely unexpected film about the life and philosophy of Ludwig Wittgenstein. The education department at Channel 4 had asked the independent producer Tariq Ali to develop a series on philosophy. Ali had suggested 'a set of one-hour dramas based on the lives, times and ideas of a set of philosophers from Ancient Greece to modern times. The original plan was to do twelve over three years.'[51] Four scripts were commissioned: *Socrates* by Howard Brenton, *Spinoza* by Ali himself, *Locke* by David Edgar and *Wittgenstein* by Terry Eagleton, Wharton Professor of English at Oxford. Ali asked Jarman if he would direct Eagleton's script.

Jarman began reading Ray Monk's invaluable biography, plus whatever he could of Wittgenstein's often impenetrable philosophy.[52] He had a clear vision of how best to visualise such a subject: 'Extreme austerity . . . no competition from objects'.[53] He thought Eagleton's script 'good', but that, if he was to direct it, it would need substantial modification, particularly in terms of its humour – or lack of it. Ken Butler was again asked to step in as Jarman's 'ghost'. In late June, Ali, Jarman and Butler travelled to Oxford to meet Eagleton and discuss how best to proceed. Jarman noted of the changes discussed at the meeting: 'Terry seemed quite happy, worried a little by the humour, but otherwise decided that Wittgenstein might be too gloomy.'[54] A week later he wrote: 'I've made huge changes to Terry Eagleton's script which makes me nervous.'[55]

The changes were indeed huge, in terms not only of humour and tone, but of content and structure. Eagleton's entirely naturalistic script was concerned more with Wittgenstein's philosophy than his life. Although it opened in Austria and had a closing sequence on the coast of Galway, where Wittgenstein briefly moved in his final days, it was otherwise set exclusively in Cambridge, locus of Wittgenstein's academic existence. It ignored such things as the philosopher's Viennese childhood, his studies in Manchester, his youthful sojourn on the banks of a Norwegian fjord, his experiences as a soldier during World War I. It observed a Wittgenstein going abstractedly about his daily life while attempting to clarify his thoughts and theories both to himself and to his contemporaries, principally Bertrand Russell, John Maynard Keynes, G.E. Moore and David Jarrett, a fictional character representing the various young men of whom Wittgenstein was fond.

Never mind that, because of its period and location, such a naturalistic script would prove difficult to shoot on the sort of budget envisaged by Ali; on the few occasions Jarman had filmed someone else's script, he had always stamped the material with his own imprimateur. *Wittgenstein* proved no exception. Jarman and Butler abandoned the use of real locations in favour of a studio-based approach. Costume, props, light and sound would be used to suggest the different settings. The changes they made to the sequence and structure of Eagleton's script were equally bold, escalating in audacity over the four months they worked on the project. Some of the points Eagleton had taken the trouble to explain they took for granted: the fact, for example, that Wittgenstein's students sat on deckchairs because he had virtually no furniture in his rooms. Other information they went to great pains to include or elaborate upon. They created the character of Wittgenstein as a boy so that he could tell his own story, thereby filling in certain biographical gaps. They introduced the Wittgenstein family, Ottoline Morrell and a young man called Johnny to replace David Jarrett. They made Eagleton's script more fantastical while simultaneously giving it a more solid grounding in biographical fact. They also made Wittgenstein's homosexuality fractionally less furtive and tortured than in Eagleton's version.

Once he took delivery of this very different script, Ali began to explore the possibility of setting it up in a more ambitious manner than originally intended. Jarman gave some initial thought to the casting, then returned to his 'tabloid' paintings at South Edwardes Square. He also executed a handful of new landscapes and paid further attention to *Narrow Rooms* and *Chroma*. As his diaries show, after the relative calm of June, illness was inexorably gathering.

14 July: 'A grim gale blew through the night, my stomach collapsed and I found myself staggering through the corridors with fouled sheets.'

19 July: 'I wish I could experience one day of good health.'
24 July: 'Is my lurking headache the heat and fumes or the
dreaded toxo? Heat and fumes.'

In August matters worsened. He noted that his eyes seemed 'fuzzy'
and that he could feel a 'moving in' at the edge of his field of vision.
Although he preferred to blame London's heat and fumes rather
than the 'dreaded toxo', it was probable either that further lesions in
his brain were again affecting his sight, or that he might be adding
another fatal link to his 'necklace' of illnesses: cytomegalovirus.
CMV tends to occur in the later stages of AIDS, attacks nerve tissue
(among other things) and, if targeting the retina, can lead to blindness. The doctor ordered a brain scan.

'I worry a little about losing my sight,' he wrote. 'I'll have to go into
journalism, perhaps I should do a Lynn Barber and interview all those
people I would wish to meet . . . my more macabre thoughts dance a
deadly tango in my eyes, ah well, it's two years since the foundations
tremored. Evil eyes. I can't imagine going blind, maybe that was the
terrible premonition read in my hand all those years ago by Umberto
Tirelli in Rome. I wonder if I could paint blind, why not?'[56]

The scan revealed nothing untoward, yet Jarman's eyesight continued to deteriorate. The next morning, while taking a breakfast
coffee in Maison Bertaux, he was told by the young woman who
served him that he had put his clothes on inside out. Later that day,
during the course of further examinations, lesions were detected on
his retina. The cause of his faulty vision had finally been isolated. It
was CMV.

The treatment for CMV was Ganciclovir, or DHPG, administered twice daily by means of a drip. The side-effects of Ganciclovir
could be horrendous. They included: 'malaise (very Victorian), sore
throat and nose bleeds, headache, dizziness, abdominal pain, consti-
pation, diarrhoea, muscular twitching, cough, pruritas urticaria
(itchiness), incontinence, and abnormal blood levels in a few
patients'.[57] Achieving a satisfactory balance between benefit and
toxicity was like walking the tightrope on which Jarman so often
found himself. He was given two options: either he could be
admitted to Bart's for the duration of his treatment, or he could stay

home and make two forays per day to the hospital. He chose to stay at home.

His diary entry for 11 August reads: 'I won't get the vision back this time, though when the bleeding in the eye is stopped I might improve slightly. Blindness is on the cards. I'm relieved that I know what is happening, the worst is the uncertainty. I think I have played this scenario back and forth nearly every day for the last six years.'[58]

The next day Jarman was connected to the drip for the first time. 'I monitor myself with my hands. I've lost ½ to ⅓ of my vision in my right eye, it's a strange sensation, I can feel it, it is like being accompanied by a shadow. HB, walking beside me, appears and disappears.'

He was nervous crossing roads and on crowded pavements. He worried how he would cope with his morning shave. 'I couldn't bear anyone else to touch my face as my skin is so irritated, even when I do it myself I hold my breath.'[59] He visited the Tate and discovered that where before he had always been able to see the next picture in a line, now there was merely a shadowy blank. And after a treatment session at Bart's,

I left the hospital in a downpour, standing at the entrance [was] an elderly woman trapped in the storm. I hailed a cab and asked if I could give her a lift, I took her to Holborn. On the way she broke into tears, she had come down from Edinburgh to see her son in the [AIDS] ward, he has had meningitis and lost the use of his legs. I hardly knew how to help as the tears flooded, I couldn't really see her sitting next to me, just the sound of her sobbing as I left her.[60]

After a week, there was talk of fitting Jarman with a permanent implant so that he could administer the drip himself at home. Then came another alternative. He could join a trial group taking the Ganciclovir orally, in the form of a pill. There were risks involved, but the group would be monitored closely and he would enjoy complete freedom from the restrictions of the drip. 'I think it's best to be adventurous,' he wrote, 'to treat this as dodgems, bright lights and the bumps.'[61]

At the same time, largely because his white blood cells were now under attack from the Ganciclovir, his neutrophil count – an indicator of the strength of the immune system – had dropped dramatically. As a result, he was taken off the AZT. In combination with a low neutrophil count, AZT was liable to make him even more vulnerable to infection.

As he watched 'the shadows closing in',[62] he experienced moments of terrible despair, both for himself and Collins. In the main, however, like his carer, he remained characteristically stoical: 'I think I have to come to terms with my blind fate, there is so much to do, I'm certain I could make a film, if Beethoven could do the 9th without hearing. There are the concerts with Simon, books, and painting, none of which need sight. I wonder how long it takes to learn Braille.'[63]

'There is so much to do.' The words are an understatement. He drove constantly to Dungeness to check on the garden, even though he could only be absent from London for the day. He kept keenly abreast of the activities of OutRage! and events on the world stage. He was enthusiastically supportive of the notion raised by the journalist Neil McKenna, a fellow member of OutRage!, that a statue be erected to commemorate the centenary of Oscar Wilde's arrest. McKenna thought the statue should be of Wilde chained and in prison garb. Jarman felt the city already boasted more than enough portly Victorians and suggested a hare by Barry Flanagan. The hare was, after all, historically a symbol of homosexuality.[64] He arranged a meeting with John Sainsbury to discuss forming a committee to carry the matter forward. He wrote to a number of potential allies, including Jeremy Isaacs, then general director of the Royal Opera House, who promised to do everything in his power to help organise the committee and see a statue erected.[65] Jarman also lent his name to Nicole Robinson's design for a production of Genet's The Maids which Michelle and Tania Wade, who ran Maison Bertaux, took to that year's Edinburgh Festival and mounted for a short run in Heaven the following January.

He was still hard at work on Chroma, now called Colour Blind, often picking up his pen late at night when he could not sleep: 'I can write quite legibly in the dark and the best thoughts seem to flood at four.'[66] He was similarly determined to advance *Narrow Rooms*. The day he had been to see his doctor about his failing eyesight was also the day he found time to ring his agent and take out an option on the book. The drama department at Channel 4 were approached and, in September, stepped smartly aboard with an offer of development money. It started to look as if the film might actually be made. Although the fallback position was always that shooting could take place in a British studio, the plan was to travel to America and do the filming there. Casting discussions were reactivated. There had never been any doubt in Jarman's mind that Collins would play the renderer. Other names mentioned included Dirk Bogarde and Faye Dunaway, who had been very visible at the Sundance Film Festival, where she had attended the screening of *Edward II* and even asked a question afterwards.

First, though, came *Wittgenstein*. When he sensed that the new script had cinematic potential, Tariq Ali showed Butler's and Jarman's reworking of Eagleton's original to Ben Gibson in the production department at the BFI. Gibson agreed with Ali's assessment and, between the BFI, the education department at Channel 4 and Takashi Asai in Tokyo, a budget of just under £300,000 was realised; enough, if everyone was extremely careful, to expand the hour-long television project into a seventy-five-minute feature. In mid-August, Jarman wrote: 'I make a decision to go for *Wittgenstein* in time and colour. The child could tell his story into the camera. Black drapes.'[67] He worked closely with Butler to expand what he liked to term their 'Loony Ludwig script' and lead it into 'the green valleys of silliness'.[68] The character of a green Martian with whom the young Wittgenstein could indulge in philosophical banter was cheerfully added to the dramatis personae.

Everything Jarman did was compromised by tiredness, not to mention the itching, bouts of amnesia so acute they induced attacks of panic, migraines so powerful he found himself unable to read, more fouled sheets. He viewed the world through 'a storm of black floaters from the retina which is flaking',[69] and would, before long, lose his sight completely in one eye. 'I have,' he said, 'this image now of me, very sick, eating dried biscuits, slowly and very deliberately. My eyes are so blurred they bring the writing to a halt.'[70]

In addition, the BFI had issued a challenge that would be hard to meet: 'To turn philosophy into cinema for £200,000 [sic] in a twelve-day shoot . . . is a tall order.'[71] Yet this transformation of television into cinema was proving immensely enjoyable. Jarman found Ali 'the enthusiast you dream of as a producer', having both 'flair and enough wickedness'.[72] Casting proceeded smoothly, as did the selection of the crew. A studio was found at 12 Theed Street, behind Waterloo: little more than 'a shoebox for pop promos',[73] but perfectly adequate.

Amid the preparations, time was even found for celebration. Jarman had recently been invited to choose a book for a Radio 4 programme. He asked the Sisters of Perpetual Indulgence if he could proffer the form of ceremony for his canonisation. They agreed, though on condition he undertook to renew his vows and undergo an appraisal of his saintly achievements. The service took place at Dungeness on 12 September.

It was a warm, sunny day. Again there was an altar in the garden, on which stood a teddy bear, a small cake, a toy duck and various other offerings. A robed Jarman was led to the altar and sat on his throne. His good deeds were enumerated, his praises sung, especially with reference to his gorgeous nose. He was asked what miracles he had performed. Slightly embarrassed, he mentioned the west wing and that the garden had flowered. He remembered visits from Fay Godwin, Beth Chatto and Clement Freud. The greatest achievement, though, was the fact of his survival: 'Here we all are again, that's a miracle.' He was crowned, the new extension was blessed, he and the sisters again went paddling in the sea. 'I know I'm not to take this too seriously,' he wrote, 'but my feelings were rather emotional.'[74]

Shooting on *Wittgenstein* began on Monday 5 October. With only twelve working days to cover fifty-three sequences, finishing on time would, as Jarman said, be a tall order, but he was greatly helped by the simplicity of his design and the presence of colleagues with whom he had worked before.

Apart from the occasional prop, the use of black drapes meant there were no sets as such. Mood and setting were created solely by means of the lighting and the later addition of sound and music;

colour by Sandy Powell's dazzlingly bright costumes, which wittily emphasised the cartoon-like aspect of Jarman's approach to his subject. A new cameraman, James Welland, joined other newcomers including John Quentin as Maynard Keynes, Nabil Shaban as the Martian and Sally Dexter as Wittgenstein's sister Hermine. For the rest, old friends proliferated, in minor as well as major roles and capacities. Karl Johnson played Wittgenstein, Michael Gough was Bertrand Russell, Tilda Swinton was Lady Ottoline Morrell, 'Kevin' Collins was Johnny, Lynn Seymour was Lydia Lopokova. Jan Latham-Koenig, whom Jarman knew from *L'ispirazione* and who also did the music, played Wittgenstein's brother Paul. Howard Sooley doubled as another of Wittgenstein's siblings and the film's resident photographer. Clancy Chassay from *War Requiem* played the young Wittgenstein, while Annie Lapaz, who had worked on both *War Requiem* and *Caravaggio*, was the art director.

The days were long and demanding. Up every morning at six, Jarman dressed in his blue overalls, heavy black coat and a favourite scarlet cap, then snatched breakfast in the Bar Italia before crossing the river to the waiting studio. He managed to keep diary notes of the day's filming for only the first two days of the shoot. Thereafter, he needed all his energies for his role as director. The days got steadily longer as the shoot progressed. At the end, they stretched to midnight. Yet by dint of sheer determination, careful planning and a minimum of improvisation – 'quota quickie masters in the day, close ups at night'[75] – the film was brought in on schedule.

The result was a short feature of considerable originality, humour and charm. It is debatable whether Jarman succeeds in fully elucidating Wittgenstein's philosophy, but he certainly manages to visualise a number of the philosopher's key concerns, and to do so with wit. He also succeeds in being most moving when the moment demands it. As Wittgenstein lies dying in his bed, Maynard Keynes quietly delivers a long speech of Eagleton's about 'the young man who dreamed of reducing the world to pure logic' and ended up being 'marooned between earth and ice'. Jarman's quirky Martian appears. 'Hail Chromodynamics, Lord of Quantum,' says the Martian. 'This is Quark, Charm and Strangeness reporting.' In his hand, he holds a prism which reflects light into the lens. The final image Jarman would ever film echoes one of his first, a poignant way of acknowledging and encapsulating what he had been attempting to do throughout his career as a film-maker: flashing coded messages of light at the viewer. As he had written of cinema in *The Last of England*, 'An archaeologist who projects his private world along a beam of light into the arena, till all goes dark at the end of the performance, and we go home. Home is where one should be, as Dorothy said, clicking her ruby slippers, there's no place like it.'[76]

Although aggrieved that the BFI had raised the stakes from television to cinema without sufficiently funding the difference, thereby exploiting everyone's goodwill, Jarman himself seemed pleased with what had been achieved. 'I have made a sophisticated comedy that more accurately reflects my state of mind than all the previous films.'[77]

He still kept his diary and was particularly proud that his handwriting, always beautiful, still looked good 'even though impatience and my blurred sight conspire to ruin it'.[78] He paid a late-night visit to the heath, returning in a cab whose driver made a determined and unwelcome effort to be asked in for a 'cup of coffee'. He went again to Richard Salmon's studio, where, with the continued help of Piers Clemmet, he painted furiously. 'I dip my hands in the paint and then claw the canvas as if I am trying to break out of the limits of my painted language. The canvas is a cage in which I perform, old Monkey as HB calls me.'[79] Despite determining to have nothing further to do with the media unless given master copies of all his interviews and the right to exploit them as he saw fit, he agreed to write a piece for the *Independent* on Robert Mapplethorpe.

Meanwhile, *Wittgenstein* was moving briskly through postproduction. On 2 November, Collins' birthday, there was a screening of the rough cut. Eagleton was present and stunned Jarman by belatedly announcing his absolute abhorrence of the liberties taken with his original script. Although Jarman fought his corner by explaining the exigencies of budget and the collaborative nature of film-making, he found the encounter deeply wounding. It almost made him wish he had never embarked on the film.

It did not, however, distract him from *Blue*, or *Blueprint*, as it was currently called.[80] He told James Mackay that he wanted to make the film as originally conceived: a blue screen totally devoid of images so that nothing would detract from 'the admirable austerity of the void'.[81] He realised that if he merged his chapter on blue from *Chroma* with his diary entries about losing his sight and being treated with Ganciclovir, this, combined with the sounds and music which Simon Turner could produce, would make a haunting soundtrack. He would have a meditation not only on the void, but on his disease. He had long wanted to make on celluloid the sort of statement about AIDS he had been making with paint. Two things had defeated him: the impossibility of visualising an unseen virus and the difficulty of avoiding sentimentality, almost inevitable in any realistic or semi-realistic treatment of the subject. With no image, simply a field of blue, and a complex soundtrack that mingled poetry with an account of losing his sight and coping with the general disintegration of his body, he had found what seemed to him the perfect way of addressing his own concerns while taking his audience on an elegiac journey towards immateriality. What had started as a homage to Yves Klein had, after many years and many incarnations, become a film about its maker.

> In the pandemonium of image
> I present you with the universal Blue
> Blue an open door to soul
> An infinite possibility
> Becoming tangible.[82]

As Jarman was deciding the final form of the film, Mackay was enjoying long overdue success on the monetary front. Armed with £10,000 pledged by the Arts Council to start the ball rolling – and with the text of the new soundtrack under his arm – he capitalised on the fact that *Wittgenstein* had brought Jarman to the attention of Channel 4's education department by ignoring the drama department and instead targeting education and the independent film and video department, of previous help with *The Last of England* and *The Garden*. Both were enthusiastic and committed funds. Takashi Asai and Brian Eno were brought into play. With the budget set at £90,000, just £9,000 was still needed. Infuriatingly, this final amount proved hard to find, until Mackay realised that the film's lack of image enabled him to approach BBC Radio 3, who would be able to broadcast the soundtrack either on its own or in tandem with the film's eventual transmission on television. By December, the entire budget was in place and Jarman (with the help of David Lewis) had readied the script for recording.

During the same period, Jarman was finishing *Chroma* and checking carefully through the unproduced film scripts that Vintage were eventually to publish. He attended a solo exhibition of his work at the Karsten Schubert Gallery in Charlotte Street, where some small landscapes plus a handful of the large paintings from the *Queer* exhibition were put on show. The exhibition attracted none of the coverage showered on him in Manchester, though it did lead to the acquisition by the Arts Council of *Morphine*, the third of Jarman's works to enter their collection.[83] He was also writing an introduction entitled 'This is Not a Film of Ludwig Wittgenstein' for the publication dreamed up by Colin MacCabe to defuse the animosity between Jarman and Eagleton: a single volume containing both scripts in their unadulterated entirety, plus a brief foreword by Tariq Ali, a preface by MacCabe and more lengthy introductions by the two principals. Verbal fireworks might have been expected, though in the event these would come later, in the press. The introductions themselves proved a model of literary *politesse*.

All this was achieved against a rising tide of illness. On 6 November, Jarman was back in hospital with a raging fever; another bout of PCP. 'I've noticed,' he wrote, 'that the diary is sinking under the weight of illness like the raft of Medusa.' This observation sparked another potential project: 'In fact the raft would make a great AIDS film, perhaps I should ask Simon [Watney] to piece it together, it could be like a fifties TV documentary or Huis Clos all at sea. The raft is such an image, I'll ask HB for some paper.'[84] He also asked for a desk and chair to be added to the now utterly minimalistic Phoenix House flat so that he could continue working there when he was discharged from Bart's. A full month would pass before this would happen. When it did, he resembled a wraith. 'Very weak and palsied, my hand shakes so the tea slops off the cup. HB says I've shrunk. I'm on the fourth hole of my belt, usually it's three. I am eating, which is a surprise as I imagined that the pills would have put paid to that, light as a feather the slightest gust could blow me away.'[85] He had lost one and a half stone.

For Christmas and the New Year, while Collins divided his time between Phoenix House and Newcastle, enjoying some much needed rest, Jarman drove to Prospect Cottage with Howard Sooley, Peter Fillingham and Karl Lydon. Despite his extreme fragility, he welcomed this long overdue chance to check on the garden. He had planned a raised bed for vegetables, which Fillingham and Lydon dug and installed. He went walking on the beach. He picked up his paints. He paid a visit to some of the Sisters of Perpetual Indulgence in Margate. He went to London for a check-up. On New Year's Day, Nigel Terry and Alasdair McGaw phoned to wish him well: 'These were my two phone calls to welcome in this New Year, as the strength ebbs, probably my last, it doesn't bring hope or happiness.'[86] Not even a couple of visiting friends or a treasured call from Collins could materially lighten his mood.

In fact he would live to see one more New Year, and through the thirteen months he had left he continued in public to put the bravest and most cheerful of faces on the torment he was suffering. Although he felt his 'inexhaustible thirst for new projects' to be 'drying up', and although he found putting 'pen to paper . . . harder by the day and less of an adventure',[87] on 4 January 1993 he was resolutely back to work, catching up on a 'wasted December'. Channel 4 appeared to be dragging their heels over *Narrow Rooms*, but this was temporarily of little concern.

The famous Géricault painting of the raft on which the survivors of the shipwrecked *Medusa* endured madness, mutiny and cannibalism before reaching land was far more firmly at the forefront of Jarman's mind. Like the playwright Joe Pintauro, he saw the story – how, because of their lowly status, certain survivors were denied access to lifeboats and forced to make do with the raft – as emblematic of the fate of people with AIDS. He was thrilled when Norman Rosenthal and Simon Watney supplied him with rare books on the painter, and embarked with David Lewis on a 'nicely acid'[88] script that took events on the raft and the passion with which Géricault tackled his subject as its starting point before following in the footsteps of *Wittgenstein* and *Pansy* and tipping into pantomime. Before long Tariq Ali had secured a promise of funding from the BBC. Meanwhile, Jarman's enthusiasm for working with Lewis had suggested yet another possibility: a 'red' sequel to *Blue*, 'a scarlet film in choking hellfire, smashing glass, madness, a horror film with HIV as a conscious beast rustling around, hysteric laughter (get Jack Orlando to do this), Borgia Ginz, Beelzebub, legions, PCP is summoned, HELL ON EARTH, red generated from sulphur.'[89] Collins had returned from Newcastle 'looking fit, furry and rested'.[90] The two of them sat down to write a piece for the *Independent on Sunday* entitled 'How We Met'.[91]

There were the unproduced scripts to correct for Century, Lewis to chivvy over the typing up of *Chroma* in order that it too could be corrected. *Blue* was being prepared for the screen and, in the course of a few half-day sessions, Jarman helped oversee Nigel Terry and John Quentin intoning the poems and diary entries that would form the spoken soundtrack. Earlier, Lewis and Marvin Black, who had worked on *The Garden*, had recorded a number of sound effects, some of them in Bart's during Jarman's last hospital stay. Simon Turner now fused voice and sound with music culled from various sources to create the final soundtrack. Once this was mixed, the credits shot and the original filmed loop of an Yves Klein painting replaced with a blue field created in the lab, Jarman's final and most idiosyncratic film was ready for release.

In January, elaborating yet again on what he had frequently said about how hard it was to tackle the subject of AIDS effectively on film, Jarman had written:

No ninety minutes could deal with the eight years HIV takes to get its host. Hollywood can only sentimentalise it, it would all take place in some well-heeled west-coast beach hut, the reality would drive the audience out of the cinema and no one viewpoint could mirror the 10,000 lives lost in San Francisco to date, so we are left with documentaries and diaries like mine and even they cannot tell you of the constant, all-consuming nagging, of the aches and pains. How many times I've stopped to touch my inflamed face even while writing this page, there's nothing grand about it, no opera here, just the daily grind in a minor key. But in spite of that we would wish our lives to be recorded in an oratorio by a Beethoven or Mozart not in the auction sale of Keith Haring tea towels.[92]

Blue is that oratorio. In *Caravaggio*, blue had been poison; now it represented a healing distillation. Jarman had transmuted the pandemonium of images that had been his boon and bane into a vibrant void in which, miraculously, he was more fully present than in almost any of his other films. Warhol-like, he had followed the path of his own experimentation in film-making to its very end; a bitter end, too, but one that avoided any sense of cul de sac. In his own words: 'The monochrome is an alchemy, effective liberation from personality. It articulates silence. It is a fragment of an immense work without limit. The blue of the landscape of liberty.'[93]

As January drew to a close, he celebrated his fifty-first birthday with a day trip to Cambridge for a screening of *Wittgenstein* at the Arts Theatre, where an audience of 'students and the remaining Wittgensteinians'[94] had gathered to pass judgement – and, as it happened, wholeheartedly applaud – Jarman's take on their city's philosopher.

The next day he was travelling to White City to record a *Face to Face* interview with Jeremy Isaacs. 'I am nervous,' he confided in his diary, 'as I expect this is the last time I will appear on TV and I want to convey some of the fun of my life and less of the gloom and doom, the balance I have achieved in *Wittgenstein* much more clearly reflects my situation than *Edward II* or for that case *Caravaggio* . . . I do hope I don't appear as washed out as I feel, thank God there is always the make-up lady between you and the lens.'[95] In the event, the make-up lady was unable to obscure the molluscum that dotted his face, nor could Jarman entirely mask his equally evident nervousness, particularly when Isaacs' gently probing questions hit the subject of anonymous sex on Hampstead Heath. However, that did not prevent him from achieving his goal. 'Fun' might be overstating the case, but he was certainly successful in conveying a sure sense of

the grace and wit with which he was facing his situation. Few who
saw the interview were unmoved by it.

Nervousness under fire was unlike Jarman and short-lived; whenever and wherever possible, insouciance predominated. Peter
Fillingham asked a friend who made pillbox hats to create a set for
Jarman and friends. Jarman gleefully chose appropriate appellations
to be emblazoned upon each one. Collins was 'Somnabulist',
Fillingham 'Postgenderist', Sooley 'Obscurantist'. For himself,
Jarman settled on a description lifted from the late fourteenth-
century poem 'Pearl': 'Controversialist'. It was in this role that he
took part in an alternative Valentine's Day carnival organised by
OutRage! Exotically attired in his Moroccan jellaba, the gold robe
from *Edward II*, Jordan's red apron from *Jubilee* and a gold laurel
wreath, he rode on an open truck from Soho Square to Old
Compton Street, which he then renamed 'Queer Street'.[96]

As *Wittgenstein* began its round of festival screenings, its director
was in line to fly to Berlin and America to promote the film. His
body, however, had other, less palatable plans for its owner. He was
now 'absolutely dependent'[97] on Collins and given to fretting terribly if his companion went away for so much as a single night. He
awoke one morning to a particularly distressing 'collapse' of his stomach. 'The whole of my dinner with Richard shat out as I opened the
door – indescribable mess. I cried as HB cleaned it up, more in fury
than anything else.'[98]

He then developed a new CMV-related lesion which dramatically blurred the sight in his left eye. The trial for the oral form of
Ganciclovir having concluded, he again needed a daily drip. In order
to allow him a degree of mobility and continued visits to Dungeness,
Bart's wheeled him into the operating theatre and inserted a port-a-
cath to enable the drip to be administered away from the hospital.
Part of him hoped he would not survive the operation. Another
part prompted the purchase of a walking stick with which 'to menace
the wandering pedestrians on the Charing Cross Road'.[99] He was
down but not yet out.

With March came the completion of *Blue*, dedicated to 'HB and
all true lovers'. Cheered, Jarman crowed in his diary: 'I think the film
is magnificent.'[100] Next came the official opening of *Wittgenstein* at

the NFT, where it formed part of the seventh London Lesbian and Gay Film Festival, before enjoying a brief run at the ICA. Colin MacCabe's hopes that publication of the BFI edition of the two scripts would put paid to any lingering rancour between Jarman and Eagleton were dashed when, two days prior to the NFT screening, Eagleton chose to make his bruised feelings public. Writing in the *Guardian*, he applauded Jarman's 'bizarrely creative imagination', then made it perfectly clear that in terms of its most important goal, the explication of a philosophy, he counted Jarman's film a failure: 'Jarman, for all his admirable radicalism, has a very English middle-class sensibility, which is light years from the austerity and intellectual passion of his subject.'[101] Although no less a figure than Ray Monk, Wittgenstein's biographer, sprang to the director's defence,[102] thereby threatening to prolong the correspondence, this footnote to the annals of cinematic vitriol was prevented from mush-rooming by the fact that one of the warring parties was more concerned with simply clinging to existence. Sunday 21 March: 'Could not get up. Burning eyes, face. Sad.' Monday 22: 'Should I give up?' Tuesday 23: 'I'm still here . . .'

There followed three weeks of complete disorientation, fever, an inability to eat and the loss of some two stone in weight: 'I couldn't write the diary, something that has never happened with the other illnesses, I felt dizzy, retired for whole days to bed and I burnt, I struggled through sleepless nights to find a cool pillow, my head scratched, my back and arms burnt, a recommended lotion [Quellada] turned my skin to salami. Brown as a berry, people in the street said "Where were you on holiday?" To one persistent one I said "Oh, just in Hell."'[103]

He put the final touches to his will and began planning his funeral. Ironically for someone who so mistrusted traditional family structures, his first will, drawn up in early 1990, benefited his blood relatives ahead of Collins. Jarman's sole 1990 bequest to his partner had been the Phoenix House flat. Prospect Cottage went to Tilda Swinton, the super-8 films and his directorial revenues from *The Last of England* and *The Garden* to James Mackay, the royalties from his books to his nephews and niece. Everything else – money in the bank, paintings and any revenue from the majority of his films –

went to his sister Gaye or, in the event of her death, his nephews and niece. With time, his attitude changed. By mid-1991, he had dropped the legacy to Swinton and decreed that, in the event of his sister's death, his residuary estate should pass to Collins. The iller he became, the more intent he grew on safeguarding Collins' interests. He viewed Collins who, in the short term at least, had effectively sacrificed his own future to Jarman's, as the person most in need of financial support. By March 1993, the will had changed to such an extent that Collins had become its principal beneficiary. The only other bequests still in place were those of the super-8 material to Mackay and the book royalties to his nephews and niece.[104]

A similar skirmish between the forces of tradition and iconoclasm characterised Jarman's funeral plans. In the late eighties, he had talked cheerily about simply wanting to disappear. He imagined his ashes being scattered either on Hampstead Heath or down the loo at Heaven, being put in Prospect Cottage, which would then be torched – or being mixed in black paint, then spread by Christopher Hobbs on a presigned canvas and sold. Another alternative was a 'state funeral' in preparation for which all the boys would be sent to saunas for a suntan 'so they can march the streets of London quite naked, bronzed, and good-looking'.[105] He had spoken too about wanting 'to be buried – the tombstone lark'.[106] He wished this funeral to be suitably solemn: featuring a muffled drum roll and Simon Turner playing his mandola. He planned to wear something 'really smashing' on his deathbed. For the rest, simplicity would be the keynote. He imagined his tombstone in black Purbeck marble, without inscription.

By 1993, his desire for a more or less traditional funeral had entirely won the day. He made comprehensive lists of who should attend. As he envisaged the event, there would be enough mourners to require a sound system 'for those outside'. The service itself would be punctuated by some of the sacred sonnets of John Donne, 'Stormy Weather', 'The Skye Boat Song', a call to arms, 'Abide with Me', a hailing by the Sisters of Perpetual Indulgence and a passage from the works of Siegfried Sassoon. He wrote an address to be delivered when his coffin was carried from the church to the grave. It began: 'To the Archbishop and synod, I have lived my life to the full, I die in Bliss, but a shadow in my sunshine day has haunted me all my days. The homophobia that has grown like a hydra since the 11th century when the Church of Rome was consolidating its power over its provincial bishops and priests. This created the world in which I lived.' It was, he said, high time that 'the Church accept life as it is rather than life as it would like it to be. I was once thinking of becoming a priest but I knew that the vocation would be a lie. I did the better thing and became an artist, an alternative spiritual path. I believe in Christ as exemplar. Love thy neighbour as thyself.' He thanked his friends for their love and help. He asked that no tears be shed 'but tears of joy. I had a life that should be made a reality for many more . . . there is nothing I wanted to do that I have not done . . .' He signed himself: 'Derek of Dungeness'.[107] In order to confirm the note of joy, he suggested a marquee for afterwards and maybe a Jamaican steel band.

He told Collins he thought he should be buried in London, either in Highgate, which was where Mario Dubsky lay, or Earl's Court; somewhere near his old stamping grounds and the more senior of his friends. The service could be held in the church at Bart's. To his surprise, Collins told him that he had been investigating the possibility of a burial in the graveyard at St Clement's, Old Romney, close by the 'spectacular yew' Jarman so loved. Jarman wholeheartedly embraced this suggestion, even buying a book on the yew because, he said, 'I want a vegetable immortality at Old Romney and thought I should get acquainted with my host. Oh silly billy.'[108]

As both a relative newcomer to the marsh and someone who did not attend church, Jarman's right to be buried in his local graveyard was far from assured. It took time for his application to be approved by the Parish Council. When it was, he was told he would have to be buried alone. This he found intolerable. He demanded that Collins be allowed to join him when the time came. An impasse seemed inevitable. If Jarman wanted to be buried locally, it looked as if he would have to settle for the larger 'overflow' cemetery at Lydd or, failing that (and providing it could be arranged), his own back garden. Paul Copson, a recent acquaintance of Jarman's who knew the people concerned, offered to intervene; successfully, too. Permission was eventually granted not only for Jarman to be buried in the old graveyard, but for Collins to join him when the moment came. Meanwhile, by visiting Memorials by Artists in Saxmundham, Norfolk, Jarman set about choosing himself a gravestone, finally settling on one of black slate.[109]

Given the extent of his funeral plans and the ferocity of his most recent illness, it is not surprising that in late March he should write: 'The idea of death is rather entrancing, getting there not that much fun, particularly for a physical toughy like myself. Life now is a little like eating the leftovers from a feast.'[110] What is surprising is that, even at this late stage, his appetite for leftovers appeared relatively undimmed.

He embarked on a final book, an account of the genesis of the garden at Dungeness. Commissioned by Thames and Hudson, who had published his *Caravaggio*, *derek jarman's garden* was to be illustrated by Howard Sooley's photographs, which everyone knew would powerfully complement Jarman's prose. He wrote in longhand, with barely a correction, as if the words had been waiting to spill out of him. The resulting book, with its short but lyrical text and luminous photographs, is testament to what many, even Jarman himself at moments, had come to see as perhaps his greatest achievement. Writing in *Modern Nature*, he had told his gay constituency: 'Before I finish, I intend to celebrate our corner of Paradise, the part of the garden the Lord forgot to mention.'[111] In horticultural terms, this is precisely what he had succeeded in doing.[112]

At the same time he was attacking his final cycle of paintings at South Edwardes Square. Towards the end of his *Queer* series, he had used hospital photographs of his eyes as the basis for a study of his CMV.[113] What he painted now was a further commentary on his disease – large, colourful canvases in which the swirling frenzy of paint has been etched with a series of angry and despairing messages: 'IMPOTENT', 'ARSE INJECTED DEATH SYNDROME', 'ATAXIA (AIDS IS FUN)', 'FUCK ME BLIND', 'SCREAM'. Jarman had said of the expressionistic landscapes he began to paint in 1991 that they were 'landscapes of the mind'. The same description could apply to the final paintings, though here the mind illustrated is in extremis. The paintings evidence none of the calm or stasis of Jarman's middle period, or of the recent *Blue*. Instead, they hark back to his very earliest work, but with an overlay of anger that is truly shocking. They are a cry of pure horror, 'the most awful paintings'[114] their creator could produce.

Because of Jarman's failing eyesight, which had recently turned him colour-blind, and because time was at a premium and the violent emotions he had unleashed too urgent to handle otherwise, the paintings were dashed off at considerable speed and with the help of two assistants: Piers Clemmet to begin with, then Karl Lydon. Peering myopically through his by now pebble glasses and speaking in a reedy whisper whose measured and often humorous tones were in complete contrast to the activity surrounding him, Jarman would perch in the old wingback chair that stood in the centre of the studio and instruct either Clemmet or Lydon in what to do. Tin upon tin of colour would be opened, mixed, then flung at the canvas with such energy that before long, the plastic sheeting covering the floor was squelchy with paint. Then would come the message, often arrived at in consultation with Clemmet or Lydon or whoever happened to be passing through the studio. Using a kitchen knife, Jarman would sometimes inscribe the chosen word or phrase himself. If he was feeling particularly weak, he would delegate the task to his assistant. Although this modus operandi was dictated purely by ill health, yet again it happened to be how Jarman had always preferred to work: communally, fast and in a manner approaching the 'sublime anonymity' of the Middle Ages.

Despite worries about how far his money would carry him, he found that 'each time I escape from death's clutches I have a rush into life, this takes the form of spending more money than I have, so hospital bankrupts me'.[115] In large part, this profligacy took the form of paying as much attention to Prospect Cottage as he did to work. He had new windows installed, the sofa upholstered and the front path cobbled. During an earlier stint in Bart's, he had read John Donne's poem 'The Sunne Rising' and noted how it compensated for 'this shadowy room where the sun never falls and light is provided by six fluorescent tubes glaring behind glass in the ceiling'.[116] To celebrate his admiration for Donne, and for this poem in particular, a group of his friends[117] placed a sculpted fragment of Donne's verse on the south wall of the cottage.

Come May, Jarman was again incarcerated in Bart's, this time – because the AIDS ward was full – in an open and extremely noisy casualty ward. Although occasionally allowed out, his existence was 'like that of a dog on an extendable lead – pulled back if too adventurous'.[118] Medical setbacks continued. At the end of April his port-a-cath had become infected, necessitating its complete removal before a replacement could be fitted. He had lost weight dramatically and was down to 9 stone 8 from 11 stone 6. With the exception of a new-found passion for fruit pastilles, he was experiencing almost constant nausea and had great difficulty in eating. As the title of one of his last paintings demonstrates, he had also been afflicted with ataxia – or, to use Jarman's term, a 'wobble' – caused by either lesions on the brain or damage to the nervous system. Compounded by his failing sight, this wobble made it almost inevitable that whenever Jarman moved, he would fall over or bump into something. Yet his hunger for life and determination to keep working still flickered fitfully.

Trips to the heath were now impossible and he no longer appeared to function sexually, though one of the final infections he picked up in hospital was sexually transmitted and he still took keen delight in sexual reminiscence. 'Peaches came in with a big smile, he had been picked up by a Spanish lad who fucked the arse off him for six hours, he's coming back tonight, three sessions rather than one. It's four years since anyone did that to me, I can't get enough of it. This tale excited us all, sex, thank heavens, can still be enjoyed. He had a great big juicy cock with plenty of precome – did not have an orgasm, he did not want to stop – when he reads this I hope he jerks off.'[119] As well as finishing the book about his garden, making his final adjustments to *Chroma* and overseeing the typing up of his diary, he now started a memoir entitled *Death in Venice*, an impressionistic account in prose and poetry of the advent of AIDS hinged around memories of his various trips to Venice and the sexual escapades each trip triggered or suggested. Like the book on his garden, he intended this project to be illustrated by Sooley's photographs, many of them featuring Jarman himself, all taken in the city where Thomas Mann's ageing composer had so hopelessly but ardently pursued the young Tadzio. Jarman wanted to reclaim and celebrate the act which had made him ill. 'A boy's arse,' he wrote in one of the poems, 'is the hole to heaven.'[120]

On a civic note of a less personal kind, he struck a most public and effective blow for the campaign to save his hospital from redevelopment. It was a campaign which, alongside many others, he had been fighting for some time, usually by means of marches. What he did now was write a letter about the threatened closure to the *Independent*. The paper took the unusual step of publishing it on its front page.

Jarman's impassioned plea that his country's heritage should not be strangled by the 'voracious cashflow snake' ('without our past our future cannot be reflected, the past is our mirror')[121] elicited a strong response. One of the many letters he received in reply put it thus: 'In view of your letter today, I feel that the final nail has been driven home and that I will no longer offer my support to John Major's party. With such clarity, you have echoed the thoughts, I am sure, of millions of Britons.'[122]

On 26 May, Jarman took his final holiday. There had been some talk of realising an old ambition and visiting the pyramids, but this would now have proved too taxing. Instead, travelling with Howard Sooley in the photographer's car, Jarman visited Monet's garden at Giverny before retracing his student steps and paying homage to the Issenheim altarpiece in Colmar. After a night spent in nearby Vernon, he and Sooley arrived early at Giverny and for a short while had the luxury of not having to share the garden with anybody but its gardeners. Jarman, who knew the site only from photographs and the paintings of its owner, many executed when Monet himself had been losing his sight, was entranced. Then the tourists 'started to arrive in horrible bright anoraks which disrupted old Monet's colour schemes'. Horrified by this sudden eruption of 'shrieking orange green and purple', Jarman decided the powers-that-be 'should introduce a dress code'. 'I wonder,' he mused, 'if I'm the only one to notice this?'[123]

On his return to Dungeness, the traveller felt very weak: 'a washed out rag of my former self'.[124] Nevertheless, in London the following weekend he appeared with Collins in *The Clearing*, a student film by Alexis Bisticas of the RCA. Set and shot entirely on Hampstead

Heath, the film shadows an unseen person searching the heath for the source of some saxophone music heard in the distance. At the end of the film's handful of sequences, we discover that the unseen person is Jarman and that the object of his search, a young man playing the saxophone in a clearing, is Collins.

A week later, Jarman flew with Collins, his sister Gaye and Sooley to Venice, where, as part of the city's Biennale, *Blue* received its world première. Immediately prior to his departure, Jarman had been confined to bed for a few days. At Heathrow he required the use of a wheelchair. Yet that evening in Venice, dressed in a white linen suit specially made for him by Nick Knightly (who, with his boyfriend Julian Cole, was very much part of Jarman's circle), he rallied sufficiently to relish every moment of the film's reception. Not in the least put out that the auditorium was far from full (according to one report, 'the glitterati were at Peggy Guggenheim's, ogling Liz Taylor as she presided over a gala dinner and auction – the fundraising 'Art against AIDS'),[125] Jarman responded to the 'overwhelming ovation'[126] of those in attendance. He 'felt like Maria Callas taking a bow at the end of an aria'.[127] With Sooley in constant attendance, taking photographs for the proposed *Death in Venice*, Jarman and party then visited Torcello and the cemetery, attended the opening of the Biennale and treated themselves to a leisurely meal in Montin's under its canopy of vines.

Back home, the jet-setting director again paid the price for being too active. He was still putting the final touches to *Chroma*, he performed a marriage ceremony at Dungeness for two lesbian friends of David Peshek, another friend, and met the pop group Suede to discuss working with them on a fund-raising concert for the Red Hot Aids Charitable Trust. But this was about the extent of his reach. There were days when a 'sleeping sickness' nailed him to his chair and he was 'incapable of doing anything but eat cherries which HB brings me'.[128] Nights passed in an equal blur as he lay itching in bed, his wasted frame wrapped in special pads against the incontinence that now had a dual cause: the ataxia as well as his perennially upset stomach.

This being the state to which his disease had reduced him, it could not have come as too much of a surprise or disappointment to him to learn that Channel 4 were withdrawing from *Narrow Rooms*. Surprise and disgust do, however, seem to have affected everyone else. In May, Christine Vachon and Steve Clark-Hall had taken the project to Cannes, started to establish co-production possibilities and were in the process of approaching or considering a range of actors, including Debbie Reynolds, Sissy Spacek and Matt Dillon. Then came Channel 4's bombshell: they were dropping the film because, they said, Collins was neither well enough known nor experienced enough to carry the role of the renderer. Collins offered to step aside, but Jarman refused to compromise. If Collins could not be in the film, then Jarman did not want to make it.

To have Channel 4 pull the plug in such an unexpected and high-handed fashion was obviously difficult to deal with; to have them do so for the reason given was even harder to swallow, particularly for Jarman. It is not surprising that feelings ran high. But once the dust had settled – and after a few attempts to find alternative finance, it settled very quickly – it was possible to see that perhaps the confrontation over Collins' suitability had worked to everyone's advantage. It allowed escape from a project which, with the best will in the world, its director could never have hoped to complete.

On 5 April, at a ceremony he had been to ill to attend in person, Jarman had been awarded an honorary doctorate by the newly constituted Middlesex University. On 9 July, in the flesh this time, he was made a senior fellow of the RCA. Dressed in a multicoloured robe capped by a large velvet hat with gold tassels, which he was required to doff to the applauding audience after being publicly eulogised, he found the occasion quintessentially 'English and dotty'.[129]

Days later,[130] he was present at the Grand Theatre in Clapham for the Suede concert given in support of the Red Hot Aids Charitable Trust. It was his task to introduce the evening. Perched in a box with Neil Tennant and Jon Savage, his scarecrow hair at distinct odds with the smartness of his white tie and black jacket, he breathlessly addressed the packed house about the need for AIDS funding and the potentially grave problem caused by twenty-one being the age of consent for homosexuals. Seemingly locked inside himself by disease, he was nevertheless in good spirits and his short speech brought cheers from the audience. Suede and their guests,

Chrissie Hynde and Siouxsie Sioux, took to the stage before a gigantic screen on which was projected an ad-hoc medley of Jarman's super-8 footage.

For some days, Collins had suspected that Jarman might be suffering another bout of pneumonia and had been urging a check-up. Jarman refused to go anywhere near a doctor. He knew that if he did, he was likely to be forbidden the next item on his itinerary – a trip to Rome for something of a Jarman junket. Prior to a fortnight in September at the new Filmmuseum in Potsdam, the *Queer* exhibition was being shown in the cool, white rooms of Rome's Palazzo delle Esposizione. In addition, there was to be a private screening of *Blue*, a series of Blue concerts and a comprehensive retrospective of Jarman's films. Not one of these events did Jarman intend to miss, though, by ignoring Collins' advice, all he ensured was his own collapse. On his first night in Rome, he was too ill to emerge from his hotel room. Instead, he stayed in bed watching television: *The Wizard of Oz*, as it happens, the very film which, in that very city, had ignited his love of cinema. He was later able to visit the exhibition, to be interviewed, to treat himself to Italian ice-cream, to eat at his favourite restaurant, the Tavolo Calda, and to visit the gardens at Tivoli. But he was utterly unable to attend either the screening of *Blue* or any of the concerts, for by then he had become delirious and had virtually sunk into a coma. He was bundled into a British Council car, driven at speed to the airport and hurried on to a plane, where he promptly shat himself. On the flight out, his spiky hair and thick glasses, his old tweed jacket and workman's overalls had raised a few eyebrows. Now an indescribable smell added spice to his appearance. The eyebrows rose even higher. The saving grace for the tramp-like cause of this panic and opprobrium was that delirium equalled oblivion. Only when safely back at Bart's did he begin to regain awareness of his surroundings.

Pneumonia was duly diagnosed and Jarman confined to bed on Andrewes Ward for the rest of the month. In August, he put in a brief and somewhat pitiful appearance at the Edinburgh Film Festival for a screening of *Blue*. The happy fact that the film was given a standing ovation and won the Michael Powell award for best British film at the festival, or the unhappy one that on Jarman's return to

London, the Camden Parkway, where his film was due to have opened, was suddenly closed, thereby depriving *Blue* of its antici- pated London release, was more than the film's director now had the energy to care about. 'One less screening to go to,'[131] was how he recorded the Parkway disappointment in his diary.

In the course of September – much of it spent in Bart's – he had two miraculously successful eye operations that temporarily halted the encroaching blindness. Whenever discharged from hospital, he ignored his distressed stomach and 'wobble' to link arms with his 'guide dog' and make his way from Phoenix House to Poons, the small Chinese restaurant in Lisle Street, where he frequently lunched. As if to celebrate this respite, *Blue* was given a last-minute release in central London before its simulcast on Channel 4 and Radio 3.[132] Radio listeners were invited to write in for a blue post- card at which to stare for the length of the broadcast, while on television the film was shown without pause for commercials, a breakthrough as far as Jarman was concerned. Of the 252 calls taken by the Channel 4 duty office after the screening, the majority expressed horror and disappointment. Ten queried problems with transmission and four declared a preference for red. Jarman's old sparring partner the *Sun* was predictably, punningly dismissive: 'It may be Blue, but it's no movie.'[133] Elsewhere, the film met with a generally positive reaction, especially from those who felt that by dis- pensing with the image, Jarman had made what amounted to a different film for each and every member of his audience; no mean feat by anyone's standards.[134]

A week after the transmission of *Blue*, Jarman heard from Potsdam that he had been awarded the first Rainer-Werner Fassbinder prize for his 'extraordinary artistic ouevre'.[135] James Mackay travelled to Berlin to collect the prize on his behalf. Paying £13,000, it 'truly put paid to financial problems' and even allowed its recipient to splash out on a treat for the staff at Bart's: he spent £500 buying them tick- ets for *Carousel*.[136] Meanwhile, the Sisters of Perpetual Indulgence were planning a celebration for the second anniversary of Jarman's canonisation. They hired a room above a London pub where, with 'hymns and hopes', they held a 'blue mass' and sang their saint's praises. It was, said the saint, 'a great evening'.[137]

He chose not to travel to Penzance, where the Newlyn Art Gallery was mounting *Dead Sexy*, a month-long exhibition of twenty-nine of his works, including some from the *Queer* series, some recent landscapes and a handful of pieces dating back to the eighties. He was conserving his energies for New York, to which city, surprisingly, he was now adjudged sufficiently fit to fly for an entire week in order to attend a screening of *Blue* as part of the New York Film Festival. As had been the case at Edinburgh, he was not well enough to do much publicity, though he did manage to mount the stage after the screening and answer questions for almost an hour. He also attended a brunch given in his honour by Jeff Hill, the film's publicist, where, asked by the photographer Bruce Weber how he and Collins had met, he launched with such intensity into the story of how the 1986 Tyneside Lesbian and Gay Film Festival had been illuminated for him by Collins' beauty and glamour that he soon had the entire room spellbound.

New York triggered other, equally happy memories and provided the chance to revisit the scenes of some of them. Mark McCormick's friend Leland Wheeler arranged a trip to the Cloisters where, despite being unable to see the flowers properly, Jarman could still identify the herbs by smell. He ate with surprising heartiness at his beloved diners and enjoyed a slap-up lunch at the oyster bar in Grand Central Station.

Back in London, his implacable and exhausting determination to continue functioning against all the odds led him to embark on his very last paintings at South Edwardes Square.[138] He was asked by the Red Hot organisation if he would make a short film to illustrate Patti Smith's 'Little Emerald Bird', the song she had written as a tribute to Robert Mapplethorpe and sung on one of the organisation's albums. A television and video version of the album was being planned, for which visuals were needed. Jarman listened to the track and readily agreed to supply them, though, since he was by now unable to attempt anything of this nature on his own, it was Collins who put together some of Jarman's old super-8 footage for the occasion.

Jarman's involvement with *Glitterbug*, his final film, was equally peripheral; so much so, in fact, that the film is more truly James

Mackay's than his. For some time, Mackay had been circulating the idea of assembling a selection of Jarman's super-8 footage into a continuous whole that would run for between thirty and forty-five minutes.[139] As early as March 1992, he had put the idea to David Curtis at the Arts Council and, in the course of 1993, had approached Alan Yentob at the BBC, who, because at that stage they were talking to Jarman about *The Raft of Medusa*, had declined it. Mackay approached Channel 4 and ZDF before returning to the BBC, this time in the shape of *Arena*, who agreed to fund the project.[140] Jarman would not live to see the film finished, but he did spend a little time helping to log his footage. He provided a whispered, breathless commentary, not used in the final film, and briefly attended a couple of recording sessions for the music Brian Eno provided for the film's eventual soundtrack.

Jarman celebrated Guy Fawkes' Night at Dungeness and saw the nearby Southlands Community Comprehensive School hold an exhibition of eighteen of his smaller paintings, six of which were displayed separately in the governors' room, where they could only be viewed by the school's pupils with parental permission. That summer, Norman Rosenthal had selected *Toxo* to hang in the Royal Academy's annual show at the invitation of the president and council. Simultaneously, Richard Salmon was quietly but persistently urging the director of the Tate, Nicholas Serota, to acquire a Jarman canvas. Serota had not yielded to Salmon's entreaties, but when – in memory of his brother, Adrian, who had died from AIDS – Nicholas Ward-Jackson offered to arrange for the Weltkunst Foundation to present the Tate with a Jarman painting that would heighten AIDS awareness, Serota instantly agreed. The painting was *Ataxia (Aids is Fun)*. To celebrate its acquisition, Serota hosted a lunch for Jarman in the Tate boardroom. The painting was given pride of place on the wall. Among the treasured friends gathered round the table was the artist Richard Hamilton, who took a number of polaroids that would later form the basis of a posthumous photographic portrait of the guest of honour. Jarman once told Peter Fillingham: 'I've never been a great painter, but I like to think I've made a bit of a contribution.' He also liked to think his contribution had been noticed. Now it had, and by one of the country's more prestigious galleries – the very gallery, indeed, whose buyer had angered Jarman at his Edward Totah exhibition in 1982 by asking crushingly, 'Who is Derek Jarman?'

Monuments to Jarman's existence were springing up in a number of places. In August, Richard Salmon's studio had provided the setting for *Here We Are John*, a filmed interview with John Cartwright of the Arts Council. A few weeks later, Jarman was introduced by Tania Wade to the artist Michael Clark, another of the regulars at Maison Bertaux, a meeting which would result in a portrait currently hanging in the National Portrait Gallery.[141] Last but not least came Takashi Asai, who had finally completed *Freeze Frame*, his bibliographic retrospective of Jarman's entire cinematic output. Asai flew in from Tokyo to deliver a copy personally to its 'director', who was, sadly, unable to focus with any clarity on the results of his Japanese distributor's labours.

At the beginning of December, Jarman had felt well enough to travel to Brussels for the world première of a one-man stage version of *Modern Nature* being mounted there by a company called De Parade. With the arrival of Asai and Christmas, that least favourite moment in the Jarman calendar, it became clear the end was not far away. Now effectively blind, Jarman was able to walk only with help and had taken to a wheelchair. Extreme forgetfulness signalled the onset of dementia. He still insisted, however, on taking part in Channel 4's *Camp Christmas*, an attempt to provide gay viewers with a variety show of their own. His depleted presence in a studio armchair accepting a sandwich from Lily Savage could hardly have lifted the spirits of those watching, but at least he had the satisfaction of knowing that his *bête noire*, the Stonewall group, were being forced to share the limelight with this most stubborn of thorns in their self-satisfied flesh. Christmas and New Year were spent at Dungeness, in the company of the usual gang. The heating was turned up high and a series of lavish breakfasts prepared in the hope that Jarman would be tempted into starting the day with a proper meal inside him. Further sustenance came in the form of as much laughter and talk as the assembled friends were capable of generating.

In January, he was barely able to move from his bed or the wing-backed chair in which he had sat to 'direct' his final paintings, now relocated by Richard Salmon to Phoenix House. He seriously considered a request from Penguin to write a book for children on AIDS and took delivery of a finished copy of *Chroma*, which, of course, he was unable to see. Speaking in the most exhausted of whispers, he gave a radio interview by telephone to mark the book's publication. Calling his health a 'low-level disaster', he confessed that 'the idea of dying is actually at this stage quite comforting, I have to say'. By Saturday 29 January, he had been readmitted to hospital, though he still insisted on being driven to Dungeness for the birthday celebration he had been planning since Christmas and the New Year.

Aware that this would be Jarman's last birthday, as many of his friends as the cottage would hold gathered for the occasion. Jarman sat in state in a chair in the 'west wing'. Fellow Dungeness resident Derek Ball cooked a fish gumbo. A large bonfire was built and, as it was lit, fireworks provided by Collins were ignited. Even though the lights inside the cottage had been doused so that the spectacle could be better admired against the backdrop of the glittering power station, the fifty-two-year-old guest of honour was unable to see a thing. Tilda Swinton knelt by his chair to describe the scene, but eventually he turned his head away and quietly asked to be left alone. After the room had emptied, he was carried to the car and returned to Bart's.

In a spidery, uncertain hand, he made his final diary entry:

Birthday.
Fireworks.
HB true love.

He had under three weeks to live and would not re-emerge from hospital. Like the mute Jerusaleme in *Caravaggio*, Collins was in constant attendance, spending his nights on the floor alongside the patient's bed. Almost every afternoon, Gaye would arrive to sit with him, listening to music on the radio or to read to him from *Chroma*. Friends who could not visit regularly phoned for news of his condition, announced by the newspapers as serious.

His doctors agreed that they would alter the balance of his drugs to see if the horrific itching could be alleviated, but Jarman now refused further medication. Apart from a saline drip and morphine, he dispensed with the cocktail of drugs which, for over three years, had helped to keep him alive. This had the paradoxical effect of bringing about a temporary improvement in his condition. Then, on 3 February, he suffered a violent seizure. Thereafter, the slightest touch, even a loud noise, more and more frequently caused his entire body to go into protracted spasm. With the nurses predicting every night as his last, he began drifting in and out of consciousness. He had long experienced difficulty eating, sorely trying Collins' patience and ingenuity with his culinary demands: blueberries one moment, a diet of rosti from Marks and Spencer the next. A matter of days before his death, he announced a desire for cheese. Collins hastily dismantled a cheese sandwich from a café to fulfil this unexpected request. The next day, Collins asked him if there was anything else he would like.

'No,' he replied.

'Why, aren't you hungry today?'

'I'm starving myself to death.'

In desperation, Collins asked if there was nothing that would tempt him to eat.

'I want the world to be full of fluffy little ducks,' was his response.[142] He never spoke again.

On Saturday 19 February, at 11 pm, after a series of wracking spasms worthy of the very worst of Umberto Tirelli's prediction and with Collins, Sooley and Lydon in attendance, Jarman's stubborn body was still at last. Yet even then, after Collins had asked the doctor whether Jarman would move again and had been told he would not, the body gave one final, defiant convulsion.[143]

For some time, it had seemed to Collins as if the man he knew and loved, a man of intense physicality and sharp wit, was simply not present in the pitiful form that lay on the hospital bed. He nevertheless asked to be allowed to wash and lay out the corpse. Then, following Jarman's own instructions, he dressed the dead man in the gold robe from *Edward II*. In further accordance with Jarman's wishes, Sooley stepped forward to take photographs.[144]

Still in its gold robe, the body was kept in cold storage at the hospital while Collins and Jarman's sister did their level best to follow the rest of Jarman's instructions. They chose a suitably simple coffin, finalised arrangements for the burial and planned the exact order of the funeral service. Everything proved problematic, especially their attempt to honour Jarman's wish that the coffin remain open until it was taken into the church. For fear of AIDS-related infection, the undertakers were adamant that it be sealed, and it was only with support from the hospital that Collins was able to convince them that the body did not pose a threat. On the morning of the funeral, the coffin was delivered unsealed to Prospect Cottage and placed in the new extension. Before setting off on its final journey to St Nicholas in New Romney, and then to the grave being dug under the shadow of the old yew tree in the churchyard of St Clement at Old Romney, its lid was removed so that various treasures could be placed inside it to ensure Jarman's comfort in the afterlife. These included the cap proclaiming its wearer a 'Controversialist', the pen without which Jarman would never leave the house, his silver razor, his spectacles, his wristwatch, a comb, a bottle of poppers, a lapis lazuli necklace he had bought when making *Blue*, a fresh fig and the jingling toy frog that, until recently, Collins had attached to Jarman's person so that he could hear him as he moved about the house.

All that might have been added was a benediction of Jarman's own from the closing section of *Blue*:

> *Our name will be forgotten*
> *In time*
> *No one will remember our work*
> *Our life will pass like the traces of a cloud*
> *And be scattered like*
> *Mist that is chased by the*
> *Rays of the sun*
> *For our time is the passing of a shadow*
> *And our lives will run like*
> *Sparks through the stubble*

> *I place a delphinium, Blue, upon your grave.*

Notes

Abbreviations

AYOR	*At Your Own Risk*
C	*Chroma*
DJC	*Derek Jarman's Caravaggio*
djg	*derek jarman's garden*
DL	*Dancing Ledge*
DV	*Death in Venice* (unpublished fragment in Jarman's papers)
FFM	*A Finger in the Fishes Mouth*
JP	The papers of Derek Jarman*
JR	The papers of Dom Sylvester Houédard in the John Rylands Library, Manchester
KP	*Kicking the Pricks* (paperback edition of *The Last of England*)
LP	The papers of Lance Jarman
MI	Transcript of filmed interview of Derek Jarman by Colin MacCabe
MN	*Modern Nature*
SF	Slade Files
SISM	*Smiling in Slow Motion***
UA	*Up in the Air*
WR	*War Requiem* (as published by Faber & Faber)

*Jarman's papers, which at the time of writing are uncatalogued, include journals, appointment diaries, letters, interviews (both transcribed and on tape), newspaper cuttings and reviews, scripts and related material, other writings, notebooks and photographs. They are currently held either by the BFI or the Jarman Estate. On occasion I have specified to what within the papers I am referring (a certain notebook, say, or a journal), but only where this has seemed essential or easy to do. Otherwise, because the papers are due to be moved and catalogued, I have simply indicated the source as 'JP': any more precise indication might no longer be valid by the time of publication. I may on occasion have attributed a quote to 'JP' when it appears in identical or similar form in Jarman's published writings. I have also (though not often, and only where absolutely necessary) altered the spelling and punctuation in some of Jarman's original writings for the sake of clarity. As a deft mythologiser of his own life, and as someone supremely careless of factual accuracy, Jarman's many accounts of his personal and family history, whether published or not, are often inaccurate or contradictory. I have tried to verify all the important facts as they appear in the body of the text (or, where this has proved impossible, to avoid including questionable information) and have not attempted to point out where these facts conflict with Jarman's own accounts unless it has seemed particularly pertinent to do so.
** At the time of writing, this diary was not published. I worked from the unedited typescript, typed by Keith Collins from Jarman's handwritten original, which is likely to differ from the published version. I have indicated entries by date, not by page number.

The principal sources for the book are: Jarman's own papers, a handful of subsidiary archives, a great many interviews, various newspaper and magazine articles. For a complete list of the people interviewed or who have contributed in some way to the book, see the Acknowledgements. I have credited any and all direct quotations taken from these interviews, but for the rest, because this account is an amalgamation of all that I was told and read, I have not cited specific interviewees anecdote by anecdote. When quoting from newspaper and magazine articles, I have indicated only the author (unless unknown) and the date rather than the page number or title of the article.

In the editing of the book, a number of cuts were made. In due course, it is my intention to lodge a copy of the unedited typescript with Jarman's papers so that students of his work can have access to additional information which, while unlikely to interest the general reader, may well be of value to the scholar.

Prologue

1 23.2.94.
2 April–May 1994.
3 18.3.94, letter from Alex Russell.
4 The *Evening Standard*, 16.5.96.
5 *Square Peg*, No. 4, 1984.

1: Family Mythology

1 Jarman is a common name in the West Country. At the time of the Black Death, weavers from Flanders fled to the West Country, where they were known as the Germans. Jarman believed the family were descended from the Huguenots, the Breton or Celtic 'German' becoming 'Jermain', then 'Jerman', then 'Jarman'. He also liked to maintain that the Breton saint St Germain de Prés was therefore the entirely suitable family saint.
2 LP for this and all letters.
3 Thereafter he was known mainly as Mike, though since there were those who continued to call him Lance, I have opted to do the same.
4 Letter dated 4.11.32.
5 DL, p. 47.
6 The job for Hartnell was the only time Betts was ever able to put her artistic talents to any professional use; otherwise, like those of so many women of her generation, they were at the disposal of her husband. This is perhaps why this potentially unconventional woman ended up becoming so suburban. By marrying, she gave up what she liked to do, turning it into a hobby instead of a career. Her husband was her career.
7 MN, p. 292.
8 KP, p. 19.

2: Beautiful Flowers and How to Grow Them

1 *Beautiful Flowers and How to Grow Them*, p. 1.
2 MN, p. 7.
3 Ibid., p. 11.
4 Ibid., p. 11. Elsewhere Davide is the grandson of the old lady in the gate house.
5 JP.
6 DL, p. 19. Lance called the priests 'Grubbies' and, when he had an audience with the Pope, refused to kiss the papal ring, shaking the papal hand instead – a story Jarman delighted in telling because of the streak of rebelliousness it indicated in a father who was otherwise so conservative.
7 Ibid.

8 Notebook dated August 1974, JP. Moselle had a cupboard full of ivory fans, so 'the cupboard with the white fans' could be a reference to those. When making *The Tempest*, Jarman at one point asked his designer, Yolanda Sonnabend, to recreate the fans from Ciano's attic.
9 DL, p. 19.
10 The name is given as Zaganovitch in KP, p. 40.
11 Jarman would later assert that at four his 'painting was as coherent as my conversation' (KP, p. 40). The only record we have of this is the Christmas card he scribbled for his parents in 1946 – hardly an old master.
12 DL, p. 40
13 Ibid., p. 40.

3: Buried Feelings

1 MN, p. 15.
2 Ibid.
3 JP. In DL, p. 49, Jarman writes: 'my first "conscious" painting was copied from the top of a biscuit tin, a watercolour of swans flying at sunset by Peter Scott.' MN, pp. 27–8, contains a further account of Abingdon and 'Jonno, the delinquent "ton-up" boy, who rode his bike round the camp, with me on the back clutching his pubic hairs for dear life through his nonexistent pockets – a game known as "pocket billiards".' See also AYOR, p. 27.
4 Lance was posted to Kidlington in 1949. The family moved first into rented accommodation in Long Hanborough, then into Kidlington itself, to another cheerless RAF house.
5 MN, p. 22.
6 JP. As with much of what Jarman wrote, there is an element of embroidery here. Although one should not underestimate the effect of the war, nor of Lance's determination to blend into middle-class English society, he had always been a hard man; his character did not transform overnight. And the children's mother was of course already English and middle-class, so neither of the children exactly needed turning into 'middle class English product'. It is also possible Jarman makes more of his father's 'creative work' than is strictly justified. Elsewhere, for instance, he talks of his father's friendship with Vivien Leigh and Syrie Maugham, for whom he supposedly made a pair of art deco candlesticks. Yet there is no record of a friendship with Syrie Maugham, and the

candlesticks are most probably the ones Lance designed at the School of Technical Training at Manston in Kent. If there is a Vivien Leigh connection, it is Uncle Teddy's: he played with Vivien Leigh in India as a child.

7 DL, p. 134.
8 Ibid.
9 Letter from Jarman to Paul Copson.
10 DL, p. 134.

4: School House and Manor House
1 Except for the duration of the Second World War, when the school moved to Underley Hall in Westmorland.
2 MN, p. 143.
3 Ibid., p. 39.
4 JP.
5 MN, p. 34.
6 JP.
7 MN, p. 34. See also DL, p. 49 for a short description of this first sketch book.
8 C, p. 17. The quote continues: 'Perhaps he lived in one of the black and white timber houses which were also illustrated in the book, and from which I made countless drawings . . . I think these drawings reflected my inner turmoil, the battle that had raged throughout my childhood, the bombers and air raid sirens, while down below was a threatened home.'
9 MN, p. 39.
10 Ibid., p. 42.
11 The incident shows the strength of Jarman's need to come first, to have his contribution acknowledged. He did, however, tend to keep his competitiveness hidden, either behind his charm, or – in this case – by writing it out. In his account of Hordle in DL, although he writes of his acute disappointment at not winning the prize, he does not go on to tell the story of the salt. As he said to James Mackay after the book's publication, 'There's enough salt in it already.'
12 DL, p. 49.
13 MN, p. 23.
14 DL, p. 49.
15 *The Founding of Hordle House*, p. 23.
16 An adaptation of the hair-raising morality tales contained in *Struwwelpeter*.
17 JP.
18 DL, p. 49.
19 JP.
20 KP, pp. 19–21.
21 MN, p. 50, where Gavin becomes Johnny.
22 AYOR, p. 20. On a tape among his

papers, Jarman also maintains he was masturbating daily at the age of nine, producing semen, and was caught doing this by the matron.
23 C, p. 92.
24 WR, p. 9.
25 JP.
26 DL, p. 44.
27 MN, p. 33.

5: Pakistan
1 DL, p. 46.
2 DL, pp. 46–7. To anyone who has seen Jarman's super-8 films, this image will seem familiar.
3 MN, p. 66.
4 DL, pp. 47–8.
5 AYOR, p. 24.
6 Ibid., p. 25.
7 DL, p. 50.
8 MN, p. 38.
9 MN, p. 292.
10 Or so Jarman always maintained. The bag is not obviously present in any of his films.
11 JP.
12 MN, p. 68.
13 KP, p. 239.
14 DL, p. 48.
15 JP.

6: A Subtle Terror Rules
1 LP.
2 *The Buildings of England: Dorset*, p. 126.
3 MN, p. 57.
4 Ibid., p. 143.
5 Or so Jarman maintained. There is no record of this test.
6 DL, p. 51.
7 Ibid., pp. 50–1.
8 JP.
9 MN, p. 143.
10 KP, p. 115.
11 Ibid., p. 125.
12 'Lay Down Your Arms' as sung by Anne Shelton.
13 JP. Later, Jarman would allow that there might have been some marginal sexual activity: 'I remember putting my hands down a boy's trouser pockets and touching him up, but that's all. I might have surreptitiously brought him to orgasm but I can't remember . . . I had sexual fantasies about some of the boys.' (AYOR, p. 35.)
14 MN, p. 63.
15 AYOR, p. 28.

16 MN, pp. 63–4. Jarman later told Colin
MacCabe that Dr Matthews reminded him of
the Wizard of Oz.

17 It has proved impossible to establish the
precise details of what took place, but there
can be no doubt that something along these
lines occurred. Jarman later told Ron Wright
that he had been 'raped'.

7: Every Man is a Special Kind of Artist

1 DL, p. 51.

2 MN, p. 61.

3 Maud Smith, the house matron.

4 JP.

5 AYOR, p. 35.

6 JP.

7 Jarman was given further encouragement
as a painter by Maud Smith, who allowed him
to paint in the sanitarium and who hung one
of his early works in pride of place above her
mantelpiece.

8 Fire runs like a seam through most of
Jarman's films, also his paintings. Now
regenerative, now destructive, the flames twist
and turn for the camera, or under the brush,
in an endlessly transformative dance. Perhaps
it was here, at Canford, late at night in the
far-flung shack, with Bach or Stravinsky on
the gramophone and only the other members
of the firing party for company, that this
intense fascination with combustion began.

9 DL, p. 53.

10 Held either in Poole or Bournemouth,
venue unknown. The date was 1959 or 1960.

11 To the parents of Dugald Campbell.
They bought *The Washerwomen*. Later the
family also acquired a still life.

12 DL, p. 53.

13 JP.

14 DL, p. 219.

15 JP.

16 Easter 1959.

17 Although he was beginning to grow out
of 'Mr Scott's pots and pans' (JP), Jarman had
not yet found a style of his own. Some would
say he never entirely did. He was, however,
narrowing the field. Despite continuing
experimentation – sticking newsprint on to a
series of yellow and brown paintings, or
coming up with a line of priests in the boldest
and brightest of reds – what he now
concentrated on were abstract landscapes.
Ever since his holidays there as a child, Kilve
had made a great impression on him, both in
itself and for its literary associations. He loved
the look and texture of the Quantocks, and

the fact that it was there that Dorothy
Wordsworth had written her journals, her
brother William much of his poetry, and
Coleridge 'Kubla Khan'. He revisited Kilve
whenever he could, making charcoal drawings
that formed the basis of many of his
landscapes.

18 JP.

19 The article appeared in the *Daily Express*,
19.5.56. The quote is taken from *Dance till the
Stars Come Down*, p. 216.

20 SF.

21 Ibid.

22 The set received better notices than its
designer's performance. The critic in *The
Canfordian* felt that what was otherwise 'a
good character study' was, on the first night at
least, marred by 'rather nervous mannerisms
and a tendency to overact'.

23 *The Canfordian*.

24 The year before Jarman had also attained
an A-level in geography.

25 MN, p. 23.

8: Metroland Student

1 14.2.63.

2 The door Jarman carved with quotes from
Chaucer for Robin Noscoe is a good example.
The door hangs in Noscoe's house.

3 Letter written on the occasion of Jarman's
designs for *Jazz Calendar* (JP). Jarman's
'perceptions' – his very idiosyncratic reaction
to the world around him – were as significant
as the legacy of any studies. The eleven-year-
old who was affected by the imperial
splendour on display at Nehru's marchpast
would always be as repelled as he was
captivated by what he learned and saw of his
country's history. As already noted, if there is
a single period to which he was drawn, it was
the Elizabethan age, an age of wealth and
stability, of philosophy and literature, but
equally of piracy, greed and the first secret
service. And of considerable sexual
ambiguity. An age to be both admired and
abhorred. It is a dichotomy that finds an echo
in Jarman's personal life. A great flouter of
authority and lover of anarchy, who could
and did pour withering scorn on the
establishment, he was also a man who
nurtured his own links with that
establishment and always seemed at home
even in the most elevated of company; a man
who could jeer at knighthoods and still
confess that one of his favourite images was
of the second Queen Elizabeth in her

coronation coach. He was the most conservative of iconoclasts.

4 DL, pp. 69–70.
5 MN, p. 194.
6 Ibid., p. 206.
7 *The Advertiser and Gazette*, 20.10.60.
8 One was a street scene, doubtless *We Wait*. The other was a slightly abstract still life.
9 In later accounts of the exhibition, Jarman airbrushes David Kunzle out of the picture. In DL, for instance, under the proud heading 'A First Newsclip', he styles himself as sole winner of the amateur prize.
10 19.5.61. There appear to have been some sales as a result of the exhibition.
11 MN, p. 192.
12 Ibid., p. 190.
13 'The Linear Quality of English Art', Easter term 1962.
14 Lent term 1963.
15 DL, p. 55.
16 KP, p. 22. See also AYOR, p. 41.
17 DL, p. 58.

9: If You're Anxious for to Shine
1 MN, p. 192.
2 Ibid., p. 265.
3 Ibid., p. 196.
4 JP. With very few modifications, this was a credo Jarman would carry to the grave.
5. MN, p. 197.
6 Ibid., p. 192.
7 Ibid., p. 197.
8 Ibid., p. 192.
9 Ibid., p. 196.
10 Jarman was at a dinner dance for Caroline Green's twenty-first birthday at the Mayfair Hotel.
11 MN, p. 196.
12 MN, p. 265.
13 It is possible that Lance also paid Jarman's rent. Father was to support son until he was in his mid-twenties.
14 SF.
15 31.1.63.
16 By 1963 the exhibition was sponsored by the *Evening Standard*. It is possible Jarman had also entered a work the year before, though I have not been able to find any record of this. He would certainly enter more work after starting at the Slade.
17 KP, p. 23. See also AYOR, p. 43.
18 DL, p. 60.
19 Ibid.
20 MN, p. 197.
21 Ibid.

22 These lyrics can be heard in the background of *Wittgenstein*, Jarman's penultimate film.

10: Meeting Mr Wright
1 While a student, Jarman did a number of odd jobs. He worked in a betting shop in Ashford, chalking odds on the board; for the Minnesota Mining Company; as a gardener in Northwood; with Michael Ginsborg at 3M, the adhesive tape company, where the two of them had to catalogue the company's stationery; and, thanks to the fact that John and Ann Colligan's father worked there, at the RNIB, the charity for the blind. At the RNIB Jarman sorted the mail that flooded in as a result of the charity's Christmas appeal. The job was overseen by Miss Punch, who helped open the eyes of her still innocent underling: 'dear Miss Punch, seventy years old, who used to arrive each morning on her Harley Davidson . . . was the first out dyke I ever met . . . She looked like Edith Piaf, a sparrow, and wore a cock-eyed beret at a saucy angle' (C, p. 114). About the only other 'identifiable' gay person Jarman had seen at that stage was Stuart Hopps, a fellow student at King's, who 'worked in the first John Steven's in Carnaby Street during his summer vacation, and came back wearing outrageous red pants with which he embarrassed the theologians' (AYOR, p. 41).
2 MN, p. 194.
3 The writer Helen Waddell lived downstairs in the back room. Because she was bedridden, Jarman and Hardy never saw her, but Jarman was familiar with her work and would later discuss filming one of her books.
4 SF.
5 JP.
6 *Private View*, p. 142.
7 Notebook dated February 1964, JP.
8 Ibid.
9 In Jarman's notebooks for 1964, in addition to a large number of poems, there are notes towards a play entitled *The Picnic* and the first act of *The Quest for George Daly*, a somewhat baffling existentialist piece featuring Herself (a woman in a mask); the Begum of Flowered Chintzes (a character Jarman would return to more than once – for example, in his poem 'Fargo 64' from *A Finger in the Fishes Mouth* and *Through the Billboard Promised Land*); a smiling man (Adonis in Infernis); and, as a first-act curtain, Herself's supposedly shocking revelation that the

George Daly on whom she has been pinning her romantic hopes 'doesn't exist'.

10 AYOR, pp. 43–4. Given that Healey Street is so close to Gloucester Crescent, one can be forgiven for wondering whether Brenda Lukey's suggestion that Jarman stay overnight – if indeed it was her suggestion – was quite as innocent as he implies.

11 Undated, the poem appears in A *Finger in the Fishes Mouth*.

12 AYOR, p. 44.

13 Letter dated 19 April 1964, from Betts to her friend Mary Rob.

14 DL, p. 60.

15 *The Gay Succession* was written by Gavin Arthur. It first appeared in *Gay Sunshine Journal 35* (1978) and was reprinted in an appendix to the Allen Ginsberg interview in the book *Gay Sunshine Interviews*, Volume 1, Gay Sunshine Press, 1978.

16 Act 1, Scene 4.

17 JP.

18 Ibid.

11: The Billboard Promised Land

1 DL, p. 63. See also KP, p. 33, and AYOR, pp. 47–8.

2 Ibid., p. 63.

3 AYOR, p. 48.

4 FFM.

5 KP, p. 36.

6 DL, p. 65.

7 JP.

8 DL, pp. 65–6. See also KP, pp. 36–7, and AYOR, pp. 49–50.

9 KP, p. 37.

10 DL, p. 67.

11 AYOR, p. 56.

12 Ibid., pp. 52–3.

13 Ibid., p. 55.

14 Ibid., p. 53.

15 Ibid., pp. 53–4.

16 Ibid., p. 42.

17 Ibid., p. 54.

18 Ibid., p. 51.

19 Ibid., pp. 19, 60.

12: Becoming Derek

1 JP.

2 Julian Harrap.

3 Lawrence Warwick-Evans.

4 Letter to Richard Rowson, January 1965.

5 JP.

6 DL, p. 76.

7 In time, Michael Snow would be added to this list.

8 As a vorticist and surreal painter as well as a film-maker, Jennings handled film in a particularly poetic manner. Films like *Listen to Britain* and *Fires Were Started* were a huge influence on Jarman, who shared with Jennings a romantic and essentially conservative love of England, plus an interest in Blake and the occult.

9 MN, p. 9.

10 SF.

11 The order is guessed at and the list is not necessarily exhaustive. There was an earlier design 'of considerable ingenuity' (SF) for *Measure for Measure*, and there may well have been two additional projects.

12 DL, p. 123.

13 KP, p. 178.

14 DL, p. 67.

15 Ibid., p. 74.

16 JP.

17 DL, p. 67.

18 Ibid., p. 74.

13: Father Figures

1 1968. The title presumably refers to Jarman's stage design.

2 KP, p. 71.

3 Nina's first marriage was to the lawyer Charles Huberich. Serge Mdivani's trophies were the silent film star Pola Negri, the opera singer Mary McCormick, and finally the heiress Louise Van Alen, on the rebound from his brother Alexis. David skipped the opera singer, but otherwise equalled Serge's score of one film star and one heiress: Mae Murray and Virginia Sinclair respectively. Alexis outflanked them both by gaining access to the Woolworth millions in the person of Barbara Hutton. Sister Roussie married the wealthy Spanish artist and muralist José Maria Sert y Badía and, it was rumoured, had an affair with Coco Chanel.

4 DL, p. 78.

5 In KP, p. 71, Jarman writes: 'I was given Ouspensky, from that came Jung.' The two volumes of Murasaki Shikibu's *The Tale of Genji* were a gift from Harwood to Jarman. Volume 1 is inscribed: 'For Derek, it's better with your shoes off.' Volume 2 is inscribed: 'For Derek, no shoes at all.' These inscriptions call to mind the occasion when Jarman, shod in 'elastic-sided Chelsea boots', walked with a shoeless Peter Orlovsky to his rooms in Kentish Town. Jarman later did some designs for Harwood's unperformed theatrical version of Blixen's *The Dreamers*.

6 DL, p. 78.
7 KP, p. 69.
8 Ibid., p. 52.
9 DL, p. 82.
10 Ibid., p. 78.

14: Swinging Decayed
1 DL, pp. 75–6.
2 Ibid., p. 95.
3 24.9.67.
4 2.10.67.
5 13.10.67.
6 KP, p. 46.
7 DL, p. 72.
8 KP, p. 41.
9 DL, p. 94.
10 Ibid., p. 84. The dates were 19–21.4.67. The director was David Gale. Set design: Albert Watson. Special effects: Richard Loncraine. Translation: Lawrence Ferlinghetti.
11 At the Arts Lab and elsewhere, Jarman would also see a number of other Warhol films over the years.
12 DL, pp. 82–3.
13 MN, p. 115.
14 AYOR, p. 56.
15 DL, p. 75.
16 The archive of the Royal Opera House.
17 Peter Brinson, 9.2.68.
18 Julian Turner, 1.2.68.
19 JP.
20 In the long run, the more carping of the critics were proved right: much as the ballet pleased the crowds in 1968, and although it has occasionally been revived, to date it has not entered the repertoire on a permanent basis.
21 DL, p. 84.
22 Enza Plazzotta later made a study of Antoinette Sibley and Anthony Dowell in the *pas de deux Friday's Child* for the Spode Factory. A limited edition of 300 pieces was produced.
23 JP.

15: This Month in Vogue
1 *Self Portrait*, p. 109.
2 DL, p. 87.
3 Programme notes.
4 *Observer*, 17.3.68.
5 John Percival, 6.3.68.
6 JP.
7 DL, p. 88.
8 Letter dated 26.3.68, JP.
9 Later the English National Opera.

10 JP. Jarman indicates that the notes were written to accompany a British Council exhibition of his designs for *Don Giovanni*. I have been unable to find a record of any such exhibition. All that is on record is that the British Council donated some of the designs to the Theatre Museum.
11 DL, p. 88.
12 *Writing Home*, p. 296.
13 Sydney Edwards, 22.8.68.
14 Desmond Shawe-Taylor, 25.8.68.
15 Writing in the *Listener* on 29.8.68, David Thompson gave Jarman's designs a particularly even-handed and thoughtful appraisal.
16 A year later, under the baton of Mackerras and with John Blatchley directing, Jarman had the chance to make some alterations to his work. The resulting reaction was warmer. Rodney Milnes, writing in *Queen*, even went so far as to say: 'The *Don Giovanni*, which opened last year's season and received a critical drubbing, is immeasurably improved. I liked Derek Jarman's decor then – but now that he has titivated both sets and costumes it has become visually one of the most interesting opera productions for many a season.' (17–30 September 1969.) Further sanction was supplied by the Arts Council, who bought some of the designs as examples of exciting new talent. But then a year after that, in 1970, *The Times* would again put back the clock: 'The production is still an eyesore . . .' (Alan Blythe, 16.2.70.)
17 DL, p. 88.
18 Ibid., p. 96.
19 Ibid.
20 In DL, Jarman writes as if he and Logan were the sole pioneers of loft-style living in London, particularly on the river, which is a slight exaggeration: a number of other painters had similar studios. It is often remarked that Jarman was aping Warhol with his new lifestyle, but interestingly, it was Anthony Harwood who – as early as the fifties – was one of the first people to pioneer loft living in New York, the city where the phenomenon originated.
21 Guy Brett, *The Times*, 26.2.69.
22 19.3.69.
23 JP.
24 SISM, 11.11.92. Jarman met Steede at the Place, where Steede was working for Robin Howard.
25 Ibid., 2.7.92.

26 Ibid., 11.11.92.
27 Jarman would later question the importance of Warhol's influence: 'I imagined Warhol had a greater influence on my work than he really had. My super-8 of Andrew kissing his friends was a spoof. Anger, Burroughs, Ginsberg and Rauschenberg were the influences – Andy, the court jester.' (MN, p. 131.)
28 JP.
29 Then called the London Contemporary Dance Company.
30 A year earlier, in 1968, Hirtenstein had accompanied Jarman on holiday to Morocco. In DL, pp. 88–90, Jarman gives a vivid account of the trip. At around the same time, in addition to visits to Paris and Italy, Jarman went as the guest of Patrick Procktor to le Nid du Duc, Tony Richardson's hamlet in the south of France.
31 MN, p. 139.
32 JP.
33 AYOR, p. 42.
34 DL, p. 16.
35 AYOR, p. 62.
36 DV.

16: The Devils
1 Jarman clearly did not count *Poet of the Anemones*, which he had designed in the interim.
2 DL, p. 97.
3 *The Devils of Loudun* and *The Devils* respectively.
4 *A British Picture*, p. 192.
5 *The Devils of Loudun*, p. 132.
6 According to Peter Logan, towards the end of the year there was another show, this time in Copenhagen, where, in order to help Olaf Gravesen start a gallery, Jarman and Logan were jointly invited to send examples of their work to hang on the walls of what was called the Panegyris Gallery. Jarman's own record of paintings sold at this time reports that the exhibition was due to have taken place in November 1969 but was 'called off'. (JP)
7 *Age and Guile*, p. 34.
8 JR.
9 AYOR, p. 72.
10 *It's Not Unusual: A History of Lesbian and Gay Britain in the Twentieth Century*, p. 170.
11 JP. Jarman did, however, have a number of firm friends in the GLF, including Dom Sylvester Houédard and Simon Watney.
12 JP.

13 KP, p. 57.
14 DL, p. 204.
15 Ibid., p. 101.

17: Oasis at Bankside
1 DL, p. 105.
2 Warner Brothers demanded substantial cuts, especially for the American market, and the film was banned in some British towns by local councils. In general, the reviews were not good, though thanks to the controversy, business was brisk.
3 DL, pp. 122–3.
4 'The Oasis' was how Jarman captioned the year in DL, p. 105.
5 DV.
6 KP, p. 55.
7 *Independent on Sunday*, 8.11.92.
8 DL, p. 107. See also KP, p. 57.
9 JP.
10 Ibid.
11 DL, p. 105.
12 Pp. 46, 47.
13 DL, p. 107.
14 Ibid., p. 93.
15 May 1971.
16 JP.
17 DL, p. 105.
18 JP.
19 Ibid.
20 *Observer*, 28.11.71.
21 DL, p. 108.
22 Ibid., p. 110.
23 Ibid.
24 Ibid., p. 111 .

18: Movietown
1 'Poem III', FFM.
2 *Through the Billboard Promised Land Without Ever Stopping*, JP.
3 DL, p. 140.
4 JP.
5 Ibid.
6 Also called *At Low Tide*.
7 DL, p. 116.
8 Ibid., p. 117.
9 Andrew Logan being interviewed by Jarman for *Interview*, April 1973.
10 AYOR, p. 75.
11 JP.
12 MN, p. 14.
13 SISM, 13.3.92.
14 DL, p. 119.
15 *An Appalling Talent: Ken Russell*, p. 229. In *Dreams of England*, p. 59, O'Pray notes: 'Given Jarman's popular reputation for excess,

the idea of him acting as a brake on the imagination of another director has a certain irony.'

19: Butler's Wharf and Beyond

1 SISM, 29.6.92.

2 Jarman liked to maintain that when Pasolini had been in London making *The Canterbury Tales*, he had inadvertently bumped into his idol on the steps of Bankside and been able to stammer how much he admired the Italian's films. While working on *Gargantua*, Jarman was afforded glimpses of two other legendary Italian directors. He saw Fellini 'at Cinecitta with his great green basilica umbrella' and he stood 'on the balcony behind Visconti while he viewed an editing copy of *Ludwig*'. (SISM, 11.11.92. See also C, p. 70.)

3 DL, pp. 123–4.

4 In his writings Jarman gives the new studio two names: Butler's Wharf and/or Shad Thames.

5 It is not surprising that Jarman should have been drawn to superimposition. In a way, this is what his entire artistic attitude was about: fusing one concern with another, adding this image to that, so that nothing is lost, everything is simultaneous.

6 Around this time, courtesy of Andrew Logan's friend Michael Davis, who organised screenings of their work at the Architectural Association, Jarman was introduced to the new wave of German film-makers such as Fassbinder, Schroeder, Herzog and Klaus Wyborny, whose *Pictures of a Lost World* bears a marked similarity to Jarman's own work, in particular *The Last of England*, in that it includes sequences of the smashed-up warehouses along the Thames. Wyborny was a keen proponent of super-8. Some of his super-8 footage appears in Herzog's *The Enigma of Kaspar Hauser* (1974). These European film-makers now joined the old favourites and such relatively recent English influences as Michael Powell, Ken Russell, David Larcher and the 'Carry On' films.

7 In C, p. 75, Jarman credits Jung's *Alchemical Studies* with introducing him to alchemy. Both his research for *The Devils* and his interest in Jung played their part.

8 JP.

9 The tablets containing the wisdom of Hermes Trismegistus were supposedly emerald in colour – like the emerald city from *The Wizard of Oz*. Jarman loved this idea. In C, p.

64, he writes: 'If the journey was long and difficult it could end in the Emerald City.'

10 A *History of Magic, Witchcraft and Occultism*, p. 82.

11 *John Dee*, p. 268.

12 DL, p. 128.

13 Ibid., p. 188.

14 There is superimposition throughout *In the Shadow of the Sun*, mainly of *Journey to Avebury* and then *Fire Island* over various of the tableaux shot at Butler's Wharf; also of *Tarot*. The film is a slow and pitiless unfolding of disturbed and disturbing dream images. On p. 76 of *Dreams of England* O'Pray writes: 'The title is an alchemical synonym for the philosopher's stone included in a book published in 1652 by Gratacolle William called *The Names of the Philosophers Stones*.'

15 DL, p. 131.

16 These same stones had been photographed by Paul Nash, long an influence on Jarman. During the early seventies, Jarman frequently gave his landscapes titles which did homage to Nash's own *The Equivalents for the Megaliths*.

17 DL, p. 126. Whether consciously or not, the words 'undisturbed in the sun' echo the title of what, over the course of the following year, was filmed here to become *In the Shadow of the Sun*.

18 Ideas to be found in the notebook include a film about twentieth-century images of ancient Egypt; a film about a female detective, to be played by Luciana Martinez, who travels by train through Transylvania to Dracula's castle; a drama with an intriguing title, *The PT Lessons of Eva Braun*; an 'art film' called *Monet's Garden* in which a gardening personality like Percy Thrower talks about the painter's garden (and his paintings) in purely gardening terms until 'at the very end mr monet comes out of the house and thanks Percy Thrower'; 'The sands of time an earth film here watch a butterfly trapped in a glass the sand pours in until the white wings flutter into stillness . . .'; a film of glass breaking; one of the country and the flowers that grow at Tilly Whim in June; a remake of the fire maze, with many more people and many more gallons of paraffin; a silent version of *The Tempest*.

The list of completed films or fragments of film is by no means comprehensive. One could add: Andrew Logan getting dressed in Downham Road; a picnic lunch in the garden of the fashion designer Rae Spencer-Cullen, otherwise known as Miss Mouse; the tea shop at 23 Tooley Street; and more.

19 DL, p. 137, and JP.

20 April 1974. There was a Klein exhibition at the Tate in March 1974.

21 For instance, the meetings of the London Super-8 Group, organised by Gray Watson at the ICA, where super-8 film-makers could meet to show each other their work and swap information; or the festivals of Expanded Cinema at the Arnolfini in Bristol in the mid-seventies and at the ICA in January 1975; plus similar small festivals in Belgium and France. There is a certain irony in the fact that Jarman's films should be shown under the heading 'Expanded Cinema'. As he wrote in a letter to Ron Haseldon, who helped organise the ICA festival in January 1975, rather than being an expansion, 'super-8 is a contraction to the point o the 20th century hieroglyphic monad'; a cinema 'of small gestures'.

22 DL, p. 128.

23 Ibid., p. 124.

24 DL, p. 132.

25 Ibid.

26 John Percival, 23.10.73. Jarman's notebooks from this time also contain designs for *Romeo and Juliet*. There is no record of what this might have been.

27 It is possible there was more than one such studio opening.

28 *Spectator*, 15.6.74.

29 DL, pp. 131–2.

30 Ibid., p. 129.

31 Letter dated 13.11.74, JP.

32 DL, p. 134.

33 *Gerald's Film* was shot in the course of a weekend Jarman and Christopher Hobbs spent with Incandela and Von Watzdorf in an eighteenth-century fishing lodge or folly on the outskirts of Stoke by Nayland. In the mid-seventies, in the marshy wooded area at the far end of the lake that adjoins the lodge, there stood a ruined boathouse, no longer there. This is where Jarman filmed Incandela, who wore the green felt hat from Pasolini's *Canterbury Tales*.

34 LP.

35 KP, p. 132.

36 Ibid., p. 131.

37 Ibid., p. 128.

38 JP.

39 To music by Sibelius.

40 *Sunday Telegraph*, 5.5.74.

41 JP.

42 DL, p. 134.

43 Ibid., p. 136.

44 Ibid., p. 134.

45 Ibid., p. 137.

46 Ibid.

47 Ibid., p. 130. Again this footage was incorporated into other films. Some of this New York footage could date from 1972, though this is unlikely.

48 Ibid., p. 136.

49 AYOR, pp. 80–1.

50 DL, p. 137.

51 JP.

52 The Hockney film is of course *A Bigger Splash*.

53 JP.

20: Features

1 MI.

2 'Sebastian, the doolally Christian who refused a good fuck, gets the arrow he deserved. Can one feel sorry for this Latin closet case?' (AYOR, p. 83.)

3 Tony Rayns, *Time Out*, 5–11 November 1976.

4 AYOR, p. 84.

5 As written, the film's final moment reads thus: 'The soldiers fire arrows one by one. One of the arrows goes through Sebastian's neck. It is sexual and ecstatic for Sebastian. He has a hard-on. It is the culmination of all his desires. Max helps Justin who can hardly stand up aim the last arrow. Justin makes a giant effort and sends the arrow through Sebastian's heart. Sebastian is in a state of orgasm.' As filmed, the scene is rather different. Although we end with the death, it is far less openly erotic than this and the emphasis is on the group who have turned on the outsider, rather than on the outsider's sexual summation.

6 Among others, investors in the film included Whaley's parents, Thilo von Watzdorf, the Marquis of Dufferin, and Ava, John Siddeley (Lord Kenilworth), possibly David Hockney, certainly Jean Boudrand, at whose house Jarman had met Whaley.

7 Jarman asked Scarfiotti if he would undertake the film's art direction. Scarfiotti declined, although, given the importance of its setting to the finished film, in suggesting Cala Domestica as a location he might well be said to have had a hand in its design.

8 This workbook is now lost. Those for the other films are in Jarman's papers.

9 It was Scarfiotti who suggested Treviglio, though as it happens, Jarman had earlier seen Treviglio at the Roundhouse in *Lila, the Divine Game* and earmarked him even then as a potential Sebastian.

10 *Ken Hicks*. Jarman liked to show this film in dreamy slow motion, as an erotic reverie – a notional reply, one could say, to the way in which Lindsay Anderson in *If* had filmed Richard Warwick going through his paces in the school gymnasium.

11 SISM, 10.11.92. Elsewhere Jarman suggests that he and Ron Wright never went any further than mutual masturbation.

12 *Troubadour* is shot through a blue gel and features two heraldic figures (Luciana Martinez and Paul Humfress) striking a sequence of poses on the battlements of Corfe Castle. Although Jarman never did cut this material together in the manner planned, from his notebooks it would appear that what he had in mind was a carefully structured film, using long static takes, in which 'a figure is seen like a shadow passing'. The film would amalgamate two different ideas, that of breaking a mirror and a ghost. As the mirror flashes into the camera, a figure would be seen in the glass, which would then smash to reveal the castle. Over all this: 'the sound of jackdaws and wind blowing'.

13 DL, p. 138.

14 This was Hermine Demoriane, who would repeat the stunt at the end of *Jubilee*.

15 DL, p. 148.

16 The film was shot Academy ratio (a 16mm ratio), then optically transferred (still in Academy ratio) to 35mm, which is normally projected at a different ratio. If the film is shown in Academy ratio, Hicks' hard-on is visible at the bottom of the screen. If, however, the film is projected in a different ratio, as it was on television, the frame is cropped and the hard-on disappears.

17 MI.

18 DL, p. 155.

19 In a similar gag, 'Oedipus' does duty for 'motherfucker'.

20 JR.

21 JP.

22 DL, p. 155.

23 Ibid. Robert Medley commemorated this scene in a large painting currently hanging in Prospect Cottage.

24 Ibid.

25 Or *Akhenaten*, in some versions or parts

of the script. Akhenaten ascended the throne as Amenhotep IV. He ruled from 1380 to 1362BC. The titles *Flight into Egypt* and *In the Shadow of the Sun* are also associated with this project, which could have been planned in 1976 rather than 1975. Jarman's papers also contain notes for *The Angel's Kiss*, the story of a knight. This is another project that presumably dates from this time. As, perhaps, does *Cleopatra*.

26 UA, p. 5.

27 Also called Tutenaten in the script.

28 UA, p. 40.

29 Ibid., p. 3.

30 Perhaps, as for many others, it had been the great Tutankhamun exhibition of 1972 that had sparked Jarman's interest in Egypt, though alchemy is more likely. Egypt as a locus of mystic correspondences and alchemical harmonies is part and parcel of a romantic tradition that goes back a good deal further than the Tutankhamun exhibition. There are those who maintain that the Rosicrucian movement of the 1600s, with which Jarman was particularly familiar, had its roots in Akhenaten's attempt to elevate the sun disc above all other gods.

31 UA, p. 28.

32 Ibid., p. 3.

33 This design concept is very similar to the one used in *Caravaggio* and *Edward II*, both of which were also designed by Christopher Hobbs.

34 Also called *John Dee The Art of Mirrors* and/or *John Dee The Art of Mirrors and a Summoning of Angels*.

35 *John Dee*, p. 268.

36 JP. According to Dee's own accounts, the angel he most usually spoke with was Uriel.

37 And later blown up to 16mm. The quotes are from one version of the script in Jarman's papers.

38 Mirrors and mirroring are integral to the script. At one point Dee pronounces: 'All mirrors contain within them the sum of their reflections, they are a book wherein we may extract much knowledge, a gateway through which we may pass.' The same speech also appears in *Archaeologies* (see chapter 22). In *John Dee*, p. 37, Deacon writes that Dee believed in the power of mirrors and 'had a theory that powerful mirrors, specially constructed, could be used for drawing magical power from the sun to transmit messages and objects to the stars and other worlds'.

Dee's words call to mind the Herbert poem and hymn, a great favourite of Jarman's – it was sung at his funeral:
> A man who looks on glass
> On it may stay his eye
> Or if he pleaseth through it pass
> And then the heavens espy.'

Or this passage from Jung's *Memories, Dreams, Reflections*: 'And what was the intellect? It was a function of the human soul, not a mirror but an infinitesimal fragment of a mirror such as a child might hold up to the sun, expecting the sun to be dazzled by it.' (P. 77.)

In *The Art of Mirrors*, the short super-8 film which part shares a title with the Dee script, a mirror flashes into the camera, dazzling the viewer with the sun's reflection. The viewer is 'looking on glass', or a mixture of glass and light, and is perhaps being invited to step through it. Jarman is exploring how the medium of film itself is allied to journeying between the temporal and the spiritual, to establishing and exploring one's own true nature.

39 Jarman asked the Arts Council for the £800 he reckoned he needed to complete some of the super-8 films he had been working on and refilm them on to 16mm so that he could lay down a soundtrack and properly distribute them. There is no record of whether this application was successful.

40 JP.

41 Ibid.

42 Ibid.

43 In full: *The Space Gospel according to the Apostles* by Ken Russell and Derek Jarman. In his notes Jarman sometimes refers to this as *Bible Story*. Russell later recycled this material as a novel, *Mike and Gabys Space Gospel* (Little, Brown, 1999).

21: Jubilee

1 AYOR, p. 113.

2 DL, p. 162.

3 Satisfying and cathartic though all this was, the last laugh, at least financially, was on Jarman – the landlords successfully pursued him through the courts for redecoration costs, which further depleted his already meagre resources.

4 DL, p. 160.

5 Some months earlier, Jarman had joined with many of the people at that summer fête in producing a personalised calendar. Each of them was pictured in the month of his or her birthday, and the whole group photographed together for the cover. Since Jarman shared a January birthday with the glamorous Chelita Secunda, they were featured on the first page. Their picture was taken on a set at Pinewood Studios. Jarman wore a black suit and a beret and carried a cane; Chelita was swathed in furs. This calendar was the closest the colourful group that swirled around the Logans ever came to consciously delineating itself – paradoxically, at precisely the moment when Jarman was preparing to leave it. Among those featured were Michael Davis, Duggie Fields, Michael Kostiff, Andrew and Peter Logan, Luciana Martinez, Little Nell, Zandra Rhodes, Eric Roberts, Rae Spencer-Cullen, Tim Street-Porter, Joan de Vere Hunt and Kevin Whitney.

6 With David Dye, Marilyn Halford, Ron Haselden, Tony Hill, Jeff Keen, Malcolm Le Grice and William Raban.

7 At the other end of the spectrum entirely, Jarman suppressed his antipathy to the advertising world and accepted an invitation from Ken Russell to design the set for Nescoré, a French brand of substitute instant coffee. In normal circumstances, or so he liked to think, Jarman would have declined such a commission, however brief, amusing and well paid, but he desperately needed the money. His account of designing this ad (DL, p. 163) dates it as 1976. However, his expenditure book for 1978–9 lists £700 for a film set for Ken. Either there was another, unrecorded job for Russell, or else the ad was done later than 1976.

8 Jarman had also earmarked Eno to do the music for *The Angelic Conversation of John Dee*.

9 Whaley and Malin had secured the cover of *Time Out* and a prominent feature in *Films and Filming*.

10 *A Bone in My Flute*, pp. 41–2.

11 Michael Billington, in the *Guardian*, 28.10.76, called the film 'an exceptionally promising first feature – one of the most striking and original to emanate from our beleaguered independent industry for some considerable time'. Although the differences of opinion between Jarman, Whaley and Humfress were fatally reflected in the finished film – as Nigel Andrews remarked in the *Financial Times* (29.10.76): 'There is no doubting the film-makers' flair and inventiveness, but one would love to see what

they did with those qualities in a more coherent context' – most of the reviewers agreed to a greater or lesser extent with Billington. The censor gave the film an X certificate and did not require any cuts. And, much to Jarman's surprise and delight, in reply to a query whether the film bore any relation to life in the forces, Lance stated: 'I was out in the Middle East before the war and it's really quite accurate' (DL, p. 165).

12 AYOR, pp. 23–4. See also DL, p. 243.

13 DL, p. 165.

14 Ibid., p. 142.

15 Alasdair McGaw enjoyed a similar nickname: Alley Cat.

16 DL, p. 166.

17 Ibid., p. 162.

18 JP.

19 Her real name was Pamela Rooke.

20 England's Dreaming, p. 93.

21 JP. See also DL, pp. 26–7.

22 England's Dreaming, p. 147.

23 DL, p. 121.

24 Ibid., p. 164.

25 While planning his second feature, Jarman made some fragmentary notes towards a three-part film (High Renaissance) that would never reach the screen. Part 3 features Michelangelo. Part 2 concentrates on Pontormo and the method by which he gains inspiration for an angel in an unfinished fresco. It comes from the face of a beautiful choirboy, who then disappears, hence Pontormo's inability to complete the fresco. Part 1 provides a similarly homoerotic explanation of how the Mona Lisa came to be painted. Da Vinci is trying to discover the secret of flight, but because this will not pay the rent, accepts a commission from an Englishman called Westminster Coote to paint Coote's wife, Mona Lisa, a moaning windbag who never stops talking. Instead of flight, Mona urges Da Vinci to invent 'toothpaste, photography, Martini bianco, coca-cola . . . There must be money in that . . . all this High Renaissance doesn't pull much punch back home at St James.' She has a cold and keeps sneezing, so Da Vinci is unable to finish the lips. 'The next day he waits for her, she doesn't arrive, a page comes with a message, he's really beautiful, Leonardo fucks him and then dressing him up in the costume of Mona Lisa, finishes the lips.' For the part of Da Vinci, Jarman envisaged Andrew Logan, with Jordan as his Mona Lisa. JP. C, pp.

100–01 contains a sanitised version of the story – plus alternative titles for the three segments. Pontormo's Unfinished Masterpiece, Michelangelo's Slave, The Smile on the Face of the Mona Lisa.

26 DL, p. 164.

27 It is sometimes implied that Jubilee grew out of Jordan's Film, the super-8 footage of Jordan in her tutu, parts of which are in the final film. This is not so. That footage was actually shot during the filming of Jubilee, whose genesis Jarman described as follows to Jon Savage: 'Jubilee was originally a super-8 film with Jordan, it wasn't anything to do with punk in that sense. It was to do with Jordan and whatever she wanted to make, but it grew in the course of early '77, while we were writing it, and it was Jordan who brought in the punk element, because we wanted musicians involved.'

28 There are no accurate figures that I can find for the final budget of Jubilee. It was most likely in the region of £75,000 – certainly between £50,000 and £80,000.

29 23.2.79.

30 In an interview with Nicholas de Jongh in the Guardian, 21.2.78, Jarman says that he got the idea of the polarities – black and white – from Jung's Sermons to the Dead.

31 UA, p. 44.

32 And Hitler's daughter in the original script.

33 UA, p. 44.

34 Jarman would explain that: 'Viv is based on myself.' (Keith Howes, Gay News, 23.2.79.)

35 Jarman once said: 'I've always loved the idea of brothers being in love or a father being in love with his son and this love being extended into actual physical contact.' (Keith Howes, Gay News, 23.2.79.) A very illuminating remark, given Jarman's strained relationship with his father. In With Chatwin, p. 198, Susannah Clapp observes that 'there are those – notably Edmund White – who think of a preoccupation with twins as distinguishing a vein of fiction by homosexuals, or about homosexual experience'. Michael O'Pray makes the point that in many of Jarman's films you find 'a narcissistic mirroring' (Dreams of England, p. 88) of either twin brothers or two men who share a particularly close relationship. At the time of Jubilee, Steve Treatment (a new friend) told Jarman that his brother was also

gay. Jarman was intrigued. Treatment
maintains that Jarman based Angel and
Sphinx on himself and his brother, and that
Jarman wanted Treatment to play Angel – but
Treatment was too shy. Personally, I would say
that the presence of twins points to a
desire/need not be alone; to have one's
existence and sexuality validated by a twin,
someone who is similar to oneself.
  36 UA, p. 56.
  37 Ibid., p. 75.
  38 JP. In *Dreams of England*, p. 12, Michael
O'Pray notes the similarities between Jarman
and Blake: 'Like Blake, Jarman was a
Londoner who believed the city physically
embodied the woes of its times – in sixteenth-
century alchemical terms, it was a microcosm.
Both created mythological systems spanning
the personal and the national . . . Both . . .
plundered the cabala, alchemy and the occult
philosophies . . . On a more personal level,
Jarman made ornate, handmade diaries,
notebooks and scripts in a Blakean fashion.
He too was a charismatic figure, living
frugally, expounding radical views, including
free love.'
  39 Ibid. See also KP, p. 188.
  40 Ibid.
  41 See *Man Enough to be a Woman*, pp.
120–21, for Jayne County's account of this.
  42 October was leader of the group Chelsea.
His song 'Right to Work' was something of a
punk anthem.
  43 JP.
  44 DL, p. 209.
  45 The blessing of the unions was only
sought after the event, when it was too late
for them to refuse co-operation.
  46 MI.
  47 The film also exists as a super-8 on its
own, *Jordan's Dance*. The other super-8 linked
to *Jubilee – Jubilee Masks* or *Jean-Marc Makes a
Mask* – features Prouveur making face casts of
Jenny Runacre and Jordan. The casts were
given as a gift to the actresses.
  48 DL, p. 176.
  49 AYOR, pp. 86–8.
  50 DL, p. 172.

22: Stormy Weather
  1 Incandela had moved to New York in May
1977 and had taken an apartment on the
fourteenth floor of a block in Lexington
Avenue. It was here that Jarman
voyeuristically filmed his two 'cats' at play. He
called the film *Art and The Pose*, or *Arty the*

Pose – we cannot be sure which. In it,
Prouveur and Incandela strike a number of
playful 'artistic' poses.
  2 DL, p. 238.
  3 JP.
  4 DL, p. 247.
  5 Ibid., p. 249.
  6 Over the next year or so Jarman also
worked on this script with Marina Warner,
who wrote an opening scene full of pseudo-
Shakespearian dialogue. Jarman took the
scene and a synopsis to the BFI. Nothing ever
came of the approach. See also Chapter 23 for
reference to a further *The Bees of Infinity*.
  7 Sometimes the 'Nec' is written 'Ne' in the
scripts.
  8 A selection of first features chosen by a
committee of Paris-based film critics.
  9 C, p. 102. See also DL, p. 11. Jarman had
of course imagined Jordan playing the Mona
Lisa in his film *High Renaissance*. At the time
he was also talking to Jenny Runacre about
her appearing in *Caravaggio*.
  10 Taking issue with this idea, the critic
Waldemar Januszczak pointed out in his
review of the film that the painting Jarman is
referring to is in fact signed 'f . . . Michele'
which probably stands for the standard *fecit*
Michelangelo, or Michelangelo made this.'
(*Guardian*, 24.4.86.)
  11 DL, p. 182.
  12 LP.
  13 DL, p. 184.
  14 3.8.78. The air commodore had been
'fined £50 at Uxbridge yesterday'.
  15 Lawyer's letter, LP.
  16 Thereafter, Lance singled Sam out for
ongoing and heavy-handed disapproval, to
the extent that when Gaye finally realised the
truth, she felt impelled to compensate for the
presents which Lance, despite his generosity
to his other grandchildren, failed to give his
eldest grandson. At Christmas and on his
birthday, Gaye would slip Sam money she
pretended had come from Lance. Jarman
made equally sure that his own presents to his
nephew were particularly handsome.
  17 KP, p. 129.
  18 MN, p. 263.
  19 KP, p. 122.
  20 MN, pp. 266–7.
  21 Ibid., p. 263.
  22 The other two films Boyd was working
on at this time were *Sweet William* and *Scum*.
  23 Jarman's fee was between £6,500 and

£10,000. The film's budget was between £150,000 and £200,000.

24 There is no mention of the sailors in Francis Rose's own account of his twenty-first birthday party in his memoir *Saying Life*.

25 Mary Blume, 14.5.80.

26 JP.

27 Never admitting to the fact that he did not really see eye to eye with Jarman, or like the script, or (perhaps) fancy playing what was really a supporting role, Gielgud wrote to Jarman on 20 November to say that he found the script 'full of ingenious compressions and imaginative ideas. But I'm afraid I couldn't agree to playing it. For one thing I have promised to play the part for the BBC Shakespeare series in the spring of next year.' It would later gall Jarman that Gielgud would agree to play Prospero for his 'rival' Peter Greenaway.

28 JP.

29 DL, p. 188.

30 Timothy Hyman, *London Magazine*, October 1980.

31 DL, p. 186.

32 Ibid.

33 Ibid., pp. 189–90.

34 The signs on the walls of Prospero's study came either from the Egyptian hieroglyphs or from Henricus Cornelius Agrippa's *Three Books of Occult Philosophy*, Jarman's copy of which lay open on Prospero's desk. Christopher Hobbs made a wand for Prospero which resembled Dee's Monas Hieroglyphica. A circle of magnifying glass surmounted by a crescent, its two juxtaposed shapes 'symbolised the unity of spirit and matter'. 'On the floor the artist Simon Read drew out the magic circles that were blueprints of the pinhole cameras he constructed in his studio . . . at Butler's Wharf, thereby making a subtle connection.' (DL, p. 188.) Further connections with Jarman's riverside studio were an Andrew Logan mirror and the silk and satin roses in the final scene, made there by the standard army of art-school helpers.

35 DL, p. 196.

36 JP.

37 *London Magazine*, October 1980.

38 DL, p. 188.

39 So low, in fact, that the first few scenes had to be reshot; they were simply *too* dark.

40 DL, p. 194.

41 In Jarman's first script for *Caravaggio*, he included a scene where Giordano Bruno is burned at the stake in Rome for heresy. In the script, Bruno is a friend of Del Monte's; in real life, Bruno conceivably knew Dee, the model for Prospero. The worlds of *The Tempest* and *Caravaggio* were only a hair's breadth apart.

42 JP.

43 DL, p. 197. Jarman loved Williams' phrase and would later want to use it as the title for the book of *The Last of England*.

44 Also known as Simon Fisher Turner.

45 DL, p. 194.

46 Paul Wells, *Art & Design*, July–August, 1996. In a 1984 interview with Toby Rose in *Coaster*, Jarman elaborates on this idea. Rose asks: 'Do you find the crew taking over?' 'No. They don't take over at all. I take over completely. What happens is the opposite from the normal film set. I know exactly what I want to do. The situation has been created so everyone can do whatever they want to do because it will be exactly what I want to happen. It's like throwing a party: you just go along and choose all the right people for your party and you stick by them, then it doesn't go wrong.'

47 DL, p. 202. William Thomas Beckford (1760–1844) was a writer, art collector and consummate party-giver.

48 Ibid., p. 197.

49 The films shown were *Savage Messiah*, all three of Jarman's own features, plus a selection of his super-8s under the title *Apprentice Work*.

50 Also showing at Berlin was *The Great Rock and Roll Swindle*, which of course included a small section of Jarman's footage.

51 2.5.80.

52 2.5.80.

53 4.5.80.

54 22.9.80.

55 DL, p. 211.

56 Ibid., p. 212.

57 Although there is no reason to suspect these facts, which are the memory of David Meyer, it has proved impossible to verify that the awards ceremony Jarman attended was held by the *Evening Standard*, or that the category in which he was placed was that of most promising newcomer.

23: Montage Years

1 *Afterimage 12*, p. 46.

2 *Dreams of England*, p. 113.

3 JP.

4 DL, p. 202.

5 KP, p. 11. The passage is an (unused)

sequence written for the film of the same name.

6 Apart from regular visits to the VD clinic, Jarman seems to have had little call for a doctor at this time. He did, however, suffer from persistent back pain, which, in the mid to late eighties, he discovered was because he had distorted one leg lifting furniture, making it slightly shorter than the other. A session of shiatsu remedied this.

7 Jarman did not have the money to buy a flat. Until 1985–6, when his annual income suddenly rose to around £25,000, he earned between £6,000 and £10,000 a year. It was enough to pay for his travel and keep him supplied with books, film and painting materials, food and the most basic of clothes – but no more.

8 DL, p. 250.

9 The fire started on the floor occupied by a group of furniture-makers, probably by accident, though there were those who said it was the work of the developers.

10 Toby Rose, *Coaster*, 1984.

11 JP.

12 The painting is reproduced in *The Male Nude: A Modern View*. It was painted in June 1982. Around now, and with Jarman in attendance, Butler filmed a tea party in a house in Cheyne Walk. This is *Ken's First Film*, listed in certain filmographies as one of Jarman's own.

13 The Falklands throne derived its name from the fact that one of its side panels read: 'Cooked Corned Beef . . . Product of Argentina'.

14 One of the features of these fragments from Heraclitus to most delight Jarman was the fact that the sayings were either part of a whole now lost, or quotations from separate sources attempting to recreate the original text. 'I like fragmented things,' was how he put it, '. . . things which have been wrecked by the storm . . . One can apply that to human beings as well, you know. I quite like people who have been through the wars' (JP). Of course, this echoes his use and rehabilitation of junk in his capes and works of art. Heraclitus believed that all things are composed of opposites. Because the opposites are constantly at war with each other, all things are in a state of perpetual flux. Jarman's own view of the world, especially as exemplified by his studies of alchemy, bore a striking similarity to Heraclitus's.

15 JP.

16 AYOR, p. 91. So dedicated to and skilled at cruising did Jarman become that he would decant a jar of Vaseline directly into one of the pockets of his leather jacket so that he always had a ready supply of lubricant.

17 DL, pp. 244–6.

18 JP.

19 DL, p. 246.

20 MI.

21 JP.

22 Ibid.

23 All in 1980.

24 15.5.84.

25 There are references in Jarman's papers to signing documents relating to *The Holy Sinner* and records of payments for it in 1983, all from Germany.

26 UA, p. 117.

27 The handwritten script of the film in Jarman's papers is dated January 1981.

28 Jarman had earmarked Adam Ant to play the part of Adam, though when, in early 1981, he sent Adam Ant two of his scripts, the singer replied: 'Dear Derek . . . thank you for sending me the scripts of your two films. Unfortunately it is impossible for me to take part in any other projects for at least the next twelve months, as I have to complete two world tours in 1981 . . . Also, I am not too sure about the type of film I want to take part in; if at all. I do not want to meddle or dabble or be considered another "singer cum actor" à la "Breaking Glass/Quadrophenia" etc. etc. . . . Much love, Adam.' The letter is dated 9.3.81.

29 Renamed Malvinas in a later version of the script.

30 UA, p. 117: 'Janet Street-Porter, an old friend, would have made an excellent Veronica'.

31 Ibid., p. 144.

32 JP.

33 *Free Association*, p. 348.

34 DL, p. 222.

35 Letter written by Berkoff, who was in Australia at the time, on 25.2.82 (JP).

36 It would be a decade before Berkoff's play was filmed. When it was, it was with Berkoff's own script and under his direction. He and Joan Collins played the warring protagonists. Jarman's script is dated December 1981. The other film Jarman was discussing with Berkoff was *Neutron*. See later.

37 October 1981. See Chapter 22 for

reference to an earlier *The Bees of Infinity*.

38 Jarman's notes for *Angelology*, a fragment of a film idea from 1988, read: 'Angels . . . are the bees of infinity, the messengers of lady wisdom, their thoughts are honeyed, sweet, dead souls they whisper, wisdom is opaque, indistinct, only discovered on earth by an archeology of soul.' (JP.) There are two more of Jarman's titles in this sentence: *Dead Souls Whisper* and *Archeology of Soul*.

39 Jarman planned to shoot *The Bees of Infinity* in a mixture of super-8 and 16mm. His notebook reads: 'The Ivory Tower and the Bees of Infinity a film on Artaud. A: 1: Seashell and pianoforte 2: Dinosaur with John the Baptist 3: the dancer 4: Van Gogh's ear 5: A small sexual ball rolling around 2 naked boys rolling on the floor 6: Swearing Christ B: 1: A painter who is van Gogh 2: A dancer who is Nijinsky 3: A singer who is Maria Callas 4: A pianist who is Schnable 5: Artaud as himself 6: John the Baptist and the dinosaur 7: A sex act/Christ' (JP).

40 JP. The script is dated 1982.

41 This image will recur in the forthcoming *Caravaggio*.

42 There are two versions of the script. I describe the second. The synopsis is taken from Jarman's notebook (JP).

43 A series of *tableaux vivants* were to be enacted in 'a large grey room of stark geometrical simplicity with three tall curtained windows through which there is a screen for back projection' (JP). Segments of Rilke's poem were to be used as the accompanying voice-over. The design of this piece somewhat suggests the later *Wittgenstein*.

44 The proposal is dated 8.5.83. The budget was £85,008.00 for a thirteen-day shoot.

45 As described in Richard Buckle's *Nijinsky*, pp. 406–8.

46 March 1984. The proposed budget was £64,000, which would allow for the film to be shot on 16mm and edited on tape. A further £1,000 would be needed if the tape was then transferred back to film for theatrical distribution. The plan was to shoot in April 1984. The proposal is reproduced in full in *Afterimage 12*. Jarman had also thought of using Michael Clark to play the part of Rupert Doone in his documentary on Robert Medley.

47 Jarman's handwritten notes for this are dated March 1985.

48 JP.

49 The outline for this is undated and unattributed. There is, however, a workbook relating to the project and that is dated August 1984. The proposal is reproduced in full in *Afterimage 12*.

50 *Jean Cocteau and Raymond Radiguet*, a handwritten fragment of script Jarman wrote with Chris Ward. Undated, but likely to be late 1984 onwards.

51 In January 1983 there is also passing mention of Stephen Blackman working on a film project with Jarman called *Reporting for Duty*. In addition, Jarman was possibly re-examining *Pure Heaven*, which is dated both June 1978 and August 1980. With Geff Rushton, there was vague – but angry – talk of making a polemical film called *Bright's Disease*: so called after Graham Bright, the MP who introduced the Video Recordings Bill in July 1983. The purpose of the bill was to curb the distribution of 'video nasties' by requiring all videos to be licensed. To Jarman, who from the start of the decade had been keeping a wary eye on how the Conservatives were attempting to control anything they found distasteful, this was part of the sinister way in which the government was seeking to erode civil liberties and force him and his ilk back into the closet. The idea behind *Bright's Disease* was to show illegal pornographic images on screen, but only for a few seconds, then to have the images being devoured by fire. There is also mention of Jarman working on a super-8 of 'Kubla Khan'. The above list is not necessarily exhaustive. There may well have been other projects Jarman either toyed with or partially developed.

52 At the time of writing there are plans afoot to film Jarman's script for *Neutron*.

53 KP, p. 182.

54 In fact the Neutron bomb was a small hydrogen bomb with a limited range, the idea being that its use could spare both buildings and nearby civilians.

55 I have been unable to ascertain with any certainty how much Kendon Films paid towards *Neutron's* development. The figure could be anything from £1,000 or £2,000 to £10,000. Jarman shared this money with Drysdale. There is a Kendon budget for £503,326 linked to the November 1980 script.

56 Among other things, Jarman and Sullivan cut an early scene in which Aeon and Topaz eat the corpse of a young child. They also cut an earlier character – an old woman who guides Aeon to his destiny and is

actually the Virgin Mary. They added the character of Sophia.

57 *Square Peg* No. 4, 1984.

58 DL, pp. 214–15.

59 Ibid., p. 209.

60 This version, the most gentle of them all, was finally published in *Up in the Air*. Two other young friends, Steve Thorn and Paul Wolfson, also helped on the early scripts. *Neutron* was a project Jarman would continue to think about – and have hopes for – for many years to come. When Tim Bevan set up Working Title, Jarman asked Bevan if he would take over the film from Don Boyd. Boyd was not prepared to allow this, though Bevan did show it to Peter Sainsbury at the BFI. Sainsbury did not care for it and never put it to the board.

61 *Rapid Eye I*, p. 268.

62 UA, p. 182. This image was added only in the 1983 rewrite.

63 UA, p. 81.

64 DL, p. 26.

65 JP.

66 *Blue is Poison* was co-written by Steve Thorn and Paul Wolfson, who had been helping with *Neutron*.

67 JP. This is Caravaggio's final voice-over, cut from the finished film, but retained – albeit with slightly different wording – in the published script, p. 101.

68 Either in April 1981 or later the same year. These changes were made in a number of linked drafts.

69 JP. The gypsy and artist are Ranuccio and Caravaggio.

70 JP. This speech survives into the finished film.

71 DL, p. 9.

72 Apart from Steve Thorn and Paul Wolfson, in 1981 Jarman worked on the script with Julian Sands and, over an intensive three-week period in May to June 1981, with Tom Priestley, the supervising editor on *Jubilee*. Also with Stephen Pickles. And he continually consulted friends such as Robert Medley, Ken Butler, James Mackay and Simon Watney.

73 DL, p. 30.

74 Ibid., p. 28.

75 Ibid., p. 31.

76 JP. James Mackay then suggested it would be possible to take this process a step further and shoot not on 16mm, but direct on to video, which was considerably cheaper. The video could then be blown up to 35mm. On 10.7.85, Mackay wrote to Colin MacCabe at the BFI, supplying a budget of £68,500 for a 100-minute film. This was to do *Caravaggio* as a video-to-film transfer. Such a drastic reduction was, however, unnecessary, for at precisely this point, funding for the film was finally found.

77 Pezzali's involvement with film was mainly in the area of the television documentary. His only previous film was *From a Far Country* (*Da Un Paese Lontano*), a life of Pope John Paul II directed by Krzysztof Zanussi. This was a co-production between Pezzali's company, Transworld, ITC, RAI and Film Polski.

78 JP.

79 Ibid.

80 Ibid.

81 KP, p. 86.

82 Interview with James Norton.

83 In early 1980, Jarman designed a short ballet called *One* for Tom Jobe, a dancer – and, in this instance, choreographer – with the London Contemporary Dance Theatre. Along with some other short pieces, the ballet toured a handful of centres in the south of England but did not have a life beyond that one short tour. In mid-1980, with the help of Christopher Hobbs, he suggested various ideas, put into effect by Steven Meaha, who had assisted on *The Tempest*, for the design of *The Secret of the Universe*, a one-act comedy of modern manners by Jonathan Gems, which played the ICA for a week at lunchtime.

84 DL, p. 224.

85 Ibid., p. 223.

86 Ibid.

87 JP.

88 *Rapid Eye I*, p. 271.

89 JP. Jarman was being given a lift on McGaw's motorbike during the making of *Jubilee* when the crash to which he refers occurred.

90 DL, p. 242.

91 Ibid., p. 226.

92 Ibid.

93 *Pontormo and the Punks at Santa Croce*. He also filmed *The Rake's Progress*.

94 DL, p. 226.

95 Bergese had been an associate choreographer of the London Contemporary Dance Theatre when Jarman designed *One*. A lesser design commission from this era was the one for a Zandra Rhodes fashion show at

Olympia in March 1983. Jarman's role was to choose the music – which he did with a colleague in the course of a single morning spent sashaying up and down the aisle of the record shop pretending to be models – compile a tape and provide a backdrop. The collection was on a mediaeval theme. Jarman supplemented the white, T-shaped catwalk with a tented arrangement of white net topped by a silver sun and moon through which the models would enter. He was then given a mere three hours to cobble the show together. 'All one really needs in the world of fashion,' he noted sourly, 'is a voice, the louder and brassier the better – ideas get in the way.' (JP.)

96 Jan Parry, 17.2.85.

97 JP.

98 It is possible that this list is not entirely exhaustive, and that in addition Jarman made a video of 'My Heart Beats' for Jimmy the Hoover and one for Troy Tate. He also did some filming for Jayne County when she was starting a new band. *Catalan* involved travelling to Spain for filming; the other videos were all made very quickly in and around London.

99 KP, p. 12.

100 *Dreams of England*, p. 127. Not having a clue how to do the pop promos when he started, Jarman rang Ken Russell for advice. Russell said, 'Just cover the song twice, then you'll be OK.' So that is what Jarman did.

101 UA, p. 81.

24: Angelic and Other Conversations

1 DL, p. 229.

2 Ibid., p. 223.

3 JP.

4 DL, p. 223.

5 Ibid., p. 229.

6 The title was in part a coded reference to *The Final Academy* exhibition at the Ritzy in Brixton, covered later in this chapter, and in part an acknowledgement of the fact that in the most recent of his paintings, Jarman was treating the male nude in a fairly classical manner; returning, as he put it, to the Academy.

7 DL, pp. 228–9. The short review in *City Limits* was by Guy Brett (26.11–2.12.82), and the review in *The Times* by Paddy Kitchen (23.11.82).

8 Proposal, Tate Gallery Archive.

9 The cape for Houédard was specially reconstructed for the show by Sandy Powell, who had worked as costume designer on a number of Jarman's pop videos. The new capes were black and made out of newsprint. The exhibition comprised some fifty pieces in all.

10 The *GBH* series was too big to have been painted at Phoenix House, so Jarman used the dining room of a flat belonging to Ken Butler's mother as a temporary studio.

11 Emmanuel Cooper, *Him*, March 1984. Elsewhere Jarman says he did actually do this painting after the Falklands War, but never exhibited it.

12 April 1984.

13 *Athanasius Kircher*, p. 21.

14 *Building Design*, 23.3.84.

15 Writing in the *Observer*, 26.2.84, William Feaver concluded equivocally: 'Jarman has such blithe effrontery no painting skills are needed.'

16 Broadcast, 9.9.84. During the course of the programme, Jarman is seen filming a short super-8 film entitled *Working for Pleasure*. He filmed this at the ICA, in the gallery where the *GBH* series was hanging.

17 7.2.84.

18 JR.

19 JP.

20 *Square Peg*, No. 4, 1984.

21 Ron Meerbeek, *Crowd*, February 1984.

22 Attallah had previously been approached by Ward-Jackson about the possibility of doing a book of essays on *Caravaggio*. The book's editor at Quartet was Paul Keegan.

23 *National Heroes*, p. 232.

24 Tom Phillips, 6.4.84.

25 DL, pp. 239–40. Anita Bryant was an American singer and active campaigner for the rights of gay people.

26 JP.

27 Martin Grimes, LCP College Magazine, 1988.

28 AYOR, pp. 114–15.

29 Ibid., p. 113.

30 DV.

31 Jane Solanus, *New Musical Express*, 25.5.85.

32 Ron Meerbeek, *Crowd*, February 1984.

33 Sean O'Hagan, *The Face*, January 1991.

34 JP.

35 Sean O'Hagan, *The Face*, January 1991.

36 Either in the second half of 1981 or early in 1982.

37 The film was called *B2 Movie* because it was first shown at the B2 Gallery, to a

soundtrack of old 78s compiled by Dave Baby.

38 Summer 1982.

39 29 September to 2 October. In addition
to Burroughs, the event featured Brion Gysin,
John Giorno, Psychic TV, Cabaret Voltaire,
23 Skidoo, Jeff Nuttall and others.

40 JP.

41 The 'Priest', They Called Him, pp.
114–15.

42 Burroughs was most likely to have been
reading from either Cities of the Red Night or
The Place of Dead Roads.

43 Jarman's 'dream' was of Jean-Marc
Prouveur and Gerald Incandela. It utilised Art
and the Pose, the footage he had shot years
previously in Incandela's New York
apartment. James Mackay now came on board
as producer. A further application was made
to the Arts Council, this time for £4,750
towards the cost of completing the film in its
new guise. The money raised was, however,
insufficient to finish the film. Mackay then
turned to the BFI, who some years later
stumped up what was necessary to complete
the film for non-theatrical distribution.

At much the same time (July 1983),
harking back in style to the 'staged' super-8s
made in the deserted lot next to Bankside in
the mid-seventies, there was a half-realised
attempt to film an enactment of the Edward
Lear nonsense song, 'The Dong with a
Luminous Nose'. This idea was Ken
Campbell's, and was partially masterminded
by Francesca Moffat, Ward-Jackson's
sometime assistant, who was keen to move
into film production. Bearing a colourful and
bizarre assortment of costumes, two super-8
cameras and enormous enthusiasm, Campbell,
Moffat, James Mackay, John Maybury, Jarman
and others spent a spirited weekend filming
on the beach at Seaton in Dorset. But
weekend enthusiasm did not translate into
celluloid reality and, as with the Dong
himself, who searched so fruitlessly for his one
true love, the jumbly girl with 'her sky-blue
hands and her sea-green hair', nothing
tangible ever came of their footage. (The
Complete Nonsense of Edward Lear, pp.
225–8.)

44 JP.

45 Ibid.

46 Sylvia Andresen and the Freunde der
Deutschen Kinemathek. Over the years,
Jarman's key supporters in Berlin were: Sylvia
Andresen, who worked with Ulrich and Erika

Gregor, Manfred Salzgeber, Wieland Speck
and Alf Bold, who programmed for the
Arsenal Kino.

47 P-Orridge as quoted in England's
Dreaming, p. 251.

48 Founded 1976. The core members were
P-Orridge, Peter Christopherson, Cosey Fanni
Tutti and Chris Carter.

49 In the Shadow of the Sun leaflet, JP.

50 According to the record sleeve: 'The
music was improvised to a VHS video cassette
of the finished film on to an 8 track tape deck
at a cost of just over £100'. It was done in a
day.

51 DL, p. 214.

52 Ibid., p. 215.

53 Cynthia Rose, 17–23.4.81.

54 JP.

55 DL, p. 216.

56 One of the German film-makers was a
young man named Padeluun – 'an artist-
mendicant with hollow Kafka eyes, shaved
head, and baggy grey trousers tied with string'.
His last job had been 'refilling the
contraceptive dispensers at the service areas
on the autobahn – after he had done the job
he would glue on the machine an immaculate
sticker in orange, blue and silver which
announced DIESE MACHINE IST MEIN
ANTIHUMANISTISCHES KUNSTWERK with the PO
box-number Padeluun Berlin.' (DL, p. 231.
According to Padeluun, the stickers were
yellow and black.) Jarman was very taken by
this artist-mendicant and his stickered
manifesto. When asked by P-Orridge to make
a new film for his group (now called Psychic
TV), Jarman made Diese Machine Ist Mein
Antihumanistisches Kunstwerk. Using a static
camera in Phoenix House, he filmed
Padeluun's sticker in a mirror so that as well as
the manifesto, you see Jarman as film-maker
making the film. He also put a sticker on the
case in which he carried around his
Caravaggio script – a private note to himself to
help him keep a sense of purpose.

57 Around now A Room of One's Own,
Sloane Square was also blown up to 16mm
with music by Simon Turner and taken by
Jarman to one of the smaller film festivals.
These festival screenings were in addition to
ongoing screenings at such places as the Film
Makers' Co-op, the B2 Gallery and the ICA.

58 DL, p. 219.

59 The television was purely a monitor.
Only when linked to a video-recorder could it

display any pictures.

60 Taken from the sleeve of the record of the soundtrack. The quote continues: 'It has no linear, entertainment or musical intent outside that function.'

61 Early members included P-Orridge, Peter Christopherson, Geff Rushton (aka John Balance), David Tibet and Alex Fergusson. Jon Savage was also briefly a part of the group.

62 The programme, broadcast on 19.2.92, was called *Dispatches Beyond Belief* and was based on a book by Andrew Boyd entitled *Blasphemous Rumours: Is Satanic Ritual Abuse Fact or Fantasy? An Investigation.*

63 JP.

64 KP, p. 142.

65 JP.

66 KP, p. 133.

67 *Afterimage 12*, p. 52.

68 He would have filmed at Curry Mallet Manor itself, except that he found it 'wrecked' (MI).

69 KP, pp. 133–134.

70 JP.

71 *Afterimage 12*, p. 64.

72 Sainsbury.

73 Ibid.

74 Sainsbury, *Three Sixty*, May 1985.

75 KP, p. 140.

76 Geoff Brown, 25.2.85.

77 The film was later distributed abroad, often with great success, particularly in Japan, and shown on television. It became a favourite of art-house cinemas and film festivals throughout the world, though without ever currying great critical or commercial favour.

78 The other film-makers were Ed Bennett, Sally Potter, Peter Wollen and Peter Greenaway, who, because he was unable to attend in person, was represented by Peter Sainsbury. The group was assembled by Ian Christie.

79 KP, p. 99.

80 Jarman was particularly struck by Konstantin Lopushanksy's *Solo*, a student film of about thirty minutes' duration set during the siege of Leningrad in the Second World War. The film included an image which would enter Jarman's filmic vocabulary, that of a room in which it is snowing.

81 Peter Wollen. See also KP, p. 97, where Jarman describes the event somewhat differently.

82 KP, p. 97.

83 Ibid., pp. 96–7. See also djg, p. 43.

84 *Afterimage 12*, p. 44.

85 KP, pp. 100–01.

86 The list of films chosen to represent British Film Year were: *Another Country; Another Time, Another Place; Chariots of Fire; The Company of Wolves; The Dresser; The Draughtman's Contract; Educating Rita; The Elephant Man; The French Lieutenant's Woman; Gandhi; Gregory's Girl; Greystoke; Heat and Dust; The Hit; Local Hero; The Life of Brian; The Long Good Friday; Merry Christmas Mr Lawrence; Moonlighting; Pink Floyd – The Wall; Tess.* And, as Academy Award winners: *Hamlet; Bridge on the River Kwai; Tom Jones; A Man for All Seasons; Oliver; Lawrence of Arabia; Chariots of Fire; Gandhi.* Jarman would have added – or in many cases substituted – the film-makers with whom he had travelled to Moscow, plus such names as Terence Davies, Bill Douglas, Ron Peck, Julian Temple, John Maybury, Cerith Wyn Evans, Sophie Williams, Ken Russell, Nicholas Roeg.

87 Whereas in *The Tempest* Jarman had made Prospero dream the film, now he himself was dreaming it. He would do the same in *The Last of England* and *The Garden.*

88 KP, p. 100.

89 When Jarman attended the AGM of the Workers' Revolutionary Party in 1980–81 in the Kensington Town Hall with Vanessa Redgrave and company, the committee sat at a long table on the stage under a large portrait of Lenin. At the time Jarman said it reminded him of the Last Supper.

90 Golden teeth recur in Jarman's work. There is reference to this image in *PPP* and we see such teeth in *Caravaggio.*

91 Including Nicholas Ward-Jackson (£1,000) and Bryan Montgomery.

92 Besides concern for the welfare of the Russians, a factor in the festival's reaction may have been that its selectors (specifically the Gregors) were 'doyens of traditional left-wing film-making in Germany' (JP). As such, they were a conduit for Russian film-makers wanting to show their work in the West. To offend the USSR might have meant the cessation of this valuable traffic.

93 Despite this furore, Mackay did screen the film at Berlin in the year of *Caravaggio,* albeit privately, and at a very small cinema. There have since been other screenings, and not only of the censored form, though it is true to say that the film is rarely seen. But then there are commercial reasons for that.

See below.

94 JP.

95 JP.

96 *New Musical Express*, 25.5.85.

97 The one painting Jarman did not attempt to recreate accurately was *Profane Love*, Caravaggio's 'venture into paedophilia'. As described by Jarman, the painting is of 'a naked twelve-year-old boy as Cupid trampling over Culture and Architecture and the Martial Arts with a wicked grin' (DJC, p. 75). In the film, the character who models for the painting (Pipo) is neither a boy nor naked; instead, he is played by a woman (Dawn Archibald) and always remains fully clothed.

98 JP.

99 DJC, p. 44.

100 Ibid., p. 15.

101 Letter dated 14.7.85, JP.

102 Michael M. Moore, *New York Native*, 22.9.86.

103 JP.

104 DJC, p. 28.

105 Ibid., p. 52.

106 All quotes JP.

107 The published script adheres fairly closely to what ended up on screen, though because it was felt the book needed extra explication, Jarman did leave in many of the voice-overs that were finally cut from the finished film. By contrast, many of the diary entries were quite heavily edited to tone down some of Jarman's continuing anger at British Film Year. Ken Butler helped with the book.

108 For the film's 'cinematography and visual achievement'.

109 *Dreams of England*, p. 149.

110 The retrospective was organised by the Film and Video Umbrella, of which O'Pray was director. It comprised all three of Jarman's features to date, plus *The Angelic Conversation* and *Imagining October*, *Broken English*, as well as two compilations of his home movies. The 'influences', largely chosen by Jarman himself, were: Anger's *Eaux d'Artifice*, Cocteau's *Testament d'Orphée*, Dreyer's *La Passion de Jeanne d'Arc*, Eisenstein's *Ivan the Terrible, Part II*, Genet's *Chant d'Amour*, Pasolini's *The Gospel According to St Matthew*, Powell and Pressburger's *The Life and Death of Colonel Blimp*, and Warhol's *Chelsea Girls*.

111 *Afterimage 12* was edited by: Simon Field, Guy l'Eclair (a pseudonym for Ian Christie) and Michael O'Pray. The two unmade projects were: *PPP* and *Nijinsky's Last Dance*.

Of Angels and Apocalypse was not the only instance of Jarman receiving acknowledgement. In May 1984, shortly after the ICA exhibition and the publication of *Dancing Ledge*, a group of architects and young architectural students known as NATO – Narrative Architecture Today – chose Jarman as the person for whom they would like to design a house. The group comprised Nigel Coates, who was an old friend of Jarman's, Catrina Beevor, Martin Benson, Peter Fleissig, Robert Mull, Christina Norton, Mark Prizeman, Melanie Sainsbury and Carlos Villanueva. Their drawings of their design for Jarman's house featured in a *Starchoice* exhibition at RIBA in Portland Place. The exhibition comprised twenty-four architect-designed interiors for personalities as diverse as David Hockney (a shower) and Lord Carrington (a sofa). Jarman made a tape for the group and met with them to discuss where he wanted the house and what he would like in it. He chose Winspit and asked for five rooms, which had to be completely enclosed. NATO's resulting design had a roof of glass bricks and a bedroom in an underground cave.

112 *The Times*, 2.5.80.

113 KP, p. 89.

114 Currently the Independent Television Commission.

115 Letter dated 2.12.85.

116 27.2.86. Churchill's letter was written in response to a leader critical of his bill that appeared on 24.2.86.

117 KP, p. 90.

118 Martin Sutton, *Stills*, April 1986.

119 Tony Rayns, *American Film*, September 1986.

120 As quoted by David Robinson, *The Times*, 12.3.86. The three programmes were produced by Thames Television. Parker's programme, which was broadcast on 12.3.86, was followed by Lindsay Anderson's *Free Cinema 1956?* . . . (19.3.86) and Richard Attenborough's *A Marriage of Convenience* (26.3.86). The series was produced by Kevin Brownlow and David Gill and directed by Jeremy McCracken.

121 JP.

122 For example, Nigel Andrews, *Financial Times*, 25.4.86, said: 'If you keep your eye on the film's guiding star, the film will mesmerise rather than baffle. That star is Caravaggio's quest for truth . . .' By contrast, Michael

Parkinson, sitting in for Barry Norman on *Film '86*, slated it and asked for his 'money back'. Waldemar Januszczak berated the film for taking too many liberties with historical fact: 'As an artistic document it is, I am afraid, a true successor to *Lust for Life*' (*Guardian*, 24.4.86). At the next BAFTA Awards, the film failed to receive a single mention, even for the design. Jarman 'wept'. (JP)

123 Alan Stanbrook, *Stills*, April 1986.
124 Spring 1986.
125 *Isis*, 1987.
126 JP.
127 Michael O'Pray, *MFB*, April 1986.

25: *The Last of England*

1 KP, p. 239.
2 May 1986.
3 In *The Last of England*, p. 175, Jarman describes the making of that film in the same terms, as a jump out of the window into the blue. The budget for *Depuis le Jour* was between £28,000 and £50,000.
4 The actress Aimée Delamaine, wrongly credited on screen as Amy Johnson.
5 23.5.87.
6 WR, p. xi.
7 *Morrissey & Marr: The Severed Alliance*, p. 252.
8 *The Queen is Dead*, a 'mock-epic assault on Her Majesty the Queen' and 'a nightmare vision of a country weakened by spiritual and moral decay', was given a similarly dizzying treatment. The more tender 'There is a Light that Never Goes Out', with its 'expression of adolescent wish fulfilment', was treated more gently. (Quotes taken from *Morrissey & Marr: The Severed Alliance*, pp. 248, 249, 251.)
9 It may also have been the case that Jarman felt slightly guilty that the services of James Mackay had been so abruptly waived on *Caravaggio*. Perhaps he wanted to make amends by working further with Mackay in the manner which, with *The Angelic Conversation* and *Imagining October*, they had started so excitingly to pioneer.
10 KP, p. 239.
11 Ibid., p. 240.
12 Ibid., p. 242.
13 Ibid.
14 JP.
15 Simon Watney, *Marxism Today*, October 1987.
16 Maureen Cleave, *Observer*, 22.2.87.
17 JP. Jarman also considered *GBH* and *Three Minutes to Midnight*.

18 KP, p. 189.
19 Ibid., p. 190.
20 DL, p. 235.
21 JP.
22 The Tate catalogue, which lists Jarman's four features. The other artists short-listed were Michael Baldwin and Mel Ramsden, who worked as Art and Language, and Victor Burgin, Gilbert and George, Stephen McKenna and Bill Woodrow.
23 JP.
24 KP, p. 235.
25 Roger Wollen. The use of found objects in these paintings harked back to the work Jarman was doing in the late sixties when he moved into the first of his riverside studios.
26 JP. Because Jarman's use of smashed glass was highly reminiscent of the way in which Andrew Logan used the same medium, these new paintings caused a degree of surprise among certain of Jarman's friends. In an odd echo of one of the principal themes of *Caravaggio*, they muttered about plagiarism; art as theft. Others saw Jarman's magpie-like appropriation of found objects as an echo of his father's kleptomania. Everyone glimpsed the restless despair at work behind the hammer blows and hectic swirls of pitch-black paint.
27 Also called *Night Life*; a new application of an old title.
28 KP, p. 129.
29 Ibid.
30 Ibid.
31 MN, p. 265.
32 KP, p. 122.
33 Letter postmarked 4.12.86, JP.
34 Mackay rented the mill from the London Docklands Development Corporation.
35 JP.
36 Jarman was never the only person behind the camera. He filmed alongside John Maybury, Cerith Wyn Evans, Richard Heslop (who shot most of the ambient footage) and Chris Hughes (who doubled as lighting cameraman and took care of the master shots). Part of the reason for the different cameras was that although they had lights on the shoot, Jarman was always scared that super-8, particularly when in colour, would not come out except in blazing sunlight. Extra cameras, some using black and white film, were a form of insurance.
37 21.11.86.
38 JP. As part of the prize, Jarman's features

were given a screening and Michael O'Pray delivered a talk on Jarman at the Tate.

39 AYOR, p. 112.

40 JP.

41 As reported by Tom Sharrat, *Guardian*, 12.12.86.

42 Ibid.

43 KP, p. 17.

44 Maureen Cleave, 22.2.87. The interview was carried out in December 1986.

45 KP, pp. 16–17. This passage is identical to one in *At Your Own Risk*, p. 7; a good example of how Jarman cribbed himself.

46 Earlier that month, Jarman had visited Harley Street to have a medical for an insurance company he was seeing about a mortgage on Phoenix House (which, with his father's inheritance, he was suddenly in a position to buy) and had detested how 'careful' he had needed to be in what he revealed of his sexuality. As someone who hated harbouring secrets, it was not in his nature to be 'careful'. Lance's estate was worth some £200,000. Jarman and Gaye each received in the region of £100,000. On 9.12.86, Jarman acquired a ninety-nine-year lease on Phoenix House.

47 JP.

48 KP, p. 24.

49 DV.

50 KP, pp. 29–30.

51 JP.

52 DV. Of course, this boy was only one of many possible sources. In his more realistic moments, Jarman would admit he could not possibly know where or when he had become infected.

53 Undoubtedly Manfred Salzgeber.

54 JP.

55 Dan Yakir, *Globe and Mail*, Toronto, 2.9.86.

56 KP, p. 39.

26: A Fifth Continent

1 William Blake, 'The Sick Rose'.

2 JP. McBean also did the stills for Jarman's segment of *Aria*.

3 *The Ruffian on the Stair* and *The Erpingham Camp*, June 1967.

4 KP, p. 48.

5 In January 1987.

6 *Sunday Telegraph*, 23.11.86.

7 WR, p. xi.

8 KP, p. 188. Jarman wrote that both *The Last of England* and *Jubilee* were dream allegories, but that whereas in *Jubilee* 'the past dreamed the future present', in *The Last of England*, 'the present dreams the past future'.

9 JP.

10 KP, p. 30.

11 Jarman first used flares in *The Angelic Conversation*. On that film, but meaning of the garden rather than the nautical variety, he had asked James Mackay to buy some flares for the scenes shot in the caves at Tilly Whim. When Mackay produced nautical flares by mistake, Jarman had initially been unwilling to use them. When he did, he so loved the result that they became one of his trademarks.

12 In the foreground of Ford Madox Brown's painting various vegetables hang from the netting on the ship. It was this that suggested the sequence with Hughes and the cauliflower.

13 Among other things, they wanted to use material from the Falklands debate and Churchill's debate on the widening of the Obscene Publications Act.

14 Letter postmarked 16.1.87.

15 KP, p. 42.

16 Ibid., p. 240.

17 Exhibition catalogue.

18 Hinney means honey or flower.

19 djg, p. 69.

20 KP, p. 239.

21 In *The Fifth Continent*, Duncan Forbes quotes R.H. Barham, writing as Thomas Ingoldsby: 'The world, according to the best geographers, is divided into Europe, Asia, Africa, America and Romney Marsh.'

22 KP, p. 181.

23 JP.

24 Ibid.

25 Other mooted titles were: *A Pandemonium of Images, The Art of Memory, Mnemosyne*. See also below.

26 JP.

27 KP, p. 66.

28 As a title, Jarman would have preferred *Dead Souls Whisper, Silence is Golden, Household Gods, Pinch Me Not, Passing the Time* or (a particular favourite) Heathcote Williams' oft-quoted phrase, *Flow with the Glue*. Jarman worked on collating the material for the book with Hirst, who was credited as editor, and with Shaun Allen. In the book's acknowledgements he also thanked Keith (Collins), Nick (Searle) and Stephen (Thrower) for 'all your help'.

29 JP.

30 Also then called *Blue is Poison, Into the Blue*, or *My Blue Heaven*.

31 Proposal dated August 1987. In the end, because *The Garden* came before *Blue*, it is to the Garden that the refugees travel.

32 This poem refers to Klein's Theatre of the Void, to which he dedicated a specially prepared edition of a Sunday newspaper.

33 21.8–3.9.87.

34 15.8.87.

35 18.8.87.

36 JP.

37 Ibid.

38 Ibid.

39 Ibid.

40 In Tokyo, Jarman and Mackay talked to Sony, then looking for suitable material to pioneer their new high-definition video system. Sony had bought *The Last of England* for release as a laser disc and seemed keen to explore how, using their new system, Jarman's brand of non-narrative, image-based film-making might be taken into the mainstream. There was the carrot of a great deal of money should the right project be found. Jarman wondered whether *Paradise Lost* might fit the bill. This adaptation of Milton's epic poem for the screen by the writer John Collier had been suggested to Jarman as a potential project by Nicholas Ward-Jackson. But Collier's script was too lavish for what Sony had in mind. Undeterred, Jarman and Mackay later began talking about altering it to suit Sony's needs, or, failing that, taking it elsewhere.

41 JP. The despairing name Jarman gave this section of his diary was 'Borrowed Time', a title also in use for his next film with Tilda Swinton.

42 October 1987.

43 John Gill, 25.11.87.

44 From 1985 onwards, Jarman had also sold paintings through Mario Amabile, who had a gallery in Tufnell Park. Richard Salmon first encountered Jarman in the sixties, though it was only in the early eighties, through Ken Butler, that he had met him properly and started to become excited by his potential as a painter.

45 Jarman saw black as the colour that binds the universe. As he told Michael Petry in *Arts Review* (27.1.89), he used it so much because 'things shine out of the darkness and so the very nature of black means that you actually see things better'.

46 Adrian Searle, *Art Forum*, March 1988.

47 Over the publication of *Spycatcher*.

48 And, one might add, Theresa Russell in Roeg's segment of *Aria*.

49 Kimmerghame, Tilda Swinton's family home.

50 In further notes Jarman again mixes ideas from old scripts, other films and daily observation with such literary influences as those two favourite Anglo-Saxon poems 'The Wanderer' and 'The Dream of the Rood'.

51 JP.

52 Though parts of it would find their way into *At Your Own Risk*.

53 JP. Jarman would execute a commemorative painting on each successive anniversary of his diagnosis.

54 22.10.87. During 1987, Jarman started to talk more and more frequently in public about being HIV positive.

55 AYOR, p. 121.

27: Sod 'Em

1 WR, p. xi.

2 Ibid., p. xi–xii.

3 Ibid., p. 2.

4 Ibid., p. 6.

5 Because this was all the payment Jarman ever received, and because the film never did go into profit, there were those who maintained he had been cheated. He himself would sometimes agree.

6 JP.

7 AYOR, p. 128. As if Clause 28 were not enough to make Jarman feel under attack, on 10.1.88 Norman Stone wrote a long and blistering article in *The Sunday Times* bemoaning the state of the British film industry. Among the films he singled out for attack was *The Last of England*. Jarman's reply to Stone was published in *The Sunday Times* on 17.1.88.

8 JP.

9 All quotes taken from the typed transcript of the debate in Jarman's papers.

10 JP, the 'Listening Wall' diary. This short private diary is named for the Listening Wall at Greatstone, 'a massive concrete semicircle built in the war so that we could hear enemy planes coming across the channel' (MN, p. 72). It is a revealing choice of name, showing the extent to which Jarman saw himself as under attack and at war.

11 Paul Callan, 27.3.88.

12 JP.

13 Ibid.

14 Ibid. Nor could Jarman entirely escape the British critics, or the paper which had carried Norman Stone's attack on him earlier in the year. 'The Sunday Times is at it again,' he wrote in his diary on 22 February. 'IJ, a man whose initials I unwillingly preserve on this page, takes up arms against the Berlin film festival, grudging me a moment in the sunlight . . . next time a newspaper comes down on the head of a critic let's put an iron bar in it and smash his head properly . . .' IJ was Ian Johnstone, who had written that 'Berlin suffers from a bad attack of the Jarmans' (*The Sunday Times*, 21.2.88). In fact he was objecting not just to Berlin making a fuss of Jarman, but equally to what he saw as the festival's neglect of British cinema and, in particular, of Tony Palmer's *Testimony*, which was not in competition, allegedly because this study of Shostakovitch had offended the Russians. This latter scenario was so like the one Jarman had faced with *Imagining October* that he might have been expected to see the connection – except that he was feeling too much under 'psychic attack' to react rationally.

15 Paul Griffith, 31.5.88.
16 JP.
17 Ibid.
18 Ibid.
19 UA, p. 185.
20 Ibid.
21 All quotes UA, pp. 186–225.
22 Eventually made by John Maybury.
23 This idea was first mooted in 1987. In June 1988, the Dungeness Leaseholders Association gave Jarman permission to make a film about Dungeness. He never did – or rather, he incorporated this impulse into *The Garden*. Jarman was currently calling his diary *The Fifth Quarter of the Globe*. The diary also mentions, or includes notes/prose poems for: *The Fifth Quarter of the Globe*, *The Bees of Infinity*, *Angelology*, *Dreamtime*, *Gnosis*, *The Hourglass and the Scythe*. All these pieces/fragments are rather despairing and bleak.
24 Michael Petry, *Arts Review*, 27.1.89. Petry added: 'I urge Nick Serota to buy one for the Tate.' Painting still provided therapy, though Jarman was also painting with a more specific purpose in mind – he had been offered a touring exhibition cum film retrospective in Europe in late 1988.
25 JP.

26 Maureen Cleave, 22.2.87.
27 KP, p. 149.
28 Ibid., p. 151.
29 JP.
30 Because Dungeness is a site of special scientific interest, there are restrictions as to what may be grown there.
31 WR, p. 8.
32 DV.
33 The film had its American première in San Francisco as part of the city's International Lesbian and Gay Film Festival.
34 Janet Maslin, 28.9.88.
35 Katherine Dieckmann, 24.1.89.
36 WR, p. 36.
37 Ibid., p. 35.
38 MI.
39 4–11.1.89.
40 4.1.89.
41 5.1.89.
42 MN, p. 16. The film was shown at Berlin in February 1989. It was shown on British television the following Good Friday, 24.3.89. In April, Faber and Faber published the script together with explanatory material by Jarman and an introduction by Boyd.
43 *Know What I Mean.*

28: I Walk in This Garden
1 Tim Clark, *Time Out*, 28.12–4.1.89.
2 Katherine Dieckmann, *Village Voice*, 24.1.89.
3 Jarman was also asked by the opera house in Lyons to direct Strauss's *Salome*. He met Robyn Archer, the Australian performer whose homage to certain favourite singers, *A Star is Torn*, might, it was thought, provide the basis of a film. He discussed filming Penelope Mortimer's novel *The Handyman* for the BBC. He watched *Sod 'Em* become the subject of lengthy deliberations with Channel 4 and the European Script Fund. He lent an ear to vague but excited talk of filming *A Midsummer Night's Dream* in Italy and considered an invitation from Philip Prowse to direct a play at the Citizens Theatre in Glasgow.
4 MN, p. 112. See also p. 183.
5 Ibid., p. 89.
6 JP.
7 MN, p. 93.
9 Ibid., p. 98.
8 Ibid., p. 99.
10 Ibid., p. 100.
11 JP.
12 MN, p. 100.

13 Ibid. p. 116.
14 *Literally*, p. 329.
15 Ibid., p. 331. The concert was positively
reviewed in the music press, but not in the
broadsheets. A video, *Projections*, was
produced of the back projections. It contained
seven of the eight songs ('Nothing Has Been
Proved' was dropped). To make up the
numbers, two new songs were added, both set
to old super-8 footage: 'Violence', set to 'A
Garden in Luxor', and 'Being Boring', set to
'Studio Bankside'. The video of the concert
itself was called *Highlights*. It comprised a total
of eight songs.
16 MN, p. 132.
17 Ibid., pp. 154–5. See also Chris Heath's
Literally for a detailed account of the concert
and tour.
18 Ibid., p. 32.
19 Ibid., p. 17.
20 Ibid., p. 25.
21 Ibid. Jarman frequently spoke about
becoming 'the object of necrophilia', and was
alarmed to discover, in 1988 or 1989, that the
newsletter of the Old Canfordian Society
prematurely reported his death.
22 Jeni Walwin in the brochure for the
1989 festival.
23 MN, p. 88.
24 Ibid., p. 117. He tarred and feathered a
bible 'open at Leviticus with a barbed wire
marker' (MN, p. 111). One of the larger
objects he painted with tar varnish was Güta
Minton's garden seat.
25 Ibid., p. 127.
26 Ibid., p. 160.
27 Hilary Robinson, *Glasgow Herald*,
6.10.89. The 'physique magazine' referred to
was in fact Jarman's copy of *The Best of
Physique Pictorial*.
28 MN, p. 167.
29 Ibid., p. 168.
30 Ibid., p. 54.
31 Ibid., p. 69.
32 *Bloodhounds on Broadway*.
33 MN, p. 75.
34 Ibid., p. 98.
35 Ibid., p. 99.
36 Of Andy Marshall, and his continuing
need for support, Jarman noted in MN: 'HB
won't let me get involved any longer. I know
he is right about this but I feel guilty.' (p.
158.) MN also makes reference to the fact
that in 1989 (or perhaps in early 1990 – the
exact date is uncertain) Jarman bought

Raimond, who was half Dutch, a houseboat in
Amsterdam. Either he wanted to see the
rather wild Raimond settled, or else he was
buying him off.
37 MI.
38 JP. See also Chapter 26.
39 Ibid.
40 Production notes.
41 MN, p. 157.
42 Ibid., p. 134. The 'ghastly video' was
Highlights.
43 Ibid., p. 151.
44 Ibid, p. 149. Entry dated 13.9.89. David
is David Lewis. Drako was the Serpent rather
than the Devil. Spring does not appear in the
final film. Graham is Graham Dowie. At the
same time, Jarman was deciding to use his
own poetry as a voice-over.
45 Ibid., p. 157.
46 Ibid., p. 165.
47 Ibid., p. 171.
48 Ibid., p. 172.
49 Ibid., p. 173.
50 Ibid., p. 174.
51 Ibid., p. 179.
52 Ibid., p. 198.
53 Ibid., p. 189.
54 Ibid., p. 190.
55 Ibid., p. 199.
56 Ibid., p. 210.
57 Ibid., p. 212.
58 Ibid., p. 211.

29: Blue Prints
1 MN, p. 218.
2 Various singers were asked to do covers of
Porter songs. There was to be both a disc and
a TV show, which was why films were needed.
After accepting Lennox's commission, Jarman
fell ill (see below) and decided he did not
have the energy to make the video. It seemed
that Lennox would have to look elsewhere.
Then it was suggested that Jarman's home
movies might provide a backdrop for the song.
They were collected from Prospect Cottage,
viewed and given the thumbs-up. Almost
without his knowing it, Jarman had provided
the film Lennox wanted.
3 Canby's *New York Times* review was of the
opinion that 'Derek Jarman has made a movie
of epic irrelevance that, when it rises to the
occasion, is merely redundant' (26.1.90). The
film soon closed. Nevertheless, as Jarman
mused in an article in *Outweek* (4.2.90, by
Karl Soehnlein), published to coincide with
the film's opening, he could at least say of his

professional standing in America: 'The situation in the States seems to be on the turn; though, of course, I've had no commercial success there and that puts me in a very weak position.' His standing as a gay activist was a great help in this regard.

4 MN, pp. 220–21.
5 Ibid., p. 251.
6 Ibid., p. 250.
7 Ibid., p. 253.
8 Ibid., p. 267.
9 Ibid., p. 258.
10 Ibid., p. 275.
11 Simon Watney was another friend to work on the script of Edward II.
12 Ibid., p. 284. Derek B. is Derek Ball, who had a house in Dungeness and became an invaluable part of Jarman's life there.
13 Ibid., p. 286.
14 Ibid., pp. 288–9.
15 Ibid., pp. 290–91.
16 Ibid., p. 291.
17 Ibid., p. 294.
18 Ibid., p. 293.
19 Ibid., p. 301.
20 Ibid., p. 304.
21 Ibid., p. 307.
22 Ibid., p. 304.
23 Jarman himself would probably not have agreed with this interpretation. On 29.11, reacting to the letters he received after the screening, he wrote: ' I had a large pile of letters from The Garden showing last Monday, all very affirmative except for one abusive one, spurred by the Independent and sent via OutRage! It said I made sadomasochistic films of self-hatred, if I do hate myself I've never noticed it. This muddle, if you show the problems say in The Garden you become a masochist. The more letters I get from these old-fashioned "gays" the more I'm glad of the queer.' (SISM, 29.8.92.)
24 Nigel Andrews, 23.8.90.
25 MN, p. 314.
26 JP.
27 MN, p. 312. Jarman's dosage was 500mg.
28 Sean O' Hagan, The Face, January 1991.
29 When Clare later published a collection of his interviews, including the one with Jarman, Jarman took exception to his introduction to the interview. Clare wrote: 'With me he is characteristically frank about his earlier promiscuity, about his decision to have an HIV test, about his subsequent celibate behaviour (although one or two things he has said since suggest that this has sadly changed).' (In the Psychiatrist's Chair, p. 160.) Clare's bracketed aside made Jarman vow never to allow the interview to be repeated.
30 JP.
31 MN, p. 8.
32 Guardian, 9.1.91.
33 Ibid., 10.1.91.
34 Although McKellen seemed to receive more public support than Jarman over this affair, Jarman was not without allies. Lindsay Anderson sent the following card: 'Dear Derek – I'm not a Guardian reader (you may be surprised?!) but a friend has sent me the cuttings, which have delighted me, and I congratulate you . . . When do you think the British lost their sense of humour?? . . . But then this has never been the strong point of Sir Ian – or indeed any of those signatories . . . Bravo anyway for sticking your neck out with such insouciance . . .! I look forward to THE GARDEN – Best always! Lindsay (Anderson).'
    There is a postscript to this. In mid-1992, in an interview with Scott A. Hunt in Christopher Street, McKellen remarked that when he came out: 'There was nobody in British life, full stop, who'd come out. Wait a minute. Derek Jarman . . . Maybe Derek Jarman. A few people on the fringes of society.' Not surprisingly, this reference to being 'on the fringes of society' prompted an angry response from Jarman: ' I will continue to criticise both McKellen and Stonewall until I see a chink of democracy in their attitudes to the rest of us' (JP).
35 Pink Paper, 16.2.91.
36 Jarman would always support OutRage! and attended their meetings whenever he could. He was involved in the full-page advertisement they ran in The Times to protest at Clause 25, helping both to draft it and to drum up celebrities to sign it. He organised charity screenings of his films for the group's benefit, bought them a fax machine and gave freely of his services as a celebrity. In answer to these and other demonstrations, the government did eventually 'qualify' what had started life as Clause 25.
37 Act 5, scene 5, lines 31–32.
38 Historians dispute the exact method of Edward's death; some that he died prematurely at all. Jarman used this uncertainty as justification for his happy

ending.

39 *There We Are John*.

40 *Queer Edward II*, p. 16.

41 Ibid., p. 22.

42 Ibid., p. 46.

43 Ibid., p. 146.

44 Ibid., p. 154.

45 Jonathan Romney, *Blitz*, June 1991.

46 13.3.91. 'Superstar Cliff Richard was besieged by a mob of foul-mouthed gays,' said the article. The *Evening Standard* also carried a piece on 12.3.91.

47 He kept the diary in a series of small, black notebooks which he could tuck into his pocket, enabling him to carry it wherever he went.

48 Proposal dated 20 November. It was for a one hour documentary, ideally with a voice-over by Jarman himself.

49 Furse had known Jarman for many years and was then doing a course in screenwriting. When he heard this, Jarman suggested Furse write a script about Lance. To have easy access to Jarman, Furse followed the example of McBride and rented a cottage at Dungeness. During the first six months of 1991, he worked up a script outline entitled *Janus*, because the script had become the story not just of Lance, but of Lance and Jarman, two sides of a single coin. The idea was that Jarman would direct the finished result. However, although Furse completed the script, it never reached the screen. Jarman was not suited to directing another person's telling of his tale. Furse wrote *Janus* for Working Title, who optioned the film rights in *The Last of England* and *Modern Nature* so as to be covered for *Janus*. In the final script, which covers a lot of familiar territory, Lance (Air Commodore Dyson) is still alive when the Jarman character (Gerald Dyson) is diagnosed. Gerald is therefore able to share this with his father, which helps effect a final reconciliation that never took place in real life. Jarman would have played the part of Gerald's dealer. He wanted Daniel Day-Lewis to play himself.

50 djg, pp. 34–7.

51 The idea for this was suggested to Jarman by the journalist Neil McKenna. Malcolm Sutherland was involved in helping to plan it, as was Antony Root at Working Title.

52 In addition to the above projects, Sarah Radclyffe remembers trying to option a Francis Bacon biography for Jarman.

53 The blue was that of an Yves Klein painting from the Tate, filmed by Steve Farrer and Anna Thew.

54 JP.

55 As the concerts unfolded, their form changed. According to Michael O'Pray, in Japan a loop of blue film was used accompanied by slide images from Jarman's super-8s. Speech came from a recording of Michael Gough reading Jarman's poetry. In Rome, John Quentin read from the text of *Blue* itself, which by then existed, and Mackay used blue gels rather than the loop, which often became snared in the projector.

56 Proposal dated 22.4.91.

57 Proposal dated 30.5.91. Simon Turner would provide the soundtrack. Jon Savage, who wrote the text for a *Bliss* portfolio put together by James Mackay, made a compilation tape of London songs through the ages for this proposal. Savage's text for the portfolio was later reproduced on the sleeve notes for *Live Blue Roma* (*The Archeology of Sound*), Mute Records.

There are other proposals in the Basilisk files for variations on these themes, all dated 1991. The film would follow the life of an 'everyman' character from birth to the attainment of the immaterial after death. Or it would be 'an elegiac testament to the colour blue' with a 'centralising thread' of narrative: two lovers, each sixty three, or one of sixty three, one young. Or it would have Jarman as 'an alchemist who . . . conjures up the film . . . The demon/angel he conjures is the ringmaster. The ringmaster is given a charge, a child whose life he looks over and guides.'

58 JP.

59 All taken from treatments one and two and the script dated September, JP.

60 Working Title were later shown the *Pansy* script and also said no. Antony Root agreed it was essentially a theatre piece. Jarman then spoke to Jonathan Kent about mounting it at the Almeida, but Kent was not keen. Jarman saw Marianne Faithfull as Dick Trace It and thought Andy Bell of Erasure would make a great Pansy. At one stage Neil Tennant was asked if he was interested in doing the music.

61 *Projections 2*, p. 93.

62 SISM, 2.7.91. Century's indefatigable publicist was Gina Rozner.

63 Ibid., 8.8.91.

64 In addition to the *Guardian* and the

Sunday Telegraph, reviews appeared in *The Sunday Times*, the *Daily Express*, the *Sunday Express*, the *Financial Times*, the *Sun* and the *New Statesman*. SISM, 12.8.91: 'HB reluctantly showed me an unpleasant review in the Telegraph, the nastiest I have ever received . . .'. This review (11.8.91) was written by Christopher Tookey and ends: 'His journals epitomise the cliquishness, preciousness, amateurish contempt for craft, and political naivety which have infantilised British experimental art for three decades, and British film-making for the last 10 years.'

65 On discovering that Peter Tatchell kept the letters he received, Jarman began to do the same. Whenever possible, he would send a reply, sometimes a copy of one of his books, otherwise a few encouraging or grateful words scribbled on the back of a postcard. As time went on and the letters began to arrive in their hundreds, replying to them became increasingly impossible.

66 This did not stop Jarman reacting quite violently to these letters: 'I'm deluged by letters of the type "Christ died for your sins." I wrote back a saintly rebuff: How stupid of him, why didn't he stay alive and die decently of old age?' (SISM, 4.1.92.)

67 *Projections 2*, p. 94.

68 31.7.91.

69 7.9.91.

70 McKellen took tea with John Major on 24.9.91. The only coverage the *Guardian* accorded the meeting was a short diary piece by Nicholas de Jongh on the following day. Preston's reply to Jarman's fax is dated 25.9.91 and is in Jarman's papers.

71 SISM, 10.7.91.

72 Ibid., 4.8.91.

73 Artist's Statement for the exhibition at the Glasgow Art Gallery and Museum, Kelvingrove, January 1992.

74 SISM, 31.5.91.

75 SISM, 31.5.91.

76 Charles Spencer, *Daily Telegraph*, 2.10.91.

77 Rhoda Koenig, *Punch*, 9.10.91.

78 SISM, 15.8.91.

79 Ibid., 17–22.9.91.

80 Letter dated 16.3, JP.

81 AYOR, p. 132.

82 *Impertinent Decorum*, p. 173.

83 Ibid., p. 174.

84 AYOR, p. 131.

85 Andrew Gliniecki, *Independent*, 23.9.91.

30: Do Not Go Gentle

1 SISM, 15.10.91. The agent was Lorraine Hamilton.

2 Minty Clinch, *Observer*, 13.10.91.

3 JP. The tapes Jarman made for AYOR indicate that in part he was finding it difficult being an AIDS survivor; he felt guilty to be outliving so many friends.

4 15.10.91. At the Curzon West End. The première was in aid of AIDS research. After the screening, there was a party at Heaven at which the Pet Shop Boys played.

5 13 October–5 November. The films shown were: *In the Shadow of the Sun*, *The Dream Machine*, *Imagining October*, *Sebastiane*, *Edward II*, *Jubilee*, *The Tempest*, *Caravaggio*, *The Angelic Conversation*, *The Last of England*, *War Requiem* and *The Garden* – plus a handful of accompanying super-8 shorts and pop promos: *Studio Bankside*, *Sebastiane Wrap*, *Sloane Square*, *Every Woman For Herself*, *Broken English*, *Catalan*, *Pirate Tape*, *The Queen is Dead* and various of the films for the Pet Shop Boys. Jarman gave a *Guardian* interview. Earlier in the year, in May, the NFT had run a short season to coincide with the publication of *Take 10*, a collection of essays on contemporary film-makers. Jarman was one of the film-makers to be thus honoured.

6 Issued by Richard Salmon in a printing of 3,000 copies.

7 17.10.91.

8 *Evening Standard*, 23.10.91.

9 Ibid., 30.10.91.

10 8.8.91.

11 *Evening Standard*, 4.11.91. Jarman gives the full text of his letter in AYOR, pp. 142–3.

12 SISM, 22.10.91

13 The Bob Angelo Penning Award, presented during the Amsterdam Gay and Lesbian Film Festival.

14 The collaborators included: Michael Christie (editor), Malcolm Sutherland, Chris Woods, and, of course, Keith Collins. Both Sutherland and Woods, a journalist, interviewed Jarman on tape. Christie, who was then working at TV AM and had met Jarman through Neil McKenna, typed up Jarman's other thoughts.

15 AYOR, p. 3.

16 Ibid., p. 61.

17 SISM, 31.12.91 and 1.1.92.

18 Jarman also thought to scramble *Pansy* with *Ubu Roi* and *The Beggar's Opera*. (SISM,

2.1.92.) He talked about doing ten pages of a play called *Fucking Queer* for Sean O'Connor. (SISM, 13.1.92.) He was approached to direct a couple of commercials and, surprisingly, said yes, though in the event he did neither.

19 SISM, 2.2.92.

20 The discussion was hosted by B. Ruby Rich. Also on the panel were: Todd Haynes, Tom Kalin, Julien Isaacs, Sadie Benning, Lisa Kennedy, Simon Hunt and Stephen Cummings.

21 SISM, 13.3.92.

22 OutRage! leaflet, JP.

23 SISM, 6.2.92.

24 Ibid., 6.2.92. Thanks in part to the presence of Somerville and Jarman, the march received wide coverage, even making the TV news. Jarman's rather sombre picture appeared in the *Guardian* on 7.2.92.

25 Ibid., 18.2.92. The Fédération Internationale de la Presse Cinématographique, the international film critics' association, awarded the International Film Critics award (FIPRESCI Prize) in the twenty-second International Forum jointly to *La Vie de Bohème* (Aki Kaurismaki, Finland) and *Edward II* 'for the vibrant sexuality combined with rigorous lyricism brought to a classical text'. The film also scooped a Teddy Bear. A year later, in February 1993, *Wittgenstein* would win Jarman his third Berlin Teddy Bear. At the time of writing, this makes him the only film-maker to have won the award so many times.

26 February 1992 was also when the brief controversy over Jarman's appearance as the spokesman for Psychic TV in a Dispatches programme caused him to fear becoming the object of tabloid scrutiny. He overcame the problem by following Jon Savage's advice and keeping his head down for a few days. He phoned Alan Beck in Brighton and asked Beck to rescue him, which Beck did by taking him to Brighton. See chapter 24.

27 SISM, 26.2.92.

28 Statement in *Queer* catalogue.

29 SISM, 22.3.92.

30 Ibid., 23.3.92.

31 Ibid., 23.4.92.

32 Ibid., 7.4.92.

33 Jarman was also one of those to call for calm in the legal battle that flared up between the *New Statesman* and the *Pink Paper* over an article by Duncan Campbell in which Campbell attacked the group Positively

Healthy for the manner in which it advocated alternative therapies as a means of combating AIDS. Jarman welcomed debate over how to tackle AIDS, but deplored that it should end in the courts.

34 SISM, 15.4.93. Francis Bacon was another figure to die at this time. The following day, Jarman and Clemmet painted a homage to Bacon at South Edwardes Square. Called *Francis Going to Work*, the painting was in response to a much-loved Bacon reproduction Jarman had owned as a youngster: *Van Gogh Going to Work*.

35 Ibid., 31.3.92.

36 Ibid., 21.4.92.

37 16.5.92.

38 SISM, 7.5.92.

39 Ibid., 19.5.92.

40 The four essays in the catalogue were by Stuart Morgan, Andrew Renton, Norman Rosenthal and Simon Watney. The interview was by Howard Smith. The filming was done by Mark Jordan.

41 Matthew Parris, 14.5.92. At this time, Jarman heard that Overlook Press in New York had made an offer for *Dancing Ledge* – an offer which soon led to the American publication of virtually all his titles.

42 SISM, 26.5.92.

43 Ibid., 7.6.92.

44 Ibid., 22.6.92.

45 The original proposal for the film scripts was for nine in all: *Sebastiane, Jubilee, Caravaggio* (already published), *Akenaten, Little England, Sod 'Em, Neutron, Bob-up-a-Down* and *Blue*. Eventually six were published, posthumously, as *Up in the Air*. The title was suggested by Collins.

46 To be scripted by Ken Butler.

47 *Narrow Rooms*, p. 173.

48 SISM, 31.5.92.

49 Ibid., 20.7.92.

50 Jarman's helpers included David Roden (also known as Gingerbits) and David Lewis.

51 Ali's introduction to *Wittgenstein*.

52 Of *Tractatus* Jarman said: 'Personally I don't have the mind to approach the book, but its incomprehensible density attracts me, particularly that which cannot be spoken.' (SISM, 30.5.92.) The book's famous closing dictum – 'Whereof one can not speak, thereof one must be silent' – is nicely reminiscent of Jarman's own motto, Silence is Golden.

53 SISM, 9.6.92.

54 Ibid., 24.6.92.

55 Ibid., 1.7.92.
56 Ibid., 10.8.92.
57 Ibid., 17.8.92.
58 Ibid., 09.8.92.
59 Ibid., 12.8.92.
60 Ibid., 13.8.92. This diary entry is used in *Blue*. A fair amount of Jarman's diary from this time found its way into the film, along with phrases lifted from his favourite books and writers.
61 Ibid., 18.8.92.
62 Ibid., 14.8.92.
63 Ibid., 13.8.92.
64 The Epistle of Barnabus, a first-century text, describes 'various proscriptions supposedly laid down by Moses. Among these was eating the flesh of the hare since, as the hare develops a new anus annually, the meat would make one a pederast.' (*Queer Companion*, p 80.)
65 A piece designed by Maggi Hambling was eventually erected in Adelaide Street in 1998.
66 SISM, 24.8.92.
67 Ibid., 12.8.92.
68 Ibid., 30.9.92. When Ali made his offer to Jarman, Jarman replied: 'I've always wanted to make a film called *Mad Ludwig*.' He was referring, of course, to Ludwig of Bavaria, who had featured as a character in some of Jarman's earliest adult writing.
69 Ibid., 9.9.92.
70 Ibid., 10.9.92.
71 Ibid., 5.10.92.
72 Ibid., 3.9.92.
73 Ibid., 5.10.92.
74 Ibid., 12.9.92. On 19.9.92, Jarman attendeda seminar at the ICA on New Queer Cinema. He was also interviewed by Simon Callow for a film on Shakespeare, then not included in the finished piece – a cause of some anger. See SISM, 18.10.92.
75 Ibid., 5.10.92.
76 KP, p. 235.
77 SISM, 18.10.92.
78 Ibid., 28.10.92.
79 Ibid., 2.11.92.
80 Soon there were other titles: *Forget-Me-Not, Speedwell Eyes, Bruises, Blue protects white from innocence, o.*
81 SISM, 19.9.92.
82 JP.
83 The Arts Council exhibited *Morphine* at the Festival Hall in the spring of 1993.
84 SISM, 6.11.92. Initially the idea was to base the script around the display of Géricault's painting that had once taken place in a tent on Salisbury Plain.
85 Ibid., 6.12.92.
86 Ibid., 1.1.93.
87 Ibid., 3.1.93.
88 Ibid. , 27.1.93.
89 Ibid., 12.2.93.The title was *Demonology or Hell on Earth*.
90 JP.
91 17.1.93.
92 SISM, 11.1.93.
93 Basilisk proposal.
94 SISM, 31.1.93.
95 Ibid., 1.2.93.
96 At around the same time, a film student by the name of Tom Stephen made *21st Century Nuns*, a short film about the Sisters of Perpetual Indulgence. Stephen interviewed Jarman for the film in the course of the carnival.
97 SISM, 1.2.93.
98 Ibid., 15.1.93.
99 Ibid., 1.3.93.
100 Ibid., 4.3.93.
101 18.3.93. Eagleton took particular exception to the 'camp Martian' and his 'wads of embarrassing whimsy'. He pointed out that this character had not been in the original script.
102 Monk wrote to the *Guardian* on 19.3.93 to point out that 'much of the "embarrassing whimsy" was written by Wittgenstein himself. In *On Certainty* paragraph 430, Wittgenstein asks us to imagine a Martian approaching him with the question, "How many toes have human beings got?"' Monk also gave the film a glowing review in the *TLS*, 19.3.93.
103 SISM, 8.3.93.
104 Jarman's sole eventual executor was Collins. The net worth of the estate was assessed at just over £100,000. A further legacy to be dropped during the course of Jarman's alterations to his will was that of the Dutch houseboat which he had bought for Gerard Raimond, and which at one point he intended to leave to Raimond.
105 AYOR, p. 118. This plan also involved turning 'the House of Commons into a backroom for the under twenty-ones for a night'.
106 JP.
107 Ibid.
108 SISM, 21.3.93. By now, the buying of books was vestigial in nature. Virtually unable

to read, Jarman entered bookshops only 'to remind me of what I would read if it were possible' (SISM, 20.3.93).

109 After considerable difficulties in clearing the necessary permissions, Jarman's gravestone was finally erected in 1996. It is inscribed with his signature.

110 SISM, 20.3.93.

111 MN, p. 23.

112 *derek jarman's garden* was published in 1994.

113 *Blind Maniac.*

114 *The Last Paintings of Derek Jarman.*

115 SISM, 11.5.93. One of the items Jarman bought was a gold Movado watch.

116 Ibid., 30.11.92. As Jarman became increasingly unable to read himself and began to rely more and more on others reading to him, he particularly enjoyed being read to from the metaphysical poets. One of the things he had always most feared about blindness was that it would deprive him of the kind of literature he liked to read. As he had reflected ruefully to Julian Cole on the occasion of first being diagnosed with toxo, when Cole had suggested Jarman ask his friends to read to him: 'I can't imagine friends of mine settling down with the biography of Augustine, stumbling through the intricacies of his war on Pelagianism as the Empire cracked up.' (SISM, p. 307.)

117 Peter Fillingham, Karl Lydon, Steve Melton and Katie Lester.

118 Ibid., 11.5.93.

119 Ibid., 17.3.93. 'Peaches' was a nickname for Steven Graham Downes.

120 DV. Jarman was currently calling his diary *Chill in Utopia.*

121 *Independent*, 5.5.93.

122 Letter dated 5.5.93, JP.

123 SISM, 27.5.93. From Giverny Jarman and Sooley drove to Chartres, then to Milly-la-Forêt, where they visited Cocteau's house and St Blaise-aux-Simples, the tiny chapel where the writer is buried. Again, Jarman was entranced. Comparing his reaction to the 'murky' cathedral at Chartres with how he felt about St Blaise-aux-Simples, he wrote: 'I think on the whole I'm a person for small places' (SISM, 27.5.93). They then crossed France to Colmar, stopping on the way at another small place, the chapel built by Corbusier at Ronchamp. This Jarman thought the most beautiful of all the buildings they visited.

124 Ibid., 3.6.93.

125 Sarah Kent, *Time Out*, 23–30.6.93.

126 SISM, 15.6.93.

127 Paul Burston, *Time Out*, 18–25.10.93.

128 SISM, 22.6.93.

129 Ibid., 9.7.93. Also honoured were: Jack Lang, Roy Lichtenstein, Issey Miyake (honorary doctors), Alberto Alessi, Patrick Caulfield, Edmund Happold, Leslie Waddington (senior fellows), Manual Cosa Cabral, Mark Fisher, Tricia Guild, Norbet Lynton, James Roddis, David Shah, John Styles (honorary fellows).

130 12.7.93.

131 SISM, 24.8.93.

132 19.9.93.

133 18.9.93.

134 In his novel *Still*, Adam Thorpe has a central character who is a film-maker planning a movie without pictures or sound. He is told that 'Japes Jarman' (p. 134) has got there first.

135 The full citation reads: 'For his extraordinary artistic oeuvre, consisting of painting, literature and cinema, whose imagery always blends passion with poetry and whose creative vision breaks the bonds of current vogues whilst maintaining an individual political and artistic position.' The prize, a glass pyramid containing a golden eyeball, is dated Berlin, 25 September, 1993.

136 SISM, 1.10.93.

137 Ibid., 1.10.93. During 1993, Jarman provided a few lines of introduction, or blessing, to *Get The Rubber Habit*, a postcard book of photographs of the sisters by Denis Doran that was published in 1994.

138 *Dipsy Do*, *Do Lalley* and *Bubble and Squeak.*

139 From *Glitterbug*, the original proposal written by Jon Savage, Mackay had gone back to an earlier image, never used in *The Garden*, and framed the idea thus: 'Two space boys discover a chest on a beach (studio against blue screen). They find the chest to contain reels of images (the S8mm films from 1972–82) and begin to examine them against the light. The images form the backdrop and eventually become the entire image. The boys try to make sense of this strange past with the help of notebooks that they also find in the chest. Words become poems and songs in the soundtrack'. (*Sound on Film*, proposal dated 4.2.93.) There was talk of Nicholas de Jongh questioning Jarman for the soundtrack.

140 Anthony Wall and Nigel Finch. The BBC contributed in the region of £120,000 for worldwide TV rights. Dangerous to Know offered a £10,000 advance for the video rights.

141 *Derek Jarman*, oil on card. There is a Lorca quote in mirror writing across the bottom of the portrait: 'Enjoy the luscious landscape of my wound – but hurry, time meets us and we are destroyed.'

142 It is anyone's guess what this rejoinder might mean. In SISM, 15.4.92, Jarman writes about waiting like 'a duck' for the change Stonewall promises it has achieved. Or he could have been referring to 'fluffers', his word for attractive young men; or the ducks he saw in St James's park on one of his last, wheelchair-bound outings. As a final utterance, this puzzling sentence was a source of mild concern to those who judged it insufficiently sonorous for a departing saint. 'Any advance on fluffy ducks?' Collins would be asked when people rang or visited.

143 The death certificate gives the cause of death as bronchial pneumonia.

144 Later Takashi Asai, who had been at the Berlin Film Festival, came to Barts with his camera and filmed the body.

Performed, Produced, Exhibited and Published Works of Derek Jarman

I have not attempted to list magazine or newspaper articles, either here or in the bibliography. Vincenzo Patanè's *Derek Jarman* and the select bibliography compiled by Chris Lippard for *By angels driven* both contain a reasonably extensive (though by no means exhaustive) list of these.

As author

A Finger in the Fishes Mouth, Bettiscombe Press, Dorset, 1972. Collection of 32 poems. Designed by John Miles. Illustrated.

Dancing Ledge, Quartet Books, London, 1984. Edited by Shaun Allen. Illustrated. (Published in America by Overlook Press & in Japan by Uplink.)

Derek Jarman's Caravaggio, Thames & Hudson, London, 1986. With special photography by Gerald Incandela.

The Last of England, Constable, London, 1987. Edited by David L. Hirst. Illustrated. (Reissued in paperback by Vintage under the title *Kicking the Pricks* 1996 & published in America under the same title by Overlook Press. Published in Japan by Film Art Sha.)

War Requiem, Faber & Faber, London, 1989. Introduction by Don Boyd. Photographs by David Bramley.

Modern Nature: The Journals of Derek Jarman, Century, London, 1991. Illustrated. (Published in America by Overlook Press, in Italy by Ubulibri & in Japan by Kinema Jumposha.)

Queer Edward II, BFI Publishing, London, 1991.Written by Derek Jarman, Stephen McBride, Ken Butler & Tilda Swinton. Edited by Keith Collins & Malcolm Sutherland. Slogans by Greg Taylor. Slogan design by Derek Westwood. Photographs by Liam Longman & Jacqueline Lucas-Palmer. Designed by Malcolm Sutherland. (Published in America by Indiana University Press & in Japan by Uplink.)

At Your Own Risk: A Saint's Testament, Hutchinson, London, 1992. Edited by Michael Christie. Illustrated. (Published in America by Overlook Press, in China by Knowledge House, in Germany by PVS Verleger, in Italy by Ubulibri & in Japan by Uplink.)

Wittgenstein: The Terry Eagleton Script, The Derek Jarman Film, BFI Publishing, London, 1993. Preface by Colin MacCabe. *Introduction to Wittgenstein & Ludwig Wittgenstein: The Terry Eagleton Script* by Terry Eagleton. *This is Not a Film of Ludwig Wittgenstein* by Derek Jarman. *Wittgenstein: The Derek Jarman Film* by Derek Jarman & Ken Butler. Photographs by Howard Sooley. (Published in America by Indiana University Press.)

Blue: Text of a film by Derek Jarman, Channel 4 Television & BBC Radio 3, London, 1993. (Published in America by Overlook Press, in Turkey by Nisan Yayinlari & in a special limited edition by Richard Salmon.)

Chroma: A Book of Colour – June '93, Century, London, 1994. (Published in America by Overlook Press, in Germany by Merve Verlag, in Italy by Ubulibri & in Japan by Uplink.)

derek jarman's garden, Thames & Hudson, London, 1995. With photographs by Howard Sooley. (Published in America by Overlook Press, in France by Thames & Hudson, in Japan by Korinsha Press, in Germany by Volk und Welt, & in Sweden by Max Strom.)

Up in the Air: Collected Film Scripts, Vintage, London, 1996. Introduction by Michael O'Pray.

As contributor

Lindsay Kemp and Company, GMP, 1987. Photographs by Anno Wilms. Introduction by David Haughton. Preface by Derek Jarman.

Today and Tomorrow, Richard Salmon, London, 1991. Perpetual Calendar illustrated with 17 colour plates of Jarman paintings.

Freeze Frame: Directed by Derek Jarman, edited by Takashi Asai, Uplink, Tokyo, 1993. Collection of stills from Jarman films with occasional captions by Jarman.

Get The Rubber Habit! The Sisters of Perpetual Indulgence, Blasé Ltd, London, 1994. Book of postcards. Photographs by Denis Doran. Foreword by Saint Derek of Dungeness.

As designer

For reasons of economy and space, in general I have only listed the cast members and technicians involved in Jarman's work as a designer where the names are likely to mean something to the general reader, or where the people involved had a connection to Jarman. I have not attempted to list work done as a student or on a semi-professional basis with friends. I have on a few occasions listed unrealised work when the project involved seemed to merit it.

Ballet

Jazz Calendar. Royal Ballet at the Royal Opera House, London, & on tour. January 1968. Sets & costumes. Choreography: Frederick Ashton. Music: Richard Rodney Bennett. Original cast included Lesley Collier, Vergie Derman, Anthony Dowell, Rudolf Nureyev, Merle Park, Antoinette Sibley, Wayne Sleep.

Throughway. Ballet Rambert at the Jeannetta Cochrane Theatre, London. March 1968. Set & costumes. Choreography: Stere Popescu. Sound & music assembled on tape by David Vorhaus.

Silver Apples of the Moon. London Festival Ballet at the New Theatre, Oxford. October 1973. Set & costumes. Choreography: Tim Spain. Music: Morton Subotnik.

Nocturne pas de deux. Item in a gala performance at the Palladium Theatre, London, in a programme arranged & presented by Petrus Bosman & Anya Sainsbury in aid of Friends of Fatherless Families. May 1974. Set & costumes. Choreography: Peter Wright. Music: Sibelius. Danced by Ann Jenner & David Ashmole.

One. London Contemporary Dance Theatre on tour. February 1980. Set & costumes. Choreography: Tom Jobe. Music: Bernie Holland.

Mouth of the Night. Mantis Dance Company at the ICA, London, & on tour. February 1985. Design. Choreography: Micha Bergese. Music: Psychic TV. Costumes: Anne Gruenberg.

Fashion

Zandra Rhodes Autumn 1983 collection. Olympia, London. March 1983.

Film

The Devils. 1971. Director: Ken Russell. Producers: Robert H. Solo & Ken Russell (Russo Productions/Warner Brothers). Associate Producer: Roy Baird. Screenplay: Ken Russell, based on the play by John Whiting & the book *The Devils of Loudun* by Aldous Huxley. Photography: David Watkin. Cameraman: Ronnie Taylor. Assistant Cameraman: Peter Ewens. Lighting: John Swan. Original Music composed & conducted by Peter Maxwell Davies. Art Director: Robert Cartwright. Assistant Art Director: Alan Tomkins. Set Designer: Derek Jarman. Set Decorator: Ian Whittaker. Property Master: George Ball. Construction: Terry Apsey. Editor: Michael

Bradsell. Production Manager: Neville C. Thompson. Costumes: Shirley Russell. Cast included: Oliver Reed (Urbain Grandier), Vanessa Redgrave (Sister Jeanne des Anges), Dudley Sutton (Baron de Laubardement), Max Adrian (Ibert), Gemma Jones (Madeleine de Brou), Murray Melvin (Mignon), Michael Gothard (Father Barré), Georgina Hale (Phillipe Trincant), Brian Murphy (Adam), Christopher Logue (Cardinal Richelieu), Graham Armitage (Louis XIII), John Woodvine (Trincant).

Savage Messiah. 1972. Director: Ken Russell. Producer: Ken Russell (A Russ-Arts Ltd. Production for MGM). Associate Producer: Harry Benn. Production Associates: John & Benny Lee. Screenplay: Christopher Logue, based on the book by H.S. Ede. Photography: Dick Bush. Cameraman: Ronnie Taylor. Assistant Cameraman: Eddie Collins. Original Music: Michael Garret. Production Designer: Derek Jarman. Art Director: George Lack. Set Decorator: Ian Whittaker. Property Master: George Ball. Editor: Michael Bradsell. Artist: Paul Dufficey. Production Manager: Neville C. Thompson. Costumes: Shirley Russell. Cast included: Dorothy Tutin (Sophie Brzeska), Scott Antony (Henri Gaudier), Helen Mirren (Gosh Smith-Boyle), Lindsay Kemp (Angus Corky), Michael Gough (M. Gaudier), John Justin (Lionel Shaw), Aubrey Richards (Mayor), Peter Vaughan (Museum Attendant), Ben Aris (Thomas Buff), Eleanor Fazan (Mme. Gaudier), Otto Diamont (Mr Saltzman), Suzanna East (Pippa), Maggy Maxwell (Tart), Imogen Claire (Mavis Coldstream), Judith Paris (Kate), Robert Lang (Major Boyle).

Gargantua. 1972–3. Director: Ken Russell. Producer: Alberto Grimaldi. Design: Derek Jarman. (Unrealised)

Advertisement for Nescoré. 1976 approx. Director: Ken Russell. Design: Derek Jarman. Set Decorator: Ian Whittaker.

Opera

Don Giovanni (Mozart). Sadler's Wells at the Coliseum, London. August 1968. Sets & costumes. Director: John Gielgud. Conductor: Charles Mackerras (though owing to the indisposition of Mackerras, the première was conducted by Mario Bernardi).

Taverner (Maxwell Davies). Royal Opera House, London. 1971–2. Sets & costumes. Director: Ken Russell. (Unrealised.)

Rake's Progress (Stravinsky).Teatro Comunale at the Teatro della Pergola, Florence. May 1982. Sets & costumes. Director: Ken Russell. Conductor: Riccardo Chailly. Production filmed by RAI (Italian television channel).

Theatre

Poet of the Anemones (Peter Tegel). Royal Court Theatre Upstairs, London. July 1969. Set & costumes. Director: Nicholas Wright.

The Secret of the Universe (Jonathan Gems). ICA, London. July 1980. Design: Derek Jarman & Steven Meaha, with special thanks to Christopher Hobbs. Director: Ian Kellgren. Choreography: Keith Hodiak. Cast included Jonathan Gems, Keith Hodiak & Jordan.

Waiting for Godot (Samuel Beckett). Queens Theatre, London. September 1991. Design: Derek Jarman with Madeleine Morris. Director: Les Blair. Presented by Phil McIntyre & Stoll Moss. Cast included: Adrian Edmondson, Philip Jackson, Rik Mayall & Christopher Ryan.

The Maids (Jean Genet; translated by Bernard Frechtman). Edinburgh Festival, August 1992, & Heaven, London, January, 1993. Design: Derek Jarman. Director: Christopher Payton. Presented by Ad Hoc Theatre Company. Costumes: Nicky Gillibrand & Nicole Robinson. Cast: Amanda Bellamy, Michele Wade, Tania Wade.

As director
Film
See Filmography.
Opera
L'ispirazione (Sylvano Bussotti). Teatro Comunale, Florence. May 1988. Design: Sylvano Bussotti. Conductor: Jan Latham-Koenig. Cast included Tilda Swinton (Futura).

As painter
Principal Exhibitions
I have not attempted to list any school exhibitions or those which were particularly informal and/or ad hoc. I have not included any exhibitions after the retrospective at the Barbican in May 1996, at the time of writing the last significant show of Jarman's work. I have not included full or comprehensive details of what paintings were exhibited at which show, or of any sales. One-man shows are indicated by *.

Michael Jarman, True Lovers' Knot, Northwood; October 1960; 25 paintings. *
Sixth International Amateur Art Exhibition, Warwick Square, London; late 1960; 2 paintings.
University of London Union Art Exhibition, May 1961; sponsored by the *Daily Express*; joint winner of first prize, amateur class, for *We Wait*. (Jarman entered more than one such University Union exhibition during his time as a student, but this is the only one of which there is a record.)
Michael Jarman, Watford Public Library; 17–31 May 1961; 40 paintings. *
Michael Jarman, Rimmell Gallery, 104 Allitsen Road, London; 28 February–13 March 1966; 43 drawings, 2 silkscreen prints, 2 etchings & 8 paintings. *
Young Contemporaries, Tate Gallery, London; 26 January–19 February 1967; thereafter on tour; exhibiting as Michael Jarman, Jarman showed *Cool Waters* & *Landscape with Various Devices* (joint winner of a Peter Stuyvesant Foundation Prize for Landscape).
Opening Exhibition, Lisson Gallery, London; 4 (or 12)–29 April 1967; with Terrence Ibbot, Paul Martin, Keith Milow & Paul Riley; 10 works.
Edinburgh Open Hundred, David Hume Tower, Edinburgh; 25 August–25 September 1967; exhibiting as Michael Jarman, Jarman showed *Landscape with Marble Mountain*.
Joint Exhibition, Lisson Gallery; September 1967; with Raymond Gringhofer, Peter Joseph & Keith Milow.
Cinquième Biennale des Jeunes Artistes, Musée d'Art Moderne de la Ville de Paris; 30 September–5 November 1967; exhibiting as Derek Jarman, Jarman showed his designs for Prokofiev's *Prodigal Son* in the theatre decor section.
John Moores' Sixth Biennial Exhibition, Walker Gallery, Liverpool; 23 November 1967–21 January 1968; exhibiting as Michael-Derek Jarman, Jarman showed *Landscape with a Blue Pool*.
Exhibition of Ballet Designs, Wright Hepburn Gallery, London; August 1968; Jarman showed his designs for *Jazz Calendar*.
The English Landscape Tradition in the 20th Century, Camden Arts Centre, London; 30 January–28 February 1969; exhibiting as Derek Jarman, Jarman showed *Landscape with a Blue Pool*.
Derek Jarman, Lisson Gallery; 16 February–late March 1969; 14 paintings, theatre designs, environmental sculpture. *
Upper Ground Works, Lisson Warehouse, 57 Lisson Street, London; 29 May (or 3 June)–27 June 1970; capes & banners & *light*. *
Panegyris Gallery, Copenhagen, Denmark; November, 1970; with Peter Logan. (Jarman's papers suggest he may not have contributed to this exhibition.)
Visual Poetries, work by Sylvester Houédard at the Victoria & Albert Museum; 10 November–5 December 1971, & on tour; Jarman contributed a floor piece entitled *Grass Poem*.
Slade Centenary Exhibition, Diploma Galleries, Burlington House, London; November–December 1971; Jarman was represented by some of his student designs for *Orpheus*. (He may then have given the Slade a design for their permanent collection, though this is unsubstantiated.)
Derek Jarman: Drawings, paintings and designs for 'The Devils', 13 Bankside, London; 17–30 November 1971; with Michael Ginsborg & Peter Logan; Jarman showed 20 pieces, including a number of capes.
Drawing, Museum of Modern Art, Oxford; 18 November–23 December 1972; Jarman showed *The Pleasures of Italy*.
Open Studio-Warehouse, Butler's Wharf, London; 13–18 November 1973; with Oliver Campion & Peter Logan; Jarman showed his Avebury paintings, some earlier landscapes & his super-8 films. (From 1973 onwards, Jarman would hold frequent showings of his films.)
New London in New York, Hal Bromm Works of Art, 10 Beach Street, New York; 2 December 1974–17 January 1975; with Laurie Rae Chamberlain, Duggie Fields, Guy Ford, Gerald

Incandela, Andrew Logan, Peter Logan, Luciana Martinez, Chris Orr, Richard Wentworth & Kevin Whitney.
American Bicentennial Exhibition, DuBose Gallery, Houston, Texas; November 1976; with Michael Craig-Martin, Mario Dubsky, Michael Ginsborg, Bill Jacklin & Keith Milow; curated by Bryan Montgomery.
Derek Jarman's Still Lifes, World's End Art Gallery, 390 King's Road, London; 22 February–22 March 1978; some capes, 8 small drawings on slate, 8 small painting, some stills from the super-8s & a variety of artifacts relating to *Jubilee*, shown alongside some of Jean-Marc Prouveur's stills of the film. *
Group exhibition, B2 Gallery, Metropolitan Wharf, London; December 1981; with Duggie Fields, Michael Kostiff, Andrew Logan, Luciana Martinez, John Maybury & Cerith Wyn Evans; curated by David Dawson; Jarman showed a selection of his recent paintings & some super-8 films.
Derek Jarman, Edward Totah Gallery, 39 Floral Street, London; 18 November–23 December 1982; 22 new paintings. *
Derek Jarman, ICA Upper Gallery, London. 3 February–18 March 1984; painting retrospective & first showing of GBH series, also season of films; Andy Marshall showed his furniture under the title *In Sheer Luxury*. Curated by Sandy Nairne. *
Charting Time: an exhibition of artists' drawings, notes and diagrams for film and video, Hatton Gallery, Newcastle Upon Tyne, 7 January–10 February 1986; Serpentine Gallery, London, 9–31 August 1986; with Mineo Aayamaguchi, Tim Cawkwell, Peter Gidal, Judith Goddard, Jeff Keen, Patrick Keiller, Mike Leggett, Jayne Parker, Marty St James & Anne Wilson, Lis Rhodes & Anna Thew; exhibition devised & selected by Steve Hawley & David Curtis, assisted by Trisha Anderson; Jarman showed certain of his notebooks.
Caravaggio Suite, 9 paintings shown at the Tate as one of the shortlisted artists for the 1986 Turner Prize; 3 November–7 December 1986; with Art & Language (Michael Baldwin & Mel Ramsden), Victor Burgin, Gilbert & George, Stephen McKenna & Bill Woodrow.
Night Life and Other Recent Paintings, Herbert F. Johnson Museum of Art, Cornell University, Ithaca, New York; 3 April–3 May 1987; curated by Richard Herskowitz; 32 paintings; the exhibition coincided with a touring film retrospective entitled *Of Angels and Apocalypse*, which had been touring the UK & which went on to play at the Walker Art Centre, Minneapolis; catalogue. *
Paintings from a Year, Richard Salmon Ltd., 59 South Edwardes Square, London; 30 October–4 December 1987; 132 new paintings. *
Derek Jarman, Dom Kulture, Studenski Grad, Belgrade; 5–15 December 1988; 18 paintings & film retrospective. * (An extensive retrospective of Jarman's films toured various European cities, including Stuttgart, in late 1988; catalogue: *The Complete Derek Jarman*.)
New Paintings, Richard Salmon Ltd., 59 South Edwardes Square, London; 6 January–3 February 1989; 30 new paintings & assemblages. *
Derek Jarman: Peintures, Accatone, 20 rue Cujas, Paris; 17 March–20 April 1989; 40 paintings accompanying a film retrospective; catalogue. *
Pintures de l'Apocalipsi, Galeria Ambit, 282 Consell de Cent, Barcelona; 4–12 July 1989; 39 paintings in a show that coincided with the Barcelona Film Festival. *
The Marsh in War and Peace, Lydd Airport & Martello Tower, Dymchurch, Romney Marsh; 8–15 July 1989; with Marion Bataille, Peter Fillingham & Luke Oxley.
Summer Exhibition, Lyth Arts Centre, Lyth, Scotland; 26 June–6 September 1989; with Marius Alexander, Chris Bailey, Shirley Farquhar, Lotte Glob, Alex Main, Jacqueline Morreau, Mike Rand & Phil Ward; 26 paintings.
Richard Demarco Gallery, Edinburgh; 4–28 October 1989; 36 paintings. *
Installation, National Review of Live Art, Third Eye Centre, Sauchiehall Street, Glasgow; 11–15 October 1989.
Luminous Darkness, Space T33, Terrada Warehouse, Tokyo; also Kyoto; 10–24 September 1990; organised by Takayo Iido, Noriko Umemiya & Takashi Asai; there was an accompanying film retrospective. 48 paintings & assemblages; catalogue. *
'*Designing Yourself*: Creativity in Everyday Life, Design Museum, London; 5 June–15 September 1991; garden installation with Peter Fillingham & Karl Lydon.
Carnegie International, Carnegie Museum of Art, Pittsburgh; 19 October, 1991–16 February 1992; with Michael Asher, Richard Avedon, Judith Barry, Lothar Baumgarten, Christian Boltanski,

Louise Bourgeois, John Cage, Sophie Calle, James Coleman, Tony Cragg, Richard Deacon, Lili Dujourie, Katharina Fritsch, Bernard Frize, Dan Graham, Ann Hamilton, Richard Hamilton, David Hammons, Huang Yong Ping, Ilya Kabakov, On Kawara, Mike Kelley, Louise Lawler, Ken Lum, Allan McCollum, John McCracken, Boris Michailov, Lisa Milroy, Tatsuo Miyajima, Reinhard Mucha, Juan Muñoz, Bruce Nauman, Maria Nordman, Giulio Paolini, Stephen Prina, Tim Rollins & K.O.S., Richard Serra, Thomas Struth, Hiroshi Sugimoto, Philip Taaffe, Christopher Williams, Christopher Wool; curated by Lynne Cooke & Mark Francis; Jarman showed stills from *Edward II*; catalogue.
At Your Own Risk, Art Gallery & Museum, Kelvingrove, Glasgow; 14 February–12 April 1992; assemblages & landscapes. *
Queer, City Art Gallery, Manchester; 16 May–28 June 1992; 28 new, large scale paintings & 16 smaller works; catalogue, which includes interview by Howard Smith & essays by Stuart Morgan, Andrew Renton, Norman Rosenthal & Simon Watney. *
New Paintings, Karsten Schubert Gallery, 85 Charlotte Street, London; in conjunction with Richard Salmon Ltd; 24 November–22 December 1992; 11 paintings. *
Screening of *Blue* at the Venice Biennale, 12 June 1993.
Toxo included in Royal Academy Summer Show, Royal Academy, London; 1993.
Queer, Palazzo delle Esposizione, Rome, 14 July–2 August 1993; then at the Filmmuseum, Potsdam, 13 August–26 September 1993; the exhibition coincided with a film retrospective & concert for *Blue*; organised by the British Council & Richard Salmon Ltd; 35 paintings. *
Dead Sexy, Newlyn Art Gallery, Penzance; 29 September–30 October 1993; with Benjamin Gay, Danielle Hart, David Miles, Pippa Oldfield, Carol Ann Pegg, Ben Rivers & Becky Troth; curated by Emily Ash; 29 paintings & assemblages.
Exhibition of 18 paintings at Southlands Community School, New Romney; 6–22 November, 1993. *
Derek Jarman: Painter, Filmmaker, Writer, Chesil Gallery, Portland, & Portland Bill Lighthouse; 23 April–22 May 1994; 32 paintings. *
Evil Queen: The Last Paintings, Whitworth Gallery, Manchester; 7 September–5 November 1994; 15 of the final paintings; catalogue. *
Derek Jarman, Drew Gallery, Canterbury; 9 October–3 November 1994; paintings & assemblages. *
Derek Jarman: Artist, Film-maker, Designer, Barbican Art Gallery, London; 9 May–18 August 1996; painting, design & film retrospective; researched by Roger Wollen; designed by Peter Fillingham; the exhibition later toured to the Hatton Gallery in Newcastle, the Sainsbury Centre in Norwich & the Centrode Cultura Antigue Instituto, Gijón, Spain; catalogue. *

Filmography

Of the various filmographies of Jarman's work in existence, few are exhaustive and many inaccurate, even three of the most extensive: Lindsey Merrison's *The Complete Derek Jarman*, compiled in 1988 on the occasion of a film retrospective in Stuttgart, Vincenzo Patanè's *Derek Jarman*, compiled in 1995, and Michael O'Pray's in *Dreams of England* (though the latter does have an excellent introduction on Jarman's work in super-8). The following is an attempt to be as exhaustive and accurate as possible. However, it does not pretend to be definitive: in super-8 at least, Jarman shot a huge amount of material over a long period of time, some of which is lost, some of which is as yet uncodified.

The super-8 material poses many problems of classification. Because the films can be (and were) shown at differing speeds, it is impossible to give accurate running times. For this reason, I have opted not to give running times at all, though with very few exceptions, it is safe to say that the super-8 films, if run at the speed at which they were shot, would last only a few minutes each.

If projected more slowly, they tend to run at between five and fifteen minutes.

Dating the super-8 material is similarly difficult. Insofar as it has been possible to ascertain them, the dates given here are the year in which the film was shot rather than the year in which it was assembled. I have also indicated alternative dates where the dating is uncertain. Within each year, if the exact chronology is vague, I have grouped films in terms of thematic or aesthetic similarities. For the feature films, the dates given are the dates on the finished print.

I have not differentiated between super-8 films which were shown and those which were not, nor between completed films and fragments; in the former case because it is impossible to know with any certainty, in the latter because many of the 'completed' films are in any case fragmentary by nature.

With regard to the titles of the super-8 films, because many of these films (particularly the early ones) were made as home movies and never intended for distribution, their titles were often not fixed: they were called one thing when made, another when exhibited. Jarman also had a habit of recycling titles, so in certain instances the same title can apply to different films. Where sufficiently well or widely documented, I have provided alternative titles.

Just as titles were recycled, so on occasion was the material. The film *Sulphur*, for example, incorporates *The Art of Mirrors* and has a lot of footage/images in common with *Arabia*; ditto *In the Shadow of the Sun*. Wherever possible, I have indicated where the material is thus linked by a system of stars: * for one strand, ** for another.

Except where a soundtrack was specially commissioned, almost all the super-8 films are silent. However, Jarman almost always showed them with music, and where I can I have indicated what that music might have been.

The casts of the super-8s are poorly documented, so the lists of participants are not always exhaustive; and in the case of most of the pop promos, it has proved impossible to ascertain full filmographical details. For the features, if the credits as they appear on screen do not mention any known participants, I have (on the few occasions this has happened, and where the details are known) added those names to the end of the credit list. I have made little attempt to correct or verify the erratic spelling of names as they appear in the credits for the features.

I have not attempted to document video release of the films, since this is something that constantly changes; but all of the features (and some of the super-8s) have been released on video at some time or another.

All films are 'UK' and are directed by Derek Jarman.

This filmography could not have been compiled without the earlier research of Michael O'Pray or the access granted by James Mackay to the material in his possession.

Abbreviations

acc accountant; *add* additional; *alt* alternative; *arr* arranged; *assoc* associate; *asst* assistant; *bb* best boy; *bw* black & white; *cam* camera; *carp* carpenter; *cat* catering; *chor* choreography; *cl* clapper loader; *col* colour; *cond* conducted by; *const* construction; *cont* continuity; *co-ord* co-ordinator; *cost* costumes; *dept* department; *des* design; *dir* director; *dist* distribution; *DJ* Derek Jarman; *dub* dubbing; *ed* editor; *elec* electrics; *eng* engineer; *equip* equipment; *exec* executive; *f* featuring; *fl* floor; *fp* focus puller; *fx* effects; *gaff* gaffer; *gp* grip; *hr* hair; *illus* illustrations; *incl* including; *ins* insurance; *loc* location; *ltg* lighting; *m* music; *man* manager; *mast* master; *mins* minutes; *mix* mixer; *m-u* make-up; *mus* musicians; *neg* negative; *off* office; *op* operator; *orig* original; *p* producer; *pc* production company; *perf* performed by; *ph* photography; *proc* processed; *prop* props; *prod* production; *pub* publicity; *rec* recordist; *rig* rigger; *run* runner; *sc* screenplay; *sd* sound; *secs* seconds; *s-8* super-8; *seq* sequence; *sh* stage hand; *sp* sparks; *spec* special; *stud* studio; *sup* supervisor; *tr* trainee; *trans* transport; *vid* video; *vis* vision; *vo* voice over; *wde* wardrobe

1971

Electric Fairy, 16mm; *des* Andrew Logan; made with the assistance of Malcolm Leigh, Alasdair McGaw & unknown young man. Now lost.

1972

Studio Bankside, aka *Bankside*, second segment aka *One Last Walk One Last Look Bankside*, s-8; made in 2 segments, the 1st col, the 2nd bw; *f* various of DJ's friends; *m* from *Zabriskie Point* or Elgar; *ph* DJ

The Siren and the Sailor, aka *At Low Tide*, s-8; col; *f* Andrew Logan, Bente Lohse, Ian; *cost* & *prop* Christopher Hobbs; *m Daphnis et Chloé*; *ph* DJ & Marc Balet

Miss Gaby, aka *Miss Gaby Gets It Together* or *All Our Yesterdays*; orig, expanded version entitled *I'm Ready For My Close Up with Miss Gaby and Mr de Havilland*, s-8; alt date 1973; col; *f* Gaby Chautin, née Longhi & unknown young man; *des* Andrew Logan; *m* Roberta Flack; *ph* DJ & Marc Balet

1973

Andrew Logan Kisses the Glitterati, s-8; col; *f* Andrew Logan & 9 friends, incl Manolo Blahnik, Eric Boman, Duggie Fields, Jenny Galer, Christopher Hobbs, Gerlinde Kostiff, Peter Schlesinger; there also exists a tape recording of Gerald Incandela interviewing the kissers in halting English to ask whether Logan gives a new meaning to the kiss; *ph* DJ

Andrew, s-8; col; *f* Andrew Logan; *ph* DJ

Red Movie, aka *Tourist Film*, s-8; col–film shot thro a red filter; *f* Gerald Incandela & unknown man; *ph* DJ

Stolen Apples for Karen Blixen, s-8; bw; *f* Gerald Incandela & unknown man; *ph* DJ

Gerald Plants a Flower, s-8; alt date 1974; *f* Gerald Incandela; *ph* DJ

Gerald Takes a Photo, s-8; alt date 1974; *f* Gerald Incandela; *ph* DJ

Tarot, aka *The Magician*, s-8; filmed in 2 sections, the 1st probably earlier (maybe 1972) than the 2nd; part 1 used in the 2nd half of *In the Shadow of the Sun*; col; *f* Christopher Hobbs & Gerald Incandela; *ph* DJ

A Garden in Luxor, aka *Garden of Luxor*, s-8; alternative date 1972; also used in *The Art of Mirrors*; col & bw; *f* Christopher Hobbs; *ph* DJ

Kevin Whitney, s-8; col; *f* Luciana Martinez & Kevin Whitney; *ph* DJ

The Art of Mirrors, aka *Burning of Pyramids*, s-8; used elsewhere, notably in *Arabia, Sulphur, Beyond the Valley of the Garden of Luxor Revisited*; col; *f* Gerald Incandela, Luciana Martinez & Kevin Whitney; *m* often by Varèse; *ph* DJ *

Beyond the Valley of the Garden of Luxor Revisited, s-8; a reworking of footage from such films as *The Art of Mirrors*, *Arabia* & *Sulphur*; col; *f* approximately 7 figures, incl Gerald Incandela, Luciana Martinez & Kevin Whitney; *ph* DJ *

Burning of Pyramids, s-8; alt date 1974; col; *ph* DJ

Death Dance, s-8; alt date 1974; col & bw; *f* 7 figures, incl Christopher Hobbs, Gerald Incandela, Tim Spain, Robin Wall & Kevin Whitney; *ph* DJ

Arabia, s-8; alt date 1974; col & bw; *f* approximately 15 figures, incl Graham Dowie, Gerald Incandela, DJ, Penny Jenkins & Andrew Logan; *ph* DJ *

Green Glass Bead Game, s-8; alt date 1974; col; *f* approximately 15 figures, incl Graham Dowie, Gerald Incandela, Penny Jenkins & Andrew Logan; *ph* DJ *

Sulphur, s-8; alt date 1974; col; *f* approximately 15 figures, incl Graham Dowie, Gerald Incandela, DJ, Penny Jenkins, Andrew Logan, Luciana Martinez & Kevin Whitney; *ph* DJ *

Journey to Avebury, s-8; alt date 1972; used in the first part of *In the Shadow of the Sun*; col; *ph* DJ

Walk on Møn, aka *The Island of Møn* or *Space Travel, A Walk on Møn*, s-8; col & bw; *ph* DJ

Shad Thames, s-8; bw; *ph* DJ

Cafe in Tooley Street, s-8; alt date 1974; *ph* DJ

Miss World, s-8; bw & shot thro a pink filter; *f* a great many, incl Gerald Incandela, Andrew Logan & Patrik Steede, *ph* DJ

1974

Fred Ashton Fashion Show, s-8; col; featuring pupils of the Royal Ballet School; *chor* Frederick Ashton *asst* Michael Pink; *ph* DJ

Bill Gibb Show, s-8; col; *ph* DJ

Duggie Fields at Home, aka *Duggie Fields*, s-8; alt dates 1973 or 1975; col; *f* Duggie Fields & unknown man; *ph* DJ

Picnic at Rae's, aka *Lunch at Rae's*, s-8; alt dates 1973 or 1975; col; *f* Rae Spencer-Cullen (Miss Mouse) & friends, incl Gaby Chautin, Duggie Fields, Andrew Logan & Jenny Runacre; *ph* DJ

Herbert in NYC, aka *New York Walk Don't Walk* or *Downtown Walk Don't Walk*, s-8; alt date 1972; col & bw; *f* Herbert Muschamp; *m* Lou Reed's *Walk on the Wild Side*; *ph* DJ

New York City, aka NYC, s-8; alt date 1972; col; *ph* DJ

Dinner and Diner, s-8; alt date 1972; bw; *ph* DJ

The Devils at the Elgin, aka *Reworking The Devils* or *Sister Jean of the Angels* or *Jean des Anges*, s-8; bw; *f* various cast members of *The Devils*; *ph* DJ

Fire Island, s-8; used in *In the Shadow of the Sun* & reworked as *My Very Beautiful Movie*; footage also used in *The Kingdom of Outremer* and *The Sea of Storms*; col; *ph* DJ **

My Very Beautiful Movie, s-8; a reworking of *Fire Island*; col; *ph* DJ **

The Kingdom of Outremer, s-8; col; *ph* DJ **

1974–1980

In the Shadow of the Sun, s-8 blown up to 16mm in 1980; col; 50 mins; *f* many of the people to appear in *Arabia*, *Green Glass Bead Game* & *Sulphur*, incl Karl Bowen, Christopher Hobbs, Gerald Incandela, Andrew Logan, Luciana Martinez, Kevin Whitney & Francis Wishhart; *m* (in s-8 form) Berlioz's *Grand Messe des Morts*; *ph* & *ed* DJ. For 16mm version: *pc* Dark Pictures; *p* James Mackay; *m* Throbbing Gristle, 1980; *rostrum cam* Marek Budzynski; *16mm blow up* John Hall; *graphics* Mark Robertson; made possible by Freunde der Deutschen Kinemathek, Berlin; Music from *In the Shadow of the Sun* released on Illuminated Records, 1984 */**

1974–76

Sloane Square, aka *Removal Party*, s-8 blown up to 16mm in 1981 & retitled *Sloane Square, A Room of One's Own*; col & bw; *f* various of DJ's friends, incl Graham Cracker, Guy Ford, Gerald Incandela, Malcolm Leigh, Alasdair McGaw; *ph* & *ed* DJ & Guy Ford. For 16mm version: *pc* Dark Pictures; *p* James Mackay; *m* Simon Turner

1975

Corfe Film, aka *Troubadour Film*, s-8; col; *f* Paul Humfress & Luciana Martinez; *ph* DJ

Ken Hicks, s-8; col; *f* Ken Hicks; *ph* DJ

Sebastiane Wrap, aka *Sebastiane Mirror Film* or *Mirrors* or *A Break from Sebastiane*, s-8 blown up to 16mm in 1981; col; *f* various cast & crew members of *Sebastiane*; *ph* DJ. For 16mm version: *m* Psychic TV

Karl at Home, s-8; date uncertain; bw; *f* Karl Bowen; *ph* DJ

Gerald's Film, s-8; alt dates 1974 or 1976; col; *f* Gerald Incandela; *m* Mahler's 5th Symphony; *ph* DJ

1976

The Sex Pistols in Concert, s-8; bw; *f* The Sex Pistols & Jordan; included in *The Great Rock and Roll Swindle*, dir Julien Temple; *ph* DJ

Sebastiane, 16mm blown up to 35mm; col; 86 mins; *pc* Distac; *p* James Whaley & Howard Malin; *dir* Paul Humfress & DJ; *sc* DJ & James Whaley; *m* Brian Eno; *dance chor & perf* Lindsay Kemp & troupe, *m* Andrew Wilson; *ph* Peter Middleton; *asst cam* Bob McShane; *sd rec* John Hayes; *sd asst* Hugh Smith; *dub mix* Mike Billing; *ed* Paul Humfress; *asst ed* Ian Murdoch & Colin Gittins; *stills* Gerald Incandela; *Latin translations* Jack Welch; *loc execs* Luciana Martinez & Jane Fields; *props* Daniel Egan; *titles* Barney Wan & Jose Aguon; *illus* Christopher Hobbs; *asst dir* Guy Ford; *prod asst* Neil Robinson; *hr for the 1st scene* Keith of Smile; *special thanks* Fernando Scarfiotti, Louise Walker, Ian Kierney, Andrew Logan & the many friends who made the first scene possible especially Robert Medley as Diocletian; filmed on location in England & Sardinia for Distac Ltd; © Distac London 1976; *proc & printed* Kay Laboratories, London; *cast* Leonardo Treviglio (Sebastian), Barney James (Severus), Neil Kennedy (Max), Richard Warwick (Justin), Ken Hicks (Adrian), Donald Dunham (Claudius), Janusz Romanov (Anthony), Steffano Massari (Marius), Daevid Finbar (Julian), Gerald Incandela (Leopard Boy); *1st scene f* Charlotte Barnes, Rufus Barnes, Sally Campbell, Graham Cracker, Michael Davis, Duggie Fields, Guy Ford, Peter Hinwood, Christopher Hobbs, Nicholas de Jongh, Jordan, Lindsay Kemp & troupe, Gerlinde & Michael Kostiff, Ulla Larson-Styles, Alasdair McGaw, Little Nell, Eric Roberts, Norman Rosenthal, Johnny Rozsa, Philip Sayer, John Scarlett-Davis, Rae Spencer-Cullen, Volker Stox, Joan de Vere Hunt, Harry Waistnage & Thilo von Watzdorf.

Ulla's Fete, aka *Ulla's Chandelier*, s-8; alt dates 1974 or 1975; bw; *f* a number of DJ's friends, incl Duggie Fields, Ulla Larson-Styles, Andrew Logan, Little Nell, Rae Spencer-Cullen, Janet Street-

Porter, Kevin Whitney (also Liliana Cavani); *m Tubular Bells; ph* DJ
Houston Texas, s-8; ph DJ
The Sea of Storms, aka *Kingdom, s-8; bw; f* figures from *In the Shadow of the Sun & Fire Island; ph* DJ
*/**

1977

Jordan's Dance, s-8; sections of this film appear in *Jubilee;* col; *f* Jordan, Steve Treatment & 2 others; *ph* DJ

Jubilee Masks, aka *Jean-Marc Makes a Mask, s-8; bw; f* Jordan, Jean-Marc Prouveur & Jenny Runacre; *ph* DJ

Art and the Pose or *Arty the Pose, s-8;* used in *The Dream Machine; bw; f* Gerald Incandela & Jean-Marc Prouveur; *ph* DJ

1978

Jubilee, 16mm & s-8 blown up to 35mm; col; 104 mins; *pc* Whaley-Malin Productions for Megalovision; *p* Howard Malin & James Whaley; *script* DJ & James Whaley; *asst dir* Guy Ford; *ph* Peter Middleton; *asst cam* Bob McShane; *sup ed* Tom Priestley; *ed* Nick Barnard; *asst ed* Annette D'Alton; *cost & prod des* Christopher Hobbs; *prod asst* John Maybury & Kenny Morris; *m* Brian Eno; *songs* 'Plastic Surgery' by Adam & the Ants, 'Right to Work' by Chelsea, 'Paranoia Paradise' by Wayne County & The Electric Chairs, 'Love in a Void' by Siouxsie & The Banshees, 'Jerusalem' & 'Rule Britannia' by Suzi Pinns (*arr* Danny Beckermann & Will Malone), cabaret-disco 'Wargasm in Pornotopia' *arr* Amilcar & Guy Ford; *sd* John Hayes; *dub mix* Mike Billing; *asst sd* Trevor Rutherford; *prod man* Mordecai Schreiber; *cont* Judi Futrille; *gaff* John Rogers; *elec* Mike Munro; *gp* Dennis Balkan; *wde* Luciana Martinez; *stills* Jean-Marc Prouveur & Johnny Rozsa; *cost* Dave Henderson; *cost makers* Richard Croft & Ralph Dyer; *hr* Keith of Smile; *prod asst* Lee Drysdale & Luciana Martinez; *spec fx* Martin Gutteridge; *trans* John Albery; *proc* Kay Laboratories; *cast* Jenny Runacre (Bod/Queen Elizabeth I), Little Nell (Crabs), Toyah Willcox (Mad), Jordan (Amyl Nitrate), Hermine Demoriane (Chaos), Ian Charleson (Angel), Karl Johnson (Sphinx), Linda Spurrier (Viv), Neil Kennedy (Max), Orlando/Jack Birkett (Borgia Ginz), Wayne County (Lounge Lizard), Richard O'Brien (John Dee), David Haughton (Ariel), Helen Wallington-Lloyd (Lady-in-Waiting), Adam Ant (Kid), Donald Dunham & Barney James (Policemen), Claire Davenport (First Customs Lady), Howard Malin (Schmeitzer), Ulla Larson-Styles (Waitress), Gene October (Happy Days), Iris Fry & Joyce Windsor (Bingo ladies), William Merrow (Maurice), Quinn Hawkins (Boy), Luciana Martinez & Prudence Walters (Borgia's escorts), the Slits (Street girls); *f* in the party scene are, among others, Nigel Coates, Graham Cracker, Duggie Fields, Lindsay Kemp & troupe, Gerlinde and Michael Kostiff, Alasdair McGaw, Johnny Rozsa; *soundtrack* released by E.G. Records on Polydor, March 1978; also 'Rule Britannia' & 'Jerusalem' as a single (Suzi Pinns)

Every Woman for Herself and All for Art, s-8 blown up to 16mm in 1981; *bw; f* Jordan; *ph* DJ

The Fountain, s-8; could be dated slightly later; col; *f* Christopher Hobbs & Jean-Marc Prouveur; *ph* DJ

The Pantheon, s-8; could be dated slightly later; col; *f* Christopher Hobbs & Jean-Marc Prouveur; *ph* DJ

Italian Street Scene, s-8; could be dated slightly later; col; *f* Italian crowd; *ph* DJ

Italian Ruins, s-8; could be dated slightly later; col; f Christopher Hobbs; *ph* DJ

1979

The Tempest, 16mm blown up to 35mm; col; 95 mins; *pc* Boyd's Company; *p* Guy Ford & Mordecai Schreiber; *assoc p* Sarah Radclyffe; *exec p* Don Boyd; *sc* Derek Jarman; *ph* Peter Middleton; *cam op* Robert McShane; *ed* Lesley Walker; *asst ed* Annette D'Alton; *electronic sd & m* Wavemaker; *rec at* Electrophon Music, London; 'Stormy Weather' *arr* Steven Pruslin, *perf* Steven Pruslin & Dave Campbell, *sung* Elisabeth Welch, *prod* Guy Ford; *m for the dance* Gheorge Zamfir & his orchestra, Delta Music; *des* Yolanda Sonnabend; *art dir* Ian Whittaker; *asst to des* Steven Meaha; *Prospero's Cell* Simon Read; *chor* Stuart Hopps; *sd recordist* John Hayes; *boom op* Trevor Rutherford; *sd ed* Sarah Vickers; *rerecord* Tony Anscombe; *wde* Nicolas Ede; *m-u* Rosalind McCorquidale; *m-u asst* Ruth Kahn; *hr* Keith of Smile; *asst to dir* John Scarlett-Davis; *1st asst* Anthony Annis; *loc org* Simon Turner & Tim Deutsch; *cont* Judi

Futrille; *gp* Denis Balkan; *cl* Graham Berry; *stills* Bridget Holm; *spec stills* Doug Luke; *casting consultant* Maggie Cartier; *gaff* John Rogers; *bb* Mike Munroe; *sp* Peter Young; *generator op* Bill Thornhill; *unit pub* Soren Fischer; *cat* Other People's Houses; *acc* Alasdair McGaw; *trans* Mobility Services; *const* Small Works Ltd; *proc* Kay Laboratories Ltd; *many thanks to* all those who took an interest, especially Morgan, Clare, Nancy, Mark, Simon, Dennis, Ian, Volker, Val, Charlotte, Alec, Thilo, Ben, Robert, Tom, Anthony, John & Mark at Smile, Christopher & all the sailors who weathered the storm; shot entirely on location in England & at Stoneleigh Abbey & Bamburgh; © Kendon Films 1979; 'This film is dedicated to the memory of Elizabeth Evelyn Jarman'; *cast* Heathcote Williams (Prospero), Karl Johnson (Ariel), Toyah Willcox (Miranda), Peter Bull (Alonso), Richard Warwick (Antonio), Elisabeth Welch (Goddess), Jack Birkett (Caliban), Ken Campbell (Gonzalo), David Meyer (Ferdinand), Neil Cunningham (Sebastian), Christopher Biggins (Stephano), Peter Turner (Trinculo), Claire Davenport (Sycorax), Helen Wallington-Lloyd & Angela Whittingham (Spirits); Kate Temple (Young Miranda); 'Stormy Weather' released as a single by Industrial Records
Broken English: Three Songs by Marianne Faithfull ('Witches Song', 'The Ballad of Lucy Jordan' & 'Broken English'), s-8 & 16mm blown up to 35mm; col & bw; 12 mins; taken from the album *Broken English* on Island Records; *p* Guy Ford for Island Records in association with Mark Miller Mundy; *ed* Dennis Ferminger; *asst* Máive Nic Suibhne; *ph* Peter Middleton & Bob McShane; *dir assts* John Scarlett-Davis & Julian Sands; *dub mix* Lou Hawks; *vid* Nick Fry, Two Boroughs Video; *des consultant* Christopher Hobbs; shot entirely on location in Great Britain; *f* Marianne Faithfull &, among others, Dave Baby, Michael & Gerlinde Kostiff, Marilyn (Peter Robinson), Julian Sands, Simon Turner & Helen Wallington-Lloyd

1981
TG Psychic Rally in Heaven, s-8 blown up to 16mm; col; 8 mins; *pc* Dark Pictures with financial assistance from the Arts Council of Great Britain; *p* James Mackay; *m* Throbbing Gristle (Chris Carter, Peter Christopherson, Genesis P-Orridge, Cosey Fanni Tutti) performing the songs 'Slug Bait-Brighton', 'Maggot Death Studio' & 'Maggot Death-Rat Club' from their album *Second Annual Report*; *ph* & *ed* DJ
Jordan's Wedding, s-8; col; *f* Jordan, Kevin Mooney & friends; *ph* DJ

1982
Rakes Progress, s-8; col; *f* the cast of the Ken Russell/Teatro Comunale production; *ph* DJ
Pontormo and Punks at Santa Croce, s-8; col; *ph* DJ
B2 Movie, s-8 transferred to vid; alt date 1981; col & bw; *f* various of DJ's friends & colleagues, incl Dave Baby, Judy Blame, Graham Cracker, Keith Hodiak, Gerald Incandela, Jordan, Alasdair McGaw, James Mackay, Scarlett, John Scarlett-Davis, Volker Stox; *ph* DJ
Waiting for Waiting for Godot, s-8 & vid; col & bw; *f* Sean Bean, Gerard McArthur, Johnny Phillips & the stage designs of John Maybury; *ph* DJ
Pirate Tape, s-8, later transferred to 16mm & vid; col; *f* William Burroughs; *soundtrack* Psychic TV; *ph* DJ
Diese Machine ist Mein Antihumanistiches Kunstwerk, s-8 short made for Psychic TV; exact date uncertain; bw; *f* DJ; *ph* DJ

1983
Touch the Radio, Dance!, vid for Steve Hale; *f* the Rational Theatre Company; *p* David Dawson; *ph* Peter Middleton; *ed* John Scarlett-Davis; *cost* Sandy Powell
Dance With Me, vid for Lords of the New Church; col; *f* Scarlett & the Neo-Naturists; *pc* Aldabra; *ed* John Scarlett-Davis & Volker Stox
Home Movie Dong, aka *The Dong with the Luminous Nose*, s-8; incomplete fragment involving, among others, Ken Campbell, James Mackay, John Maybury & Francesca Moffat
Willow Weep for Me, vid for Carmel; 16mm; col; 2 mins 30 secs; *f* Jack Birkett & others; *pc* Aldabra; *cost* Sandy Powell
Dance Hall Days, vid for Wang Chung; col; *pc* Aldabra; *cost* Sandy Powell

1984
Working for Pleasure, s-8; bw; filmed at ICA gallery & *f*, among others, Christine Binnie from the

Neo-Naturists, Judy Blame, Ken Butler, Michael Clark, James Mackay & Andy Marshall; *ph* DJ & others

Wide Boy Awake, vid for Billy Hyena; 16mm; col; 3 mins 45 sec; *pc* Aldabra; *p* Luc Roeg; *des* Christopher Hobbs; *cost* Sandy Powell; © RCA Records

Catalan, vid for Jordi Valls; 16mm, col; *des* Christopher Hobbs; later incorporated into a film about Psychic TV for Spanish Television, *La Edad de Ora*, first broadcast March 1984

Barcelona, s-8; col & bw; *f* Christopher Hobbs, Genesis P-Orridge; *ph* DJ

What Presence, vid for Orange Juice; 16mm; col; 4 mins 15 sec; *f*, among other, Jayne County; *pc* Aldabra; *cost* Sandy Powell; © RCA Records

The Dream Machine, s-8 blown up to 16mm; 35 mins; 4 films by DJ (*Art and the Pose*), Michael Kostiff, John Maybury & Cerith Wyn Evans; linking footage by Tim Burke

Oxford Medley Show, s-8; col; *ph* DJ

Imagining October, s-8 & vid blown up to 16mm; col & bw; 27 mins; *p* James Mackay; *cam* DJ, Richard Heslop, Cerith Wyn Evans, Carl Johnson, Sally Potter; *crew* Stuart Dolin, Chris Hughes, Francis Stevenson; *ed* Cerith Wyn Evans, Richard Heslop, DJ, Peter Cartwright; *m* Genesis P-Orridge & David Ball; *text* Shaun Allen & DJ; *artwork* Christopher Hobbs; *exec p* Francesca Forbes Moffat, Fierce Vision; *f* John Watkiss (the painter), Angus Cook, Peter Doig, Toby Mott, Steven Thrower & Keir Wahid (the soldiers), Peter Wollen

Tenderness is a Weakness, vid for Marc Almond; 16mm; col; *pc* Aldabra; *p* Elizabeth Trafford; *ph* Denis Crossan; *ed* Peter Scemmel; *art dir* Annie Britten; *cost* Sandy Powell

1985

The Angelic Conversation, s-8 edited on to vid & blown up to 35 mm; col & bw; 78 mins; *prod* with the financial assistance of the BFI; *p* James Mackay; Shakespeare's sonnets read by Judi Dench; *cam* DJ; *2nd cam* James Mackay; *ed* Cerith Wyn Evans & Peter Cartwright; *sd ed* Richard Anstead & Peter Christopherson; *sd fx* Adrian Fogarty; *prod man* Stuart Dolin; *prod asst* Christopher Hughes; *titles* Sally Yeadon & Dave King; *crew* Kenneth Bolton, Steve Radnall, Alice Stepanek & Andy Wilson; *stills* Alistair Thain; 'How to Destroy Angels' *perf* Coil, courtesy L.A.Y.L.A.H. anti-records; 'Sea Interludes' from *Peter Grimes* (Benjamin Britten) *perf* the chorus & orchestra of the ROH, Covent Garden, *cond* Colin Davies, courtesy Phillips Records, published Boosey & Hawkes Ltd; *orig m* Coil (John Balance, Peter Christopherson, Steven E. Thrower); *vid post prod* Research Recordings; *vid transfer* Colour Video Services; *sd* Videosonics; *thanks to* The Olympus Optical Co (UK), Research Recordings, ICA, Andy the furniture maker, Shaun Allen, Chris Bligh, Ian Christie, Jo Comino, David Curtis, Ian Dickens, Andi Engel, Pam Engel, Alex Graham, Christopher Hobbs, Jocelyn James, Jem Leigh, Andy Powell, Peter Sainsbury, Jon Savage, Henry Stein, Anne Whitfield, John Cartwright, Peter Grey; © Derek Jarman 1985; *cast* Paul Reynolds & Philip Williamson with Dave Baby, Timothy Burke, Simon Costin, Christopher Hobbs, Philip Macdonald, Toby Mott, Steve Radnall, Robert Sharp & Tony Wood

Windswept, vid for Bryan Ferry; 16mm; col; 4 mins 8 secs; *pc* Aldabra; *ph* Gabriel Beristain; *cost* Sandy Powell; *chor* Stuart Hopps; © EG Management

1986

Caravaggio, 35 mm; col; 93 mins; *pc* BFI in association with Channel 4 & Nicholas Ward-Jackson; *p* Sarah Radclyffe; *sc* DJ from an original idea by Nicholas Ward-Jackson; *des* Christopher Hobbs; *ph* Gabriel Beristain; *cost* Sandy Powell; *ed* George Akers; *orig m* Simon Fisher Turner *asst by* Mary Phillips; *casting* Debbie McWilliams; *extras casting* Simon Turner; *deaf & dumb teacher* Paul Treacy; *prod man* Sarah Wilson; *prod asst* Jules Bradbury; *run* Yvonne Little & Simon Wallace; *project development* James Mackay; *paintings* Christopher Hobbs; *art dir* Mike Buchanan; *prop mast* Tim Youngman; *sh* Mark Russo; *const* Constructivist, Alastair Gow, Susan McLenachan, Robin Thistlethwaite; *scenic artists* Annie Lapaz & Lucy Morahan; *run* Josh Jones & Charlie McGrigor; *wbe sup* Annie Symons; *wde run* Karen Sherwin; *m-u* Morag Ross; *m-u asst* Miri Ben-Shlomo; *1st asst dir* Glynn Purcell; *2nd asst dir* Simon Mosely; *3rd asst dir* Patricia Aldersley; *floor run* Belinda Bemrose & Luke Losey; *fp* Noel Balbirnie; *cl* John Mathieson; *cam dept tr* Mike Barber; *gp* Tony Haughey; *2nd cam op* Steve Tickner; *2nd cam asst* Phil Bough; *cont* Heather Storr; *stills* Mike Laye; *gaff* Larry Prinz; *sp* Mickey Donavan & Tony Hare; *stunt co-ord* Jim Dowdall & Gareth Milne; *stunt perf* Tracey Eddon; *sd rec* Billy McCarthy; *boom swinger* George Richards;

sd dept tr June Prinz; *dub ed* Budge Tremlett; *dub mix* Peter Maxwell; *asst eds* Nicola Black,
Anuree de Silva, Matthew Whiteman & Alistair Bates; *mus* Bill Badley, Steart Butterfield, Lol
Coxhill, Charlie Duncan, Brian Gulland, Stuart Hall, Julia Hodgson, Timothy Hugh, Neil Kelly,
Chi Chi Nwanoku, Jocelyn Pook, Rodney Skeaping, El Tito, Veryan Weston; *singers* John
Douglas-Williams, Charles Gibbs, Mary Phillips, Nicholas Robertson, Angus Smith; *music
recorded at* Berry Street Studios; *music eng* Richard Preston; *cat* The Good Eating Company; *ins*
Bailey Martin & Fay International Ltd; *ltg equip* Film Lighting Services; *re-recorded at* De Lane
Lea Sound Centre; *sd fx* Studio Sound, Italy; *footsteps* Beryl Mortimer & Ted Swanscott; *titles*
Frameline; *film stock* Fuji, *proc* Technicolor; *shot* entirely at Western Half Warehouse of
Limehouse Studios, London; *special thanks* to Peter Sainsbury, Maria Liljefors, Simon Costin,
Stephen Brown, Sarah Walsh, Paul Treacy, Ian Shipley Books, Belinda Scarlett, Susie Giblin,
Penny Beard, Jill Parker, Paul Minter, Sarah Sankey, Tina Winters, Stephen Lewis, Andy Wilson,
Matthew Hamilton, Nigel Lowry, Cath Pater-Lantucki, Patricia Lester, Kuko Steiner, Michael
Carter, Ben Wilson, Mike Fowkes, Daniel, Dominic Penrose, Antonia & Panayiota Savvides,
Circolo Gramsci, Bar Italia, Rory Keegan, Nikos & Kyriacou Sozou, Phil McDonald, Mr
Marinelli, Claudia Nicolaou, the Presto, Bill Craster, Margaret Matheson, the BFI print room,
Shirley Hobart & Andy Chapman, Limehouse Studios, John O'Keefe, Michael Barnett & Ron
Payne, Frances, Frankie, Gloria & Len, Ken Butler, Cob Stenham, Suso Cecchi D'Amico,
Steven Pickles, Atilio Lopez, Sally Sutton, Aileen Seaton, Niako, Tony Covell, David Cooper,
Martin Duncan, Chris Palmer, Nobby Roker, Les Spring, St Peter's Italian Youth Club, Venus
F.C., Willy Landels, Paul Reynolds, Kevin O'Shea, Bob Storer, Museum of Instruments, Royal
College of Music, London, & Working Title Ltd; *cam & lenses by* Moviecam, *supplied by* cinefo-
cus, London; *for the BFI: exec p* Colin MacCabe; *exec in charge of prod* Jill Pack; *prod acc* Sheryl
Leonardo; *and many thanks to* Liz Reddish, Andy Powell, Leslie Eyles, Behroze Ghandi, Willy
Maley, Eliza Mellor & Jennifer Howarth; *cast* Nigel Terry (Caravaggio), Sean Bean (Ranuccio),
Garry Cooper (Davide), Dexter Fletcher (Young Caravaggio), Spencer Leigh (Jerusaleme), Tilda
Swinton (Lena), Nigel Davenport (Giustiniani), Robbie Coltrane (Scipione Borghese), Michael
Gough (Cardinal del Monte), Noam Almaz (Boy Caravaggio), Dawn Archibald (Pipo), Jack
Birkett (Pope), Una Brandon-Jones (Weeping Woman), Imogen Claire (Lady with the Jewels),
Sadie Corre (Princess Collona), Lol Coxhill (Old Priest), Vernon Dobtcheff (Art Lover), Terry
Downes (Bodyguard), Jonathan Hyde (Baglione), Emil Nicolaou (Young Jerusaleme), Gene
October (Model peeling fruit), Cindy Oswin (Lady Elizabeth), John Rogan (Vatican Official),
Zohra Segal (Jerusaleme's grandmother), Lucien Taylor (Boy with guitar), Simon Turner (Fra
Fillipo); *guests at Giustiniani's party include* (even if not always visible on screen) Dave Baby,
Judy Blame, Tim Burke, Roger Cook, Michael & Gerlinde Kostiff, Willy Landels, Luciana
Martinez, Patrick Procktor, Jon Savage, Chelita Secunda, Yolanda Sonnabend; *Caravaggio 1610
- Sound Sketches for Michele of the Shadows* (by Simon Turner) released by Cherry Red Records,
1986
Short film-clip for star-studded 'Action Against Aids' gala charity performance of Walter
Reynolds's *Young England* at the Adelphi Theatre, London, 18.05.86; s-8; *ph* Chris Hughes
Promo for Matt Fretton, s-8; *p* James Mackay for Rick Rogers; *ph* DJ
The Queen is Dead: Three Songs by The Smiths ('The Queen is Dead', 'There is a Light that Never
Goes Out', 'Panic'), s-8 edited onto vid & blown up to 35 mm; col & bw; 13 mins; *pc* Rough
Trade; *p* James Mackay, Mayo Thompson, Peter Walmsley & Yvonne Little; *f* various of DJ's
friends & colleagues; *ph & ed* DJ, John Maybury, Richard Heslop, Chris Hughes & Sally Yeadon
Ask, vid for the Smiths, s-8; col; 3 mins; *p* James Mackay; *cost* Sandy Powell; *chor* Stuart Hopps; *ph
& ed* DJ, Chris Hughes, Cerith Wyn Evans
Whistling in the Dark, vid for Easterhouse, s-8; col & bw; 4 mins; *p* James Mackay; *ph & ed* Richard
Heslop, Chris Hughes, DJ, Cerith Wyn Evans, Peter Cartwright
1969, vid for Easterhouse, s-8; col & bw; 5 mins; *p* James Mackay; *ph & ed* Richard Heslop, Chris
Hughes, DJ, Cerith Wyn Evans, Peter Cartwright

1987
Depuis le Jour, sequence in *Aria*, s-8 & 35mm; colour & bw; 5 mins; *p* Don Boyd for LightYear
Entertainment/Virgin Vision; *seq p* James Mackay; *m* Gustave Charpentier from his opera *Louise*;
sung Leontine Price, RCA Italiana Orchestra, *cond* Francesco Molinari-Pradelli; *f* Aimée

Delamaine (incorrectly credited on screen as Amy Johnson), Tilda Swinton (Young Girl) & Spencer Leigh (Young Man); *s-8 ph* Chris Hughes; *35 mm ph* Mike Southon; *prod des* Christopher Hobbs; *ed* Peter Cartwright & Angus Cook; *cost* Sandy Powell; *special stills photog* Angus McBean; *asst assoc p* Yvonne Little; *asst to dir* Cerith Wyn Evans; *cam asst* Philip Sindel; *cl* Kelvin Richards; *sd playback* Matthew Evans; *gp* Malcolm Sheenan; *gaff* Tommy Moran; *elec* Richard Holborow & Glen Gilbert; *scenic artist* Raymond Harris; *hr des* John Egan; *m-u* Morag Ross; *cat* Moving Menu; *cam equip* Samuelsons; *ltg & stud* James Electrical, London; *vid post prod* Air TV Facilities, London; *telerecording* Colour Video Services, London; *casting* Debbie McWilliams; *tour org* Rick Rogers; *prod run* Nick Searle & Adam Elliot; filmed on location in Scotland & Cornwall & studio, London; other sequences *dir* by Nicolas Roeg, Charles Sturridge, Jean-Luc Godard, Julien Temple, Bruce Beresford, Robert Altman, Franc Roddam, Ken Russell & Bill Bryden; © LightYear Entertainment, LP. & Virgin Vision, 1987

The Last of England, s-8 & vid blown up to 35 mm; colour & bw; 87 mins; *pc* Anglo International Films for British Screen, Channel 4 & ZDF; *p* James Mackay & Don Boyd; *prod des* Christopher Hobbs; *cost des* Sandy Powell; *ltg des* Christopher Hughes; *sd des* Simon Turner; *assoc p* Yvonne Little & Mayo Thompson; *ph* DJ, Christopher Hughs, Cerith Wyn Evans & Richard Heslop; *stills* Mike Laye; *riot ph* Tim Burke & Richard Heslop; *prod acc* Chris Harrison; *prod asst* Elizabeth Burn; *commissioning eds* Dagmar Benke & Alan Fountain; *cam asst* Nick Searle; *gen asst* Hector Chronos & Adam Elliott; *wde asst* Paul Treacy & Pam Downe; *sd rec* Mathew Evans & Chris Gurney; *m-u* Thelma Mathews & Wendy Selway; *hr des* John Egan; *asst* Cleo Mathews; *ltg gaff* Melvin Benn; *elec* Richard Holborow; *rig* John Cassidy; *generator op* Don Springhall; *special fx* Tony Neale; *trans capt* Rick Rogers; *unit run* Russell Millard & Gerard Raimond; *researcher* Jo Comino; *telecine eng* Tom Russell; *ed* Peter Cartwright, Angus Cook, John Maybury & Sally Yeadon; *m mix* Richard Anstead; *eng* Johannes Dell; *sd ed* Budge Tremlett; *asst ed* Melanie Ryder; *dub mix* Peter Maxwell; *asst mix* Mick Boggis; *sd fx artistes* Bill Garlick & Felicity Cottrell; *m arr* Simon Turner; *m perf* Brian Gulland, El Tito, Simon Turner, (vocals) Claudine Coule, Martyn Bates, (harp) David Snell, (strings) Sally Herbert, Audrey Riley, Jocelyn Pool, Annie Stephenson, Bill McGee; *add m* 'Refugee Theme' by Barry Adamson, *perf* Barry Adamson & Martin Micarrick; 'Terrorists' by Andy Gill, *perf* Andy Gill & Dean Garcia; 'Disco Death' by Mayo Thompson & Albert Oehlen, *perf* Mayo Thompson; 'The Skye Boat Song' *sung* Marianne Faithfull; 'Pomp and Circumstance' by Edward Elgar, *perf* the Scottish National Orchestra, *cond* Gibson; 'La Treizième Revient' & 'Deliver Me' by Diamanda Galas; *pic ed* Air TV; Air TV *facilities man* Jane Smith; Videosonics *stud man* Peter Hoskins; *re-record* De Lane Lea Sound Centre; De Lane Lea *stud man* Richard Paynter; *superscan telerecording* Colour Film Services; Colour Film Services *lab man* Ted Shorthouse; *titles* Les Latimer Opticals; *ltg equip* James Electrical; *off-line ed* Tiny Epic; *pub* PSA Public Relations; *thanks to* Mark Alder, Gill Beckett, Jim Bryce, Stephen Cassidy, Ian Cooke, Daniel Clegg, Cordelia de Peon, Joanie de Vere Hunt, Graham Dowie, Tony Eliakas, Steve Farrer, Lisa Foster, Jane Gould, Amy Louise Johnson, Jordan, Rod Lay, Agnes Laye, Emily Goodrum Laye, Maybelle Laye, Selina Laye, Suzette Llewellyn, Philip McDonald, Alasdair McGaw, Claire Muller, Michael O'Pray, Henrietta Payne, Paul Reynolds, Andrew Smith, Anna Thew, Steve Thrower, Louis Tomlin, Zoran Vidinic; *and* Bryanna Barwick, Jim Carter, Ian Boyd, Paul Cable, Lindy Campbell, Paul Campbell, Clovis, Ian Christie, Diane Croft, Linda Daniel, Michael Gibbs, Lyn Goleby, Stella Haddon, Sally Herbert, Len & Lilly James, Dick Jewell, Janet Jones, Rena Kay, Roger La Haye, Daniel Landin, Daniel Miller, Yvonne Mitchell, Carole Myer, Fred Nunney, Louise Philippe, Richard Preston, Manfred Saltzgeber, Bernard Simons, Ursula Stein, Philip Symes, Geoff Travis, Charles Trowers, Peter Walmsley, Nicholas Ward-Jackson, Fred Weinal, Li & Dennis Weinrich, Anne Whitfield, Rapier 33; *with special thanks to* Air TV, Colour Video Services, De Lane Lea, James Electrical, Sony UK Ltd, Videosonics, Animal Actors, Alaska Studios, Bapty & Co, The British Council, The BFI, The Editors Collective, The Film Clinic, Kodak Laboratories London & Stuttgart, P.S.A. Public Relations, Small Unit Film & TV Caterers, Tiny Epic, Willis Faber Dumas; *locations* HPC Logorent Ltd; made in England; © 1987; *cast* includes Gerrard McArthur, John Phillips, Gay Gaynor, Mathew Hawkins, Spencer Leigh, Tilda Swinton, Spring; *vo* Nigel Terry; soundtrack issued by Mute records as a cd; laser disc issued by Sony

Out of Hand, vid for The Mighty Lemon Drops; s-8 & 16mm; col; 3 mins & 36 secs; *pc* Anglo

International; *p* James Mackay; crew included Richard Heslop & Chris Hughes

I Cry Too, vid for Bob Geldof, s-8 & 8mm video; col; 4 mins & 30 secs; *pc* Anglo International; *p* James Mackay *f* Bob Geldof, Dawn Archibald & Spencer Leigh; crew incl Chris Hughs & Cerith Wyn Evans; *cost* Sandy Powell

In the Pouring Rain, vid for Bob Geldof, s-8 & 8mm video; col & bw; 4 mins & 30 secs; *pc* Anglo International; *p* James Mackay *f* Bob Geldof; *crew* incl Chris Hughs & Cerith Wyn Evans; *cost* Sandy Powell

It's a Sin, vid for The Pet Shop Boys, 35mm; col; 5 mins; *pc* Anglo International; *p* James Mackay; *f* Chris Lowe & Neil Tennant, Duggie Fields, Richard Logan, Ron Moody, Gerard Raimond & others; *ed* Peter Cartwright, *asst* Angus Cook; *des* Christopher Hobbs; *cost* Sandy Powell; *crew* incl Chris Hughes, Yvonne Little, Cerith Wyn Evans

Rent, vid for The Pet Shop Boys, 35mm & s-8; col & bw; 3 mins & 30 secs; *pc* Basilisk; *p* James Mackay; *f* Chris Lowe & Neil Tennant, Margi Clarke & others; *des* Brian Ackland-Snow; *cost* Sandy Powell

1988

L'ispirazione, s-8 ed on vid & blown up to 35mm; col; *p* James Mackay; *f* Tilda Swinton, Spencer Leigh; *ed* John Maybury & Peter Cartwright; *ph* DJ

1989

War Requiem, s-8 &35 mm; col; 93 mins; *pc* Anglo International Films; *p* Don Boyd; *sc* DJ; *ph* Richard Greatrex; *des* Lucy Morahan; *ed* Rick Elgood; *cost* Linda Alderson; *vid ed* John Maybury; *assoc p* Chris Harrison; *prod man* Sarah Swords; *hair & m-u* Peter King & Peter Owen; *exec p* John Kelleher; *exec p (Decca)* Herbert Chappell; *execs in charge of prod (BBC)* Alan Yentob & Eben Foggitt; *marketing & pub* Matthew Freud Associates; *orig recording courtesy* Decca Record Co Ltd, England, cat no. 414 383-2, Benjamin Britten *War Requiem*, opus 66 (*poems* Wilfred Owen; *sung* Dietrich Fisher-Dieskau (baritone), Peter Pears (tenor) & Galina Vishnevskaya (soprano), the Bach Choir, London Symphony Orchestra Chorus, Highgate School Choir & Melos Ensemble; London Symphony Orchestra *cond* Benjamin Britten); *casting dir* Susie Figgis; *asst casting dir* Abi Cohen; *prod co-ord* Elizabeth Burn; *assts to dir* Julian Cole & Keith Collins; *unit pub* Kate Williams; *1st asst ed* Guy Bensley; *2nd asst ed* Emma Lawson; *asst vid ed* Keith Collins; *on-line vid ed* Steve Crouch; *telecine op* Nigel Shaw; *1st asst dir* Sarah Swords; *2nd asst dir* Mark Harrison & Marc Munden; *3rd asst dir* Ian Francis; *fp* Roger Bonnici; *cl* Steve Brook-Smith; *key gp* Nick Ray; *gaff elec* Billy Pochetti; *elec* Steve Roberts, Nigel Woods & John O'Callaghan; *cam dept tr* Anthony Radcliffe; *sd rec* Garth Marshall; *steadicam op* Peter Cavaciuti & John Ward; *asst cost des* Annie Symons; *cost dept asst* Rebecca Du Pont; *art dir* Michael Carter; *asst art dir* Vicki Burton; *art dept asst* Gill Mumford & Andrew Sidoli; *art dept run* Kevin Rowe; *const* London Film Construction; *carp* Josh Jones; *scenic artist* Annie Lapaz; *rig* Drew Meldon; *sh* James Parry-Jones; *const run* James Ward & Stuart Wood; *grass by* Daniel Reuben Harvey; *thanks to* Penny Beard, Danny Gallagher, Helengai Walsh; *hr & m-u assts* Caroline Bass & Carol Robinson; s-8 unit: *ph* Christopher Hughes; *cam op* Paul Bettell; *cam asst* Seamus McGarvey; *war footage co-ord* Lynn Hanke, Nick Hadcock, Sarah Swords & Richard Stirling; *Okinawa seq* Martin Friedman; *war footage cam* Tim Cooper, Nick Downie & Ken Guest; *loc finder* Derek Brown; *fight arr* Jim Dowdall; *can-can chor* Richard Stirling; *unit driver run* George Barbero; *unit run* Philip Rose; *prod off asst* Nick Hadcock & Sue Cleary; *thanks to* Donna Allbury, Marina Baker, George Barbero, Stan Barton, Daniel Bier, Charles Black, David Black, Til Bruggemann, Tim Burke, Julian Cole, Keith Collins, Rex Conyer-Silverthorn, Harvey Cooper, Peter Crotty, James Cunningham, Patrick Cunningham, Leonard Davis, Gabrielle Dellal, Nick Delves, Graham Dowie, Kate Epps, Antony Evans, Ed Farely, Steve Farrer, Richard Feeney, Kevin Flint, Alexander Fodor, Ian Francis, Colin Fryer, Brendan Gallagher, Philip Gay, Alex Giles, Greg Gossett, Jane Gould, Jeff Hammond, Paul Harrison, Joseph Harrower, Chris Hartin, Alexander Hood, Christopher Hughes, Sarah Humble, Ronnie James, Pamela Kane, Erei Kene, Thomas Kett, Paul Mackie, Ian Macpherson, Stephen McBride, Jane McDermott, Philip Macdonald, Hussein (Alasdair) McGaw, D. McKella, Toby McLellan, Sarah McMenemy, Josh McMullen, Charlie Malcolmson, Ewan Marshall, John Mathieson, Mary Mathieson, Robert Meldon, John Moorhead, Charles Morgan, Marc Munden, Keith Murkin, Philip Murphy, Roy Murray, Christopher Owen, Jean

Parslow, Anthony Peake, Anthony Powell, Sandy Powell, Gerard Raimond, Lucy Readett-Bailey, David Roberts, Duncan Russell, Simon Ryan, Clifford Sadler, Douglas Sherlock, Charles Simpson, Donald Smith, Graham Stanford, Kathleen Stowe, Annie Symons, Francesca Thyssen, Jimmy Tippett, Paul Treacy, Richard Trice, Toby Uffindell-Phillips, Christopher Underhill, Ronis Varlaam, Zoran Vidinic, James Ward, Felicity Webster, Prudence Webster, Verity Webster, Peter Whitaker, Paul White, Jean Woodman, James Woollam, the Bach choir; *cost* Berman & Nathan; *cam equip* Samuelsons; *ltg equip* Samuelsons; *trans* Hamish Bell & Cine Trucks; *film lab* Studio Film Labs; *cutting rms* Mercury Cutting Rooms; *on-line digital vid ed* Soho 601; *off-line* P.E.C.; *spec fx* Amy Effects & Ace Effects; *titles & opticals* Tony Long Opticals; *neg cutting* Mike Fraser Ltd; *ins* Willis Wrightson; *cat* For Goodness Sake; *special thanks to* Christopher Hobbs, Imperial War Museum, BBC Enterprises, Grip House, Tattooist International Ltd, Better Sound, Pinden Quarry, Bapty's, The Royal British Legion Poppy Appeal, Mark Westaway, Nancy Braid, Richard Thomas, Bob Storer, John M. Sherry, Colin Fryer, the administrative staff of Darenth Park Hospital, Mary Jane Walsh, Dr John Gaynor, Layla Cook, The Ugly Agency, Maureen McDonald; © Anglo International Films 1988; *stills* David Bramley; *cast* Nathaniel Parker (Wilfred Owen), Tilda Swinton (Nurse), Laurence Olivier (Old Soldier), Patricia Hayes (Mother), Rohan McCullough (Enemy Mother), Nigel Terry (Abraham), Owen Teale (Unknown Soldier), Sean Bean (Enemy Soldier), Alex Jennings (Blinded Soldier), Claire Davenport (Charge Sister/Britannia), Spencer Leigh (Soldier 1), Milo Bell (Soldier 2), Richard Stirling (Soldier 3), Kim Kindersley (Soldier 4), Stuart Turton (Soldier 5), Lucinda Game (Nurse 1), Beverley Seymour (Nurse 2), Linda Spurrier (Nurse 3), David Meyer (Businessman), Clancy Chassay (Young Wilfred), Jody Graber (Enemy Child), Liberty Ross (Young Girl), Leo Ross, Joe Baxter, John Jagger & Alicia Ligenza (Other Children)

Backdrops for Pet Shop Boys Concert, 8 short films made as backdrop projections for the 1989 Pet Shop Boys Tour; songs covered: 'Opportunities', 'Heart', 'Paninaro', 'Nothing Has Been Proved', 'It's a Sin', 'Domino Dancing', 'King's Cross' & 'Always on my Mind'; s-8 & 16mm blown up to 70mm; col & bw; credits as per *Projections* or *Highlights*

1990

Highlights: Pet Shop Boys on tour; film of the Pet Shop Boys in concert at Wembley Arena, July 1989; incorporating the 8 films made as backdrop projections for the Pet Shop Boys Concert & covering the songs 'The sound of the atom splitting', 'It's a sin', 'Shopping', 'Love comes quickly', 'Domino Dancing', 'Rent', 'King's Cross', 'It's alright'; s-8 & 16mm transferred to vid; col & bw; 33 mins approx; *pc* Basilisk for Picture Music International & Areagraph; *f* Neil Tennant & Chris Lowe, Courtney Pine (saxophones), Danny Cummings (percussion), Dominic Clarke (keyboards), John Henry, Michael Henry, Juliet Roberts, Carol Thompson (all backing vocals), Geron 'Casper' Canidate, Hugo Huizar, Derek 'Cooley' Jackson, Robia Lamorte, Tracy Langran, Marion Jill Robertson (all dancers); concert *staged & dir* DJ; *ltg dir* Patrick Woodroffe; *cost des* Annie Symons; *m-u des* Pierre Laroche; *m-u* Lynne Easton; *hr* Leonard Hughes; *wde sup* Alan Keyes; *wde asst* Tobias Kenyon & Pinkie Braithwaite; *live sd eng* James Ebdon; *ltg eng* David Hill; *monitor eng* Steve McCale; *rig* Mark Armstrong & Rory McKewan; *stage carp* Robert Earls; *projectionist* Steve Farrer; integrated back projection films *dir* DJ; *pc* Basilisk for Areagraph Ltd; *p* James Mackay; *prod des* Christopher Hobbs; *cost des* Annie Symons; *prod man* Yvonne Tucker; *dir's asst* Keith Collins; *prod acc* Chris Harrison; *prod asst* Nick Searle; *p's asst* Jo Coriat; *asst dir* Julian Cole; *ph* Chris Hughes; *cam op* Seamus McGarvey & Steve Farrer; *m-u* Thelma Matthews; *hr* John Egan; *des asst* Sophia Caldwell & Kevin Rowe; *wde asst* Pam Downe & Kathy Fanthorpe; *casting* Simon Turner & Adrian Carbutt; *stills* Liam Longman; *gaff* Keith Osbourne; *elec* Glen Gilbert & Chris Bailey; *rig* Robert Peek; *unit driver* Julian Ayers; *ed* Peter Cartwright & Adam Watkins; *asst ed* Keith Collins; *on-line ed* Nigel S. Hadley & Colin Napthine; *vid graphics* Clive Davis; *telecine* Tom Russell; *thanks to* Christian Campus, Margie Clarke, Rene Eyre, David Jones, Ian Jones, Les Hannibal, David Lawson, Gordon Lowton, Rod Lay, Luciana Martinez, Diana Mavroleon, Dino Pereira, Claudia Pottier, Andrew Purdy, Liz Ranken, Stephano Spagnoli, Donald Smith, Spring, Maribel Warwick, Peter Williams; *ins* Ruben Sedgwick; *ltg equip* James Electrical; *cam equip* Cine Europe; *animals* Animal Actors; *cat* Eejay Caterers; *digital on-line* Soho 601; *telerecording* C.V.S.; *70mm* Technicolor; *filmed at* James Electrical Studios & on location at Benjy's Nighclub, London; the film *pc* Basilisk for Picture Music International; *p* James Mackay;

dir DJ; *dir post prod* Keith Collins; *ed* Peter Cartwright; *exec p* Martin Haxby; *prod exec* Martin Smith; *prod man* Yvonne Tucker & Lana Topham; *prod acc* Chris Harrison; *asst dir* Mathew Evans; *prod asst* Nick Searle; *p's asst* Jo Coriat; *ph* Chris Hughes; *cam op* John Simmons, Stephen Ley, Frank Meyburgh, Bob Penderhughs & Seamus McGarvey; *steadycam* John Ward; *eng man* Richard Rose; *VT eng* Simon Shirley; *vision eng* Gareth Maynard & Graeme Robson; *sd eng* Neville Young & Daniel Clarke; *live sd mix* David Jacob; *sd crew* Mick McKenna, Peter Stevens, Les Kingham & Chris Mying; *m-u* Thelma Mathews; *hr* John Egan; *wde* Pam Downe; *stills* Liam Longman; *gp* Alan Rank & Philip Jones; *driver/rig* Alan Wright & Bob Wheeler; *run* Hector Chronos, David Lewis, Gareth Jones & Geoff Hammond; *ob unit* Lynx Video; *sd mobile* Rolling Stone Mobile; *gp equip* Grip House; *on-line ed* Rick Waller; *digital on-line ed* Nigel S. Hadley; *facilities* Editors Collective, Livingstone Studio, Hilton Sound, Ultrasound, Carlton TV, Soho 601, TWTV; *filmed at* Wembley Arena

Red Hot and Blue vid of Cole Porter songs sung by various artistes; extracts from Jarman's library of home-movie footage used for Annie Lennox singing 'Every Time We Say Goodbye', *dir* Ed Lachman

The Garden, s-8, vid & 16mm blown up to 35 mm; col; 92 mins; *pc* Basilisk in association with Channel 4, British Screen, ZDF & Uplink (in association with Sohbi Corporation & Space Shower TV); *p* James Mackay; *ph* Christopher Hughes; *orig m* Simon Fisher Turner; *ed* Peter Cartwright; *prod acc* Chris Harrison; *prod man* Nick Searle; *prod asst* Jo Scarlett Coriat; *prod adviser* Simon Goldberg; *stud prod man* Sarah Swords; *asst dir* Matthew Evans; *2nd asst dir* David Lewis; *3rd asst dir* Ian Francis; *cam* Steve Farrer, Richard Heslop, Christopher Hughes & DJ; *add ph* David Lewis, James Mackay, Nick Searle; *cam asst* Seamus McGarvey; *cl* Guillame Lemoine; *gp* Glynn Fielding & Mick Duffield; *prod des* Derek Brown & Christopher Hobbs; *asst art dir* Michael Carter; *const man* Robin Thistlethwaite; *scenic artist* Annie Lapaz; *art dept asst* Kevin Rowe, Jonathan Wells & Martyn Wilson; *casting* Debbie McWilliams & Michelle Guish; *extra casting* Simon Turner; *stills* Liam Longman; *unit pub* Toby Rose; *asst to prod* Duncan Petrie; *gen asst* Hector Chronos, Adam Holden, Toby Kalikowski & James Norton; *gaff* Keith Osborne, Richard Holborow & Chris Bailey; *elec* Clive Freeth; *generator op* George Cowan; *rig* Drew Meldon; *sd rec* Gary Desmond; *cost* Annie Symons; *wde asst* Pam Downe & Catherine Fanthorpe; *m-u* Thelma Mathews; *m-u asst* Ayesshu Nuriddin; *hr des* John Egan; *hr asst* Billy Shabir; *asst ed* Keith Collins; *digital on-line* Nigel Hadley; *telecine* Tom Russell; *sd ed* Nigel Holland; *sd eng* Marvin Black; *asst sd ed* Richard Fetties; *foley artists* Bill Garlick & Beryl Mortimer; *synclavier op* Andy Kennedy; *dub mix* Peter Maxwell; *asst dub mix* Mick Boggis; *strings arr* Dean Broderick; *music rec* Marvin Black & Richard Preston; *mus* Martyn Bates, Dean Broderick, Glen Fox, Paul Jayasinma, Andrew Okrezeja, Melanie Pappenheim, Ian Shaw, David Sinclair, Brian Springbacrou, Tito, Hugh Webb; Balenescu Quartet: Alexander Balenescu, Tony Hinnigan, Jonathan Carney, Kate Musker, with Mark Horn; *thanks to* Barry Andrews, Angella, Marvin Black, Yolande Brenner, Andrew Brooks, Andrew Campsey, Hector Chronos, Graham Dowie, Drako, George Eustathio, Helen Eustathio, Eve, Rene Eyre, Steve Farrer, Lucinda Gane, Jane Gould, Chris Hughes, Iris Jackson, David Jones, Spud Jones, Michael Kavides, Annie Lapaz, the Laye family, Liam Longman, Pino Maestri, Seamus McGarvey, Vincenzo Magrino, Maria, Maureen, Rohan McCullough, Pino Mivo, Sarah Pasquali, Oscar Phillips, Claudia Pottier, Jessica Purcell, Domenico Sartoni, Thomas Sartoni, Andronllo Sozou, Kyriacou Sozou, Nicos Sozou, Spring, Alexandra Symons; Robert Styles, Zoran Vedinik, Andreas Vernazza, Maria Vernazza, Jonathan Wells & Peter Williams; *special thanks to* Derek Ball, Paul Cable, Andrew Catlin, Conchita & Alex, Dee Croft, Collette Dicker, Barry Edson, John Gleeson, Akiko Hada, Martin Harradine, Roger La Haye, Roger Inman, Len & Lily James, Helen Leicester, Carole Myer, Richard Paynter, Joyce Pierpoline, Simon Pizey, Peter Rackham, Simon Relph, Jules Rogan, Ursula Stein, Alison Thompson, Clare Timms, Fred Weinel, Keith Williams, Animal Actors, Berman & Nathan, the British Council, Cine-Europe, Colour Film Services, De Lane Lea, Cory Waste Management, The Editors Collective, Dungeness Power Station, For Goodness Sake, The Film Clinic, Julia's Meadow, Halls Aggregates, Film Stock Centre, Kodak Laboratories, Nick Scott Associates, Film Service Transport, The Oddball Jugglers, Geoff Axtel Associates, Oasis TV, Osborne Sound, The Pilot (Dungeness), Redwood Recording Services, Ruben Sedgwick Insurance, The Sales Company, The Travel Company, Soho 601, The Sound Suite, TWTV, VTR; *commissioning ed* (ZDF)

Dagmar Benke; *exec p* (Uplink) Takashi Asai; a superscan tape to film transfer by Colour Film Services; filmed on location at Dungeness & London & at James Electrical Studios; © Basilisk; principal *cast* Tilda Swinton (Madonna), Johnny Mills & Kevin Collins (Lovers), Pete Lee-Wilson (Devil), Spencer Leigh (Mary Magdalen), Jody Graber (Young Boy), Roger Cook (Christ), Philip Macdonald (Judas); with Dawn Archibald, Milo Bell, Vernon Dobtcheff, Michael Gough, Maribelle La Manchega (Spanish dancer), Jessica Martin (Singer), Orlando (Pontius Pilate), Leslie Randall, Mike Tezcan, Matthew Wilde; the voices of Michael Gough, Tilda Swinton & Stephen McBride; soundtrack released on Mute Records

1991

Edward II, 35 mm; col; 90 mins; *pc* Working Title in association with British Screen & BBC Films; *p* Steve Clark-Hall & Antony Root; *cost* Sandy Powell; *m-u chief* Morag Ross; *prod des* Christopher Hobbs; *m* Simon Fisher Turner; *ed* George Akers; *ph* Ian Wilson; *sc* DJ, Stephen McBride & Ken Butler, based on the play by Christopher Marlowe; *exec p* Sarah Radclyffe, Simon Curtis & Takashi Asai; *assoc dir* Ken Butler; *sd rec* George Richards; *art dir* Rick Eyres; *1st asst dir* Cilla Ware; *sc sup* Pearl Morrison; *prod man* Sarah Swords; *prod co-ord* Mairi Bett; *2nd asst dir* Ian Francis; *3rd asst dir* Jeremy Johns; *fl run* Daniel Bevan & James Norton; *prod run* Jason Goode & Julian Woolford; *acc* Rachel James; *acc asst* Debbie Moore; *fp* Kenny Byrne; *cl* Ros Naylor; *gp* Malcolm Huse; *cam dept tr* Tristam Cones; *stills* Liam Longman; *dub mix* Peter Maxwell; *asst dub mix* Mick Boggis; *sd rec* Bill McCarthy; *boom op* Peter Murphy; *sd jobfit tr* Andrew Griffiths; *asst ed* Laura Evans; *2nd asst ed* Hermione Byrt; *dub ed* Ean Wood; *asst dub ed* Mike Crowley; *ed jobfit tr* Jake Martin; *wde sup* Paul Minter; *wde s/b* Clare Spragge; *wde run* Kate Temple; *m-u asst* Miri Ben-Shlomo; *prop mast* David Balfour; *s/b props* Pat Harkins; *art dept asst* Chris Roope; *gaff* Norman Smith; *bb* Peter Lamb; *elec* Dave Brown, Steven Read & Colin Powton; *chor* Lloyd Newson & Nigel Charnock; *fight dir* Malcolm Ranson; *asst fight dir* Nicolas Hall; *add casting* Ian Francis; *crowd casting* Lee's People; *const man* Steve Ede; *s/b sh* Derek Ede; *s/b carp* David Lee; *s/b rig* Dave Tubbs; *s/b painter* William Lowe; *rig* Nigel Crafts; *carp* James Muir; *pub* Frontline; *m perf* Simon Fisher Turner, Dean Broderick, Richard Preston, Melanie Pappenheim & Glen Fox; *rec & mixed* Shrubland Studios, London, Elephant Studios, Wapping, using 'Fisher Prestonics'; *eng* Richard Preston; *sd re-record* De Lane Lea, London; *titles* Peter Watson Assoc; *gp equip* Grip House, London; *trans* Rabbit Car Hire; *lab* Bucks Laboratory, Slough; *grader* George Howard; *sd transfer* Anvil, Denham; *ltg equip* Mr Lighting, London; *cam supplied* Samuelsons, London; *orig on* Eastman Colour Film Kodak; *special thanks* Susie Figgis, Lynn Beardsall, Nigel Eddington, Dean Andrews, Leigh Blake, Catri Drummond, Sunita Singh, Annie Symons, Lee Towsey, Nigel Holland, Graham Sharpe, Wendela Scheltema, Cinnamon Day, Modern Travel and Stereo & Mono; *cost & toile for fittings scene lent* Amy & Grace Ltd; *gowns* John Kravsa; *add gowns* Clare Spragge & Heather Joiner; *clothes donated* Paul Smith, Joe Casely-Hayford, Katherine Hamnett, Hermes, Expectations; *cost supplied* Morris Angel, Berman & Nathan, Rose Noire; *completion guarantor* Completion Bond Co Inc; *dist* The Sales Co; filmed at Bray Studios, England, by Edward II Ltd; © National Film Trustee Company, 1991; *cast* (in order of appearance) Steven Waddington (Edward II), Kevin Collins (Lightborn), Andrew Tiernan (Gaveston), John Lynch (Spencer), Dudley Sutton (Bishop of Winchester), Tilda Swinton (Isabella), Jerome Flynn (Kent), Jody Graber (Prince Edward), Nigel Terry (Mortimer), Jill Balcon, Barbara New, Andrea Miller, Brian Mitchell, David Glover, John Quentin, Andrew Charleson (Chorus of Nobility), Roger Hammond (Bishop), Allan Corduner (Poet), Annie Lennox (Singer), Tony Forsyth (Captive Policeman), Lloyd Newson & Nigel Charnock (Dancers), Mark Davis & Andy Jeffrey (Sailors), Barry John Clarke (Man with Snake), John Henry Duncan & Thomas Duncan (Altar Boys), Giles de Montigny, Jonathan Stables, Michael Watkins, Robb Dennis (Soldiers on Guard), David Oliver, Chris McHallem, Chris Adamson, Danny Earl (Thugs), Kim Dare & Kristina Overton (Wild Girls), Trevor Skingle (Gym Instructor), Christopher Hobbs (Equerry), Sandy Powell & Kate Temple (Seamstresses), Andrew Lee Bolton (Masseur), Liz Ranken, Renee Eyre, Sharon Munro (Sexy Girls), Daniel Bevan, Ian Francis, James Norton, Tristam Cones (Youths); Elektra Quartet: Jocelyn Pook (viola), Abigail Brown (violin), Sonia Slany (violin), Dina Beamish (cello); with members of OutRage! & the Sisters of Perpetual Indulgence

1993

Wittgenstein, 35 mm; col; 75 mins; *pc* Bandung for Channel 4, the BFI & Uplink (Japan); *p* Tariq Ali; *sc* DJ, Terry Eagleton & Ken Butler; *assoc dir* Ken Butler; *ph* James Welland; *cost* Sandy Powell; *m dir* Jan Latham-Koenig; *ed* Budge Tremlett; *art dir* Annie Lapaz; *m-u & hr* Morag Ross; *sd rec* George Richards; *prod man* Anna Campeau & Gina Marsh; *exec in charge of prod (BFI)* Eliza Mellor; *exec p* Ben Gibson (BFI) & Takashi Asai (Uplink); *1st asst dir* Davina Nicholson; *2nd asst dir* Richard Hewitt; *sc sup* Pearl Morrison; *fp* Denzil Armour-Brown; *cl* Debbie Kaplan; *gp* Johnny Donne; *2nd cam asst* Araf Khan; *boom op* Orin Beaton; *sd ed* Toby Calder; *dub mix* Paul Carr; *m mix* Andre Jacquemin; *wde sup* Penny Beard; *wde asst* Michael Weldon; *hr & m-u asst* Miri Ben-Shlomo; *prop buyer* Kate Stubbs; *art dept s/b* Melanie Oliver & Kevin Rowe; *art dept asst* Karl Lydon, Ruth Naylor, Peter Fillingham, Mandy Barnes & Madeleine Morris; *scenic artist* Matthew Parsons; *carp* Jonathan Wells & David Williams; *stills* Howard Sooley; *titles* Steve Masters; *prod asst* Gordon Baskerville; *prod sec* Polly Hope; *gaff* John Turley; *bb* Cephas Vazquez-Howard; *rig* Drew Meldon; *stand-in* Sky Macaskill; *unit run* Emily Caston & Trevor Williams; *cat* Ademola Falola; *m perf* Jan Latham-Koenig (piano), Paul Barritt (violin), Judith Hall (flute); *special thanks to* Karen Brown, Colin MacCabe, John Krausa & London Film Construction; © Channel Four Television Co Ltd 1993; *cast* (in order of appearance) Clancy Chassay (Young Ludwig Wittgenstein), Jill Balcon (Leopoldine Wittgenstein), Sally Dexter (Hermine Wittgenstein), Gina Marsh (Gretyl Wittgenstein), Vania del Borgo (Helene Wittgenstein), Ben Scantlebury (Hans Wittgenstein), Howard Sooley (Kurt Wittgenstein), David Radzinowicz (Rudolf Wittgenstein), Jan Latham-Koenig (Paul Wittgenstein), Anna Campeau, Roger Cook, Michael O'Pray, Tony Peake, Michelle Wade & Tania Wade (Tutors), Nabil Shaban (Martian), Karl Johnson (Ludwig Wittgenstein), Michael Gough (Bertrand Russell), Tilda Swinton (Ottoline Morrell), Donald McInnes (Hairdresser), Chris Hughes, Hussein (Alasdair) McGaw, Budge Tremlett (Prisoners), Aisling Magill (Schoolgirl), Perry Kadir (Artist's Model), John Quentin (John Maynard Keynes), Kevin Collins (Johnny), Lynn Seymour (Lydia Lopokova), Stuart Bennett, Steven Downes, Peter Fillingham, David Mansell, Ashley Russell, Fayez Samara (Students), Samantha Cones, Sarah Graham, Kate Temple (Cyclists), Layla Alexander Garrett (Sophia Janovskaya)

Blue, 35mm; col; 79 mins; *pc* Basilisk Communications & Uplink in association with Channel 4, Arts Council of Great Britain, Opal & BBC Radio 3; *p* James Mackay & Takashi Asai; *m* Simon Fisher Turner; *sc* DJ; with the voices of John Quentin, Nigel Terry, DJ & Tilda Swinton; *assoc dir* David Lewis; *sd des* Marvin Black; *mus* John Balance, Gini Ball, Marvin Black, Peter Christopherson, Markus Dravius, Brian Eno, Tony Hinnigan, Danny Hyde, Jan Latham-Koenig, Marden Hill & The King of Luxembourg, Miranda Sex Garden, Momus, Vini Reilly, Kate St John, Simon Fisher Turner, Richard Watson & Hugh Webb; *add m* 'Triennale' *written & perf* Brian Eno, 'Scheherazade' from 'The Masques' by Szymanowski *perf* Jan Latham-Koenig, 'Summertime' by Marden Hill & The King of Luxembourg, 'Disco Hospital' *written & perf* Coil & Danny Hyde, 'Fermina' *written & perf* Vini Reilly, 'Gnossiennes' by Erik Satie *perf* Jan Latham-Koenig; *sd post prod* The Sound Suite; *m rec* Brian Eno's Wilderness Studio; *m rec eng* Markus Dravius; *rerecord* de Lane Lea Sound Centre, London; *rerecord mix* Paul Hamblin; *titles* General Screen Enterprises; *col* Technicolor; *ins* Ruben Entertainment; *rec equip* Fostex (UK) Ltd; *thanks to* Karen Brown, Paul Cable, John Cartwright, David Curtis, Roger Eno, Steve Farrer, Chris Gacon, Jane Geerts, Brendan Griggs, Lorraine Hamilton, Jeremy Howe, Chris Hughes, Andre Jacquemin Recording, Jordan, Liam Longman, Dave Magna, Sabino Martiradonna, Christine Neocleous, Richard Paynter, Duncan Petrie, Penny Pitts, Richard Preston, Pete Rackham, Pete Ratcliffe, Anthea Norman-Taylor, Rod Stoneman, John Willis, Rodney Wilson, the doctors & nursing staff at St Bartholomew's & St Mary's Hospitals, the British Council; *prod co-ord* Angela Connealy; *legal advisor* Simon Goldberg; *prod acc* Chris Harrison; *assoc p* David Lewis; 'for HB and all true lovers'; *Live Blue Roma (The Archeology of Sound)*, recorded at the Palazzo delle Esposizione, Rome, July 1993; *perf & written* Simon Fisher Turner, Marvin Black, James Mackay, John Quentin, Markus Drays, Ian D. Smith; *words* DJ; *p* Ian D. Smith for Basilisk Communications Ltd; released on Mute Records

Little Emerald Bird, vid for Patti Smith, s-8; col; 2 mins 4 sec; *pc* Basilisk Communications; *p* James Mackay; *f* Graham Cracker, David Dipnall & other figures from Jarman's library of s-8 footage; *ed & compiled* Keith Collins & Andy Crabb

Projections, release on vid of Jarman's backdrop films for the 1989 Pet Shop Boys tour; col & bw; 46 mins; songs covered: 'Opportunities', 'Heart', 'Paninaro', 'It's a Sin', 'Domino Dancing', 'King's Cross', 'Always on my Mind', 'Violence' (to an excerpt from *A Garden in Luxor*), 'Being Boring' (to an excerpt from *Studio Bankside*); *pc* Basilisk Communications; *p* James Mackay; *project man* Michael Christie; *ed* Peter Beswick; other credits as per integrated back projection films & the film under *Highlights*

1994
Glitterbug, s-8 blown up to 35mm; col & bw; 60 mins; *pc* Basilisk Communications & BBC; *p* James Mackay; *m* Brian Eno; *assoc dir* David Lewis; *ed* Andy Crabb; *telecine* Tom Russell; *BBC Arena series ed* Nigel Finch & Anthony Wall; *special thanks* Opal Ltd & Dangerous to Know; © Basilisk Communications 1994; video distributed by Dangerous to Know with an accompanying 16 page booklet

Select Bibliography

Publications
Auty, Martyn, & Roddick, Nick, (eds), *British Cinema Now*, BFI Publishing, London, 1985.
Baxter, John, *An Appalling Talent: Ken Russell*, Michael Joseph, London, 1973.
Bennett, Alan, *Writing Home*, Faber & Faber, London, 1994.
Bersani, Leo, & Dutoit, Ulysse, *Caravaggio*, BFI Publishing, London, 1999.
Bland, Alexander, *The Royal Ballet: The First 50 Years*, Threshold Books, London, distributed by Sotheby Parke Bernet, 1981.
Bland, Alexander, *The Nureyev Image*, Studio Vista, London, 1976.
Booker, Christopher, *The Neophiliacs: The Revolution in English Life in the Fifties and Sixties*, Pimlico, London, 1992.
Boorman, John, & Donohue, Walter, (eds), *Projections 2: A Forum for Film Makers*, Faber & Faber, London, 1993. Includes *Freewheelin' Gus Van Sant Converses with Derek Jarman*.
Boorman, John, & Donohue, Walter, (eds), *Projections 41/2: Film-makers on Film-making*, Faber & Faber, London, 1995. Includes *Notes on Derek Jarman* by Michael Almereyda.
Boyd, Andrew, *Blasphemous Rumours: Is Satanic Ritual Abuse Fact or Fantasy? An Investigation*, HarperCollins, London, 1991.
Bracewell, Michael, *England is Mine: Pop Life in Albion from Wilde to Goldie*, HarperCollins, London, 1997.
Brett, Guy, *Exploding Galaxies: The Art of David Medalla*, Kala Press, London, 1995.
Bruce, Michael, with Billy James, *No More Mr Nice Guy: The Inside Story of the Alice Cooper Group*, SAF Publishing, Wembley, 1996.
Buckle, Richard, *Diaghilev*, Weidenfeld & Nicolson, London, 1979.
Buckle, Richard, *Nijinsky*, Weidenfeld & Nicolson, London, 1971.
Burton, Peter, *Parallel Lives*, GMP, London, 1985.
Button, Virginia, *The Turner Prize*, Tate Gallery Publishing, London, 1997.
Caughie, John, with Kevin Rockett, *The Companion to British and Irish Cinema*, Cassell, London, 1996.
Caveney, Graham, *The 'Priest', They Called Him: The Life and Legacy of William S. Burroughs*, Bloomsbury, London, 1997.
Charters, Ann, (ed), *The Portable Beat Reader*, Viking, New York, 1992.
Christie, Ian, & Elliot, David, (curators), *The Director's Eye: Drawings and Photographs by European Film-makers*, Museum of Modern Art, Oxford, 1996. Exhibition catalogue.
Clapp, Susannah, *With Chatwin: Portrait of a Writer*, Jonathan Cape, London, 1997.
Clare, Anthony, *In the Psychiatrist's Chair*, Heinemann, London, 1992.

Clark, Ossie, *The Ossie Clark Diaries*, edited & introduced by Lady Henrietta Rous, Bloomsbury, London, 1998.

Clarke, Mary, & Crisp, Clement, *London Contemporary Dance Theatre: The First 21 Years*, with photographs by Anthony Crickmay, Dance Books, London, 1988.

Collick, John, *Shakespeare, Cinema and Society*, Manchester University Press, Manchester, 1989.

Cook, Pam, & Dodd, Philip, (eds), *Women and Film: A Sight and Sound Reader*, Scarlet Press, London, 1993.

County, Jayne, with Rupert Smith, *Man Enough to be a Woman*, Serpent's Tail, London, 1995.

Crisp, Quentin, *Resident Alien: The New York Diaries*, HarperCollins, London, 1996.

Crossley-Holland, Kevin, (transl), & Mitchell, Bruce, (ed), *The Battle of Maldon and Other Old English Poems*, Macmillan & Company, London, 1965.

Crow, William Bernard, *A History of Magic, Witchcraft and Occultism*, Abacus, London, 1972.

Curtis, David, (ed), *A Directory of British Film and Video Artists*, John Libby Media, University of Luton, Luton, 1996.

David, Hugh, *On Queer Street: A Social History of British Homosexuality 1895-1995*, HarperCollins, London, 1997.

Davies, Anthony, & Wells, Stanley, (eds), *Shakespeare and the Moving Image: The Plays on Film and Television*, Cambridge University Press, Cambridge, 1994.

Deacon, Richard, *John Dee: scientist, geographer, astrologer and secret agent to Elizabeth I*, Frederick Muller, London, 1968.

Del Re, Gianmarco, *Derek Jarman*, Editrice Il Castoro, Milan, 1997.

Demoriane, Hermine, *The Tightrope Walker*, Secker & Warburg, London, 1989.

Dominic, Zoë, (photographs), & Gilbert, John Selwyn, (text), *Frederick Ashton: A Choreographer and his Ballets*, George C. Harrap & Company, London, 1971.

Dwyer, Simon, (ed), *Rapid Eye I*, Annihilation Press, London, 1993. Includes *Through a Screen Darkly, The Derek Jarman Interview* by Simon Dwyer.

Dyer, Richard, *Now You See It: Studies on Lesbian and Gay Film*, Routledge, London, 1990.

Ede, Harold Stanley, *Savage Messiah*, Gordon Fraser Gallery, London, 1971.

Eldridge, Mona, *In Search of a Prince: My Life with Barbara Hutton*, Sidgwick & Jackson, London, 1988.

Eno, Brian, *A Year with Swollen Appendices*, Faber & Faber, London, 1996.

Dunning, T.P., & Bliss, A.J., (eds), *The Wanderer*, Methuen, London, 1969.

Faithfull, Marianne, with David Dalton, *Faithfull*, Michael Joseph, London, 1994.

Farson, Daniel, *The Gilded Gutter Life of Francis Bacon*, Century, London, 1993.

Field, Simon, L'Eclair, Guy, & O'Pray, Michael, (eds), *Afterimage 12, Derek Jarman Of Angels & Apocalypse*, London, Autumn 1985.

Findlater, Richard, (ed), *At the Royal Court: 25 Years of the English Stage Company*, Amber Lane Press, Ambergate, 1981.

Forbes, Duncan, *The Fifth Continent: the Story of Romney Marsh and its Surroundings*, Shearwater, Hythe, 1984.

Friedman, Lester, (ed), *British Cinema and Thatcherism: Fires Were Started*, University of London Press, London, 1993.

Fritscher, Jack, *Mapplethorpe: Assault with a Deadly Camera*, Hastings House, New York, 1994.

Gardiner, James, *Who's A Pretty Boy Then? One Hundred and Fifty Years of Gay Life in Pictures*, Serpent's Tail, London, 1997.

Garfield, Simon, *The End of Innocence: Britain in the Time of AIDS*, Faber & Faber, London, 1994.

Gent, Lucy, *Great Planting*, Ward Lock, London, 1995.

Gill, John, *Queer Noises: Male and Female Homosexuality in Twentieth-Century Music*, Cassell, London, 1995.

Godwin, Fay, (photographs), & Ingrams, Richard, (text), *Romney Marsh*, Wildwood House, London, 1980.

Godwin, Joscelyn, *Athanasius Kircher: A Renaissance Man and the Quest for Lost Knowledge*, Thames & Hudson, London, 1979.

Gomez, Joseph A., *Ken Russell: The Adaptor as Creator*, Frederick Muller, London, 1976.

Gott, Ted, (ed), *Don't Leave Me This Way - Art in the Age of Aids*, National Gallery of Australia,

Canberra, 1994. Exhibition catalogue. Works by a number of artists. Includes Jarman's *Blood*.

Hacker, Jonathan, & Price, David, (eds), *Take Ten: Contemporary British Film Directors*, Clarendon Press, Oxford, 1991.

Haeffner, Mark, *The Dictionary of Alchemy from Maria Prophetissa to Isaac Newton*, The Aquarian Press, London, 1991.

Heath, Chris, *Pet Shop Boys, Literally*, Penguin Books, London, 1991.

Heymann, C. David, *Poor Little Rich Girl: The Life and Legend of Barbara Hutton*, Hutchinson, London, 1985.

Higgins, Patrick, (ed), *A Queer Reader*, Fourth Estate, London, 1993.

Higgins, Patrick, *Heterosexual Dictatorship: Male Homosexuality in Postwar Britain*, Fourth Estate, London, 1996.

Higson, Andrew, (ed), *Dissolving Views: Key Writings on British Cinema*, Cassell, London, 1996. Includes *The British Avant-Garde and Art Cinema from the 1970s to the 1990s*, Michael O'Pray; *Derek Jarman's The Tempest and Edward II*, Colin MacCabe.

Hillman, James, & Moore, Thomas, (ed), *A Blue Fire: The Essential James Hillman*, Routledge, London, 1989.

David Hockney by David Hockney, edited by Nikos Stangos, Thames & Hudson, London, 1977.

Howes, Keith, *Broadcasting It: An Encyclopaedia of Homosexuality on Film, Radio and TV in the UK 1923-1993*, Cassell, London, 1993.

Howes, Keith, *Outspoken: Keith Howes' Gay News Interviews 1976-83*, Cassell, London, 1995. 'Published in memoriam Derek Jarman (1942-1994)'.

Huelin, Gordon, *King's College London 1828-1978: A History Commemorating the 150th Anniversary of the Foundation of the College*, University of London King's College, 1978.

Hultén, K.G. Pontus, *The machine as seen at the end of the mechanical age*, The Museum of Modern Art, New York, 1968.

Huxley, Aldous, *The Devils of Loudun*, Chatto & Windus, London, 1961.

Hyde, Maggie, & McGuinness, Michael, *Jung For Beginners*, Icon Books, Cambridge, 1992.

Isaacs, Jeremy, *Storm Over 4: A Personal Account*, Weidenfeld & Nicolson, London, 1989.

Jivani, Alkarim, *It's Not Unusual: A History of Lesbian and Gay Britain in the Twentieth Century*, Michael O'Mara Books, London, 1997.

Jordan, Stephanie, *Striding Out: Aspects of Contemporary and New Dance in Britain*, Dance Books, London, 1992.

Jordan, Stephanie, & Grau, Andrée, (eds), *Following Sir Fred's Steps: Ashton's Legacy*, Dance Books, London, 1996.

Julien, Isaac, & Savage, Jon, (eds), *Critical Quarterly – Critically Queer*, Volume 36, Number 1, Blackwell Publishers, Oxford, Spring 1994.

Jung, C.G., *Memories, Dreams, Reflections*, recorded & edited by Aniela Jaffé, translated by Richard & Clara Winston, Collins & Routledge & Kegan Paul, London, 1963.

Jung, C.G., *Alchemical Studies*, translated by R.F.C. Hull, Routledge & Kegan Paul, London, 1983.

Jung, C.G., *Aion: Researches into the Phenomenology of Self*, translated by R.F.C. Hull, Routledge, London, 1991.

Jung, Carl G., & M.-L. von Franz, Joseph L. Henderson, Jolande Jacobi, Aniela Jaffé, *Man and his Symbols*, Arkana, London, 1990.

Kahn, Charles H., *The Art and Thought of Heraclitus: An edition of the fragments with translation and commentary*, Cambridge University Press, Cambridge, 1979.

Kavanagh, Julie, *Secret Muses: The Life of Frederick Ashton*, Faber & Faber, London, 1996.

Kirschbaum, Leo, (ed), *The Plays of Christopher Marlowe*, Meridian Books, Cleveland, 1962.

Koudelka, Josef, (photographs), *Gypsies*, Aperture Inc., New York, 1975.

Kuhn, Annette, *Family Secrets: Acts of Memory and Imagination*, Verso, London, 1995.

Lack, Russell, *Twenty Four Frames Under: a Secret History of Film Music*, Quartet Books, London, 1997.

Langdon, Helen, *Caravaggio: A Life*, Chatto & Windus, London, 1998.

Laughton, Bruce, *The Euston Road School, A Study in Objective Painting*, Scolar Press, Aldershot, 1986.

Lear, Edward, *The Complete Nonsense of Edward Lear*, edited & introduced by Holbrook

Jackson, Faber & Faber, London, 1947.

Leyland, Winston, (ed), *Gay Roots: Twenty Years of Gay Sunshine, An Anthology of Gay History, Sex, Politics, and Culture*, Gay Sunshine Press, San Francisco, 1991.

Lippard, Chris, (ed), *By angels driven: The films of Derek Jarman*, Flicks Books, Trowbridge, 1996.

Livingstone, Marco, *David Hockney*, Thames & Hudson, London, 1981.

Lloyd, Christopher, *In My Garden*, Bloomsbury, London, 1993.

Lucas, Ian, *Impertinent Decorum: Gay Theatrical Manoeuvres*, Cassell, London, 1994.

Lucas, Ian, *OutRage! An Oral History*, Cassell, London, 1998.

Lucie-Smith, Edward, (ed), *The Male Nude: a Modern View*, catalogue of an exhibition organised by François de Louville, Phaidon, Oxford, 1985. Includes a reproduction of Medley's *Sunday Morning*, 1982.

Lucie-Smith, Edward, *Artoday*, Phaidon, London, 1995.

MacCabe, Colin, *The Eloquence of the Vulgar: Language, Cinema and the Politics of Culture*, BFI Publishing, London, 1999.

Mann, Thomas, *The Holy Sinner*, translated by H.T. Lowe-Porter, Secker & Warburg, London, 1952.

Martin, Judith, *Miss Manners' Guide to Excruciatingly Good Behaviour*, Hamish Hamilton, London, 1983.

Mathews, Tom Dewe, *Censored*, Chatto & Windus, London, 1994.

Medley, Robert, *Drawn from the Life: A Memoir*, Faber & Faber, London, 1983.

Merrill, James, *A Different Person*, HarperCollins, San Francisco, 1994.

Merrison, Lindsey, *The Complete Derek Jarman*, Arbeitsgemeinschaft Kommunales Kino e. V., Stuttgart, 1988.

Meyers, Jeffrey, *The Enemy: A Biography of Wyndham Lewis*, Routledge & Kegan Paul, London, 1980.

Monk, Ray, *Ludwig Wittgenstein: The Duty of Genius*, Jonathan Cape, London, 1990.

Moore, Oscar, *PWA: Looking AIDS in the Face*, Picador, London, 1996.

Morrisroe, Patricia, *Mapplethorpe: A Biography*, Macmillan, London, 1995.

Mulvagh, Jane, *Vivienne Westwood: An Unfashionable Life*, HarperCollins, London, 1998.

Murray, Timothy, *Like a Film: Ideological Fantasy on Screen, Camera and Canvas*, Routledge, London, 1993.

Nash, Margaret, (ed), *Paul Nash: Fertile Image*, Faber & Faber, 1951. With an introduction by James Laver.

Newman, John, & Pevsner, Nikolaus, *The Buildings of England: Dorset*, Penguin Books, 1972.

O'Pray, Michael, *Derek Jarman: Dreams of England*, BFI Publishing, London, 1996.

Park, James, *Learning to Dream: The New British Cinema*, Faber & Faber, London, 1984.

Patanè, Vincenzo, (ed), *Derek Jarman*, Quaderni del Circuito Cinema, 55, Ufficio Attivita Cinematografiche del Comune di Venezia, Venice, 1995.

Percival, John, *Nureyev: Aspects of the Dancer*, Faber & Faber, London, 1976.

Petrie, Duncan J., *Creativity and Constraint in the British Film Industry*, Macmillan, London, 1991.

Petrie, Duncan, (ed), *Screening Europe: Image and Identity in Contemporary European Cinema*, BFI Publishing, London, 1992.

Petrie, Duncan, (ed), *New Questions of British Cinema*, BFI Publishing, 1992.

Petrie, Duncan, (ed), *Inside Stories: Diaries of British Film-makers at Work*, BFI Publishing, 1996.

Pinney, Michael, *River In Light*, Bettiscombe Press, Bettiscombe, 1971.

Pinney, Michael, *Clothes in a Museum*, Bettiscombe Press, Bettiscombe, 1971.

Pinney, Michael, *Nota Bene*, Bettiscombe Press, Bettiscombe, 1972.

P-Orridge, Genesis, *GENESIS P-ORRIDGE ESOTERRORIST selected essays 1980-1988*, OV-Press, Denver, 1989.

Poynor, Rick, *Nigel Coates: The City in Motion*, Fourth Estate in conjunction with *Blueprint* magazine, London, 1989.

Procktor, Patrick, *Self-Portrait*, Weidenfeld & Nicolson, London, 1991.

Pugh, Peter, et al, edited by Guy Nickalls, *Great Enterprise: A History of Harrisons & Crosfield*, Harrisons & Crosfield, London, 1990.

Purdy, James, *Narrow Rooms*, published as a Gay Modern Classic with an introduction by Paul

Binding, GMP, London, 1985.

Raeburn, Michael, (introduction & commentaries), *Vision: 50 Years of British Creativity*, Thames & Hudson, London, 1999.

Rathbone, Michael, *Canford School 1923-1983*, Canford School, 1983.

Rees, A.L., *A History of Experimental Film and Video: From the Canonical Avant-Garde to Contemporary British Practice*, BFI Publishing, London, 1999.

Richardson, Tony, *Long Distance Runner: A Memoir*, with an introduction by Lindsay Anderson, Faber & Faber, London, 1993.

Rilke, Rainer Maria, *Duino Elegies*, the German text with an English translation, introduction & commentary by J.B. Leishman & Stephen Spender, The Hogarth Press, London, 1975.

Rimmer, Dave, *Like Punk Never Happened: Culture Club and the New Pop*, Faber & Faber, London, 1985.

Robertson, Bryan, & Russell, John, & Lord Snowdon, *Private View*, Thomas Nelson & Sons, London, 1965.

Rogan, Johnny, *Morrissey & Marr: The Severed Alliance*, Omnibus Press, London, 1992.

Rose, Sir Francis, *Saying Life*, Cassell & Company, London, 1961.

Rosenfeldt, Diane, *Ken Russell: a guide to reference and resources*, George Prior Publishers, London, 1978.

Russell, Ken, *A British Picture: An Autobiography*, William Heinemann, London, 1989.

Russell, Ken, *Mike and Gaby's Space Gospel*, Little, Brown, London, 1999.

Rushdie, Salman, *The Wizard of Oz*, BFI Film Classics, BFI Publishing, London, 1992.

Savage, Jon, *England's Dreaming: Sex Pistols and Punk Rock*, Faber & Faber, London, 1991.

Savage, Jon, *Time Travel: Pop, Media and Sexuality, 1977-96*, Chatto & Windus, London, 1996.

Shikibu, Murasaki, *The Tale of Genji*, 2 volumes, translated by Arthur Waley, Allen & Unwin, London, 1965.

Sinclair, Andrew, *Francis Bacon: His Life and Violent Times*, Sinclair-Stevenson, London, 1993.

Skurka, Norma, & Gili, Oberto, *Underground Interiors - Decorating for Alternate Life Styles*, Quadrangle Books, New York, 1972.

Sleep, Wayne, *Precious Little Sleep*, Boxtree, London, 1996.

Spalding, Frances, *Dance till the Stars Come Down: A Biography of John Minton*, A John Curtis Book, Hodder & Stoughton, London, 1991.

Spalding, Frances, *Roger Fry: Art and Life*, Paul Elek, Granada Publishing, London, 1980.

Stewart, William, *Cassells' Queer Companion: A Dictionary of Lesbian and Gay Life and Culture*, Cassell, London, 1995.

Street, Sarah, *British National Cinema*, Routledge, London, 1997.

Strinati, Dominic, & Wagg, Stephen, (eds), *Come On Down?: Popular media culture in post-war Britain*, Routledge, London, 1992.

Summers, Claude J., (ed), *The Gay and Lesbian Literary Heritage: A Reader's Companion to the Writers and their Works, from Antiquity to the Present*, Henry Holt, New York, 1995.

Thomson, David, *A Biographical Dictionary of Film*, André Deutsch, London, 1994.

Thorpe, Adam, *Still*, Secker & Warburg, London, 1995.

Thurston, Herbert, & Attwater, Donald, (eds), *Butler's Lives of the Saints*, Burns & Oates, London, 1956.

Tilley, Sue, *Leigh Bowery: the Life and Times of an Icon*, Hodder & Stoughton, London, 1997.

Vaughan, David, *Frederick Ashton and his ballets*, A & C Black, London, 1977.

Vaughan, Keith, *Journals 1939-1977*, John Murray, London, 1989.

Vermorel, Fred, *Fashion & Perversity: A Life of Vivienne Westwood and the sixties laid bare*, Bloomsbury, London, 1996.

Walker, Alexander, *National Heroes: British Cinema in the Seventies and Eighties*, Harrap, London, 1985.

Watson, Peter, *Nureyev: A Biography*, Hodder & Stoughton, London, 1994.

Webb, Peter, *Portrait of David Hockney*, Chatto & Windus, London, 1988.

Whately-Smith, Peter, *The Founding of Hordle House*, 1981.

Wilson, Colin, *Ken Russell: A Director in Search of a Hero*, Intergroup Publishing, London, 1974.

Wollen, Roger, *Derek Jarman: A Portrait*, introduction by Roger Wollen, with contributions by

Matt Cook, Christopher Lloyd, Stuart Morgan, Michael O'Pray, James Cary Parkes, Peter Snow, Yolanda Sonnabend, Gray Watson; Barbican Art Gallery & the Hatton Gallery in association with Thames & Hudson, London, 1996.

Wright, Horace J., & Wright, Walter P., *Beautiful Flowers & How to Grow Them*, T.C. & E.C. Jack Ltd, London, 1926.

Yates, Frances A., *Giordano Bruno and the Hermetic Tradition*, Routledge & Kegan Paul, London, 1964.

Yates, Frances A., *Theatre of the World*, Routledge & Kegan Paul, London, 1969.

Yates, Frances A., *The Rosicrucian Enlightenment*, Routledge & Kegan Paul, London, 1972.

Yates, Frances A., *Shakespeare's Last Plays: A New Approach*, Routledge & Kegan Paul, London, 1975.

Yates, Frances A., *The Occult Philosophy in the Elizabethan Age*, Routledge & Kegan Paul, London, 1979.

Yates, Frances A., *The Art of Memory*, Pimlico, London, 1992.

York, Peter, *Style Wars*, Sidgwick & Jackson, London, 1980.

Film, television & radio

Certainly towards the end of his life, Jarman appeared on or contributed to a significant number of radio and television programmes. Aside from his own, he also featured in a number of (mainly short) films. I have listed only those shows or films where his contribution seems to me sufficient (or sufficiently noteworthy) to merit it. I have listed only one of the programmes made about him after his death. Films that were never broadcast or shown, or which are in private hands, are marked by a *.

Abbreviations:

dir director; *p* producer; *pc* production company; *pres* presenters; *ed* series editor; *sp* series producer

A Self-Portrait Filmed For Me by Mike Davis, super-8 film of Jarman having his hair cut; James Mackay Collection; circa 1973. *

Shad Thames, super-8 segment filmed by Gerald Incandela & featuring Jarman, parts of which appear in *Glitterbug*; James Mackay Collection; 1973. *

High Noon, super-8 short by Robin Wall, featuring Derek Jarman & Michael Davis; 1973–5. *

A Bigger Splash, includes a brief appearance by Jarman; *dir* Jack Hazan; 1974.

The making of *Sebastiane* as filmed by Hugh Smith; James Mackay Collection; 1975. *

Nighthawks, includes a brief appearance by Jarman as an extra; *dir* Ron Peck & Paul Hallam; 1978.

South of Watford, profile of Jarman; *pres* Ben Elton; *p* & *dir* John Scarlett-Davis; *sp* Michael Chaplin; first broadcast 9 March 1984.

Six of Hearts: Andy the Furniture Maker, television programme about Andy Marshall & his furniture in which Jarman appears; *p* Mark Cellier; *dir* Paul Oremland; first broadcast 29 November 1986.

Ostia, student film by Julian Cole in which Jarman plays Pasolini, David Dipnall the Angel of Death; 1986. *

Behind Closed Doors, 14 min film by Anna Thew in which Jarman makes a brief appearance in the final scene; among those involved with the film were Steve Farrer, Richard Heslop, Yvonne Little, James Mackay; 1987.

Prick Up Your Ears, brief appearance by Jarman as Patrick Procktor; *dir* Stephen Frears; 1987.

Dead Cat, student film by David Lewis in which Jarman plays a medicine man; among the others involved with the film were Alan Beck, Andy Crabb, Genesis P-Orridge & Andy Tiernan; 1988. *

The Media Show, Jarman in interview about Clause 28; *dir* Bob Collins; first broadcast March 1988.

Talking Cinema: Derek Jarman in conversation with Simon Field, ICA Video; 35 mins; 1988.

Know What I Mean, television profile of Jarman; *p* Phillip Bartlett & Laurens C. Postma; *dir* Laurens C. Postma; A Yo-Yo Film Production for Channel Four; first broadcast 11 May 1989.

In the Psychiatrist's Chair, Jarman in conversation with Anthony Clare; BBC Radio 4; first broadcast 15 August 1990.

Jarman in interview with Colin MacCabe at Dungeness; 1990. *

The Making of Derek Jarman's The Garden, *dir* Takashi Asai for Uplink/Space Shower; 1990.

Film of Jarman filming *The Garden, dir* Yoshiharu Tezuka; James Mackay Collection; 1990. *

A Chip off the Block of Paradise, profile of Jarman with interviewer Rosemary Hartill as part of the TVS series *The Human Factor; dir* Bob Franklin; *sp* Andrew Barr; first broadcast 25 November 1990.

Building Sights, Jarman on the subject of Robin Noscoe's Garden House in Wimborne; *p* Ruth Rosenthal; *dir* Keith Collins; first broadcast 1991.

Derek Jarman: A Portrait, profile produced for *Arena; p & dir* Mark Kidel; *s ed* Nigel Finch & Anthony Wall; first broadcast 18 January 1991.

The Media Show, short profile of Jarman when making *Edward II; dir* Basil Comely; first broadcast 7 April 1991.

Dig, includes short section on Jarman & his garden; *pres* Carolyn Marshall; *p* Gill Fickling; *dir* Denman Rooke; *sp* Norrie Maclaren; a Tartan Television Production for Channel Four; first broadcast 26 April 1991.

Saint Derek, short film about the anniversary of Jarman's canonisation in September 1992; *dir* Peter Fuller. *

Face to Face, Jarman in interview with Jeremy Isaccs; *p* David Herman; *dir* Janet Fraser Crook; first broadcast 17 March 1993.

L'Amore Vincitore, Jarman in conversation with Roberto Nanni on the occasion of his *Queer* exhibition in Rome; 1993. *

The Clearing, student film by Alexis Bisticas in which both Jarman & Keith Collins appear; 1993. *

There We Are John, filmed interview of Jarman by John Cartwright at Richard Salmon's studio; *p* Guy Landver & Hannah Wiggin; *dir* Ken McCullen; British Council; 1993.

The Last Paintings of Derek Jarman, short study of Jarman's final paintings & Jarman at work on them; *pres* Mark Radcliffe; *p & dir* for Granada Television by John Piper; original Jarman footage researched & *dir* Mark Jordan; *sp* Colin Bell; first broadcast 1994. (Mark Jordan also filmed around Jarman on the occasion of his *Queer* exhibition in Manchester in 1992. *)

Introduction to *A Night With Derek* as broadcast on Channel Four; *dir & p* Richard Kwietniowski; *p* Peter Murphy; includes interviews with Keith Collins, Sarah Graham, Maggi Hambling, Nicholas de Jongh, Andrew Logan, Tony Pinching, Sandy Powell, Richard Salmon, Ian Shipley & Clem Crosby, Sister Latex of the Immaculate Protection, Howard Sooley, Tania Wade, Simon Watney, Elisabeth Welch, Toyah Willcox; Alfalfa Entertainment for Channel Four; first broadcast 20 February 1995.

Acknowledgements

I owe a great many thanks to a great many people. Keith Collins gave tirelessly of his time and encouragement, read the typescript and made sure I had unfettered access to Jarman's papers and effects. So too did Gaye Temple and, through her, other members of Jarman's family and certain family friends.

Roger Wollen allowed me to use the extensive research he undertook when mounting the retrospective of Jarman's work at the Barbican in 1996. Michael O'Pray was always on hand to answer my many questions and read the typescript. Others to read the typescript and provide invaluable comment were Simon Watney and Peter Cartwright.

Una Hurding first introduced me to Derek Jarman; without that introduction, this book would never have been written. My then agent Jennifer Kavanagh set the ball rolling quite splendidly; my current agent David Miller has given so generously and wisely of his time and advice that I shall always be in his debt. Among a number of friends and colleagues who provided a similar service, Laura Morris was crucial in giving me the confidence to believe I was vaguely equal to the task ahead.

The number of people at Little, Brown to have contributed to the book are many; pre-eminent among them are Alan Samson, Richard Beswick, Duncan Spilling, Alison Menzies, Diana Russell, Linda Silverman and Caroline North, whose unerring eye, exceptionally hard work and great forbearance helped turn a hopelessly unwieldy typescript into these pages.

Equal forbearance (and enormous support) has been shown by my family and friends.

With apologies for any names I have neglected to include, and for the fact that a mere list cannot accord particular thanks where they are perhaps due, those I interviewed or contacted in connection with the book were:

Edward Adie, John Adie, Rupert Adley, Tariq Ali, Shaun Allen, Jonathan Altaras, William Andreae-Jones, Takashi Asai, Charles Atlas, Dave Baby, Brian Baggott, Marc Balet, Dorothy and Peter Bargh, Phyllida Barlow, Charlotte Barnes, Rufus Barnes, Lionel Bart, Dr Basden, John Baxter, Keith Baxter, Jeremy Beal at Quartet Books, Alan Beck, Lutz Becker, Alan Bennett, Sarah Benson of the Herbert F. Johnson Museum of Art, Micha Bergese, Richard Bernstein, Madeline Bessborough, Christopher Biggins, Leigh Blake, Judy Blame, Conrad Bodman and the staff of the Barbican Art Gallery, Jean Boudrand, Val Bourne, Don Boyd, Guy Brett, Hal Bromm, Dennis Brown, Stephen Buckley, Paul Buckmaster, Michael Bukht, Peter Burton, Martin Butcher at UCL, Ken Butler, Dugald Campbell, Naomi Campbell, Caroline Cator (née Green), Georgia de Chamberet at Quartet Books, Stephen Chaplin at the Slade, Gaby Chautin (née Longhi), John Chesworth, Ernst Chin, Ian Christie, Michael Christie, Peter Christopherson, Ossie Clark, Steve Clark-Hall, Paul Clements, Jonathan Clowes, Nigel Coates, Professor Bernard Cohen at the Slade, Ann Colligan, John Colligan, John Colson, Roger Cook, Paul Copson, Beverly Cork, Jayne County, Bruce Cratsley, Quentin Crisp, Marilyn Croft, Adrian Curry at Zeitgeist Films, David Curtis, Peter Curtis, Peta Dalrymple, Robert Darling, Andrew Davis, Michael Davis, David Dawson, Ray Dean, Hermine Demoriane, the staff of the Devon Records Office, Exeter, John Dewe-Mathews, Thomas Dillow, Peter Docherty, Peter Dockley, Euphrosyne Doxiadis, Nicholas Dromgoole, Lee Drysdale, Janet Eager of The Place, Maggie Ellenby, Brian Eno, Randy Fahey, Lynn Farleigh, Peter Fillingham, John Fleming, Guy Ford, Roger Ford, Duggie Fields, Michael Fish, John Furse, Robert Gates, Nicholas Georgiadis, Constantine Giannaris, Ben Gibson, Roma Gibson at BFI Publishing, John Gielgud, W.S. Gilbert, Peter Gill, Michael and Robby (née Nelson) Ginsborg, Adrian Glew and the staff at the Tate Gallery Archive, Simon Goldberg, Brad Gooch, Mary Gosling, Diana Grace-Jones, Beryl Grey, Martin Grimes, David Gwinnutt, Stella Halkyard of the John Rylands Library, Maggi Hambling, Lynn Hanke, Noël and Winnow (née Colyer) Hardy, Dorothy Harling (née Bargh), Julian Harrap, Graham Harris, John Harrison, Michael Harth, David Haughton, John Hayes, Diana Helve, Jeff Hill at Clein & White, R.F. Hill, Susan Hill, Peter Hinwood, Robin Hirtenstein, Christopher Hobbs, Timothy Holderness-Roddam, Stephen Hollis, Stuart Hopps, Paul Huxley, Gerald Incandela, Jonathan Ionides, Jeremy Isaacs, Terence James, Jim G. Jarman, Roger Jones, Nicholas de Jongh, Jordan, Mark Jordan, Roderick and Liz Kalberer, Tom Kalin, Brenda Kaye, Ian Kellgren, Lindsay Kemp, John Kennedy, Jonathan Kent, Michael Kostiff, George and Jessica Lack, Mark Lancaster, Paul Langley, Ulla Larson-Styles, George Lawson, Malcolm Leigh, David Lewis, Matthew Lewis, Peter Lewis, Susanne Lindgren, Maud Lloyd, Keith Lodwick of the Theatre Museum, Andrew Logan, Peter and Diane Logan, Nicholas Logsdail, Max Loppert, Rupert Lord, Ian Lucas, Brenda Lukey, Karl Lydon, Jim Lyons, Colin MacCabe, James Mackay, Ewen MacLeod at the Arnolfini, Gayrie MacSween, Gerrard McArthur, Gavin McEchern, Alasdair McGaw, Robin McIver, John McLoughlin, Howard Malin, Paul Manousso, Andy Marshall, Patricia Martin at the Lisson Gallery, Moyra Masters, David Medalla, Robert Medley, Gina Metcalf, Patricia Methven and the archive at King's College, David Meyer, Peter Middleton, Robin Middleton, John Miles, Robert Mill, David Miller, Simon Midgley, Keith Milow, Peter Minshall, Janet Moat at the BFI, Ray Monk, Norman Morrice, Paul Morrissey, Peter Murphy, Herbert Muschamp, Adam Nankervis, Diana Neutze, Ken Newlan, Melissa North, James Norton, Robin and Phyll Noscoe, Michael O'Pray, Padeluun, Saffron Parker at the BFI, Ron Peck, Burnel Penhaul, John-Paul Philippe, Henry Phillips and the staff of Hordle House, Tony Pinching, Michael Pinney, Susan Pinney, Misha Popov, Sandy Powell, Jane Pritchard (archivist for Rambert Dance Company, English National Ballet and The London Contemporary Dance Theatre), Professor Richard Proudfoot of King's College, Philip Prowse, Jean-Marc Prouveur, James Purdy, Eugene Rae of the Royal College of Art, Sarah Radclyffe, Gerard Raimond, Margaret Ranicar, Philippe Rasquinet, Peter Ratcliffe, Tony Rayns, Dries Reyneke, Paul Reynolds,

Patricia Rianne-Lloyd, B Ruby Rich, Colin Richardson and the archive at *Gay Times*, Jasper Ridley, Mark Rimmell, David Rintoul, Mary Rob, Brian Robinson, Geoffrey Rogers, Rick Rogers, Harvey Rose, Norman Rosenthal, Johnny Rozsa, Royal Opera House archive, Richard Rowson, Jenny Runacre, Geff Rushton (John Balance), Joy Russell, Ken Russell, Shirley Russell, Anya and John Sainsbury, Peter Sainsbury, Richard Salmon, Chelita Salvatore, Jon Savage, George Saxon, John Scarlett-Davis, Richard Shone, Bryn Siddall, Ira Silverberg, Wayne Sleep, Maud Smith, Peter Snow, Jeffrey Solomons, Yolanda Sonnabend, Howard Sooley, Timothy Spain, Wieland Speck, Yana Spence, Nikos Stangos, John Stevenson, Volker Stox, Tim Sullivan, Cordelia Swann, Nina Swayne, Moira Tait, Sheridan Tandy, Peter Tatchell, Amy Taubin, Maggie Taylor, Peter Tegel, Neil Tennant, Anna Thew, Lynne Tillman, Steve Treatment, Leo Treviglio, Betty Tuck, Yvonne Tucker (née Little), Richard Turley, David Usborne, Christine Vachon, Una de Vere (née Gray), John Vernon, Vincent Vichit-Vadakan, Christopher Marsden of the V&A Archive and Registry, Thilo von Watzdorf, Desmond Vowles, the staff of University College London records office and archive collection, the staff of London University library, Ronald Waldron, Claudia Walker, Louise Walker, Robin Wall, Nicholas Ward-Jackson, Marina Warner, Richard Warwick, Lawrence and Pat Warwick-Evans, Simon Watney, Gray Watson, Bruce Weber, the staff of the West Country Studies Library, Exeter, James Whaley, David Whately-Smith, John and Diana Whately-Smith, Peter and Dorothy Whately-Smith, Leland Wheeler, Kevin Whitney, Ian Whittaker, Robin Wicker at Canford, Douglas Williams, Fiona Williams, Marilyn Williams, Peter Wollen, Isobel Womack, Marcus Wood, Patrick Woodcock, Penelope Woolley (née Jenkins), Nicholas Wright, Nikki Wright, Laetitia Yhap, Caroline Zaleski.

I have made every effort to trace copyright holders. My apologies for any omissions, which will be rectified in future editions.

My thanks to Quartet Books for permission to quote from *Dancing Ledge*; to David Higham Associates for permission to quote from Dylan Thomas's 'Do Not Go Gentle Into That Good Night', from *Collected Poems*, J. M. Dent; and to Thames & Hudson for the kind loan of their film for many of the colour photographs.

Material quoted from *Modern Nature*, *At Your Own Risk*, *Chroma*, *Kicking the Pricks* and *Up in the Air* by permission of the Random House Group.

Index

NB: *Works not by Derek Jarman are followed by the originator's name in brackets. Throughout the index the abbreviation DJ is used for Derek Jarman and s-8 for super-8 film.*